In the Images of Development

Urban and Industrial Environments

Series editor: Robert Gottlieb, Henry R. Luce Professor of Urban and Environmental Policy, Occidental College

For a complete list of books published in this series, please see the back of the book.

In the Images of Development

City Design in the Global South

Tridib Banerjee

Foreword by Manuel Castells

The MIT Press
Cambridge, Massachusetts
London, England

This book was set in Stone Serif and Stone Sans by Westchester Publishing Services. Printed and bound in the United States of America.

Library of Congress Cataloging-in-Publication Data

Names: Banerjee, Tridib, author.
Title: In the images of development : city design in the Global South / Tridib Banerjee.
Description: Cambridge, Massachusetts : The MIT Press, [2021] | Series: Urban and industrial environments | Includes bibliographical references and index.
Identifiers: LCCN 2020005066 | ISBN 9780262044707 (hardcover)
Subjects: LCSH: City planning--Developing countries. | Urbanization--Developing countries. | Urban policy--Developing countries.
Classification: LCC HT169.5 .B44 2020 | DDC 307.1/216091724--dc23
LC record available at https://lccn.loc.gov/2020005066

10 9 8 7 6 5 4 3 2 1

In memory of my parents Leela and Banikanta,
my roots in the Global South

and to my family:

Frances
Josh and Victoria
Joya and Harris
Shaan
Nathan
Luca
and
Leland

Contents

Foreword

Cities are meaningful forms. Meaning is constructed by culture. Culture is diverse because is produced by history. Thus, in a globalized world the image of the city varies depending on context. Yet, cities are connected in a network of multiple interdependencies. So, every city is at the same time local and global, and so are the images that convey this new spatial reality. This raises an extraordinary challenge for urban designers in a rapidly urbanizing planet: how to make sense of the cacophony of signals emerging from the past and from the blueprint of the future in a multicultural fabric. It is not a minor issue. Because of the growing sense of alienation of human beings facing an unprecedented experience of uncontrolled social, economic, and spatial change, urban design must set codes of identification. These codes are protocols of communication in an otherwise meaningless expanse of undifferentiated habitat. Rather than opposing traditionalism to modernism, or giving up to postmodernism, the restoration of spatial meaning requires starting from history and cultural specificity. Then proceeding with proposing new layers of forms associated with the new functions of cities. Relying on the support of new technologies that allow shaping environments and adapting cities to the needs and representations of their citizens. Yet, never forgetting the fundamental principle of what makes a spatial form a good city form, in the normative tradition masterfully established by Kevin Lynch: cities are images that live in our brains and construct our experience. Thus, urban design is as important for the quality of our lives as is functional urban planning.

Tridib Banerjee has spent his brilliant career rethinking cities in the Global South from this perspective, broadening the approach to urban development beyond the predominant instrumentalist view of how to manage megalopoles.

This elegantly written book brings together his research, insights, and planning practice in the understanding of how history, old and new, makes cities, and how urban design could contribute to shed light in the new urban experience to escape from the darkness currently descending on our blue planet.

Manuel Castells
Emeritus Professor of City Planning, University of California, Berkeley
2004 Awardee of MIT's Kevin Lynch Prize

Preface

The literature on development and globalization of nations, regions, and cities is well endowed with studies, theories, and conjectures. Remarkably, relatively little of this pertains to actual urban form and physical design of cities as outcomes of development and globalization. Urban form and structure are significant considerations in thinking about the urbanism of cities. But the existing development and globalization literature is limited in explaining the urban form of actual cities and their contemporary transformations. We know that cities are historical palimpsests that reveal the occasions for change, as well as the inertia of continuity in their urban form. Put differently, *people live in cities*, and their everyday lives and daily commerce are situated in urban spaces and places, in what constitute the built environment. The future growth of cities—mainly in the developing world—and their "ecological footprints" will have an enormous effect on the consumption of energy, water, and other resources. While there is a substantial body of literature on the history of cities, relatively little focuses on the images of development that have shaped historic transformations in the urban form of cities in the Global South, and that may presage endogenous possibilities for their future design. In the absence of such discourse, the design of developing cities continues to be a project of the West led by non sequitur "signature" architecture, or just gratuitous mimicry of exogenous urban form, indulged by global capital.

This project is conceived to fill some of this void by linking the idea of development with that of urbanism, urban form, and urban design. The primary focus of the book is on contemporary cities in the developing world and their intrinsic prospects in city design. But the arguments will be critical and retrospective in part, going back to the urban legacy of the developing world at the beginning of the colonial era, and tracing the economic, political, and ideological forces that influenced the colonial and postcolonial development up to the present time. The book is comparative in scope, as it draws from relevant experiences of different cities in the developing world. It concludes with some essential notions of future city design that are grounded in the critical challenges we face today: sustainable development, equity, environmental and social justice, and diversity. The book can be best seen as the opening of a long overdue conversation among the design, development, and planning scholars and practitioners and those interested in the urban development of the Global South.

The Timing: Why Now?

One important aim of this book is to contribute critical materials to broaden and inform the conversation regarding the future of cities of the Global South in the face of unrelenting globalization and explosive urban growth. The timing is right for several reasons. The world urban population has grown to be 4.2 billion in 2018 and expected to reach 6.7 billion by 2050. In other words, 68 percent of the world population will be urbanized by 2050, from the current level of 55 percent. The bulk of this urban growth is expected to be in Global South; three countries—China, India, and Nigeria—will account for 83 percent of this growth by 2050.[1] The contemporary urban transformation of countries such as China, India, and those in the Arabian/Persian Gulf and Southeast Asia, instigated by their phenomenal economic growth in recent years, has raised many questions about the livability and sustainability of cities in those countries as well as the rest of the developing world. And such questions are not solely the province of academics, policy makers, and researchers. General interest stories about cities are appearing with increasing frequency in popular magazines and leading newspapers. I know from my recent visits to China, India, and the UAE that the residents who have to live in these cities are deeply concerned about the impact of increased automobile traffic, air and water pollution, and the shortage of decent shelter, all resulting from the explosive growth of their cities. In the search for answers from within and without, there is little consensus on how to manage the unprecedented environmental and human consequences that will be produced by this juggernaut of global economy. Academic seminars and discussions about models of more livable and sustainable cities abound, but the scale and haste of urban development continues to outpace the local capability to manage the existential crises in health, justice, and livability. In one of the chapters in this book, titled "The Faustian Imperative," I focus on the unprecedented urban growth and development in emerging economies such as China, India, and United Arab Emirates. In this discussion I draw from Marshall Berman's seminal 1982 treatise on modernity, *All That Is Solid Melts into Air,* in which he develops the metaphor of the second transformation of Goethe's Faust as the developer, where the drive for modernity and prosperity consistently trumps synoptic thinking and the possibility of sustainable options. China and India may represent the leading edge of this drive for modernity and development, but other large, populous countries with expanding economies and mass consumption are not far behind. Similar problems will soon be faced by other countries in Asia, Africa, and Latin America that are poised on various rungs of the development ladder.

In particular, I hope this book will draw the attention of organizations that guide and fund much of the development and modernization projects worldwide, such as the World Bank, UNDP, USAID, and foundations dedicated to improving life in the developing world. The outreach efforts and publications of the bank and other development agencies have so far directed little attention to: the issues of urbanism, urban form, and design; the livability of developing cities and the related questions of inequality; and the growing concerns for environmental and social justice. Hopefully this book will engage them in this conversation.

The project for this book required bridging two very different traditions: writings on development, which are mainly grounded in social sciences; and writings on urban form and appearance, much of which are rooted in the aesthetics, humanities, and design traditions. My academic career trajectory in research, teaching, and practice has consistently straddled these traditions. This project has been nourished by sustained conversations with colleagues and students from different corners of the world who have confronted me with new questions and helped me consider new ideas and alternative propositions.

Origins of the Project

The original inspiration for this project came many years ago from my mentor Kevin Lynch, who believed that a book on the design of cities in developing countries was urgently needed and urged me to take on this project. Subsequently a similar nudge came from my University of Southern California (USC) colleague Manuel Castells (formerly at the University of California, Berkeley), who also strongly endorsed this project. Over the years, as I presented my ideas at various conference presentations and invited lectures, I received similar words of encouragement. I was motivated by suggestions from several international scholars and professionals, including Alessandro Balducci of Milano Polytechnic, Matthew Carmona of University College London, Pietro Garau of Sapienza University of Rome, Haarry den Hartog and Richard LeGates of Tongji University, Balaji Parthasarathy of the International Institute of Information Technology Bangalore, Klaus Kunzmann of TU Dortmund University, Lu Bin of Beijing University, Sun Fengqi and Wu Liangyoung of Tsginhua University, photographer Fang Wang of Potsdam, Anastasia Loukaitou-Sideris of UCLA, and my USC colleagues Vinayak Bharne, Clara Irazábal, and Martin Krieger.

Additional impetus came from many years of teaching courses relevant to this book. The long trajectory of this project began during my 1979–1980 sabbatical at Stanford University, where I designed a graduate seminar on the topic of Third World cities and development. On returning to USC, I designed and taught an undergraduate general education course titled "Third World Cities" that fulfilled the non-Western and diversity requirement for USC undergraduates. The course drew large numbers of students and was used as a model for courses at other universities. Subsequently I was invited to design and teach "Comparative International Development," a graduate-level planning core course built on the earlier course. The absence of appropriate textbooks in both instances has been a constant reminder that I should proceed with this project. I hasten to add, however, that this book was not written as a textbook for any of these courses. But I certainly hope that it will be considered for graduate or upper-level undergraduate courses focusing on the broader and comparative themes of the culture of cities, globalization and development, urbanization, urbanism, urban planning, and city design, with a comparative focus on the developing world.

There are several features of this book that distinguish it from a "how to" handbook. First, I did not intend it as a collection of recipe knowledge of design solutions culled from the current practices in the West that might be appropriate for the Global South. That would have run counter to the very premise of the book which explores endogenous approaches to city design. Second, the book suggests a critical synthesis of the literature on development and the literature on city design, two distinct tracks in urban literature that rarely cross paths. This synthesis provides the groundwork for framing critical questions about the design and development of the cities of the Global South. Third, the narrative begins with an interpretation of the multiple legacies of the precolonial cities and the endogenous images of ideal city form. This review suggests that sustainability, a much-discussed concept today, was intrinsic to the genius of their canonical urban form. Fourth, it offers a critical retrospective of the urban development of the Global South, arguing that it has been essentially a project of the West not only through the colonial years but also in the contemporary postcolonial, and increasingly globalized, phase of urban development. Fifth, it offers a conceptual framework for thinking about cities along certain critical dimensions and mapping the effects of development on urban form. Sixth, the book is meant to be comparative in scope, spanning multiple eras and multiple places that should engage broad readership from both the Global North and the Global South. Finally, the book concludes on a prospective note, anticipating multiple scenarios of city development and a selected collection of native possibilities of city design in the Global South.

I should make two other disclaimers. First, this book is not about any single city or a particular region. At least, it is meant not to be that way. But unquestionably there is more here from Asia than other regions of the Global South. My coverage of cases from the African continent, especially sub-Saharan Africa, is limited. Similarly, the coverage of Latin American cases is also not exhaustive. This bias or oversight is essentially a reflection of my personal travel experiences, which have not been as encompassing as I would have liked.

Second, I have tried to connect the images of city design with the notion of development at the level of a discourse in political economy. This has necessarily kept the coverage of development at a macroeconomic level. Readers with an economistic bent might find this lacking insofar as the discussions do not address economics of land, location of firms and businesses, or the pro forma of profit and "penciling out" that dictates investment in real estate development. There is no question that real estate development has increasingly become an important sector of private investment and the global economy. In fact, the State in the emerging economies has become a key player in real estate contributing to oversupply, defying fundamental market principles, and ignoring negative environmental and social externalities such as loss of natural resources, global warming, and gentrification and displacement. The "ghost towns" from China to Turkey featured in the media are cases in point.[2] But I have not ignored these dimensions of development; in fact, they are the essential critiques of this book. What I have not done, I must admit, is praise the value production in the economics of the land market through design that serves the rentier class in a global economy; nor have I conceded the subservience of planning to the market in painting the ideal portrait of development.[3]

Acknowledgments

I should conclude by expressing my heartfelt thanks to institutions and individuals who supported and helped in the research and production of this volume. My research began in the late 1970s, when I received a United Parcel Service Foundation sabbatical grant for a visiting associate professorship administered by the Department of Civil and Environmental Engineering of Stanford University. In the 1990s two UNDP contracts gave me the opportunity to visit Iran and India on professional assignments. The assignment to Iran involved designing for resiliency, especially developing post-earthquake mitigation measures for historic cities such as Rasht after the Manjil earthquake. The assignment to India, under UNDP's Transfer of Knowledge through Expatriate Nationals

(TOKTEN) program, required that I work on a plan for the National Capital Region, design proposals for the Kashmiri Gate and Connaught Circus station area developments as part of the Delhi Metro Rail project, and develop alternative schemes for the planned New Town (Rajarhat) near Kolkata. A decade later another trip to India, under the auspices of the US State Department's public diplomacy program, allowed me to interact with administrators, engineers, planners, and concerned citizens about urban development challenges in India, not just for big cities such as Mumbai and Kolkata, but also for lower-order provincial capital cities such as Raipur, Ranchi, and Agartala. These visits were useful in terms of experiencing the ground-level challenges of city design and modulating the theoretical and academic thinking that shaped the intellectual armature of the book. They also helped me collect new materials and embellish the content of the book.

The initial writing of the manuscript did not begin until 2005, when I received a Rockefeller Foundation Bellagio Scholar in Residence grant. Valuable ideas and feedback came from fellow residents, particularly Carl and Jane Smith, urban historians from Northwestern University. In the years following, the experience of teaching international planning studios in China, Mexico, Morocco, India, and Argentina further enriched my thinking about this book. I should also acknowledge the Harvey Perloff Visiting Chair award from UCLA, and my appointment as a visiting Honorary Professor at the School of Geography and Planning at Cardiff University, which gave me additional opportunities to hone some of the ideas and propositions presented in this book. In 1999 I was appointed to the Irvine Chair of Urban and Regional Planning in my school at USC, and I owe a note of thanks for the funding available from the Irvine Foundation. More generally, I should note the sustained institutional support from the Sol Price School of Public Policy, and the university more generally. Finally, I must gratefully acknowledge a capstone grant from the Provost of USC that helped offset some of the costs of student help, royalty payments, reproduction of illustrations, related travel, and the like.

I thank my graduate students, at both the master's and doctoral levels, whose association influenced my thinking about this book. My role as a faculty advisor of Matthew Westfall's award-winning documentary *On Borrowed Land*[4] intensified my awareness of the plight of the urban poor in the developing world: their eviction, exclusion, and gentrification from the land previously settled by squatters. Stephen Horton, as a teaching assistant for the undergraduate course on "Third World Cities" offered useful insights, especially from southern Africa. Rafael Pizarro, now at American University of Sharjah, offered insights from Latin America, while helping teach the same class. Shin Lee of Cardiff University and HaeRan Shin of the Bartlett School of the University

College of London offered important critical insights. I should note that my thinking for this book was further enriched by interactions with many doctoral students as part of supervising their dissertations on the Global South. They are Mohamad Alnowaiser (1983), Ali Kiafar (1986), Nozizwe Makgaleme (1991), Yohansen Eid (1992), Chenxia Li (1992), Jeong Ho Moon (1994), Gazala Pirzada (1997), Kiran Lalloo (1998), Chungki Kwon (2001), James Steele (2002), Emel Ganapati (2005), Rafael Pizarro (2005), Hussam Salama (2010), Surajit Chakravarty (2010), Jia Lu (2013), Sangmin Kim (2014), Francesca Piazzoni (2019), and Huê-Tâm Jamme (2020). More recently, others helped develop early drafts of the manuscript. Ferdinand Lewis, now at University College Groningen, Meredith Drake-Reitan, now at USC, and Felicity Hwee-Hwa Chan, now at Nanyang Technological University Singapore, helped from the preparation of the initial prospectus to reading early drafts of various chapters. Hussam Salama of the German University in Cairo gave useful feedback on chapters 6 and 12. Amer Moustafa, formerly of the American University of Sharjah, has given me several entertaining and insightful tours of Dubai.

Many graduate students assisted in preparing the manuscript. Priscilla Appiah did a rather thorough edit of an initial draft. Grace Kim helped with substantive research and bibliographic references. Rachel Mills-Coyne provided timely assistance in preparing the final manuscript. Saumya Lathia helped out in finalizing the images and the manuscript more generally. I owe them all a big note of thanks. I am particularly grateful to Samirita Dabade who provided valuable help in finishing the charts and graphs, tracking down references, and finalizing the photographic images during the final stages of the manuscript preparation. All graphics that show the author as the source, are actually done by Samirita. These include figures 2.2, 2.3, 2.4, 2.5, 2.6, 5.6, 6.1, 6.13, 6.16, 8.1, and 13.16. I am very fortunate to have her help in the production of the final manuscript.

Among my colleagues, Martin Krieger and Vinayak Bharne read the entire manuscript and gave good advice. Hassan Radoine from Mohammed VI Polytechnic University in Morocco gave some constructive feedback on the chapter on Fès. Anastasia Loukaitou-Sideris from UCLA and Clara Irazábal from University of Missouri had also read some chapters and offered helpful feedback. I remain deeply grateful for their critical insight and encouragement.

I have benefited from the questions and comments I received from the faculty and students of many different universities in the US and abroad where I was invited to speak and where I presented many of the ideas. My early thoughts got vetted in these forums and matured from the feedback. These occasions included the Mike Wolfe Lecture at the University of Washington, the Himi Jammal Lecture at the University at

Buffalo, the Sapienza University of Rome, the Medina Forum at American University of Sharjah, the Hearst Lecture Series at California Polytechnic State University, Baumer Lecture at the Ohio State University, and lectures at Cornell University, University of Dortmund, Polytechnic University of Milan, Indian Institute of Management (Joka) in Kolkata, School of Planning and Geography at the Cardiff University, the Bartlett School of the University College London, Universidad Autónoma del Estado de México, Fudan University Department of International Economics in Shanghai, Tsinghua University School of Archtecture, Beijing University Department of Environment, Bandung Institute of Technology in Bandung and Universiti Malaya in Kuala Lumpur. Discussions following these lectures always gave me critical but constructive suggestions that helped shape the content of this book.

I remain indebted to many individuals—students, colleagues, and professionals—for their comments, critiques, and constructive feedback. I also acknowledge the useful critiques and caveats from the reviewers of the initial manuscript, although I may not have been able to incorporate all their suggestions without significantly altering the flow and cadence of the book. I thank Robert Gottlieb, series editor, Beth Clevenger, the acquisitions editor, and Anthony Zannino of the MIT Press for their help in finalizing the manuscript. I also thank Anne Healey and Deborah Grahame-Smith for their assistance during the copyediting and guidance during the production process.

Finally, this book wouldn't have been possible without the affection and encouragement from my dear wife, Frances, who read many versions of the manuscript including the copyedits and gave me critical but constructive advice throughout this process.

1 Looking Back from Vila Dunia

> Amid Roman sarcophagi, and genuine exotic plants, and remade baroque stairways, you pass Neptune's Pool, a fantasy Greco-Roman temple peopled with classical statues including (as the guidebook points out with fearless candor) the famous Venus rising from the water, sculpted in 1930 by the Italian sculptor Cassou, and you reach the Great House, a Spanish-Mexican–style cathedral with two towers (equipped with a thirty-six-bell carillon), whose portal frames an iron gate brought from a sixteenth-century Spanish convent, surmounted by a Gothic tympanum with the Virgin and Child. The floor of the vestibule encloses a mosaic found in Pompeii, there are Gobelins on the walls, the door into the Meeting Hall is by Sansovino, the great hall is fake Renaissance presented as Italo-French.
>
> —Umberto Eco, *Travels in Hyperreality*[1]

Vila Dunia (meaning "global village" in Bahasa Indonesia) is a privately developed gated community located in the Gegerkalong Hills, on the outskirts of the city of Bandung. The sales catalog offers four different styles of two-story detached townhouses mimicking the facades of nineteenth-century townhouses in London, Paris, Amsterdam, and Rome. In 2001, units were selling for 500,000,000 rupiahs (equivalent to about US $50,000 at the historical exchange rate).[2] As I marveled at this tableau of house forms, taking many pictures, my amused hosts suggested that if I found this new development intriguing, I must visit two gated communities being built on the fringes of greater Jakarta.[3]

I took their advice and visited these developments. Kota Wisata ("Tourist City") and its companion Legenda Wisata ("Tourist Legend") are much larger and more exuberant in design than Vila Dunia.[4] Legenda Wisata is stocked with enough phantasmagoria to qualify as a residential Disneyland. A huge Sphinx on the median divider guards the entrance, and the main avenue leading up to the sales office is lined with alabaster statuaries representing tableaux from various classical epics, including a scene from the *Ramayana*.

The neighborhoods are fashioned after images of faraway—mainly European—places and times. The ensemble also includes vignettes of traditional Kyoto and contemporary Florida, California, and Washington, DC. Indeed, these neighborhoods come as a complete package, with ambience, architectural icons, and landscapes associated with the chosen place and era. The neighborhood called Kyoto has houses with Japanese gardens furnished with small stands of bamboo, moss-covered rock sculptures, and carefully shaped bonsai plants.

Across the highway, the Kota Wisata complex is a variation on the same theme. The house types are more cosmopolitan and include models named after Beverly Hills and Miami Beach. The Kota Wisata sales office itself is a striking landmark, with colorful forms and icons reminiscent of *Alice in Wonderland* (figure 1.1). Inside there is a large model of the complex's town center, which is designed to resemble an archetypal nineteenth-century European town square.

Figure 1.1
Sales Office, Kota Wisata.
Source: Author, 2003, with permission from SINARMAS.

The master plan of Kota Wisata suggested that there was still a lot more to come, since the development was only about half finished at the time of my visit (figure 1.2). Completed neighborhoods are closer to the main entrance from the highway. Closest to the gated entrance are neighborhoods labeled Monaco, Madrid, and Denhaag, followed by Kyoto and a neighborhood dubbed "the Victorian." To the left of the main approach are areas called America and California. Nested inside California is a smaller area called Melrose. Farther up are the neighborhoods Paris, Florence, Amsterdam, and Vienna. The plan showed sites reserved for a future high school and a medical center beyond these neighborhoods. Almost directly opposite is the city center, where the developers proposed to build various recreational facilities: a Movie World, a country club called Palace of the Lost City, replicas of London's Tower Bridge (already built) and the Sydney Opera House, an International Village, and water features named the Blue Lagoon and Jurassic Lake.

Could it be that these ersatz vignettes of a global archaeology are merely a quest for a global identity? Is there an internal logic to this tableau of hyperreality? Recall that Kota Wisata means "tourist city"; we can imagine its neighborhoods and buildings as part of a simulated global tour, a collection of faraway places and historic times brought to one's own front door. It shouldn't come as a surprise that the slick sales pamphlets look more like travel brochures. Note also that some of these places are imaginary and fictional, and indeed an urban simulacrum that conflates the real and imagined, like in a Hollywood back lot (figure 1.3). The eclectic architecture of the shopping area is seemingly built in 7/8 scale—as in Main Street, Disneyland—to create a "Gulliver effect."[5] This Disneyscape makes sense in light of the fact that these developments are targeted for the weekend-home market of affluent Jakartans, especially those with young children.

Kota Wisata and Legenda Wisata are not the only examples of such urban imaginaria in the Global South.[6] Similar gated communities are cropping up throughout the developing world, typically at the edges of sprawling metropolises. From Shanghai to Mumbai, these images of fantasy from around the globe are being built for the cosmopolitan nouveau riche of the developing world, such as the "overseas Chinese" or the "NRIs" (Non-Resident Indians). Geographer Anthony King notes the deep irony in the symbolism of many of these global images that represent "Constructed Dream Cultures of (or for) the NRI" with names like "Bel Air, La Hacienda, Villa Del Mar, Belvedere, Riviera, Manhattan, as well as a rich sprinkling of Anglicized pseudo-aristocratic names—Burlington, Somerville, Sinclair."[7] In a clearing of dense forest in Powai, an upscale neighborhood on the outskirts of Greater Mumbai, incongruously stands Hiranandani Gardens, a new development of high-rise residential towers mimicking classical colonial architecture (see figure 1.4). Salah El-Shakhs, a development planner, writes about

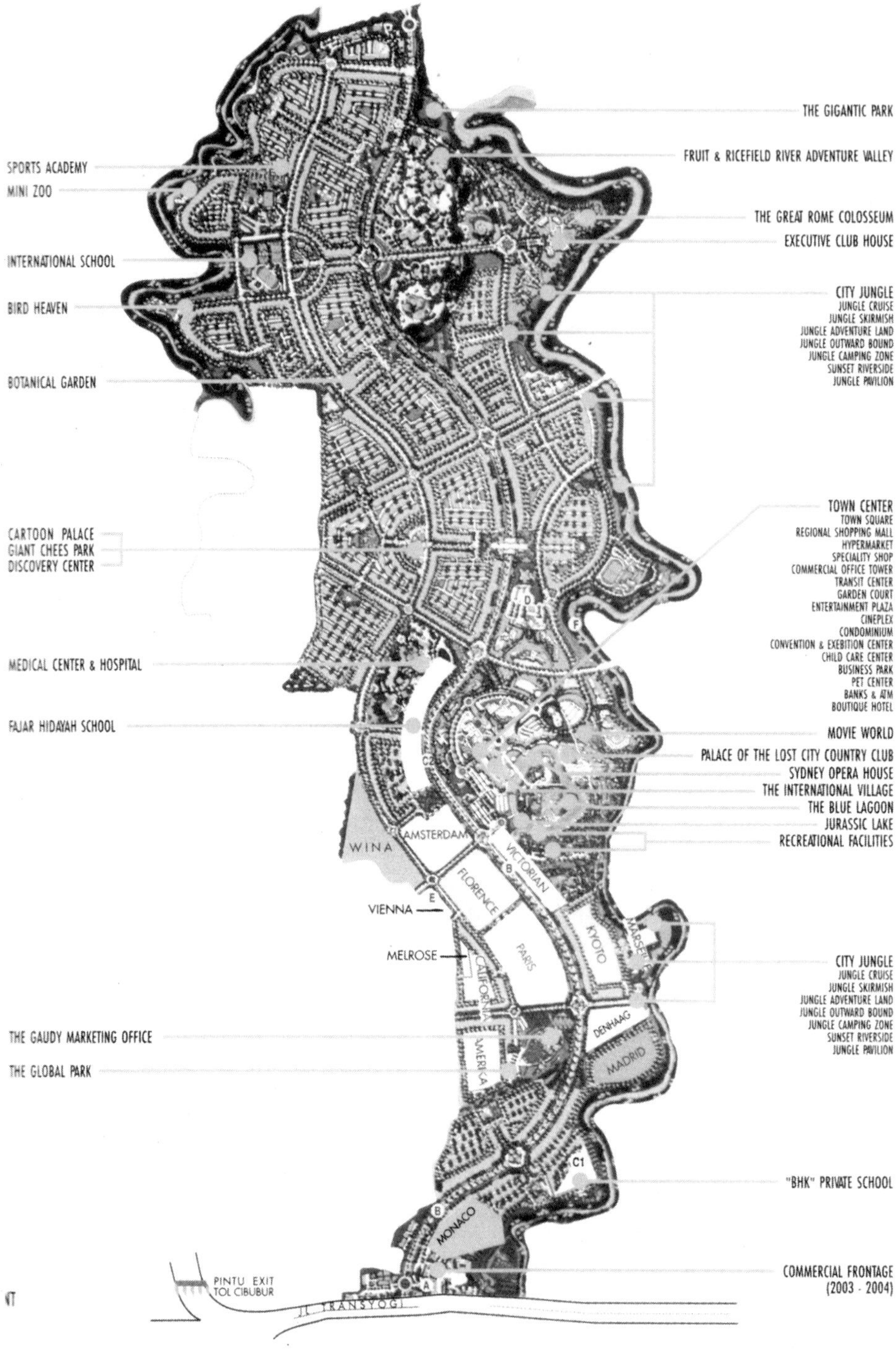

Figure 1.2

Master plan of Kota Wisata.

Source: Author, 2003, with permission from SINARMAS.

Figure 1.3
The town center or a Hollywood backlot? Legenda Wisata.
Source: Author, 2003, with permission from SINARMAS.

similar developments in Cairo: expensive residential suburbs complete with golf courses and country clubs in the middle of the desert, with names such as Dreamland, Greenland, and Beverly Hills.[8] A recent issue of *The Economist* included a picture of what it called "Turkey's oddest ghost town"—the Burj al Babas housing development in northern Turkey. It consists of 700 identical French châteaus with ancillary retail and community spaces, all sitting empty because the developer, the Sarot Group, has gone bankrupt.[9] In Indonesia there are Southern California–inspired developments that urban planners Robert Cowherd and Eric Heikkila refer to as "Orange County, Java."[10]

Other ironies and incongruities abound. The Emirate of Dubai is transforming its fragile desert landscape into housing complexes and shopping malls designed with a global theme but lacking an endogenous urbanism. These developments include offshore artificial islands shaped like giant palm trees, in which the fronds are linear strips of luxury housing.[11] In erstwhile communist Beijing in 2000, Starbucks Coffee opened

Figure 1.4
The Hiranandani project in Powai, on the outskirts of Greater Mumbai, is designed in the classical colonial style.
Source: Author, 2007.

a store inside the Forbidden City, the historic palace complex of the Ming dynasty (see figure 1.5), although it was discontinued after a few years. These absurdities of hyperreality seem to proliferate throughout the Global South. In 2015 a scale replica of the London landmark Big Ben, called "Kolkata Time" (figure 1.6.), showed up in the middle of a traffic rotary in Kolkata on the access road to Lake Town, a residential district, off a major arterial to the airport.

In Yamoussoukro, the capital of Ivory Coast, a huge church—a replica of St. Peter's Basilica in Vatican City—stands incongruently in an empty and poor rural landscape (see figure 1.7). Considered the world's largest church by some measures, the basilica was constructed in the 1980s to memorialize President Félix Houphouët-Boigny at his birthplace, Yamoussoukro, which he designated the capital in 1983. At an estimated cost of up to $600 million, the basilica cost almost one-twelfth of country's 1985 GDP.

Figure 1.5
Starbucks Coffee in the Forbidden City, Beijing (closed in 2007).
Source: Courtesy of Ajay Agarwal, 2005.

The pace and scale of development constitute another striking feature of this new urban transition. Take contemporary Shanghai, for example. In a single decade Shanghai has added an entire new city to itself, called Pudong (meaning "east of the river"), on the low-lying agricultural land east of the Huangpu River. The area now includes new housing, industrial parks, a brand new international airport, and a shiny new downtown—the Lujiazui Financial and Trade Zone. At the same time, the original city—called Puxi, or "west of the river"—is a palimpsest of indigenous, colonial, and socialist legacies, now expanded horizontally and vertically to include over 3,000 high-rise buildings (20 stories or higher), a new 16-line subway network 705 kilometers in length, several new bridges across the river, a new system of ring roads and freeways, and a maglev train (the first in the world) that connects the new airport to a local destination within Pudong. While Rome might not have been built in a day, it seems that Pudong and much of modern Shanghai certainly was.

Figure 1.6
"Kolkata Time," Kolkata.
Source: Courtesy of Surajit Chakravarty, 2019.

But Shanghai has not stopped there. To accommodate its metropolitan expansion, it launched a plan dubbed "One City, Nine Towns" in 2001 and began building satellite towns in the images of iconic European cities.[12] Architects and planners from the UK, France, Italy, Germany, Sweden, Netherlands, and the like were invited to design these towns as ersatz neighborhoods of cities such as London, Paris, Rome, Stockholm, and Amsterdam, with contemporary as well as iconic features of Western urbanism and lifestyle.

Figure 1.7
The Basilica of Our Lady of Peace in Yamoussoukro, Ivory Coast.
Source: L. Romano (De Agostini Picture Library). By permission of Getty Images.

The obsession with mimicry in city design is seemingly not limited to provincial and local authorities.[13] Recently the Chinese global technology giant Huawei (which reported 2018 revenue of $105 billion) opened a sprawling 2,700-acre campus in Dongguan. The campus includes twelve replicas of different European towns connected by tram lines.[14]

While the pace and scale of Shanghai's transformation may be unprecedented in urban history, other megacities in China, and indeed in other parts of the developing world, are also undergoing spectacular metamorphoses.[15] These changes may represent capital accumulation, modernity, prosperity, mass consumerism, and technological renaissance, but the subtext of the transformation comprises several narratives.

Narratives of Development

One of these narratives has to with the question of identity and authenticity. Let us consider the Indonesian example. The symbols of globalism that are expressed in such names as "Vila Dunia," as well as in the Disneyland-like tableaux of replicated cityscapes, suggest a rejection or absence of endogenous sources of modern expression. At best it implies a reluctance or inability to explore possibilities within Indonesia's traditional forms and symbols. It is also possible that this "continental" design is a marketing strategy, a sales gimmick conjured by developers and architects to appeal to the emerging cosmopolitan preferences and tastes of the local nouveau riche.[16] When asked about this choice, the young developer of Kota Wisata and Legenda Wisata responded that these Western prototypes are established paradigms of modern living in the West, and that they seem to work.[17] His response seemed to imply that a good copy is better than a bad original, as the saying goes. Nevertheless, the question begged here is whether these developments preempt authentic expressions of modernity that remain latent, stifled, or confused in a time of transition. Are the inexorable forces of globalization obviating city design that is endogenous, authentic, and distinctive?

One may also wonder whether the absence of autonomous faces and images of development and modernity is a structural problem in the developing world. There might be two positions on this point. The first would be a Kiplingesque assertion that links this structural inability to the inherent inferiority of the cultures of the developing world, with their dark-skin origin and genetic makeup. Today few will make such prejudiced claims openly, although such hypotheses may lurk in some Western minds. Scholars such as anthropologist Jared Diamond and development economists Andrew Mellinger, Jeffrey Sachs, and John Gallup have attributed the handicap to the larger geographical circumstances of these countries.[18] The second position, likely to be presented by some Third World scholars, is that if there is such a structural deficiency, it is the outcome of a deliberate process of "development of underdevelopment," an inexorable outcome of decades and centuries of colonial exploitation and hegemony, as Latin American political theorist Andre Gunder Frank argued.[19]

A complementary view is offered by literary theorist Edward Said's critique of the legacy of Orientalism in representations of the non-Western world. Contemporary scholarship in postcolonial and subaltern studies, inspired by Said's work, would support the position that vestiges of Orientalism still dominate the images of development as pursued in both theory and practice. One might argue also that stereotypes expressed by the terms "underdeveloped," "backward," and "traditional," commonly used to describe developing countries, are an integral part of this legacy. These aphorisms have continued to be the presumptive basis of development discourse and indeed have become institutionalized in contemporary development theories and practices.[20] Such abstractions as "bell curves" of development,[21] stages of development,[22] and modernization as the enactment of values[23] are cases in point. Recently, physical transformations of the cities and countryside in "emerging-market" economies have been shaped by not only Western images but also Western purveyors of development, design, engineering, and planning. Even where local actors are involved, their imagination is limited to the Western palette of options.

A second and related narrative of the images of development has to do with a pervasive sense of loss of place, community, tradition, and cultural continuity that permeates contemporary writings on urbanism and urban design. This is of course not unique to the developing world; it is a global phenomenon. Critical writings on contemporary urban development in the West have eminently articulated this loss, although much of it has to do with the banality of new developments and urban sprawl.[24]

The third narrative concerning the images of development has to do with the increased inequality, polarization, and segregation of urban populations in space and, in a sense, time. Although segregation and inequality remain a worldwide urban pattern, reflecting in part a structural feature of the global economic order,[25] inequality in the developing world remains much more pernicious and prevalent because of the legacies of the colonial past and enduring differences in religion, ideology, ethnicity, gender, and culture. No doubt integration with the global economy has exacerbated the inequality effect inherent in capitalism, as the economist Thomas Piketty[26] has argued. Differences are compounded further by extreme poverty and, in some instances, by a total absence of democratic rights and civil society.

Consequently, city authorities now have to deal with a new generation of slums and squatters, even in economies that are considered to be the "emerging markets." The erstwhile egalitarian China, while experiencing spectacular growth in recent decades, is now one of the most unequal countries, with a Gini coefficient approaching 50, a 15-point increase since 1990.[27] While this inequality is not manifested in visible slums and squatter settlements, save from some itinerant homeless sleeping in pedestrian passages and tunnels, it has resulted in huge informal housing market. According to urban planner Annette Kim, approximately one million people live in bomb shelters and basements in Beijing in conditions of extreme overcrowding.[28] In Brazil scholars have reported new growth in favela population and residential segregation,[29] which, interestingly, has been occurring without significant rural-urban migration, the primary cause for the earlier emergence of favelas.[30]

The fourth narrative of development images concerns the sense of uneasiness about the sustainability of the scale and the pace, if not the inexorability, of such urban transformations. According to the 2017 UN Population Division report, the world population is expected to reach between 9.4 and 10.2 billion by the middle of this century, and a majority of that population—more than 5 billion—will be living in cities. In fact, the urban population worldwide will double in that period.[31] Furthermore, as the developing nations grow more prosperous and as their citizens become eager participants in a global consumer culture, the "ecological footprints"[32] of cities will no doubt expand at an unprecedented rate. As biologist Paul Ehrlich has pointed out, the lifetime ecological pressure of a child born in Nepal is typically one-sixth of that of her counterpart living in a suburb of San Francisco.[33] As this disparity decreases due to increasing levels of mass consumption, and the ecological pressures of development intensify, we will increasingly face such questions as the following: Will there be enough water to sustain such urban growth? Will there be enough energy to sustain urban lifestyles and emerging consumer societies? Will these countries be able to finance the infrastructure and urban services necessary to support their population growth? What might this level of consumption do to global warming or environmental pollution? Do we have any idea as to how, or more importantly, where to dispose of the mountains and rivers of waste these cities would inevitably generate?[34] Do we have enough habitable space for the future residents of these cities, or will urban sprawl continue to consume valuable agricultural land and other natural resources? These are, to be sure, troubling questions. Responses often tend to be passionately polarized between doomsday scenarios and technological fixes.[35] Real answers, meanwhile, remain elusive.

Finally, the narrative of globalization in the images of development introduces new debates about continuity and change, thanks to innovations in information and communication technologies and the rise of the network society.[36] The idea of a global marketplace and a global economic order continues to pervade economic thinking on development.[37] Accordingly, the technical order of market and capitalism may have trumped the moral order of development for some time.[38] The attendant images of development have flourished without much concern for development's environmental or human consequences. One may suspect that the imperative of a moral order is beyond the ken of the technical order mindset. Others might assert that some scenarios for ideal economic development subsume such imperatives. Accordingly, the technical order conjoins the moral order with the belief in an ideal human condition defined in terms of democracy, modernity, market liberalism, and institutional rationality, which remain the basic tenets of the liberal Western project of development and modernization. Authenticity and identity in the expressions of new urban development, and the sense of loss associated with the disappearance of traditional place and community, are not themes that are likely to be debated in the literature on development economics and policy. Yet inequality and polarization are certainly intrinsic to this literature. So has been the concept of sustainability, thanks to the recently raised international institutional conscience.[39]

Not all development thinking is necessarily economistic. Cultural, institutional, political, and social perspectives on development encompass some of the larger concerns about its human consequences, encouraging us to think about alternative images of development.

Accordingly, authenticity and identity; place and community; inequality and segregation; growth and sustainability; and localism versus globalism, climate change, and global warming are some of the central themes of the dialectic that defines the contemporary discourse on development and change. Moreover, the intellectual locus of these issues quite conspicuously runs through the collective domains of urban planning and design and the images associated with development. All of these themes involve urban space—the ways in which it is produced, organized, differentiated, and consumed.[40]

The practice of urban planning and design obviously plays an important role in the production, organization, and differentiation of urban form. We find today considerable disagreement among planning academics and practitioners about how aggressive a role planners might or should play in shaping the production of urban form.[41] Many seem to believe that planning's days of visionary heroism are indeed over and that planners must simply follow the imperatives of either the market or politics.[42] I demur to this diminished role of the planner and to the image of the planner as antihero. Here I take the position that not only do planners and designers have an imperative to be normative today, but also their normative views must address the sustainability and human consequences of development. Thus the normative, even visionary, position that I am arguing is fundamentally different from the Platonic approach[43] previously rejected by social scientists as deterministic and megalomaniacal. Unlike such romantic and arbitrary approaches, the normative position should be grounded in critical perspectives on globalization and an understanding of how the built environment and the "culture of cities"[44] are related to the development and underdevelopment of nations.

Looking Back from Vila Dunia: Three Arguments

One of the difficulties of writing about the contemporary urban transformation in the developing world is that it is changing at an ever-increasing pace. It is almost impossible to get a fix on this moving target. Yet in a sense the old French proverb seems to hold: *Plus ça change, plus c'est la même chose* (the more things change, the more they remain the same). Thus the legacy of hunger, disease, famine, natural disaster, poverty, and the gap between the haves and have-nots still endure on a global scale amid the shiny and glittering images of prosperity and development. This paradox of stasis and flux sets the stage for this inquiry. What follows, then, are three essential and interrelated arguments that define the approach and the perspectives presented in this book.

The first argument is that the Western predilections for the built environment—its spatial organization, three-dimensional form, and urbanism—have always set the benchmark for judging the state of development (or underdevelopment). In common parlance and media coverage, development is associated with shiny office towers, "intercontinental" hotels, shopping malls, single-family detached homes, freeways, mass transit systems, and the like. But it is more than that. It is the urbanism of modernity, industrialization, and mass consumption—the landscape of a market economy characterized by efficiency, order, and cleanliness. In contrast, underdevelopment is associated with traditional settlements, slums and squatter settlements, narrow streets with animal- or people-powered vehicles, and the absence of piped water and adequate sanitation. According to Western standards, these represent an urbanism that is chaotic, uncertain, provisional, and unclean. Western images of the built environment remain implicit in national development policies in the developing world. For example, in the 1980s the Saudi government moved residents from indigenous settlements of Unayzah to modern planned communities because these indigenous settlements, with their adobe construction and narrow lanes, were icons of a backward, rural society, inconsistent with the kingdom's self-image of prosperity and modernity.[45]

To be sure, the built environment mirrors many of the contradictions of development driven by Western images. Economic growth has also brought income disparity, segregation, pollution, traffic congestion, crime, and loss of familiar places, provoking such questions as these: Must economic development lead to income inequality and class segregation? Is it inevitable that development will always result in decline of the public realm, loss of a sense of community and place, privatization of public life, a growing deficit in parks and open spaces, unequal access to public services, and the like? Does development necessarily mean relinquishing the past, cultural heritage, and historic urban form? What are the environmental costs of urban growth? Is the devastation of nature and ecosystems inevitable? What about the health and livability costs? How can developing cities be efficient in resource utilization while sustaining future growth? These issues frame the substantive themes pursued in this book.

The second argument is about the notion of "image" as a vision for what development might or should accomplish. In ancient times, cosmic and spiritual models of the ideal city guided the layout and ordering of urban space.[46] Today secular notions of modernity, economic rationality, accumulation of capital, and global consumerism have driven the design and development of the new urban space in much the same way that ancient images shaped premodern city form. We need to better understand the secular challenges of the contemporary images of development, and their ideological roots and imperatives.

As the urban outcome of economic development begins to look like built environments of the Global North—with suburban sprawl, gated communities, freeways, and shopping malls—concerns abound regarding questions of livability, social justice, and sustainability. This outcome is seen as an inexorable effect of growing consumerism, prosperity, and globalization. But the point often missed is that this new landscape is also the result of a larger project of development and modernization that began two centuries ago, and mainly in the images of Western capitalism, secular democracy, and market liberalism. While the communist antithesis challenged capitalism for a while, it proved to be only a provisional dialectic.[47] Market liberalism and capitalism dominate development thinking today. Yet the institutions of secular democracy still remain a difficult and distant target in many parts of the developing world.

The third argument concerns the causes of the developing world's dearth of endogenous expressions of modernity—what philosopher Charles Taylor called "alternative modernities."[48] What is common in developing landscapes is either a mimesis of the Western urban form and icons in an ersatz Disneyland-like setting of mass consumption, or a collection of expensive signature architecture produced by internationally renowned architects commissioned by multinational corporate clients.[49] Some of this ensemble comes with creative flourishes, and even with some aesthetic merit. But by and large it remains what architect Michael Sorkin refers to as "variations on a theme park."[50] In either case, these spaces are a non sequitur compared to the "thick" cultural narratives of the indigenous that evolved over many centuries.[51] Of course, globalization is the usual suspect, but the process had begun much earlier than commonly assumed. This new urban transformation is part and parcel of a script written by the Western project of modernization that began during the colonial hegemony of the late nineteenth century.

In this third argument about normative images of development, Said's critique of Orientalism is apropos. Like the work of Orientalists, images of development grew out of the Western project of modernization and development. The relevant academic works have also supported and promoted the basic tenets of Western liberal and secular democracy as the model of modern institution-building and development. The process has been further aided and abetted by the grants and loan policies of international agencies such as the United States Agency for International Development (USAID), the International Monetary Fund (IMF), and the World Bank, and reflected in their own images of development. The script for contemporary urban transition and development is a part of the larger narrative of development and modernization. The ideology of the West in technical assistance has occasionally led to innovation with local expertise, but only under exceptional circumstances.[52] There are no endogenous or alternative models of development—save perhaps the orthodox Islamic theocratic tendencies and the communist mode of production, now expired.

Notes on the Methodological Approach

In his preface to what is perhaps the most authoritative study of contemporaneous India, AbūRaihān Muhammad ibn Ahmad al-Bīrūnī, the famous Islamic scholar of the Middle Ages who is also known simply as Alberuni, spoke of the difference between hearsay and the account of the eyewitness. As far as historical authenticity goes regarding a particular event in time, Alberuni wrote, "hearsay does not equal eyewitness" but he argued, making a case for his own methodology, hearsay would be preferable to the eyewitness,

> ... for the object of eye-witness can only be *actual* momentary existence, whilst hearsay comprehends alike the present, the past, and the future, so as to apply in a certain sense both to that which *is* and to that which is *not* (i.e. which either has ceased to exist or has not yet come into existence). Written tradition is one of the species of hearsay—we might almost say, the most preferable. How could we know the history of nations but for the everlasting monuments of the pen?[53]

Although Alberuni was known to be a strong believer in objectivity and truth, his statement presaged the current tension between the positivist Chicago School tradition of urban studies and the more postmodern approach to understanding urban phenomena (as claimed by the incipient Los Angeles school), in which interpretation and narratives take precedence over data analysis and model building.[54] The synoptic thinking I am advocating for designers and planners is to be grounded in this hearsay approach, because very little of the effects of globalization on urban form—especially along the dimensions I have suggested—can be supported by the "eyewitness" metaphor.

So, where does one begin? In other words, which time period, which narrative, or which historiography must we focus on in order to understand the design challenges for the Global South? The concept of globalization has considerable currency these days, both in academic fields and in contemporary media. While some academic fields link the era of globalization to postmodernity and postcolonial development, more commonly the literature seems to associate itself with the emergent global economic order and the flourishing of information and communication technologies. For the purposes of this endeavor I propose that globalization is not something that began near the end of the previous century with the "Thatcho-Reaganite" policies of the 1980s, or with the market liberalism and structural reform brought about by the World Bank in the 1990s. Indeed, one could argue that, to the extent that the process of globalization involves intercontinental flows of capital, culture, people, and information,[55] it actually began many centuries ago (going back to perhaps the era of Imperial Rome or even post-Hellenic Greece, and much later involving the Mauryas, the Gandharas, and the Mongols in Asia and the Ottomans in Europe and Africa) and has undergone several phases.

We do not need to begin that far back to trace the contemporary effects and consequences of globalization on urban form and space. It will suffice to note that the history of globalization has two parts: the conquests and dynasties of the old world and the discovery of the new world and subsequent mercantile trade and formal colonization by the European countries. This book involves the second phase only. The colonial era of globalization is particularly relevant because the colonial rule dictated the order of some of the cities and influenced the potential of development of other cities. One could also argue that the history of the colonial era is significantly different from the earlier phase of globalization because it had a distinct political economy that was shaped by the rise of capitalism, markets, and property rights; the Industrial Revolution; and ultimately the development of modern institutions of governance. For our purposes it will suffice to define the history of globalization according to the time frame—taking 1600 onward as the beginning of early colonization established by geographer Alan Thomas and his colleagues in their comprehensive and authoritative history of the "Third World."[56]

The next challenge is how to delimit the corpus of relevant literature that provides the intellectual antecedents of this proposed inquiry. There is a growing industry of globalization literature, but all of it is quite contemporary and eclectic and thus may not be an appropriate starting point for an argument based in the history of development, although I will dip into that pool of literature from time to time. I will begin my major argument with two very distinct bodies of literature. One has to do with the concept of development, the other with the topic of urban form and design.

The first section of the book will be devoted to reviewing academic and intellectual contributions to our understanding of the relationship between development and urban form. I will begin by reviewing theories of development and their implications for understanding the production of urban space and form. Conversely, I will consider the literature on urban form in order to explore whether concepts of development may help us understand transformations in urban form and responses in city design.

There is a strong disciplinary divide here. The development literature represents the works of social scientists, mainly economists, but also political scientists, sociologists, geographers, anthropologists, and academics from such professional disciplines as planning, public policy, public administration, and international relations. Within that literature are occasional (though growing) sprinklings of scholarship from the humanities, but their influence is limited. The urban form literature, meanwhile, has evolved within the allied design disciplines—architecture, planning, and landscape architecture—with some help from urban historians, cultural geographers, and anthropologists. However, the divide between the two literatures remains deep and wide.

There is another interesting disjunction between these two bodies of literature. While the development literature has unavoidably, but not exclusively, focused on developing countries with contributions from scholars of the developing world, the urban form literature is heavily weighted toward the developed, and primarily Western, countries and is based mainly on the writings of Western scholars. Scholarly materials written in such non-Western languages as Chinese, Farsi, Arabic, Korean, and Bahasa Indonesia are rarely translated and remain largely inaccessible to the Western audience. Much of the literature in Spanish and Portuguese from Latin American countries also remains outside the orbit of the Anglo-American axis of urban discourse. I have made a conscious effort to include, as much as possible, materials from non-Western scholars as well as translated materials from non-English sources.

In *Orientalism*, his incisive critique of the Orientalists' work, Said pointed out the one-sided nature of this scholarship.[57] He discussed scholars and practitioners' complete unawareness about the thoughts and knowledge of the very cultures and people they were representing—including the views those people held regarding the colonial interlopers. Said revealed how self-serving, albeit arguably unwitting, the Orientalists were in supporting and sustaining colonialist political aims. In a subsequent book, *Culture and Imperialism*, Said further expanded the scope of his critique to include the entire developing world, especially those regions of the world under extended periods of colonial rule and imperialism.[58] These works of Said have had a significant impact on critical studies and have shaped postcolonialist studies in a major way. Although the target of Said's critique did not include any significant work of urban historians, we should be mindful of his critique when we consider well-known Western scholarly works on the cities of the developing world.

Take for example the term "Islamic City," which is commonly used to refer to cities in predominantly Muslim cultures and is currently under close scrutiny from urban scholars.[59] The argument here is that in this construction of cities of the Muslim world as "Islamic," there is an implication that the cities were an artifact of spiritual doctrines, and that because of this fact they ignore secular aspects of Muslim culture. Furthermore, since the overall urban form of most of these cities is inherently medieval, with the exception of the mosques and the madrasas (the two most important religious elements), the urban form of the so-called Islamic cities is undistinguishable from that of the walled cities of medieval Europe, or that of the non-Muslim dynasties of the Indian subcontinent. Many of these scholars of Muslim countries also worry that in a climate of fundamentalist zeal, the notion of "Islamic City" may legitimize political aims and thus serve the purpose of religious zealots in power.

I will revisit the Saidian critique in depth throughout the book because it promises a platform to integrate the literature of development—especially that concerning political economy—with the literature on urban form. I will present the criticisms of Said's work as well. More importantly, I see Said's work as a counterpoint to the more critical and disparaging views of the developing world as captured by Rudyard Kipling or his contemporary counterpart, V. S. Naipaul, a sardonic critic of the Global South.[60]

Organization of the Book

The materials presented in the forthcoming chapters are organized in three sections, each containing three to four chapters. The first section is devoted to reviewing academic and intellectual contributions to our understanding of the relationship between development and urban form. This section reviews theories of development and implications of development for urban space and form. The literature on urban form may help us understand how development transforms urban form. Arguments in this section attempt to bridge the disciplinary divide between development and urban form and propose a framework for conceptual integration of the effects of development on urbanism and urban form.

The second section of the book is mainly retrospective, beginning with the state of cities of the Global South at the time of colonial invasion and expansion. This discussion includes an argument establishing the parity of these cities' urban form with that of their contemporaneous Western counterparts. One of the chapters is devoted to parallel urban forms and their economic and technological determinants, and the developmental images that have historically shaped some of those urban outcomes. One chapter in this section is devoted to case studies of colonial urban development and the structural distortions brought about through both the distribution of urban systems and the internal organization of cities. This includes the colonial planning and design traditions that were shaped by nostalgic adaptations of the ideal form of the home countries. These chapters also discuss the beginning of the subaltern identity of indigenous urban space and how the institutions of the modern colonial state shaped the contemporaneous images of development.

The third section of the book focuses on the status of city design and development in the postcolonial era. One chapter is devoted to the legacy of new towns and the different visions of modernity and rationality that shaped many of these cities. Another chapter examines alternative paradigms of development in including the legacy of communism in shaping postcolonial cities. Some of these chapters focus on the segregation and dualism, poverty and inequality, exacerbated by the imperatives of the global economic order; they also discuss the recent growth of urban sprawl, shopping malls, and the ersatz entertainment or amusement complexes of the new prosperity. The chapter titled "The Place of Medina" considers the challenges of preserving traditional and historic urban places such as the medinas of the Middle East and the *hutongs* of China, and the form and prospect of their future survival. Still another chapter focuses on large-scale urban developments in prospering economies and implications of the breakneck pace of such development for sustainability and cultural continuity. These chapters expound further upon the central argument that Third World city design is being shaped by "images of development" that are imposed by a global economic order, and that such design is thus enabling a subaltern relationship with the indigenous. The final chapter is devoted to the possibilities of images of endogenous modernities and how—and under what circumstances—such outcomes can be obtained.

I Development and Urbanism

2 The Fable of Bell Curves

> It is very likely that, in the middle of the eighteenth century, the average standard of living in Europe was a little bit lower than that of the rest of the world. This is due to the high level achieved by the Chinese millennium, and the relative importance of that country in the rest of the world (some 36 percent). Till the years 1815–20, the impact of the industrial revolution was negligible for what would later become the developed world. There was still a parity of average income levels between the two regions, since at its outset the industrial revolution concerned only a small fringe of the future developed countries, and growth was very slow in the beginning.
>
> —Paul Bairoch, "The Main Trends in National Economic Disparities since the Industrial Revolution"[1]

Throughout human history, the meaning of development—whether manifested in ideal settlement forms or in some abstract shared concept of a good society—has always been driven by aspirations for a higher state of being. In contemporary times, the seemingly abstract concept of development as a process is often guided by symbolic representations of that process—images of development, as it were—reflecting a belief in universal truth and norms.

The concept of image has both positive and normative connotations within the context of development. For example, an image as a picture, a reflection, or even a mental map[2] is a positive concept even though there are different degrees of verisimilitude in their content.[3] In the normative sense, images may capture imaginations, ideals, dreams, and visions. They may be socially constructed, spiritually grounded, or advanced by entrepreneurs of nation building. In the development literature, however, one encounters the word "model" more often than the word "image," because a model is a positive concept but one that suggests greater empirical legitimacy. However, what is constructed as a model often comes to be viewed as the Holy Grail, and as a result the positive becomes normative.

Notions of Development

The most common image of development is one of growth and change, implying evolution, movement, transition, and progress. Conversely, the most common image of the absence of development is one of reflux, retardation, and stagnation. What is not made explicit is that development is a turbulent process that implies uncertainty, disruption, and discontinuity—"a chain of disequilibria," as development economist Albert Hirschman famously noted.[4]

But does development also imply transcendence? Some theories of development seem to imply that there is an ultimate stage of transcendence, like in the Maslovian hierarchy of needs.[5] Thus, in the stage theory of development proposed by economist Walt Rostow, for example, we see explicit reference to a transcendent level—that of mass consumerism—which nations must aspire to achieve.[6]

Development theorists today would emphasize the concept of development as a vector, where direction and magnitude of progress from an initial state are more important than a specific target or vision. An image of steady progress may be more relevant than one aimed at transcendence. In the early years of the Chinese communist development, large inspirational posters that were hung in brigade headquarters, in workers' canteens, and on city walls showed workers with their heads high and gazes fixed on the horizon (see figure 2.1). As anthropologist Elizabeth Croll points out, the message of these images was this: Don't look at what is immediately in front of you; always look toward the far horizon, toward the bright future that lies ahead, because metaphorically the foreground—the immediate experience—was pretty bleak and depressing, with little to inspire one's confidence in the future.[7] The irony of this visual rhetoric, of course, is that with every forward step the horizon recedes, like a mirage. The Maoist vision soon faded,[8] as it did not promise a transcendental state by Western capitalist standards, but only an improvement in living standards that would lift workers out of the immediate experience of poverty. It promised equality, if only equality of poverty, as some detractors suggested.

Halfway into the last century it became a common practice to refer to the Western industrialized nations as "developed," as though they had all matriculated to a particular plateau yet to be reached by the "underdeveloped" countries of the Third World. In recent years, it has become a more polite practice to refer to developing countries as "less developed countries" (or LDCs) and to developed countries as "more developed countries" (or MDCs). The larger and growing economies of the LDCs are now called "emerging markets." These new terms also suggest a more nuanced appreciation of

Figure 2.1
"March bravely forward along the glorious road of Chairman Mao's May 7th directive." Images of development—the communist era. May 1971.
Source: By permission of the University of Westminster Archive.

development as a continuum rather than a set of discrete phases.[9] This shift in perspective recognizes several facts about development.

First, development may not necessarily mean transcendence or matriculation from one state of being (underdeveloped) to another (developed). We may instead think of development as a continuum that may include many different paths and phases.

Second, the term "underdeveloped" is not only pejorative but also naive as many countries so labeled boast a rich history of culture and civilization that predates many Western countries that are considered "developed" today. Furthermore, such labels implicitly devalue culture and understate the possibilities for endogenous images and paths of development.[10]

Third, the shift in language recognizes that many previously poor nations have become quite prosperous and successful in recent years. These countries, ranging from the "four tigers of Asia" (Hong Kong, Singapore, South Korea, and Taiwan) to the "emerging markets" countries (which include China, India, and Indonesia), can hardly be called underdeveloped today. The latter are the subject of a weekly report on indicators by *The Economist.* Similarly, the BRIC rate of growth (the average growth rate of the BRIC countries, Brazil, Russia, India, and China) has become a conventional benchmark of economic growth worldwide.

Fourth, there is a growing recognition that all may not be well in the Western industrialized nations. Critics of the West may argue that none of the Western industrialized nations have achieved a stable state of development, even in strictly economic development terms, and there are serious concerns in many Western countries about worsening income inequality, a shrinking middle class, deteriorating environmental quality, a perceived decline in ethical and moral values, and a sense of widespread social maladies and malaise. There are frequent reports in the media about how the West is "sliding toward the Third World," how New York is beginning to look like Calcutta (Kolkata),[11] or how Los Angeles has become the "Capital of the Third World."[12]

Fifth, even in terms of objective measures, some parts of the developing world are doing better than certain social groups within the developed world. For example, as economist Amartya Sen points out, the life expectancy of the people of Kerala, a progressive province of India, a LDC, is higher than that of the African American population in the United States, an MDC.[13]

Sixth, even if we are convinced that there are some policy benefits to be gained from monitoring the progress of countries by some standard of development, the question of measurement persists. There was a time when GNP per capita (in dollar equivalent) was the sole indicator of development; but the threshold between more developed and less developed was arbitrary. The dollar measure did not take into account the purchasing power of local currencies, nor did the accounting of GNIs include domestic- or informal-sector activities, which comprised a sizable portion of productive economic activities in developing countries.[14] Further, such a narrow indicator ignored whether a country was ruled by a despot or had guaranteed basic human rights. Nor did it capture whether countries had huge income disparities, whether they tolerated the oppression of women and inequality in educational opportunities, or whether the poor had access to basic shelter and services. True, we are getting smarter about these measures as they become more complex, sensitive, and comprehensive: GNI per capita is now modified by purchasing power parity (PPP) of local currencies; there is growing demand for a "green" GDP (i.e., one that takes into account the cost of natural resources in the accounting of GDP); and the United Nations Development Programme (UNDP) now tracks human development indicators with the Human Development Index (HDI). It also has a gender-based development index (Gender Empowerment Measure, or GEM), and a search for a sustainable development index is underway. Yet fundamental misgivings remain about whether any of these metrics can objectively measure development and thereby judge a country without prejudice.

Finally, even in strictly materialistic terms, there are growing misgivings about judging development solely by the Western standards of consumer society, if that development is not sustainable in regards to social equity, the interests of future generations, environmental protection, continuity of cultural heritage, and the like. Perhaps under a more optimistic scenario, nations will redefine and renegotiate their own ideal states. Active societies will seek and set new and higher standards of collective achievements, and perhaps even the criteria for judging progress itself will inexorably change or will be subject to challenge. Technological advances will also continue to set the bar higher. Nations will be judged not by the Nietzschean criterion of the progress of the leading edge but rather by the corresponding mobility of their trailing edge.

While developing countries may have to be increasingly circumspect about using Western societies as their role model, contemporary discourse on development still revolves around two parallel themes of Western origin: economic progress and modernization. Embedded in these themes are the notions of industrialization, urbanization, Westernization, and globalization. Of the two themes, economic progress has been the more dominant thus far and has profoundly shaped our images of development. Development has usually meant economic development, and even today this view continues to influence the contemporary discourse in planning and public policy.

Ideas and Images of Economic Development

In his comprehensive survey of the literature, economist Heinz Wolfgang Arndt has suggested that the notion of economic development is a relatively new idea, one that gained currency mainly after the Second World War.[15] Colonial powers were responsible for the exploitation and underdevelopment of their colonies for decades, and in some cases centuries.[16] Development itself was not part of their initial agenda.[17] In other words, development is essentially a postcolonial idea. The idea did not come of age until the former European colonies became independent nations and found themselves bankrupt and mired in poverty. Given the dire status of their postcolonial economies—still largely rural, primary-resource producing, and dependent on colonial powers for their limited export capability—the imperatives of development became critical.

Contemporary thinking about economic development has been dominated by two competing ideas, each having a strong influence on images of development:

(a) Development as a *natural process*, as in the notion of an "automatic society" based on Adam Smith's celebrated concept of the "invisible hand"

(b) Development as a *deliberate process* requiring a collective will and a strong and "visible" hand of government

These two views are ideologically contradictory and continue to compete in the development-planning arena today. The deliberate-process approach was more popular in the early years of the postcolonial era. Lately, the market process appears natural, so the natural-process approach commands neoliberal thought.[18]

According to Rostow, the idea of development began in Western Europe.[19] While agreeing with Rostow's claim, Arndt also notes that considerable uncertainty remains about the exact moment or event in the history of modern Western civilization that led to germination of the idea of development. It could have been one of many momentous circumstances that contributed to a formal acceptance of the concept of development. Not that it really matters where the origin of economic development ultimately lies, but as Said has pointed out in a different context, this Western history totally ignores the parallel reality of the non-Western culture.[20] In particular, it overlooks the areas of philosophy and sciences, especially the knowledge of astronomy, mathematics, and medicine that flourished during this millennium, and even earlier, in China, India, and the Arabic-Islamic world. Drawing from economic historian Joel Mokyr,[21] sociologist and communication theorist Manuel Castells enumerates other inventions and technological capabilities of China: the use of blast furnaces to cast iron in the second century BCE, the iron plow in the sixth century CE, the water clock in the eleventh century, the spinning wheel in the thirteenth century (about the same time as in the West), the adoption of water power and the use of the hydraulic trip hammer by the eighth century, and the invention of the compass in the tenth century (making ocean travel easier for Chinese vessels). Gunpowder, explosives, paper, and printing were some of the other inventions that made China more technologically advanced than the West.[22] These are impressive development achievements of premodern times that are often ignored in the postcolonial images of development.[23]

It is noteworthy that the colonial expansion of the Western world does not quite figure among the critical circumstances listed by Arndt or Rostow as the causes of development and underdevelopment. This blind spot still remains. A recent study by economist Jeffrey Sachs concludes that geography—climate and access to seas—is the most significant cause of underdevelopment but overlooks the possible effects of the colonial exploitation as a contributing factor. Ironically, such terrestrial shortcomings of the colonies notwithstanding, colonial powers extracted considerable primary resources from many of these geographically deprived countries that supported the mercantile and industrial economies of the colonial era.[24] Beginning with trade and mercantilism, and later shifting to industrial capitalism, the colonial era remains an important narrative in the development of Western capitalism.

The emergence of capitalism—first mercantile, then industrial—did not, however, bring about economic development, especially in the early stages from the thirteenth to sixteenth centuries, as noted previously. Development as a natural process—the "automatic society" scenario—did not work. Accumulation of wealth certainly occurred due to the avaricious instincts and initiatives of the ruling class, but capitalism by itself did not produce economic development as we know it today, at least not with a focus on the elimination of poverty and distributive justice through progressive taxation and other state actions.[25] In those days the Western liberal democratic state as we know today was largely absent. The idea of development as a deliberate process was yet to be articulated.

The Theory and Ideology of Capitalism

In eighteenth- and nineteenth-century Europe, where ideas of market liberalism came to dominate public philosophy, capitalism itself was seen as a form of societal development. The notion of an "automatic society" based on Adam Smith's celebrated concept of the "invisible hand" of the market was too compelling an idea. Avarice and acquisitive behavior were morally reprehensible in every form of precapitalist (mainly religious) ideology, including Christianity, but through the ideology of capitalism they became acceptable and respectable for the first time. As Hirschman has shown, the concept of greed was transformed from that of a "disruptive" passion—one of the seven deadly sins—to one of "steadying" interest.[26] Indeed, it was through acquisitive behavior that the image of commerce evolved into that of a civilizing force—*le doux commerce*.[27]

This view was rationalized further in theories of capitalism that proposed that there could be a "science" of acquisition, which provided powerful images indeed. Acquisitive behavior could be measured, modeled, and formally studied, it was argued, and in this secular scientific approach, moral questions were unwelcome or irrelevant. Economic historian Robert Heilbroner points out, however, that in Adam Smith's writings "the interplay of material progress and moral decline takes the form of a subtle dialectic that invests his work with its remarkable depths."[28] But this dialectic disappears completely in the scientific theories of capitalism. Once science had rationalized the human instinct for accumulation and profit into a basis for capitalist development, the image of economic growth became intrinsic to capitalism. As political theorist Theodore Lowi has argued, capitalism was not just an ideology and a theory; it also became a public philosophy.[29] Accompanying that philosophy was the popular image of economic growth as an automatic outcome of individual enterprise, liberty, and property rights sustained through democratic processes and market mechanisms.

While the theory of capitalism envisaged an automatic economy that promised economic growth, more jobs, and lower prices, it begged the question if an automatic economy necessarily led to automatic society.[30] Since the automatic society failed to materialize from the workings of capitalism, argued Lowi, "the industrializing societies had to develop institutions that would, as a regular matter, adjust themselves and their members to the requirements of capitalism."[31] Consequently administration became "a necessary part of capitalism and capitalist society," even though "it never was incorporated into capitalist ideology."[32] The invisible hand seemingly required visible interventions.

The Visible Hand Philosophy

By the turn of the nineteenth century a profound shift in public philosophy had occurred, from that of the "invisible hand" to a "visible hand" doctrine. Administration and management became more visible functions and forces in managing the affairs of the capitalist economy and the market mechanism. The new public philosophy asserted a positive role for government.[33]

In the context of developing economies, the interest in economic development initially grew out of what Arndt refers to as the "reactive nationalism" of the political leadership of countries such as China, India, and Japan. The new public philosophy of the West no doubt helped to inspire the strong statist visions of the postcolonial leadership of the developing world more generally. After decades—centuries in some instances—of colonial rule, humiliating defeat in wars, and other forms of subjugation, the image of economic development appealed to the postcolonial leaders as one of autonomy and independence. This embrace of the image of economic development was the catalyst for modernization even though there was considerable tension within the leadership of these countries regarding the balance of traditional values and modernity.[34] The Meiji restoration in Japan, Sun Yat-Sen's initiatives in China, and the Nehru-Gandhi dialectic on postindependence nation-building in India are notable examples of economic development as a deliberate process. Most other developing countries—such as Egypt, Indonesia, and Iran—would in time similarly embrace this image of economic development as the image of independence, although not without moral anguish and internal conflict.[35] As Arndt points out, in almost all of the instances above, the goals of development were shaped by the leadership's yearning for autonomy from political hegemony, for national prestige, and for the elimination of poverty, rather than by an incontrovertible vision of economic prosperity and a Western-style mass consumer society.[36] In the Indian dialectic of development, for example, the Gandhian position actually celebrated poverty as a politically potent image of autonomy, emphasizing traditional values and eschewing secular goals of prosperity and progress in the images of the industrialized West.

Global Inequality

By the middle of the twentieth century, as European colonial powers relinquished control of their former colonies, the appalling income gap between the Western industrialized nations and the former colonies became apparent. For example, in the 1950s per capita incomes for the developing countries were estimated to be around $50 to $100, as compared to $1,000 or more for the developed countries,[37] a tenfold to twentyfold advantage. Twenty-five years later, in 1976, the average GNP per capita for the poorest thirty-four countries was only $150 (in 1976 dollars), compared to $6,000 for the industrialized countries,[38] a doubling of the previous advantage. A quarter-century later, that gap had increased by another 50 percent.[39] As figure 2.2 shows, inequality in the distribution of the world's wealth has steadily increased since the beginning of the nineteenth century.

It is perhaps impossible to do an accurate audit of the capital transferred from colonies, much less determine what portion of that might have been invested in the rebuilding and expansion of European cities. Observers argue that the capital accumulated from colonial trade and primary resources obtained from colonies, even at a favorable rate, accounted for a very small portion of the growth of these European countries' national economies, and that much of that capital accumulation—the new wealth of the West—was obtained through the marvels of the industrial revolution. Eurocentric authors dismiss the contribution of the colonies as insignificant—economic historian Patrick O'Brien, for example, claims that it was no more than 2 percent of the European GNP in the late eighteenth century.[40] Furthermore, they would argue that the tax revenues obtained from the colonies were invested mainly in the governance and maintenance of the colonies' internal security, as well as in colonial infrastructure development. Arguing that the controversy over the role of colonial trade in the Industrial Revolution will never be settled by quantification or historical scholarship, O'Brien observes that in this debate "the 'perspective of the world' for Europe emerges as less significant than the 'perspective of Europe' for the world."[41]

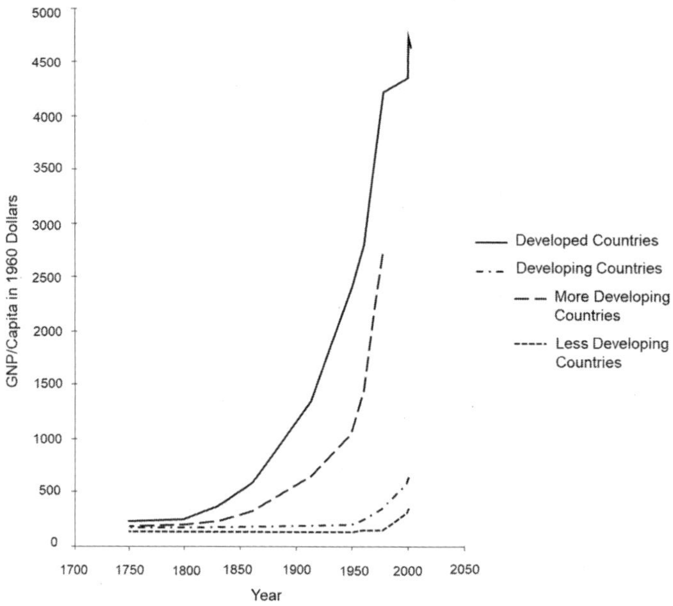

Figure 2.2

The growing disparity in economic growth from colonial times.

Source: The data used to map the trend from 1750 to 1977 are derived from Bairoch (1981), table 1.3. The 1999–2001 data are from World Bank (2000/2001, 2002, 2003), table 1.

This position, however, is contested by the more "world-centric" view.[42] Estimates of the capital transfer from the colonies to the colonizing countries are by no means insignificant. Geographer Alan Thomas and his colleagues estimate that between the seventeenth and nineteenth centuries some 60 billion pounds, or 90 billion dollars in 1991 prices, were transferred from developing countries to developed countries.[43] This may not be a significant amount in today's dollars, but even in 1989 this amount was close to about 60 percent of the combined GDP of sub-Saharan Africa.[44] While it might be difficult to estimate amounts invested specifically in urban development of the colonies, there can be little doubt that much of the capital was mainly invested in infrastructure needed to facilitate export of primary resources such as cotton, jute, minerals, and timber. As Sen points out, while the British invested in such infrastructure, and mercantile development, they were remarkably "hesitant in the fields that were the pillars of British industrial establishment, to wit, cotton textile, iron, and steel."[45] The colonialists had very little interest in investing in industries that would compete with the mainstay of their industrial economy.

A more detailed accounting of the wealth transfer is shown in table 2.1, summarizing the information compiled and presented by Thomas and his colleagues under what they refer to as the "pillage" and "plunder" of the Third World.[46] They define the process as "the accumulation of resources with little or no exchange: resources, goods and labour are taken by force."[47] Their examples include the forced labor in agriculture and mining in Latin America and "the slave trade and the Spanish looting of Aztec and Inca civilizations."[48]

Although this estimate may be partial and rough at best, it seems to support the "development of underdevelopment" argument presented by political theorist Andre Gunder Frank in comparing the wealth of more developed countries (MDCs) with that of less developed countries (LDCs).[49] Revisiting the debate over the contribution of the colonial "periphery" to Europe's industrial development, Frank reiterates the same argument.[50]

Table 2.1
Estimates of wealth transfer from the Third World

Colonial period	Category of pillage and plunder	Estimated amount
1600–1810	From the Americas: 22,000 tons of silver and 185 tons of gold to Spain [a]	(1) £300 million [c] (2) £1,700 [d]
1750–1810	From Brazil: 800 tons of gold to Portugal [b]	
1601–1700	Slave trade	(3) £1.3 million [c]
1650–1780	Dutch East India Co. profits from remittances, dividends, and spices from Indonesia, Malaysia, and the Philippines	(4) £60 million [e]
1710–1810	Slave trade: 6 million slaves [c]	(5) British profit: £75 million [f][g] (6) French profit: £50 million [h]
	Profit from slave labor production	(7) £200–300 million [i]
1750–1800	Land taxes paid by the Indian peasantry to the British	(8) £100 million [j][k]
1800–1890	Opium trade to China [c]	(9) £1 million per year [l], hence a total of £80 million
1811–1870	Slave trade: 1.9 million slaves [c]	No estimate available
Total		£866- 966 million (or £60 billion in 1991 prices) [c]

Note: Estimated amounts are for transfers during the sixteenth through nineteenth centuries according to Thomas et. al. (1994).

Source: [a] Hamilton (1929); [b] Frank (1973); [c] A. Thomas et al. (1994); [d] Mulhall (1889); [e] Colenbrander, cited in Mandel (1971); [f] Barratt Brown (1963); [g] Stein (1979); [h] Rinchon (1938); [i] Wiseman, cited in Mandel (1971); [j] Furber (1948); [k] Habib (1975); [l] Greenberg (1951).

Counterfactually, it is difficult to imagine today where the LDCs would stand in economic terms in comparison to the MDCs if they were never colonized. Could they have offered formidable competition during the industrial revolution? Could they have prospered by supplying primary resources at fair trade terms? Or was that highly unlikely given their declining share of the world's production with the dawn of the industrial economy of the West, and their unfavorable climate and geography, as suggested by economists Mellinger, Sachs, and Gallup?[51] A "bad karma"—one might conclude. Nevertheless, since the industrial production process is capital-intensive, there should be little doubt about the critical role that colonial wealth played in the initial infrastructure development of an incipient industrial economy. It is reasonable to assume that the rise and expansion of the modern Western industrial city benefited from capital transfer from the colonies.

It would follow, then, that cities of contemporary LDCs and MDCs were not significantly different in their material wealth and living standards before the dawn of the colonial era. To get an empirical handle on this assumption, let us consider available historical data on the distribution of the world product by groups of countries that are considered more developed or less developed as shown in table 2.2. This table is constructed from data presented in the 1984 World Development Report[52] and extended to 2000 with data from the same source.[53] It is quite evident here that two centuries ago, the share of world products among today's LDCs and MDCs was much closer than recent years, with the LDCs having a 44 percent share of world products. Still this is particularly remarkable, considering that the "pillage and plunder" beginning in the seventeenth century as documented by Alan Thomas et al. amounted to a capital transfer of some 60-68 billion pounds or roughly 100 billion dollars to the west from the colonies.[54] The table also shows how the developing countries' share of the total world product declined steadily from 44 percent at the turn of the nineteenth century to a mere 17 percent at the middle of the twentieth century—precisely the period of the greatest colonial expansion and rule of the developing world—with some modest recovery of that share in the

Table 2.2
Growth and share of world production (billions of dollars): 1800–2000

Countries	1800	1900	1950	1980	2000
More Developed Countries (MDC)	129	786	2183	9259	24722
Less Developed Countries (LDC)	101	184	447	2461	6614
Percentage share of LDC of the total world production	44	19	17	24	21

Source: World Bank (1984).

post-colonial era. The 1984 World Bank report also points out that in that same period—between 1800 and 1980—the world population share of developing countries more or less remained the same, at about 75 percent.

Despite the early parity between these LDCs and MDCs,[55] per capita income difference would worsen by the beginning of the nineteenth century, and subsequently become much worse by the end of the twentieth century (see figure 2.2).[56] A somewhat different picture emerges if we consider the systematic analysis of historical data as compiled by economic historian Paul Bairoch in 1960 US dollars and prices modified by estimates of local prices and prevailing exchange rates.[57]

The graphs shown in figure 2.3 are based on Bairoch's price- and exchange rate-adjusted data. They demonstrate different trajectories of product shares. Here we see that the developing countries had the lion's share of the world product, some 75 percent in 1750, but it began to decline with the beginning of colonial expansion to about 20 percent by the middle of the last century.[58] According to Bairoch's data, at the end of the colonial era, the share of the developing countries looks much better today—almost twice the percentage—than that shown in table 2.2. Nevertheless, Bairoch attributes the reversal of product shares and the widening of the gap between the developed and developing countries at the beginning of the last century to industrialization and indeed the industrial capitalism of the West. At the same time, the World Bank report further demonstrates that during this period the developing world experienced an explosive population growth while the West benefited from its demographic transition and thus a higher rate of GDP growth per capita. This transfer paralleled the spectacular expansion of the European colonial empires.[59]

Thus in 1800, at the beginning of the colonial era, developed countries were behind developing countries, but by the midpoint of the twentieth century, the developed countries had accumulated almost four times as much product at the end of the colonial era (see figure 2.3). Unquestionably, this is in part a result of the industrialization and growth of productivity in those Western developed countries. But many Third World scholars have argued that the West's capital accumulation had taken place at the cost of the underdevelopment of the formerly colonized countries.[60] Some Western scholars contest this argument or else remain ambivalent.[61] But the widening gap between the colonizing and colonized countries during this period remains an uncontested fact.

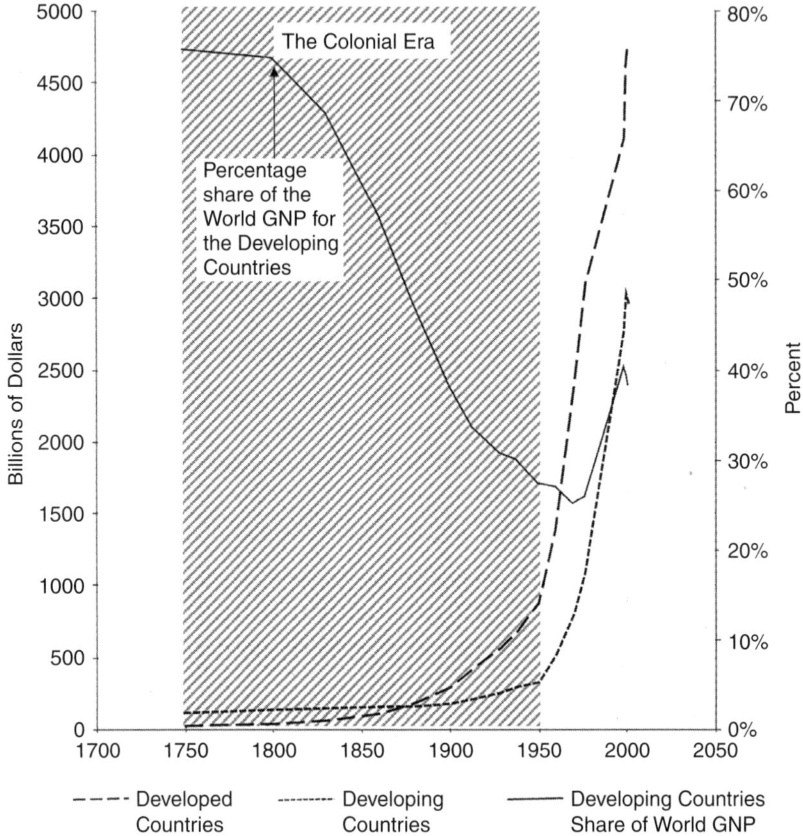

Figure 2.3

Historical trend of the growth and share of PPP-based GNP. Shaded area indicates the colonial period. *Source*: Data for 1750 to 1977 are from Bairoch (1981), table 1.2. These numbers are in 1960 dollars and indicate "real GNP" adjusted for local price differences at the prevailing exchange rates. The 1999–2001 data are obtained from World Bank (2001, 2002, 2003) and show GNP measured at purchasing power parity (PPP) and hence are equivalent to Bairoch's "real GNP." The World Bank data are not adjusted to 1960 dollars, so a logarithmic scale is used to display the shift in the magnitude of the data. Furthermore, the World Bank's accounts for low- and middle-income countries are taken as the proxy for developing countries.

Size and Prosperity of Cities

To the extent that average income can be seen as a proxy for the overall standard of living and prosperity of cities, it would seem that cities and the urban conditions generally of today's developed and developing countries were at par throughout most of the past millennium. In fact the urban condition for some developing countries may have been qualitatively better than that in Europe. As Manuel Castells points out, invoking the scholarship of economic historian Joel Mokyr, "around 1400, when the European Renaissance was planting the intellectual seeds of technological change that would dominate the world three centuries later, China was the most advanced technological civilization in the world."[62]

However, while the data on the wealth of cities, especially historical data, are not readily available, it is possible to use population size as a proxy for the relative wealth of cities. As noted by the fourteenth-century Arab philosopher of history Ibn Khaldun of Tunis, "the inhabitants of a more populous city are more prosperous than their counterparts in a less populous one."[63] As a historic corollary, the size of urban agglomerations is commensurate with political power, control, and influence, as sociologist Gideon Sjoberg has argued.[64] Table 2.3 shows the largest urban agglomerations in the world by century from 1000 CE to 2000 CE. Where the historical references sometimes include dynasties rather than countries, the modern country where the city is located is shown in parentheses. Thus, Chalukyas, Moguls, Byzantium, and the like are references to the dynasties or periods that are associated with those urban agglomerations. Corresponding numbers are the population size of these agglomerations by millions. The urban agglomerations that belong to what has been traditionally considered less developed countries are highlighted in bold. Urban agglomerations that belonged to the modern colonial powers are underlined.[65] What is remarkable about this table is that of one hundred agglomerations listed by ten centuries (not counting year 2000), some sixty-nine are from what would be considered LDCs by today's accounting. From the eleventh through seventeenth centuries—the early phases of the colonial era—seven to eight of the top ten agglomerations are from the LDC group at the beginning of each of these centuries. With the expansion and consolidation of the colonial powers in the eighteenth, nineteenth, and twentieth centuries we see a reversal in the composition of the top ten cities. In the eighteenth- and nineteenth-century lists, only four cities are from today's LDCs and, not surprisingly, at the peak of colonial expansion (the beginning of the twentieth century) none of the top ten are from LDCs.

At the beginning of the thirteenth and the fourteenth centuries, Hangchow (Hangzhou) was the largest urban agglomeration in the world, with a population of 255,000

Table 2.3

Ten largest cities of the world: 1000–2000 CE

	1000	1100	1200	1300	1400	1500	1600	1700	1800	1900	2000
1	Cordova, Spain 0.450	**Kaifeng China 0.442**	**Hngchow China 0.255**	**Hngchow China 0.432**	**Nanking China 0.473**	**Peking, China 0.672**	**Peking, China 0.706**	Cnstntnpl Turkey 0.700	**Peking, China 1.100**	London Britain 6.480	**Mexico City Mexico 26.300**
2	Cnstntnpl Byzntm (Turkey) 0.450	Cnstntnpl Byzantm (Turkey) 0.350	**Fez, Morocco 0.250**	**Peking, China 0.401**	**Cairo, Egypt 0.450**	**Vijayngr, India 0.500**	Cnstntnpl Turkey 0.700	***Peking, China 0.650***	*London, Britain 0.861*	New York USA 4.242	**Sao Paulo, Brazil 24.000**
3	**Kaifeng, China 0.400**	**Cairo, Egypt 0.200**	**Sian, China 0.300**	**Cairo, Egypt 0.400**	**Vijayngr India 0.350**	**Cairo, Egypt, 0.450**	**Agra, Moguls .0.500**	**Isfahan, Persia 0.600**	**Canton, China 0.800**	Paris, France 3.330	Tpkyo/ Yokohama Japan 17.100
4	**Sian, China 0.300**	Constntnpl Byzantm (Turkey) 0.200	**Cairo, Egypt 0.200**	**Canton, China 0.300**	**Hangchow China 0.325**	**Hangchow China, 0.375**	**Cairo, Turkey (Egypt) 0.400**	London, England 0.550	Constntnpl Turkey 0.700	Berlin, Germany 2.424	**Calcutta India 16.600**
5	Kyoto, Japan 0.200	**Canton, China 0.200**	Kyoto Japan 0.200	**Nankin, China 0.285**	**Peking, China 0.320**	**Nanking China 0.300**	Osaka, Japan 0.400	Paris, France 0.530	Paris, France 0.547	Chicago USA 1.717	**Greater Bombay, India 16.000**
6	**Cairo, Egypt 0.150**	**Marrakesh Morocco 0.150**	**Pagan Burma 0.180**	Paris, France 0.228	**Canton, China 0.300**	**Canton, China 0.285**	**Canton, China 0.350**	Yedo, Japan 0.500	**Hngchow China 0.500**	Vienna, Austria 1.662	NYC/New Jersey USA 15.500
7	**Hasa, Qarmatns 0.150**	**Bagdad, Seljuks (Iraq) 0.150**	**Nankins, China 0.180**	**Fez, Maghreb (Morocco) 0.200**	Paris, France 0.275	**Tabriz, Persia (Iran) 0.250**	Yedo, Japan 0.350	**Delhi, Moguls (India) 0.500**	Yedo, Japan 0.492	Tokyo, Japan 1.497	**Shanghai China 13.900**

8	**Hangchow China 0.140**	**Hangchow China 0.150**	Kamakura Japan 0.175	Kamakura Japan 0.200	**Tabriz Persia 0.200**	Paris, France. 0.225	Kyoto, Japan 0.350	**Ahmdabd Moguls (India) 0.380**	Naples, Naples (Italy) 0.430	St. Petersburg Russia 1.439	**Seoul, Republic of Korea 13.500**
9	**Angkor, Cambodia 0.130**	**Canton China 0.140**	**Angkor Cambodia 0.150**	**Soochow China 0.160**	Kyoto, Japan 0.200	Constntnpl, Turkey 0.200	**Hangchow China 0.350**	Osaka, Japan 0.370	**Soochow China 0.392**	Philadlphia USA 1.418	**Rio de Janeiro, Brasiil 13.300**
10	**Bagdad, Persia (Iran) 0.125**	**Kalyan, Chalukyas (India) 0.125**	Palermo, Sicily (Italy) 0.150	**Sian, China 0.150**	**Soochow China 0.175**	**Gaur, Bengal (India) 0.200**	**Lahore, Moguls (Pakstan) 0.350**	Kyoto, Japan 0.350	Osaka, Japan 0.380	Manchester, Britain 1.255	**Delhi, India 13.300**

Source: Jones and Kandl (1982); United Nations (1989).

and 432,000, respectively, although according to historian Jacques Gernet, Hangzhou's population had exceeded the million by 1275.[66] Gernet's description includes quotes from noted travelers of that time, Marco Polo and Oderic de Pordenone, who described with awe and admiration the layout of the city, its great avenues, buildings, and markets with traders from all over the world, as well as the exciting urbanism of the city's daily life, which set it apart from all others.

While the causes of the pitiful condition of the developing countries and their widespread poverty at the end of the colonial era will no doubt be debated for years to come, it is well established that colonial coffers were drained by the time the Western powers made their retreat. There was a general consensus among the world community that the financially bankrupt former colonies were desperately in need of development, to be funded by the West (and, of course, to be developed in the images of the West).

Initially, humanitarian and philanthropic aid poured into many of these countries to forestall epidemics or famines, but the international aid to fight hunger and poverty was episodic, insufficient, and limited. However, the politics of the Cold War, and the fear of the spread of communism, made both the aid and the sustained economic development assistance for developing countries a major imperative for the Western countries. Development of the former colonies became a major project of the West.

Kuznets and the Rehabilitation of Trickle-Down

As it became apparent that the "trickle-down" process was not working, development theorists were quick to point out that this process was a "myth."[67] Economist W. Arthur Lewis argued that economic growth is fundamentally "an inegalitarian process," as demonstrated "in the classical models of Smith, Ricardo and Marx."[68] The well-known historical study of modern economic growth by economist Simon Kuznets also came to very similar conclusions.[69] Unlike Marx, Ricardo, and Smith, however, Kuznets tried to rehabilitate the trickle-down hypothesis by describing progress in the relationship between economic growth and inequality with an inverted "U"-shaped curve (or bell curve), which came to be known as the Kuznets curve (see figure 2.4). Drawn from the history of the economic growth of the Western countries in modern times, the Kuznets curve showed that inequality increases at the early stages of economic growth, levels off at the middle stages, and then declines at the advanced stages. Perhaps the most important thing to keep in mind about Kuznets's work is that he was not describing a "natural" process as such, but one that in fact required direct public intervention and institutional change. Kuznets offered several explanations for the bell curve relationship, including demographic transition, urbanization, progressive taxation,

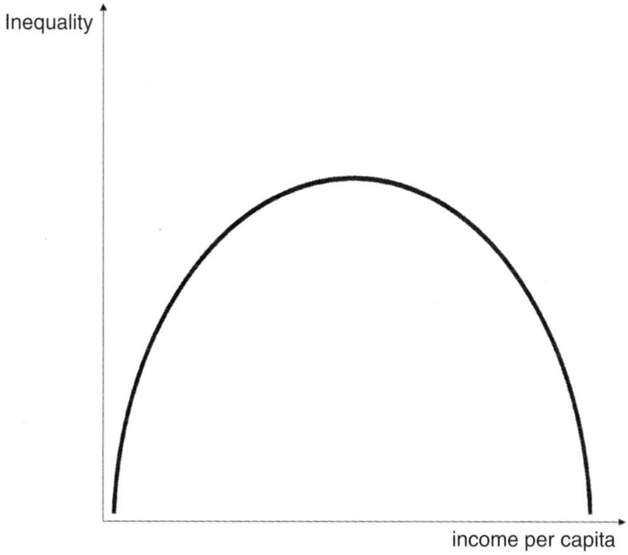

Figure 2.4
The Kuznets curve.
Source: Author.

development of political institutions, and income transfer through various social programs. The Kuznets model seemed to suggest that a trickle-down process might have a chance, but only within a "visible hand" scenario rather than the scenario of an automatic, self-guiding society. But even this "visible hand" scenario will require time, and therefore a lot of patience from the nations still at the very early stages of their development.

It turns out that there might have been a whiff of transcendence in Kuznets's articulation of the rites of passage of economic development. That is, developing countries must keep their eyes trained on a very distant horizon, like the hopeful workers depicted in Chinese Cultural Revolution posters. In the mid-seventies economist Montek Ahluwalia tried to determine empirically the exact inflection point on the Kuznets curve in terms of GNP per capita, using cross-sectional data from different countries.[70] The study found that relative inequality worsened over a phase of development marked by a transition in per capita GNP from $75 to $750 (in 1970 dollars). In the late seventies, these numbers were not very promising for the poor countries, showing that for "an economy experiencing growth in per capita GNP at the rate of about 2.5 percent per year, this transition would take about a hundred years."[71] Economist Thomas Piketty has questioned the Kuznets curve as optimistic and only a "normative theory." He further observes that Kuznets's work was a product of the Cold War, an attempt to keep the poor countries within the "orbit of the free world" with the promise of redemption.[72]

Thus, despite transcendent promises of deferred gratification and ultimate redemption, the scenario of unavoidable pain and necessary patience implicitly exhorted by the Kuznets curve–based image of development was not particularly helpful or comforting in the turbulent political world of development. Plagued by problems of widespread hunger, poverty, malnutrition, and unemployment, most of the developing world was not in a position to wait for fifty or a hundred years to reach the inflection point when things start to get better. They wanted immediate results.

Counter-Images of Development

As Arndt points out in his historical review of economic development, from the end of the Second World War to the mid-sixties, the amount and the rate of economic growth in former colonies was almost the sole consideration in development planning initiated by the West. This Western image of development was one of industrialization, modernization, higher productivity, higher rates of savings, capital formation, and the like.[73]

It is important to note, however, that not all newly independent countries bought into this theory. Indian prime minister Nehru believed in the imperatives of industrialization and modernization, but not necessarily in free international trade.[74] Indian leaders pursued a policy of import substitution, believing that economic self-sufficiency would sustain political autonomy. Meanwhile, dependency theorists from halfway around the globe were advocating similar concepts of development for Latin America. The UN-sponsored Economic Commission for Latin America (ECLA) argued that the economic backwardness of Latin America was a result of its economic dependency on the industrialized nations of the Northern Hemisphere and the political hegemony that inevitably resulted from this asymmetrical relationship.[75] In mainland China, meanwhile, Mao questioned the assumption that industrialization is a necessary prerequisite of economic development and instead emphasized the importance of the agricultural sector and rural economic development, allowing modernization only as necessary to increase agricultural productivity.[76]

Although import substitution, dependency theory, and the Maoist vision arose as counterpoints to the Western images of development, by the mid-1960s even Western development theorists had begun to question economic growth as the sole driver of development. It was apparent that even when newly industrializing countries showed impressive economic growth, they did not eliminate poverty within their borders. Moreover, economic growth seemed to exacerbate the gap between the rich and the poor.[77]

A flaw in the image of economic growth as development was its reliance on a "trickle-down" process of development. Development economist Michael Todaro defined "trickle-down" as "the notion that *development* is purely an 'economic' phenomenon in which rapid gains from the overall growth of *GNP* and *per capita income* would automatically bring benefits (i.e., 'trickle down') to the masses in the form of jobs and other economic opportunities."[78] In this view, as Todaro explained, problems of poverty, unemployment, and income distribution are necessarily of lesser concern than GNP and per capita income. The trickle-down theory was remiss about poverty and inequality.

Redefining Development: The Basic Needs Approach

By the end of the sixties considerable soul searching was underway. Development economist Dudley Seers perhaps articulated best the question that seemed to reverberate in the minds of many scholars and experts: "Why do we confuse development with economic growth?"[79] He suggested that the idea of development should be considered on its own terms, that it is basically a "normative" concept, and that fundamentally it has to do with improving the human condition, human dignity, and human performance. Thus, rather than focusing on the growth in per capita GNP, he said, we should ask three questions: "What has been happening to poverty? What has been happening to unemployment? What has been happening to inequality?"[80] If all three showed improvement, Seers argued, some development performance can be claimed.

This was an argument that larger social objectives, rather than economic growth, should guide development programs. During his tenure as president of the World Bank (1968–1981), Robert McNamara passionately argued that the elimination of poverty must be the most significant goal and indicator of development. Thus, development programs should be guided by essential human needs, including nutrition, decent shelter, potable water, basic health care, education, and jobs. This particular position came to be known as the "basic needs" approach to development planning.[81] Some years later, and inspired by Amartya Sen's arguments about human capability and freedom as the essential purposes of development, UNDP would promote its Human Development Index (HDI) as the metric of development projects and outcomes.[82]

In reality, the basic needs approach did not make a widespread impact on development planning. However, it did spark a new "structuralist" approach to development that argued that income distribution, equity, and institutional reform must be considered as essential tenets of development alongside economic growth. This model of development had a greater appeal in the development communities than the old image based purely on economic growth. Catchphrases like "growth with equity" or "redistribution with growth"[83] captured the emergent thinking about development and tempered the earlier image of development as purely economic growth.

Neoliberalism: Renewed Faith in the Invisible Hand

McNamara's newly enlightened view of development did not get much time to flourish. In the 1980s, influenced by the political ideology of US president Ronald Reagan and UK prime minister Margaret Thatcher, the political pendulum swung back to the earlier orthodoxy of market liberalism, although with a new name: "neoliberalism." This Thatcho-Reaganite-era approach celebrated the marvel of the free market economy, and it was asserted and extolled by international aid agencies and financial institutions such as USAID and the World Bank. Buttressed by the successes of the newly industrializing countries (or NICs) and the "four tigers of Asia" (Hong Kong, Korea, Taiwan, and Singapore), there was considerable optimism about the economic magic of free trade. By the end of the decade, the collapse of the Soviet Union and East European communism and the end of the Cold War, coupled with China's embrace of the market economy, further reinforced the new orthodoxy. The Thatcho-Reaganite crusade to downsize big government began to spread to developing countries and to reshape the images that led international development. The World Bank, having emerged as the single most influential force in the development of the Global South, became the principal messenger of the new orthodoxy. The bank became, and remains today, an unrelenting promoter of privatization, deregulation, currency reform, creation of markets for public goods, and the dismantling of trade barriers. This campaign was not subtle; developing countries had to fall in line to get their loans approved.

The Fable of Bell Curves

Fables are tales, usually short, that are used to teach a moral. According to dictionary definitions, they might not be based on facts; they might be shared myths or legends, or allegories involving animals, inanimate objects, or supernatural events. They may even be untruths. We all know about Aesop's fables, for instance. Here I want to introduce what might be called the fable of bell curves. I hasten to add that, unlike other fables, the bell curves in development thought are neither fictional nor untruths. Most of them are based on empirical data and credible analysis. What make them fables are their implicit morals. Fables are normative, and the bell curves are fables because they too are normative. The moral of the fable of bell curves is one of equilibrium, sacrifice and patience ("things are going to get worse before they get better"), and, ultimately, deliverance.

In an address presented at the annual conference of the Regional Science Association in 1980, urban theorist William Alonso aptly summarized the most significant and persistent images that have influenced postcolonial development thought. He described five parallel trajectories of development as "bell shapes in development"[84]—that includes the renowned Kuznets curve and four derivatives (see figure 2.5). Alonso proposed that the other four bell curves had to do with measures of economic growth, population growth, urban primacy, and interregional disparity. He pointed out that there is an internal logic to this group of bell curves, as they represent a set of interrelationships that presume historical trends of economic and population growth and concomitant transformations of settlement systems.[85] The Kuznets curve, however, is about changes in income inequality with economic growth measured in per capita income. The bell-shaped economic growth curve suggested by Alonso is a bit confusing, since no specific measure is suggested, while the x-axis is presumably income per capita as suggested in the Kuznets curve. Assuming that Alonso meant "economic development" one could use urbanization as a useful proxy, since Kunets himself had suggested urbanization is a major factor in the shaping of the income inequality bell curve.[86] As we will see urbanization and development nexus remains a major topic in policy debate.[87] Currently the Chinese government is seeking urbanization as a way to eliminate rural poverty, for example. Accordingly, I have chosen urbanization as a proxy for Alonso's bell shape of economic growth.

The image of development suggested by the bell curves represents a natural process—absent, however, of the structural interventions that Kuznets saw as essential to achieve the outcome. It is this omission that makes the bell curves a fable with an aphoristic quality, despite their complexity and interrelated dynamics.

The Bell Curves in Space

Geographers, who have an intellectual interest in all matters of space, often rightly complain that economists show a lack of concern for space, as if economies revolve around the tip of a needle.[88] Indeed, this is generally the case in the literature on development economics even though "land," along with "labor" and "capital," remains one of the major factors in macroeconomic analysis. I will now focus on aspects of spatiality that are implicit in, or derived from, the images of development described above. The literature on land economics and economic geography offers several insights about spatial implications of economic growth and development.[89] It is possible to find

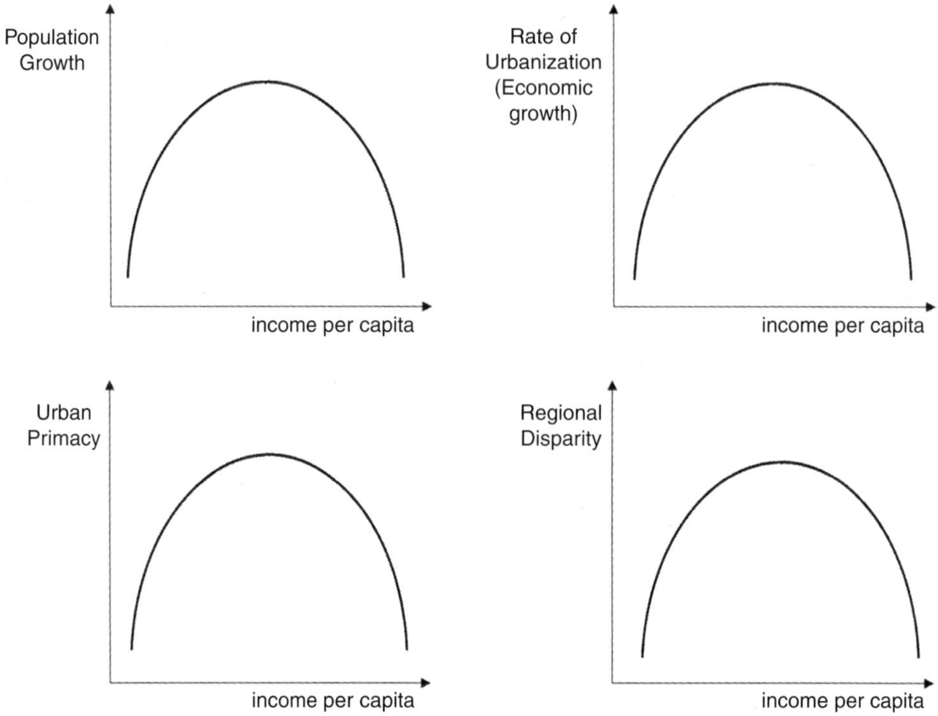

Figure 2.5
The other four bell curves.
Source: Author.

connections between development thinking and spatial processes on at least at three levels: sectoral, structural, and organizational.

Sectoral-Level Processes: Urban versus Rural

The spatial dimension of economics begins at the sectoral level, albeit in strictly functional terms. Here, space is initially recognized as the differentiating factor between urban and rural sectors of an economy. From that very simple image, it is only a small conceptual leap to the conventional economic triad that consists of primary (agricultural), secondary (industrial), and tertiary (service) sectors. This triad provides spatial distinctions that help to analyze not only a variety of urban processes—such as productivity differentials in labor, labor mobility, and demographic changes—but also structural transformations involving the urban and rural sectors of an economy. These constructs have helped to associate industrialization with urbanization, and to link sectoral transformation with spatial transformation as an important dynamic of development and economic growth.

Unfortunately, the economic development literature is vague on the subject of how urbanization actually spatializes; the specific aspects of urban form, such as size, shape, form, and organization of the space of urban settlements, are often excluded from this discourse. Thus, when development economist Michael Lipton discussed "urban bias" in national development, he used the word "urban" strictly as a social and economic concept, without any acknowledgement of the spatial nature of rural-urban differences.[90]

Since urbanization seemed to inevitably parallel development, a normative position of presumed causality began to coalesce in the development literature. In time it seemed to some experts that a strategy of deliberate urbanization was imperative for successful development.[91] However, this causal link between urbanization and development was challenged when the explosive urbanization of Latin America in the fifties and sixties yielded neither concurrent nor consequent development. The term "overurbanization,"[92] which describes a rate of urban conversion of population that far exceeds the rate of industrialization, was commonly used to suggest the pathological nature of such urban growth without concomitant development. Even today, this "chicken and egg" debate continues, although the nature of causality remains far from resolved. While acknowledging countervailing trends in the data, economists Patricia Annez and Robert Buckley, along with economist John Quigley, seem to give a nod to urbanization as a driver of economic development.[93] While the earlier Chinese development policy questioned that assumption, most recently the Chinese policy makers have accepted urbanization as the policy tool for eradicating rural poverty.

Structural-Level Processes

The structural aspects of spatial transformation associated with economic development are a relatively small subset within a fairly extensive body of literature related to urbanization and national settlement systems. Perhaps the most comprehensive effort to place economic development in the context of cities was in the work of economic historian Paul Bairoch, who tried to examine the relationship between the city and its economy, or economic development, to be more precise.[94] Truly global in scope, Bairoch's work analyzes the decline and growth of urban systems throughout the world and over different periods, in the form of a historic commentary. Unfortunately, this otherwise remarkable material lacks a substantial discussion of the spatial implications of macroeconomic theories or policies.

The relationship between urban growth and structural transformation of the economy, however, has been well documented in historical data.[95] Because industrialization was the prime mover of the economic growth of the Western world, economic development in those countries involved a major structural change. With the transition from an agricultural to an industrial economy, there was a major shift in population from rural to urban areas. The urbanization process was closely related to the rate of industrialization, and over time the urbanization rate increased with economic development, leveled off at the transitional stage, and then declined at the advanced level of economic development, thus tracing Alonso's bell curve trajectory of economic development. This bell curve then suggests the spatial implications of macroeconomic processes.

Spatial Dimensions

In contrast to Bairoch, the empirical works of regional economists such as Johann von Thünen,[96] François Perroux,[97] Walter Christaller,[98] and Brian Berry[99] laid the foundation for examining the effects of economic activities in space in more precise and formal terms, through the development of the idea of urban hierarchies and the distribution of cities in space. Drawing on evidence from the Western industrialized world—the US, UK, and Germany—these scholars argued that a well-articulated system of cities[100] is an antecedent to economic diffusion and a balanced spatial development. It followed therefore that most developing countries, especially Latin American ones, showed high urban primacy and a total absence of a balanced urban hierarchy.[101] There were several problems with this assumption, however. First, even though countries such as China and India seemed to have well-distributed systems of cities, they were not doing well in terms of economic development or the spatial diffusion of economic growth. Second, many Western developed countries—France being an eminent example—demonstrated an annoyingly (to these theorists) high level of urban primacy, while being prosperous nonetheless.[102] In order to address these contradictions, the theory of urban primacy had to be turned on its head.

Revisions to the urban structure argument proposed that instead of being seen as antecedent, the idealized urban hierarchy should be seen as an outcome of economic development. After all, this is how the urban hierarchy developed in the Western exemplars.

A study by urban planner Salah El-Shakhs showed a bell-shaped relationship between economic development measured by GNP per capita and a measure of primacy.[103] Just like income inequality, urban primacy is low at the early stage of development but increases with development, reaches a peak at the transitional level, and finally declines through the mature stage of development. Urban economist Harry Richardson called the process one of "polarization reversal" and provided an explanation, which goes as follows: scale economy and the absence of initial infrastructure leads to increasing urban concentration at the early and transitional stages of development, but with infrastructure investments and diseconomies of scale in principal urban centers a reversal of that trend ultimately occurs.[104] With greater diffusion and decentralization of urban population and economic activities, urban primacy ultimately declines. Regional economist Jeffrey Williamson similarly offered another bell curve to show how regional disparities will behave the same way.[105]

The Sixth Bell Curve of Development

Now we have been hearing of a sixth bell curve, popularly referred to as the environmental Kuznets curve, or EKC (see figure 2.6). Here the assumption is that a nation's environmental quality will decline at the initial stages of economic development but will eventually improve with technological progress, institutional innovations, and mitigation measures that will be brought about by economic development.

The possibility of an inverted U-shaped relationship between development and environmental quality was initially hinted at in the 1992 World Development Report,[106] which drew from a 1991 Organization for Economic Cooperation and Development (OECD) study that tracked the pollution levels in member countries over the previous

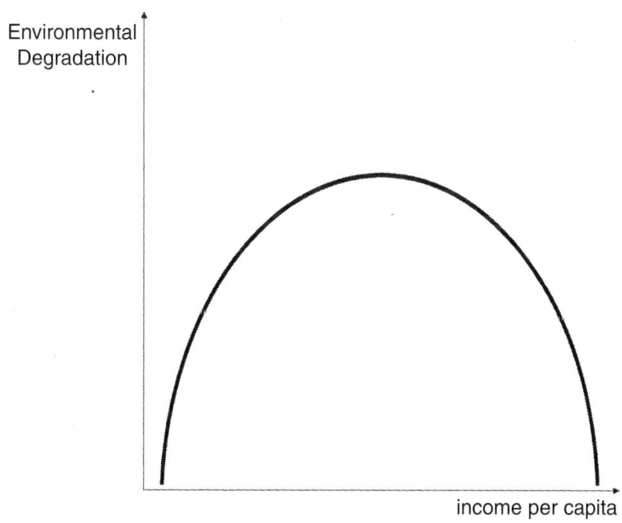

Figure 2.6
The environmental Kuznets curve (EKC).
Source: Author.

three decades.[107] The OECD study showed that a vast improvement in environmental quality—reduced emissions of sulfur oxides, nitrogen oxides, and particulates; reduced environmental concentrations of the insecticide DDT, polychlorinated biphenyls (PCBs), and mercury; and even an increase in forested areas and protected lands—had been achieved in the OECD countries since 1970 as a result of sustained economic growth. These gains were possible because of antipollution policy measures taken by these countries at a cost of some 0.8 percent to 1.5 percent of GDP since 1970. A World Bank background paper published in 1992 showed similar improvements in certain environmental indicators—access to safe water and adequate sanitation, and reductions in the urban concentration of particulate matter and sulfur dioxide—with parallel increases in per capita income, based on data obtained from some 149 countries.[108]

However, the 1992 World Bank report also found that the theoretical inverted U-shaped relationship did not quite hold for many of the other indicators. For example, municipal waste volume and carbon dioxide emissions increased with growth; river quality declined with growth; and deforestation remained unaffected by growth.

Studies focusing on both theoretical and empirical arguments continue to emerge, and indeed, controversies rage as to whether there is, or even could be, such a thing as an environmental Kuznets curve. Some economists are enthusiastic about the EKC hypothesis that "environmental damage first increases with income, then declines" with development.[109] Their enthusiasm stems from the fact that if the EKC hypothesis is true, then development versus environment becomes a "false dichotomy" in the long run, as the 1991 World Development Report asserts.[110] In addition to the 1991 OECD study and the 1992 World Bank background paper, several empirical studies show that the EKC relation seems to hold, with inflection points corresponding to specific income levels for three pollutants and deforestation,[111] for four types of airborne emissions,[112] for three types of air pollutants in Mexico,[113] and for deforestation in Latin America, Africa, and Asia.[114]

On the theoretical side there are two lines of argument regarding the EKC. One is a strictly economic argument postulating that at the lower level of development the environmental goods are plentiful and prices and consumption are low; then, with development, consumption increases, demand for resources goes up, and environmental losses increase; but with regulation and technological innovation, further environmental degradation is abated.[115] The other line of argument suggests that the EKC "can be derived directly from the technological link between consumption of a desired good and abatement of its undesirable byproduct."[116] According to this perspective, the EKC is independent of growth, institutions, externalities, and political economy. This is a universalistic "automatic society" argument, as it sees the inverted U curve as being obtained by state interventions in the form of regulations and investment in environmental quality improvements. The World Bank position is closer to this point of view.

Detractors of the EKC hypothesis have questioned its validity from both empirical and theoretical perspectives. They have pointed out various caveats and findings that are counter to previous claims. Economists Majid Ezzati, Burton H. Singer, and Daniel M. Kammen, for example, argue that the EKC relationship can only be obtained under very specific conditions and that many factors are involved in the economic-environment relationship.[117] Others have questioned the data, models, and analytical design or have suggested that the scale of analysis should be global rather than strictly local.[118]

A few additional general observations are in order. First, most of the empirical studies regarding the sixth bell curve have focused on pollution and deterioration, but few have focused on aspects of nonrenewable resources, nonrestorable losses in biodiversity, and other such aspects of environmental quality. Second, the studies almost always measure economic growth according to GDP per capita, often without even adjusting it for standard PPP factors, or "green" GDP (accounting for the environmental cost of development).[119] Third, and more critically, there is no sense of any threshold of environmental degradation against which the shape of the curve can be judged or evaluated. For the income inequality curve, there are available estimates of GDP per capita for the points of inflection,[120] but for the EKC we have no sense of the level of development at which a similar inflection in the "ecological footprint" or the depletion of environmental resources can be achieved.

Bell Curves as Normative Models

All the images of development described above are results of positivist empirical analysis. They are based on historically observed trends in the dynamics of economic and population growth, and the associated trends in structural transformations in space. Considerable documentation exists in support of each of these bell curves, and as Alonso pointed out, there is an internal logic to the bell curves and interrelationships between them that can be explained by historical changes and evolutionary processes in the structure of human societies.

While the bell curves are products of positivist analysis, they are also normative in a profound sense, because they are deeply rooted in the economistic belief in equilibrium. The fable of bell curves is based on the assumption that initial turbulence and distortions in a closed system will modulate to a steady state. Thus, bell curves are a counterpoint to Hirschman's notion of development as a "chain of disequilibria." Also implicit in this fable is the idea that the curves represent natural processes that may not necessarily require intervention. The greatest lure of the environmental Kuznets curve, considering the noninterventionist position of the World Bank, is that there is no such thing as "limits to growth."[121] While a no-limits image of development is good news for global capitalists, agents of the market economy, economists of a neoliberal bent, and kindred libertarian academics, the problem with this image is that there might be a long wait. For example, the inflection points for some of the pollutants in the environmental Kuznets curve have been estimated to range from PPP-based $3,000 in 1985 dollars to PPP-based $25,000 in 1985 dollars, depending on the pollutant and countries or regions tracked.[122] Even for rapidly developing China and India, that target remains quite distant, while the presence of such pollutants, meanwhile, continues to exacerbate both the local and global environmental crisis.

3 Modernity and Other Images of Development

> Very many people across the world suffer from varieties of unfreedom. Famines continue to occur in particular regions, denying to millions the basic freedom to survive. Even in those countries which are no longer sporadically devastated by famines, undernutrition may affect very large numbers of vulnerable human beings. Also, a great many people have little access to health care, to sanitary arrangements or to clean water, and spend their lives fighting unnecessary morbidity, often succumbing to premature mortality....
>
> Moving to other deprivations of freedom, a great many people in different countries of the world are systematically denied political liberty and basic civil rights. It is sometimes claimed that the denial of these rights helps to stimulate economic growth and is "good" for rapid economic development.
>
> —Amartya Sen, *Development as Freedom*[1]

While classical economic theories presented economic growth as development, their sociological counterparts focused on modernization as the social, cultural, and organizational antecedents of development. In this view the process of modernization was complementary to the classical economic views of development. Adam Smith's observation about the specialization and differentiation of an economy with sustained growth was paralleled by sociological expectations of increased organizational complexity associated with development. The Western predilection for conflating modernization and development underlies political scientist Edward Banfield's concern about whether "the non-Western cultures of the world will prove capable of creating and maintaining the high degree of organization without which a modern economy and a democratic political order are impossible."[2]

Sociologist Alejandro Portes presented two theoretical arguments about development as modernization: "social differentiation" and "enactment of values."[3] "Social differentiation" sees modernization as a structural transformation of traditional folk societies from a feudal-agricultural order to a capitalist-industrial order. "Enactment of values" sees modernization as a fiundamental shift in values that brings about a change in a person's disposition that leads to adaption of values associated with modernity.[4] Sociologists like Emile Durkheim saw the process of modernization as one of differentiation and integration, leading to "higher social forms."[5] Others, such as sociologist Ferdinand Tönnies, saw the social differentiation model of development as a loss of the individual sense of identity and community.[6] Anthropologist Robert Redfield's distinction between the moral order and the technical order of development reflected a similar ambivalence.[7]

The second branch of modernity theory focuses not so much on societal and structural transformation, but on values, instincts, beliefs, and worldviews. Modernization, according to this theory, involves a fundamental shift in an individual's thinking and values. Other Western scholars have come to identify the model of "modern man" with distinctive personality traits and value orientations that, not so incidentally, are dominant in Western societies. Sociologists Alex Inkeles and David Smith offered one such list of criteria for defining modern man.[8] To this basic list of nine items Portes added another seven characteristics commonly associated with modern man (see table 3.1).[9]

Portes, however, saw several shortcomings in this theory. First, the assumption that individuals have the agency and drive to obtain such a transformation, unfettered by larger structural and external constraints, may not be tenable. Second, the emphasis on consumption values puts a materialistic cast on development, which is unwarranted

Table 3.1
Characteristics of modern man

Inkeles and Smith (1974)	(1) Readiness for new experiences and openness to innovation
	(2) Disposition to form and hold opinions
	(3) Democratic orientation
	(4) Planning habits
	(5) Belief in human and personal efficacy
	(6) Belief that the world is calculable
	(7) Stress on personal and human dignity
	(8) Faith in science and technology
	(9) Faith in distributive justice
Portes (1976)	(10) Participation in organizations and electoral processes
	(11) Ambitions for self and children and willingness to take risks
	(12) Secularism – not receptive to religious or ideological positions
	(13) Use of information
	(14) Consumption orientation
	(15) Urban preference
	(16) Geographic mobility

and countermands larger sustainability goals. Third, the model of modern man is created as a counterpoint to a contrived and mythical notion of traditional man. There is no reason to think, for example, that people in traditional societies would be opposed to the idea of distributive justice or be closed to new experiences or information. So-called primitive populations have shown enormous ingenuity in adapting to or coping with external and alien stimuli, as the film *The Gods Must Be Crazy* shows with good humor.[10]

When the Indian government proposed to convert its measurement system from the colonial foot-pound-second (FPS) measures to the metric system in the early 1960s—when the national literacy rate was around 63 percent—detractors worried that the poor and uneducated masses would be confused and exploited as a result. Yet, and quite surprisingly for the skeptics, even the remote markets of rural India almost instantly adapted to the metric measures of length, volume, and weight. Similarly, the poor and the "traditional" masses of India have shown a propensity for democratic processes, with over 60 percent of eligible voters voting in national elections.[11] The secular and Westernized Chinese of Taiwan and Hong Kong still adhere to the ancient rites of *feng shui* in their daily life. Other such contradictions are seen in the Middle East, where wealthy oil-exporting countries are rapidly modernizing their built environments and raising standards of mass consumption, while clinging to traditional norms and values drawn from tenets of Islam.[12] Furthermore, the rise of religious fundamentalism in advanced Western societies continues to contradict some of the key premises of the modernization theory.[13]

The tension between modernization-as-Westernization and traditional norms, values, and standards of living continues to haunt the developing world. It can be seen in the growing disparities between urban and rural settings. This tension is also often manifested in the ironies of the recent transformations in the built environment: ersatz and faux urban form mimicking the West; historic settings obliterated by an indifferent global real estate industry. The narrative of loss extends to the wanton destruction of nature and scenic resources, impairing the traditional nexus of sustainable urban form and ecological balance.

The tension is not just about modernization, but also about modernity and modernism itself. In an important commentary on modernism, anthropologist and political scientist James C. Scott examines the institutions of the modern state and critiques the limitations of the technical and scientific order on which state authority is based. He discusses why these institutions are incapable of nurturing humanity, traditions, and the organic character of a society of individuals.[14] Philosopher Charles Taylor has argued that most critical writings on modernity present the subject as an "acultural" process "which any and every culture can go through—and which all will probably be forced to undergo."[15] This position underlies the earlier notion of modernization as an inexorable "enactment of values" and the implicit link between modernization and development. This theory had gained traction in the wake of rapid globalization and the emergence of what communication theorist Manuel Castells refers to as "the network society."[16] Taylor, however, demurs. He argues that this view distorts and misrepresents the modernity of the West by misclassifying and narrowly construing its achievements. Furthermore, he notes that this position typically assumes that modernity essentially involves the shedding of traditional beliefs and values. Taylor argues that this theory neglects the fact that the difference between modern society and its premodern forebears is not a difference in belief systems, but one of a "background understanding against which our beliefs are formulated."[17] In other words, the difference between modern and premodern societies may not necessarily represent a fundamental break from values and institutions rooted in a particular culture. Accordingly, the transformation represented by modernity cannot be independent of culture, and indeed it is best to think of it not as a universal model, as promoted by the West, but more in terms of the variable possibilities—"alternative modernities"—embedded in different cultural traditions and experiences.[18] In a monograph documenting the colonial transformation of Delhi, urban designer Jyoti Hosagrahar makes a similar case for what she calls "indigenous modernity."[19] Finally, modernity as enlightenment remains not just an incomplete project of the West; the whole development process itself, argues anthropologist Arturo Escobar, "is the last and failed attempt to complete the enlightenment in Asia, Africa, and Latin America."[20]

The Orientalist Premise

To complete the critical arguments about the prevailing images of development as modernization, it is necessary to consider the arguments of Said in his critique of "Orientalism," the rich scholarly enterprise that flourished during the colonial era, embellished by works of arts and literature.[21]

Orientalism was primarily a scholarly enterprise that included works of European geographers, historians, linguists, philologists, and others who systematically chronicled, categorized, and interpreted the history and culture of "the Orient"—namely, Egypt and other Islamic countries of the Middle East and parts of India. This community of scholars, called Orientalists, created and shared a particular worldview about a geographical region hitherto unknown to Western scholarship and the public in the West.

The paradigm of Orientalism was not limited to the work of a community of scholars; popular literature, art, and drama of the time also exaggerated, distorted, and romanticized this worldview. The cover of Said's *Orientalism* features a painting by the renowned French artist Jean-Léon Gérôme titled *The Snake Charmer (1879)*, which depicts a naked boy with a python draped around his body, entertaining a tribal chief and his underlings sitting at the *kiblah*, or prayer wall, inside a mosque. The painting is an Orientalist distortion in several ways. For one, Muslims (and many other cultures) would consider it a cause of utmost shame to be naked in public.[22] It is especially heretical inside a mosque, where the precepts of Islam forbid any form of secular entertainment. Architect Nezar AlSayyad makes the same argument, and using computer simulation he shows that the wall in Gérôme's painting is most likely a copy of the mosque of Aqasunqur, also known as the Blue Mosque of Cairo.[23] Said's strongest critiques addressed such irreverent fictions and exaggerations in Western arts and literature regarding the Middle East, myths concocted for the intrigue of the naive Western audience.

Finally, and not insignificantly for Said, the Orientalist scholarship and other literary and artistic work flourished within the context of a subaltern relationship between Europe and its colonies. Orientalist perspectives either reinforced or passively collaborated in the political control and domination of the colonies by the ruling powers. In other words, arts, politics, and scholarship inextricably linked to propagate the myth and mystique of the Orient as a way of defining "the other," the one to be dominated, ruled, and ultimately civilized in the images of the West.

To reiterate the principal argument here, all development theories represent specific images of development, and while initially constructed from scholarly work, these images soon become normative models and take on a hegemonic and preemptive role in shaping development policy. Since the source of this scholarship is almost always Western, the historical processes documented to construct its models are also typically those of the Western nations, to recall Kuznets. Furthermore, in promoting these Western models of development as a prescription for poor countries, a hegemonic relationship is imposed on recipient countries. The condition of the developing countries thus is defined against the benchmark of contemporary Western lifestyle and standards of development.

Contemporary transformation of cities in emerging economies continues to follow the script of the West, abetted by the Western purveyors of development, design, engineering, finance, insurance, and planning. Even where local agents are involved, their imagination seemingly is limited. Local "knockoffs" of Western originals abound. The architecture and urban design of the developing world continue their subaltern relationship with the West, oblivious to the contradiction, incongruence, and discontinuity in the emerging landscapes, which are no less grotesque and fictional than Orientalist "exotic" artworks from the turn of the nineteenth century.

One wonders: Might it be too late for the Orientalist dialectic, as argued by Said, to play a role in the urban planning and design of the Global South? Has this discourse already been preempted by the forces and agencies of globalization[24] and the rise of the network society?[25] Consider, for example, the work of Hassan Fathy,[26] the renowned Egyptian architect who received much praise and accolade for designing buildings in the vocabulary of traditional and indigenous architecture. Using a Saidian frame of analysis, architect James Steele has demonstrated that Fathy, while well known for his contribution to developing an architectural style of "alternative indigenous modernity,"[27] actually suffered from an Orientalist and highly romanticized view of the indigenous settlement form of his native Egypt.[28] This insight poses an important caveat in pursuing endogenous alternatives to development images.

Competing Images of Development

While the bell curves and the theory of modernization dominated development thinking, alternative models emerged from the discontent with the project of the West. Three such models are particularly relevant: development as autonomy from dependency; development as sustainability, an idea that has gained considerable traction these days; and more recently, development as freedom, which emphasizes a capability-based approach.

Development as Autonomy from Dependency

The dependency and underdevelopment theorists presented a theoretical counterpoint to the classical views about development as economic growth. It grew out of the deliberations of the Economic Commission for Latin America (ECLA), set up by the UN in the 1940s to examine the causes of Latin American underdevelopment. The commission came to the conclusion that the Latin American countries had three choices for their future development paths: revolution, continued dependency, or autonomous development. Since revolution was not a viable option given the Cuban experience, and a continued dependency relationship was simply untenable, the ECLA emphasized autonomy from dependency as the best approach to development.[29]

When scholars and political observers began to be circumspect about the term "underdeveloped," commonly used to describe countries in the Global South, economist Andre Gunder Frank proposed, somewhat sardonically, that the term "underdevelopment" was quite appropriate in describing the status of the developing countries.[30] This was so, he argued, because underdevelopment of most developing countries was a result of a deliberate process. Development and underdevelopment are the two faces of the same coin; they are causally linked and not independent phenomena. Calling this process "development of underdevelopment," Frank argued that throughout colonial history, development of the Western industrial countries occurred at the cost of underdevelopment of the colonized countries. The wealth that fueled and sustained the Industrial Revolution and the industrial economy of the West was accumulated from the surplus value created by colonized and indentured labor and resources of the colonies in the Global South. By the beginning of the twentieth century the world economic order was organized into two groups: a "core" consisting of prosperous and industrialized nations of the West and a "periphery" of primary-resource-producing countries of the Global South.[31] The periphery became increasingly "dependent" on the core countries for their economic survival. The dependency relationship continued even after the end of the colonial era. Politically hegemonic relationships with the core countries further encumbered the periphery countries' sense of autonomy. According to this scenario, the only sensible path to development was autonomy from dependency.

Political theorist Ronald Chilcote explains the roots and derivatives of the dependency theory as originally grounded in a Leninist view of imperialism.[32] Frank's view of "development of underdevelopment" basically consolidated multiple essences of the dependency theory. Later, with the emergence of transnational and multinational corporations dominating the world economy, a mutant narrative of "new dependency" became relevant. Finally, and in view of the economic successes of some of the developing countries doing business with the West, still another narrative of "dependency and development" seemed apropos, conceding that countries could actually benefit from dependent relationships.[33]

The dependency theory had a major effect on the thinking of scholars and practitioners from developing countries. Its proponents ("Dependistas," as they were called) faced criticisms from various angles. For instance, supporters of market liberalism argued that import substitution policies inspired by the dependency theory were doomed to failure from the very beginning and brought very little prosperity and overall development. Also, they argued that dependency may not necessarily lead to underdevelopment, pointing to countries such as Canada that are in similar economic relationship.[34] The emerging global economy added fuel to this argument. The Marxists have recently argued that by pitting countries against countries in a dependency relationship, the Dependistas have missed the fundamental issue of class struggle between the labor and the capital classes at a global scale.[35]

Despite these political-economic critiques of the dependency theory, and its subsequent fall from grace in the development discourse, two major legacies of this theory are relevant to our current discussion of the images of development. The first legacy has to do with the notion of "dependent urbanization," an alternative argument to the neoclassical images of urbanization and primacy as portrayed by at least two related bell curves: those of urban primacy and regional disparity. The second legacy involves the extension of economic—and, of necessity, political—dependency to the arena of cultural dependency. Both have important implications for urban form and the design of developing cities. Let us consider these in that order.

Dependent Urbanization Dependent urbanization has three features, according to Castells: overurbanization, urban primacy, and dualistic urban form.[36] To these one could add still another related feature, "tertiarization," or the rise of the service sector.[37] These traits famously manifested in the urbanization of the Latin American countries.

Contemporary urbanization in Latin America had an early start. By 1920 the average urbanization level for Latin America had already reached 20 percent and was approaching 25 percent. By the middle of the last century its urbanization level had already exceeded the 50 percent mark and was approaching the level typical in the Western industrialized countries. This level, however, is yet to be achieved by a large number of Asian and African countries.

Reasons for the early start of the urbanization cycle in Latin America are embedded in the colonial and postcolonial development history of these countries. The rapid tempo of urbanization between 1940 and 1960 resulted from external influences, which had begun to shape the postcolonial economic development of Latin America toward the end of the nineteenth century and the beginning of the twentieth century. Conventional wisdom suggested that the growth of industry, commerce, and demand for urban labor typically triggered rural-urban migration, leading to rapid urbanization in Latin America.[38] At least this was the narrative of urbanization in the industrial West. But the ensuing urbanization in the developing world did not quite follow this script. Instead what occurred was a form of "tertiarization"—comprising mainly an informal economy—and the proliferation of slums and squatter settlements. Extreme inequality in income and land distribution—a legacy of colonial times—and the collapse of the rural economy from the expanding agribusinesses of a global economy seemed to explain much of this uneven development.

Of course, colonial rule in Latin America started and ended much earlier than most countries of the developing world. By the middle of the nineteenth century, most Latin American countries had obtained their independence, yet there was little change in the urban hierarchy they had inherited from the colonial times. Economic relationships of colonial days still prevailed with regard to the export of agricultural and mineral products and the import of largely industrial products, with this activity concentrated in a few established port cities. Foreign capital and agro-export interests, as well as the foreign control of domestic transportation (railroads) and shipping, dictated national policies favoring continued development of existing capitals and port cities. This polarized and uneven spatial development continued through the initial decades of the twentieth century. Then the First World War caused a major disruption in cross-Atlantic trade, necessitating domestic manufacturing of certain products and marking the first stage of industrialization in Latin America.

Arrival of European immigrants in the latter half of the nineteenth century sustained the initial growth of cities. They had few opportunities to become farmers and rural property owners because of the established *latifundistas* (owners of large rural farmlands), who had acquired and consolidated their holdings through earlier colonial allocation rules. Thus, cities were the immigrants' default destination. According to urban planner Jorge Hardoy, immigrants accounted for as much as 50 percent of the population in some of the major cities of Latin America by the middle of last century.[39] European investment and immigrant energy led to the founding of new urban settlements for the first time since colonial times. Even though these newer cities never gained enough population or importance to match the existing large cities, they marked a major increment of urban growth.

Finally, it was the global crisis of the 1930s, following the Great Depression in the US, that would trigger Latin America's explosive urban growth—characterized as hyper-urbanization by some—in the forties through the sixties.[40] The global economic crisis, however, exposed the inherent weaknesses of the domestic economy, which was still largely dependent on foreign imports for many consumer products. This led to a second wave of industrial expansion in Latin America aided by new foreign investments from Europe and the US and national policies of import substitution.

There is no question that the economies of some of these countries underwent a significant transformation from a largely export-based agricultural economy to one dominated by the industrial and service sectors. However, the industrial expansion in Latin America did not generate a commensurate increase in factory jobs. The share of industrial employment in the total labor force did not increase greatly in the fifties and sixties. In fact, it has remained virtually unchanged since then. There are several explanations for this seeming inconsistency of an industrial expansion without an accompanying proportionate increase in the industrial labor force. Castells has argued that industrialization means modernization and increased labor productivity, often at the cost of a labor-intensive crafts sector; hence, net gain may not be significant.[41] Furthermore, because of the extreme inequality in the distribution of land, there has been little opportunity for the expansion of small-scale and labor-intensive agriculture.[42] Moreover, modernization of large-scale, export-oriented agribusiness did little to expand employment opportunities in the rural sector. The net result of this dynamic of labor surplus in the agricultural sector was the massive migration of the rural poor to the cities of Latin America. Based on a study of sixteen Latin American countries, sociologists Alan Gilbert and Joseph Gugler have argued that the rate of rural out-migration was strongly related to the distribution of farm size.[43] In other words, rural out-migration was highest for those countries where more than half of the farmers were *minifundios*, or small landholders, but where more than half of the land was held by *latifundios*, the large landholders.

Urbanization resulting from massive rural migration led to a large expansion of the "service" or "tertiary" sector. Anthropologist Lisa Peattie has called this process "tertiarization."[44] The nature of work in this sector involves many different things—domestic help, peddlers, petty tradespeople, ragpickers, and day laborers, for instance. Much of this work is only "a disguised form of unemployment."[45] Work of this nature is now officially recognized as the "informal sector" by many Third World governments, after an International Labor Organization (ILO) report made a strong case for considering the informal sector in national economic planning and policies.[46]

More generally, the term "overurbanization" refers to the phenomenon of rapid urbanization without a commensurate expansion of industrial employment, as is typical of much of Latin America. Castells defined that concept as "a level of urbanization higher than that which can 'normally' be attained, given the level of industrialization."[47] Overurbanization is not an exclusively Latin American phenomenon. Developing economies in other regions experienced a similar pattern of urban growth.

Theorists from different fields, and from outside of mainstream economics, had a different take on the colonial transformation of the settlement systems in the developing world. Anthropologist Richard Morse argued that Latin American countries had a perfectly balanced system of cities before the colonial era, and that it was the colonial economy that produced uneven spatial development.[48] This argument generally resonated with observations of other scholars,[49] although not all who examined the rank-size distribution of cities in various colonial systems reached a similar conclusion.[50] Scholars inspired by sociologist Immanuel Wallerstein's world-systems approach,[51] however, argue that the economic relationship between core and periphery during colonial and postcolonial periods is primarily responsible for this uneven spatial development.[52] Collapse of the rural economy, rural poverty, and consequent rural-urban migration—all of which are attributed to the exogenous forces of economic development—contributed to the development of distorted urban systems.[53] In a similar vein, and drawing from dependency theory, scholars explored the possibility of a dependent urban hierarchy. Castells, for one, argued that overurbanization and urban primacy essentially are outcomes of dependent urbanization.[54]

Cultural Dependency The second legacy of the dependency theory is "cultural dependency." According to this argument, the hegemonic relationship sustained by economic dependency ultimately touches and transforms cultural processes. Studies by communication theorist Everett Rogers and his colleagues demonstrated that until recently, Latin American television broadcasts were heavily dependent on reruns of American television shows.[55] Today, it is increasingly evident that the "rise of network society"[56] and the information and communication technology revolution has made this cultural transformation inexorable. Indeed, culture itself has become an agent of globalization.[57] Images transmitted through films, television shows, music, and popular magazines of the West are increasingly shaping entertainment, fashion, and preferences for consumer goods worldwide. What sociologist Fredric Jameson calls "the cultural logic of late capitalism" has now permeated countries of early capitalism.[58] In his dissertation Rafael Pizarro argues that the "Hollywood Urban Imaginarium"—the imagery in Hollywood movies that routinely use the homes, backyards, front lawns, and shopping malls of American suburbia as backdrops or central themes[59]—has profoundly shaped the preference for American-style suburban living in Latin America.[60]

Thus, the notion of cultural dependency may help explain aspects of the design of the postcolonial built environment, preempting any expectations of an indigenous modernity such as suggested by Taylor.[61] The work of Said[62] offers another argument and frame of analysis for explaining what might be called "dependent design" of the emerging urban landscape.

Development as Sustainability

The image of sustainable development—its meaning or a precise definition—remains elusive, despite the appeal and popularity of such a concept. Scholarly and professional writings emphasize the balance between economy, environment, and equity.[63] Lacking a precise meaning or definition, the concept is often socially constructed; sustainable development policies thus emerge out of an awkward marriage of science and politics. Standards of sustainable development are often politically negotiated rather than scientifically determined.

The tension between economic growth and conservation of nature continues to haunt the sustainability discourse within international aid agencies. A provocative internal memo written in 1991 by Lawrence Summers, then chief economist of the World Bank (presumably to challenge his staff to think outside the box), captured this tension.[64]

His main argument was that since the poor Third World countries yet to industrialize have considerable surpluses of clean environmental resources—air, land, and water—it will be a rational option for them to absorb the pollution of the Western industrial countries, for a price, of course. In other words, poor countries could sell "pollution rights" to Western industrial economies and in return obtain much-needed capital for development. Certainly this would make economic sense, if the human costs and consequences were not so great.

The concept of sustainable development, nevertheless, is a positive one. At the level of everyday practice and policy, many have accepted the definition proposed by the Brundtland Commission,[65] which emphasizes consideration for future generations as an operational concept, while working for an equitable balance between the economy and the environment. Definitions of "sustainable" of course vary depending on the scale at which the word is used as a qualifier. Thus, the meaning of sustainability may vary subtly if we are talking about communities or national development.[66] For example, at the scale of community, participation can be integral to sustainability. I have taken the position here that the concept of sustainability should balance the economic imperatives of development with principles that are derived not just from ecology, but also from anthropology.

Like ecologists, anthropologists have viewed "development" mainly as damaging and disruptive to the natural order of things. They have been concerned about development as "that process of technical change and colonial and commercial expansion that was tending to destroy these various cultures—and sometimes the very tribal groups who were the bearers of the cultures."[67] But in the arena of development planning, this view is seen as too romantic and not unlike the way ecologists worry about the destruction of fragile ecosystems or species. Ecology and anthropology both derive their values of conservation from an augmented sense of time inherent in the natural and cultural history of human habitat. Development, as anthropologist Lisa Peattie points out, "was for anthropology an aspect of the history of culture, of the story of the human species—the last few minutes of the long story that begins with paleontology and human evolution and goes on through ... the reconstruction of ancient civilizations."[68]

The challenges of sustainable development from the anthropological perspective are best captured in the reflections of Peattie, who was involved in interdisciplinary efforts in development planning.[69] She speaks of the work of her father, anthropologist Robert Redfield,[70] who made a distinction between the "moral order," which are the values inherent in traditional societies, and the "technical order" of the modern era—that of market, state, and corporations—which dominates contemporary thinking about development. As discussed in the earlier review of the modernization literature, the moral order of traditional societies—the "moral familism" of backward societies, to invoke political scientist Edward Banfield[71]—was seen as inadequate to launch a successful development enterprise. Peattie concedes that the development process is destined to be an artifact of the technical order, yet since development touches every aspect of human life, and since development involves human institutions, organizations, and social relationships, the moral order of societies must not be compromised. Furthermore, anthropologist Stephen Lansing shows, in his study of the Asian Development Bank (ADB) irrigation project in Bali, that ancient moral orders such as the rituals of Balinese water temples often had deep ecological bases.[72] The ADB project was symbolic of the technical order, as the experts attempted to increase agricultural production by introducing new technology. The project nearly resulted in a major environmental disaster by disrupting the ecologically rooted practice of irrigation encoded in the traditional moral order of temple rituals administered by a priest. As James C. Scott also argues, weaving the moral order into the dominant technical order of development remains the critical challenge for development planning. The concept of sustainable development epitomizes this challenge.[73]

While very few of the development visions that evolved outside of mainstream Western economic theory included a conscious consideration of space, there is one notable exception. No review of this field would be complete without the Maoist vision of development, with its very specific prescriptions for urbanization and spatial development. At a time when most developing countries lacked consistent urbanization policies, China had a very clear policy of urbanization and the development of its settlement system. Mao rejected the contemporary and conventional Western notion that urbanization is a precursor of development and modernization. Suspicious of cities as exploitative of the countryside, and thinking of them as "parasitic" in both economic and cultural senses, Mao argued for a policy of "walking on two legs," meaning a balanced simultaneous development of both rural and urban areas. He believed in modernization, but one that is not limited to cities; he instead promoted rural industrialization alongside a bottom-up approach to development. While balance in rural and urban development was promoted, it did not necessarily involve sustainability according to our contemporary discourse. As a Chinese poster of that era shows (see figure 3.1), nature was seen as hostile to development. Thus, development necessarily meant taming nature, building dams, dredging canals, terracing mountains, and changing nature services in achieving goals of development.

Development as Freedom

Finally, it is necessary to consider the work of Amartya Sen, especially his book *Development as Freedom*,[74] because his ideas offer possibilities for alternative policy measures

Figure 3.1
"Man's determination will triumph over nature," states the slogan on the building in the foreground of this Chinese propaganda poster (n.d. 1940–1990).
Source: By permission of the University of Westminster Archive.

and innovative institutional approaches to development. Sen begins his treatise on development as freedom by examining different concepts and measures of income.[75] He asks whether income should necessarily be considered the most relevant "space of inequality" in thinking about development. Asking the question "Inequality of what?" he challenges the utilitarian presumption that income is the sole means of achieving welfare. He similarly criticizes the Rawlsian emphasis on an equality of primary resources as inadequate, while nonetheless acknowledging the merits of the Rawlsian principles of justice. He points out that income by itself may not guarantee well-being or buy happiness for an individual, and that the goal of development should instead be freedom, especially "positive freedom" as defined by philosopher Isaiah Berlin.[76] Accordingly, the relevant space of equality, Sen argues, should be the functionings of individual members of a society, and the aim of development should be to maximize the capabilities that allow people to achieve their functionings. The way to meet that goal would be to remove or eliminate the "unfreedoms" that prevent people from achieving their desired and necessary functionings: lack of access to health care, to sanitary facilities, or to clean water.[77]

The development as freedom approach is a very different paradigm than the fable of bell curves. While normative, it is an individual-based approach to development thinking, profoundly rooted in the ethical and moral philosophy of freedom and justice. If the fable of bell curves represents the technical order of development thinking, Sen's approach represents the moral order. The difficulty with Sen's approach, as his detractors have pointed out, is that it remains on a theoretical plane and is difficult to translate into policy. The aggregation of individual functioning requirements and the allocation of resources to different capabilities remains a vexing puzzle. Sen's ideas about capability might have remained at an abstract level were it not for a growing body of scholarship that includes philosopher Martha Nussbaum's work on gender and development.[78]

With this perspective, it is even possible to revisit the environmental Kuznets curve and think of environmental pollution and resource depletion as "unfreedoms" to invoke Sen.[79] Thus human capability is stifled by the ill health effects of pollution, and individual functionings and freedoms are hampered by the deprivation of natural resources and amenities. The bell curve fable does not offer any positive directions for policy formulation. But the development as freedom framework may help formulate tangible policies for the environment, such as keeping the bell curves of environmental deterioration shallow and short in duration, thereby minimizing the effects of environmental unfreedoms.

Implications for Form and Spatial Organization of Cities

At the level of spatial organization of cities, most development theories remain mute, with the notable exceptions discussed above. The only other commentary on this subject comes from Castells, who suggests that the dualistic urban form of developing cities is the third feature of dependent urbanization, thus connecting dualism with dependency and colonial legacy.[80]

As I proposed earlier, the aim of this book is precisely to articulate a missing dimension of spatial organization and urban form that correlates the development history of Third World cities with the broader images of development that have guided their courses. The following chapters will be devoted to this exploration.

4 Urban Form and Urbanism

> The form of the metropolis, then, is its formlessness. Those who work within the ideological limits of this regime have only a quantitative conception of improvement: they seek to make its buildings higher, its streets broader, its parking lots more ample: they would multiply bridges, highways, tunnels, making it ever easier to get in and out of the city, but constricting the amount of space available within the city for any other purpose than transportation itself. Frank Lloyd Wright's project for a skyscraper a mile high was the ultimate reduction to absurdity of this whole theory of city development. The ultimate form of such a city would be an acre of building to a square mile of expressways and parking lots. In many areas this is rapidly approaching fulfillment.
>
> —Lewis Mumford, *The City in History*[1]

If the literature on development has remained distant from urban form, how has the literature on form connected with the idea of development? This is a reasonable inquiry, and here I explore answers to this question. To be sure, the literature on urban form is quite extensive and constantly growing. What follows is a selective review, but presented within a comprehensive taxonomy.

Urban Form in Space and Time

We can define urban form essentially as the three-dimensional built environment of an urban area: the spatial arrangement and organization of buildings, structures, streets, and open spaces. Architects often refer to this arrangement as the "figure-ground" patterns (of solid and void) as they appear in the "plan" view like the famous Nolli maps of Rome, or the maps of pre– and post–World War II Berlin presented by urban historian Hans Stimmann, which continue to inspire architectural fascination with the gestalt of urban form.[2] But these are only a partial representation of urban space; they do not capture the uses and activities in space and the various sensory and sensuous experiences derived from quotidian life experiences. The natural features that define the context of human settlements—hills, rivers, valleys, canyons, lakes, coastlines, and the like—also influence the shape and the spatial organization of urban areas. These are also intrinsic to urban form.

Our understanding of urban form would be incomplete without an appreciation of the historical evolution of places and populations, and the dynamics of urban change. Thus, a temporal dimension is also intrinsic to this definition. Students of urban history and preservation have always looked at the built environment as a transcript of social, economic, and political transitions and transformations. How to tell time from the built environment, or timing places, have been the focus of some scholarly work. The title of Kevin Lynch's book *What Time Is This Place?* captures this interest in time and form.[3]

Urban Form and Urbanism

Beyond the spatiality and temporality of urban form we must also consider the more expansive, if less tangible, notion of "urbanism." The term "urbanism" extends the realm of interpreting urban form beyond spatiality and temporality in several ways.

> First, it offers a focus on the qualitative aspects of the city's soul, for the lack of a better term. I consider Jonathan Raban's interpretive representations in *Soft City* or Italo Calvino's urban *imaginaires* in *Invisible Cities* to be examples of this particular dimension.[4] Their works represent an important aspect of understanding the urban experience, through subjective, emotive, interpretive, and imaginative expressions of its essence.
>
> Second, cities have not only different "looks" but also different "feels" and "paces." Behavioral scientists have tried to define and study what psychologist Stanley Milgram referred to as the "atmosphere" or ambience of a city.[5] He and others believed that these seemingly evanescent urban qualities could be subject to empirical research. Experiments were designed to collect measurements of public behavior—from the speed of walking to the willingness to help strangers—as indicators of the atmosphere of cities. The roots of this inquiry go back to the sociological concepts of "gemeinschaft" and "geselleschaft" that were advanced in the late nineteenth century by sociologist Ferdinand Tönnies, and subsequent discussions on urbanism as "a way of life."[6] The notion of heterogeneity is a major leitmotif in these concepts of urbanism. As sociologist Peter

Langer points out, four very different images of the city as an "organized diversity"—bazaar, jungle, machine, organism—still persist in the literature.[7]

Finally, the term "urbanism" also captures the theme of many comparative, historiographic, and critical studies of the physical city that draw from various branches of the humanities and social sciences, including cultural geography, urban history, political economy, critical studies, and comparative literature.[8] The aim here is to consider urban form of developing economies as an outcome of development processes. Here the focus, however, remains on the physical city.

In table 4.1, I propose a schema for organizing different approaches—as embedded in the relevant literature—to interpret urban form. The intent of the schema is mainly taxonomic and illustrative, as an attempt to identify the major traditions and emerging directions in inquiries into urban form. It identifies key concepts for each approach and the principal authors and proponents associated with such concepts. The remainder of the chapter will include brief reviews of these approaches. The intent here is to examine how this literature contributes to our understanding of the relationship between the idea of development and urban form.

This classification reflects a progression that is consistent with the evolution of my own personal awareness of the field and the literature. Not unexpectedly, the ordering of various approaches enumerated in table 4.1 also follows a rough chronological sequence:

1. *The Documentary-Archetypal*: consists of a rich, varied, and established literature on the history of urban form that is the oldest in vintage.
2. *The Normative-Romantic*: reflects intuitions closely linked to the historical tradition and has often derived its inspirations from the historic ideals of urban form.
3. *The Positive-Analytical*: represents the literature that began in the sixties with the infusion of social sciences into the field of planning. Until then, the subject of urban form was mainly descriptive and analytical, but became a subject of positivist analysis under the growing influence of social sciences.
4. *The Experiential-Behavioral*: Kevin Lynch's seminal work on mental maps of cities led to a convergence of interests in the experiential city between such disciplines as geography, psychology, and planning, which is represented by this category.
5. *The Political-Economic*: consists of a political-economic approach that includes radical planning theories and critiques of contemporary urbanism and urbanization, which became quite influential in the seventies. Critical explanations of urban form found their base in a neo-Marxian tradition, focusing mainly on Third World development and urbanization.

Table 4.1
Principal approaches to the study of urban form

	Key Concepts		Authors	
Categories	Western Context	Non-Western Context	Western Context	Non-Western Context
Documentary-Archetypal	Urban Pattern, Visual Form, Industrial City, Suburbia	Islamic City, Indigenous City, Colonial City	Kostof, Gallion & Eisner, Peets, Morris, Mumford, Bacon, Reps, Spreiregen, Gutkind, Sitte, Krier, Fishman, Jackson (J. B.), Geist	Morris, Crane, O'Connor, Mumford, Evenson, Abu-Lughod, Kheirabadi, Gaube, Qadeer, Madanipour, Skinner, Lapidus, Wu
Normative-Romantic	Good City Form, Ideal City, Performance Characteristics, Garden City, Neighborhood Unit, New Urbanism	Cosmic Models	Lynch, Goodman & Goodman, Alexander, Appleyard, Sert, Jacobs, Rykwert, Mumford, Howard, Le Corbusier (see chapter 7), Congress for New Urbanism, CIAM,* Krier	Ardalan, Doxiadis
Positive-Analytical	Spatial Structure and Organization, Urban Morphology	Informal Economy	Lynch & Rodwin, Alonso, Wingo, Webber, Moudon, Hillier	Geddes (see Epilogue), Santos, Castells, Doxiadis
Experiential-Behavioral	Image, Memory, Orientation, Social and Psychological Functions of Environmental Form	Image, Memory	Lynch, Appleyard, Milgram, Downs, Michelson	Stea, Gulick, Lynch, Appleyard, Low
Political-Economic	Global City	Dualism, Shared Space, Mode of Production, World Systems Theory	Castells, Friedmann, Harvey, Lefebvre, Soja, Scott, Hayden, Feinstein, Sassen, Davis, Beauregard, Tajbakhsh, Zukin	Armstrong & McGee, Santos, Castells, Bairoch, Graham & Marvin
Symbolic-Interpretive	Semiotics, Communication Theory of Urban Form, Cyber-City	Anthropology of Form, Postcolonial Theories	Castells, Gottdeiner, Rapoport, Rykwert, Sennett, Mitchell, Boyer, Meier, Duncan	Abu-Lughod, Rapoport, Wright (A. F.), Çelik, Holston, Nas, King, Evenson, Peattie
Critical-Discursive	City as Text, Rhetoric of Landscape, Modernity and Postmodernity, Feminist and Gender Theories of Space	City as Text, Rhetoric of Landscape	Boyer, Dear, Hiss, Sorkin, Sennett, Jackson (K.), Jackson (J.), Jameson, Benjamin, Meinig, Scott, Foucault, Cosgrove, Buck-Morss, Friedberg, Davis, Hayden, Sandercock, Fraser, Friedberg	Abu-Lughod, AlSayyad, Çelik, Low, Campanella, Bosker

**Note*: CIAM is the French acronym for Congres Internationaux d'Architecture Moderne

6. *The Symbolic-Interpretive*: more recent, although its roots are in the experiential city tradition and are supplemented by scholarship in fields such as cultural anthropology, semiotics, political theory, and critical studies.
7. *The Critical-Discursive*: represents the contemporary discourse on urban form. It situates urban form at a confluence of critical writings from various disciplines on contemporary culture and society.

The schema of table 4.1 has some pedagogic logic to its ordering. For a student of urban form, lessons should begin with a historical survey of city development, even if it is descriptive at best. From the descriptive tradition then flows the normative and experiential approach to understanding city form. That transition is very much a part of the training of architects, urban designers, and planners. The positivist approach seemingly could serve those interested in urban form in a social scientific way. The interpretive and critical-discursive approaches are more common at advanced levels of study.

In table 4.1 I differentiate the work that has grown out of the developing nations context from work that is mainly of Western origin. But this former type is relatively small. The "Documentary-Archetypal" category concerns Third World cities the most, and it includes writings by both Western and non-Western scholars. Also, under the "Political-Economic" and "Symbolic-Interpretive" categories, there is a considerable amount of work on the Global South cities. In fact, some of the major theoretical contributions of this approach are based on writings on the political economy of development and underdevelopment. I also note a growing body of literature in the symbolic-interpretive tradition. The contributions of the remaining approaches are indeed rather spindly when it comes to the developing world, and are primarily Occidental in origin and disposition. In the following section I explore whether or to what extent images of development are implicit in the seven different categories of urban form literature.

1. The Documentary-Archetypal Tradition

This literature is quite extensive. Its content is descriptive and in part taxonomic. Some aspects are analytical while others are interpretive, often expounding on the timeless aesthetics and archetypes of historic urban form. While some are comprehensive, covering the whole spectrum of Western civilization, for instance from prehistory to the Renaissance or to the modern industrial period,[9] others are focused on a particular period, country, culture, or even city.[10] Cases in point are the following: urban historian John Reps's study of early American settlements; work on Iranian cities by urban historian Heinz Gaube, geographer Masoud Kheirabadi, and urban planner Ali Madanipour, or on French colonial cities of North Africa by architectural historian

Gwendolyn Wright; studies of so-called Islamic cities by architect Nezar AlSayyad and urban planners Hooshang Amirahmadi and Salah El-Shakhs; architect Steen Eiler Rasmussen's classic work on London, and sociologist Janet Abu-Lughod's studies of individual North African cities like Cairo or Rabat.[11]

Much of these annals are representations of the physical city mixed in with important historic events and episodes. The accounts may also include relevant social, cultural, and technological changes brought about by mutations and evolutions of urban form. Beyond archival accounts, emphasis in this literature is on inventorying and cataloging the shape, size, physical characteristics, and spatial organization of elements of urban form. Much of this effort is devoted to describing the anatomy of the physical city and identifying prototypical elements and their archetypes.[12] Architect Rob Krier's inventory of archetypal urban spaces is a case in point.[13] At the most elementary level this category is archaeological in origin. Urban forms of antiquity—like the Mesopotamian city of Mohenjodaro in the deserts of Sindh, or the Incan city of Machu Picchu in the soaring heights of the Andes—are reconstructed from their excavated remains. Other reconstructions are products of intellectual excavations into written records or iconic representations: old maps, paintings, etchings, and so forth.

Interpretations of urban form in this tradition are usually of three types, although they are not necessarily mutually exclusive. One such type can be described as *morphological*, a term often used in the literature[14] to refer to the systematic and taxonomic nature of these studies. The term "morphology"—the study of form and structure of plants and animals—is borrowed from the biological sciences,[15] and it has an objective and analytic aura to it. This approach is quite popular in the architectural studies of building typology.[16]

The second category represents the *subjective* tradition, focusing mainly on the aesthetic and visual aspects of urban form. Strongly rooted in architecture and art criticism, this literature focuses mainly on the archetypal or epitomized elements of urban form in an attempt to derive and promote the essential principles of good design. Writings of architect-planners Edward Bacon, Hans Blumenfeld, Elbert Peets, Camillo Sitte, and Paul Spreiregen are examples of this tradition. Works of this genre continue to inspire the rhetoric and intentions of modern urban design.[17]

In the third line of interpretation, urban form is treated mainly as an *artifact*,[18] the way a Ming vase or a Sumerian urn is seen as a product of the arts, technology, and material culture of a particular period. Functions and purposes of various elements of urban form—such as the wall, the gate, the public square, houses, and the street—are described in detail, with emphasis on the functions and purposes of these elements.

Historian John Summerson wrote about the "city as an artefact" in discussing the role of urban historians.[19] In expounding the concept further, architectural historian Anthony Garvan argues that if cities are seen as an artifact in the way that anthropologists or archaeologists refer to material objects and tools, then "it is an artifact of the whole culture and not of its economy, social standing, politics or any other aspects of urban life taken singly or alone."[20]

2. The Normative Approach

In a treatise on the performance characteristics of good city form, Lynch begins by examining the historical roots of the ideal city in different cultures.[21] He refers to one class of these representations as "cosmic" models, because they tried to link the form of the city and its component parts to exalted notions of God, the cosmos, or nature. This is particularly true of non-Western images of the good city, as was the case in ancient Aztec, Chinese, Hindu, or Incan cities. In these cases, notions of ideal city form were derived from external sources of reference and inspiration, rather than an internal order of administration and social interaction as in Plato's or Aristotle's prescriptions for the ideal city. In Western culture a spiritual order of the normative city was implicit in Saint Augustine's *City of God*. But this was ultimately an intellectual reasoning for the role of *civitas* in the moral landscape of the Christian concepts of human existence. Even here the normative city was one of a secular order without any religious or spiritual symbols or prescriptions for the spatial structure and organization of the city.

Lynch notes, however, that the cosmic or the divine order that inspired some of the ancient ideal city forms often reflected nothing more than the power relationships intrinsic to the prevalent social order. Thus, the location of a pyramid or the height of a ziggurat in an Aztec or Incan or Babylonian city simply reflected the power and control of the priest. The priority locations for palaces and temples in ancient cities was similarly justified as a political rationale couched in terms of divine order, with kings and priests presented as agents of that order's cosmic authority. The cosmic or divine order is the basis for the normative city.[22] This is self-evident in historic representations of the ideal city, and seemingly continues in the contemporary debate over secular versus ecological values,[23] or in the tension between the technical order versus the moral order of development, as discussed in the previous chapter.[24] A form of anthropocentrism in the name of divine order prevailed in the ideal settlement forms of some non-Western cultures. As architect Alexander Tzonis points out, the Dogon settlement forms of sub-Saharan Africa reflected the human anatomy, in the image of the highest form of divine creation.[25] The ideal Hindu city form also contained an ordering that derived its logic from human anatomy.[26] In contrast, the form of ideal Chinese cities, related to a larger cosmic order, organized the city according to cardinal directions, the position of heavenly bodies, and principles of maintaining harmony (yin and yang) with land, water, and air.

Visions of the normative city have persisted throughout history and into the recent past. Some of these visions grow out of social utopias of the previous centuries, while others are futuristic architectural extrapolations of technological change and possibilities. Noteworthy are Archigram's "plug-in city," Frank Lloyd Wright's "Broadacre City," and Paolo Soleri's "Arcosanti." In reviewing the underlying values of those ideal cities Lynch notes the irony that while social utopias typically lacked viable visions of built form, physical utopias like architect Paolo Soleri's models of self-contained, ecologically nondisruptive cities lacked the social relationships that create viable communities. Images of the normative city thus fail to reconcile visions of a good city with visions of a good society or development.[27] Noting that it is not easy to conflate visions of a good city with visions of a good society, Lynch commented, "Only in antiutopias can we find examples where physical oppression abets social oppression in a very direct and circumstantial way. Hell, at least, is vivid and convincing. Indeed, it is difficult to unfold a coherent vision of a desirable new society in a desirable new world."[28]

In his writings Lynch tried to combine ideas of a good society with that of good form, emphasizing "performance dimensions" of good form rather than a particular model of cities or social relationships. He thus avoided the pitfall that swallowed earlier utopias, and spoke instead of the normative city as one that satisfies the essential criteria of good human environments: access, fit, equity, control, sense, and the meta-criteria of efficiency and justice.[29] Contemporary literature contains the work of other noted visionaries. The "garden city" concept of British town planner Ebenezer Howard and his US followers—including urban planners Clarence Stein, Lewis Mumford, and Henry Churchill—was seen as a way to combine nature and open space into regional form as an antidote to the inhumanity of the industrial city. Earlier the Goodman brothers'[30] treatise on alternative secular visions of the ideal city produced an important discourse on the normative city. Also noteworthy is Christopher Alexander's "pattern language" for designing good urban places—a lexicon derived empirically from past examples of successful places. This approach, however, offers no normative guidance or vision for the composition of possible patterns.[31]

Although none of the contemporary models of the good city discussed here addresses the realities of the developing world, one could argue that to the extent that the global economic order is inexorably driving much of the developing world toward a shared and universal experience of the urban condition, many of these normative criteria of good urban form should apply across cultures. This approach might be a better alternative to the blind mimesis commonly seen today.

3. The Positive-Analytical Approach

By the second half of the twentieth century social sciences had a major influence on the field of city and regional planning. Normative visions and aesthetic intuitions rooted in architecture and landscape architecture became the target of social scientists. They blamed the debacles of urban renewal, public housing, new towns, and inner-city freeway development on the megalomaniac—and physically deterministic—visions of architects and planners.[32] They exhorted planners to spurn their obsessions with the physical city and to be cognizant instead of the city as a complex network of social and economic systems. They admonished planners to be aware of the human consequences and power politics of planning decisions. They further implored planners to make rational decisions using intelligence derived from objective information about the city and its problems, and to move from a world of intuitions and beliefs to one of facts and knowledge.[33]

Positivist canons of social sciences brought a new enthusiasm for empirical studies of various facets of the city. Analyses, measurements, and models of urban systems and activities created a new trend in planning. Benefit-cost analysis, factorial ecology, gravity model, location quotient, and other quantitative approaches to understanding urban outcomes became essential tools in the planner's toolkit. Urban economists like William Alonso began to look at the spatial organization of cities in terms of land rents, density gradients, and population density, and to explain various spatial formations in those terms. Ideas such as monocentric versus polycentric urban form emerged from these studies.[34] Social ecologists added other models of urban form and growth.[35] Lynch proposed initial taxonomies of urban form based on conventional wisdom about the shape, patterns, and organization of activities and movements systems.[36] The nomenclature included such form descriptors as radial, linear, radiocentric, and dispersed sheet. With his Massachusetts Institute of Technology colleague the planning theorist Lloyd Rodwin, Lynch further attempted to formalize a new set of descriptors for representing the form characteristics of the city by combining aspects of the physical form and typical activity patterns that occur in adapted urban spaces.[37] About this same time, planning academic Melvin Webber launched a parallel effort to explain the interaction of urban space and activity patterns.[38]

While imaginative and creative, these taxonomic approaches did not yield any immediate promise of theory building. The task of measuring, storing, and analyzing the data on physical form alone proved quite daunting, beyond what is typically available as land use or circulation data. For another, it was not clear how these taxonomies and measurements would lead to theory or policy.[39] Attempts at building formal theories such as the one developed by Lynch and Rodwin were more of an algorithm for testing alternative form outcomes.[40] More significantly, earlier enthusiasms for the positivist approach were dampened by a realization that the experiential reality of urban form is more complex, and fundamentally intractable, than previously presumed. Author Jonathan Raban's notion of the "soft city," Christopher Alexander's concession that the "city is not a tree," and Melvin Webber's argument that planners should be aware of a "non-place" urban realm, were all testimonies to this growing awareness.[41]

There was another important dimension missing from the positive-analytical approach: its contribution to the understanding of how urban form can be seen as a development outcome, or for that matter, how one may derive normative implications from such analysis. What can we say about the performance of various patterns of city development? Does the "radial" form obtain greater distributive justice than the grid form, while the grid might be more environmentally efficient than the radial form? Is the polycentric form Pareto superior to the monocentric form? And so forth.

With the availability of information technology's new tools, there is new interest in positivist and empirical studies of urban form.[42] Shape, size, grain, pattern, and organization of buildings and spaces, and even the historic evolution and mutation of urban form, have become the focus of studies of urban morphology. The new interest in urban form stems from recent debates on urban sprawl and the compact city and public health initiatives emphasizing the built environment.[43] Positivist searches for formal measures and indicators of the physical form of sprawl are currently underway, mainly by economists and geographers armed with the new tools of geographic information system (GIS), satellite imagery, and fractal theory.

It should be apparent from table 4.1 that there is little in the positive-analytical tradition that draws from the non-Western urban context, both in terms of concepts and authorship. The only exception is probably the work of sociologist-planner Patrick Geddes, who is known for his advocacy of scientific planning and his belief in social data and relevant information,[44] including the developing context of colonial India. Later, architect-planner Constantin Doxiadis's notion of *ekistics*, the science of human settlements, found applications in new town plans in the developing world.

4. The Experiential-Behavioral Approach

Another significant influence of the social science approach on the study of urban form was the new focus on the individual as the "user," the "man on the street," or the "human subject." There was growing interest in how users experience, perceive, understand, and remember the physical city from their interactions with the everyday environment. Previous practices of city design drew from aesthetic principles of the earlier Baroque era nurtured and propagated by the Beaux Arts tradition. The layout of buildings, streets, open spaces, squares, courts, and gardens reflected formal geometry, order of symmetry, and proportions. How such spaces are actually experienced and understood as people move through them was not a paramount concern in this Platonic design. In contrast, with a nod to the Aristotelian tradition, Kevin Lynch asked laypeople to talk about their experiences of the physical city and to draw maps of their "images" of the city.[45] He proposed that the shared elements of these personal images constitute a consensus or a "public" image. He further proposed that the content of such images suggested five essential categories for organizing the city experience in memory: edges, districts, landmarks, nodes, and paths. Lynch's work had a major effect on the practice of design and gave it a legitimacy previously lacking in the eyes of social scientists. His taxonomy created a new idiom of urban design. Practitioners, however, overlooked Lynch's theoretical explanations of imageability—identity, structure, and meaning—and his hope that this methodology would offer a medium of conversation hopelessly lacking between the experts and the public in earlier efforts in city design (and even today perhaps), thus encouraging a new kind of Aristotelian city design.[46]

In the academic world Lynch's work triggered a major interest in such fields as environmental and social psychology, sociology, and in particular human geography. Academics found a renewed interest in studying "cognitive maps," a term originally coined by psychologist Edward Tolman in a well-known and counter-paradigmatic article titled "Cognitive Maps in Rats and Men," published more than ten years before Lynch wrote his book.[47] Although Lynch drew extensively from the works of anthropologists and geographers—because of his interest in orientation—it is not clear if he was aware of Tolman's work.[48] Nevertheless, academics from other fields replicated Lynchian studies of urban images and cognitive maps in cities around the world, including some from the developing world. Some notable examples are sociologist John Gulick's study of Tripoli and Baghdad; a study of slum dwellers' images of the city by geographers P. P. Karan, W. A. Bladen, and G. Singh; urban planner Donald Appleyard's study of residents of Ciudad Guyana; and Lynch and his colleagues' comparative study of children in cities of Argentina, Australia, Mexico, and Poland.[49] Some of these studies show that the Lynchian nomenclature, surprisingly, has had easy application to non-Western cities and could be used even in environments of poverty and low literacy. While these collective images may not have added significantly to our understanding of the structural characteristics of urban form and their development, a few of these studies did suggest some cultural differences in imageability. One such insight has to do with culturally based signification and meaning.

Of his three postulates of imageability—identity, structure, and meaning—Lynch focused mainly on identity and structure. He conceded that meaning was too difficult to elicit from maps or conversations, because it is often embedded in a personal biography of experiences that eludes easy articulation. Lynch's concern was mainly with the visual qualities of urban form that contribute to "legibility." Identity and structure in urban form, he argued, offer that promise. These qualities help us read the city better, and serve as the syntax of the urban form. Identity of individual elements is typically derived from their visual uniqueness or dominance in the landscape. From his study of Arab cities, Gulick posited further that identity does not necessarily have to be visual only, as an important footnote to Lynch.[50] He noted that smaller neighborhood mosques—those without unique architectural style or visibility—show up regularly in the cognitive maps of residents, because of their social and religious significance associated with the quotidian life and habitus.

Although Lynch himself considered meaning largely in the context of legibility, which is to say the extent to which it helps us to read the city better and make it "imageable," more recently his work has received a more sympathetic interpretation from political theorist Fredric Jameson.[51] Jameson argued that the difficulty people have in forming a coherent image of the city is a reflection of a deeper sense of alienation that citizens have about their environments in advanced capitalist societies. Although Jameson does not specifically refer to the personal meaning of place, the implication here is clearly that the contemporary city in advanced capitalist societies lacks places of personal meaning. This view reverberated in the writings of geographers Yi-Fu Tuan and Edward Relph, who have spoken of "placelessness" becoming a hallmark of modern Western industrial societies. Lynch probably would have agreed.[52]

Other studies have shown that images of the city significantly reflect group differences based on ethnicity and socioeconomic status.[53] Thus, we might expect to find a significant difference in the sense of alienation in the images of slum dwellers versus the images of upper-class elites, and indeed Appleyard's study in Ciudad Guyana showed such differences between poor indigents and the prosperous professional class all too clearly.

5. The Political-Economic Approach

Another, and perhaps more significant, influence of social sciences from the non-Western perspective is the political-economic branch of studies and writings related to development and urban form. The political-economic perspective has always presented alternative and competing explanations of development and underdevelopment, as well as of the processes that shape urban outcomes. More generally, this literature attempts to explain the spatial structure and organization of societies as historical outcomes shaped by economic imperatives and political processes. It tends to focus on conflicts, contradictions, hegemonies, ironies, and disequilibria (as opposed to the equilibrium-oriented predilections of the conventional and positivist economic models) as outcomes of these processes. This literature is apt to point out structural inequalities and injustices as consequences of political-economic processes inherent in the development experience and its attendant urban conditions.

The political-economic literature has straddled both the larger development phenomena and also the more immediate concerns of urban scale. Historically, the division of this literature between non-Western and Western typologies followed differences in scale. While the non-Western branch of the political-economic literature tended to focus on larger development issues involving global forces and hegemonic circumstances, the Western branch focused more on contradictions evident in the nature of urban processes, and the internal structure and organization of the city. But the divide between Western and non-Western branches in this literature is becoming less and less discrete. Generally, the literature on the non-Western side has focused more on the structure and organization of developing cities, while the Western branch is becoming more engaged in the effects of global economic relationships on the regional space and urban hierarchy.[54] It will be possible, and appropriately so in the context of globalization, then to draw from both of these branches in advancing our understanding of the relationship between development and form.

The work of sociologist Henri Lefebvre is particularly relevant here. In some ways it might be inappropriate to pigeonhole his work with this particular theme, other than for the fact that some of his writings have a Marxian lineage. The corpus of his work straddles the symbolic-interpretative and critical-reflective approaches as well. His writings on urbanization—"urban revolution," in his words—connect cities with development and modernization. Similarly, his treatise on the social production of space describes an essential trialectic between lived space (social practice), physical field (spatial practice), and conceived space (mental field), which also might be seen as developmental and evolutionary.[55]

One such early synthesis came from Manuel Castells, who attempted to combine theories of development with arguments about urban space and form.[56] In expanding the application of dependency theory to explain what might be commonly referred to as "uneven spatial development" typical of the developing world, Castells argued that dependent urbanization is manifested in three ways: overurbanization, urban primacy, and dualistic urban form. The first two are the legacies of the bell curve previously discussed. The dualistic urban form argument, however, directly links the notion of development—or underdevelopment, to be precise—to structural transformations in urban form.

Dualistic urban form refers to a fundamental discontinuity in developing cities characterized by an older traditional district, usually poor and lacking in adequate infrastructure and urban services, coexisting in a subaltern relationship with a modern, prosperous, well-serviced, and Westernized urban district. Others have referred to this dualism in the context of African cities as "dual city," or in the case of Latin America as "cities of peasants," or "peasants in cities."[57] The latter two examples are anthropological in source, reflecting the influence of Clifford Geertz, who through his study of contemporary Indonesian society coined the term "technological dualism."[58] The idea of a dualistic economy became popular after the International Labor Organization (ILO) formally institutionalized the concept of an "informal sector" of the economy, one that exists parallel to the mainstream "formal" economy.[59] The ILO subsequently urged national governments to reckon with the contribution of the informal sector in the developing economy. More recently, even stronger advocacy for the informal sector has come from libertarian economists such as Hernando de Soto[60] of Instituto de Libertad y Democracia in Peru, arguing for deregulation of such activities to increase their market freedom. Interestingly, until then this notion of a dualistic economy had pretty much remained in the subconscious of conventional discussions of economic development and structural change, including Marx's own writing, where the anomalies of developing countries were filed away under that well-known classification that Marx called the "Asiatic mode of production."

While this isomorphic relationship between dualistic economies and dualistic urban form is apparent throughout the developing world, recent literature shows that distinctions between the formal and informal may not be as discrete as early abstractions suggested. Instead it is best to view the dichotomy in a spatial and temporal continuum, with the modern and formal sector on one end and the traditional and informal sector on the other.[61] It is particularly difficult to map the presumed dualism of economic activities in space,[62] and the difficulty of the task itself further corroborates the insidious nature of this relationship. Nevertheless, the idea captures the polarized life experiences in developing cities.[63]

What is important to note here is that it is the legacy of the Dependistas[64] that has led to attempts like that of Castells to link spatial formations and economic systems with dependent global economic relationships. This theme received further embellishment from the works of geographers Terence McGee, Warwick Armstrong, and Milton Santos, who offered more detailed political-economic explanations for the disjunctions and associated ironies in the developing economy, its urban form, and the larger spatial formations at the regional and national scales.[65]

The idea of a dualistic urban form suggests spatial arrangements where large urban areas are differentiated from each other in services, traditions, structures, and activities, and this separation touches upon one of the four concerns addressed in the introductory chapter: segregation. Spatial segregation of people by tribes, guilds, castes, or regional or ethnic origins has existed throughout the indigenous histories of many non-Western cultures, predating their colonial history. These separations were also a way of managing and ordering diversity, as discussed by anthropologist Louis Dumont in his treatise on the Indian caste system.[66] While stratification may have been present in such precolonial ordering of urban space, it was neither as dualistic nor as bigoted as the dual cities of the colonial times. The sharp contrast between the indigenous traditional city and the "European" city that would be built outside the traditional city was unprecedented. The dependency relationships argued by the political-economic theories are not entirely satisfactory in deciphering the dualistic form. We need to turn to a different branch of literature that attempts to embellish the skeleton that the political-economic approach presents.

6. The Symbolic-Interpretive Approach

This literature falls into two generally discrete branches, albeit with some overlap. The scholarship involving the symbolic meaning of urban form and space has evolved in several phases. One such phase is an extension of what I have described previously as the historic/archetypal literature. That phase was an early attempt to read the meanings of the built environment. The works of architect-anthropologist Amos Rapoport and architectural historian Joseph Rykwert are cases in point, where the authors tried to interpret the symbolic meanings of spatial arrangements and built forms derived from cultural practices and traditions.[67] Drawn mainly from anthropological research, these studies were the first attempts to draw us beyond the initial taxonomic and representational enterprise. An important addition to this tradition is the recent work of Richard Sennett, in which he links the organization and function of public forums and spaces with the public culture and practices of the ancient Greeks.[68] This subset of the symbolic-interpretive literature includes considerations of both Western and non-Western cities and settlement forms.

The second and later phase of this literature is more contemporary and responds to the improvements of communications technology and attempts to link its effects on social behavior and urban form. Planning academic Richard Meier's work in the sixties was the earliest and most pioneering of this type, but it did not yield a tangible framework for the analysis and understanding of urban form.[69] Rather, Meier's attempt to equate levels of development in terms of "communication density," as measured by access to such modern technological devices as telephone, radio, television, and the like introduced an inherent bias in cross-national comparisons, since one could argue that the richness of nonverbal and symbolic communication common in traditional societies are totally absent from this model. Recently the explosive growth in information and communication technology innovations has drawn several important observations. Notable among these, and relevant to our immediate interest, is Castells's arguments about the rise of the new network society, where we should be reckoning with spaces of flow and the spaces of places in conceptualizing contemporary urban form.[70] Both architect William Mitchell and planning academic Christine Boyer have discussed the effects of the Internet and communication technology on the way we use and think about urban space. If Boyer's commentaries about the "cybercity" are related to the changes in the sensuous experiences of the city, Mitchell's conjectures are about the growing irrelevance of the experienced city of social and physical contact. Cities will be psychologically abandoned as we all become "cyborgs," the residents of a "city of bits." Although such conjectures ostensibly concern Western cities for the time being, no doubt soon the oracle would apply (with growing information technology penetration) to the rapidly developing economies and their cities.[71]

The works of anthropologists, historians, geographers, and sociologists focus directly on cities of the Global South from the colonial period to contemporary times. Urban sociologist Janet Abu-Lughod's sociopolitical interpretation in the context of the globalization of Middle Eastern cities (Cairo in particular) is a case in point.[72] Similarly, a growing corpus of important works focusing on the colonial urban development in India,[73] Morocco,[74] and Algeria[75] have sharpened our understanding of the way urban form evolved during the colonial period, and the symbolic meanings of colonial spaces and forms so created. Anthropologist James Holston's analysis of the effects of modernity in the postcolonial urban design of Brasília, and architectural historian Norma Evenson's work on Chandigarh, Brasília, and the contemporary cityscapes of Indian cities are important commentaries on postcolonial development.[76]

7. The Critical-Reflective Approach

The literature in this final category actually consists of three streams of thoughts. Works of some of these authors straddle several categories while sharing common themes. First, most of these works are rooted in the tradition of the humanities—critical, reflective, synoptic, and sometimes ironic—although individual authors may have their initial intellectual grounding in the social sciences. Second, although some of these writings may have empirical content, in the sense that they are based on observations and experiences, they tend to fall outside the usual positivist canons of social sciences that apply even to individual case studies. The intellectual underlayment of this approach derives from alternative notions of knowing (i.e., outside positivism) that draw from intuitions, personal insights, and tacit knowledge.[77] Third, the arguments and analysis tend toward a narrative style of reporting, involving anecdotal as well as historiographic materials. These arguments may draw liberally from the visual and performing arts, including cinema, music, paintings, and photographs, and also from various literary works, including poetry and fiction.

Fourth, many of these works are redolent of what can be called postmodernist writings. Some are more antimodernist than postmodernist in the sense that they challenge and deconstruct modernist premises that still dictate policy, design, and development decisions worldwide.[78] Others are simply ante-modernist, or non-modernist, in the sense that they represent a scholarly tradition of reflection and argument, as in philosophy, that endured through modernism as a cognitive paradigm.

Fifth, the writings attempt to decipher political intentions, social implications, and human consequences of particular organizations and arrangements of urban space and form. If some of the literature discussed earlier in this chapter is about the city as text—its language and syntax—this last group is mainly about understanding the subtext.

Sixth, and finally, although this literature is not explicitly visionary or normative, it is implicitly indulgent of the types of intervention and heroic action that could further the cause of democratic control and humanistic qualities in the design and structural organization of urban space.

The first subset of the political-economic literature includes critical and interpretive writings on urban space, focusing on the losses of humanity and a sense of place in contemporary urban settings. It bemoans the alienation of urban space according to the users of such space (or the "fall of the public man," to quote the title of Richard Sennett's well-known book); privatization and commodification of public life and space; the rise of the inauthentic and phantasmagoric landscape; and the atrophying of the public realm. Works of architect Michael Sorkin, urban critic Margaret Crawford, political theorist Mike Davis, and the like further add to this critique.[79] We might also include in this group those writings that are not necessarily critical of the trends or dominant forces, but are nevertheless interpretive of the larger structural forces that explain particular urban form and space outcomes. Works of geographer D. W. Meinig, landscape architect J. B. Jackson, urban historian Kenneth Jackson, author Tony Hiss, and political theorist

James C. Scott are also noteworthy.[80] While they may not explicitly attempt to connect the form outcome with development paradigms, many facets of change associated with development, particularly capitalist development—globalization, market liberalism, material culture, and the like—remain targets of their critiques. Recently, however, writings are focusing on the unprecedented urban transformation in the developing world; much of it focuses on China from a critical perspective. Works of the journalist Bianca Bosker and the urban planners Thomas Campanella and John Friedmann are cases in point.[81] Others are willing to celebrate this transformation, as reflected in a recent volume edited by urban planner Ananya Roy and anthropologist Aihwa Ong.[82]

The second group in this literature seemingly has a Marxian origin, and is a derivative of the Frankfurt School, interested in the philosophical underpinnings of the material culture of capitalist development. Urban form and urban space became a focus of these theorists' interest along with other icons of consumer culture and entertainment. Perhaps the most celebrated work in this regard is Walter Benjamin's *Das Passagen-Werk* (*The Arcades Project*), inspired by the late-nineteenth-century redevelopment of Paris and the new pedestrian spaces created for shopping and simple flânerie.[83] Subsequent analyses by critical theorists Susan Buck-Morss and Anne Friedberg and political theorist Fredric Jameson, among others, have focused on the ironies and contradictions in such consumer spaces in contemporary culture, drawing from earlier intellectual explorations.[84]

Finally, the last group in this literature represents an ensemble that is broadly concerned with human diversity in urban space and form, but more specifically with feminist concerns and the gender implications of urban space and form. This group is critical of the contemporary political, economic, and in the case of some developing countries, religious order that has restricted the rights, access, and uses of urban space by women and in some instances excluded women from the public realm and public space. Sociologist Nancy Fraser, for example, points out that the public space of Greek cities, which we all celebrate as the ideal configuration of public realm and space, was actually a very male domain.[85] Women were systematically excluded from both the public realm and public space, consigned to the confines of domestic space. Slaves were excluded as well. Authors in this literature have argued that the contemporary, or for that matter the historic, built environment is a product of male choices, and they advocate gender diversity and equality in the design of planning of such spaces.[86]

The diversity issue is the theme of other writings, stemming from the context of globalization and increasing labor mobility. Themes typically discussed in the literature are the ironies and incongruities in architectural expressions; social exclusion and segregation in urban space; cultural differences in the norms and uses of urban space;

cultural and social identities and markers in the urban landscape; and the social conflicts and tensions that arise from such outcomes. The works of planning academics Nezar AlSayyad, Teresa Caldeira, Clara Irazábal, and Ananya Roy have addressed some of these themes.[87]

Closing Observations

This review, skeletal as it is—a book-length manuscript is necessary to do justice to the authors and their concepts—is aimed at identifying the critical concepts that are derived from (or can be linked to) theories of development. However, other than the political-economic approach, and to a lesser extent the critical-discursive approach, there are few obvious examples of this link. The other reality about the state of the art, as should be clear from table 4.1, is that the literature on urban form in a non-Western context has been relatively sparse compared with the Western context, both in terms of theoretical concepts and the density of contributions. One may note also that the majority of the authors represented in the non-Western column of table 4.1 are themselves of Western origin. This suggests the caveat that there may exist a Western bias in this literature overall–as forcefully argued by Edward Said's theory of Orientalism—even though much of the literature reviewed is of very recent origin, and not of the vintage and intellectual paradigm Said had considered.[88]

The typology of literature presented previously is not particularly useful in mapping the urban outcomes of development. Instead the schema presented in table 4.2, I suggest, may serve as an organizing framework appropriate to map effects of development on the urban phenomena. The conceptual categories presented here suggest an existential continuum from the very endogenous core (represented by the location, site, and climate of a city) to its icons, images, and brands that can be exogenously obtained or influenced.

To begin, moving from the bottom to the top, we should understand and respect how nature has shaped and defined the origin and development of cities. I have chosen the term ***nature services***, admittedly with a slight economistic touch, to capture the resources and constraints of nature that influenced the location, size, and form of cities. One thinks of water—surface or ground—as a determinant of form. Rivers in ancient times determined the location of cities and indeed shaped eras of human civilizations known by their names: Indus Valley, Nile Valley, and Yangtze Valley most famously. Cities in the desert landscape were located near the principal supply of ground water—*wadis* in Arabic. Cities like Sa'naa and Shibam in the deserts of Yemen or Jaisalmer in the western Thor desert of Rajasthan are cases in point. When the supply of water

Table 4.2
A schema for mapping urban outcomes of development

Identity	Icons, brands, power, prestige, functional identity
Habitus	Habits, rituals, feels, dispositions, rhythms
Urbanism	Atmosphere, pace of life, diversity, density, differences
Social ecology	Location of residents as differentiated by income class, race, status
Form	Built environment—its organization and structure
Sensorium	Sound, smell, wind, heat, cold
Nature services	Location, geography, climate, topography

ended, for natural or man-made reasons, cities died. Fatehpur Sikri—a new city built by the Moghul emperor Akbar in 1569—had to be abandoned, according to popular belief, because the supply of water declined. These are all stories of sustainability and carrying capacity, a matter of great import today. Historians have documented how nature's services have shaped urbanization and the economy across the world. Historian William Cronon's classic treatise on the development of Chicago and the Great West, and historian Carl Smith's more recent work on how water infrastructure influenced the urban form of Philadelphia, Boston, and Chicago, are relevant examples from the Global North.[89] In modern times the effects of development on nature services is often annihilating, as evident in the development of the Chicago metropolis, which displaced its original prairie landscape.[90] This was less so in premodern times. Thus, the Aztecs had learned to build around the delicate system of lakes to preserve the precious source of water in the valley of Teotihuacan (where Mexico City is located). After the Spanish conquest of the Aztec Empire in 1521, Spanish engineers decided to build a system of canals and dams to prevent floods and meet the demand for colonial urban development—an intervention into the nature services that continues to exacerbate the water crisis today in the metropolitan region of Mexico City.[91] Anthropologist Stephen Lansing relates a similar tale in Bali, where experts from the Asian Development Bank caused a major ecological catastrophe by trying to introduce multiple crops to a landscape in which the allocation of water for farming was traditionally managed by temple rituals.

Every city has a unique ***sensorium***—the system of senses[92] that includes not just sights, sounds, and smells but also heat, cold, rain, wind, fog, dust, and pollutants. It is in part a gift of climate and geographical location, but also in part a result of development or underdevelopment. An example of the effect of development on an urban sensorium is the pollution from cars and factories that has led to debilitating smog in Beijing and other cities of the Global South today. An example of the effect of underdevelopment is the smoke in Delhi from the burning of dry leaves and twigs by the urban poor for cooking and keeping warm, which adds to the natural fog that envelops Delhi in the winter months. Fog in San Francisco divides the city into two distinct parts.

Sounds can be associated with identity and habitus: periodic calls to prayer in Riyadh or Cairo, the blowing of conch shells at dusk in neighborhoods of Kolkata, Bollywood songs blaring from loudspeakers in the streets of Old Delhi, and so on. Street noise may suggest verve and vitality, but also disorder and disclaimer. "Please blow horn" is typically painted at the back of trucks and buses in India that typically hog multiple traffic lanes, thus contributing to high decibel levels in the sonic landscape. The orderly traffic in the limited-access ring roads of prosperous suburban Delhi seems much quieter than the busy streets of Kolkata, famous for the blaring cacophony of traffic. A higher level of development seemingly produces a quieter street sensorium. Absence of street noise from traffic struck US visiting planners as remarkable when they arrived in China in the summer of 1980. According to a Western photographer visiting Vietnam, the "sound of silence" was the sound of socialism.[93] Smells contribute to the sensorium as well. The smell of freshly brewed coffee in the financial district of San Francisco, or the stench of lumber-processing plants in Tacoma, Washington, are two extremes. Elsewhere the scent of incense and fresh flowers in the approach to mosques or temples subtly define the boundaries between the sacred and the profane. In a recent book on Kolkata, the author describes the many aspects of the city's evanescent urbanism, but also the enduring and "'unmistakable bouquet' of urine"[94] emanating from the underserviced public realm of poverty.

The sensorium is further embellished by the animals in the urban landscape—camels, cows, dogs, mules, and monkeys, to mention a few that are found in many Indian cities—who are domesticated, revered, tolerated, protected, and also abused, in a peculiar mix of values in the moral landscape of the urban society. The smells and sounds of the urban sensorium are thus made unique by the barking of famished street dogs fighting for scraps of food in the middle of the night, or the cawing of scavenger crows, or the cacophony of birds returning to the street trees at the end of the day, occasionally punctuated by a few melodious notes from a *kohelia* (equivalent to a nightingale). Gratuitous derivatives of such sensoriums are mosquitoes, flies, and pests. The upper class filters this sensorium by staying in air-conditioned homes and vehicles. The poor remain in the mix.

The ***form*** of the city, its three-dimensional disposition of usable space, is obtained from aggregate building form; its passages, alleys, and streets; and its open spaces and natural elements—to the extent not tamed by development. Form is impacted by rules of property ownership, subdivision, and exchange; rights to improve upon the land; and public easements for movement of goods, people, energy, water, and waste, whether derived from indigenous practices or changing technological possibilities. Guanajuato, a colonial silver-mining town in central Mexico, is a classic example of how natural features, in this case a river valley, can shape the form of the city. Its organic and winding shape follows the course of the river; level areas at the floor of the valley were used for locating important public buildings and larger upper-income houses, with the houses on the slopes decreasing in size and quality along a declining income gradient (see figure 5.1 in the following chapter).

The ***social ecology*** of the city, the spatial organization of its residents by class, income, and ethnicity, is often considered primarily a market outcome suggesting a trade-off between accessibility and consumption of space. Central locations have high accessibility and thus fetch highest land rent, which declines as one moves further out, allowing consumption of larger land area while increasing transportation cost and travel time. The market outcome may not always explain the social ecology, as can be seen in the inner-city ghettoes of the Global North or the peripheral slums of the Global South. The social ecology of Guanajuato discussed above itself is a contradiction to the rent-gradient theory. Human ecologists have tried to offer alternative explanations and models of the social ecology of the city that include canons, or sentiment and symbolism, but are not necessarily tied to the concept of development.[95] Development certainly alters the social ecology in fundamental ways, often imposing a new order of market once the requisite institutions—FIRE (or finance, insurance, and real estate)—are in place. This may lead to a new social ecology characterized by polarization, segregation, and social exclusion.

The term ***urbanism*** has become fashionable these days. In the Anglophone world the concept of urbanism that sociologist Louis Wirth[96] first introduced, associating it with population size, density, and heterogeneity, still remains a bit of an enigma. The literature on planning and design is now teeming with the term, with various qualifiers—some sixty-one according to one recent count.[97] But very few of these works capture the effects of development on the emerging "urbanism" of cities around the world, and the Global South in particular. Not included in this litany are such concepts as "transitional,"[98] "splintering,"[99] or "improvised,"[100] all of which pertain to transforming urbanism in the developing world. The concept of urbanism may be connected to size, density, and diversity of urban population and the resulting norms of behavior or social relationships. Thus, anomie, autonomy, and withdrawal are associated with classical sociological interpretation, whereas pace of life, avoidance, and apathy are some of the recent interpretations from social psychology. Cities of Global South are associated with a continuum of dualistic urbanism—that of formal and informal economies. With development the urbanism of formal economy begins to dominate the informal. Incipience of a consumer society characterized by malls, supermarkets, cars, and parking lots displaces the traditional neighborhoods through development and gentrification.

The notion of ***habitus*** is even more ephemeral than urbanism. The influential concept, introduced (but not clearly defined) by sociologist Pierre Bourdieu, still remains somewhat ambiguous. According to one definition it "refers to the physical embodiment of cultural capital, to the deeply ingrained habits, skills, and dispositions that we possess due to our life experiences."[101] Intuitively one could argue that it is a derivative of urbanism, but also a product of all of the other dimensions of the urban experience. Thus, the pulse of quotidian life and rituals, as well as seasonal rhythms of life that are endogenous to culture, are some of the essential features of this habitus. For instance, the call to prayer five times a day in a Muslim city defines the rhythm of quotidian life and is an integral part of habitus. Similarly, in the Hindu quarters of an Indian city, one sees the collective morning prayers facing the rising sun, and with the setting sun celebrating day's end by blowing into conch shells and lighting lamps and burning incense, thus creating a smoky, fragrant, and acoustic sensorium. In Kolkata, Bengalis are conscious of not four but six seasons and formally celebrate the arrival of monsoon and many *pujas* (religious festivals). These *pujas* lead to seasonal "festivalization" of urban space and public life.[102]

Both Lynch[103] and Lefebvre[104] discussed the rhythms of city life and the "images of time" as intrinsic aspects of city atmosphere. One could also imagine the construct of habitus in author Italo Calvino's renowned novel *Invisible Cities*, or in author Jonathan Raban's exposition *Soft City*, or more recently, in the context of Global South, in author Suketu Mehta's *Maximum City: Bombay Lost and Found.*[105] Feature films such as Roland Joffé's *City of Joy*, Mira Nair's *Salaam Bombay*, and Danny Boyle's more recent *Slumdog Millionaire* are examples of cinematic portrayals of the construct.

The effect of development on *habitus* has yet to be fully articulated. However, in their parallel inquiries on time and rhythm both Lynch and Lefebvre addressed such transformation engendered in modernity and urban development. Seemingly they both referred to how social rhythms lose their connection to natural cycles, as sociologist Claire Revol notes: "Time tends to be more and more 'abstract'—the term found in both Lefebvre and Lynch."[106] With the proliferation of information and communication technology and digital media, our *habitus* has become confused, as space and time get increasingly conflated. Thus, one can be on public time, participating in a conference call while drying hair in the privacy of home; or one can carry out an intimate conversation, on private time, while standing in a crowded public space, such as the concourse of Grand Central Station in New York.

Finally, we turn to ***identity***, a term Lynch used purposefully in defining the concept of city imageability, referring to the features in urban form that are unique and distinctive.[107] Often these features become iconic, a brand, and themes of picture postcards or contemporary websites. The Duomo of Florence, the Eiffel Tower of Paris, and the House of Parliament of London are notable examples. Features of the aggregate urban form can also shape the identity of a city. Thus, 40 kilometers of continuous arcades of Bologna create a spatial identity for the city along with its red tiles and red exterior paint, earning it the "red city" title (also an oblique reference to the city's legacy as the headquarters of the Italian communist party). Similarly, the dominant color of the roofs or walls has defined the identity of many Moroccan cities—Rabat as a green city, Marrakech as the rose or red city, Chefchaouen as the blue city, and so on. The color blue defines the identity of much of Jodhpur in India. Many of these examples of identity are endogenous in origin, emanating from natural features or cultural practices.

In the cities of Global South extant identities have been challenged and in some cases altered by exogenous forces from invading dynasties and the colonial powers. Today identity plays a key role in the development process as countries complete in a global economy and cities try to gain in ranking in the hierarchy of world cities. This search for identity is an essential component of the image of development. Exuberant architecture and urban design imported from the West become the medium for this new identity or "branding." Burj Khalifa, claimed to be the tallest building in the world, is one such identity-forming structure in Dubai, as are the TV towers in Pudong, the CCTV tower in Beijing, the Freedom Tower in Riyadh, the Petronas Twin Towers in Kuala Lumpur, and the triple-tower Marina Bay Sands hotel in Singapore. These buildings are typically designed by "starchitects" from the West, such as Norman Foster and Rem Koolhaas. It is in the new urban architecture of Global South that development is reflected in the mirror of the West, in the images of the West, and signifying development essentially as a project of the West.

II Precolonial and Colonial Legacies

5 The Canonical City

> The cosmology of Chinese cities was made up of elements drawn from the core ideology of the Great Tradition—enriched at times by borrowing from the Little Traditions of the peasant villages, *but scarcely at all by elements of alien civilizations*. This core ideology was perpetuated by literate elite, which survived the vicissitudes of time and clung to the body of norms embodied in its Classics.
>
> —Arthur Wright, "The Cosmology of the Chinese City"[1]

The search for ideal city form engaged human imagination through the ages in both Western and non-Western cultures. Cities built according to ideal archetypes, however, were very few and limited to the capitals of kingdoms and dynasties. Iconic of power and wealth, they also reflected the culturally rooted visions of the ideal society, imagined and debated by the elites and intelligentsia.[2]

The obsession with ideal city form was often fueled by the hubris of imperial rulers. Author Italo Calvino captured the anxieties of a new ruler about his legacy in city design in his imagined conversations between Marco Polo and Kublai Khan, the great fourteenth-century Mongol ruler.[3] In the fourteenth century Khan built the city of Dadu according to canons of city design that had evolved over millennia, and it was Khan's Dadu that would precede the imperial city of Beijing of the Ming dynasty as it is known today. Calvino portrays Khan as an anxious ruler, obsessed with cities of distant lands, "visited in thought but not yet discovered or founded: New Atantis, Utopia, the City of the Sun, Oceana, Tamoé, New Harmony, New Lanark, Icaria." In Calvino's narrative the great Kublai Khan tells Marco Polo: "'You, who go about exploring and who see signs, can tell me toward which of these futures the favoring winds are driving us.'"[4] A twenty-first-century Khan might have asked instead: If development is fundamentally a transcendental process, how would urbanism reflect that process?

The aim of this chapter is to advance the argument that the visions of ideal cities and their canonical forms symbolized contemporaneous images of good society, and implicitly the aim of development. The search for the ideal form in China continued through many centuries, if not millennia. The ideal city and norms of good city form were a part of the intellectual discourse of those times—from Zhu Xi and Manasara in the non-Western world to Plato and Saint Augustine in the Western context. The ideal form of cities reflected perfection, order, and organization, and thus the very identity of a good society. The design of imperial cities captured the quintessence of dynasties and their legacies.

These ideal urban forms were canonical for an era, but typically endogenous to particular cultures and geographical regions. Their evolution was shaped by the moral, ethical, and spiritual values that had evolved within respective cultures.

Organic Cities

The canonical cities are part of a larger reference class that has been defined variously as "pre-industrial," according to sociologist Gideon Sjoberg;[5] "pre-rational," as argued by architectural historian Alex Tzonis,[6] "Oriental," as termed by political theorist Max Weber,[7] and "premodern," as suggested by anthropologist G. William Skinner.[8] Writing about imperial China's urban development, Skinner was wary of such taxonomy as being simplistic. He conceded, however, that a more conscientious classification involving political-economic functions could get also quite complicated and overbearing.[9]

Nevertheless, it is worthwhile to consider another conceptual and overarching dichotomy of cities that is relevant to our discussion here: the concepts of "orthogenetic" and "heterogenetic" cities offered by anthropologists Robert Redfield and Milton Singer.[10] A fundamental distinction between the orthogenetic and heterogenetic cities lies in Redfield's concepts of the "moral order" and the "technical order" as the guiding principles of societies.[11] Drawing on Redfield's proposition, anthropologist Diana Eck associates orthogenetic cities with the "moral order" and heterogenetic cities with the "technical order." For the former, "their primary self-image is that they reproduce the cosmological order and make it accessible on the human plane," while for the latter, "their primary self-image is that of action and work. They hum and produce; they order power, production, and wealth."[12] Orthogenetic cities, argues Eck, "create and sustain the ethos and order of a whole culture."[13] She mentions Rome, Banaras, Jerusalem, Kyoto, and Beijing as examples of orthogenetic cities, in the sense that "their names become virtually synonymous with that culture."[14] In contrast, heterogenetic cities do not signify any particular orthodoxy and may in fact reflect the inherent heterodoxy of the culture they represent: "Such cities gather up the complexity and divergence of a culture, not in harmony, but conflict, even though it be creative conflict."[15] She refers to Los Angeles, Mumbai, Jakarta, and Tokyo as examples. Indeed, one could add to that list many of the contemporary "global" or "world" cities of today's developed and developing worlds. Orthogenetic cities are clearly premodern in origin, while all modern cities are necessarily heterogenetic.

With modern times and the modernization of traditional economies, we have seen the transformation of "orthogenetic" cities into "heterogenetic" cities. In Eck's examples, cities of the orthogenetic class all have premodern origins, while those in the heterogenetic class are mainly products of modernity. Many cities of premodern times also belonged to the heterogenetic class with attributes of a technical order, but of a different sort than that of industrial cities of the modern era. In an essay on canonical Hindu cities, anthropologist Holly Baker Reynolds argues that in contrast to Madurai, which was a city of "moral order," the coastal Chola city Kaverippumpattinam, or Pukar, evolved into a port city of a "technical order" with two distinct parts—one of trade and the other of traditional spatial organization.[16]

One could use the terms "precolonial" or "premodern" to define the evolution of urban form that was shaped mainly by endogenous forces and ideas. I would argue further that although the orthogenetic cities were all situated in precolonial times, in many ways the genesis of the heterogenetic cities of the modern era began with the dawn of the colonial era. Thus, while a moral order defined the images of precolonial cities, it is the technical order—with all its contradictions, conflicts, and tensions—that has defined the cities of the colonial and postcolonial eras.

The overlay of moral versus technical order on precolonial and colonial times can only be approximate. Strictly in terms of urban form, it is possible to think of three basic categories of precolonial cities: "open" cities without walls, and "closed" or "walled" cities of two types—organic and planned. The broad distinction, of course, is one between walled cities and unwalled, which simply grew out of villages and market towns surrounded by agricultural land. Architectural historian Spiro Kostof presents Nowdushan in Iran as a classic exemplar of these unwalled or "open" cities.[17] If we accept Jean François Sobry's famous saying *"la ville sans mur n'est pas une ville"* (the city without a wall is not a city),[18] Nowdushan of course would not qualify. This distinction notwithstanding, forms of these cities were inherently organic. Indeed, the vast majority of cities and townships of the precolonial vintage fall in the unwalled category, having grown out of small villages surrounded by farmland and trading posts located at the crossroads of travel. They reflect economic and technological changes over time, as well as their climates, geographies, and local political histories. We may think of them mainly as heterogenetic cities, but a product of nature services nevertheless. Guanajuato, a former silver-mining town in central Mexico, is a case in point, an example of an organic unwalled city whose shape and form was defined by the slopes of the valley along the course of a river. (See figure 5.1.)

Within the category of walled cities one could broadly identify two types: the ordered or "planned" walled city (like Beijing of the Ming dynasty in China), and the organic city that is similar in genre and vintage to the organic forms of medieval cities (like Jaisalmer or Jodhpur in India). (See figure 5.2.)

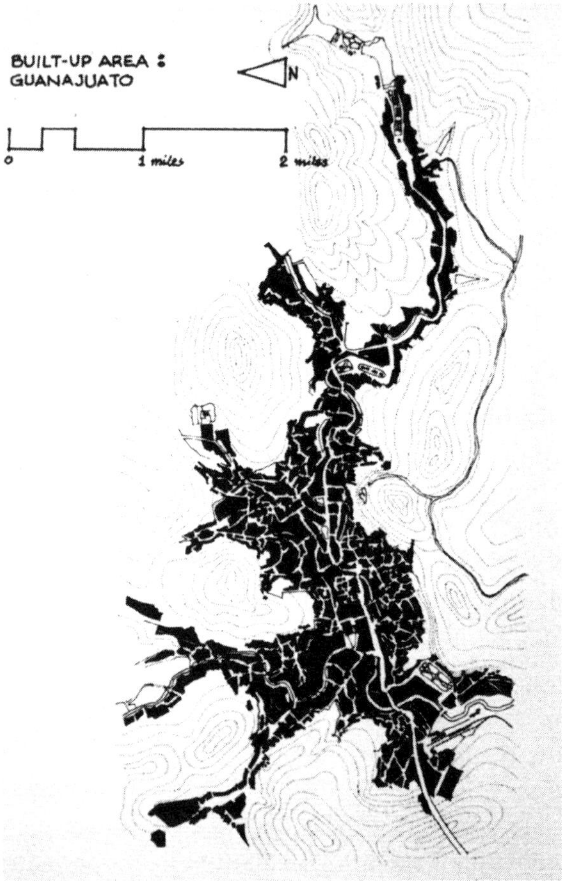

Figure 5.1
The organic urban form of Guanajuato, Mexico, around the middle of the last century.
Source: Author.

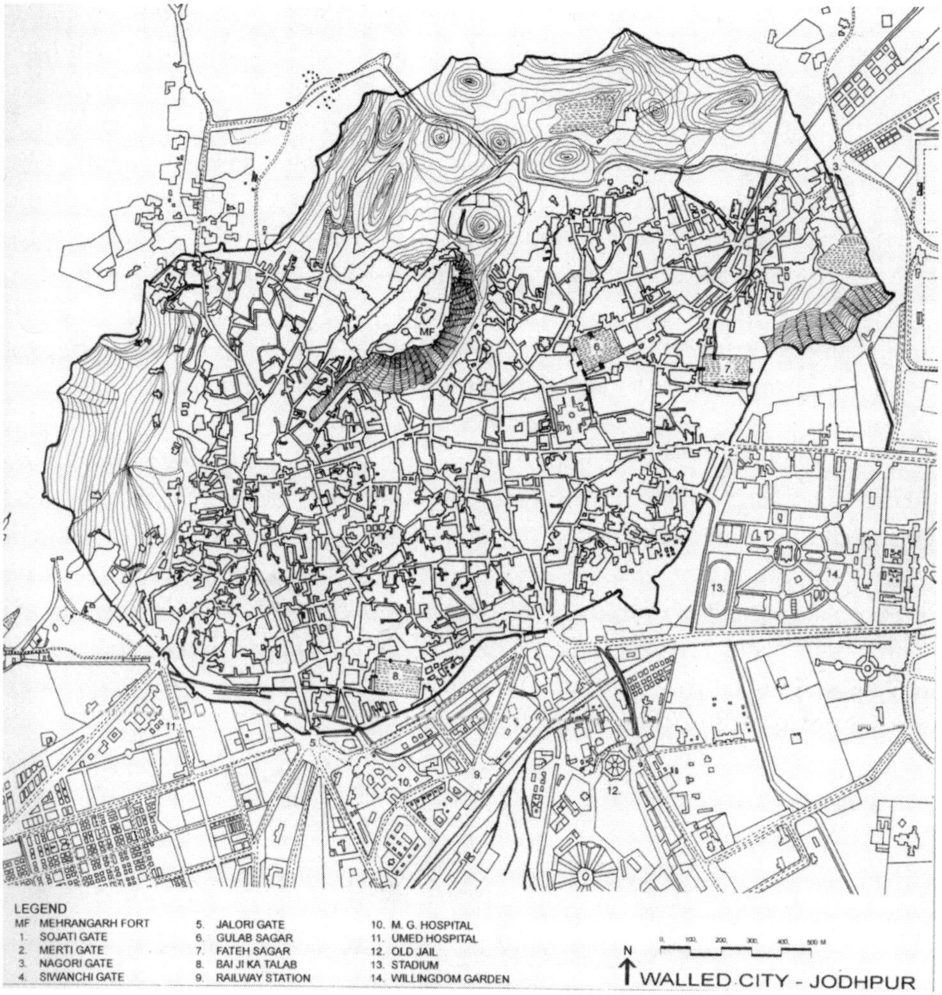

Figure 5.2

The urban form of Jodhpur, Rajasthan, India.

Source: Courtesy of Kulbhusan Jain.

The form of precolonial cities—whether canonical or organic—was primarily endogenous. This is not to say that ideas and influences did not travel across cultures and geographic regions even in precolonial times, when, for instance, agencies of trade, religious campaigns, and imperial conquests facilitated such diffusion. Examples of such diffusion of ideas in the planning and design of cities abound: the canonical urban form of Chinese cities influencing the ninth-century plan of Kyoto in Japan is a case in point; early-eighteenth-century Jaipur in India, designed according to Navagraha, or "the mandala of nine planets"[19] (see figure 5.3), is also reminiscent of the Chinese canonical form, suggesting a common reliance on the cosmic model. Similarly, the Indian cosmic model is known to have influenced city design in other regions of South Asia.[20] Similarly, Persian design traditions and designers significantly influenced Moghul architecture and garden design in India.

It is also likely that there might be other canonical principles—products of a technical order—that dictated the structure and organization of space within both open and organic cities. This makes sense if we accept the meaning of canons not just as authoritative and ideological dogma, but also as accepted ways of doing things that grew out of local knowledge, or *mētis*—a Greek word that connotes a mix of wisdom and cunning—involving age-old practices of building construction and space design based on constraints of climate, geography, and natural resources, as suggested by anthropologist and political scientist James C. Scott.[21]

The Quest for Ideal Form

The quest for an ideal settlement form was intrinsic to premodern, or "prerational," cultures, according to architectural theorist Alex Tzonis.[22] The notion of a "divine model" had dictated much of the methodology for designing medieval cathedrals symbolizing perfection, harmony, truth, and purity. Inspiration for good design came from the ordering and natural relationships of measures, numbers, ratios, rhythm, and weight. According to Tzonis, Saint Augustine defined the act of design as "an "unfolding" of the divine model that represented "truth and harmony."[23] Elemental shapes and forms like the circle, the square, the cube, and so on were seen as the proxy for divine models and used widely in the design of buildings and spaces. These principles of geometry, commonplace in antiquity and biblical times, endured through medieval and Renaissance design, and also in other non-Western cultures, as the geographer Yi-Fu Tuan points out.[24]

Even in the case of so-called primitive societies there were examples of self-conscious design that refute the argument of "unselfconscious design" suggested by architectural

Figure 5.3
The planned city of Jaipur, India, a variant of the 3×3 organization common in canonical Chinese cities. Here the 3×3 order had to be adjusted because of topographic exigencies.
Source: Courtesy of Kulbhusan Jain.

theorist Christopher Alexander to describe their organic form.[25] Drawing from anthropologists' field research[26] of Dogon settlements of sub-Saharan Africa, Tzonis argues that the form of such settlements was guided by a cosmological order embodied in a system of models and myths. Similar to medieval Western culture, the Dogon people also used a divine model to organize settlements. Here, the divine model was the human body itself, a metaphor that has also been used in medieval and Renaissance architecture to extrapolate the essence of pure forms and shapes.[27] It was also integral to principles of city design in India according to *Vastû Shīlpa* , or the art of settlement form.

Significantly, Tzonis's discussion of prerational design and the search for a "divine model" bridges two very different worlds. It suggests a more universal impulse for finding a model of built form representing purity, perfection, order, stability, harmony, security, certainty, and perhaps eternity. Yet the ideal city was not always based on the tenets of a divine model. There are a number of instances where the canons of ideal city form emphasized secular principles of size, symmetry, organization, and efficiency. Typically, it was the concept of a politically feasible optimal size that occupied the ancient Greek philosophers, for instance. Plato thought the city should have a finite size and suggested a population size of 5,040 that should be maintained at a steady state by in- and out-migration of population and rules of inheritance.[28] Aristotle, while also believing in optimal city size, was more circumspect about specifying a specific number. Instead, he thought that the optimal size of the city should be guided by the requirements for living a good life in a political community where the tenets of successful participatory democracy required personal contact. Thus, the optimal Aristotelian limit of city size was the threshold at which personal contacts among citizens became unfeasible.[29]

The canons of ideal city layout proposed by Hippodamus, an architect, for Greek cities of the fifth century BCE, comprised orthogonal grid-iron patterns and emphasized shape over size, the latter to be determined by resource constraints of the site and its hinterland.[30] This was one of the earliest recognitions of sustainability in the manner of carrying capacity or "ecological footprint"—a nod to the importance of nature services.

Medieval cities were dictated by considerations of military defense and human scale more than by pure geometric form. With the dawn of the Renaissance came a whole new wave of ideal city forms of symmetrical geometrical shapes: the octagonal ideal city form proposed by Giorgio Vasari; the design for the fifteen-century ideal city of Sforzinda by Antonio Filarte; a square fortified city plan by Girolamo Maggi; Francisco di Giorgio's radial plan for a hilly site with a spiral connecting street; Fra Giaconda's proposal for an ideal city of radial form based on aesthetic principles; and so on.[31]

In recognition of the constraints of radial street patterns and their sharp corners, Italian architect Vincenzo Scamozzi proposed an ideal city that brought back the gridiron street pattern, overlaid onto a circular form. Albrecht Dürer's ideal plan for a rectangular city further underscored the return to the orthogonal form.[32] These examples of geometric form and organization were all inherently secular in their canonical obsessions, as they were generally preoccupied with the defensive imperatives of the medieval and Renaissance eras.[33]

It is worth noting that many of the schemes for ideal cities were never actually built. Filarte's concept of the ideal city, one that he claimed was an improvement upon Vitruvius's original model from the military point of view, had some following in newly founded cities of the early Renaissance period.[34] As Kostof points out, this "logic of defense" led to the popularity of the radial form in sixteenth-century Europe, and some of the built examples of the ideal city—such as Philippeville in Belgium, Palma Nova in Italy, and Hamina in Finland—were examples of this military logic.[35] By and large, the canonical city remained a theoretical possibility in the imaginations of artists, architects, scholars, and philosophers. The ideal form of the city was integral to the quest for aesthetics and order in organization of the city.[36]

In discussing theories of good city form, Lynch spoke of three normative guides: the cosmic model, the city as a machine, and the city as an organism.[37] Of these three, the machine and organism models are heterogenetic and products of the modern era, and not pertinent to our discussion of canonical cities of the premodern era. The cosmic model was orthogenetic, and as a "magical model of the universe and the gods" it linked "human beings to those vast forces and a way of stabilizing the order and harmony of the cosmos."[38] This thinking was particularly influential in the images of the canonical city in China and India.[39] What follows is a review of these two canonical traditions.

Canonical Cities of China

Although conventional wisdom about archetypal Chinese cities abounds, historiographies of Chinese cities actually show that there were vast differences in the ways Chinese cities evolved over several millennia. While acceding that premodern Chinese cities did present a distinct cultural type, G. William Skinner cautions against archetypal reductionism, emphasizing the variation in the evolution of Chinese cities.[40] Not only were these cities influenced by historical and geographical differences in administration and location, but they also reflected different philosophical interpretations of the canons of city building. Evolving forms of Chinese cities have always been a challenge to a particular orthodoxy, and thus represented an ongoing discourse on alternative possibilities of canonical form. This discourse is uniquely endogenous to Chinese culture, and essentially developmental in nature.[41]

Architectural historian Liangyong Wu of Tsinghua University has carefully documented the evolutionary nature of Chinese cities—the capital cities, to be exact. Drawn to the same scale, these patterns, from the ideal royal city of Kaogongji of the seventh to eighth centuries BCE to the Ming-Qing Beijing of the eighteenth century CE, reveal some consistency in form: the rectangular shape; orientation with cardinal direction; grid pattern of streets; and axial layout. However, there were considerable variations in their size and internal organization, and in the specific aspects of the basic rectangular form.[42]

Nevertheless, if the long historiography of Chinese capital cities are imagined as a musical composition, certain leitmotifs of form become quite apparent, and these features are identified and discussed in many scholarly works.[43] Nancy Steinhardt, an East Asian scholar, may have given us the most systematic accounting of the invariant features and components of the Chinese capital cities.[44] These persistent features are as follows: four-sided and right-angled enclosures, sometimes as a nested set of an outer and an inner wall; one or more gates piercing the walls for access; gates opposite to each other, aligned so as to create major axial streets; almost always a central gate at the south side of the enclosure; defensive projections of the wall to protect the gates; lookout towers at the corners of the outer walls and atop the main gates where troops were housed; major east-west and north-south axial streets; and so forth. The majestic Qianmen Gate (see figure 5.4) of the historic walled city of Beijing remains an isolated reminder of the southern edge of the historic Ming city.

These imperial cities also had several archetypal buildings and spaces that remained invariant through time. For example, the palace and its location within the walled city, and its various architectural components and features, were essentially paradigmatic and comprised a basic set of planning principles.[45] All imperial cities had walled areas set aside for government offices. Called the administrative or imperial city, this area was distinct from the palace city, where the imperial palace was situated. Located at the center of the city, the palace city had a long and ceremonial access path, usually along the main north-south axis, called the imperial way. Other components of the archetypal imperial city consisted of various altars (of soil and grain, of heaven, of agriculture), temples, ritual buildings and spaces, gardens and parks, market spaces, and the like.[46] Many of these elements are an integral part of what Wright refers to as the "cosmology" of the Chinese city, with traditions going back to the early Chinese cities of the Chou dynasty, from the twelfth to sixth centuries BCE. These traditions also included good site-planning principles that considered the availability of water, location with respect to adjacent mountains and rivers, and so on. Nature services were an important determinant of urban form.

Figure 5.4
The majestic Qianmen Gate, a solitary reminder of the Ming dynasty wall.
Source: Author, 2009.

Nine imperial cities—four primary and five occasional[47]—represent the canonical cities of China. While numerous other cities have demonstrated shared properties of form and design, especially amongst various provincial capitals, many others have deviated from the norm. The mutations often resulted from geographical and regional variations, as cultural geographer Sen-Dou Chang pointed out in his analysis of the morphology of Chinese walled cities.[48] In fact, even the canons of imperial city design, which had evolved in the context of the dry, flat plains of northern China, had to be compromised during and after the Han dynasty, when the Chinese empires expanded to the south.[49] For example, city building in the Yangtze River valley was difficult because of mountainous regions, different climatic conditions, and large bodies of water. These difficulties were encountered in the design of Luoyang and Nanjing, which underwent several iterations of canonical layout over the years. The occasional imperial capital of Hangzhou, a

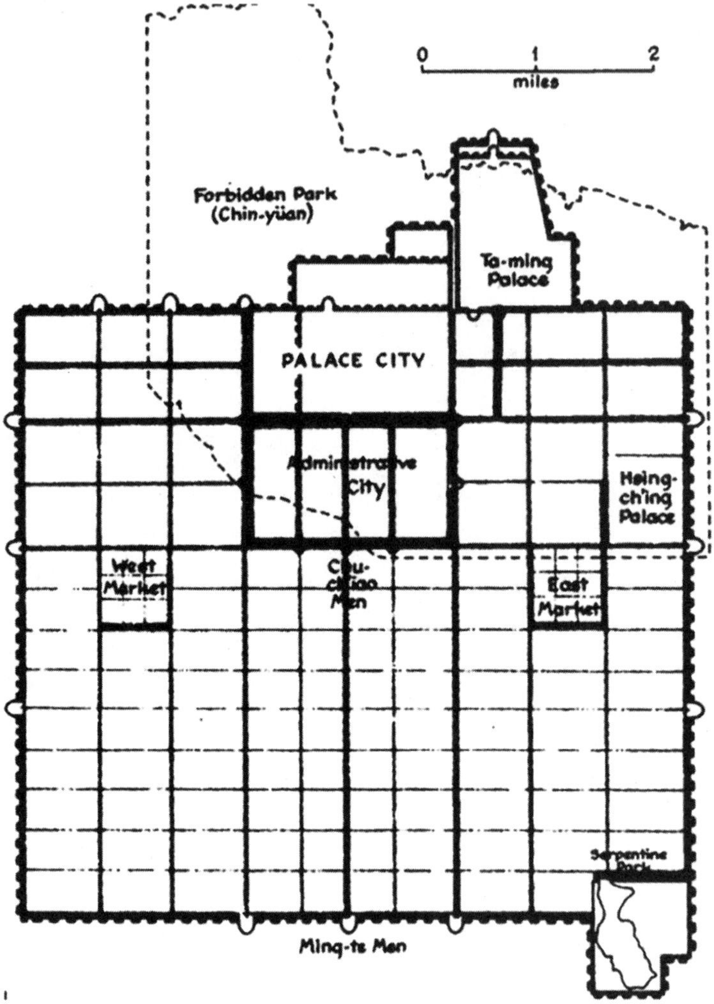

Figure 5.5
Early canonical design, Chang'an.
Source: Lynch (1981), p. 14, with permission from the MIT Press.

prosperous and cosmopolitan city at the time of the Mongol invasion, presented particular difficulties in terms of site conditions.[50] As Wright pointed out, the city, located on a narrow isthmus limited by the Che River to the east and West Lake to the west, could not remain loyal to the canonical form.[51]

These historical vicissitudes in the ideal Chinese city form notwithstanding, two important immutable aspects of Chinese city design are noteworthy. First, from ancient times the design of imperial cities had always played an important role in Chinese cultural and political historiography. With the concentration of power, authority, knowledge, and wealth within its walls, the imperial city was both the symbolic and the functional center of the kingdom. It represented the highest achievements of its people and the society at large. Often ideal cities remained a goal never fully realized. Nowhere was this more apparent than in the case of Wang-Ch'eng, the royal city of the Eastern Chou, which was supposed to be laid out according to the classic canonical design. Archaeological excavations show very little correspondence between how the city was built and its ideal form.

Second, despite wide variations in the layout and size of the imperial cities, they followed canonical design rooted in the Chinese images of an ideal city—the cosmic city. These canons of imperial city design remained relatively invariant through time, even though the design and location of new imperial cities were subject to constant tinkering in terms of the siting and organization, and also the size, which may have been a function of the growth and decline of the resident populations of the capital city. Often these canons were subject to alternative philosophical interpretations, ranging from Confucianism to *feng shui*.[52]

How did the Chinese know what was a good city, or what was an ideal city form? Or which site characteristics would be ideally suited for building an ideal city? There might be several answers to these questions. In ancient times the answer was simple—the city must reflect the larger cosmos to which it belongs, and to which it must connect. As suggested by many authors, this original cosmic model was subsequently followed by other divine and secular interpretations of the ideal city that evolved over time.[53]

The roots of the cosmological models go back to an ancient belief system that incidentally was not limited to Chinese culture. Similar beliefs were widely shared by Indian, other Asian, and Mesoamerican cultures. According to geographer Paul Wheatley, ancient cultures perceived the world as more than textures, forms, and spaces; it "was perceived schematically in term of an extra-mundane, sacred experience."[54] In this belief system only the sacred mattered and the "purely secular—in so far as it could be granted to exist at all—was the purely trivial."[55] Rituals were important because the rites dramatized the universal order and its origin, and to the extent that the canons served a type of rites of geomancy, they "sought to establish an ontological link between the realm of the sacred and the realm of the profane."[56]

The ideal form of the city, according to Eliade, was conceived in the images of a "Celestial Archetype," and the aim of city design was to create a parallel between the Macrocosmos and the Microcosmos.[57] The principal mechanism for obtaining such a link was the ritual celebration of the symbolism of the center—the *axis mundi*—and the use of cardinal orientation to define a sacred territory within a profane space.[58] The classic canonical city was based on this premise. The space enclosed within the four walls represented the universe, oriented in the cardinal directions, with the intersection of main axes defining the symbolic center—"The Pivot of the Four Quarters," as the title of Wheatley's book[59] so aptly captures—where the imperial palace was located as the symbolic link to heaven. The centrality of the imperial palace in the layout of the seventh-century Chinese city would become canonical in subsequent editions of the imperial city.

Over time the Chinese canonical city began to evolve, absorbing multiple systems of beliefs, values, and ethical principles. The orthodoxy of the original "cosmo-magical" principles endured but got variously embellished along the way. As Chinese cities evolved, other belief systems further embellished the original canons of city design. According to the Chou belief system, "the universe was peopled with divinities, spirits, and forces" that could be controlled only by "worship, sacrifices, and propitiatory rites," as Wright notes. This type of "primitive organicism" included not only respect for natural forces that were presided over by gods, but also respect for ancestors, who served as proxies for divine connections. In this worldview, "gods, men, and nature, the living and the dead—all were seen as interacting in a seamless web."[60] Thus, as we discussed earlier, altars, temples, ancestral halls, and tombs—as well as the rites of sacrificing animals in the process of city building—were all added to the canons of city design, reflecting influences of nature services and the relevant habitus.

Toward the end of the Eastern Chou dynasty the effects of Confucianism, Taoism, universalism, the school of Dual Forces, and the school of Five Elements all added layers of new interpretations of the ancient canons; consequently, city-building practices incorporated a "large and heterogeneous body of lores, practices, and ideas"[61] by the beginning of the unified empire. From Wright's historiography of the cosmology of Chinese cities, we learn that by the Han period these canons were synthesized into four basic dimensions: archaism, or codification of some of the Chou principles according to the Confucian idealization of ancient practices; organicism, which involved aspects of the human and natural worlds, but not in a primitive sense; centralism, or the emperor, the kingdom, and the country as the center of the universe; and moralism, which gave the emperor the moral right to rule. This ideology would further formalize the canons in site selection and preparation, orientation, layout, location of important structures, and the like in the design of the city.

Feng shui and its geomantic principles seem to have influenced the next phase of evolution of the cosmology of the imperial city. Wright hypothesizes that the influence of *feng shui* took hold as the Chinese empire expanded to the more varied climate, geography, and landscape of the southern regions, where city building was challenged by limitations of available sites and other natural constraints, making the larger cosmic principles difficult to implement.[62] Seemingly, *feng shui* principles were expected to mitigate the limiting conditions of building sites. I suppose that in today's terms, these principles for achieving balance and harmony with natural forces could be considered as parallel to the notions of "sustainable development."

Some observers have suggested that the ideal and canonical imperial city did not consummate until China's late imperial period.[63] In fact it was the Ming dynasty Beijing—embellished, modified, and appended through a process of ideological predilections, philosophical debates, and practical vetting—that finally came to represent the canons of city building that were conceived in the Chou dynasty a millennium earlier (see figure 5.6). This historiography reveals culturally rooted and completely endogenous developmental thinking that attempted to perfect the canonical city design in the image of the cosmic model.

Canonical Cities of India

The Hindu precepts of canonical city design had two very distinct features: a cosmic referent and a hierarchical order of social organization. The first of these features attempts to replicate the cosmic order through ideal city design, in the same manner as the Chinese, and even the Mesoamerican, canonical cities.[64]

The second feature of the canonical Hindu city involves a hierarchical ordering and organization of space based on the *varna* (literally, color) or caste system, in a tradition of what anthropologist Louis Dumont refers to as "Homo Hierarchicus."[65] While hierarchy of status, power, and authority also existed to some extent in the Chinese and even Mesoamerican cultures, it was never as refined and rigidly practiced in the design of cities as in the Indian case.

Let us then consider in turn these two features of organization and order—spatial and social.

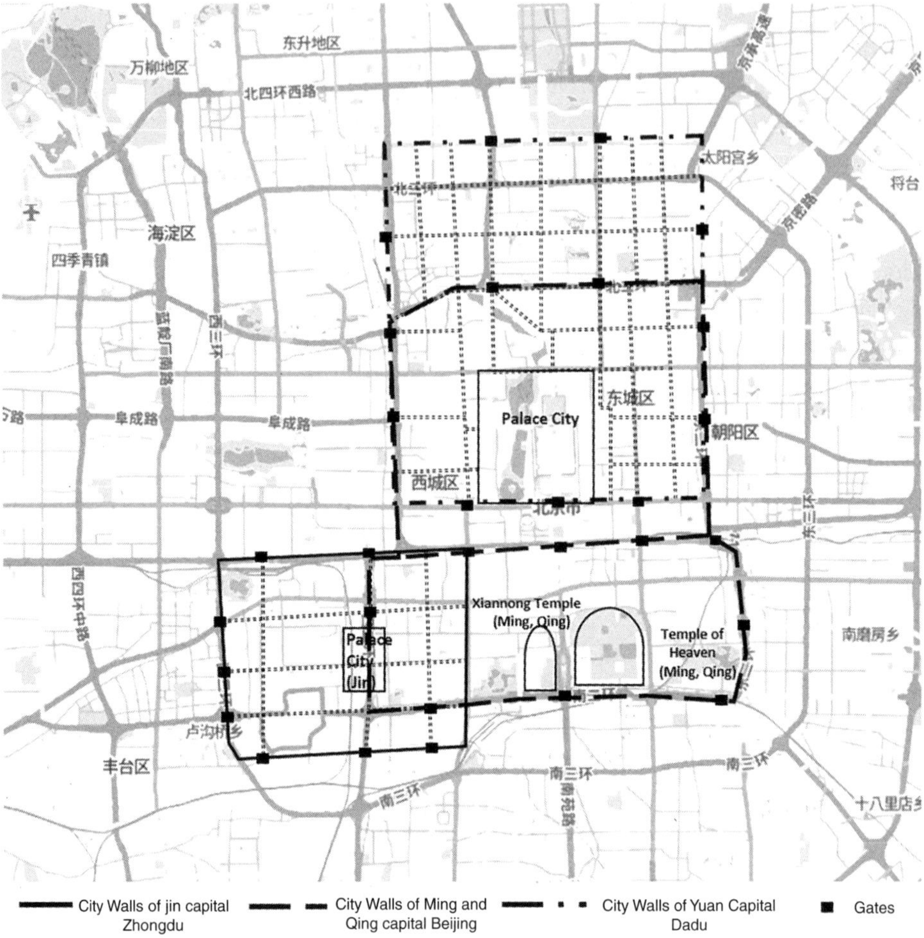

Figure 5.6
Traces of multiple dynastic capitals in Beijing: Zhongdu (Jin dynasty), Dadu (Yuan dynasty), and Beijing (Ming and Qing dynasties).
Source: Redrawn on OpenStreetMap based on L. Wu (1999), p. 7.

(a) Spatial Organization

Madurai in southern India has come to be recognized as the quintessential example of the canonical Hindu city. Like its Chinese counterparts, Madurai is laid out in images of the cosmos. Today one can construct an image of ancient Madurai as a reflection of the Hindu cosmic organization from ancient Tamil literary works dating back to the early third century CE.[66]

Also like its Chinese counterparts, Madurai had gone through several distinct phases of mutation. Its earliest description refers to it as the city of the Pandyans in the early third century CE, and describes it as a well-fortified city of high walls with towering gates, surrounded by a water-filled moat. The narrative is much less specific about the spatial organization inside the city walls, although its authors "make clear that the city is not designed on utilitarian principles."[67] It is an orthogenetic city *par excellence*. But the narrative also mentions a large market for traders, various temples and places of worship, residential areas set aside for different occupations, and broad streets near the center of the city where judges, merchants, royal advisors, and artisans typically lived. (See figure 5.7.)

A somewhat later description of Madurai from the fifth century CE comes from the epic *Cilappatikāram*, adding additional details, although the basic configuration remains the same. The description of this epic city includes two main gateways—one in the east and other in the west—and a thick wall of impenetrable vegetation surrounding the moat. Inside the walls the four different castes had designated streets, with temples dedicated to the guardian deities of each. The center of the city belonged to the palace and the king in a manner very similar to the canonical organization of the Chinese imperial cities.

The epic *Cilappatikāram, however,* endows the centrality of the king and palace with three different meanings of the role and stature of the king. The first meaning is associated with the notion of the king as a warrior-hero who is protector of his subjects. The second meaning is that of a valiant king—"the lord of the eight directions"—who through rituals and sacrifices becomes "identified with the attributes and activities of the gods who are represented in the ritual by various principals and functionaries."[68] Finally, the third view of kingship is one of moral authority, with a concomitant "image of Madurai as a city of the moral order."[69]

Unlike the Chinese imperial city, where the centrality of the royal palace remained uncontested and invariant through late imperial China, Madurai would mutate from a palace city to a temple city as its temples gained in importance, endowing it with its special sense of sanctity by the twelfth and thirteenth centuries. This transformation into a sacral city occurred during a major rebuilding of Madurai—ravaged by battles with Muslim invaders—under the auspices of the Nayak dynasty. Under the Nayak regime, the spatial layout of the city followed the principles of the *vāstuśāstra*, or the Indian art and science of architecture. As Diana Eck explains, the term Vāstu refers to a site or place, its meaning derived from its root vas, or to dwell. Furthermore, she observes that the basic tenets of mandala plan are derived from *Mānasāra Śilpa Śāstra,* the authoritative treatises on science and arts of settlement design. The *mandala* plan

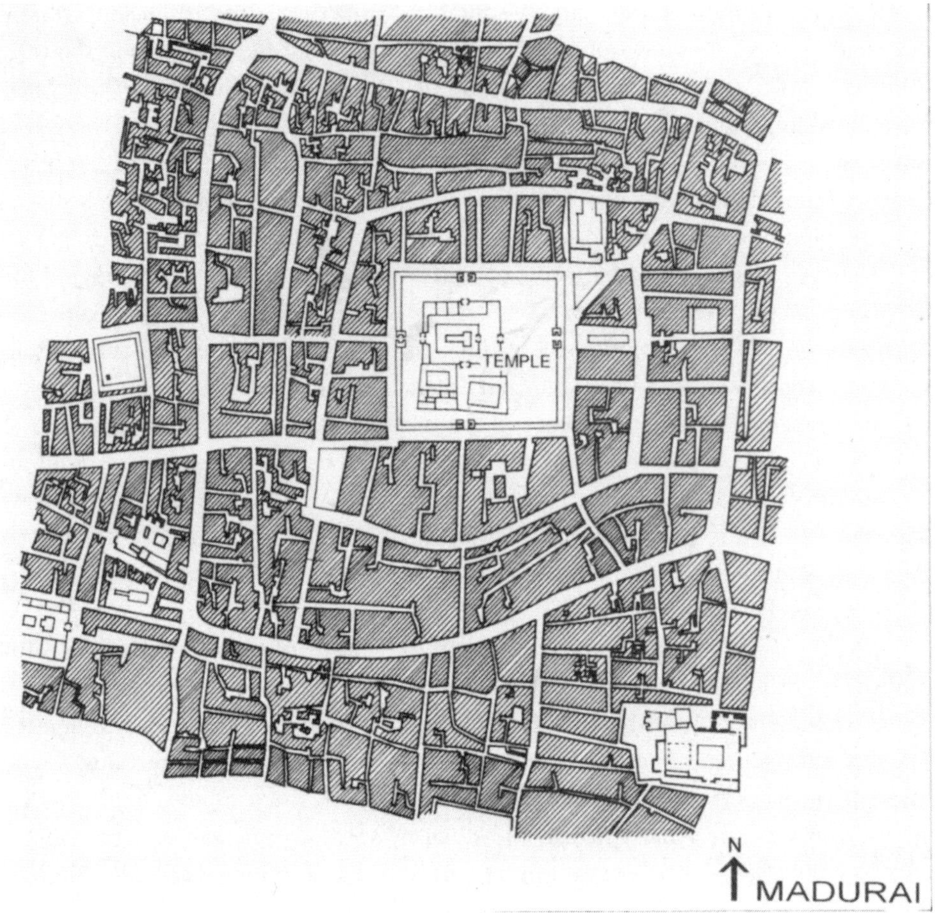

Figure 5.7
Plan of Central Madurai, India, with the temple in the center. The spatial layout was established following the principles of *vāstaśāstra*.
Source: Courtesy of Kulbhusan Jain.

ultimately defines the social order and organization of the city by prescribing dwelling locations for various castes.[70]

The *Mānasāra Śilpa Śāstra* offered a whole catalog of *mandalas* consisting of six main and some twenty-six minor models. The difference in these *mandalas* was a function of the number of grid blocks obtained by subdividing the basic area—usually a square—designated as the site or *vāstu*. Of the *mandalas*, the most fundamental was the *vāstu-purusa-mandala*, where the term *purusa* implied the spirit or the essence of the site (see figure 5.8).[71]

Figure 5.8
A *vāstu-purusa-mandala*.
Source: Lynch (1981), with permission from the MIT Press.

The design of medieval Madurai was clearly based on these canonical principles. The layout and organization reinforced and embellished the original "cosmic city" model, but in the process created a "city of local sacrality."[72] It added some architectural elements, such as *gopuras*, or gateways representing the *meru* (divine mountain), and also a street layout that allowed ritual circumambulation before reaching the center. As a framework for ritual acts within the cosmic form, the city is endowed with a liturgical quality, as anthropologist Jeffrey Meyer has suggested in the case of imperial Peking.[73]

While the Hindu and the Chinese canonical cities share many morphological similarities, there are also some significant ideological and philosophical differences. In discussing Chinese and Indian architecture, architect Nelson Wu draws some rather broad conclusions about the ideological differences underlying the canonical organization of space in the Chinese and Hindu traditions. He argues that the Chinese "sees himself, in an idealized manner of course, not at all fixed in the center of his world, but longingly looking out beyond his walls."[74] He sees the Chinese as one who "focuses his eyes on the ground instead of heaven," and creates his own knowledge and controls, organizes, and measures the world around him. In contrast, his Indian counterpart is looking toward heaven and is "the seeker of enlightenment who makes the eternal pilgrimage from the periphery to the center."[75] Elsewhere, in referring to the canonical forms, Wu observes, "The infinite universe of India revolves around the cosmic axis. On the other hand, the Chinese universe is actually a cube."[76] This conclusion, however provocative, is contrary to the earlier scholarship on Chinese cities.

There is a difference in the interpretation of the role of the center in the Chinese and Indian city-building traditions. For instance, the central position occupied by the imperial palace in China ("always keeping man at its center"), according to Wu, established the inherent anthropocentrism of the Chinese canonical city: "It is an image of man's society."[77] In contrast, the location of the temple—with its towering architectural feature, representing the mythical *meru*, the "Mountain of God"—at the center of the Indian city epitomized the link between earth and heaven. Notes Eck, drawing from Eliade, "The center is a place of hierophany ... where the divine of transcendent dimension breaks through into this world of daily life."[78]

The interpretation of the center is where Wheatley demurs with Wu's assertion that the Chinese walled city is different in every respect from the canonical Indian city. Wheatley argues that while regional, historical, and cultural overlays might have produced many differences in their appearance, the images of the canonical cities in these two cultures share very similar notions of ordering of space and "a common 'astrobiological' mode of thought."[79] Cardinal directions of the east-west axis tracking the movement of the sun, and the north-south axis anchored by the pole star, represented one such mode. Another was the center of these axes—whether occupied by a palace or a temple—the *axis mundi* "incorporating a powerful impulse to centripetality."[80] In that view, the canonical city in both contexts represents a "terrestrial image of the cosmos" by cardinal orientation, axiality, and emphasis on the strong architectural features of the gates.[81]

In any event, Wu's observation portrays the Chinese as immensely secular, pragmatic, egotistical, rationalist, materialistic, nonreflective, and overachieving people. Indians, in contrast, can be seen as otherworldly, spiritual, nonrational, reflective, brooding, disengaged, and underachieving people. While this may resonate with common stereotypes, especially in view of the hugely successful and impressive Chinese economy and the emergence of China as a global power, this is not a fair characterization of the respective cultures or the images that shaped their canonical urban form.[82]

(b) Social Organization

Let us now consider the other facet of the doctrines of ancient town planning in India as stipulated in Manasara, a classic Hindu treatise (part of Shilpa Shastras) on building and settlement design, and the tenets of social hierarchy that date back presumably to the Vedic times. Here we see a long tradition of Indian settlement planning,[83] which includes everything from edicts for planning the system of settlements and their proper hierarchy to standards and principles for designing streets and buildings. The precepts of town planning or "site planning" were often conflated with the precepts of what historian Binode Behari Dutt calls "folk-planning"—a concept comparable to modern notions of "social planning" or "social engineering."[84]

The ancient Indian town-planning principles are a part of a larger body of knowledge or treatises known as *VāstuVidyā* or *Vāstu.* The most common authoritative source for ancient Indian town-planning principles in written form are the canons of *Silpasastras*, which were laid down by Manasara and Mayamuni of the fifth or sixth century CE in southern India. According to Manasara, "the place where men and gods reside is called Vāstu."[85] The Bengali word *basati* (meaning a human settlement), or its degenerated version *bustee* (meaning an urban slum), today are derived from the same Sanskrit root *vas*, which means to reside, or to settle. The word *Vidyā* refers to science or knowledge, and the word *Sāstra* means a treatise. This body of knowledge representing the arts and science of settlements is actually quite comprehensive, including civil and military engineering, architecture, furniture design, and even sculpture and iconography.[86] According to Dutt, many of the ancient principles of town planning predated Manasara and had their roots in Kautilya's *Arthasastra* (roughly equivalent to the modern concept of economics), dated around the fourth century BCE.

It is in the canonical domain of spatial organization that ancient Indian physical-spatial planning and folk-spatial planning converge, thus prescribing the ideal social ecology of cities. The schemes of this canonical domain essentially specified the appropriate locations for castes and occupations according to a social hierarchy handed down from Vedic times. Thus Brahmans (or priests), the highest caste or *varna*, along with royal teachers, were to occupy spaces near the center, where temples and palaces were located. The Kshatriyas (or warrior class), along with state functionaries and merchants selling flowers and perfumes, were to be located in the next ring, followed by the Vaisyas (or business class), along with soldiers and merchants of less refined products. Sudras ("the servants or have-nots"[87]), along with artisans and manufacturing laborers—as well as stables and other housing for animals of conveyance—were to be located in spaces further away from the center.[88] The class of people who collected and disposed of human waste and dead animals; cleaned toilets, streets, and gutters; and cremated the dead, were considered impure and thus "untouchable" and consigned to residual spaces outside the city limits. Alongside the religious implications, this model obviously had considerable secular land use implications as well, since it specified in detail the locations of such activities as burial grounds, shops and hospitals, crafts and manufacturing, entertainment, and even brothels.

There is a bewildering variety of sources and interpretations of the planned social ecology[89] of cities as Dutt reviews them, many with seemingly arbitrary, inconsistent, and nonsensical edicts that may not always make rational sense to the contemporary mind. It is apparent, however, that they were all derivatives of the original *vāstu-purusa-mandala*, the cosmic grid that assigned deities and constellations in different cells according to their cosmic role and significance, with Brahmā at the center. In all of the above there seems to be a rationale for what I have referred to as the planned social ecology of cities.[90] Furthermore, the allocation of space to castes or guilds would have reflected the numerical size of various groups, and thus the social composition of the city's population. So the rationale for this canonical form, then, is one of ordering the corporate life of cities according to human and occupational diversity. Given this ecology, what would be a more ideal form than the original *vāstu-purusa-mandala* inspired by a larger cosmic order?

The rationale of efficient corporate life and specialization led to a socially stratified urban life reflected in city form, which privileged people and space according to a hierarchy of *varna* and occupation. While caste mobility may have been possible theoretically with changes in one's occupation, in reality such inter-caste mobility was discouraged and the caste boundaries were quite rigidly enforced. An assertion of fundamental inequality—that people are born unequal—and its attendant unequal rights and privileges were intrinsic to the concept of *varna* and class. Despite the persistence of these practices over many millennia, however, they remain anathema to the modern secular Indian state and its egalitarian and democratic institutions shaped after Western liberal democracies.[91]

There is a significant corpus of social and anthropological scholarship on the origin, evolution, and social purpose of the Indian caste system. The seminal work of anthropologist Louis Dumont in particular is worth noting here, even though he does not address the urban ecology of the caste system.[92] Dumont makes important distinctions between *varna* and caste, and between hierarchy and power. He argues that *varna* may have racial origins going back to the time of the Indo-Aryan invaders. The relationship between hierarchy and power was related more to the system of *varna* than it was to caste. The system of caste, on the other hand, is a matter of "one fundamental conception," namely, "the opposition of the pure and impure." "This opposition," argues Dumont, drawing from philosopher Célestin Bouglé, "underlies hierarchy, which is the superiority of the pure to the impure, underlies separation because the pure and the impure must be kept separate, and underlies the division of labour because pure and impure occupations must likewise be kept separate."[93] Thus the impure becomes subaltern to the pure. The gradation, separation, and division of labor that sustains the caste system is part of the "fundamental conception" of the pure and the impure that pervades all aspects of daily and periodic life in Hinduism, including the ritual of bathing and washing as an act of purifying. One can easily see the spatiality of such practices in the canonical forms and even in the everyday experiences of the built environment in contemporary India, where spaces are in effect given a denomination according to purity (similar to nuisance factors—noise, pollution, odor, etc.—used according to modern notions of land use and zoning), and where liminality—boundaries, transitions, thresholds, and crossings[94]—between the pure and the impure, between the sacred and the profane,[95] become important spatial markers (see figure 5.9, which shows a sign posted outside a Hindu temple in Jaipur that prohibits menstruating women from entering).

Figure 5.9
The ancient practice of liminality based on gender (still in practice), currently contested by the feminist movement in India.
Source: Author, 1994.

Thus placed in the conception of purity, the planned social ecology implicit in the town-planning and folk-planning of ancient Indian cities offers still another, and perhaps more synoptic, rationality for the canonical image of the ideal Indian city. (See figure 5.8.)

The semiotics of space in the endogenous images of the ideal have consistently differentiated between social groups and have privileged some classes or groups by orders of power, purity, caste (or occupation), and gender. In the classic canonical model of the Hindu city, the untouchables were not even allowed inside the city. They were not included in the hierarchical ordering of space, even though their utilitarian presence was necessary and unavoidable. Consigned to spaces of abjection, to invoke philosopher Julia Kristeva, the untouchables were the ultimate alterior, or the "other."[96] In addition, drawing on postcolonial theorist Gayatri Chakravorty Spivak, who argues that the postcolonial reasoning has been remiss about women's location as the subaltern, one could argue that while feminine subalternity was nested within the larger colonial subalternity, it was not just an outcome of colonial times but in fact integral to the precolonial order of things, albeit exploited and exacerbated by colonial institutions.[97]

The question remains as to whether this privileging of people and space by the ordering of caste or *varna* was a precursor to the dualism and subaltern spaces that began in colonial times and accepted as given. I will address that point in chapter 7.

6 Piety, Community, Autopoiesis, and Aesthetics

> Sefrou, this thousand year old town ... is hardly representative, in the statistical sense, of Morocco, much less of North Africa, the Middle East, or the Muslim world. Nor, though it includes within it almost all the elements of a classic medina in their classic forms—mosques, walls, baths, impasses, bazaars, fountains, caravansaries, shrines, citadels—is it any sort of ideal type of Islamic city. Its use is neither as a sample of something nor as an epitome of something, but as an instance of something: a case in point.... Examples instruct, they do not prove.
>
> —Clifford Geertz, "*Toutes Directions*: Reading the Signs in an Urban Sprawl"[1]

Djema el-Fna is the main public square inside the historic walled city of Marrakech. Roughly triangular in shape with sides measuring 200 to 150 meters, the space itself is unremarkable, surrounded by equally unremarkable buildings two or three stories tall with a red stucco exterior typical of this historic medina and much of the city beyond. Unlike other medieval squares, these buildings are not high enough to create a sense of enclosure. The storefront shops and terrace restaurants comprise a commercial edge that draws the hustle and bustle of tourists and usual denizens. To the northern end of the square is the entrance to the covered *souk* that winds its way through various sections specializing in pottery, textile, carpets, copperware, jewelry, and so on, before finally ending at the Ben Youssef Mosque and the Ben Youssef Madrasa, built in the twelfth century CE. About 200 meters to the west of the square is the famous late-twelfth-century Kutubiyya Mosque, built by the Almohads. The mosque is well known for its old and well-preserved minaret. In premodern times this space was mainly pedestrian save perhaps for occasional animal-drawn carriage. Today, the edges of the square have acceded to the imperatives of automobile traffic.

The name *Djema el-Fna* has a variety of intriguing meanings in Arabic. In one sense it means "assembly of the dead," a likely reference to the public executions once held there. Another interpretation is "assembly of nothing." The space is a great emptiness when the day begins, true to one meaning, but transforms into a busy square by midday. At dusk when the muezzin calls the faithful to prayer, and later into the evening, Djema el-Fna becomes an assembly of the very-much-alive, and a celebration of life. Reportedly some one hundred thousand people—residents and visitors—gather here every evening, a glorious bedlam of hawkers, storytellers, dervishes, acrobats, minstrels, magicians, and medicine men that delights locals and tourists alike. Shouts and laughter, drumbeats and music mix with the smoke and aroma of kebabs cooked over open fire. The Arabic expression *neshem al hawa* ("let's go smell the air") takes on its fullest meaning in this cacophony of sounds, sights, and smells, where the elusive notion of conviviality in public life[2] becomes palpable in this quintessential urban sensorium.[3] The script for this theater—the assembly of the alive—has continued to defy its original purport through time.

Founded in the eleventh century CE, the medina of Marrakech is a medieval city whose form has evolved through the reconstruction efforts of several dynasties. Today Djema el-Fna stands at the center of the medina—an ensemble of spaces and structures comprising mosques, souks, tightly packed residential quarters with courtyard housing, the palace, and *qasbah*, the walled enclosure to the south that includes the complex of the royal palace and also the *mellah* (the Jewish quarter).[4] (See figure 6.1.) Does the urbanism of Marrakech represent a possible archetype that captures an endogenous image of development?[5]

Consider the twin cities of Rabat and Sale, which are separated by the Oued Bou Regreg river some 300 kilometers to the northeast on the Mediterranean coast. While the walled medina of Rabat is much smaller compared to Marrakech, it has many similar features: ancient walls and gates, a lively souk, tightly packed residential quarters, several mosques scattered throughout, and an adjoining and discrete citadel or *qasbah*. Yet for all these similarities, the Rabat medina does not have a public square like Djema el-Fna. For that matter, neither does the walled medina of Sale, on the other side of the river from Rabat. Although larger and older than Rabat, it too lacks a significant central public square.

About 150 kilometers to the southeast of the coastal Rabat-Sale lies the historic city of Fès, in the heart of the Middle Atlas region of Morocco. Founded some 800 years ago, the walled medina of Fès continues to function as a medieval city with its guilds, narrow pedestrian streets, various mosques, madrasas, and a very lively souk.[6] While Fès shares many of the features of the other cities we reviewed, the city's fame is derived from the Quaraouiyine mosque, one of Islam's most important mosques, which is located in the center of the medina. The mosque is surrounded by a dense collection of courtyard houses, shops, and narrow alleys, resulting in a juxtaposition of solid and

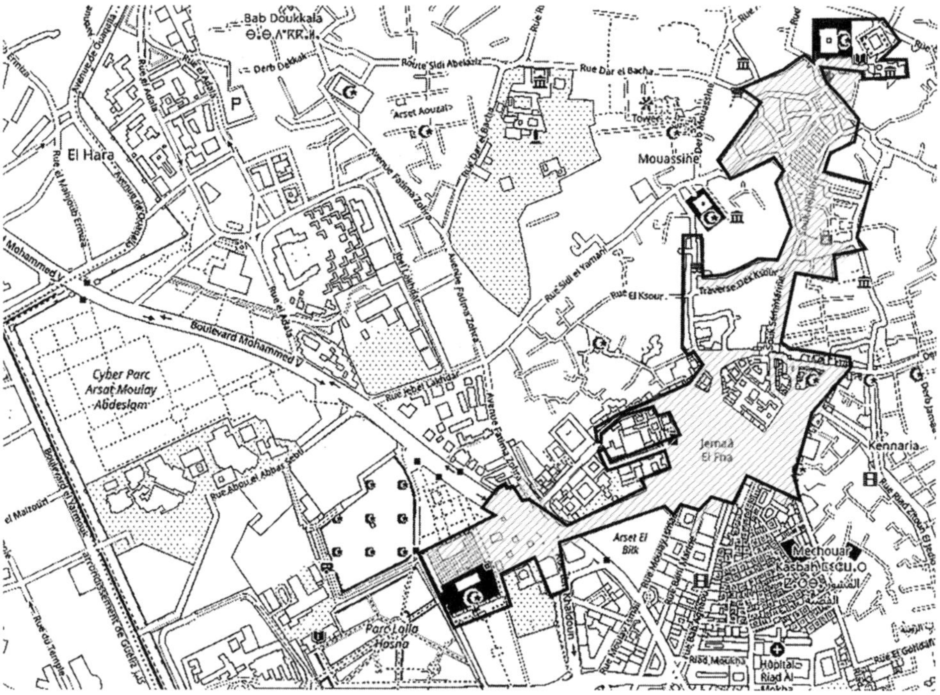

Figure 6.1

The walled medina of Marrakech with *ville nouvelle* (the colonial city) to the west of the wall. *Source*: Redrawn on OpenStreetMap, © OpenStreetMap contributors, licensed as CC BY-SA.

void typical of indigenous urban form of the preindustrial city. In the aerial view of the tightly packed Quaraouiyine district, its ancient alleys and streets appear only as cracks and fissures in the dense urban form. The grain of the medina's urban texture is defined by the void of the courtyards of the individual houses that share walls and connect seamlessly to each other. On maps, the alleys and streets of this intense urban form seem to disappear as surely they become easements of tunnels and passages providing access to the houses (see figure 6.2).

This dense pattern of solid and voids hosts a continuum of a network of private and public realms. This continuum begins in the private quarters of the courtyard houses and ultimately connects them to the public realm of souks, mosques, and other community spaces through a hierarchy of courtyards, easements, passages, impasses, alleys, and streets that connect the house to the neighborhood, and the neighborhood to the larger city. This hierarchy of private and public realm also reflects the "gendering" of space in these cities, where the private realm is associated with women and the public

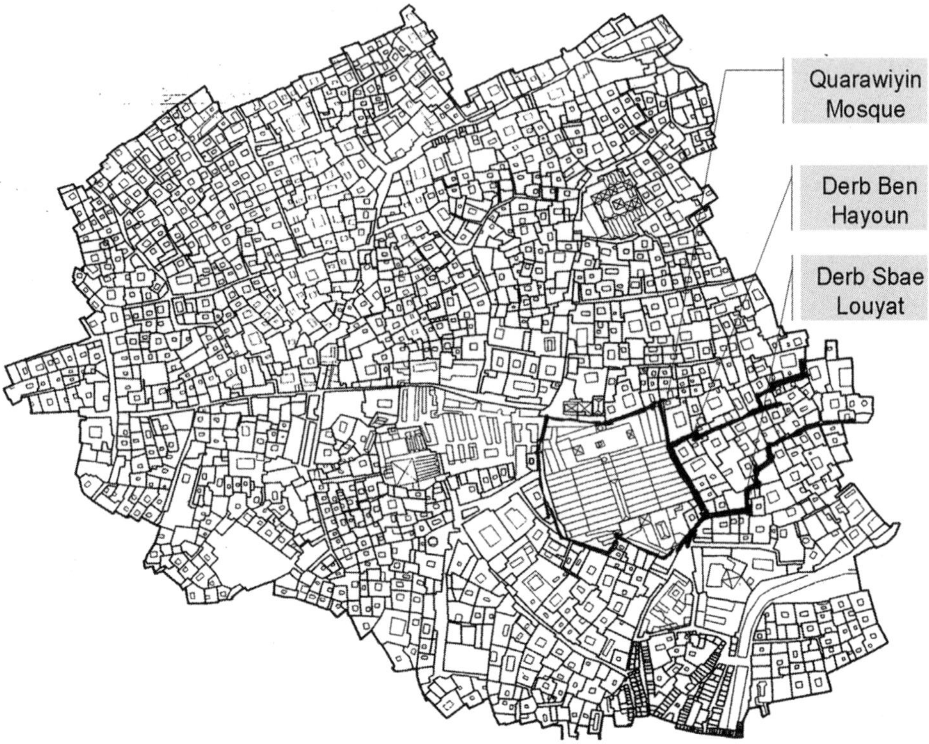

Figure 6.2
Urban form of Fès medina: The Quaraouiyine district with the Quaraouiyine mosque and the surrounding alleys and passages.
Source: Drawn on a map from ADER. Courtesy of Hassan Radoine.

realm, with men.[7] These are essentially spaces of proxemics,[8] comprising propinquity, and other sensory contacts. The conduct of the quotidian life in such high propinquity environments intensifies social contact and thereby contributes to the sense of place and community in the medina. It also plays a role in defining the unique urban sensorium of these cities, and in turn the relationship of the senses to the context of daily life.

A central open space typical in European or Latin America cities, however, is not common in Morocco. Marrakech is an exception. There is no central assembly space here in this historic city of Fès within its tightly packed organic composition of solids and voids. As Islamic scholar Titus Burckhardt pointed out, the interior courtyard of the Quaraouiyine mosque is the largest space open to sky in the Fès medina (see figure 6.3).[9] There are some clearings outside the dense urban fabric that are still inside the old walls and near

Figure 6.3
Courtyard of the Quaraouiyine mosque.
Source: Author, 1999.

some of the gates, like Bab al Ftouh, and Bab Bou Jeloud, where horses and camels rested in former times, now serving as parking spaces for tour buses and taxis.

The topography of the Fès medina gives its urban form the shape of a bowl or large hollow. This unique characteristic offers simultaneous transitions in several dimensions: One has a clear intuition of progression from the outside to the inside, from the public to the private, from the secular to the spiritual, and to invoke Eliade, from the profane to the sacred.[10] In varying degrees this simultaneous senses of inside-outside, private-public, and spiritual-secular is present in many other walled medinas of Morocco and Arab cities, such as the ones discussed previously, albeit nowhere as clearly experienced as in the urban form of Fès.

The "Islamic City": An Orientalist Concoction

Through the last two centuries the term "Islamic city" has been commonly used to describe not only the medinas of Morocco but also the hundreds of other cities throughout the Middle East, North Africa, and the Indian subcontinent that were established or adapted during the spread of Islam. Much of the academic writings on these cities—especially that by Western scholars—uses the term "Islamic cities" indiscriminately, and not only in academic writings but also in the popular press, textbooks and documentaries.[11] Furthermore, the concept of the Islamic city has been defined in terms of very specific elements of urban form that seem to remain invariant from city to city: mosques, *madrasas*, walls and gates, souks or bazaars, *hamams* or public baths, citadels and palaces, courtyard houses, organic street patterns, and so on (see figure 6.4).[12]

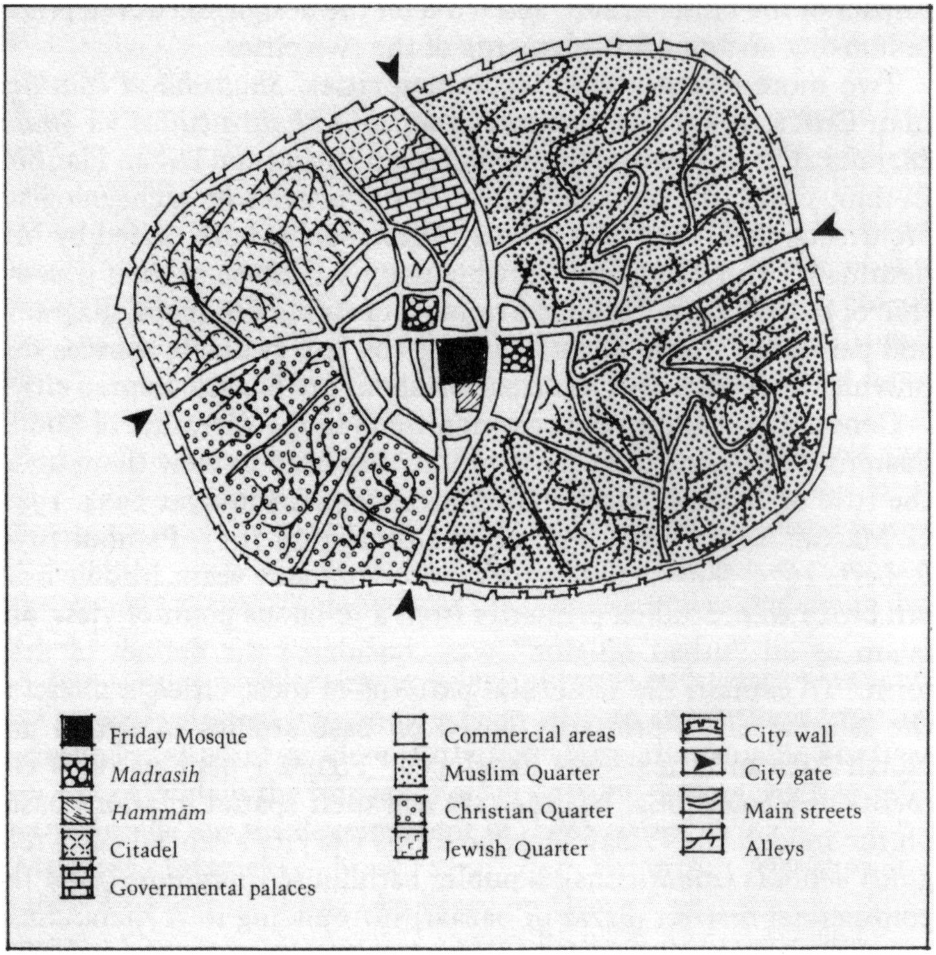

Figure 6.4
A typical Islamic city.
Source: Kheirabadi (1991), p. 4. Courtesy of Masoud Kheirabadi.

Some of the earliest twentieth-century work reinforcing those images is found in French Orientalist William Marçais's characterization of Islam as an urban religion.[13] He argued that cities represented the quintessence of the civilization that grew out of this religion. His brother Georges Marçais developed this argument further by identifying the Friday mosque as the central feature of these cities along with other archetypal elements, such as the differentiated residential quarters and commercial areas and the hierarchy of trades (hence land use) in relation to the proximity to the mosque.[14] If a skeletal framework of an Islamic city archetype came out of this scholarship, it was subsequently given shape and form in the case studies of North African cities by experts like historian Roger LeTourneau, Islamic scholar Jacques Berque, and other authors of that time. This elemental concept of the Islamic city, referred to as the "Maghrebi stereotype" by architect Nezar AlSayyad, however, did not capture the spatial organization and urban form of cities of Syria and Palestine, or Iran, many of which had even earlier Greco-Roman origin.[15]

In case studies of Aleppo and Damascus historian Jean Sauvaget documented the gradual adaptation of existing pre-Islamic cities to serve functions of the emerging culture and urbanism under Islam.[16] Mosques transformed and replaced churches and temples. The orthogonal grid city of the Greek lineage metamorphosed into a more irregular urban form, typical of organic cities of that era, in a counter-Haussmannian fashion, as it were.

That is, if we could imagine the urban form of modern Paris, a product of the nineteenth-century reconstruction in a baroque modernist design, in reverse had slowly regressed back to its original medieval urban form. Although the degeneration of the grid had begun by the end of the Byzantine era, Sauvaget suggested that the most radical alteration of the earlier Greco-Roman cities occurred during the Islamic era because of the decentralized and neighborhood-based institutions of governance.

This historiography of the adaptation of earlier cities to new Islamic institutions led to a new representation of an Islamic city stereotype, which was then formalized in the work of Orientalist scholar Gustave von Grunebaum.[17] AlSayyad argues further that these formal archetypes of the so-called Islamic city continued to have enormous influence on subsequent scholarship, including that produced by native scholars.[18] Subsequent scholarly works either continued to embellish the theme established in the von Grunebaum archetype, like historian Heinz Gaube's work on Iranian cities, or else at best attempted to validate that archetype, as was the case with city planner Sam Noe's work on Delhi and Lahore.[19]

Islamic City: The Contesting Views

The question "Is there an Islamic city?" asked in an article by sociologist Dale Eickelman continues to haunt the scholarship on the urbanism, urbanization, and urban design in the Muslim world especially as it confronts the sweeping effects of globalization and modernity.[20] Contemporary efforts to define a design vocabulary that is expressive of the authenticity and identity of Muslim culture beg this very question. Beginning in the later years of the last century, many scholarly writings contested the notion of an archetypal Islamic city.[21] Some of the earliest scrutiny of the concept began in a book edited by historians Albert Hourani and Samuel Stern. The contributors questioned generalizations based on a small sample of North African cities, or whether guilds were a characteristic of Islamic cities, and that the "Round City" of Baghdad[22] represented a major exception to this traditional archetype.[23]

In the late 1980s the Orientalist archetype of the Islamic city received critical scrutiny again from sociologist Janet Abu-Lughod.[24] Alarmed by contemporary attempts in some Middle Eastern countries to define the form of the Islamic city and thus derive the essential principles, if not canons, of city design and city building from these Orientalist archetypes, Abu-Lughod presented a critical treatise addressing such scholarship. Urban planners, she thought, were influenced, "whether wittingly or not, by a body of literature produced by Western Orientalists purporting to define the essence of the Islamic city."[25] She questioned "the criteria of authority, chains of authenticity, and the construction of reality" in this scholarship. She argued that the idea of the Islamic city was constructed by a series of Western authorities who drew upon a small and eccentric sample of premodern Arab cities on the eve of Westernization, but more than that, they drew upon one another in an *isnād* of authority."[26] While conceding that there may indeed be such a thing as "Islamic essence" (equivalent to habitus in Bourdieu's term) in these cities, she argued that the Orientalist approach has largely been a taxonomic exercise to define something that was alien to the Western repertoire of city form. Furthermore, architect Nezar AlSayyad makes the case that the unique features of the Islamic city thus identified were very much influenced by the Orientalist scholarship of an earlier era, which had begun to define Islam as the "other" against the template of the Western cities and civilization.[27]

But was the form of the so-called Islamic city all that alien to the Western repertoire? After all, one could argue that the basic urban form of the Islamic city—its organic disposition and densely packed urban texture, it walls and gates—was no different from that of many preindustrial medieval cities of that era. While mosques and madrasas replaced churches and monasteries, most other elements remained pretty much the same.[28] In his more recent critique of the Orientalist literature, historian André Raymond points out that the Orientalists failed to realize that their notions of the traditional (i.e., "Islamic") city and the European medieval city "were two aspects of the same reality."[29] In making this point he draws from the work of geographer Eugen Wirth, who argued, having shown that the irregular street pattern and dead end alleys, courtyard houses, residential quarters (and the walls and gates, we might add), were quite common to medieval and Mediterranean cities, both Muslim and Christian, and it is only the souk or the bazaar that could be considered intrinsic to the Muslim cultural heritage.[30] According to Raymond, Wirth suggested that the term "Islamic city" be replaced by the more generic term "Oriental city," arguing that "Islam seems to be more the *inhabitant or occupant* of Middle Eastern urban systems than the *architect*."[31] This critique could have also included many cities in the Indian subcontinent as examples that looked remarkably similar in form to the Maghreb and other Middle Eastern cities, sans perhaps the mosques and the souk. The twelfth-century Jaiselmar, or the fifteenth-century Jodhpur, the well-known Hindu cities in the arid hills of Rajasthan, are cases in point.[32]

Others have argued that it may not be possible to speak of an archetype of Islamic city for the entire Muslim world encompassing some 1.2 billion people spreading from the Middle East to the far reaches of the Indonesian archipelago.[33] Similarly, AlSayyad and architect Masoud Kheirabadi, among others, have also pointed out the inherent tenuity of an Islamic city archetype that is based mainly on case studies of Syrian and North African cities.[34]

Thus, the archetype of the Islamic city remains a figment of a Western scholarly imagination, as AlSayyad has argued.[35] How can the idea of an Islamic archetypal city, which is contested even in the narrower context of Arab cities, be applied even more broadly to the rest of the Muslim world? In fact, as AlSayyad has demonstrated, in the early years of the spread of Islam, artifacts of Islamic culture were grafted onto existing pre-Muslim cities, and in later years city design and city building were "inextricably linked to the lives and actions of those who controlled and governed these cities," namely the emirs, caliphs, and sheikhs.[36] These men of power who built the cities in the name of Islam were often influenced by functional imperatives such as defense, trade, and commerce, and also not uncommonly, simple fiat. Consider the founding of a new city, Fatehpur Sikri, in 1569—later abandoned—by the third Mogul ruler Akbar in northern India. The new city was built to celebrate the birth of a prince and also as the home of Salim Chisti, whose auspicious oracle about the birth of the prince made the emperor forever grateful.[37] But this new city, designed as formal orthogonal plan of courtyards and buildings along a major axis—and vaguely reminiscent of earlier Hindu temple complexes of India—had very little correspondence with the traditional Arab-Muslim city (see figure 6.5).

Figure 6.5
The mausoleum of Salim Chisti, inside the courtyard of Jama Masjid in Fatehpur Sikri. Architectural features—*chhatris* (cupolas), deep cornices, bracketed columns, and screens—are all adaptations of traditional Hindu architecture.
Source: Author, 2004.

By the time Islam had spread to the Indian subcontinent and beyond, the Orientalist notion of the Islamic city became increasingly tenuous, even though some features of the Arab-Muslim city persisted in many of these cities, the historic walled city of Ahmedabad in Gujarat, founded in 1411 CE by Sultan Ahmedshah, being a case in point. Like Fatehpur Sikri, other cities developed under the Mogul rule—Agra, Shahjahanabad (now old Delhi), Lahore, for example—had very little in their design that approached anything canonical, other than the orientation of the *qibla*, the praying wall in a mosque. In a comprehensive review of the legacy of Muslim cities in Southeast Asia, cultural scholar Jeyamalar Kathirithamby-Wells[38] pointed out that very few of these cities contained any of the characteristics suggested by historian Albert Hourani.[39] She concluded that Islam did not bring about any fundamental changes in the Southeast Asian cities, many of which had existing urban patterns derived from the Hindu canonical form.[40] Kathirithamby-Wells concludes, however, that the practice of Islam did bring about some changes in the urbanism and habitus of the existing cities. Functionally, for example, the introverted and reflective Hindu-Buddhist cities metamorphosed from essentially orthogenetic to more extroverted heterogenetic cities open to foreign trade and receiving international influence.

Revisionist Claims on the Islamic City

The anti-Orientalist view has faced some backlash as it is seen as a criticism of the very concept of an Islamic city. Many conferences and symposia have been convened to restore the legitimacy of the "original" model of the Islamic city, or at least to establish how hadith or Shariah have codified certain design and planning principles of Islamic cities.[41] Unfortunately, in their enthusiasm for the authentic, these scholars overlook the fact that such images of development were originally constructions of Western scholarship. Thus, the anti-Orientalist position that challenged what Abu-Lughod referred to as the "historic myth" is now subject to revisionist thinking, and that mainly among the community of Muslim scholars.[42] According to AlSayyad, the revisionist critique includes two types of response from scholars of Islamic studies: the "philosophical-spiritual" and the "political-nationalist." It is important to note, however, that there is a significant difference between the philosophical-spiritual and the political-nationalist approaches toward restoration of the concept of an Islamic city. The former resorted to interpretations of the city form in philosophical and spiritual terms, as in the works of Ardalan and Bakhtiar, noted previously.[43] The latter variety included scholarship that, according to AlSayyad, was "mainly sponsored by countries with strong political ideologies or because their writing has a distinctive nationalistic tone."[44] He cites the works of architects Saleh Al-Hathloul and Besim Hakim, among others, as cases in point.[45]

The Philosophical-Spiritual Approach

Of the two paths, the "philosophical-spiritual" is the more intriguing from the perspective of images of development, as in the case of the work of Ardalan and Bakhtiar, for example. These scholars, who draw from the Sufi tradition, and who are obviously influenced by the transformation of Espahan during the Safavid era, suggested a more dynamic adaptation of the original Islamic city stereotype, even going so far as to suggest it as a representation of a cosmic model.[46] However, what they actually offered in their interpretation is a developmental image of the dynamics of city growth and change, idealized as a natural process over time, but curiously without any reference to Shariah or hadith.[47] Instead, they derive the imperatives of good design—in art, architecture, and city development—from the Sufi tradition's idealization of pure geometric forms that are inherent in nature, and idealized throughout human history. Thus the concentric urban form—whether circular (as in eighth-century Baghdad; see figure 6.6) or square (as in pre-Islamic Herat in Afghanistan, established by Alexander the Great; see figure 6.7)—is the ideal plan in this interpretation. Implicit in their argument is the case for maintaining the unity and harmony with nature and cosmic order, to obtain an ideal state of being epitomized as in the "mandala."[48] In the circular plan of Baghdad, as built by Caliph Al-Mansour in 762 CE, these scholars saw a reaffirmation of these ancient ideals, observing that "the advent of Islam witnessed a profound extension of these ancient concepts."[49] Note again their making references to "mandala" and

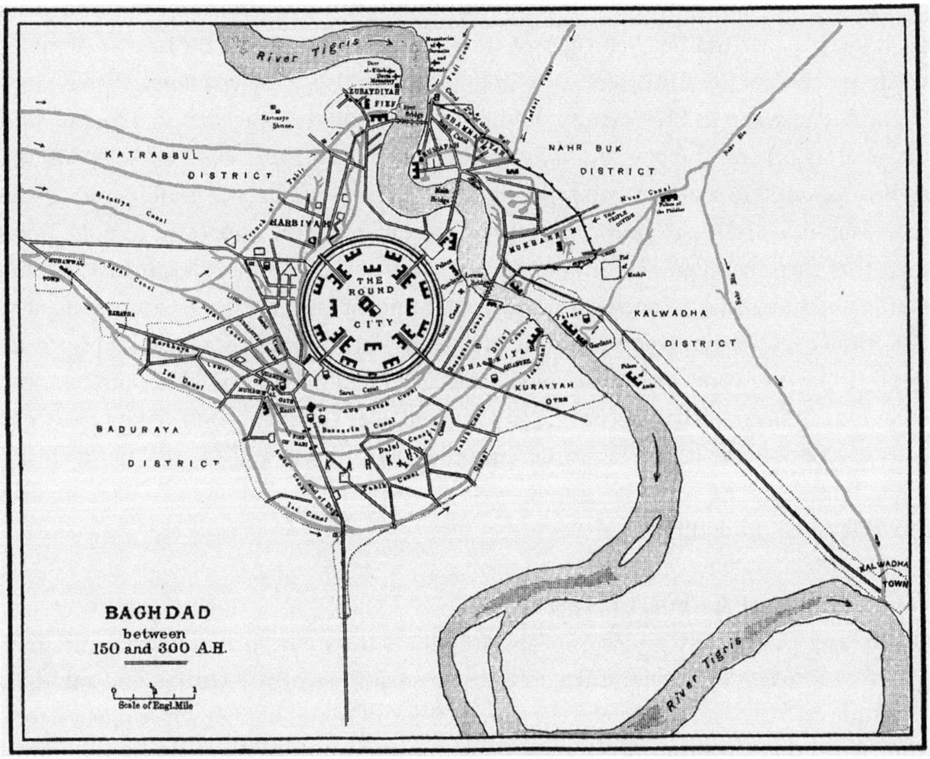

Figure 6.6
The Round City of Baghdad (between 767 and 912 CE).
Source: William Muir/Wikimedia Commons/Public Domain.

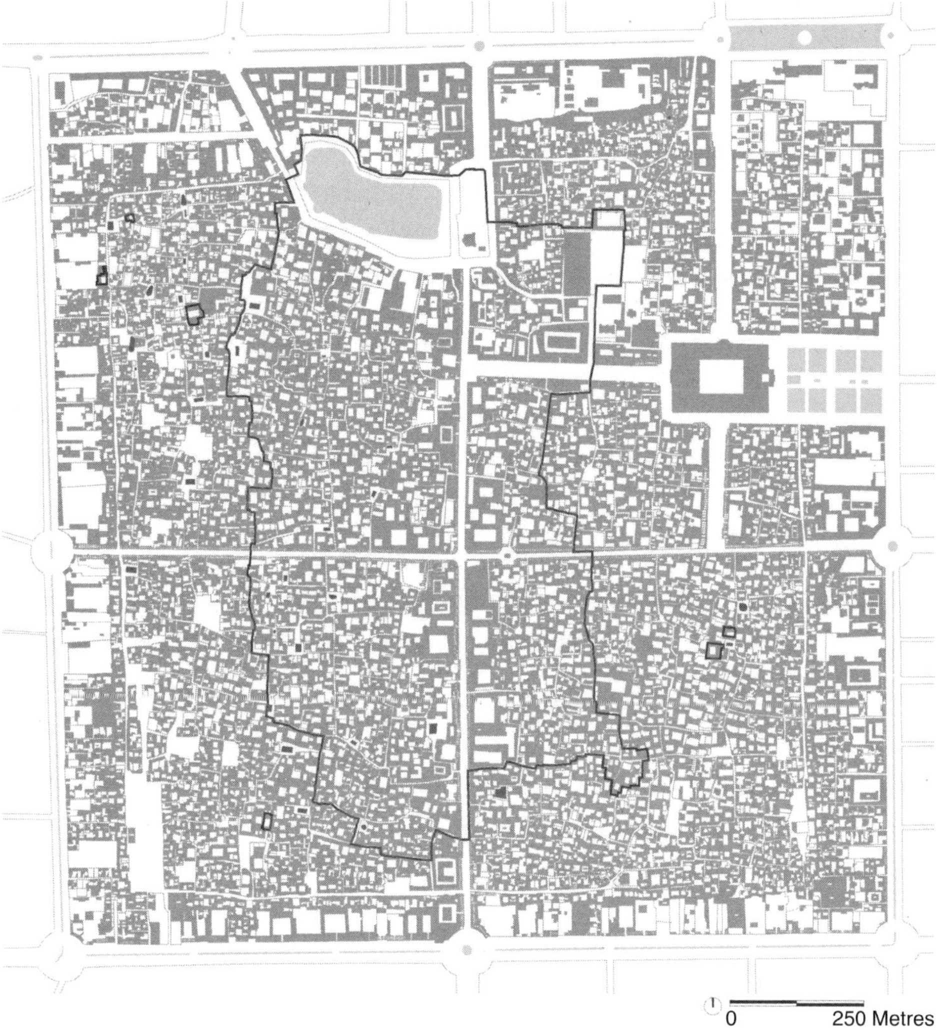

Figure 6.7
Herat, Afghanistan: Ideal city form of pre-Islamic origin.
Source: IMG42187 © Aga Khan Trust for Culture. By permission.

the ancient cosmic model. Indeed, in this sense the ideal form, order, and shape are not all that different from the Chinese and Indian search for the cosmic model and order covered in the previous chapter.

The Political-Nationalist Approach

In contrast to the "spiritual-philosophical" approach, which as we have seen draws from a very broad interpretation of ideal form, the revivalist approach to defining the Islamic city—the "political-nationalist" according to AlSayyad—tries to enumerate specific design principles and neighborhood planning guidelines based on Islamic laws. These include regulations and guidelines related to individual buildings, streets, air rights, easements, and the like, as also elaborated in the work of Hakim.[50] This work uses the city of Tunis, considered an Islamic city according to an earlier Orientalist construction, as the example.[51] Hakim's analysis connects these principles to specific Qur'ānic verses and hadiths. This documentation and cataloguing do not, however, add up to overall principles for city design. In fact, as anthropologist-architect Amos Rapoport points out in his review of Hakim's book, the author does not offer any explanation of the "why"s for these laws, or the "cultural rationale" of these principles.[52] Nor does he offer any insights about how these laws and principles may have been modified through regional variations. The author also does not sort out distinctions between the elements that are Middle Eastern in character from those that are Islamic or those that might be a local variation. Commenting on Hakim's work in particular, historian André Raymond notes that such "renewed efforts to define an urban 'doctrine' from the fundamental texts of Islam" have not been particularly compelling, because most of these Qur'ānic dictates have limited applications to matters of privacy and collective life in a neighborhood.[53]

Is There a Canonical Muslim Urban Form?

In discussing developmental images of ancient Chinese and Indian cities in the previous chapter, I argued that city design was driven in both those cases by ideal canonical forms, derived in each instance from interpretations of the cosmos. I also argued that the cosmic model of the canonical city represented an image of development that was meant to mirror the larger order of the cosmos in city form and its spatial organization, thus obtaining perfection and purity in the social formation and order within the city walls. The question here is whether the search for an archetypal Islamic city was also based on such a clear developmental premise.

The morphological approach taken by AlSayyad may be a good place to begin. While he sees the central focus of his work is on the emergence of cities with Islamic identity,[54] he structures his inquiry as an exploration into the question whether "there is a form for the Muslim city, particularly urban." His inquiry seeks to understand the larger question of what indeed a "Muslim city" might be.[55] In his attempt to systematically describe the anatomy of Arab Muslim cities,[56] he chose a positivist approach, and a methodology derived from an earlier treatise on urban form by planning scholars Kevin Lynch and Lloyd Rodwin.[57] Using such categories as elements of form, adapted spaces, and flow systems and their quantity, density, focal organization, and spatial distribution—all part of an abstract analytical system proposed by Lynch and Rodwin—AlSayyad deconstructs the urban form of Arab Islamic cities by examining two well-known examples of this genre: Cairo and Aleppo.[58] While carefully avoiding any Orientalist, ideological, or canonical predisposition for a particular archetype, AlSayyad's analysis does yield certain invariant characteristics of the Arab Islamic urban form—many of which, ironically, were used in the Orientalist construction of the "Islamic City." However, AlSayyad's secular and profoundly modernist analysis attributes these features to historical, geographical, and sociocultural roots of Arab Islamic cities. It is not clear whether his analysis leads to the definition of an archetypal form, distinct from the one previously identified by the Orientalist scholars, and which is simply that of a traditional medieval city as argued by historians Oleg Grabar and André Raymond.[59] It is apparent, however, that while suggesting certain paradigmatic traits of the Arab Muslim cities, AlSayyad does not claim any canonical properties that are derived from the precepts of Islam, nor for that matter, from any secular imperatives of the various caliphates in the evolution and the subsequent mutation of those cities.

Even when we turn to historical authoritative writings on the culture, institutions, and social organizations of the Arab Muslim civilization, there is little that suggests anything broadly canonical about the design of cities. Consider, for example, the writings of Ibn Khaldun, a fourteenth-century Arab philosopher[60] of Tunisian origin, whose writings—especially *The Muqaddimah*, or "Prolegomena to History"[61]—contained concepts similar to the ideas of many eighteenth-century European thinkers, such as Auguste Comte, Fredrich Hegel, and Karl Marx. In the realm of political thought, Ibn Khaldun is considered "the Islamic version of Machiavelli."[62] He devotes a whole section of the second volume of *The Muqaddimah* to urbanization, urbanism, and "*Requirements for the planning of towns and the consequences of neglecting those requirements*."[63] Khaldun's discussion of cities and urbanization emphasizes the role of dynasties and rulers in building cities, their monuments, fortification, the historical process of the rise and fall of successive civilizations, growth of cities, as well as the conquest and rebuilding of existing cities in history. Perhaps more insightful is his discussion of urbanism, which can almost be read as a precursor to contemporary social thought regarding cities, although written some six hundred years ago. As sociologist Fuad Baali has argued, these writings are very similar to Louis Wirth's argument for "urbanism as a way of life," along with related arguments of sociologists Emile Durkheim, Georg Simmel, and Max Weber.[64] Thus, Ibn Khaldun's discussion of *badawa* (primitive and usually nomadic life) and *hadara* (the life in cities) is parallel to the contemporary concept of the folk-urban continuum of Robert Redfield or the *gemeinschaft* and *gesellschaft* dichotomy of sociologist Ferdinand Tönnies.[65] Although Khaldun's discussion does not take any normative position, the imperative of development as urbanization in a secular sense remains implicit in his treatise on urbanism, unlike antiurban sentiments in turn-of-the-century American reformist writings on cities.[66]

Ibn Khaldun's treatise on the "requirements for the planning of towns," which is of more direct interest to us, is essentially about the optimal location characteristics of towns and cities, rather than their internal layouts. It does not offer us anything as prescriptive as the geomancy of the Chinese and Indian cities in their cosmic models, or the spatial organization of social groups according to some established hierarchy as prescribed in Manasara's *Vastû Shīlpa*, which we considered in the previous chapter. Instead it emphasizes such environmental concerns as the flow of air—stagnant air leading to disease, etc.—and availability of water. Ibn Khaldun talked about access to resources necessary for the construction of cities and their future expansions—especially the importance of having building materials like wood and stone nearby. He could very well have been speaking about sustainable development, emphasizing the importance of nature services and minding the "ecological footprint" of cities before choosing a site to build one. Today we might celebrate him as an early proponent of sustainable development. Consider the following excerpts from Ibn Khaldun in chapter 4, section 5 of the second volume of *The Muqqadimah*, which pertain, respectively, to defense, health and hygiene, economy, and sustainability:

> In connection with the protection of towns against harmful things, one should see to it that all the houses of the town are situated inside a protective wall. Furthermore, the town should be situated in an inaccessible place, either upon a rugged hill or surrounded by the sea or by a river, so that … it will be difficult for an enemy to take the town, and its inaccessibility and fortress (character) will be increased many times …
>
> … one should see to it that the air where the town is (to be situated) is good, in order to be safe from illness. When the air is stagnant and bad, or close to corrupt waters or putrid pools or swamps, it is speedily affected by putrescence as the result of being near these things, and it is unavoidable that (all) living beings who are there will speedily be affected by illness.
>
> The place should be on a river, or springs with plenty of fresh water should be facing it.
>
> Another utility in towns, for which one must provide, is good pastures for the livestock of (the inhabitants). Each householder needs domestic animals for breeding, for milk, and for riding.

> Furthermore, one has to see to it that there are fields suitable for cultivation. Grain is the (basic) food. When the fields are near, the (needed grain) can be obtained more easily and quickly.
> Then, there also is (the problem of) a woods to supply firewood and building material.
> One should also see to it that the town is situated close to the sea, to facilitate importation of foreign goods from remote countries.[67]

It is noteworthy that these requirements do not make any reference to Shariah or hadith or any other such authoritative doctrines of Islam. These are strictly secular principles grounded in common sense. Furthermore, there are frequent references to a generic "one," as in "one should" or "one has to," which presumably imply the ruler or the founder of the town—the caliph—who would make the essential site selection and planning decisions.

The Sacred Direction

None of the principles of city planning laid out by Ibn Khaldun are particularly canonical, or necessarily would lead to a canonical urban form. There is, however, an awareness of the "sacred direction"[68] in the Muslim communities, since a pious Muslim must pray five times a day facing Mecca, where the Ka'bah, or the "House of God," is located.[69] Therefore, the qibla, or the praying wall in every mosque, should (theoretically at least) be oriented toward Mecca.[70] And since mosques are the most common features of the public realm of Muslim cities, the qibla orientation, in the aggregate, must influence their spatial structure and organization, as one would expect. This is a reasonable enough proposition, as was argued by geographer David King, and led Near East scholar Michael Bonine to systematically explore the directions of the qiblas of the major mosques of Morocco more broadly, and more specifically in selected Moroccan cities—Fès, Meknes, Marrakech, Rabat-Sale, and Taza—and their effects on their respective spatial structure.[71] His analysis showed that the qibla directions varied from dynasty to dynasty by significant amounts, and differed even more dramatically from the correct qibla direction according to the Great Circle Route (see figure 6.8). Sometimes there are variations in qibla orientations within the same city, as in Fès, but one could also find internal consistency in other cities like Taza, Meknes, or Marrakech. As for the main question pursued in his study, Bonine concludes that "the close correspondence of the *qiblas* with the street patterns (and hence the main axes) exists in most cases" (see figure 6.9 for an example). However, he also found a remarkable correlation with ground slope patterns and street and qibla directions, leading him to conclude further: "Only when an appropriate main slope oriented toward the *qibla* could be found would the streets and religious architecture also be aligned with the

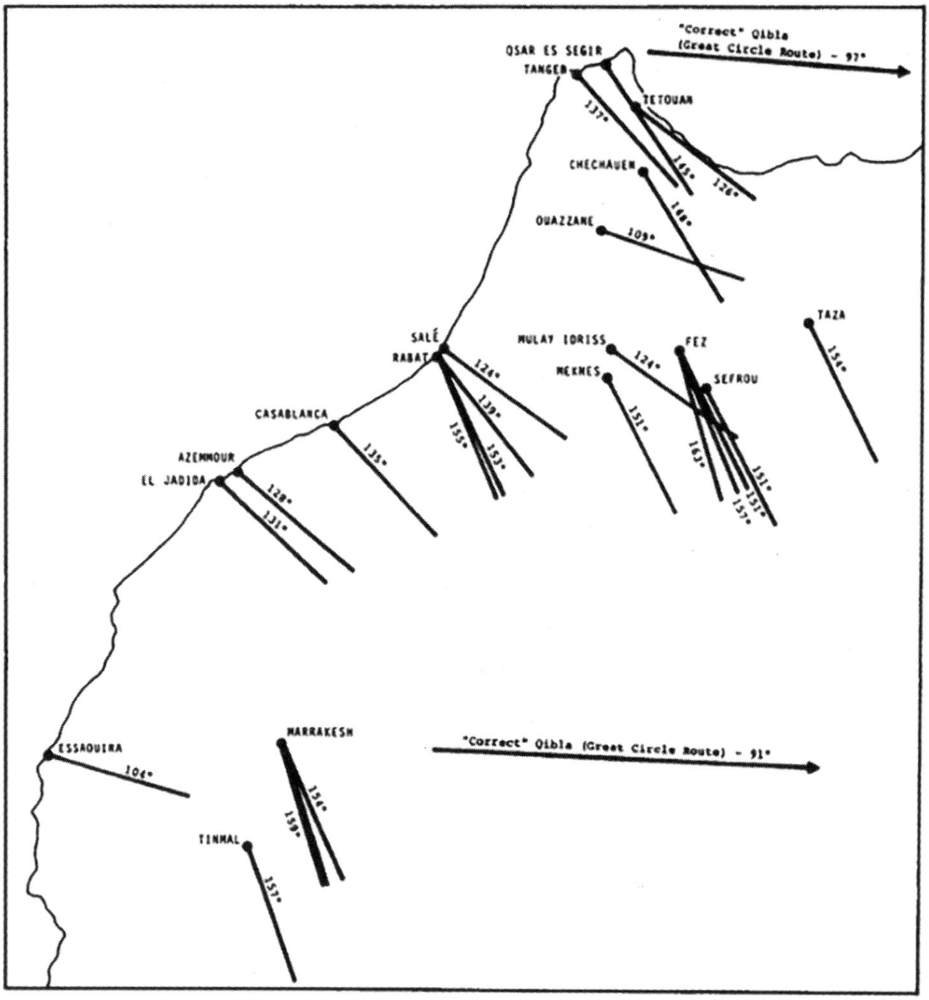

Figure 6.8

Variations in the qibla directions of major Moroccan mosques.

Source: Bonine (1990), p. 53, with permission from Brill Academic Publishers. Permission conveyed through Copyright Clearance Center, Inc.

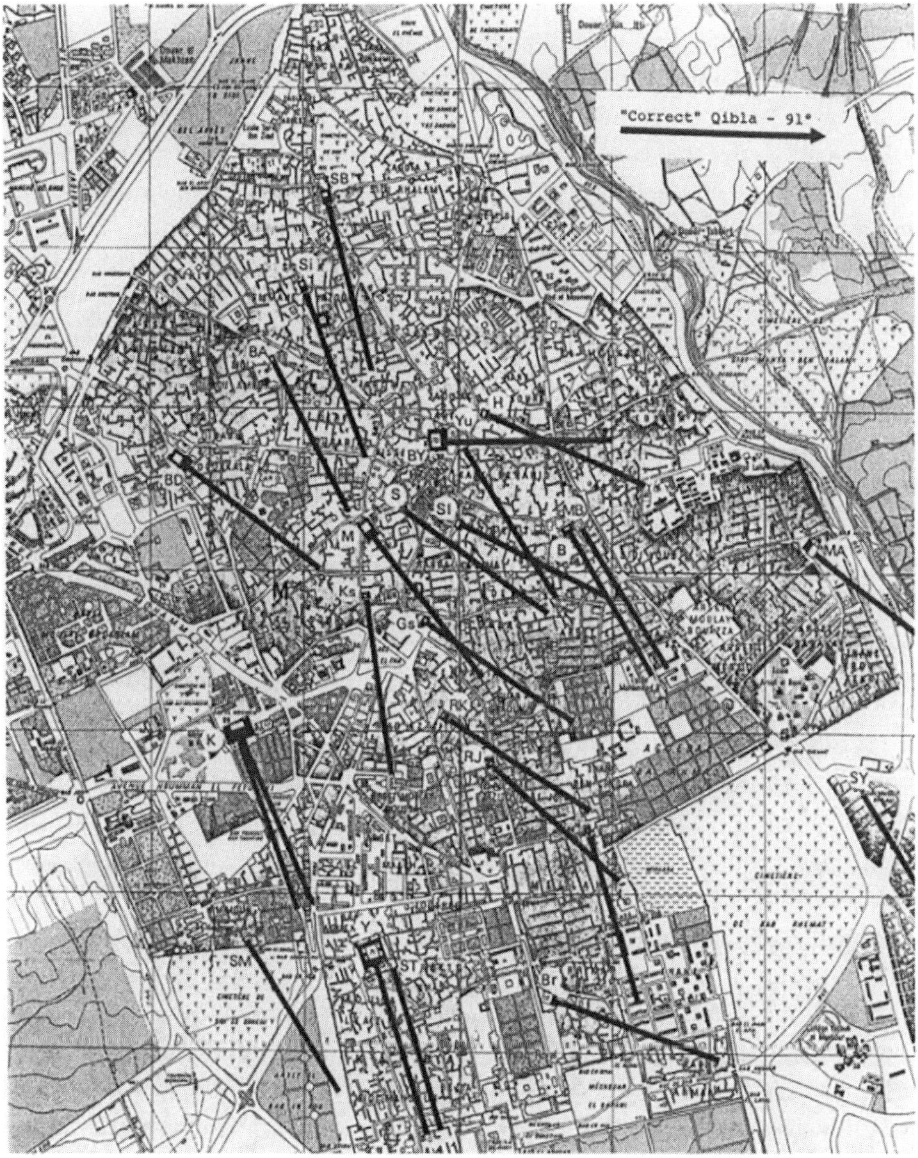

Figure 6.9
Variations in the qibla directions of mosques of Marrakech.
Source: Bonine (1990), p. 63, with permission from Brill Academic Publishers. Permission conveyed through Copyright Clearance Center, Inc.

sacred direction."[72] While these conclusions may be tentative, they raise the intriguing possibility that the act of city founding by caliphs was quite deliberate and that the site selection process itself was dictated by the sacred direction, geodesic inaccuracies (by modern standards) notwithstanding.[73]

Perhaps the most dramatic and famous example of how the qibla orientation influenced the structure and design of a Muslim city is evident in the layout of the seventeenth-century Safavid Espahan. In the twelfth year of his reign, emperor Shah Abbas undertook a major urban renewal project, almost Haussmannian in scope, in an area of the city previously known as Naqsh-i Jahan. The principal features of this urban design included: a large rectangular open space some 200 meters wide and 600 meters long called Maydan-i-Shah (see figure 6.10); a major mosque called Masjid-i-Shah (see figure 6.11); a three-story pavilion called Ali Qapu attached to the adjoining palace complex; and a smaller mosque across the open space from Ali Qapu called Masjid-i-Shaykh Lutfullah, which was used by women of the royal family; and the entrance to the historic bazaar at the northern end of the square. Organic and linear in form, the bazaar serves as a major link between the new complex designed by the Shah Abbas with the historic and famous Masjid-i-Jami, and the old palace and Maydan-i-Qadim near the mosque. It also ties together many other smaller mosques, madrasas, and caravansaries along its winding route.

The idea of a central open space like Maydan-i-Shah is not new in the Persian-Iraqi regional context. *Maydans* (or *maidans*) were commonly built for horse races and other recreational events, although they were usually located on the periphery of the city. The old *maydan* in Espahan was at the center of the old city next to the Masjid-i-Jami and the palace. The new *maydan* was designed to hold such recreational events, and primarily as a polo field with the pavilion of Ali Qapu serving as the viewing platform for the shah and his entourage.[74]

What is interesting about this urban design is the longitudinal axis of Maydan-i-Shah, which is rotated 11°25′ to the west from true north. This is no accident. Clearly this shift in the longitudinal axis was done to align the qibla directions of the two new mosques Masjid-i-Shah and Masjid-i-Shaykh Lutfullah, which are connected to the perfect rectangle of Maydan-i-Shah at a 45-degree angle (see figure 6.10). This is consistent with the Persian architectural and geometric decorative design tradition, as architectural historian Eugenio Galdieri points out.[75] Note also that this qibla direction is consistent with that of the older Masjid-i-Jami and other, but not necessarily all, mosques in the city. In addition, in order to accommodate this shift the palace complex and the garden had to be awkwardly adjusted to fit the axis of Chahar Bagh and the gardens of the Vazirs, which are laid along a perfect north-south axis.

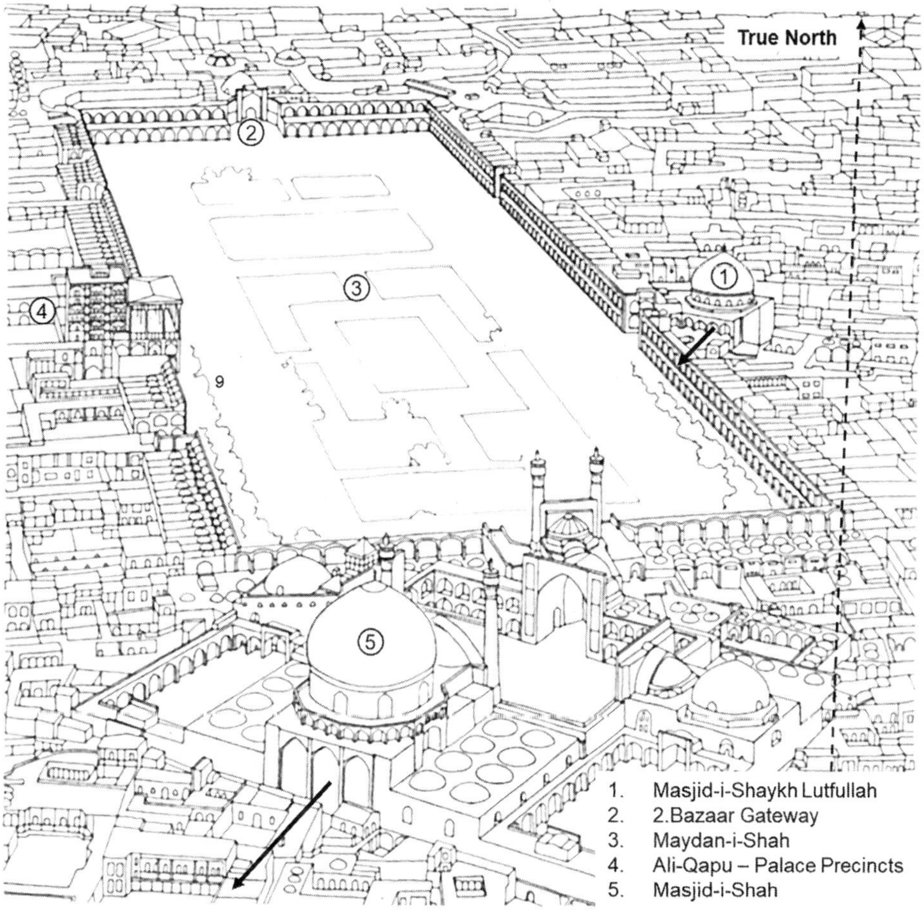

Figure 6.10
Sketch of the Maydan-i-Shah and the orientation of the two mosques.
Source: Tavassoli and Bonyadi (1992), figure 1-11. Courtesy of Mahmoud Tavassoli.

It is not entirely apparent whether the qibla direction had much to do with the structure of the urban form of Espahan prior to Shah Abbas's urban design of the Maydan-i-Shah complex and its associated street improvements. Historian Heinz Gaube's analysis shows that street patterns of the tenth-century Espahan and its older version did not suggest any association with the qibla direction. In fact it was the Shah Abbas's redevelopment that brought a major part of Espahan in alignment with the new *maydan*, and only indirectly to the qibla direction. Elsewhere Bonine has argued that the orthogonal

Figure 6.11
Interior courtyard, Masjid-i-Shah.
Source: Author, 1993.

form of many Iranian cities has resulted from the rectangular layout of farmlands, their slopes, and irrigation systems.[76] As farmland became urbanized, housing development pretty much followed the farm grid as in the case of Nowdushan near Yazd.[77] On the other hand, there are other examples of Iranian cities that suggest that qibla direction did play a role in the alignment of major streets and axes adjacent to major mosques in many important Iranian cities. The works of architectural historians Mahmoud Tavassoli and Naser Bonyadi clearly show such patterns in cities like Shiraj and Yazd (see figure 6.12).[78] Bonine comes to a similar conclusion in his study of selected Moroccan cities, although topography and slope seemingly, he argues, were the main determinants of their overall urban form.[79]

In the Indian subcontinent cities founded or developed by Muslim rulers do not seem to have such apparent structural patterns. Cities like Ahmedabad, or Shahjahanabd (known as old Delhi these days), or the new city Fatehpur Sikri near Agra discussed previously do not suggest such tendencies. Nor for that matter have we seen any such propensity in the South East Asian cities under Muslim rulers.[80] So, it seems that

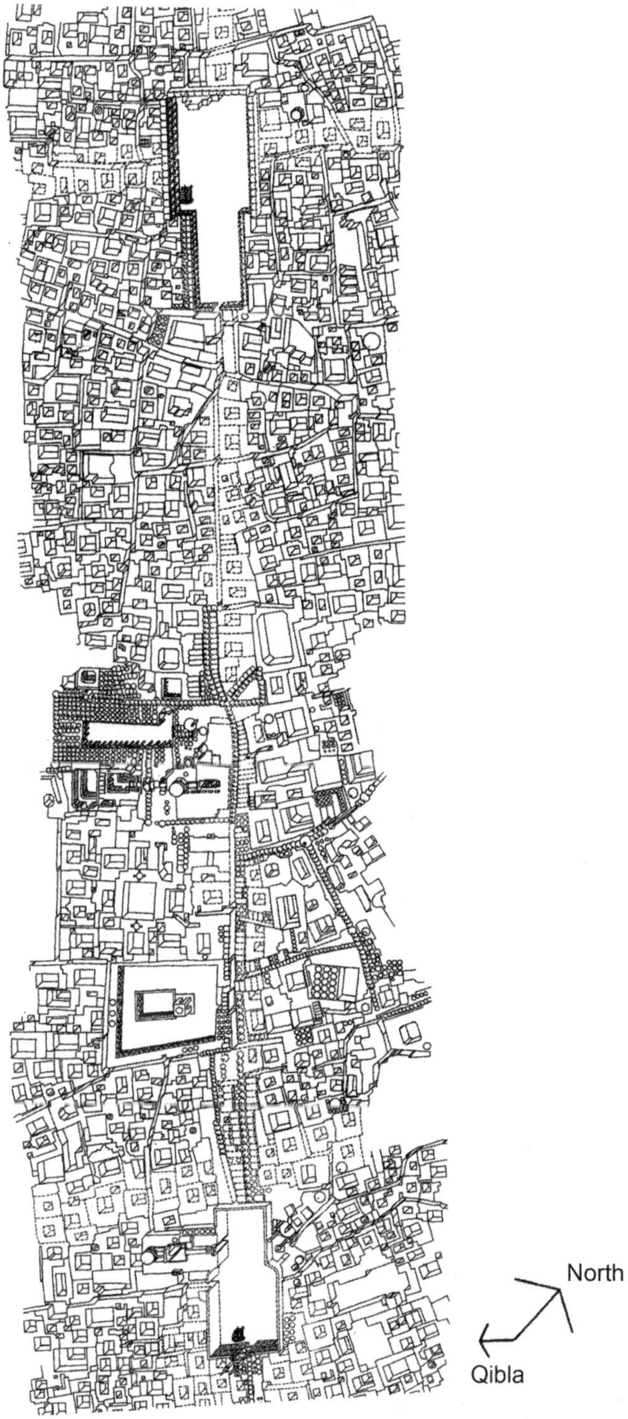

Figure 6.12

Yazd, Iran. Depicted are main elements of the historic city complex: mosques, madrassa, bazaar, and open spaces.

Source: Tavassoli and Bonyadi (1992), figure 2-11. Courtesy of Mahmoud Tavassoli.

while the sacred direction may have shaped the structure and organization of parts of some of the important cities, it has not played the kind of canonical role that cosmic models have played in the ideal Indian and Chinese cities. Furthermore, even where qibla orientation played a role, it did not have a totalizing and dogmatic influence on the structure of cities; at best it only had a partial, nudging effect. Possibly this is why the sacred direction does not come up in AlSayyad's morphological analysis of Arab-Islamic cities, or in the anti-Orientalist critiques of Abu-Lughod and Raymond.[81]

Piety and Community

What then does this extensive and complex literature on Muslim cities and culture offer us in the way of understanding images of development that were endogenous to Islam? In the previous chapter I argued that in the cases of Chinese and Indian cities the cosmic model was the primary organizing ideal, if not a proxy, for obtaining a good society. In the case of Muslim cities, on the other hand, we have not found any such organizing model, other than the sacred direction. It is true that these cities share some common elements, but their particular arrangements and organizations have been dictated by climate and topography or altered by secular forces, economic motives, or the idiosyncrasies of caliphates and dynasties. Indeed there seem to be more exceptions to the rules than the rules themselves in these cities of Islamic heritage. Yet it is difficult to imagine that a thirteen-centuries-old religion embraced by one-fifth of the world's population over three continents in countless towns and cities would not engender endogenous images of development. I will argue in the following text that while we might not be able to find a canonical model of the cities of this genre, there is ample evidence to claim that the endogenous ideal of Muslim cities has always been a normative one, derived from the twin values of community and piety rooted in Islamic beliefs. It is not the text but the subtext of Muslim cities that we must read, to understand the normative city. A superficial reading of built form alone may not always reveal this normative dimension, unless we fully appreciate the social, cultural, and religious institutions that wrote the subtext of these cities.

To begin this argument, we should go back to Abu-Lughod's critique of the Orientalist approach to Islamic city. She seemed to argue that if there is such a thing as "Islamic essence," which is often palpable to many observers, it would have to be understood at many different levels, of which historical urban form is but one. Abu-Lughod spoke of her visit to India in search of the Islamic city, and of being surprised to see how easy it was to distinguish the Muslim from the Hindu neighborhoods, as far as the public spaces were concerned.[82] She also noted that "circumspect behavior" of women in public, dictated by imperatives of privacy, was less noticeable in the Hindu than in the Muslim neighborhoods, because of different norms of privacy among the two cultures.

The above narrative of Abu-Lughod is a poignant description of the urban sensorium—sights, sounds, smells, and social contacts—that surrounds us at a micro-scale of the built environment, and usually in the public realm of streets, alleys, markets, and public places. We began this chapter with a description of the urban sensorium of Djema el-Fna in Marrakech, but one could have easily included other examples, like the bazaar in Espahan, Khan Khalili in Cairo, or Chawry Bazar in old Delhi. In her discussion of the Islamic "essence," Abu-Lughod discussed several other aspects of the urban experience that encompass both urban form and urbanism of the Arab Muslim city: the territoriality of different ethnic and religious groups; the role of the neighborhoods as an important component of civil society; the gendering of spaces according to the Islamic laws of privacy. The Islamic essence, she seems to suggest, then can be seen as the outcome of the variable and historic processes derived from the laws, norms, and precepts of Islam.

According to the schema introduced previously in chapter 4, one could argue that the habitus of a Muslim city would be the ultimate developmental outcome in the images of the two essential norms of Islam: community and piety. Habitus in any context is not independent of outcomes at the level of everyday sensory experience, nor from the historical processes that lead to particular urban forms and urbanisms. In Muslim cities, habitus develops from images and practices of Islam between cultural and geographical differences as surely as it does between institutions and political histories, as between the five pillars of faith and the common marketplace. All of these over time have been expressive of—and been expressed into—the norms of Islam. Indeed, Eugen Wirth, whom I quoted previously,[83] was partially right, in that one can argue that Islam was at once both the inhabitant and the architect of these cities, but only in the normative, not the canonical, sense.[84] Much of the literature on Islamic cities—from the Orientalist tradition to the more contemporary revisionist approach—have focused on identifying the canonical patterns in the urban form but failed to appreciate the scale of the ideology of Islam. Its cultural and political struggles throughout history may have actually obviated a canonical outcome. Islam is a normative, social developer of its cities, not a canonical, cosmic one. Let us consider why that might be the case in the following text.

Non-city or Autopoietic City?

It will be recalled that while the Orientalist studies of the Islamic city declared Islam to be an "urban religion," because they believed that the Muslim faith can only be practiced in cities, Max Weber in his classic treatise on cities declared the Islamic city essentially an incomplete or partial city, if not a "non-city."[85] In a manner not unlike Marx's dismissal of the "Asiatic mode of production" (the family-oriented, traditional, and informal characteristics of the developing economies, which didn't quite neatly fit into his overall treatise on capital), Weber found the Near Eastern cities were not quite cities in the fullest sense because they were lacking in some of the five criteria he used to define a city: "fortifications; markets; a court administering a partly autonomous law, distinctively urban forms of association, and at least partial autonomy."[86] He had argued that other than the fortification and markets, the Islamic cities lacked autonomy or even a partially autonomous legal system, and also any formal structure of civil society,[87] unless we count the Orientalist claim that guilds were a form of socio-religious professional societies, a claim contested by other scholars.[88]

Conceding the absence of civil society, formal organization of urban associations, or autonomous municipal governance in Islamic cities, some authors have noted that Islamic cities did have a management system but it was highly decentralized and the government played a minimal role.[89] Seemingly, the cities functioned as a self-organizing system, from the ground up, or as Bianca noted: "Its coercing mechanisms worked from within, so to speak, and needed little or no institutional support."[90] The city was autopoietic.

As for civil society, there was one notable exception, however, which is the institution of *waqf*—typically interpreted in English as an "Islamic trust" or a "pious foundation."[91] This institution historically evolved through royal decree, a sense of piety, and public philanthropy.[92] In a comprehensive review of the origin, development, Islamic identity, spread, and administration of the *waqf* system, economist Timur Kuran argues that the institution was used quite effectively in the provision of public goods and services in the absence of Western-style centralized municipal administration or governance.[93] Its functions typically included everything from maintaining soup kitchens to road maintenance and provision of public fountains. Thus the *waqf* system not only provided public services but also social welfare, which according to some scholars may have led to "the Islamic world's long economic descent by fostering a large class of indolent beneficiaries.[94] Questioning the Weberian view that in the absence of a municipality the waqf system could only serve as an inferior alternative to municipal service provision, Kuran argues that if the Islamic city seemed to lack order, efficiency, and organization—hence a "non-city" or at least inferior to the contemporary European cities in the Western mind—it did not mean that the residents of those cities found their habitat necessarily chaotic. A decentralized system may have been more efficient in the local service delivery at a finer grain and more responsive to local demand based on local knowledge. In any event, while small *waqfs* were of miscellaneous origin, larger trusts established by the royal or wealthy families were subject to state directives and priorities in their coverage and target areas. Noting that the system worked well in premodern times, Kuran is critical of its institutional rigidities, and thus its failure to stimulate an active civil society or to generate an abundance of social capital. In this secular critique, rooted in modern and economistic images of development, Kuran concludes that the *waqf* system "may well have contributed to turning the region into an underdeveloped part of the world."[95] Nevertheless, it is clear that in premodern times the *waqf* system was an important institutional innovation in self-governance. Indeed, the Islamic city may have been the earliest example of a "voluntary city," an idea whose time seems to have come, as recently claimed by contemporary neoliberal economists.[96]

This model of Islamic cities as a self-organizing system would be consistent with the highly organic and seemingly disorderly urban form, which historian Richard Bulliet had seen mainly as a "characteristic of a society without wheels."[97] In any case, by Western standards these cities were considered backward and underdeveloped. As historian Leon Carl Brown pointed out, "the colonial ethnographers considered the confusing ... maze of narrow, winding streets, and blind alleys" a reflection of the "allogical" [*sic*] disorder of the "indigenous mentality."[98] Such Western stereotypes notwithstanding, it is quite possible that this organic outcome in urban form resulted from a combination of *waqf*, hadith, and the role of *ulama*[99] in local governance and the administration of justice.

Scholars of Islamic cities have always been intrigued by the question of how the planned orthogonal cities of pre-Islamic times, like the Greek cities of Damascus and Aleppo, have undergone what I have referred to earlier as a counter-Haussmannian transformation. In these instances grid cities of wide boulevards were gradually converted to the organic street pattern of narrow width. Bianca, echoing the arguments of Bulliet, suggests that the main arcaded ceremonial avenues designed for horse-drawn carriages in Roman times were slowly appropriated by the merchants of the primarily pedestrian Muslim city who erected stalls and booths in the middle of those wide boulevards and public spaces, eventually filling all the space except what was necessary for pedestrian circulation (see figure 6.13).[100] Processes similar to this also explain how the residential quarters with organic street patterns completely trumped the orthogonal street patterns of large blocks. Bianca argues, "Since the street layout in the private quarters was no longer controlled by a central civic authority ... individual houses, for reasons of family links, social convenience or simply lack of space, tended to grow together into large clusters which interrupted, privatized, or simply swallowed the existing street network."[101] Another example of such transformation is the case of medieval Cairo, which witnessed a gradual deconstruction of the formal Roman-style orthogonal

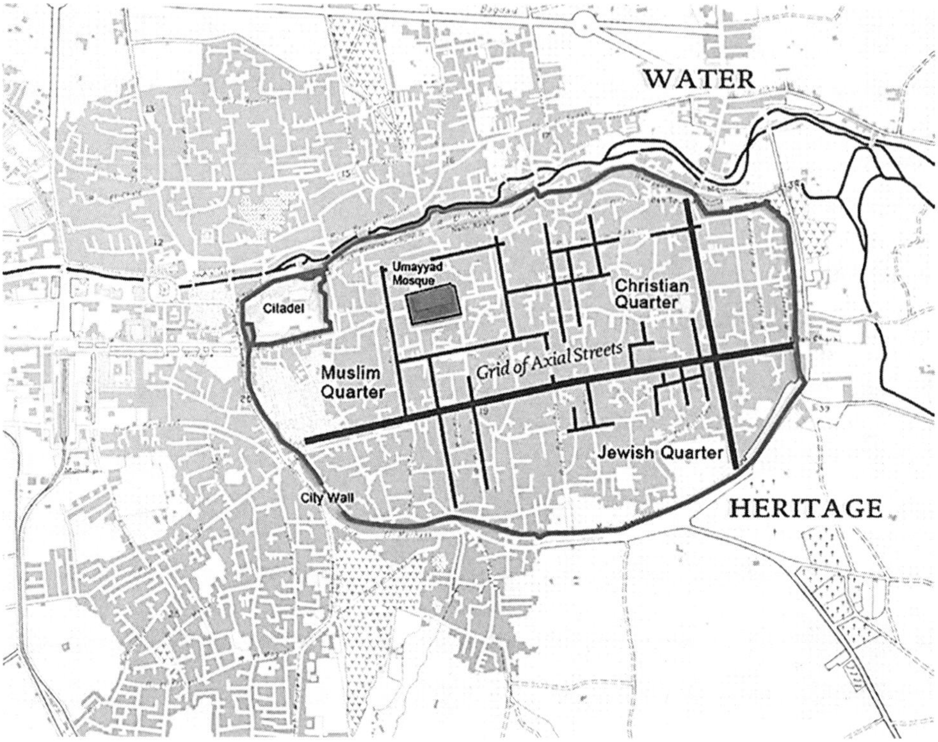

Figure 6.13
The counter-Haussmannization of Damascus: Transformation of the Apollonian order of the Greek city to the Dionysian order of the autopoietic city. Axial streets of the Greek era are highlighted on the base map.
Source: Base map and data from OpenStreetMap and OpenStreetMapFoundation, © OpenStreetMap Contributors, licensed as CC BY•SA.

public space between the two royal palaces established by the Fatimid founders of Cairo in the late tenth century CE. Known as Bayn al-Qasrayan (meaning the space between two palaces), this space did not last that long, although the expression still endures in the name of the street (and made famous by author Naguib Mahfouz's *Palace Walk* trilogy,[102] which follows the original Fatimid north-south axis that connected Bab-al-Futuh and Bab Zuwayla.[103] This space was quickly filled in the Ayyubid period, through a resettlement of the Fatimid capital city of Cairo, following nationalization of the properties belonging to the Fatimid rulers. In a series of illustrative drawings AlSayyad shows the physical change and explains the social process: "It is likely that, as masses moved in and began to erect temporary structures wherever they could, their haphazard buildings encroached on the wide streets of the city, and its large gardens and open spaces gradually disappeared."[104]

This surrender of the formal order of the Apollonian spaces to the informal order of the Dionysian spaces[105] that have come to characterize much of the archetype of the Islamic city, in effect, reflects the essential tensions embedded in the urban outcome of this genre. This tension has to do with the secular aesthetic and political forces represented by the caliphates and the laws and principles of Islam and the related values of piety and community.

I derive this argument from some of the historical analysis by historian Ira Lapidus and related theological reflections of historian Marshall Hodgson.[106] In his analysis of the relationship between state and religion, Lapidus points out that the regime of the caliphs, "the successors of the Prophet," while championed by the *ulama*, endured through the middle of the tenth century, when "they claimed authority in legal and doctrinal matters and the right to defend the Muslim community against heresy."[107] In the phase following that, the caliphs strayed from their strictly religious role to the more secular trappings of the pre-Islamic tradition involving patronage of the arts, architecture, literature, philosophy, and science. Shah Abbas's urban design of Espahan that included the monumental Naqsh-e Jahan Square and the Chahar Bagh garden are cases in point. The essential framework for an urban design that establishes an order in geometrical forms is well captured in the Tavassoli and Bonyadi study of Shiraj, Iran (see figure 6.14).

Expansion of the caliphate authority from a strictly religious to a broader cultural, political, and institutional authority was only a part of the larger process of social differentiation within the Arab Muslim community, when ethnic and tribal ties were gradually replaced by sectarian forms of identities based on religious and communal associations, like the major sects such as the Shias and Sunnis, or that of Sufism. The *ulama*, or the religious scholars who led the sectarian associations, would challenge and ultimately seize the religious authority of the caliphates and claim their "complete authority over the communal, personal, religious and doctrinal aspects of Islam."[108]

This social, political, and institutional differentiation and ultimately the tension leading to the bipolar structure of the Muslim communities—between the elitist, secular, and political authority of the caliph on the one hand, and the pious, doctrinal, and ideological authority of the ulama on the other—in many ways, I argue, has defined the normative tension symbolized by the form of Islamic cities. Hodgson characterizes this tension as being of one between corporatism versus populism. He sees the rise of ulama, or what he calls "*Shariah*-mindedness," as a communitarian and populist challenge to the corporatism and elitism of the state and the caliphate authority.[109]

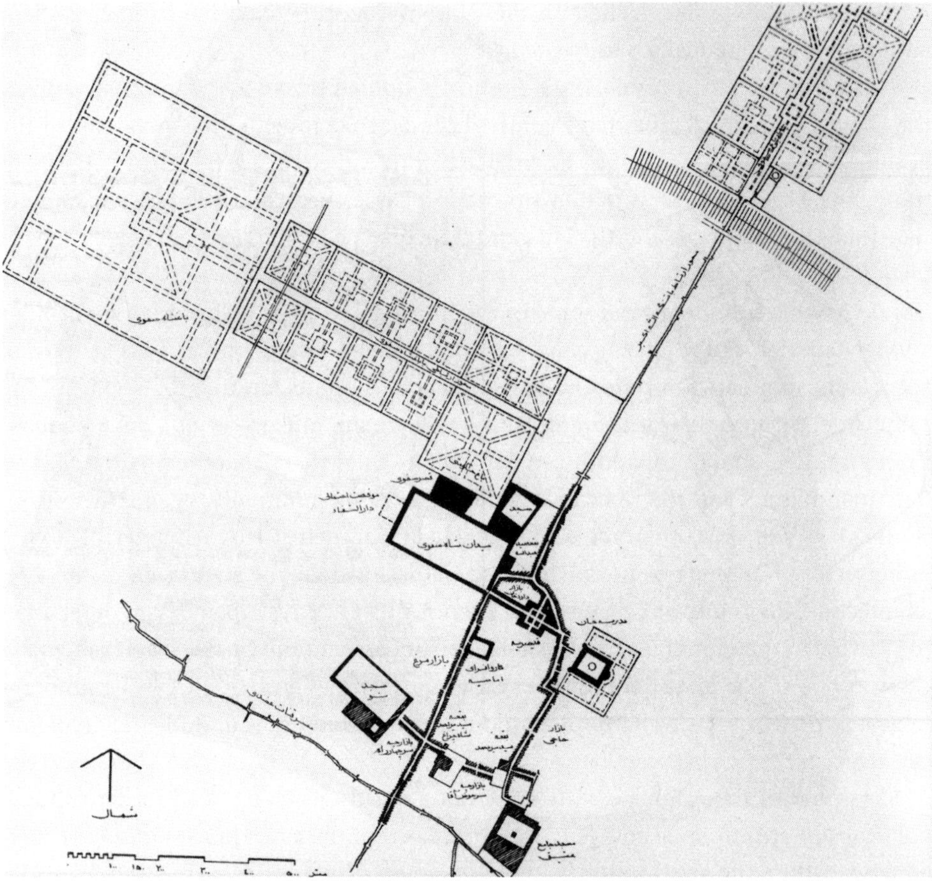

Figure 6.14
Essential urban form elements of seventh-century-CE Shiraj, Iran, suggesting order in urban design. *Source*: Tavassoli and Bonyadi (1992), figure 2-22. Courtesy of Mahmoud Tavassoli.

Hodgson points out further that the egalitarian and populist bias of Shariah in many ways is very similar to the neoliberal market-oriented values commonly shared in the Western liberal democracies. The culture of market, which did not favor anyone by rank or lineage, was consistent with the populist values of the Shariah. It is no accident that the souk was a distinctive feature of the Islamic city, and always existed in close proximity of mosques and madrasas. This market orientation was consistent with the international mercantile economy that flourished in the Middle Ages.[110] It is fair to assume that if Shariah-mindedness found market processes consistent with its populist and individualist values, it would follow that the ulama would oppose more centralized and corporatist planning by the state authority.

Regarding the urban form of Islamic cities, we can recognize this tension between the ulama and the caliph, between the market and planning, between the corporatist power of the state and the populist tendencies of self-governance and autopoeisis. As Hodgson saw this tension in the elite expressions of aesthetic values in art, architecture, and urban design on the one hand, and the prosaicism, iconophobia, and "aridity" on the other in Islamic cities.[111] This tension shaped the habitus operating in the dynamic between Islamic precepts, culture, history, institutions, daily life, and urban form. Almost every city ruled or founded by a caliph had a separate citadel or *qasbah* and a palace complex that often had architecturally distinctive buildings and elaborate gardens.[112] Mosques renowned for their visual dominance in the cityscape or for their architectural beauty were constructed under the sponsorship of caliphs and rulers. But in the main the architecture and urban design came to flourish only in later periods of Islam, because, as Ibn Khaldun noted many years ago, "Religion forbade them to do any excessive building or to waste too much money on building activities for no purpose."[113] Some of the most famous examples of Islamic urban design—the Round City of Baghdad, Chahar Bagh and the Maydan-i-Shah complex in Espahan, or the new city of Fatehpur Sikri outside Agra—came out of the whims and imaginations of these rulers (see figure 6.15). The only formal attempt to establish a canonical form for Islamic city—the Round City of Baghdad—also came from a caliph.

The Haussmannian transformation of parts of old Espahan and the attempt to realign the streets to follow the sacred direction undertaken by Shah Abbas was also another such example. It is not that these attempts did not have normative aims, but they were not always derived from Shariah or hadith, or on recommendations of ulama. Some of the best examples of gardens (such as the Shalimar garden of Lahore or Chahar Bagh in Espahan) and architectural monuments (Mogul mausoleums like Humayun's tomb in Delhi, Akbar's tomb in Sikandra, and Taj Mahal in Agra) were secular in purpose and built almost in defiance of the orthodox tenets of Islam.[114] (See figure 6.16.)

Finally, the concept of habitus gives us a useful way to think about the gendering of spaces. Recent writings of feminist scholars have begun to articulate the relationship between the Islamic norm of women's privacy and the corresponding gendering of space, facilitated by the organic form of narrow and crooked alleys, passages, and impasses of the traditional Islamic city. Abu-Lughod, for example, has pointed out that "one of the reasons why the older pattern of city building has been maintained in many sections of Arabo-Islamic cities, even today, is that it is still well adapted to the

Figure 6.15
Hawah Mahal in Fatehpur Sikri, the city Akbar built near Agra in India but later abandoned because of a shortage of water.
Source: Author, 2004.

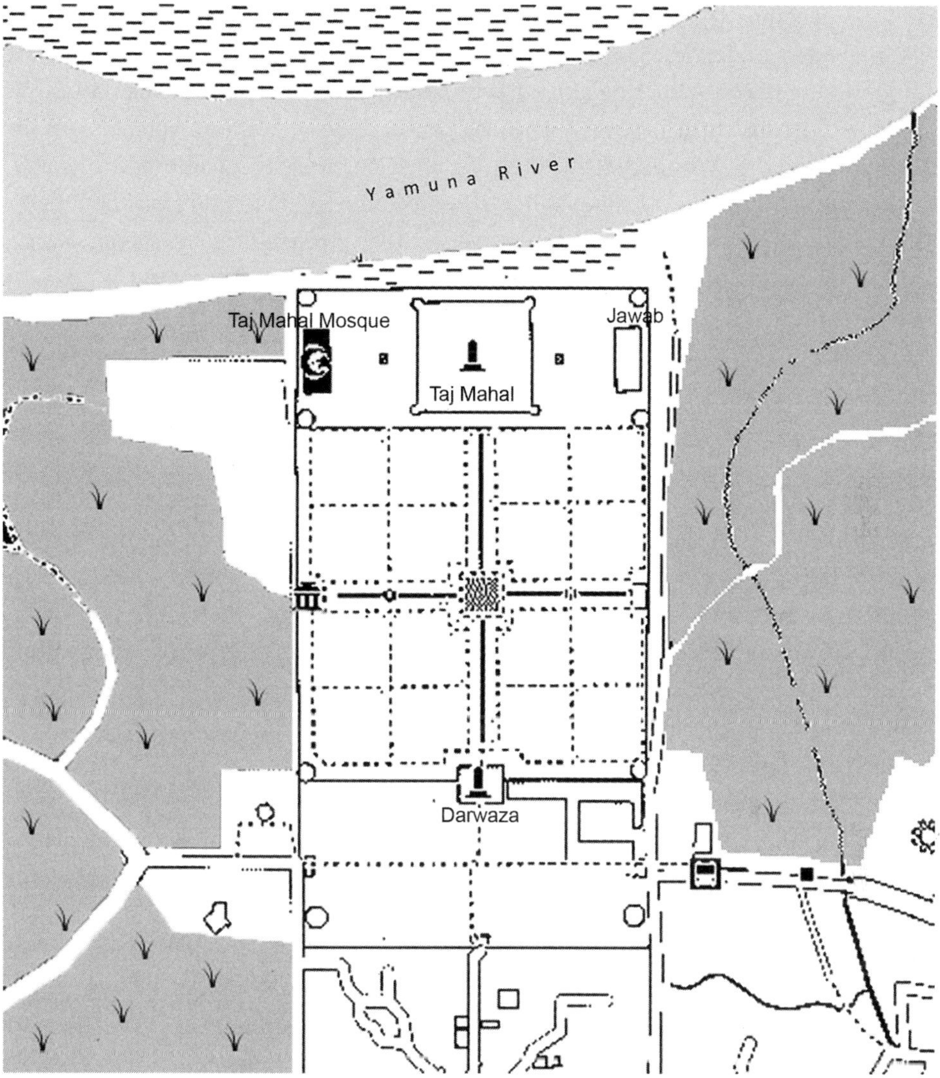

Figure 6.16

The mosque (top left) to the west of Taj Mahal, with an identical structure to the east of the mausoleum (top right), called *jawab* (or echo), without any functional purpose, but constructed strictly for symmetry and aesthetics of the site design.

Source: Author. Redrawn on OpenStreetMap. Base map and data from OpenStreetMap and OpenStreetMapFoundation, © OpenStreetMap Contributors, licensed as CC BY•SA.

complex demands of the visual privacy for females."[115] She notes that the Shariah and hadith offered guidelines about the location of windows in this regard, and the mutual responsibility of contiguous neighbors to respect each other's visual privacy needs.[116]

The gendering of the space, while rooted in the Islamic norm of women's privacy, also poses another tension within these cities, concerning inequality and hierarchy between sexes. Sociologist Fatima Mernissi, for example, argues that spatial boundaries "divide Muslim society into two sub-universes: the universe of men (the *umma*, the world religion and power) and the universe of women, the domestic world of sexuality and the family."[117]

The "Public Universe of *Umma*" (or the Islamic scholars) is a primarily male one in which women's position is at best ambiguous. The "Domestic Universe of Family," which does not exclude the male members of the family, can be assumed to be mainly a domain of women. However, whereas the male universe is guided by the principles of "Equality, Reciprocity, Aggregation, Unity, Communion, Brotherhood, Love, Trust" among its members, the principles guiding the relationship between family members are based on "Inequality, Lack of Reciprocity, Segregation, Separation, Division, Subordination, Authority, Mistrust."[118] We should note, however, that while the privacy norms for women were rigidly enforced in the spatial layout and design of courtyard houses of the upper-class families where women did not have to enter the male public realm of *umma*, women from poorer households did not have the option, and had to be in the public, and so cover themselves to maintain visual privacy, to make themselves invisible in the male gaze. Notes Mernissi: "Traditionally, women using public spaces, trespassing on the *umma* universe, are restricted to few occasions and bound by specific rituals, such as the wearing of the veil."[119]

So, we see that the populist notion of community in the Shariah-minded ideology seemingly did not have a place for women. Many Western feminist scholars have pointed out that even in the Western tradition, in the Habermasian notion of an ideal public sphere, the public realm had always been predominantly a male domain.[120] Even in modern times, by the end of the nineteenth century, upper-class women in European cities were not expected to be in public space on their own. In this sense the gender inequality in space privileges was not exclusively an Islamic norm. Nevertheless, the normative city in the Muslim world has had a long history of ideological struggles and tensions, including some inherent contradictions in the form of gender inequality.

7 The Colonial Project

> The settlers' town is a strongly built town, all made of stone and steel. It is a brightly lit town; the streets are paved with asphalt, and the garbage cans swallow all the leavings, unseen, unknown, and hardly thought about.... The settler's town is a well-fed town, an easygoing town; its belly is always full of good things. The settler's town is a town of white people, of foreigners.
>
> The town belonging to the colonized people, or at least the native town, the Negro village, the medina, the reservation, is a place of ill fame, peopled by men of evil repute. They are born there, it matters little where or how; they die there, it matters not where, nor how. It is a world without spaciousness; men live there on top of each other, and their huts are built one on top of the other. The native town is a hungry town, starved of bread, of meat, of shoes, of coal, of light. The native town is a crouching village, a town on its knees, a town wallowing in the mire. It is a town of niggers and dirty Arabs.
>
> —Frantz Fanon, *The Wretched of the Earth*[1]

The endogenous models of city design of the preindustrial, premodern, and precolonial times were grounded in cosmic or spiritual concepts of goodness, perfection, order, balance, community, piety, aesthetics, and hierarchy, all reflecting contemporaneous ideals of good society. The colonial era saw the insertion of exogenous Western ideas representing very different principles of order, organization, and aesthetics. This transmutation was not benign. The colonial transformation of the native landscape was a deliberate act of the colonizers to assert control, power, and superiority. The result was a dualistic landscape juxtaposing the native town with the newly constructed "European" town designed in the colonizers' images of their respective homelands. Privileged, and endowed with greater resources, colonizers' spaces required massive capital investments, financed by surplus values generated from local labor and primary resources. These spaces stood in stark contrast with the native urban form and urbanism.

Subaltern Spaces

The term "subaltern" is normally used to define individuals, species (as in biology), propositions (as in logic), or social classes (as in postcolonial and subaltern studies) "of inferior rank or position" or of subordinate status.[2] Much of the postcolonial subaltern studies derive their inspiration from Marxian scholar Antonio Gramsci's theory of hegemony that discussed the circumstance of subordination of individuals or groups ("*classe subalterne*") in which "the subjects are deprived of their self-reliance as persons as well as citizens" and which "denotes both a factual condition of powerlessness and a representation of oneself as an impotent hostage in the hands of an ineffable destiny."[3] The word "subaltern" seems apt to define the spatial consequences of colonial urban development. The subalternity of colonial development was not just imagined in the semiotics of form and space, but also evident in the fundamental structural transformations that continued through the postcolonial era of city development. Extant spaces and forms became subaltern as colonial development produced new urban spaces and forms in the images of the West, asserting superiority, domination, and innovation. Precolonial urban spaces and formations that had their own canons and norms, internal logic, hierarchy, sustainability, and inertia became subservient to an alien design in a moment of conquest and subjugation.[4] However, any discussion of subaltern spaces of the colonial era must necessarily address the question of spatial relationships and hierarchy that existed in the indigenous cities of the precolonial era. To the extent that dominant subaltern relationships involve unequal space privileges, one may ask: were not there great inequalities in the canonical spatial ordering of the ideal Chinese or Indian city, especially in the latter by *varna*[5] or caste? Or for that matter, in the implicit gendering of urban space and the public sphere in the cities of Muslim culture? Indeed, as we have seen in the previous chapters, the ecologies of both organic and ideal cities were very much shaped by a need to negotiate an order in diversity, with spaces of highest value and amount occupied by the rulers, priests, and influential traders. Spaces privileged by location, size, and endowment inevitably placed all other spaces and their occupants in a subaltern relationship.

The semiotics of space in the endogenous images of the ideal have consistently differentiated between social groups and have privileged some classes or groups by orders of power, purity, caste (or occupation), and gender. In the classic canonical model of the Hindu city, the untouchables were not even allowed inside the city. It was not just an outcome of the colonial times, but in fact integral to the precolonial order of things, albeit exploited and exacerbated by colonial institutions.[6]

This concession, however, does not necessarily make the subalternity and alterity of the colonial times, like slavery, any more legitimate or righteous. Indeed the subaltern spaces of colonial cities are obtained from a power relationship that was established through wars, conquests, and ultimately domination and subjugation. It is not a result of the historical processes of integration and ordering through canonical texts and institutions as in the case of the Hindu caste system, or in the customary gendering of the Muslim societies. There was a fundamental difference between the subaltern relationships of the colonialists and natives and those that were endemic to local cultures and institutions. For this hierarchy and inequality was not an exogenous outcome but an integral part of the endogenous model of development that goes back to settlement forms of primitive tribes.[7]

While this general point has been aptly made, by several writings on colonial urban form and development,[8] a broader conceptual framework has been missing about the intentions and practices of the subaltern spatiality of the colonial cities. To the extent that the success of any colonial project depended on conquest and subjugation of the indigenous culture by an exogenous and alien force, expressions such as "forms of dominance," as in the title of AlSayyad's 1992 book, is an inevitable conclusion drawn in describing the colonial urban outcome.[9] Another popular trope embedded in postcolonial writing is the characterization of the colonizing power and the colonized subjects as one of masculinity versus femininity, as in the Indian case.[10] As urban theorist Zeynep Çelik has deftly demonstrated, similar interpretation is possible in the semiotics of the French colonial representations of Algiers, perhaps rather dramatically captured in those famous sketches of Le Corbusier, where the *casbah* or the old city is shown as the head of a traditional burka-clad woman.[11] Still a third model—the "culture contact" model—advanced by cultural geographer Anthony King in perhaps one of the earliest attempts to describe the spatiality of colonial urban development in India, takes a more benign view of the subaltern relationships.[12] In contrast to the more confrontational dominance-subjugation model, King viewed the emergence of colonial urban form as a partial synthesis in a dialectical sense of two very different exogenous and endogenous cultures. Nevertheless, these models of colonial architecture, urban form, and urbanism have yet to be located within a larger metanarrative of the historical processes of which they are a part.

The Colonial Project: Metanarratives

One of the premises of this book is that the development of the Global South has been a "civilizing" project of the West, guided by its own images of development and without regard to cultural resources and legacies of the colonized. This "civilizing" project had begun in the colonial era, and at least three metanarratives support this proposition: Orientalism, Diffusionism, and Modernism.

(a) Orientalism

The seminal work of Edward Said provides the foundation for this metanarrative, which according to historian Gyan Prakash "has lived a seditious life,"[13] and persistently transgressed disciplinary boundaries of Western scholarship and thus inserted an indeterminacy of its authority. Most significantly, argues Prakash, it is "this indeterminacy that has served as a provocation to rethink the modern west from the position of the Other, ... in exploring the implications of demonstration that the East/West opposition is an externalization of an internal division in the modern West."[14]

Since Said published his seminal work on "Orientalism," there has been a significant body of intellectual and scholarly response to his work, some critical, others simply stimulated by his arguments. Considered postcolonial paradigm, this literature comprises works of humanist scholars, many from the Indian subcontinent, that critically examine the life experiences of the indigenous society and their cultural and political relationships under British rule. While engaging, this literature remains mute regarding spatial and urban form implications of the subaltern status of the native population.

(b) Diffusionism

The construction of the subaltern "Other" is a necessary artifact of the colonizers' worldview, where the Other is necessarily an inferior, undeveloped, primitive, or empty culture incapable of developing on its own. This conclusion would follow from the metanarrative presented by geographer James Blaut (1993), who argues that the "colonizer's model of the world" was based on the presumption that while culture change can be either endogenously obtained or exogenously induced, most countries are incapable of endogenous development. This is essentially a "diffusionist" view, which asserts that most examples of extant technology in the New World benefited from earlier epochs of globalization. Such views would argue that "the great pre-Columbian civilizations of the Americas must be, ultimately, the result of transpacific or transatlantic diffusions, because these civilizing traits (agriculture, temple architecture, writing, and so on) were found much earlier in the Old World than the New, and Native Americans probably were not inventive enough to think up these things on their own."[15]

We should note that like the critique of Orientalism, the critique of the diffusionist model of Western scholarship is also seditious, challenging the authority of disciplinary knowledge, and thus complementing each other. While the anti-Orientalist critique focused on the Western construction of the "Other," in the critique of diffusionist theory, as Blaut argues, there is a distinct dichotomy of an inside and an outside or more poignantly, a core and a periphery—echoing the dependency model previously discussed.

Figure 7.1
The colonizer's representation of the native landscape in a sketch showing the Mumbai peninsula looking east. Note that it is shown as empty and unpopulated.
Source: By permission of the British Library. © British Library Board.

The features of this diffusionist point of view, according to Blaut, are the following: a belief in the progress and modernization of Europe as the core, while the "outside" or the periphery remains stagnant and undeveloped. Accordingly, the superior intellect and values of the Western man propels this progress, while the absence of similar intellect and values in the periphery keeps it stagnant. It is natural then to expect that the only way the periphery could develop is from the diffusion of innovations and progressive ideas and values from the West. As quid pro quo the periphery, recipients of the European innovations and ideas, reimburses the core with primary goods, surplus labor values, and other forms of material wealth.[16]

Like Orientalism, the diffusionist scholarship essentially contributed to the cause of colonialism by collecting information of the native society, and by structuring, cataloging, and classifying indigenous society and culture. The process of diffusion in fact was achieved through the actions and agents of colonialism—missionaries, soldiers, technicians, and bureaucrats. According to Blaut, "classic diffusionism arose in tandem with classic colonialism,"[17] with attendant theories that supported and justified the colonial enterprise. Thus, the European concept of private property and property rights were

Figure 7.2
A newly constructed mansion of the colonial rulers in Baruipur, again sitting in a landscape empty of people and flora—odd given the concentration of population and the humid and fertile context of the Gangetic plain.
Source: By kind permission of the Victoria Memorial Hall, Kolkata, India.

concepts introduced and institutionalized in colonized areas. These Western institutions were necessary also for colonial appropriation of property, and subsequent taxation to generate revenue. Another version of this doctrine involved what Blaut calls the "myth of emptiness." The colonized territory was represented empty of population and settlements, thus lacking any territorial claim, property rights, or sovereignty of the indigenous population. This presumed emptiness often was the themes of early colonial renderings of the native landscape (see figures 7.1 and 7.2). It served the interest of colonial appropriation of land and natural resources without remorse. "Oriental" despotism was another such doctrine used to justify military intervention for the greater cause of liberating the people, but also to eliminate sources of armed resistance.

(c) High Modernism

This last metanarrative pertains to the emergence of the modern state, initially in the West, and its subsequent transference to the colonies. The emergence of the modern state, with all of its apparatuses and institutions, was a major phase of the modernization drive. In his classic *Seeing Like a State*, James C. Scott has effectively argued how legibility of the physical, social, and cultural landscape was critical for the governance of a country, particularly a colony as vast as the Indian subcontinent. It was particularly challenging where multiple nature services, principalities, religions, languages, and cultural practices with unclear boundaries, rights, and customs managed to coexist in a historical dynamic of change and continuity. All of these precolonial trappings seemed too messy, and "illegible" for governance purposes. The agency of a modern state was particularly critical and necessary to rule a large subcontinent with a limited supply of British soldiers and administrators.

The legibility drive included such initiatives as simple counting heads (the census, that is), as well as measuring, organizing, ordering property rights, and developing a basis for collecting taxes. Thus, the revenue necessary to govern a large state like the colonial India had to come from various sources, including property taxes. The administrative state thus had to be organized not just to collect the revenue but also to guarantee public safety, administer justice, and defend itself from the local insurgencies and the like.

The philosophical basis of establishing a modern state in India was rooted in the British liberal democratic tradition. But what this political modernity delivered was a profound culture of bureaucracy, which remained a major obstacle to economic development in the early years of postcolonial India. The modern state became a bureaucratic state involving multiple checks and balances. An ordinary sales transaction typically would be done in "triplicate," with two layers of carbon paper inserted to obtain two copies. Of course, things have changed in India with the rapid adoption of information technology, including the current biometric ID system called Aadhaar, which has already covered close to a billion people. This is another example of the "seeing" need of the modern state, which this country seemingly has achieved with some aplomb. And that is well reflected in the most recent election that involves some 900 million voters with a polling station guaranteed within walking distance of every citizen. The Western project of modernizing traditional states has seemingly worked in the case of India.

Colonial Intentions, Images, and Methods

The history of colonization is quite complex and varied, depending on the era, region, duration, territorial extent, and national origin of the colonial powers. In the limited space of this chapter it will not be possible to consider in depth the differences in the Spanish, Portuguese, British, French, Dutch, or Italian regimes of colonization. One could argue, however, that the intents, images, and methods of colonial city building and the production of subaltern spaces evolved in five distinct phases: control and domination; consolidation; assimilation; conversion; and finally, reform.

In the early phase of control and domination new spaces and institutions were created often by obliterating traditional urban form and structure or superimposing an entirely new form on the existing indigenous space. This early stage of colonial development often involved sequestering indigenous space and landscape and consigning the native population to separate and segregated settlements. Demoted to subaltern status, these spaces were subject to surveillance and panoptic control, in a Foucauldian sense,[18] by surrounding the indigenous settlements with a *cordon sanitaire*.

The consolidation phase involved building new infrastructure, new cities, that continued to relegate existing settlements to subaltern status, often by design, if not neglect. The new spaces of the colonizers were designed and built in the images of the European motherland, reflected nostalgia, denial, and romanticism, ignoring local climate and ecology. In the documentary *The Africans*, political scientist Ali Mazrui would refer to these spaces of colonial diaspora as a mere "European fantasy."[19]

The third phase involved assimilation through culture contact. In his treatise on colonial urban development, Anthony King discusses at length the "culture contact" model and the emergence of what he calls a "Third Culture" that included socialized natives—necessary, albeit in a subaltern role, for the administration and management of vast colonial territories of the Indian subcontinent. Paralleling this assimilation and consolidation were missionary projects involving proselytism and conversion to Christianity, as well as education of the native population and introduction of Western leisure and entertainment. This would result in new spaces of worship, learning, and recreation. Finally, the last phase would involve well-meaning and benevolent interventions in the spaces and institutions that included infrastructure development, and belatedly in the areas of public health and other social services,[20] but not necessarily changing their subaltern status.

It should be noted, however, to the extent that the colonial development and reconstruction could not touch every corner of the national landscape, especially for such a vast colony like the Indian subcontinent, the spatial changes were more strategic and symbolic, limited to building capital cities and administrative centers, port cities, and military cantonments. Defense and trade largely motivated infrastructure development. But other institutional changes, like property ownership, land surveys, and a taxation system, had more far-reaching and transformative effects on the colonial space.[21] What follows are specific examples from five different colonial regimes: Spanish, British, French, and Italian.

The Spanish Legacy

In the summer of 2006 the Banamex Cultural Foundation of Mexico held an exhibition titled "Imágenes de los naturales en el arte de la Nueva España" in its eighteenth-century Mexican Baroque headquarters in the historic center of Mexico City. Comprising a collection of paintings from the sixteenth to eighteenth centuries—many by unknown artists—the exhibition was a vivid tableau of the conquest, subjugation, and ultimately transformation of the indigenous people, spaces, and culture of Mexico. These paintings showed the inexorable imprint of the colonial power—in organization of space, in ordering of people, and in the conversion of indigenous culture through proselytism—over a period of some three hundred years. Particularly touching are the two tableaux—*La conquista de Mexico* by an anonymous painter and *Encuentro de Cortés y Moctezuma* by Juan Correa—which show respectively the valor and gallantry of the Aztecs fighting the invading army, and the subaltern symbolism in the meeting between Cortés and Moctezuma.

The scene of this historic encounter is set against the famous Aztec city of Tenochtitlan, a magnificent city of temples and palaces laid out around a central plaza. Cortés was so impressed with this urban design that he wrote to his superiors in Spain about it and chose to establish the new colonial city using the same site and layout. The current Plaza de la Constitución, or Zócalo—a majestic public space—is the very site where the core of the Aztec city design was supplanted by the new colonial city design (see figure 7.3). All the precolonial buildings are gone, demolished unceremoniously by the conquistadors. The only exception is the recently excavated foundation of the Templo Mayor, which is an archaeological site today. A cathedral (Catedral y Sagrario Metropolitano) was built at the site of the Aztec pyramid to the north of the plaza (see figure 7.4). To the east of the plaza, exactly where Moctezuma's palace was located, Cortés built his new palace—today a government building (Palacio Nacional), the seat of the federal executive.[22] Major hotels and department stores with ground-level colonnades now surround the plaza, replacing various other structures of the precolonial city, which were demolished at the time the new city was founded.

Around 1524 Cortés's surveyor would lay out the grid city with the original Aztec plaza, now called Zócalo, at the center. Turned roughly 20 degrees to the east of true north, the grid of the colonial Mexico City followed the alignment and orientation of the earlier Aztec city. Some fifty years later it was to become the harbinger, indeed the

Figure 7.3
An early painting of Plaza Mayor (the Zócalo) of Mexico City (circa 1695) by Cristóbal de Villalpando. *Source*: Cristóbal de Villalpando/Wikimedia Commons/Public Domain.

"urban template,"[23] for the future colonial cities in the Americas, which came to be known as the Laws of the Indies cities.

In 1573 Philip II formally codified the town-planning principles and instructions for the purposes of establishing new colonial towns and settlements. Known as the *Ordenanzas de Descubrimento y Población* (or "Discovery and Settlement Ordinances"), the royal instructions included various recommendations for selecting the appropriate site, but also how to lay out the city.[24] Much attention was paid to the design and placement of the central plaza and its orthogonal form and optimal dimensions. The edict stipulated that the "four corners of the plaza face to the four principal winds, because in this way the streets leaving the plaza are not exposed to the principal winds, which would be of great inconvenience."[25] The ordinances even suggested that principal streets of the town should radiate from the middle of each side and two from each corner, thus

Figure 7.4
The imposing Catedral y Sagrario Metropolitano, located at the northern end of the Zócalo, Mexico City.
Source: Author, 1974.

creating the basic orthogonal framework of a grid city. The fifteenth- and sixteenth-century town-planning principles and antecedents in Italy, Spain, and Portugal influenced these principles of city design.[26]

These laws would dictate the founding of many hundreds of cities throughout Latin America and even southern regions of the United States over some 250 years. In addition to the layout of the gridiron streets, the main plaza, and the surrounding blocks, the laws also prescribed the "segregation of noxious activities, the form of the wall, the disposition of common lands, the distribution of city lots and farms, and even the uniform style of the buildings."[27] In summarizing the Spanish settlement efforts, urban historian Jorge Hardoy makes several observations, of which the following are worth noting.[28] First, while they had a predilection for an ordered and geometrical city plan, they did not necessarily have a canonical "urban model," the so-called Laws of the Indies notwithstanding. Second, locational attributes were important, but they were obvious enough not to require any formal legislation. Third, the royal edicts were seemingly unconcerned about the existing indigenous settlements, and yet these settlements had significant influence on the location and design of many colonial cities. Finally, the Laws only formalized what was already being practiced, often based on the city founders' personal knowledge and experience.

Nevertheless, the Laws included instructions for the location and hierarchy of institutions and administration. The cathedral and churches received the prime *solares* (or town lots) next to the plaza, followed by government buildings—town hall, customs house, military arsenal, and the like. Vaguely reminiscent of the canonical Hindu city organized around caste or *varna,* the spatial organization of the Spanish colonial city had its own caste system involving the subaltern indigenes.[29] This subalternity of the new "caste" system was reflected in the founding of two types of colonial towns—pueblos de españoles and pueblos de indios—one for the conquerors, and the other for the conquered. The Laws of the Indies were applied scrupulously in both instances, but with more success in the case of the former, where the new colonial city was organized spatially according to class and rank. Since the vestiges of previous indigenous caste system were banned, the native city was not spatially ordered according to social status. Its only identity was one of subaltern class and space, subject to religious teaching and other modes of socialization.

The founding of the early cities involved certain rituals.[30] It "began with the planting of a pike, the utterance of a challenge, and the cutting of weeds, an act of possession," followed by the erection of a gallows, "and only then was the cross raised and the founding mass celebrated."[31] When Pizarro founded Lima after the conquest of the Incan capital of Cuzco, the native population was confined to a *cercado,* or walled enclosure, while the new city was under construction.[32]

Today these plazas resulting from the Laws of the Indies play an iconic role in the civic functions and the public life and identity of most Latin American cities. The Plaza Bolívar in Bogotá is a case in point (see figure 7.5).

The British Legacy

The British colonial history is a complex evolution of social, political, and cultural relationship of the settlers with that of the natives. As argued by historian Thomas Metcalf, ideological tensions and contradictions continued throughout this process.[33] Indeed, as we will see, many of these ideological tensions repeatedly influenced establishment of the urban colonial footprint in India.

Drawing from the "culture contact" theory inspired by anthropologist Bronislaw Malinowski's work on culture change,[34] Anthony King discussed the evolution of

Figure 7.5
Plaza Bolívar, Bogotá.
Source: Author, 2015.

colonial urban form and spatial organization in a larger context of cultural adaptation and change. What intrigued him was Malinowski's observation that the product of the culture contact process is not necessarily a hybrid one that retains institutional elements of both, but one that engenders an entirely different culture.[35] This "colonial Third Culture" then, according to King's analysis, is an outcome of "culture contact" between the selected representatives of the "First Culture" (the metropole), such as the officials of the crown, the military, the bureaucrats, the "box-wallahs" (or businessmen), and their families; and the "Second Culture" of the indigenous society, as represented by the various ethnic groups and regions of the Indian subcontinent. The Third Culture is a new culture altogether, with some limited overlap with the "Second" or the indigenous culture, but little with the "First" or the "Selected First Culture." King further argued that the colonial urban development in India had to be understood by comparing the institutions of this "Third Culture"—government, religion, law, kinship, economic and social systems, knowledge and values, and the like—with those of the indigenous culture.

In pursuing the "Third Culture" approach to colonial urban development King accepts the premise of asymmetry of power and the subaltern role of the indigenous culture. The culture contact, he argued, is a relationship of "*dominance-dependence* where the ultimate source of social, economic, and political power rests in the metropolitan society, with physical force being the ultimate sanction in the colonised society."[36] The spatial organization of the colonial cities fully reflected this asymmetry, creating subaltern spaces at several levels through segregation and separation. Typically, the British colonial landscape consisted of a military "cantonment" and a "civil station" (or "civil lines") next to it, but separate from the indigenous "native" city. These features became paradigmatic—but not necessarily canonical—in most major cities of colonial India. Thus, not just Delhi, but also Mumbai, Chennai, Kanpur, Allahabad, Agra, and Kolkata retained this tripartite schema of the colonial city. Separation of the native city or the "Black Town"[37] by distancing the new developments, especially the cantonment, from the indigenous city was commonplace, in a manner similar to the idea of *cordon sanitaire* used in the French colonial cities.[38] Where indigenous populations like the local *sepoys* had to live with the British army, the living quarters and associated facilities were totally segregated. This practice continued even through the twilight years of the colonial rule in India, while the British were still planning the new imperial capital in Delhi.[39]

The Third Culture perspective on the British colonial development, however, is only partial for several reasons. For one, King's emphasis on the emergence of the Third Culture—in contrast to Malinowski's focus on the endogenous[40]—does not include the effects of institutions of exogenous origin, such as taxation, jurisprudence, property rights, and religion, on the subaltern indigenous culture. Nor does it take into account the resistance from the native population to such exogenous influences.[41] Missing too in this analysis is the colonizers' strategic acceptance of such recalcitrant indigenous institutions as the caste[42] or the *zemindary* system, and incorporating them into the scheme of colonial administration. Second, there is a presumption of proximity between the Third and Second Cultures, to the extent that the Third Culture recruited a small portion of the indigenous population. In reality, the difference was much deeper, creating a permanent structural dualism within the indigenous population. A case in point, as historian Thomas Metcalf points out, is the Bengali *babu* class (or *bhadralok* in Bengali), many of whom were educated in the images of the British, and who functioned as the principal professionals and bureaucrats in the service of the Raj.[43] Finally, the Third Culture premise does not include any discussion of what Metcalf refers to as the "ideology of the Raj" and the tensions within the British government and the intellectuals about the purpose and imperatives of colonialism. This tension no doubt was reinforced by sustained culture contact, limited integration in army and civil service, and also growing resistance to various British imperial undertakings. Perhaps one of the most comprehensive and scholarly historical analyses of the British rule in India, Metcalf's work suggests that India was always a major enigma for the British. Its complex culture, traditions, faith, social structures, and value systems remained alien and intractable to them despite important scholarly work on India's cultural and political history. Even after three centuries of colonial experience the "the idea of India"—as captured in the title of a book by political historian Sunil Khilnani—remained elusive.[44] Consequently there were always tensions and contradictions within the British predilections, policies and actions. The "ideologies of the Raj,"[45] according to Metcalf, were ultimately shaped by political philosophies, administrative imperatives, strategic needs, and pragmatic reasoning that sought to justify imperialism.[46] In this process the attitude toward the natives of subaltern status oscillated between ideologies emphasizing polar opposites of the inherent similarity (or equality) of all human beings, and the intrinsic difference between the British and the Indians. Historian Suhash Chakravarty captured this tension in the British ruling class in his book *The Raj Syndrome*.[47] In his discussion of the perspectives of the imperial class, he quotes an exchange between Lord Irwin, then the Viceroy of India, and Horace Alexander, a British historian: "Rule'em, I say, rule'em, if you are going to rule'em. Look after'em of course; give'em schools, if they want education—schools, hospitals, roads and railways. Stamp out the plague, fever, and famine. But let them know you are top dog. That's the way to run an Eastern country."[48]

It is possible to collapse this complex political history into three distinct phases. The first phase involved the questioning of the expansion and exploits of the East India Company in the late eighteenth century, and the attempts to define the imperatives for the governance of India according to the British institutions. Principal advocates were intellectuals like politician Philip Francis and political theorist Edmund Burke.[49] Even by the end of this period and through the beginning of the nineteenth century there was considerable tension about the appropriate form of governance—whether it should be done according to the laws grounded in the British tradition, or in the tradition of the "Oriental despotism" of benevolent and enlightened rulers. This tension reflected the larger ambivalence about whether to treat the native population as similar or different from the ruling class.

Perhaps the most critical period of ideological development was the period following the Industrial Revolution and the rise of liberalism as a political ideal on the British mainland in the early nineteenth century. The liberal point of view "conceived that human nature was intrinsically the same everywhere, and that it could be totally and completely transformed, if not by sudden revelation as the evangelicals envisaged, then by the workings of law, education, and free trade."[50] John Stuart Mill was a principal figure in advancing the arguments of liberalism emphasizing the inherent value of liberty in governance, different from earlier Benthamite philosophy of utilitarianism.

The liberal thinking on governance focused on modern institutions like property rights and legal systems as the basis for development. By deemphasizing indigenous traditions and cultures, the liberal view proposed inherent similarity in human beings, and thus rationalized the imperative of imperialism as one of liberating the indigenous population from the yoke of despotism and traditional values that repressed liberty.

In the third phase of the ideological development of the British Raj, the lofty ideas of modernity and liberalism that emphasized the universality of the human abilities and reasoning were gradually supplanted by a deliberate construction of the differences that existed between the people of the Indian subcontinent and Europe in cultural, racial, and even personality traits. It is not apparent in Metcalf's account whether this tendency was a result of the systematic resistance to the British rule that began with the 1857 Battle of Plassey, ultimately leading to the freedom movement led by a political leadership deeply influenced by these earlier liberal values of equality and liberty. But it was evident that administrative and military exigencies required not only the "creation" but also the "ordering" of this difference. The "seeing" needs of the modern state[51] required classifying the native population by caste, ethnicity, religion, anatomical features, and the like.[52]

There should be no doubt that the construction and ordering of difference was an attempt to define the subaltern in more than one way. The British considered native customs and institutions like *sati*[53] and *bala-bibaha*[54] as backward and deplorable practices and a sign of underdevelopment.[55] The native population, largely peasant, were seen as simple and childlike people who needed civilizing by a benevolent and paternalistic government. The rule of India by now was based on an "imperial ideology by insisting that Indians, like children, required a long process of tutelage before they could participate in the governance of their country."[56]

Beyond the official acts of categorizing and census taking of the differences, there were also literary and popular writings that advanced a gendering of the subaltern relationship. Thus, it was always a difference between the "rational" Europe and the "sensual" India, a masculine colonial power controlling a feminine colonized people. The Indian male was characterized as effeminate, and the women were generally degraded.[57] Similar expressions were apparent also in the French colonial view of the native Arab population of their colonies. The ordering also involved spatial segregation, separation, and distancing between the European and the native populations. In part the distancing grew out of a sense of vulnerability, a fear of contamination, from being close to the native population and their "dirt and disease"—as aptly captured in the French expression *cordon sanitaire*—leading to a paradigmatic urban form. The form engendered by the distancing can "best be imagined as a set of nested boxes, each walled off from the larger Indian world outside."[58] In addition to the cantonment and civil lines as broad urban districts, hill stations and bungalow residences were the other two elements of British retreat from the heat and humidity of the subcontinent.[59] This was the context for the larger city design and urban-planning imprint of the colonial city.

The Imperial Kolkata

The Portuguese were the first to establish a trading post along the bank of the Hooghly River in the mid-sixteenth century some 100 miles upriver from the Bay of Bengal. By the middle of the next century the Dutch and the French had already established similar trading posts nearby along the west bank of the river.[60] The British were late. In 1690, more than a hundred years after the arrival of the Portuguese, Job Charnock, at that time governor of Bay of Bengal, was finally able to obtain a trading license from the Mogul rulers on behalf of the East India Company to develop a settlement in the vicinity of three existing villages. each specializing in religious, commercial, and trading activities. Unlike other trading posts, he chose a site on the east bank of the river, seemingly a wrong choice in retrospect, since the vast portion of contemporary India lies to the west of the river, causing logistical headaches in modern times.[61]

This modest beginning of Kolkata did not necessarily presage its future prosperity as a port city, or for that matter its emergence as an imperial city in the second half of the nineteenth century. Nor was the city laid out in the three-part paradigm discussed previously, which was used more deliberately in the planning of New Delhi after 1911, when the capital was officially moved from Kolkata to Delhi. By the time Kolkata had become the imperial city its urban form generally followed the larger colonial paradigm. The first act toward building the colonial city was largely a defensive one. A formidable fortress—Fort William—was constructed in 1712 on the bank of the river where it is widest, with a two-tiered rampart of Baroque design mimicking such fortified medieval cities as Palma Nova or Lucca. Vast expanses of open space that now comprise the premier public open space of the city—the Maidan—isolated the fort on the other three sides, thus creating the necessary *cordon sanitaire*. Beyond this dedicated open space began the first settlement of the European city, occupying the space between the three original indigenous settlements. A 1742 plan of Kolkata showed a fenced area beyond the fort noting that "within the Compass of the Pallisades [*sic*] lived the Europeans and Christians."[62] This "fenced city" included the Armenians and the Portuguese who had arrived earlier than the British and had already built churches in the northern edge of this exclusive area. As historian Pradip Sinha pointed out, this was the beginning of the separation and segregation between the Europeans and the natives, the dualism of the White Town and the Black Town, and the subaltern spatiality that continued throughout the colonial era.[63]

Soon the fences would disappear and a transitional zone—mainly commercial in nature around preexisting trading posts—would emerge to the north and northeast of the previously "fenced city," allowing interpenetration of the Europeans and the native population. The prosperous native business class, which was responsible for the development of this large commercial area of many specialized "bazaars," lived further north in their own palaces and mansions (see figure 7.6). Many native settlements of poor workers remained immediately outside the White Town as the Europeans needed domestic help and other service workers nearby. The areas to the east and the south of the Maidan would begin to be populated by sumptuous mansions built in classic European style on large lots. The bungalow architecture that King discussed had yet to evolve. Street names such as Auckland, Middleton, Park, Camac, Cornwallis, Lindsay, Ripon, Russell, Marquis, and so forth, or place names such as Eden Garden, Belvedere, Hastings, and Garden Reach, were commonplace. Some still endure and are vaguely reminiscent of the European neighborhoods that flourished in nineteenth- and early-twentieth-century Kolkata.[64] As the maps of that period show, the difference in the density, organization, and building footprint of the native and the colonial city was quite striking indeed (see figures 7.7, 7.8, and 7.9).

By the late eighteenth century the core of the colonial administrative complex had begun to take shape about a mile to the north of the fort. The Writers' Building was completed in 1777 to house the clerical functions of the East India Company, later to be used as the executive offices of the colonial government (see figure 7.10), and after independence, as the headquarters of the West Bengal state government. From the late eighteenth century to the mid-nineteenth century other buildings—the Anglican churches of St. Andrew's and St. John's, the Town Hall, the Customs House, the Mint, and other administrative buildings—were built in locations around the Tank Square (later Dalhousie Square, renamed BBD Square after independence[65]) in the vicinity of the Writers' Building. These civic buildings involved major capital investments and were built in the images of the European homeland, reflecting a classical architecture in the Palladian tradition (see figures 7.9 to 7.11).

Even more expensive, monumental, and nostalgic architecture was still to come. At the end of the eighteenth century Marquis Wellesley, the then governor-general, decided to construct a monumental Government House "that would be a true symbol of power and authority, a headquarters fit for a mighty empire"[66]—a sentiment not unlike that of Cortés in Mexico or Pizarro in Peru in building their imperial cities a few

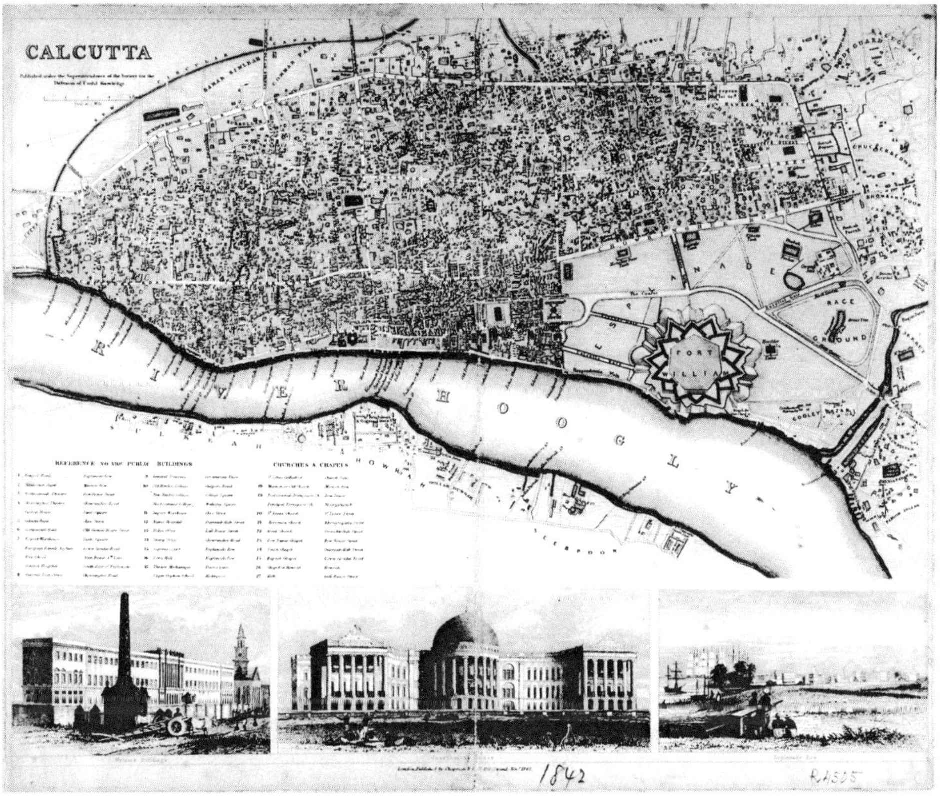

Figure 7.6

A map of early-nineteenth-century Kolkata showing a dualistic urban form. Sketches at the bottom of the map show important new buildings—the governor's mansion, a church—against the contrasting and largely empty native landscape.

Source: By kind permission of the Victoria Memorial Hall, Kolkata, India.

centuries earlier. This new edifice, completed in 1802, was an exact copy of the Keddleston Hall in Derbyshire designed by Robert Adams. The price tag of some £179,000 that included the cost of land and site improvements apparently was neither expected nor quite appreciated by Wellesley's bosses, "the court of directors," in London.[67] The building was erected by clearing some fine existing and recently constructed residential structures, serving as the southern end of a north-south civic axis with the Writers' Building across the BBD Square at the other end (see figure 7.6, middle of the bottom row). This axis serving the visual connection between two most important colonial buildings was a nice touch of classical urban design that would be interrupted in the

Figure 7.7
A painting showing the mixed urbanism of colonial Kolkata (circa eighteenth century).
Source: By kind permission of the Victoria Memorial Hall, Kolkata, India.

Figure 7.8
A painting showing the emerging waterfront of eighteenth-century colonial Kolkata. Proximate landscape shows mansions owned by wealthy local residents, the colonial townscape farther down the river.
Source: By kind permission of the Victoria Memorial Hall, Kolkata, India.

Figure 7.9
Photo showing the emerging urban form and urbanism of Old Court House Road.
Source: By kind permission of the Victoria Memorial Hall, Kolkata, India.

Figure 7.10
A recent view of the Writers' Building, Kolkata.
Source: Author, 2012.

Figure 7.11
St. Andrew's Church in contemporary Kolkata.
Source: Author, 2019.

postcolonial years by a nondescript modernist tower housing the telephone exchange, a bureaucratic decision, oblivious of the earlier intentions of colonial civic design.

Through the nineteenth century, the exogenous landscape of the White Town comprised such institutions as the racecourse, several clubs, a few cemeteries, and more churches, the most significant being St. Paul's Cathedral at the southeastern edge of the Maidan, constructed around the middle of the nineteenth century. Contemporary Park Street is a legacy of that era (see figure 7.12). About fifty years later, in an adjoining site at

Figure 7.12
Colonial-era commercial and residential buildings with street-level arcades on Park Street in Kolkata. *Source*: Author, 2019.

the southern edge of the Maidan, another grand edifice—perhaps the most distinguished in British colonial history—would arise to commemorate Queen Victoria, who managed to cultivate a special bond with her Indian subjects. Initiated by the then governor general Curzon, and designed by William Emerson, at that time president of the Royal Institute of British Architects, the Victoria Memorial was completed in 1906 (see figure 7.13). Dubbed immediately as the "Taj of the Raj," this building was also constructed in the classical Palladian style, reminiscent of Belfast City Hall in Northern Ireland, according to some critics (see figure 7.14). Emerson's design was considered "a mixture of English Baroque and Indo-Saracenic with some Islamic and Hindu features."[68]

By this time the colonial legacy and its "civilizing project" had a profound effect on the urban form, and indeed the urbanism of Kolkata. Even V. S. Naipaul, a strident critic of India, had succumbed to a bit of nostalgia about the urbanism of Kolkata during his visit in the early sixties, conceding that the city vaguely reminded him of London.[69]

Lutyens' Delhi

Five years after the Victoria Memorial was constructed, the British decided to move the capital of imperial India to Delhi, a city with a long history of serving as the capital for

Figure 7.13
The Victoria Memorial in Kolkata today.
Source: Author, 2018.

many dynasties in the past. King George V made the announcement at his coronation *durbar*[70] held in Delhi. The decision to move the capital to Delhi was a major symbolic act. The location was seen as more central, strategic, and symbolically important, having served as the capital of many previous dynasties, dating back to Indraprastha of the fifteenth century BCE and the Mogul empire, which the colonial powers replaced. It would have been a major lapse if after three hundred years of colonial rule the British Empire had failed to establish a significant presence in Delhi. Thus the move, although expensive and somewhat controversial, was unavoidably exigent.

It fell on the then Viceroy Lord Hardinge to carry out the planning and the building of the new imperial capital. A special Town Planning Committee was given the

Figure 7.14
Belfast City Hall, Northern Ireland.
Source: Author, 2013.

task to organize the planning process and find an appropriate town planner to lead the work. After much deliberation and lobbying by interested parties, Edwin Lutyens, a well-known British architect, was chosen by the viceroy to plan the new city, even though he had little planning experience. As it would turn out, his strong views were often in conflict with those of his client. Where to locate the new capital was the focus of a number of initial studies and surveys. The civil station and the cantonment were already in place to the north and northeast of the walled Mogul city of Shahjahanabad.[71] Locating the new capital to the north did not seem possible because of space constraints. Other sites immediately south or west of the walled city and near the river were rejected on the grounds of drainage issues.[72] Ultimately it was the sloping terrain of the Raisina Hills or the ridge to the west that dictated the location of the residence of the viceroy and the visual terminal of a monumental east-west axis—Kings Way (now called Rajpath)—extending toward the river Yamuna to the east. Immediately in the front of the viceroy's residence, the axis was flanked by the two wings of the Secretariat buildings—housing the offices of the executive branch of the government. Lutyens himself designed the viceroy's residence, while his colleague Herbert Baker, also a very

Figure 7.15

A Mughal miniature-style painting by Marjorie Shoosmith showing Lutyens and Baker presenting the model of the proposed Viceroy's House and the Secretariat in New Delhi to Lord Irwin, then the viceroy to India. Color reproduction from the *Illustrated London News*, 1931.

Source: By permission ©British Library Board.

1. His Excellency the Viceroy.
2. Sir Edwin Lutyens, R.A. (presenting "Viceroy's House").
3. Sir Herbert Baker, A.R.A. (presenting the Council House).
4. Sir A. M. Rouse, Chief Engineer, carrying plan of New Delhi.
5. The Hon'ble Sir Bhupendra Nath Mitra, Member, Industries and Labour.
6. The Hon'ble Sir John Thompson, Chief Commissioner, Delhi Province.
7. Mr. J. L. Sale, P.W.D.
8. Mr. H. J. Donkin, P.W.D.
9. Mr. A. G. Shoosmith, Architect.
10. Mr. H. E. Parker, P.W.D.
11. Sardar Bahadur T. S. Malik, P.W.D.
12. Mr. H. A. N. Medd, Architect.
13. Mr. W. R. Mustoe, Superintendent, Horticultural Division.
14. Mr. F. T. Jones, P.W.D.
15. Lt.-Colonel C. O. Harvey, Military Secretary to the Viceroy.
16. Major W. P. A. Bradshaw, A.D.C.
17. "Max" and "Mina."
18. Lt.-Colonel W. W. Muir, Comptroller of the Viceroy's Household.
19. Mr. G. Cunningham, Private Secretary to the Viceroy.
20. Major A. D. Vigors, Commandant of the Viceroy's Bodyguard.
21. Her Excellency the Lady Irwin.

Figure 7.16

A key to the individuals depicted in the painting in figure 7.15.

Source: By permission ©British Library Board.

successful architect, was commissioned to design the executive office buildings and the legislative assembly (see figures 7.15 and 7.16).

Lutyens's plan for the new imperial capital followed the Baroque order and symmetry that inspired the layout of Versailles, Baron Haussmann's surgery of medieval Paris, Pope Sixtus V's design for Rome, and Pierre L'Enfant's plan for Washington, DC. Many observers have likened the main east-west axis, a wide ceremonial boulevard to the Champs-Élysées in Paris. As an architect, Lutyens liked the classical style with simplified modernistic lines. It is not surprising that lacking a background in town planning he would choose a more formalistic approach—a Baroque design—to the layout of the city. Thus, the Government House, the Secretariat buildings, and the Parliament House complex to the west, Connaught Circus—a major business and commercial node to the north—and a monument that establishes a visual terminal point to the east formed the three corners of an equilateral triangle of roughly two kilometers each side, fitting inside a larger hexagon whose corners served three additional points of radiating streets.

The similarity of Lutyens's plan for Delhi with L'Enfant's plan for Washington and Haussmann's reconstruction plan for Paris is not entirely accidental. Impressed by the layout of Washington, the viceroy sent for plans for these cities to serve as a guide. Lutyens himself explicitly considered such comparisons, not knowing then, ironically, that this similarity in design would presage the political isomorphism between the oldest and largest democracies in the world.[73] Other than a convergence of views about the Baroque layout in the tradition of the "City Beautiful" movement, Lutyens and Hardinge had considerable difference about the planning and design of the new capital and its major buildings (see figure 7.17).

This was not just simply a matter of aesthetic sensibilities; it was symbolic of the ideological differences that characterized much of the British rule. Hardinge, and indeed the King Edward VII and Queen Victoria before him believed in ruling India as compassionate rulers with appreciation and understanding of the indigenous culture, and if not for benevolence at least for strategic reasons of governance. Lutyens, on the other hand, represented the elite class who had very little appreciation for the indigenous architectural style or aesthetics, or for that matter, the existing landscape and urban form. Thus, as Khilnani points out, the plan of New Delhi completely ignored the historical connection of the city with the river.[74] While Hardinge wanted the new city to make visual connections with the historical sites in the area, much in the way Pope Sixtus V conceived the sixteenth-century design of Rome, Lutyens only responded to it somewhat mechanically. Later, however, he would admit that Lord Hardinge's insistence on maintaining vistas of Indraprastha (or Purana Qila)—the location and ruins of earlier dynasties—and the Jumma Masjid (the Friday mosque)

Figure 7.17

Map of New Delhi by Marjorie Shoesmith in an Indian style. Color reproduction from the *Illustrated London News*, 1931. This pictorial map shows the layout and location of the new British capital (commonly known as Lutyens' Delhi) with respect to the walled city of Shahjahanabad (to the extreme right). Note the *cordon sanitaire* between the walled city and the new, and retreat from the river. *Source*: By permission ©British Library Board.

of Shahjahanabad, led to the equilateral and hexagonal street patterns that form the core of the New Delhi plan.

The disagreement between the viceroy and his architect was much more intense when it came to choosing the architectural style. Hardinge, and indeed the king himself, wanted the architecture of the Government House and other buildings to be a marriage of the European classical style and the traditional Indian architecture. But Lutyens, basically an ur-modernist, had nothing but disdain for the traditional Indian architecture and had very low opinion of the previous works of British architects in India who tried to combine Indian elements with classical architecture. He found them gaudy and grotesque.[75] When Hardinge wanted him to use pointed arches, he disagreed vehemently and refused to modify his preference for circular arches. His design for the Government House finally included some traditional Indian elements, like *chujjahs*

Figure 7.18
The Secretariat complex, a legacy of the architecture and civic design of Baker and Lutyens.
Source: Author, 1994.

and *chhattris*[76] and the base of the main dome reflecting some of the features of a Buddhist *stupa*. Herbert Baker, his associate, who designed the Secretariat complex, was more willing to adapt his architecture to the wishes of his client.

Despite Hardinge's best intentions and ideas, the plan for New Delhi became an expression of Baroque monumentality that had very little sense of continuity with the existing urban form or urbanism. Unfortunately Lutyens's urban design concept for the main civic axis turned out to have a major flaw. The location of the two wings of the secretarial building flanking the approach to the Government House came under criticism as soon as the construction began. Located on the highest point of the Raisina Hills, the Government House served a magnificent visual terminus for the ceremonial axis from a distance, but as one approaches this building it begins to disappear from the visual field as one arrives at the bottom of the hill, where the Secretariat buildings dominate the landscape, a design lacuna that endures even today, as pointed out by civic designer Gordon Cullen.[77] (See figure 7.18.)

Ironically, the British New Delhi would come to be recognized as Lutyens' Delhi, rather than Hardinge's Delhi even though Hardinge was, according to Lutyens, the "father of the equilateral and hexagonal plan."[78] Beyond the monumental architecture, urban design, and Baroque layout, Lutyens' Delhi would leave still another legacy that will be reflected in the organization of its residential quarters and housing types. Quite early in the planning process Lutyens drew a sketch in which he showed the placement of housing types reflecting racial segregation, which "was made even more emphatic by placing bungalows of junior European officials on rising ground above junior Indians (labeled 'thin white' and 'thin black'), with the residences of senior officers still higher."[79] In the final version of the social organization of the plan, a combination of the rank and occupational hierarchy of Edwardian India was combined with race and subaltern status of the local population.[80] Plots of land were allocated according to status, which also reflected land price. However, this segregated arrangement was a far cry from the lofty liberal values of Bentham and Mills. The legacy of Lutyens' Delhi was a new caste system based on race and subalternity, something that Abu-Lughod refers to as "urban apartheid" in the case of Moroccan cities.

The French Legacy

The shape of the French colonial intervention was not all that different from that of the British colonial imprint, and it was impelled by very similar motives that drove British imperialism in India in the waning years of the late nineteenth and early twentieth centuries. It is not clear the extent to which the French imperialist project underwent the kind of ideological dilemmas that the British struggled with in reconciling the contradictions between liberal values and imperial mandates. But it is apparent that, like the British imperial rule, there were tensions over the hegemony of the metropole in authorizing every colonial administrative decision.[81]

The essence and ideology of the French colonial urban development was inherent in the planning and layout of certain cities, implemented under the leadership of agents responsible for the larger colonial project. These individuals had power, authority, and visions steeped in the ideology and worldview of the larger metropole. These visions, however, reflected limited understanding of the endogenous culture and tradition. Nevertheless, their approach to designing the colonial city lent a material reality to the romanticism and prejudice associated with most colonial projects of the West. Like

Job Charnock and Marquis Curzon in Kolkata, or Lord Hardinge and Edwin Lutyens in New Delhi, Louis Hubert Lyautey, résident géneral of the French protectorate of Morocco from 1912 to 1925, led such a "civilizing effort." During these years he transformed the urban landscape of Morocco by constructing colonial additions outside the walls of the indigenous cities in the images of the West.

Although in a sense the colonial transformation of the Moroccan cities was similar to the British colonial development, it was also different. First, the transformation involved several cities simultaneously. Second, it happened through a central edict and associated institutional changes. Finally, it happened over a relatively short time. This change was dramatic enough to prompt Abu-Lughod to characterize it as a case of "urban apartheid,"[82] confirming, unambiguously, the essence of segregation and the subaltern relationship of the native population compared to that the colonizers.

The French colonial apartheid-type outcome began with an aesthetic impulse[83]—conserve the traditional Moroccan walled cities. A French aristocrat of refined tastes, Lyautey apparently appreciated the rich heritage of the Moroccan culture, including its urbanism, and while having a vision of bringing order and harmony in these cities, he felt strongly that the indigenous city should remain untouched, not just in physical form but also in its social content and institutional structures.[84] As architectural historian Zeynep Çelik pointed out, this sentiment no doubt reflected the "arabizing" policies of Napoleon III. Thus, conservation of the *casbah* in Algiers was unavoidable because "the needs of the French were different from those of the indigenous people."[85]

Typically, the new European city was constructed on vacant land outside the walled city. The result was the classical dualistic urban form that segregated and separated the natives of subaltern status from the colonizers. This was a part of the grand vision of Lyautey, patronizing and paternalistic, as we have seen in the case of Britain's attitude toward its Indian subjects. He wanted to construct in Morocco "a strong edifice, ordered and harmonious, ... where men, so unlike in origins, dress, occupations, and race, continue, without abdicating any of their individual conceptions, their search for a common ideal, a common reason to live."[86] One could read this remarkable statement as a vision of a multicultural society, but the result was an "urban apartheid," as Abu-Lughod had argued.[87]

Instituting this spatial insularity and segregation was a political choice with strategic advantages. Clearly, a Haussmannian intrusion into the existing indigenous city—as was done in Algiers—would have been aesthetically degrading, and more importantly could have fomented resentment among the native population for disrupting their social and institutional fabric. Furthermore, keeping the natives contained within the walls of the medina separated by open space improved the panoptic surveillance and military control.[88]

Finally, the spatial segregation was seen as having a hygienic function, because it would allow the Europeans to avoid direct contact "with the indigenous elements of the lower class, whose physiological misery and filthiness would be important factors in the spread of epidemics."[89] This was the essence of the idea of creating a *cordon sanitaire* that was also effectively used by the British in India. Concerns for contamination and disease similarly motivated the British policy of segregation. So, the subaltern spatial relationships of the indigenous medina with the colonial settlements were formalized in three ways: nonintervention in the historic medina, creation of a *cordon sanitaire* separating the indigenous city from the new colonial city, and creation of a European city in the images of the colonizers' homeland.[90]

An architect named Henri Prost translated the ideology of Lyautey into specific master plans for the European quarters in several cities: Fès, Marrakech, Meknes, and Rabat being the major ones. The general pattern was the same, the modernist layout of the European city with wide boulevards and geometric layout of the Baroque legacy.[91] The *cordon sanitaire* was most effective in the case of Fès and Meknes, with the help of existing natural features like small river valleys. In the case of Rabat it was too late to acquire large easements because the Europeans had already started subdividing the land immediately outside the wall. Seemingly the same circumstances prevailed in Marrakech, where only a partial *cordon sanitaire* could be achieved.

Visually and cognitively the images of this dualism were quite different. If we consider Kevin Lynch's three criteria—identity, structure, and meaning—the new European town may have seemed more imageable, at least in the Western mind, because of its structure and order, even though it lacked identity and meaning from the native's perspective.[92] The European mind on the other hand found the form of the medina totally illegible, lacking order and structure, but to the native it had its own imageability derived from identity and meaning, as sociologist John Gulick had pointed out in his study of the images of Arab cities.[93]

Algiers

Compared to the colonial transformation of the Moroccan cities under Lyautey, which happened with relative ease and speed, the transformation of Algiers that began some fifty years earlier was much less expedient, and as it turned out, more invasive. Despite ideological emphasis on conservation, in the early stage of colonial control, the French "diced and sliced the city, appropriating and demolishing indiscriminately."[94] The target of the slicing and dicing was the marine quarters in the lower casbah, known as the "public city" because of the spaces of public life like souk, mosques, and later, military and administrative quarters. The upper casbah, or the private city of some fifty ethnic neighborhoods, was spared such intervention, at least initially.

Urbanists Marcello Balbo and Guido Moretti documented the historic transformation of the casbah and the growth of the colonial city surrounding the native city from 1830 to 1895.[95] Figure 7.19 shows the colonial transformation in the urban fabric of the casbah during this period. Figure 7.20 shows four historical snapshot sketches the authors prepared of this remarkable transformation in a span of sixty-five years. Military necessities required the initial intervention by clearing out a large part of the historic fabric in order to create a *place d'armes*, as shown in the 1833 map, followed by street widening for north-south connections. The construction of the new colonial city began soon thereafter to the south of the casbah along the coast. Because of the difficult topography, the rectilinear grid had to be adjusted to negotiate the steep terrain. The layout of the new colonial city had begun to establish a new order, scale and geometry very different from the organic urban form of the casbah within the Ottoman walls. After the initial intervention and improvements of the casbah the colonial authorities shifted their attention to the planning and design of the new urban additions. The physical condition of the old city deteriorated through neglect. As argued by Algerian sociologist Djaffar Lesbet,[96] this process eventually led to a system of self-governance and civic activism that transformed the casbah into an *espace contre* (or "counter space"), symbolizing the opposition to colonial power.[97]

By 1880 obsession with defense led to a new fortification circumscribing the new colonial city and enfolding the original native city. But the antipodic relationship between "the casbah and French Algiers, crystallized further by the former's "counter space" character, destroyed any possibility of overall harmony in a situation distinct to French colonial urbanism."[98] To paraphrase Fanon, there was never a chance for any conciliation, the *intramuros* locations notwithstanding, because of their mutual exclusivity.[99]

In another fifteen years the colonial development extended much further south beyond the new wall. Meanwhile, necessities of the colonial economy and mercantile prosperity had led to significant transformation of the marine quarters. At the turn of the century, the French colonial architecture and urban design went through another phase of development overtures for Algiers that included visionary schemes of Le Corbusier for the city and the marine quarter.

As we have seen in the case of British India, the ideology of power and a sense of superiority often represented the subaltern with a myth of femininity. As Çelik has pointed out, this was true in the case of Algiers as well. In the writings of French travelers, writers,

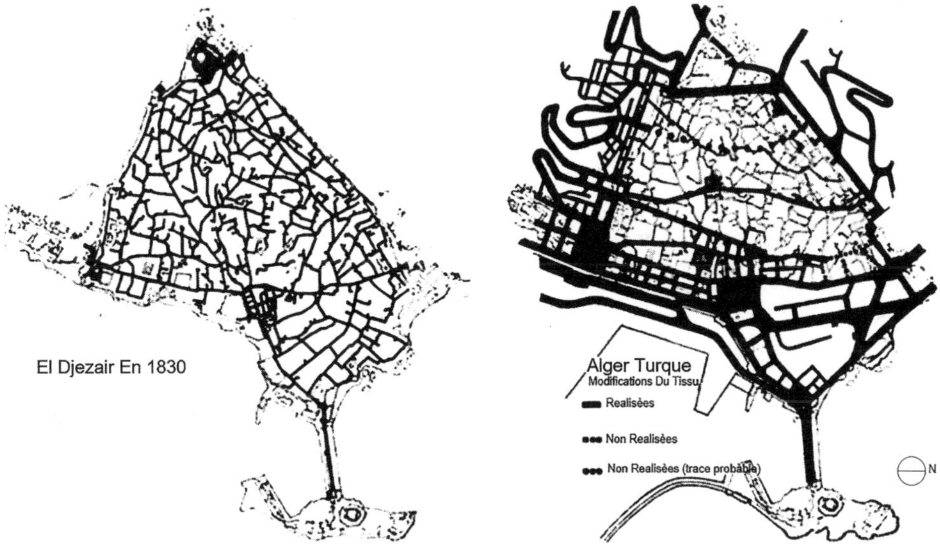

Figure 7.19
Indigenous walled city or casbah of Algiers—the organic form (above) and the Haussmannian surgery of the colonial times.
Source: Balbo and Moretti (1973), figure 19, with permission from Marcelo Balbo and Guido Moretti.

intellectuals, administrators, and military officers, Algerian women became the "key symbols of the colony's cultural identity."[100] This trope will be extended to the traditional cities, especially the casbah, and none other than Le Corbusier himself developed this metaphor in describing the exotic, private, and organic nature of the casbah's urban form, and represented this mythology in his sketches from his *Poésie sur Alger* (see figure 7.21).[101]

Italian Legacy

Compared to French, British, and earlier Spanish colonial history, the Italian record was limited both in space and in time. Geographically its major colonial territories in Africa included Tripolitania, Cirenaica (or Cyrenaica), Eritrea, and Somalia, which Italy controlled from the late nineteenth century through the first half of the twentieth century. In addition, Ethiopia was an Italian protectorate from 1889 to 1896.[102]

The colonial project helped unify Italy and also helped it assert its claim on modernity and on becoming a modern political power. Despite the popular perception of the Italians as humane or at least benign colonizers, the record shows very similar patterns of exclusion, segregation, alterity, and hegemony that all other colonial powers had

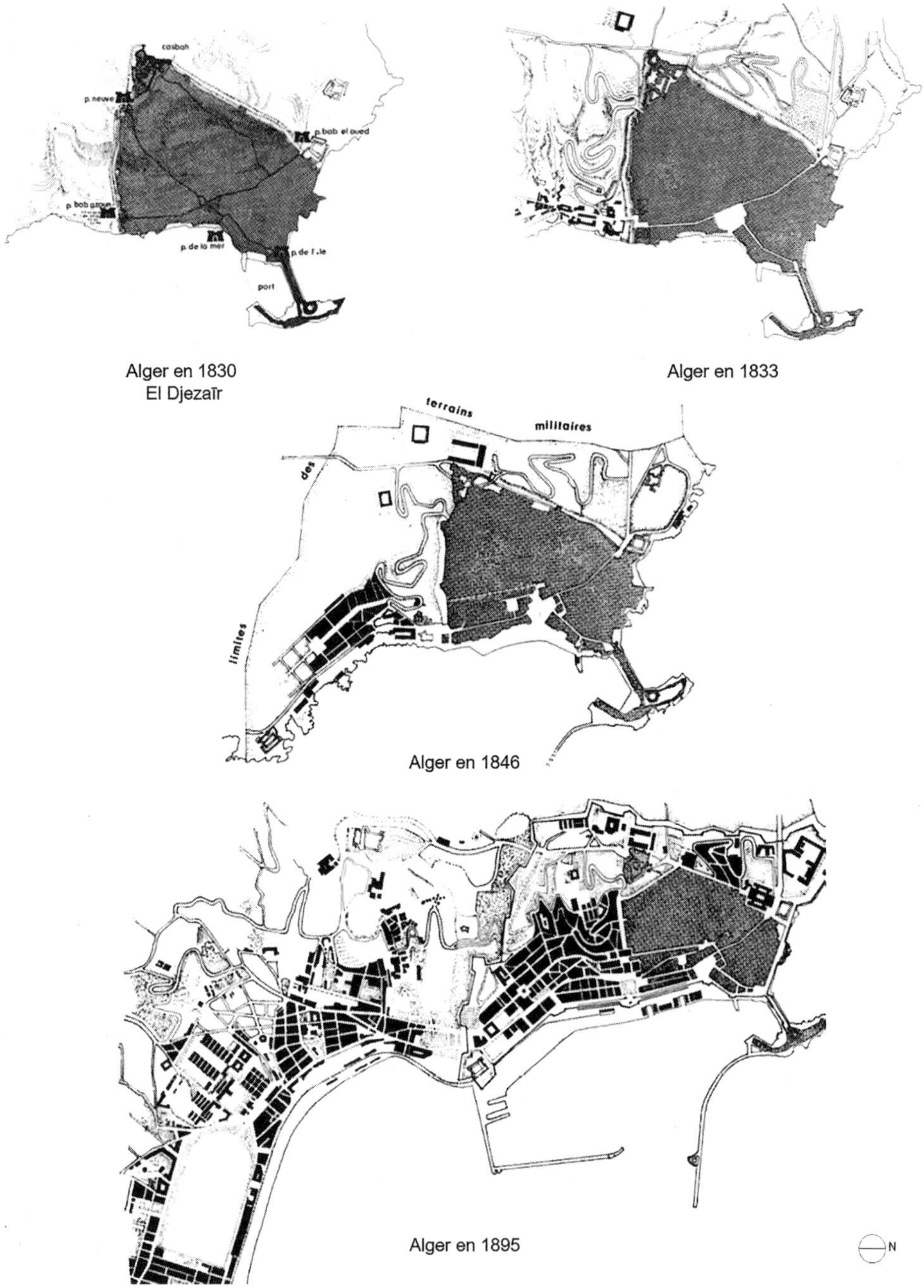

Figure 7.20

The nineteenth-century urban transformation of colonial Algiers, and the increasingly subaltern role of the indigenous city, insulated by a *cordon sanitaire*.

Source: Balbo and Moretti (1973), figures 11 and 18, with permission from Marcelo Balbo and Guido Moretti.

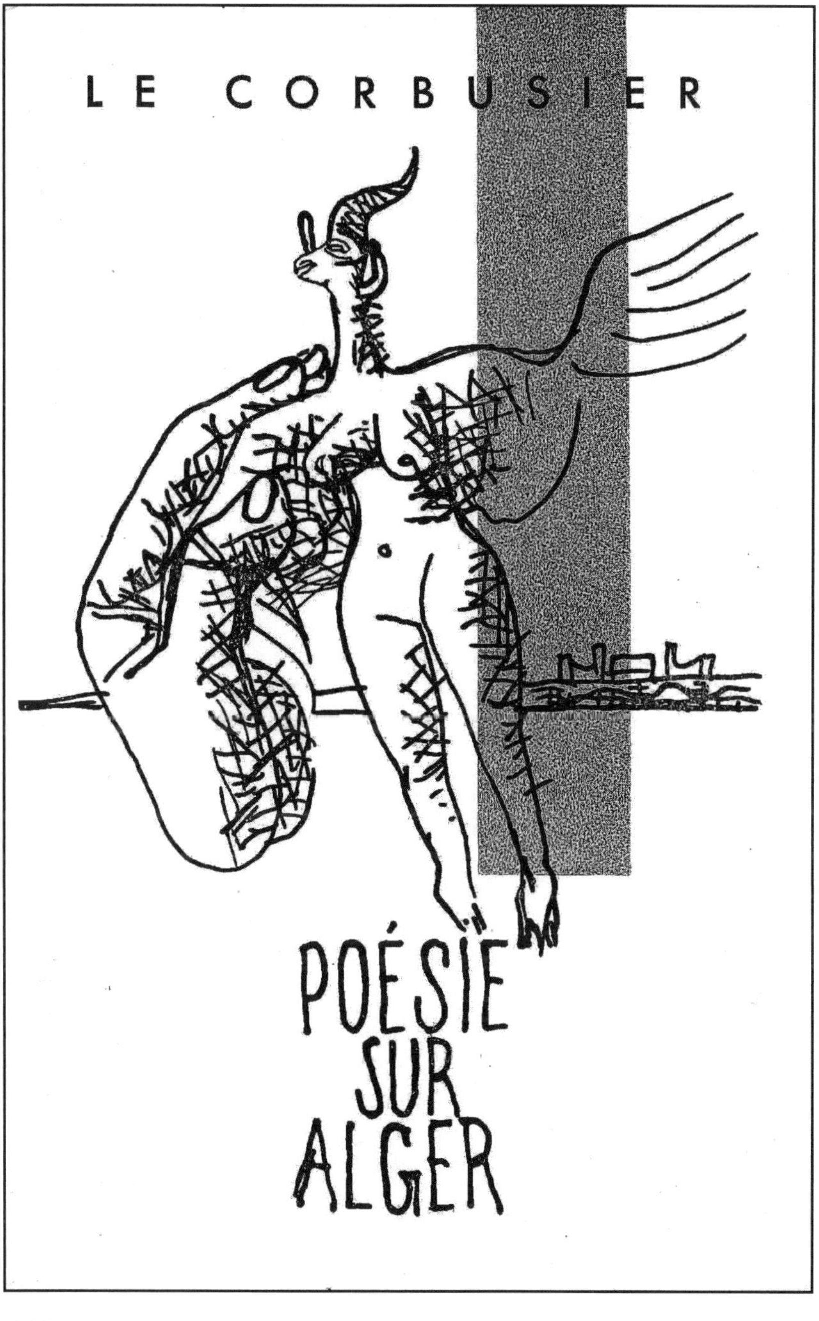

Figure 7.21
Le Corbusier's sketch for the cover of *Poésie sur Alger*.
Source: By permission of Fondation Le Corbusier.

displayed.[103] It is also apparent that skin color played an important role in the "othering" of the colonized. Libya was considered much closer to the homeland, because of its lighter-skinned Arab population, but also because of its history as a former Roman colony. Its status as a protectorate rather than a colony served a strategic purpose—to create an alliance with the Arab-Muslim world to thwart the colonial ambitions of the British and the French.[104] There was no strict segregation between the Italians and the indigenous population, the Arab housing typology was similar to Roman *domus*, and the colonial residential architecture reflected interpretation of the traditional style.[105]

It is possible that the Italians in the metropole saw their colonial project as humanitarian and civilizing, according to the shared Western images of how the colonies might develop. Rural and agricultural development was a major tenet of their colonial policies, as the Italians planted vineyards and olive groves in the desert land and arid climate using innovative techniques of afforestation.[106]

The benevolent and benign image of the colonial regime in part reflected a much less aggressive or invasive regime. As urban historian Ruth Ben-Ghiat and cultural anthropologist Mia Fuller point out, Italy could never approach the scale of profits realized by the colonial ventures of Britain or France. Italy was a relatively minor colonial power and because of its limited resources and absence of private investment many of the professional ambitions for various settlement schemes never materialized.[107] This is probably why the Italians showed much greater restraint in protecting the indigenous walled city of Tripoli, for example. Because of its Roman past it was seen as a familiar environment not requiring any major intervention. Also, unlike the British and French city design, there was no obvious *cordon sanitaire* separating the native city from that of the colonists. In East Africa, however, as the Italians applied their modern town-planning laws in developing master plans for the new types of land use required of a colonial economy—manufacturing, storage, business quarters, and the like—segregation between the "native town" and the "settlers' town" became all too obvious. Nevertheless, an earlier colonial plan for Addis Ababa shows a clear separation between the two towns, and the subaltern nature of the Native Town is even legible in the street grid and the "grain" of the urban form.[108] The 1936 plan proposed by Le Corbusier similarly ignores the endogenous urban form in imposing his modernist design. (See figure 7.22.) The plan for Harar similarly shows the clarity with which the design principles of the colonial plan relegated the native town—*Vecchia Harar*—to a subaltern status. Similar patterns were evident also in plans for cities like Benghazi.[109]

In the early part of the twentieth century the Italian architectural and urban design efforts were principally devoted to the shaping of the new business and civic centers

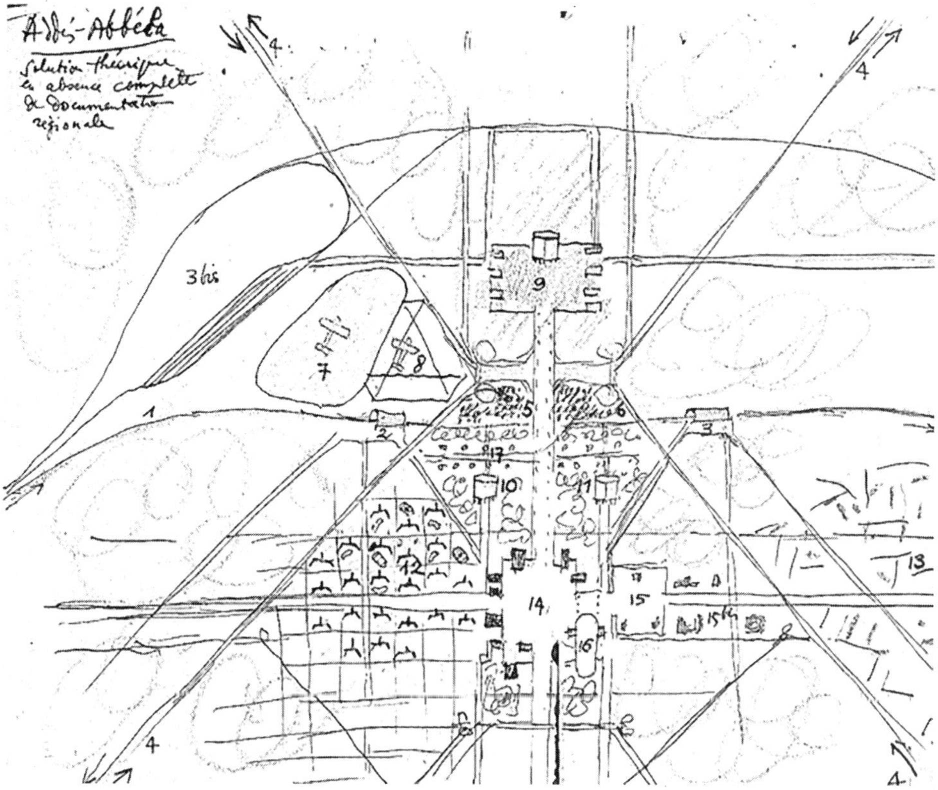

Figure 7.22
Le Corbusier's 1936 plan for the colonial Addis Ababa.
Source: By permission of Fondation Le Corbusier.

in the principal colonial cities. Markets and squares of the traditional North African cities were designed in the images of the European motherland. These civic and public spaces often included arcades similar to those in Italian cities like Bologna, and architecture reflecting some modernist derivatives of the classical style with occasional touches of simplified local architectural tradition. These spaces and buildings constructed during the 1920s and 1930s Fascist regime were a part of the Italian strategy of asserting authority and control over the Libyan cities. While the planners attempted to segregate the Europeans and the natives in separate residential districts, according to historian Krystyna von Henneberg "hybrid civic spaces" were "technocratically created 'organic' (or pseudo-organic) spaces, usually in the form of piazzas, marketplaces, and fairgrounds."[110] She further argues that the hybridity of design was an attempt to attract multicultural users and controlled mingling in an orderly way.

Perhaps one of the more symbolic expressions of the hybridity of the Italian colonial modernism was the construction of the Tripoli Trade Fair, inaugurated in 1927, four years before the better-known international colonial exposition opened in Paris. As argued by Patricia A. Morton, the mission of architecture often was to display the contrast and differences between Europe and its colonies, the civilized and the savage, the developed and the underdeveloped.[111] The "representational divide" of the Paris Colonial Exposition was symbolized by two types of pavilions, the ones containing the tableaux of French civilization, constructed in the classical or Art Deco style, and those containing colonial artifacts, designed in the indigenous style. By making this difference explicit, the architecture of the Paris exposition in effect symbolized Europe's civilizing mission: "The *mission civilisatrice* was the responsibility of the civilized white race to bring enlightenment and progress to the benighted savages of the world in the form of colonization."[112] The Tripoli Trade Fair exposition, in contrast, while symbolizing similar hybrid architecture, attempted to display "the empire in its kinder, gentler incarnation."[113] Most of the colonial pavilions in this exposition were syncretic architecture with ersatz icons of the indigenous Islamic tradition.

Summing Up

The colonial era had a profound effect on the form, structure, and hierarchy of cities in the developing countries. It marked a major disruption and disjuncture from the traditional institutions, norms, and uses of space. While the colonial era ushered in modernity—in institutions, in technologies, in belief systems—which had even deeper social and psychological effects than what is manifested in the physical form, the transition has been violent, oppressive, hegemonic and polarizing. In every instance, the colonial era meant domination, control, and subalternity of the indigenous people and their spaces. Where the liberal conscience of modernity questioned the very morality of the colonial enterprise, the cognitive dissonance was rendered mute by invoking the noble aim of civilizing the savage and liberating the oppressed.

In the arena of spatial and urban development, it is possible to discern several recurring themes that capture the nature and extent of the colonial order and organization, despite the inherent cultural and historical differences among the various colonizing powers. These generic themes can be described under the following headings.

(a) Transformation of the Existing Settlement System

One of the most significant impacts of the colonial project is the distortion and uneven spatial development of the precolonial, indigenous landscape. Historian Richard Morse discussed how the evenly distributed system of cities of precolonial Latin America was distorted into a primate distribution in the colonial times as the new port cities gained importance with the growth of the colonial mercantile economy.[114] Urban primacy, and later overurbanization, increased, as the mercantile economy yielded to the new industrial economy, increasing rural-urban productivity difference and the attendant income gap.

The four major megacities of India today—Chennai, Delhi, Kolkata, and Mumbai—were either founded or transformed by the colonial power, overshadowing earlier precolonial cities. The French colonial rule had a similar impact on the existing hierarchy of cities in Morocco and the Maghreb more generally. The rank-ordering of the twenty-five largest cities of the world by century shows clearly that the cities that dominated in the precolonial era were typically interior rather than coastal cities, and are now all but forgotten in terms of their contemporary significance (see table 2.3).

(b) Beginning of an "Urban Apartheid"[115]

Spatial segregation and isolation of the native population from the European settlements, often by creating a *cordon sanitaire* for security and health reasons, and sometimes in the pretext of conservation of existing culture, led to a de facto apartheid, or at best a new order or caste system. This caste system corresponded to the various orders of subalternity among the population. This was in fact the beginning of a dualistic urban form.

(c) Colonial "Urban Romanticism with the European Motherland"[116]

The conquest of the colonies of alien and intimidating landscape, ecology, and climate challenged the European settlers to seek the familiarity and comfort of the motherland. This often led to romantic recreations of buildings and landscapes, often incongruous in the native setting, but serving nevertheless the purpose of inspiring awe among the natives, and thus claiming the superiority of the ruling class.

In the postcolonial years the physical traces of this era, while enduring in some form, are becoming increasingly invisible. In some instances this is a result of a decolonization process—a deliberate erasure and rewriting of the text of the city—as buildings and statues are taken down, or the streets and squares are renamed. Today, one has to make a special expedition to find the remains of the Dutch colonial Batavia in the sprawling and teeming metropolis of Jakarta. The colonial buildings still line the waterfront Bund in Shanghai, but the colonial enclaves have long lost their identities as high-rise towers sprouted all over those neighborhoods during China's real estate boom. Much of British Kolkata still remains, but it is increasingly declining in significance with the peripheral growth of the metropolis. The same is true of Lutyens' Delhi, which is seemingly shrinking in size and importance as the urban sprawl of Delhi continues outward. These postcolonial urban transformations will be the focus in the next section of the book.

III The Postcolonial Era

8 Postcolonial Utopias

> Le Corbusier's concept of city planning appealed to the modernizing vision of Jawaharlal Nehru, the builder of modern India. Nehru wanted Chandigarh to be the symbol of forward-looking new India, a city of prestige, a city of progress, reflecting the pride of Punjab and the pride of new India. He said: "Let it be the first large expression of our genius flowering on our newly earned freedom." Thus a historic role, a representational role, was cast upon Chandigarh right from its inception.
>
> —K. R. Narayanan[1]

According to the dictionary, utopia is an ideal place or state of perfection that offers the best of human experience. Another sense of the word is that it is something impractical, a pipe dream, something that can never be achieved. This second meaning corresponds to the Latin meaning of the word—"noplace"—or the similar Greek meaning that combines *ou* (not) and *topos* (place) that may also mean "nonplace." Of course, this is not the intention of utopian thinking in community design and planning. Yet this was precisely what the modernist design of postcolonial new capitals achieved: nonplaces. These new capitals became icons of progress, of modernity, and a clean break from the traditional way of life. They represented a search for an appropriate image of development, at least an exemplar or a model, if not a catalyst of change, as anthropologist James Holston has argued in his critical treatise on Brasília.[2] The intentions, the associated mythology, and most importantly, their design, made these new capitals postcolonial utopias. The design, production, and evolution of new capitals became the epitome of the postcolonial urban development. Abuja in Nigeria, Brasília in Brazil, Chandigarh in India, Dodoma in Tanzania, and Islamabad in Pakistan are cases in point. In addition, capitol complexes would be built in such cities as Port Moresby in Papua New Guinea, Colombo in Sri Lanka, Kuwait City in Kuwait, Dhaka in Bangladesh, and Putrajaya in Malaysia—all "in search of national identity," as planning historian Lawrence Vale observed.[3]

Some observers commented in jest that the two most important symbols of the postcolonial autonomy and independent nationhood were a national airline and a new capital. By the seventies, World Bank economists declared new towns an elite profligacy and refused to finance them any further.

Meanwhile, Chandigarh and Brasília are the two new capitals whose planning and architecture have long captivated the design professions, while provoking critical commentaries from the humanities and the social sciences. Much has been written about the history of planning, design, and development of these cities, and about their contemporary realities. These narratives underscore the curious irony of why the Western images of modernity serve as proxy for development and continue to guide and influence a postcolonial search for autonomy and identity.

Chandigarh

The end of the colonial era in the Indian subcontinent in 1947 came with the "partitioning" of the British colony into a primarily Hindu India, and a Muslim Pakistan. The state of Punjab was one casualty of this partition, as the line of nationhood was drawn through the state dividing it into two parts. Lahore, the principal city of previously undivided Punjab, became part of Pakistan, making it apparent that the Indian side of Punjab needed a new capital for political exigency. Because Lutyens' Delhi was already in place, finished barely three decades earlier, the case for another new capital for the republic was out of the question. The new capital for Punjab created an appropriate proxy to showcase the modern face of the new nation.

In India disaffection for Lutyens' Delhi—the new colonial city completed less than two decades before the British left India—continued to simmer in the collective consciousness of the independence movement through the waning years of the colonial rule. The alien street layout of Baroque style, the classical neo-Palladian architecture, the arrogant domination of the natural landscape, the dismissal of the historic connection between the city and the river, and the deliberate distancing from Shahjahanabad, the old walled city, were all seen as symbolic of power, domination, and control. For someone like Gandhi, the cities of the colonial era represented simultaneously the symbol of India's subaltern status, and also an antithesis to traditional life and values represented by its villages, where 80 percent of the population lived at that time. According to Sunil Khilnani, a professor of politics, "He recognized the extent to which the British Raj was a creature of its cities, and knew how little they meant to the lives of most Indians."[4]

Gandhi's well-known antipathy for cities, however, was not necessarily shared by the other leaders, who believed in cities as the prime movers of modernity and progress. While rejecting the colonial city—especially New Delhi—as pompous, sterile, and lacking urbanity, Nehru for one, spoke lovingly of the traditional Indian cities: "There is the spirit and the genius of an ancient city, where almost every stone tells you a story, where history is embedded even in the dirty lanes ... it has a definite and positive atmosphere which you can feel in your bones."[5] As Khilnani points out, Nehru apparently made a distinction between the modernity of the colonial city which he saw as "inauthentic" and a modernity that is "genuine, productive, and universal" represented by cities of modern industry and commerce.[6]

It is this quest for the authentic, productive, and universal modernity that would lead to Nehru's patronage and ownership of the planning, design, and development of the new capital of Punjab.[7] This association of Chandigarh with Nehru's image of modernity is commonly assumed and indeed attributed to some of the oft-quoted statements of Nehru, especially the one from his first visit to the location: "The site chosen is free from existing encumbrances of old towns and old traditions. Let it be the first large expression of our creative genius flowering on our newly earned freedom."[8] This rhetorical endorsement, seemingly contradictory given his earlier praise of traditional Indian cities, may actually have to do with the political impossibility of selecting the other two candidate sites near two existing urban centers—Ambala and Ludhiana—and the fact that the Chandigarh site was more central, further away from the Pakistani border. The site was also the least expensive. Despite his strategic endorsements and oversight of various stages of Chandigarh's planning process, Nehru was not responsible for the initial choice of either the site or its famous architect, Le Corbusier.

The planning of Chandigarh was already underway for almost two years when Le Corbusier arrived in India. Albert Mayer, an American planner, prepared the initial master plan. His associate, the talented architect and urban designer Matthew Nowicki from Poland, added further refinements to the Mayer plan. Mayer had met Nehru two years before independence and discussed his views about future city planning in India, which Nehru approved, while urging him to think of "model villages" that would emphasize "good housing, sanitation, and community structure."[9] Nehru's suggestion must have resonated well with Mayer's predilections for urban village concepts rooted in the ideology of the Garden City movement. Mayer subscribed to the ideas originally championed by architect-planner Clarence Stein in his classic paradigm for new towns that incorporated the concept of the superblock, and the "neighborhood unit" principle developed by urban planner Clarence Perry.[10]

Responding to Nehru's exhortations to plan the city and community utilizing Western technology, "without breaking up the old foundations" of India and to "fit it into Indian resources and Indian conditions,"[11] Mayer proceeded to develop the plan for Chandigarh drawing from his convictions about the Garden City paradigm.[12] The principal organizing element, not surprisingly, was the residential unit, albeit not quite in the Perry model of "neighborhood unit," advanced for the New York regional plan, and in sufficient variety to fit the socioeconomic classes and diversity of an Indian city. The second organizing principle drew from the site characteristics—topography, rivers, and streams—to structure the residential spaces, the circulation and open space systems, and the various functional foci of the new city. Finally, the plan considered social customs and traditions of the region in thinking about spaces for bicycle traffic, schools, shopping areas, and the like within these districts. The result was a "fan-shaped" plan—dictated largely by the natural courses of two existing rivers to the east and the west—with curvilinear streets and informal organization (see figure 8.1). This layout, vaguely

Figure 8.1
Albert Mayer's original plan for Chandigarh.
Source: A schematic redrawn from Evenson (1989), Plate No. 1.

reminiscent of Frederick Law Olmsted's 1869 plan for the residential suburb of Riverside, clearly represented a break from the Baroque traditions of geometrical order that influenced the layout of many colonial cities, including New Delhi, or for that matter the rational modernity of the American grid already rejected by the Garden City movement. Conscious of the vehicular traffic problems of American cities, and fond of the pedestrian culture of traditional Indian cities, in his plan Mayer isolated the high-speed vehicular traffic from the slow-moving traffic, thus containing the quotidian life of the pedestrian culture largely within the neighborhood space.

Proposing a major break from the traditional Indian city, where the center has traditionally always been reserved for the administrative or religious authority and power—temple, mosque, or imperial palace—Mayer's plan proposed to locate the capitol complex at the northern edge, at the top of the map, and outside the organized structure of the city. This gesture and the plan more generally, thought architectural historian Norma Evenson, echoed the concept of *Ville radieuse* advanced earlier by Le Corbusier.[13] Using an organic metaphor and a romantic stretch of the imagination, historian Ravi Kalia thought that the placement of the capitol was "analogous to that of the head in relationship to the body," and that "Mayer was reaffirming the allegorical reference to the Indian caste structure in the story of *Purusha* (the Cosmic man), in which his head represents the Brahmin (the priest-thinker), his arms represent the *Kashtriya* [*sic*] (the soldier), his thighs represent the *Vaishya* (commoner), and his feet represent the *Sudra* (the slave)."[14] In the canonical model of the Indian city discussed previously, it will be recalled that the *vāstu-purusa-mandala* (*mandala* of Vastu-Purusha) shows the central square in this ideal layout is devoted to Brahmā as the highest order of hierarchy. If anything, it is the earlier Chinese canonical cities, like the 700 CE Chang'an (modern Xi'an) or the 800 CE Kyoto (influenced by the Chinese model),[15] that can be imagined as the precursor of the Mayer plan, and as we will see, the subsequent plan for Chandigarh by Le Corbusier.

Le Corbusier arrived in India in 1951, having been selected by two officials of the Punjab government—P. N. Thapar and P. L. Verma—who went abroad, ironically at the urging of Mayer himself, to initially look for talented architects who could give the shape and form to the architectural projects that would define the identity of the new town.[16] This was a historical moment indeed in the annals of modern city planning and urban design. "Twice in the 20th century," writes Khilnani, "India has been visited by architectural megalomaniacs," referring to the fact that Le Corbusier's work began "barely 20 years after imperial New Delhi was completed to Lutyens's plan."[17]

Unquestionably Le Corbusier was a talented architect who began his career in paintings and sculptures of the cubist genre. In his architecture he gave new forms and expressions of modernity exploiting contemporary materials and the construction technology of reinforced concrete. In his thinking about city design Le Corbusier tried to combine the technical order of modernity with the natural order of life and humanity, some of which were no doubt derived from the International Congress of Modern Architecture (CIAM) discourses in the first half of the last century. While producing brilliant design that created a whole new paradigm of modern architecture, Le Corbusier's life and work also represented what architectural theorist Charles Jencks refers to as "tragic" and a "concomitant failure" of modernity—"everyone today is well aware that a house is both more and less than 'a machine for living in,' that city planning cannot be over-simplified into four different functions."[18]

Le Corbusier, however, thrived on the criticism and rejection of his many city design and planning visions over a period of years before he was invited to design Chandigarh.[19] After having done seven different schemes for Algiers,[20] and also plans for Stockholm, Moscow, Buenos Aires, Montevideo, Rio de Janeiro, Paris (several), Zurich, Antwerp, Barcelona, New York, Bogotá, Saint-Dié, La Rochelle-Pallice, and Marseille, none of which was ever accepted or implemented, the invitation to plan Chandigarh was a major redemption of Le Corbusier's talented but tormented career as an architect, sculptor, and painter. It was an enormous boost to his ego, despite the meager financial reward offered by his poor Indian clientele.[21]

Contrary to the common belief that Le Corbusier scrapped the earlier Mayer plan and began afresh, his plan actually retained many features of the previous scheme: location of the capitol complex at the top of the layout; placement of the developed area between the two river courses; location of the central business district; the course of a natural stream as an open space corridor; the residential sector as an organizing principle; basic dimensions of the new sectors close to the average size of the Mayer plan; and a hierarchy of street system designed to accommodate the slow moving vehicles typical of Indian streets. The plan proposed by Le Corbusier standardized the sector dimensions to 1,200 meters by 800 meters, proportions ostensibly inspired by the distances between the Tuileries, Place de la Concorde, and Place l'Étoile and glorified by Le Corbusier in his design rhetoric, its arbitrary nature and irrelevance to the Indian context notwithstanding.[22] Earlier, Mayer had reasoned similar dimensions based on walkable scale, which Le Corbusier also endorsed. However, he further reasoned the legitimacy of these dimensions as multiples of 100 meters by 100 meters Spanish "*cuadras*" and that bus stops in Paris are typically spaced 200 meters apart.[23] As noted earlier, the main organizing principle proposed by Le Corbusier involved the "V7"(*les sept voie*) hierarchy of movement system, which further embellished and rationalized—drawing from the CIAM principles—Mayer's idea of separating the pedestrian and slow-moving vehicles from the fast-moving ones. Thus the plan evolved on the basis of the best practices—the "images"—of Western industrial economies, infused with the ideals of the Garden City[24] and the CIAM movement.[25] Ironically, both had their roots in the intellectual opposition to the urbanism and urban outcomes of the contemporary industrial economies.[26]

A January 1999 symposium celebrating 50 years of Chandigarh (the site was selected in early 1948, immediately after India's independence on August 15, 1947) brought together an impressive collection of international architects and planners, with a sprinkling of humanists and social scientists.[27] The talks and seminars in this celebration included the usual homage to Le Corbusier and his associates, and also reflections on the architecture, planning, and urbanism of the city—some nostalgic, some romantic, and some critical—but in the main reconfirming the social, indeed largely professional, construction of Chandigarh as "a mythical place," a city based on "the myth of liberation, of escape from empire, and Modernism," as one participant aptly put it.[28]

The mythology of Chandigarh, one could argue, is an artifact of the search for an image of development that the leadership of India—Prime Minister Nehru, in particular—was trying to define. The inaugural address by K. R. Narayanan, the president of India, on this celebratory occasion captured this sentiment quite succinctly (see the epigraph to this chapter). In this speech Narayanan also invoked another oft-quoted saying by Nehru, who wanted a city "unfettered by the traditions of the past," which seemed to inhere in Le Corbusier's "high modernist"[29] vision of the new capital promised to deliver while embedding "in the matrix of the Indian civilization standing tip-toed at the door-step of the modern age."[30] Indeed, Le Corbusier's rather blunt but poignant rhetoric about the elusive image of development reflects his own patronizing view on this matter:

> India had, and always has had a peasant culture, which has existed for thousand years! India possesses Hindu temples ... and Muslim temples [*sic*] ... whose architecture is very geometrical. India also possesses Maharaja's palaces and gardens, but India has not created an architecture for modern civilization (offices, factory buildings). India jumps suddenly into the second era of modernization. Instead of sinking into the groupings and errors of the first era, we will be able to fill our mission: to give India the architecture of modern times (modern techniques, modern mind, the adaptations to surrounding conditions that are extreme over there).[31]

In other words, Le Corbusier found India lacking a "modern mind" and thus an endogenous image of modernity. And this he proposed to remedy in the planning and design of Chandigarh, as a demonstration of what the image of modernity would look like in the circumstances—climate, culture, and society—of India. But he did not promise endogeneity.

Apparently Le Corbusier delivered what Nehru was looking for—an icon of modernity and progress—which he didn't find in the earlier plan by Albert Mayer and its more idyllic Garden City image, never mind that Le Corbusier's reformulation of the Mayer plan was not that drastic.[32] Indeed, the existence of the Mayer plan may have spared Le Corbusier from having to start from scratch, a daunting task for someone who was essentially an architect, with naive views of urbanism and cities. Le Corbusier's "Voisin Plan" for Paris epitomized his attempt to build the future city of modernity with geometric clarity by erasing the old, organic, complex and incomprehensible (to him) text of medieval Paris. Since the Mayer plan had already offered some clarity and structure in organizing the life and functions of the proposed city, Le Corbusier's own contribution to the Chandigarh plan (see figure 8.2) was limited to rather schematic embellishments on the original proposal. The "genetic code" of current Chandigarh can be easily traced to the original Mayer plan. The Garden City legacy still continues in the official branding of Chandigarh by its Union Territory government[33] as the "city of gardens."

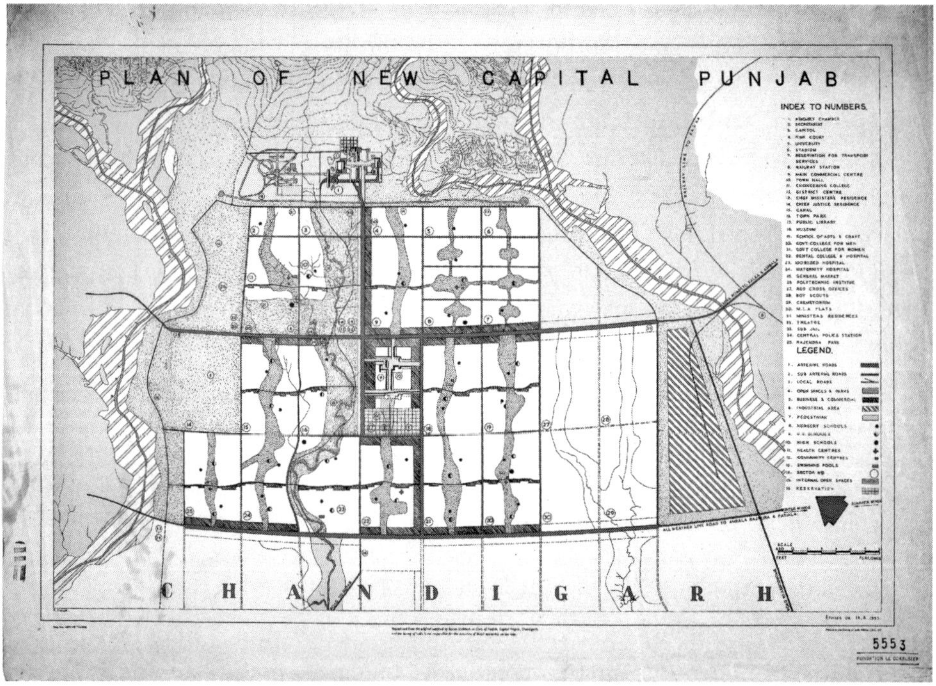

Figure 8.2
Le Corbusier's plan for Chandigarh.
Source: By permission of Fondation Le Corbusier.

Regardless of how credit is ultimately apportioned, there is no question that the plan of Chandigarh was influenced by two parallel and more or less contemporaneous modern movements in planning—the Garden City paradigm of Anglo-American vintage, and the CIAM principles of a broader international, and mainly European, origin. Two very different and contradictory ideologies of Mayer and Le Corbusier—both imported from the West—struggled to define a vision of modernity unique to India. While Mayer tried to capture the endogenous urbanism of Indian cities, Le Corbusier was largely dismissive of the endogenous urbanism alien to him. The mythology of Chandigarh was born out of these conflated Western ideologies.

In this imported image, the urban heritage of India—its sensorium, its form, its urbanism, and indeed its habitus—was conveniently ignored, or at worst dismissed. It will be recalled that in a previous quote Le Corbusier had reduced the urban tradition of India to architecture of palaces, gardens, and temples. In all of the Le Corbusier's travels in India, *charpais*,[34] cows, arid plains, and shade trees seemed to be his most memorable elements to capture the essence of India, as evident from his sketches and writings. There was very little mention of the urban tradition or habitus of Indian cities. In his mind the verve of Indian cities, like the medieval quarters of Paris or the casbah in Algiers, was messy and incomprehensible that can only be cured by the clarity of the grid, the separation of traffic, and spatial ordering of land use and residential areas.

This clarity, hierarchy, and order that Le Corbusier sought to achieve in defining the image of modernity for urban India unfortunately led to class segregation and social exclusion of the poor from the planned city. The sectors of Chandigarh were allocated by official rank and social class, thus institutionalizing a practice begun in colonial times as in the Lutyens plan for imperial Delhi. The practice reminds us that the order of *homo hierarchicus*[35] in this exogenous model remained recalcitrant to the institutions of democracy and egalitarianism that are supposed to be intrinsic to the images of modernity and development. While the social ecology of traditional and even contemporary Indian cities endures mixing of classes,[36] the planned ecology of Chandigarh showed little tolerance for such mix, reminiscent of the social order of ancient cities. In particular, the planners—the grand master included—failed to make provisions for the workers who toiled hard to dig the trenches, lay the bricks, pour concrete, and pave the roads of this new city. Migrant workers from the poor rural countryside did not have a place to stay. So, they created their own informal settlements—*jhuggies*[37]—in the marginal spaces of public rights of way, or in the fringes of the construction sites. As architect Madhu Sarin pointed out in a well-documented study, barely ten years after the construction began, many of the temporary shanties had become permanent settlements by the roadside along with an active informal economy—roadside teashops and *dhabas*.[38] These intrusions of informality and poverty were offensive to the wealthy, powerful, and the elite who considered them to be "eyesores" that corrupted the aesthetic order of the city. Of course, many of these settlements now have been removed and consigned to walled enclaves or peripheral land.

It would be unjust to deny Le Corbusier's effort to define an indigenous modernity in his architectural forms. He and his colleagues undertook careful studies to develop design innovations like deep louvers (or *brise-soleil*) and overhangs and recessed doors and windows to minimize exposure to sun and the harsh climatic conditions of the region. The unique and rather striking architectural form he proposed for the buildings in the capitol complex—the high court, the assembly, and the secretariat—reflected these considerations (see figure 8.3). Yet large glass windows behind the louvers still do not make sense from the climatic point of view, nor in particular does the urban design of the capitol complex, a composition of buildings and spaces in an elegant geometry in the plan view, where these buildings are separated by vast empty spaces paved in cement and fully exposed to the blazing Punjab sun for most of the year. Why Le Corbusier would not want to plant some shade trees, whose functions he seemingly appreciated, should not be a mystery (see figure 8.4).

After all, trees would have masked his architecture and corrupted the distant views and visual compositions he so fastidiously planned. In fact, nature usually played a

Figure 8.3
The capitol complex, Chandigarh, looking west toward the Assembly Building (foreground) and the Secretariat Building (background), both designed by Le Corbusier.
Source: Courtesy of Deepak Bahl, 2019.

Figure 8.4
The Supreme Court, the third building in the capitol complex designed by Le Corbusier, looking east from the Secretariat Building across a vast expanse of concrete.
Source: Courtesy of Deepak Bahl, 2019.

very minor role, was often missing, and probably not welcome in most of Le Corbusier's architectural creations, urban projects, and in his sketches. What is impressive, however, is that after seventy years, the Chandigarh administration, which takes much pride in its gardens, has only recently moved to make the capital complex a more hospitable and humane public realm by sensitive landscaping that offers some shade and respite for the peons who had to deliver paperwork from one building to the other in the oppressive heat of northern India (see figure 8.5).

The reputation of Chandigarh as a "designer city" may be fading, but the original pattern still endures. The city has expanded enormously in two different directions from its originally planned twenty-three sectors to some eighty-one sectors. Much of this has extended into Mohali, the adjoining town to the southwest in the state of Punjab. Another twenty-one sectors have been added in Panchkula, to the east beyond the Industrial Area and the Sukhna Choe river in the state of Haryana, all religiously

Figure 8.5
A view of the Assembly Building—arguably an architectural jewel.
Source: Courtesy of Deepak Bahl, 2019.

adhering to the sector concept and its original dimensions as the basis of planning (see figure 8.6).

The planned open spaces inside the sectors serve their functions well for all residents, as does the designated sector-specific local commercial areas. It is not clear that there is much interaction between the sectors as Le Corbusier had imagined through the continuous green corridors weaving through the centers. Nevertheless, the streets internal to the sectors designed to serve local traffic, slow moving vehicles and pedestrians, as well as the neighborhood open spaces and community facilities seem to work well both in the poorer and more affluent sectors. In the wealthy sectors, however, original houses are now being unceremoniously demolished and replaced by mansions of larger footprints. Gone are the carefully controlled exposed brick and concrete architecture, replaced by pseudoclassical hyperreal[39] sandstone and marble facades of the mansions of the *nouveau riche* in Chandigarh, now the most prosperous city in India.[40]

Despite the order and control of the plan, sectors have developed their own ecology and specializations. Sector 17, the designated central business district, which has rather sterile modern architecture and large and empty public spaces, has become more animated and intensively used. A jumble of signs now masks the dull and drab exteriors

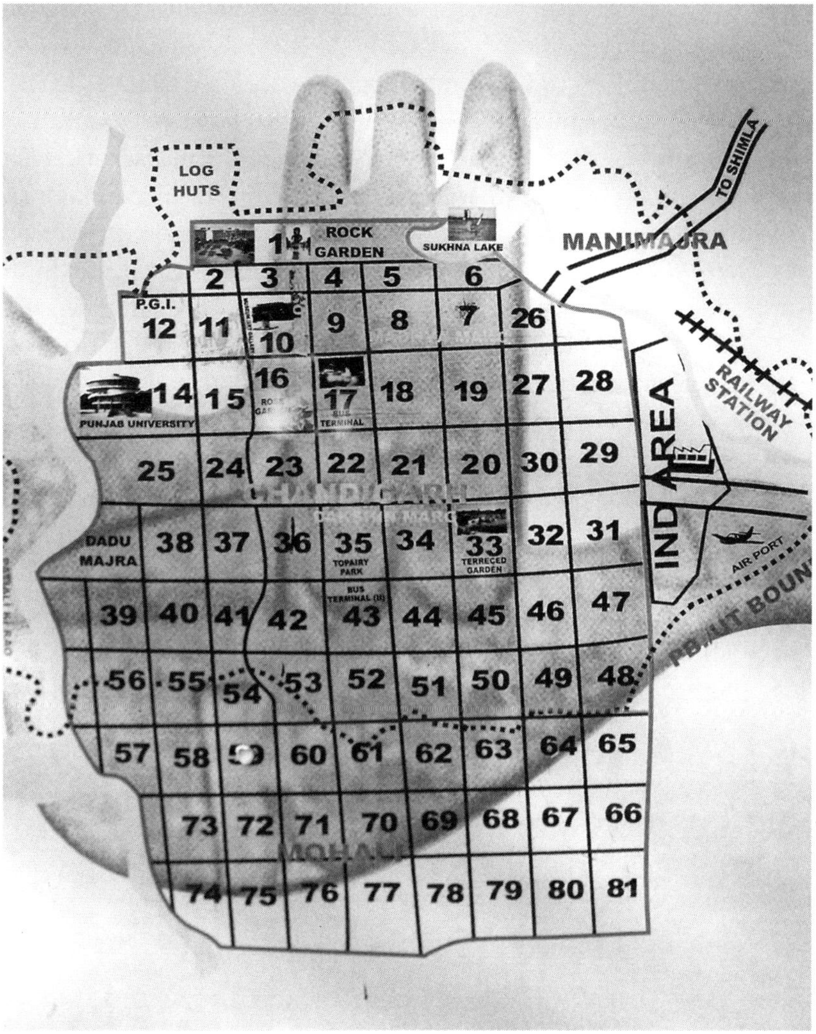

Figure 8.6

A schematic poster of contemporary Chandigarh, showing its expansion to include eighty-one sectors, growing from twenty-three in the original plan, superimposed on Le Corbusier's "open hand" ("*la main ouverte*") edict.

Source: Photo by author, 2004; original source unknown.

of the original modernist architecture. The public spaces are used for many different types of behavior settings.[41] The city authorities have converted the designated green areas into an impressive system of parks and open spaces (see figure 8.7). The major arterials are wide and function well to convey growing automobile traffic. However, streets separating the sectors do not have active building faces and lack street life. They are flanked by wide strips of open spaces on both sides, which continue to remain targets of "transit-oriented development"[42] or student design projects that propose to bring the street life back in Chandigarh like any other functioning cities in India or elsewhere.[43] Indeed the streets of Chandigarh lack the usual chaos, disorder, and verve of what Michael Sorkin saw as the "democratic" order of traffic in the streets of urban India.[44] In the early years of Chandigarh, a visitor from another city commented that Chandigarh was "quiet like a hospital ward."[45] Even today one might still consider the

Figures 8.7
A view of the linear park system based on the green corridors along existing streams as imagined in the original plan.
Source: Author, 2004.

city to be quiet and clean, almost antiseptic as a hospital ward, compared to the bedlam of typical Indian cities.

Brasília

Brasília was a postcolonial utopia deferred. It became a reality more than a century and a quarter after Brazil obtained its independence from the Portuguese in 1822. The postcolonial era in Brazil had begun, like most other Latin American countries, some hundred years before the decolonization occurred in Africa and Asia. But as the dependency theorists had argued, these postcolonial years were an era of dependent development where the "north" maintained a hegemonic relationship with Latin American "south," placing the entire continent into a subaltern status.[46] Furthermore, the dependent capitalism had failed to deliver the *doux commerce* promises of capitalism—the civilizing effect of market forces—because of what Albert O. Hirschman refers to as the "feudal shackle" of the Latin American societies.[47] According to this thesis vestiges of the feudal structure had gotten in the way of fulfilling the promises of the "bourgeois revolution," resulting in what economist Paul Baran referred to as "comprador bourgeoisie" or what was termed "lumpenbourgeoisie" by sociologist Andre Gunder Frank.[48]

The Brazilian desire for an inland capital was understandable in this context, because its major cities—Rio de Janeiro and São Paulo—were originally artifacts of uneven colonial spatial development, their coastal locations dictated by exigencies of trade, shipping, and imported labor of mercantile capitalism.[49] Their dominant role in the colonial urban hierarchy was further exacerbated by its dependent relationship and the consequent massive rural migration to cities in the first half of the twentieth century.

The idea of Brasília, however, goes back to the late-eighteenth-century colonial years, when many visionaries wanted to transfer the capital from the coast to the uninhabited virgin territories in the interior and at a more geographically central location. As anthropologist James Holston points out, this vision was shared by men of different and opposing ideological bent, and with different interests and political aims—from revolutionaries to colonial agents—"as a means of populating, developing, and securing Brazil's vast interior."[50] But it was not until the late nineteenth century, some seventy years into the postcolonial era, that the "idea of Brasília" would be finalized in the form of a constitutional decree that dedicated a 14,400-square-kilometer land to be found somewhere in the Central Plateau. The rationales for the move were several: more effective territorial control over the whole country; safety from future and possible attacks from sea; economic development of the interior, connecting the capital with other cities in the Brazilian system of cities by establishing axes of growth; achieving national integration; and so on.[51]

It would take another sixty years for this vision to become a reality. Juscelino Kubitschek was elected president in 1955, and the new capital and achieving national integration were two of his major campaign promises. Regional development of interior regions was a major strategy of his administration, and construction of the new capital and the infrastructure improvements needed for this purpose promised an enormous infusion of capital to the sparsely populated region selected for locating the new capital. Thus, the "idea of Brasília" was integral to the visions of economic growth and development, and to the images of modernity. Skeptics, however, questioned the feasibility of the project, and the very idea itself. This was countered by a clever campaign that "combined new world mythology and development theory in linking the foundation of a capital city with the foundation of a new Brazil,"[52] drawing from the images and visions entertained throughout the Brazilian history.

Since the presidential terms were limited to five years, Kubitschek was anxious to get the project underway and completed before the end of his term. Given the exigencies of the task, a specific site was chosen quickly, and arbitrarily, one might add. He then turned to Oscar Niemeyer, an old friend, to develop a plan for the new city. As architectural historian Norma Evenson observed, the choice of Niemeyer suggested "from the beginning that Brasília was to be an architect's, rather than a planner's city,"[53] an observation that could very well have applied to the case of Chandigarh as well. Niemeyer, a talented architect known for his modernist sculptural forms, agreed to design some of the main buildings of Brasília but also was persuaded by the Institute of Brazilian Architects to invite an international competition for the plan of the new capital.

The competition was formally announced by NOVACAP (Companhia Urbanizadora da Nova Capital do Brasil) in September 1956, with submissions due six months later by the middle of March the following year. Some twenty-six entries were received, and the individual schemes proved to be variations on the modernist concept of urban design popular among architects in those days. According to Evenson, those principles included such things as segregation of urban functions and activities; systems of traffic separation; residential superblocks with a mix of housing and apartment blocks; and unified design based on a sense of order and rational organization,[54] similar to the planning and design principles of Chandigarh formulated less than a decade earlier. Holston would succinctly characterize this urban design paradigm as the "CIAM city"—an artifact of the CIAM principles—which ultimately would dictate the final design of Brasília.[55] (See figure 8.8.)

Figure 8.8
Contemporary Brasília, aerial view.
Source: JPL, NASA, Creative Commons.

The design concept that won the competition was a rather minimalist and reluctant—as the designer noted with some modesty later—submission of few sketches and a schematic by well-known Brazilian architect-planner Lúcio Costa.[56] The jury liked the "monumentality" of Costa's scheme that seemingly trumped all other submissions. Costa's plan proposed a simple scheme of a cross defined by a monumental axis of civic and government functions, intersected by a residential axis gently curved to touch the base of an inverted equilateral triangle that would include housing and other quotidian necessities of shops, schools, recreation, and the like.

Ironically, as Vale notes, while the mythology of Brasília was very much linked to defining a postcolonial identity of progress and development, Costa himself invoked "colonial tradition" as a source of inspiration.[57] He called Brasília not a product of regional planning but a priming action for regional development—echoing Kubitschek's legitimizing rhetoric—as "a deliberate act of conquest, a gesture of pioneers acting in the spirit of their colonial traditions."[58] The symbolism of the cross—indeed, one can even read it as a crucifix[59]—while not incongruent in a predominantly Catholic country, certainly seemed to subordinate Brazil's secular tradition.[60]

In an insightful anthropological analysis of the history of Brasília's design, Holston argued that Costa's minimalist and modest entry in the competition using the symbolism of the cross was in effect an ingenious ploy to introduce a modernist design ideology that was steeped in communist ambitions.[61] The other competition entries, while detailed and thoughtful, remained oblivious of context or history true to the tenets of modernist design that typically decontextualizes and dehistoricizes form. In contrast, Costa's choice of a religious icon and his reference to historical antecedents of the "idea of Brasília" in his report was no happenstance. It was a deliberate attempt to establish a mythology that he knew would appeal to the jury headed by Oscar Niemeyer, and also would not alarm the political power structure wary of communism. The "hidden agenda" of Costa's plan ultimately was to create, as Holston argues, "both a rational and a critical utopia." It was rational in the sense of "a means and process of development," and critical at the same time "as an image of a future radically different from the present."[62] But the notions of both the rational order and the critical alternative were influenced by the design philosophies of Le Corbusier and embedded in the CIAM principles of the Athens Charter.[63]

Brasília's design reflected the essentialist doctrine that "the keys to city planning are to be found in four functions: housing, work, recreation (during leisure) and traffic."[64] The monumental civic axis devoted to the location of government buildings was the zone of work; the residential axis combined housing with recreation and leisure, served by parks, open spaces, and other community facilities; and broad avenues and the axial highway were designed to carry through traffic (see figure 8.9). Thus, the organizing principles of the city were very similar to the Chandigarh plan.[65]

The design of Brasília attempted to present an alternative to the typical city transformed by industrial capitalism overlaid on earlier colonial and medieval cities. These cities were seen as exploitative of the labor class, unequally distributing physical resources and amenities, causing major public health problems, lacking a coherent organization, or serving efficient circulation of traffic. While most of the other ideological attributes of this tradition were manifest in the overall master plan and urban design of the city, the anticapitalist and egalitarian ideology was specifically incorporated in Costa's plan for residential superblocks, or *supercuadras*. The aim of the *supercuadra* design was to

Figure 8.9
A panoramic view of Brasília.
Source: Cinthia Martins Dos Santos Peixoto/EyeEm. By permission of Getty Images.

achieve social integration of various ranks and statuses of the bureaucracy by providing a mix of housing options within each unit. Furthermore, open space and recreational and other public amenities were to be provided at the superblock level according to a fixed standard, ensuring equal distribution of necessary amenities.[66] In the design of the housing types, there was scale difference in the quantum of housing available to different echelons of government employees, while being masked by the uniform modernist veneer of the building façades. The residential design of Brasília was an antithesis to the social ecology of typical cities characterized by stratification, segregation, and huge disparities in basic services and economies. But the idea that upper-echelon bureaucrats will socialize at the level of neighborhood parks or soccer clubs with lower-grade clerks and peons, while separated by official ranks at the workplace, was a bit romantic. The social utopia embedded in the residential design was quickly abandoned in the social life of housing in these *supercuadras*, very much in the manner the sectors got differentiated by rank and class in Chandigarh.

What proved to be even more limiting about this social utopia is that this egalitarian vision was based on a truncated spectrum of social classes. Costa's blueprint for a social utopia did not have a place for the poor who live in depressed rural areas or favelas of Brazilian cities, and typically forsaken from the mainstream planning as "marginals" or as a product of "culture of poverty."[67] The abject poor were carefully edited out, with a design decree that excluded favelas from the planned new capital.

The social reality of Brazil, a country with a high-income inequality—a Gini coefficient close to .49 in 2014, one of the highest in South America and the Global South more generally[68]—ultimately trumped the physical and social utopia of Brasília. While the government recruited bureaucrats and the white-collar workers to staff the government bureaus, NOVACAP was busy recruiting the workforce that will construct the new city. Most of these workers came from the poor rural areas. Just as in the case of Chandigarh, the workers did not have any place to live in Brasília, and workers' temporary shacks cropped up in the vicinity of the construction sites, some occupying land designated for *supercuadras*. Eventually they were removed, but they were allowed to form permanent settlements outside the planned city, thus confirming, if not the myth, certainly the reality of marginality.[69] This was a political embarrassment and prompted the Kubitschek administration to direct NOVACAP to build formal settlements outside Brasília. As the subsequent migration of the poor to Brasília continued, determined to keep the migrant population outside the new city, the government started to build satellite cities in the periphery of Brasília. While in 1960 the population of the Plano Piloto (the original planned city) made up only half of the total population of the Federal District, by 1980, when it had reached its planned capacity, it accounted for only less than a quarter of the total population of the district.[70]

If regional development and national integration were the aims of founding Brasília, it succeeded in reinforcing the contemporary reality of dualism of formal and informal, core versus periphery, the privileged versus the marginals of the Brazilian social structure. Holston refers to the perversion and denouement of the modernist utopia as the "Brazilianization of Brasília."[71] According to political scientist David Epstein, "the city is a monumental urbanistic and social disaster ... a Potemkin village in the midst of a sea of poverty, corruption, disease, and despair."[72]

Those Brazilians—mainly bureaucrats and government workers—who were privileged to live in Brasília suffered from what they called *brasilite*—"meaning 'Brasíl(ia)-itis,' a term used to describe the trauma of living in Brasília."[73] The experience of living in Brasília, in the modernist architectural utopia of Costa and Niemeyer, was indeed traumatic for these first residents as Holston reports from his interviews with them. They found the modernist facades boring and monotonous, and standardization of housing as anomic. They rejected the social mixing in *supercuadras*, but above all they missed the "street life." What the CIAM paradigm could not deliver is the essence of the sensorium, urban form, urbanism, and the habitus of cities—in this instance, that of traditional Brazilian cities.[74] In creating this alien urban form—resembling the fuselage and wings of an airplane—the organization of monumental spaces, axial symmetries, spatial layout of *supercuadras*, and futuristic architectural forms—inspired by Le Corbusier's numerous but thankfully unbuilt projects that attempted to free the ground space by minimizing building footprint—the designers obviated the familiar street and the social life of street corners. This alien urban form achieved by what Holston refers to as "The Death of the Street"[75] inverted the gestalt of the figure-ground relations between buildings and spaces, thus eliminating the usual dialectic[76] between the public and private spaces that are commonplace in contemporary cities. However, as is always the case, current residents seem to express satisfaction with the social and public life in the sector.[77]

Deconstruction and Denouement

Although I have used both Chandigarh and Brasília as examples of postcolonial utopias that were conceived and produced in the images of development, there is a significant difference between the two. Chandigarh was seen, at least in Nehru's eyes, as an exemplar of what postcolonial India may look like. The plan of the city and the design of the buildings were supposed to present an alternative image, that of development and modernity. Yet this image was mired in a profound ambivalence between tradition and modernity embedded curiously in Nehru's own thinking. While he wanted the new design to be "unfettered" by constraints of the past, mindful of the chaotic and dysfunctional form of Indian cities on the one hand, he also wanted to capture the rich urbanism and habitus of traditional cities on the other. He also wanted the planning and design of Chandigarh to be a hands-on training process for young Indian architects and planners, working at the atelier, as it were, of great Western architects and planners. It will be recalled that at the time of India's independence there was only one arts and crafts–oriented nondegree school of architecture in India,[78] which trained only a handful of architects, and no city planners, in a country of some 360 million.[79] Building design and town planning was strictly a domain of civil engineers, and of the public works tradition, guided mainly by the town and country planning ordinances imported and implemented by the colonial authority.[80]

While Le Corbusier's influence produced some talented architects and urban designers, and while his high modernist style superimposed on Mayer's Garden City model produced a hybrid urban form reflecting Nehru's ambivalence, it remained a utopia of placelessness. Of course Chandigarh was not intended to be an agent of social change, and indeed it reproduced the Indian tradition of *homo hierarchicus*[81] in its carefully segregated sectors reinforced by the bureaucratic order inherited from the colonial era. While failing to capture the habitus and urbanism of the traditional Indian city, it merely reproduced the hierarchy of the social order.

In the case of Brasília, the high modernist design was not a question of being just a mere icon of a modern state; it was conceived as an agent of social change. The aim was to demonstrate a kind of social change that requires inverting the current social order and the process of development, by creating an egalitarian city, where there would be equality in access to amenities and public facilities in a Rawlsian sense.[82] The urbanism, habitus, and the sense of place of the traditional Brazilian city was ignored, if not rejected, as a symptom of the capitalist social order. Hence Brasília also became a utopia of placelessness.

These two new cities were similar in their utopian visions. Neither of them had any sense of the dynamic of change and processes—institutional, social, and temporal—that necessarily impinges on the evolution of cities. The modernist plans of Chandigarh and Brasília tried to defy the larger social reality, and failed to anticipate growth, change and the liabilities of social order. Exemplars of a new order by themselves could not change the contemporary social order or limit future growth and change. The essential utopian premises of these two cities have been challenged and subverted by institutions, bureaucracies, insurgencies, and informalities from the very beginning. Over last fifty years, as the population size of the original city has been surpassed by marginal growth by a factor three or more, the original postcolonial utopias have shrunk in size and importance. They have gone through a process of deconstruction and denouement that Holston described as the "Brazilianization" of Brasília. And Chandigarh has gone through a similar process of "Indianization" of a high modernist city. These high modernist utopias ultimately became the icons of the failure of development to anticipate change and disorder endogenous to the environment.

The Monochromatic and Silent City

To some political theorists, the fall of the Berlin Wall and the dissolution of the Soviet Union symbolized the end of history—in the sense that these events marked the end of a dialectic of competing ideas about alternative political economies—as capitalism trumped socialism once and for all. The aim of this essay is not to challenge this position, although intellectual demurrals still may exist in the world of ideas.[83] The intent here is to accept it as a premise *fait accompli*, and to focus on the nature of the urban legacy shaped by the ideology and institutions of the socialist era. Indeed, while the era of socialism may have ended, or at least metamorphosed into a form of capitalism under a thin veneer of low-key and largely perfunctory communist ideology, the urban legacy of the fifty-plus years of socialist rule in various parts of the world no doubt will continue for a while. Yet, it is possible that the legacy of socialist urban form may soon become an endangered species as the inexorable forces of global capital continue to transform the urban heritage of the socialist era. Thus before they become extinct we may want to reflect on the urban forms and spaces of the socialist legacy. This reflection may help us understand how images of development in a political ideology may influence the urban outcome and its design and planning. Let us begin by first considering China shortly after the end of the Cultural Revolution. We focus here on the urbanism, habitus, and identity of socialist cities—a distinct alternative outcome of the postcolonial era, and yet one that was shaped by an ideology of modernization, not necessarily rooted in capitalism.

Shanghai, August 1980

In the summer of 1980, a group of American planning academics and practitioners was invited by the China-US People's Friendship Association to visit six Chinese cities and participate in planning seminars with local planners. Ostensibly the aim of the visit was to exchange ideas, and familiarize local planners with contemporary Western (American) ideas and innovations in planning, and in turn for the Chinese to highlight the accomplishments of socialist city planning. For the US planners it was an opportunity to have a peek into the remarkable transformation of China in the previous three decades under the Maoist vision of development.

It seems appropriate to share the first impressions of these US planners arriving in Shanghai, a premier socialist metropolis at that time. Urban designers Donald Appleyard and Rai Okamoto, two members of this visiting group, were asked to report on the visit to Shanghai, summarizing their impressions, events, and meetings with local academics and planners.[84] Their description by and large captures my own memory of our first arrival in communist China, and its premier industrial city. Although the Appleyard-Okamoto report talked about the occasional soundings of horns to clear the throngs of pedestrians, others remembered how quiet the streets were. Some years later, photographer David Allen Harvey recalled the "sound of a socialist city" when he had first visited Hanoi in 1989 on an assignment: "It was silent. It was all bicycle traffic or people walking, so there wasn't much on the streets to hear. To me that's the sound of a socialist city."[85]

But is the silent street a function of socialism alone? One could argue that the absence of motorized traffic noise was a function of underdevelopment and technological backwardness typical of poor cities like Shanghai and Hanoi. Except that this argument does not really hold, if one considers contemporaneous poor cities of noncommunist economies like India. The sensorium of the streets of major Indian cities are well known for the bedlam and the cacophony of noise that emanates not just from traffic but also from the quotidian urban life: the hawking of street vendors and the cajoling of shop owners; the constant chatter of arguments, greetings, and conversations; Bollywood music blaring from the loudspeakers of tea shops; shouts of street performers; barking street dogs and the cawing crows; high-pitched singing of *bauls* and similar roaming minstrels; the wail of beggars; periodic calls to prayer in the vicinity of mosques, and so on. This cacophony is one of public life, of discourse, deviance and disorder, of permissiveness and individualism that one can also hear in the bazaar of Espahan or Tehran, in the Khan Khalili of Cairo, or in the evening market of Djema el-Fna of Marrakech. These are the sounds of a market economy, of selling, buying, and bargaining; but also of cultural diversity, entertainment, social encounters, and public life in general. One can almost imagine a similar cacophony frozen in the old Chinese paintings of the traditional street scene that show acrobats, story tellers, traders, shoppers, and so on. Yet this quotidian sound of the street seemed to be totally missing from the streets of socialist Shanghai or Hanoi. Indeed, "the sound of socialist city" has a deeper meaning, suggesting an overall ambience shaped by an ideology of equality, collective ownership, socialist mode of production, and an authoritarian order.

One of the lasting impressions I had from this trip to China, one that was not addressed by the Appleyard and Okamoto report, was the absence of color in the streetscape. As I recall, the plane trees—whose lush canopy shaded the streets and helped lower the temperature by an average 5 degrees Fahrenheit, mitigating the overall heat-island effect—provided the only color in the cityscape of Shanghai, save perhaps for occasional billboards with socialist exhortations about the dangers of smoking or safe ways of crossing streets, painted walls of ancient temples and gardens, or some fading vestiges of the colonial buildings (see figure 8.10). This was by and large true for almost all the Chinese cities we visited at that time.[86] These cities lacked not only the cacophony of sounds but also the cacophony of colors that typically characterize the landscape of a market economy.

In the case of Shanghai and its sister cities, the lack of color was in part a reflection of the absence of a consumer culture and its accoutrements of billboards, store displays, neon lights, etc. In addition, the low-cost utilitarian plastered cement exterior of buildings that created the street walls were also a part of the monochromatic cityscape.

Figure 8.10
A street scene of the urbanism of the communist Shanghai against the built form obtained from the colonial era (circa 1980).
Source: Author, 1987.

There was little color on the exterior of the buildings, except occasional exposed brick exteriors in the millions of square meters of housing—mainly in six-story walk-ups—built during this period (see figure 8.11). The color of cement was the primary color. In this egalitarian palette color was a luxury and unaffordable given the other exigencies of shelter, food, and health care. The end result was a city without sound or color—a quiet and monochromatic city!

Essential Traits of Socialist Cities

How are socialist cities different from their capitalist counterparts in the structure, organization, urbanism, and design of their built environment? Drawing primarily from the experience of East European countries, sociologist Ivan Szelenyi argues that the socialist project has produced a unique urban outcome—both in terms of urbanism and urbanization—and that it is possible to differentiate socialist cities from capitalist cities in several important ways: in the pattern and rates of urbanization; and in their

Figure 8.11
Communist-era egalitarian housing—six-story walk-ups in Minghan, a satellite city of Shanghai. *Source*: Author, 1980.

urbanism.[87] Thus, one sees less urban primacy[88] or overurbanization.[89] Rather, we see underurbanization, a term Szelenyi uses to indicate a lack of concomitant population growth consistent with the rate of urban job creation as more typical. Szelenyi uses the concept urbanism, as sociologists like Ferdinand Tönnies, Georg Simmel, and later Louis Wirth previously had, "in terms of the density and diversity of human interaction (and institutions), anonymity, the breakdown of traditional community and its replacement by society, and the tendency of urbanites to be marginal and creative."[90]

Szelenyi builds his arguments by considering the ecological approach in social theory, which associates urban outcome—urbanization and urbanism—with industrialization, albeit modified by social organization and relationships as intervening variables. In contrast, the historicist approach argues that social organization and relationships influence urban outcomes, with industrialization as an intervening variable. Szelenyi concludes that both the Marxian and Weberian views rely on historical processes and antecedents as independent variables that influence urban outcomes, rather than the more conventional ecological, and (we might add) positivist approach, thus implicitly advocating a synthesis of the Marxian and Weberian positions. In arguing how socialist cities are different from capitalist cities, he draws essentially from the mode-of-production argument and focuses on the concept of "urbanism," which he finds to be absent from socialist cities.

The absence of urbanism in the socialist urban outcome, according to Szelenyi, has three distinguishing traits: absence of diversity; absence of concentration; and absence of marginality. In other words, socialist cities are characterized by uniformity, diffusion, and conformity. Ironically, these are also the characteristics of contemporary urban sprawl and suburbia that critics consider a bane of the market landscape of the advanced capitalist economies.[91] Absence of diversity, according to Szelenyi, is manifested in "the relative scarcity of urban services, shops, restaurants, ads, and street vendors"[92] that thrive in most market economies, whether advanced capitalist or poor developing. The absence of concentration, as he explains, is a function of absence of a land market, since most of the land is under public or collective ownership. He argues that "there is less pressure to economize with space in inner cities under socialism"[93] and that it liberates planners to pay more attention to matters of aesthetics and public realm and be generous in the allocation of inner-city space for public purposes and collective welfare.

Finally, regarding marginality or lack thereof, he points to the absence of "negative" marginality in the form of poverty visible in capitalist cities. Homelessness, panhandling, prostitution, slum housing, and even squatter settlements are totally absent from socialist cities because of their egalitarian ideology and attendant welfare system.

Parenthetically, when Oscar Lewis defined the concept "culture of poverty," he was quite specific about noting that it was a product of capitalist cash economies and a characteristic not found in socialist countries.[94] At the same time socialist cities also seem to be missing other forms of "positive" marginality or creative and innovative deviance in the form of alternative lifestyles, bohemian or artists' colonies, ethnic neighborhoods, gay communities, and the like. In other words, there is less tolerance for such deviant behavior in the socialist context and greater control for conformity in behavior and expressions, including freedom of speech. Economist Robert Heilbroner points out that one of the positive aspects of capitalist economies is the incentive for creativity and innovation, including opposition to the capitalist system itself.[95] This point of the missing urbanism of diversity is probably one of the more critical arguments Szelenyi makes in his essay.

A fourth trait can be added to Szelenyi's three from the literature on dependent urbanization. Castells has argued that in addition to overurbanization and urban primacy, a dualistic urban form is typical of many Third World cities located in a dependent economic relationship with industrialized nations of the West.[96] This dualism is in many instances a vestige of colonial urban development[97] mirroring the technological and cultural dualism[98] and that of the formal and informal economies.[99] Like the phenomenon of marginality, the cultural, economic, and technological dualisms are also absent in the socialist cities.

The mode-of-production argument may not fully explain the socialist urban form outcomes. For it does not include the institutions, the leadership, and the individual or collective visions and imaginations that shaped the normative choices made about the organization of urban spaces and the design of the built environment. What were the compelling images of socialist development that shaped the design and planning of cities like postliberation Beijing, Berlin, and Bucharest? The answer, I argue, lies in the commitment to modernity of the socialist regimes.

The communist or socialist project of alternative development is also a product of modern times. The same possibilities and promises of modernity embedded in the same matrix of scientific and technological knowledge and imagination that has guided capitalist development elsewhere in the West also inspired the images of socialist development and the socialist project of building egalitarian cities and communities (see figure 8.12).

While the legacy of the socialist cities may be interpreted through the mode-of-production filter offered by Szelenyi, they are also important testaments of the experience of modernity. Accordingly, several points should be noted.

Figure 8.12
A Chinese poster invoking the modernist vision with the slogan "Great new prospects for starting to build socialist modernization" (n.d. 1940–1990).
Source: Reproduced with permission of University of Westminster.

First, the socialist planning and reconstruction of cities represents an important epoch in the ongoing project of defining urban space and form in particular images of development. In this case the vision was one of egalitarianism and modernity. No doubt the specific urban outcomes of the socialist projects have been shaped by their particular inheritance of culture and economy, but the leitmotifs of socialist planning and design are common to all.

Second, Szelenyi has argued that the legacy of the socialist cities may be best interpreted through the mode-of-production filter, and the freedom of planning unencumbered by the usual constraints of private property ownership and rights. However, this premise alone may not fully explain the appearance and design of socialist cities. To limit it to the mode-of-production filter would deny the preeminence of the modernist visions that inspired and impelled the design of urban form and space.

Third, one of the important instincts of this modernist urban design was to deny the traditional and indigenous form, which socialists associated with lack of progress, decadence, and exploitation. Just as Marshall Berman has argued in his critique of modernity by using Goethe's Faust as the hero of development, socialist urban planning and design had very little regard for the cultural heritage and traditions of cities. In affirming the triumph of socialism, historic urban fabric was destroyed to create monumental spaces of public buildings and squares. The saga of urban redevelopment in Beijing—the destruction of the historic approach to the Forbidden City in Beijing, the demolition of most of the hutongs that defined the urbanism of the Ming-Yuan city in a Haussmannian fashion—are a testament to this high modernism. Interestingly, the new aesthetic order of modernity nevertheless suggested continuity of traditional and iconic elements in the cityscape (see figure 8.13).

Fourth, the inspiration for these megalomaniac spaces—the monumental scale, the grand axis, the symmetry, the superhuman scale—presumably created to instill a sense of pride and accomplishment among the citizens of socialist republics—all came from the very bourgeoisie adaptation of the Baroque and neoclassical order.[100] Thus, the scale and symmetry of Tiananmen Square reflected the same civic design ideals popular at the end of the nineteenth and the early twentieth centuries: the Baroque order of Haussmann's Paris, Daniel Burnham's plan for Chicago, and the various expositions that were staged to celebrate the industrial accomplishments of that time.

Fifth, and finally, there is also an element of agency of leadership that has to be reckoned with in examining socialist cities. Yet this has been an important feature of the modern socialist state as discussed by James C. Scott in his case study of Tanzania's experiment initiated by Julius Nyerere. These projects almost always were driven by an

Figure 8.13
"Make our cities more beautiful," exhorts a more recent Chinese poster.
Source: Reproduced with permission of University of Westminster.

authoritarian megalomania, like that of Mao in Beijing, the GDR planners in Berlin, and of course most famously that of Nicolae Ceaușescu in Bucharest.

Today, at the fading of the communist vision, the capitalist reconstruction effort fueled by the spirit of neoliberalism and market forces of the global economic order has begun to initiate a new transformation—either as market-based overlays and new uses of existing urban spaces, or alternatively as incremental changes brought about by private property ownership and rights. In retrospect, however, we should be asking whether these socialist urban outcomes may be seen as examples of alternative modernities, as Charles Taylor[101] argues, or as examples of the Faustian impulses of development that Berman[102] so eloquently describes as the essence of modernity? These are the questions we must continue to address at the end of history as long as we continue to plan and design our cities in the images of development shaped by the imperatives of the new modernity of globalization.

9 Import of Design Paradigms

> With this lesson from the past what is to be the attitude towards the anachronism of New Delhi? Can the Capital City of India afford to preserve the present aristocratic density or should it accept this density as a desirable norm and develop a huge, sprawling Delhi in which two storeys is the average height? Quite clearly the centre of Delhi must be made available to many more people and the question is really how best to do this, not shall it be done at all.
> —Gordon Cullen, "IXth Delhi"[1]

Western images of development continued to shape much of the postcolonial design, planning, development, and redevelopment of existing urban settlements in the Global South. Initially these imported paradigms came in the valises of world-famous architects with modernist visions. The following phase involved the transfer of Western planning paradigms for urban growth and containment.[2] It came less in the form of the megalomaniac ideologies of internationally known architects, and more in the form of institutional and technical assistance involving interdisciplinary professional teams. While some of this assistance produced innovative concepts of planning relevant to the indigenous context, such as the 1962 Basic Development Plan for Kolkata, most were not grounded in the political reality of the local context.[3] The following are some relevant vignettes of how the Western professional practice of urban development shaped the emerging urban and metropolitan form of the developing world in the postcolonial era.

Satellites, Sectors, and the Neighborhood Unit

The idea of building new capitals to assert the dawn of a new postcolonial era resonated widely among the political leadership. Following the precedents of Brasília and Chandigarh, other nations had followed suit—Islamabad in Pakistan, Tema in Ghana, Abuja in Nigeria, for example. However, in almost all instances the search for an indigenous image of modernity was left to the interpretations of Western architects and planners.[4] The political leadership did not have faith in domestic design professionals, whose professional identity and capability were seen as limited. In India a formal professional degree program in architecture did not begin until the early fifties—the first class graduating in the late fifties from a five-year degree program.[5] Meanwhile, the very concept of new towns, not just capital cities, came to dominate the postcolonial urban development agenda for years to come.

The imperative to build new towns had several conflated rationales. First, as the postcolonial era experienced initial waves of refugee movements in the Indian subcontinent, and later, as rural-urban migration burgeoned throughout the developing world, managing explosive growth of very large cities became a major concern.[6] The rapid influx of transnational refugees and domestic rural migrants quickly outpaced and overwhelmed the original infrastructure and housing capacity of these cities. Between 1951 and 1961, for example, Kolkata's urban population grew from 4.6 million to 5.7 million. By 1981 the population had reached 9.2 million.[7] Because the new arrivals were poor or had very limited resources, there was little market response to accommodate this new demand for housing and infrastructure. It was assumed that the best way to handle this growth was to create new towns outside the existing cities. The problem, however, was that local and national governments had little financial resources, and in the absence of private capital for new industries and company towns, these new towns were limited in number and at best were opportunistic.[8]

The second popular rationale for new towns had to do with the decentralization of economic activities at a national scale, and thereby minimizing the regional disparities of income within a particular country. This interventionist thinking was inspired by the concept of "growth poles" popularized by the work of economic geographer François Perroux.[9] Although Perroux's original idea was strictly limited to the sectoral context, that is, to identify and promote the growing sectors of the economy, it quickly took on a spatial dimension, and a rationale for policy intervention at a regional scale. Thus, to defy the scenario of the fifth bell curve[10] of development, it was presumed that by decentralizing economic activities in such spatial growth poles it would be possible to stimulate the economy of depressed regions and improve upon a particular Williamson Index[11] of regional disparity, by invigorating economic growth in depressed regions of a country. The new towns were very much a part of this scenario, with usual expectations about economic growth poles.

The third rationale for new towns was associated with decentralization of the population at a metropolitan or regional scale, mainly in the form of satellite cities in the periphery of the core city. Originally inspired by the Garden City movement expounded by Ebenezer Howard and promoted in both the UK (Letchworth and Welwyn being the most notable examples) and the US (Radburn, Garden City, Greendale, and so on), they became an integral part of the policy for decentralizing London's population growth in the postwar years. A ring of new towns (Crawley, Basildon, Hemel Hempstead in the first generation and Milton Keynes and Thamesmead during a later cycle) were subsequently built outside the green belt surrounding London. Other versions of such towns include Marne-la-Vallée outside Paris,[12] and Vällingby outside Stockholm, to name a few.[13]

The idea was appealing to Europeans. The green belt would contain the urban sprawl of the already-congested industrial city of London, and the new towns outside the green belt, connected by commuter trains, would provide healthier living space where families could bring up children in a safe and clean environment. However, these earlier postwar British new towns proved to be rather sterile and uninspiring places lacking the verve and vitality of a major metropolis—a phenomenon that would come to be known as the "new town blues."[14] Nevertheless, the satellite city idea continued to entice the postcolonial developing world.

Still, a fourth rationale for new towns was to create a new pole of growth within the immediate urban or metropolitan region, to relieve pressures on the exiting and older cities with overtaxed infrastructure. Where opportunities existed for building such growth poles in the vicinity of the existing city—across, say, a river or a bay—as we have seen in the case of Pudong in China or Navi Mumbai in India, building new towns has always presented an appealing strategy to accommodate urban growth.

Finally, a fifth rationale for new town planning and design was to create these modern settlements to house population previously living in indigenous traditional settlements. We have seen this in the Unayzah province in Saudi Arabia, where the population living in historic indigenous settlements—but without modern plumbing, electricity, or appliances—was relocated to new planned communities with modern amenities and facilities.[15] These new settlements served as icons of progress, an effort by the Kingdom in this instance to get rid of any backward images associated with such traditional modes of living.

New towns and satellite cities have always appealed to the urban design and planning in the socialist tradition, because these projects offered an opportunity to begin from scratch, unencumbered by the legacies and spoils of the capitalist development. New towns were seen as a possibility to demonstrate the promises of communism and its egalitarian goals, their plan showing a new spatial organization based on the socialist mode of production and a collective form of ownership and community life. But here we will limit our discussion to the Chinese fascination with satellite cities in the postliberation planning, especially in the context of containing city size and organizing the metropolitan form of important cities. What is particularly remarkable here is that this model, which was made famous by the British new town policy of a postwar capitalist economy, was adopted rather widely in the metropolitan planning of the socialist world, including the Soviet Union and its allies. In carrying out the satellite cities program, the Chinese even followed some of the British ideas about "expanded towns" where new satellite city plan was grafted on to existing small towns and settlements. Jiading in the Shanghai metropolitan area is a good example of a satellite city conceived as an expanded town concept.

The idea of building new towns to contain and accommodate future growth of existing dense and congested primate cities was pursued vigorously in Egypt, especially in planning for the greater Cairo region. New towns called Sadat City, Tenth of Ramadan, and Fourteenth of October, were built 70 to 100 kilometers away from the core city of Cairo, in the middle of a barren desert landscape, and often not well serviced by infrastructure provisions. In some instances, these cities, initially designed for the low- and moderate-income public as bedroom or dormitory suburbs, sat empty for many years as people found the environment inhospitable, sterile, and most importantly, requiring long commutes to work.[16]

In other parts of the Middle East, as the countries blessed with oil revenue became wealthy, new imperatives for modern settlements for their prosperous class ensued. With growing demand for foreign workers in construction and various service sectors, older and depopulated inner-city neighborhoods began to be repopulated by the poor immigrant labor class, typically male and imported from the Indian subcontinent, the Philippines, and less affluent Arab countries. This immigrant population typically settled in the historic core of these cities. This infusion of expatriate population paralleled the simultaneous decanting of native population to the peripheral settlements planned and built to modern standards of space consumption and fitted with appliances and amenities appropriate for the modern world. And of course this modern urban form included new requirements of multiple car ownership and parking.

Clearly the ideological antecedents of these planned new towns were the trinity of such modernist concepts as the Garden City, the neighborhood unit, and the superblock, as we have previously discussed in the case of Brasília and Chandigarh. In postcolonial urban development, however, the fundamental principles of new town design morphed into many variants. For example, Clarence Perry's neighborhood unit concept (based on grade-school children's walking radius)—which presumed coterminality of the communities of place and grade schools—and the idea of a "superblock" to minimize pedestrian-vehicular conflict were transformed into the paradigm of "sector" as the basic organizing principle of space. In the late forties the American Public Health Association institutionalized the neighborhood unit concept as the basis for residential planning standards, in a publication titled *Planning the Neighborhood*.[17] Soon it became the holy grail of residential planning standards, and popular worldwide, never mind that the concept was framed in the context of the post–World War II American suburban developments comprising single-family homes, typically at seven dwelling units per acre, or 30 to 35 people per acre. In a recent book urban planner Sanjeev Vidyarthi has argued that the neighborhood unit concept became the basis for new town planning in India, not just in Chandigarh, where it was introduced by Albert Mayer, but also in Bhubaneswar, Orissa, championed by German architect Otto Koenigsberger, and subsequent new towns like Gandhinagar near Ahmedabad in Gujarat. He has argued further that this fundamentally American concept had been used to organize the planning structure of Delhi's master planning efforts, and in planning incremental planned developments in many Indian cities, including Jaipur.[18]

The second related paradigm was a hierarchical organization of streets based strictly on the notion of different scales of movement, especially movements by automobiles, while recognizing the need for separate systems of pedestrian circulation. The traditional concept of the street as a public realm, a space for social contact, flânerie (including its many non-Western variants), shopping, or entertainment was excised from this new utilitarian paradigm.

Even with the sensitivity to pedestrians and slower traffic implicit in the planning ideas of Mayer and Le Corbusier, as discussed in the previous chapter, streets and roads were simply seen as channels of movement and circulation. As Holston pointed out in his critique of the modernist design of Brasília, the "death of the street" was an inevitable outcome of the rational order of the modernist utopia.[19] But it was more than that. It was an early concession to the rational ordering of modernity and the imperatives of the new technology of mobility where spaces of flows irreversibly trumped spaces of places, to use more contemporary "network society" constructs suggested by Castells.[20]

While the obsession with new towns and satellite cities declined as the costs and criticisms mounted, the planning predilection for sectors as the basis for organizing new increments of urban growth continued unabated. The urban sprawl of the postcolonial development—consisting of vast areas of slums and squatter settlements, private subdivision of greenfield, and the incremental peri-urban growth commonly characterized as the "desakota" phenomenon[21]—is unplanned, uncontrolled, and unregulated. But a large part of the postcolonial urban sprawl is also the result of very specific planned increments of urban areas in the form of residential sectors. What began in Brasília and Chandigarh as an integral component of a modernist utopia became gradually institutionalized in the planning of many cities in the developing world. Much of the urban sprawl of postcolonial Delhi, planned and developed by the expertise of the powerful Delhi Development Authority (DDA), is a case in point.

The saga of the modernist ideas of new settlement planning would remain incomplete if we did not consider, if briefly, the role of the Greek architect Constantin Doxiadis in further promoting the paradigm of sectors and the hierarchy of movement system. A visionary thinker, Doxiadis proposed to bring scientific and rational order to town planning and city design by promoting the idea of "ekistics," or the science of human settlements. He imagined that this science would flourish from research and analysis of human settlement systems as they evolved historically, and as they might transform in future years to come.[22] He conceptualized an "ekistics grid" composed of different scales and components of human settlements for cataloguing and compiling such research and analysis. Although Doxiadis's ekistics movement proved to be short-lived, failing to ignite any enduring following, some of his ideas about the future urbanization patterns of the world may have proved prescient. He predicted, for example, that the future urbanization worldwide would lead to what he called "ecumenopolis," consisting of continuous and linked urban agglomerations at a global scale. While there were only a few examples of such possibilities in his time—the Randstad in the Netherlands, the "megalopolis" of the eastern seaboard of the US, and perhaps the Ruhrgebiet in Germany—the prospect of large transnational megaregions preempting older urban hierarchies in a national space has become quite real today. Chinese planners for example are now expecting, if not actively pursuing, ten urban agglomerations of fifty million people each, to accommodate the bulk of China's future urban growth.[23] In India the Mumbai-Delhi urban-industrial corridor is being imagined today as one such megaregion. Recent writings on "planetary urbanization" by geographer Neil Brenner and others have begun to identify the form and organization of this phenomenon.[24]

Doxiadis's ideas of dynamic communities were limited to notions of scale, structure, and organization. Although there were discussions of the hierarchy, size, and organization of communities, emblematic of structural modernist thinking, there was very little discussion of the humanity of place, or how people use spaces and endow them with meaning. The discussion was limited to abstractions of form only, and absent of considerations of the sensorium, the urbanism, the habitus, or the identity of place as discussed elsewhere in this book.

Also lacking was the sense of environmental sustainability and the "genius of the site" in an ecological sense in the concept of the science of human settlement. Despite Doxiadis's intuitions about the spatial consequences of urbanization at a global scale, and his efforts to anticipate the future of human settlements by engaging well-known experts from various disciplines in well-publicized retreats[25]—one such gathering was held in Delphi, and romantically referred to as the "oracle of Delphi"—the environmental problems we face today such as global warming, shortage of water, poverty, and disease did not quite figure in those ruminations about the future of human settlements.

This blind spot in modernist thinking was eminently displayed in the new town plans that Doxiadis and his associates were drawing up for many corners of the world. Here we will address perhaps the most eminent example of the projects of Doxiadis and associates—the plan of Islamabad, the new capital of Pakistan. The 1959 decision to build a new capital of Pakistan close to the old city of Rawalpindi in the Potwar Plateau almost 1,400 miles from the coastal city of Karachi,[26] gave Doxiadis an opportunity to apply some of his modernist visions of town planning. The key idea was that of "dynapolis," a schema for an axial growth of the city and its center, rather than the historic patterns of concentric growth that, in Doxiadis's view, often choked future expansion of the central business district and led to decentralization. In the case of Islamabad, the growth of the new city was expected to occur along an axis parallel to the growth of the existing city of Rawalpindi, whose growth was also expected to occur in such an axial manner.

Interestingly, this plan never considered an integration of the old city and the new, conceding perhaps the inability of the modernist principles of planning and city design to meld with the messy legacy of the traditional city reflecting the earlier colonial planning practice. This may have also reflected the desires of the power elite who did not want the new seat of administration and authority to get corrupted by the informality of the old city, and possibly preferred a clean break.[27] This separation of the parallel axes of the Islamabad-Rawalpindi "dynapolis" is reminiscent of the colonial legacy of excluding the indigenous city from the European city, as in New Delhi, and according to architect Stan Nilsson, embraced also by the postcolonial elite in the Indian subcontinent.[28]

The chosen direction of the axes was southwesterly, away from the rugged mountains and where space was available for future growth. The basic form of the Islamabad plan consisted of a square grid defining the sectors with their sides measuring 2 kilometers, a dimension almost twice that of the sectors in Chandigarh proposed by Mayer and Le Corbusier. The basic grid advanced by Doxiadis was to contain some thirty to forty thousand persons subdivided into a hierarchy of successive lower-order "communities" of decreasing sizes corresponding to Doxiadis's "scientific logic" of communities. In justifying this rigid order of square grids, Doxiadis liberally invoked indigenous examples from the Indian subcontinent as precedents—Mohenjo Daro and the Lahore Fort in Pakistan; Fatehpur Sikri and the Red Fort in Delhi in India, and so on—all of which ironically represented "a flexibility of scale and a liberty in the space concept which makes his own grid look like a lifeless pattern."[29]

The sectors were used to effectively stratify and segregate social and income classes, just like in Chandigarh, in the grand tradition of the British colonial planning. Every piece of real estate was allocated according to a formula that included eleven categories of income and bureaucratic rank complete with plot size and a program for the housing design, which Nilsson saw as a class continuum between "Peons and Nabobs."[30]

The rigid geometric grid defied the natural terrain and drainage pattern, the flora and the extreme climatic circumstances of the site. The plan remained oblivious of the ecological constraints and potentials of the site, and the resulting possibilities of the built form that were apparent in the existing settlements. The modernist instinct for a scientific rationality, based on a very limited understanding of how cities work, and a naive ordering of space based on arbitrary hierarchies of communities and circulations, had no patience for indigenous form or nature. Bulldozers—some five hundred of them, obtained from the Soviet Union as technical assistance—leveled the undulating hills and outcroppings, filled the valleys and *nullahs* (the natural drainage channels)—to make room for wide avenues, boulevards, and the construction sites of the new township.[31]

For most critics, Islamabad remains a dull, sanitized, and lifeless city—a haven for the upper class and political elites. Like other examples of modernist planning, it lacks the verve and urbanism of traditional cities. Streets some 100 feet or so wide are flanked by one- or two-story housing units of various types. Surrendered to the imperatives of motor vehicles, the public realm of the street remains inhospitable to any public life in the harsh climate, when the summer temperature can reach close to 50 degrees Celsius (122 degrees Fahrenheit). These imported images of city design were visions and projects of the Western expertise, but they were neither sustainable nor sufferable in the indigenous context. Other projects of Doxiadis and those of a similar genre shared the same liabilities.

Planning for Growth and Renewal: The Rational City

The involvement of Ford Foundation experts in the planning and design of two major cities in India—Delhi and Kolkata—is an important case of Western technology transfer because they brought with them a new model of planning that involved multidisciplinary teams with a strong predilection for social and economic analysis, rather than the physicalist approach typical of previous instances. Although urban and regional planning was not on the Ford Foundation's initial agenda—its original mission was to assist rural and institutional development in the postcolonial India—by the late fifties it found itself engaged in a major planning effort for the Delhi metropolitan area that led to the Delhi Master Plan of 1962. In the mid-fifties, the government created several agencies with the explicit task of planning and developing the capital city: the Delhi Development (Provisional) Authority and the Town Planning Organisation.[32] The following year, the Ford Foundation organized a team of American experts to advise the Delhi planning and development work that had just begun. The Ford Foundation appointed Albert Mayer of the Chandigarh fame, then a New York–based architect and planner, to head the team.[33] The team included a formidable group of renowned experts, who saw their work as unique in trying to combine many different facets of planning—physical, social, economic, and regional—and thus possibly creating a new paradigm (a "prototype," according to Mayer) for planning in other cities in India.[34]

Despite this interdisciplinary and objective approach to planning, and an ethos grounded in the democratic ideals and social equity, the American images of the future of Delhi as presented in the master plan didn't quite fit the Indian reality or expectations about the future of their capital city. This was eminently evident in the writings of local academics and planners once the master planning process was complete.[35]

In those days, in the middle of the last century, the dominant paradigm of the American planning was the rational model, or at least a type of pragmatic rationality, as planning theorist Niraj Verma has suggested.[36] The corresponding image was one of an efficient and orderly city. In the words of planning historian Christine Boyer, planning in America was about "dreaming the rational city,"[37] which seemed to capture the postcolonial efforts worldwide. A hallmark of this rational city approach was to segregate land use, and to control density and overcrowding.[38] Later observers like urbanist Jane Jacobs, sociologist Richard Sennett, and anthropologist Constance Perin would critique planners' penchant for segregating land use, and their inability to deal with the urbanism and verve of settings where uses and incomes mix quite easily, as in the older preindustrial cities.[39]

To the Ford Foundation planners, the old walled city of Shahjahanabad presented a classic antithesis to the American penchant for rational order and organization. Its legacy of preindustrial organic urban form—narrow streets and alleys; overcrowded eighteenth-century courtyard houses; a bewildering mix of shops, wholesale outlets, craft workshops, warehouses, foundries, markets, food vendors, mosques, temples; and a public realm teeming with pedestrians, animals, bicycles, *tongas*, cycle-rickshaws, and the like—was too messy, unclean, and unhealthy for American sensibilities, reflecting ironically the earlier colonial instinct to isolate and distance the city considered subaltern. According to modern American planning standards, the old walled city would be considered blighted, and a prime candidate for renewal and rehabilitation. As expected, the Ford Foundation team recommended de-densification of Shahjahanabad, involving removal of industries that did not belong to the residential areas according to the American images, a partial clearing of what they generally considered a "slum," and rebuilding with new modern uses and residential structures according to the principles of urban renewal.[40] Gentrification of the old city was clearly the subtext of this proposal.

The Ford Foundation planners also deliberated over how the future growth and development of the Ninth Delhi—the capital of the Indian republic[41]—should take place, and the territorial boundaries of such growth. The Delhi Master Plan (see figure 9.1) envisaged containing the future growth of Delhi and distributing surplus growth to satellite cities connected by public transportation. This scenario included moderate-density residential growth in modules of self-contained sectors with their own commercial and public amenities. The plan recommended future industries be located in industrial estates

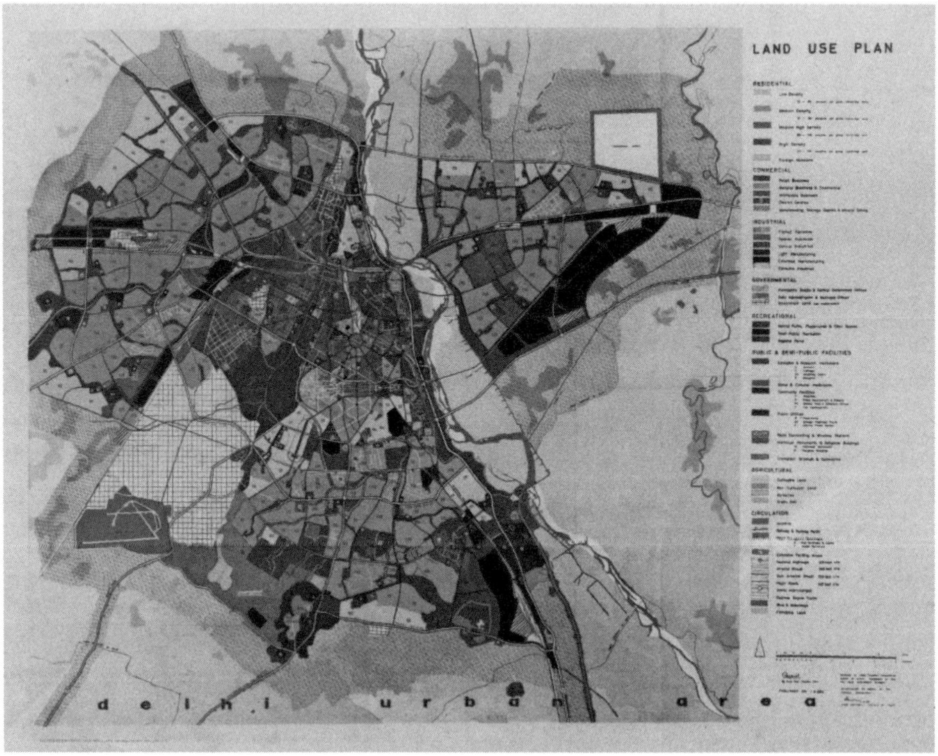

Figure 9.1
Delhi Master Plan of 1962, prepared by the Ford Foundation team.
Source: Ford Foundation Archives, Catalogued Reports. Report #000523. Courtesy of Rockefeller Archives Center.

east of the Yamuna River. The overall philosophy was for Delhi to become a polycentric city, despite existing commercial activities concentrated in the old city and the popular Connaught Place of the colonial city in close proximity. The image of the rational city was based on a policy of decentralization and segregation of land use, obviating the usual disorder of the typical Indian city.

What was particularly disappointing to Indian observers was that the plan failed to address the legacy of a dualistic urban form inherited from the colonial era, and to offer a unifying and integrative image. The image of rational city, in the end, was an abstraction expressed in such policy measures as: exclusionary land use, density and floor area ratio; sectors and satellites; industrial estates; and so on. The plan failed to deliver any distinctive icons or compelling visual images of a modern Indian city, much to the disappointment of local observers. While the national government had built many cultural and civic buildings since independence they remain scattered throughout the city, the plan having failed to identify a civic center or core, a major indictment for the nation's capital. Besides its colonial civic design—within "Lutyens' Delhi"—the city lacks a coherent image, or a sense of place. The wide streets are not particularly pedestrian-friendly, missing the street life and sensorium that is characteristic of most Indian cities. Other than the major arterials, very few local streets are named and building addresses are by sectors, sections, and parcel numbers, often presenting a major challenge for the first-time visitor, as in the case of Chandigarh.

At the outset of the master planning process Albert Mayer wanted the expertise of an urban sociologist not merely for sociological analyses, but for advice on involving community organizations in the planning process. Although this overture toward community participation was in itself a major break from the conventional colonial practice, it remained merely a gesture and was not pursued for budgetary reasons. Nevertheless, the draft Delhi Master Plan was released to the public in July 1960, "for the purpose of inviting objections and suggestions." The DDA also released an outline of the plan in three languages—English, Hindi, and Urdu—along with relevant maps, charts, and narratives for the benefit of the general public, the press, and the members of parliament. After the three-month period allowed for filing objections and comments, the agency received almost six hundred responses from the public, co-operative housing societies, industrial associations, local bodies, the Delhi administration, and various ministries and departments of the government of India.[42] This overture represented the lowest rung of the "ladder of citizen participation"[43] and served as a weak substitute for the kind of participation Mayer originally had intended. But it did provide a public discussion of a plan unprecedented in the local culture, even though the discourse was limited to technocrats, experts, interest groups, and the local power elite.

At about the same time as the Delhi Master Plan was underway, the Ford Foundation was financing a pilot project in community development in urban areas in the US. Inspired by the success of rural community development programs, the aim of the project was to build what today we refer to as "social capital."[44] It was hoped that with this induced social capital the looming problems of slums and infrastructure deficit could be addressed through self-help programs. Thus, the goal was to promote community life and civic engagement by organizing citizens development councils of 250 to 400 families living in the same locality, forming neighborhood councils, improving local bazaars, training workers of *mohalla* (neighborhood) committees, and the like.[45]

By the end of the sixties, and perhaps because of its involvement with the planning of two major cities—Delhi and Kolkata—the Ford Foundation's agenda had incorporated urban and regional planning issues on a broader scale and in the context of overall national development. Meanwhile, even at the end of the sixties, Douglas Ensminger, head of the Ford Foundation mission in India, had not lost sight of the original question posed by Nehru: '"How are the disadvantaged groups in 550 thousand villages to be brought into the mainstream of India's development?"'[46] He argued that in the past twenty-two years of independence this question represented "the most burning issue" in India's development. He proposed three key planning concepts necessary to address this very issue: (1) integrated area development, involving a rural district or region; (2) growth centers, focusing on existing small town or large villages with potentials for becoming development nuclei serving clusters of 50 to 100 villages; and (3) viable rural-urban communities, which would build on rural-urban linkages, rural industrialization, and so forth. Although Ensminger makes no reference to it, it is clear that the latter idea was very similar to the Chinese policies of rural industrialization and modernization of their agricultural economy under the Maoist vision of balanced development.[47] The Ford Foundation's effort would continue to support such research and projects,[48] and the infusion of such thinking would be quite apparent in the case of the Kolkata metropolitan planning. Certainly, it is impossible to attribute any particular share of credit (or blame) to the Ford Foundation initiatives for the subsequent changes in the government policies. Nevertheless, it is interesting to note that since 1979 there has been in place an Integrated Development of Small and Medium Towns (IDSMT) under the auspices of the Ministry of Urban Affairs and Employment. Some 945 towns in almost all states and territories had already benefited from this program. In 1992 a constitutional amendment (the 74th Amendment) now requires integration of spatial and socioeconomic planning in India.[49]

The Legacy of Civic Design

The criticism that a strong visual image or civic design component was missing in the Delhi planning approach prompted the Ford Foundation team, somewhat late in the game, to invite Gordon Cullen, a well-known British civic designer. Cullen's ideas were rooted in the urban aesthetic tradition of civic design. His visionary and imaginative sketches were typically illustrative, without any site plan or implementation details. Upon his arrival in Delhi, Cullen immersed himself in studying the legacy of colonial architecture and civic design, the form of the indigenous walled city, and its planned isolation from the British city. Perhaps his most significant contribution was to propose a civic center—the missing soul of the city—in the *cordon sanitaire* that was created by the British to isolate the old city from the British city. He examined the Old Delhi surroundings of the Jama Masjid and their possible connection to the colonial heritage of New Delhi. His sketches in figure 9.2 capture some of his preliminary explorations. This was also a gesture toward unifying the indigenous and the colonial city and thus mending the heritage of duality in urban form.

Cullen devoted his attention to the future development of the capitol complex and the placement of buildings along the central axis and around the Secretariat and Parliament House, and other general ideas for the development of the colonial city (see figures 9.3 and 9.4). He further imagined possibilities for continuous pedestrian spaces, sunken and shaded courtyards, while maintaining vistas and visual linkages. He also proposed schemes for infill development within the large blocks of Lutyens's street layout. Although sensitive to the indigenous palette of urban form and urbanism, and in many ways innovative as design concepts, ultimately none of Cullen's ideas were included in the master plan and thus were never implemented. Civic design—indeed, the image of the city—was an afterthought in the rational order of American planning and remained an empty exercise.[50]

When the Ford team was brought to Kolkata to prepare that city's Basic Development Plan (BDP), its primary concern was infrastructure improvements, so that Kolkata could be habitable. Issues of restructuring urban and metropolitan form were not explicitly discussed, although specific infrastructure improvement programs carried out by the Kolkata Metropolitan Development Authority would have profound impacts on the metropolitan form as we are seeing today. Nevertheless, even with their hands full with the agenda for the Basic Development Plan, the Ford team tried to generate some piecemeal images of a future Kolkata. Again Gordon Cullen was asked to develop possible images for Kolkata's developing cityscape. Although he was given some specific

Figure 9.2
Gordon Cullen's sketches of the Jama Masjid in Old Delhi and its vicinity. The sketches show new developments in the distance and a shopping arcade in the foreground.
Source: Ford Foundation Archives, Catalogued Reports. Report #002224_004. Courtesy of Rockefeller Archives Center.

assignments, such as the redevelopment of the New Market area, or the approach to Howrah Bridge, it is not clear that his work was ever taken too seriously in the institutional context of Kolkata's planning. Today we know that this was a bias typical of the American planning dominated by social sciences. Matters of appearance or design were considered a frill, sort of window dressing.[51]

Although Cullen never addressed issues of larger city design or the changing urban form, he was perceptive enough to capture much of Kolkata's urbanism in some of his sketches and writings. His proposals, attractive as they were in his stylish renderings, were actually images of Western style shopping streets, apartment and office towers, corporate plazas, public squares and the like, built around the existing edifices of the colonial era. These were transplanted images of affluent Western mass consumption grafted to a local urbanism (see figure 9.5 to 9.6). If colonial Kolkata reminded the

Figure 9.3
New developments around the colonial-era Parliament House as imagined by Gordon Cullen. *Source*: Ford Foundation Archives, Catalogued Reports. Report #00224_01. Courtesy of Rockefeller Archives Center.

noted author V. S. Naipaul of classic London, Cullen's proposals would have extended this resemblance through the postcolonial years.[52]

What was missing in Cullen's vision for Kolkata was an understanding of the political economy of a poor Third World city. The level of corporate and municipal investment taken for granted in these images of Kolkata was totally out of step with reality. In his New Market–Chowringhee area renewal proposal Cullen proposed a series of interconnected public spaces lined with shops, cinemas, and restaurants, accessible from nearby apartment and office towers (see figures 9.7 and 9.8). These are essentially images of Oxford Street, Piccadilly Circus, or the St. James, or the more contemporary fashionable mixed-use developments popular in American and European cities today, coproduced by the public and private sector. Cullen of course had difficulty reconciling his images of civic design with the social reality of Kolkata. He realized that the civic

Figure 9.4
Cullen's vision for development around Rajpath, New Delhi.
Source: Ford Foundation Archives, Catalogued Reports. Report #00224_002. Courtesy of Rockefeller Archives Center.

spaces he imagined could very well be taken over by squatters and pavement dwellers. So he reasoned that these spaces should be owned by the private sector and locked up at night, just like the well-maintained facilities of the private clubs and corporate headquarters. There was no room for squalor and poverty in Gordon Cullen's cityscape of Kolkata.

Indeed, Cullen may have been ahead of his time! In these proposals he advocated a "privatization" of the "civic spaces." Today such spaces are being created in many American cities—New York, Los Angeles, San Francisco—by offering zoning bonuses to downtown developers, a practice that has become a contested issue in contemporary design and planning.[53]

Cullen's comments in the epigraph for this chapter point to his inability to capture the very public and permissive nature of Kolkata's urbanism, and the very humanity of

Figure 9.5
Cullen's vision for redeveloping the Dalhousie Square (now BBD Bagh) area in Kolkata. Looking north along Old Court House Road with the St. Andrew's Church of the colonial era as the main vista.
Source: Cullen (1966), B6. Courtesy of Santosh Ghosh.

Figure 9.6
Another sketch from Cullen's proposal looking west with the portico of St. Andrew's Church to the right.
Source: Cullen (1966), B6. Courtesy of Santosh Ghosh.

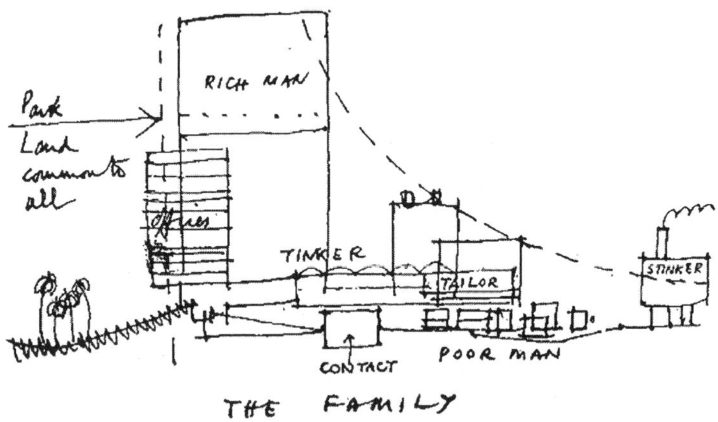

Figure 9.7
A schematic section showing the future mixed-use redevelopment possibilities along the Chowringhee.
Source: Cullen (1966), B9. Courtesy of Santosh Ghosh.

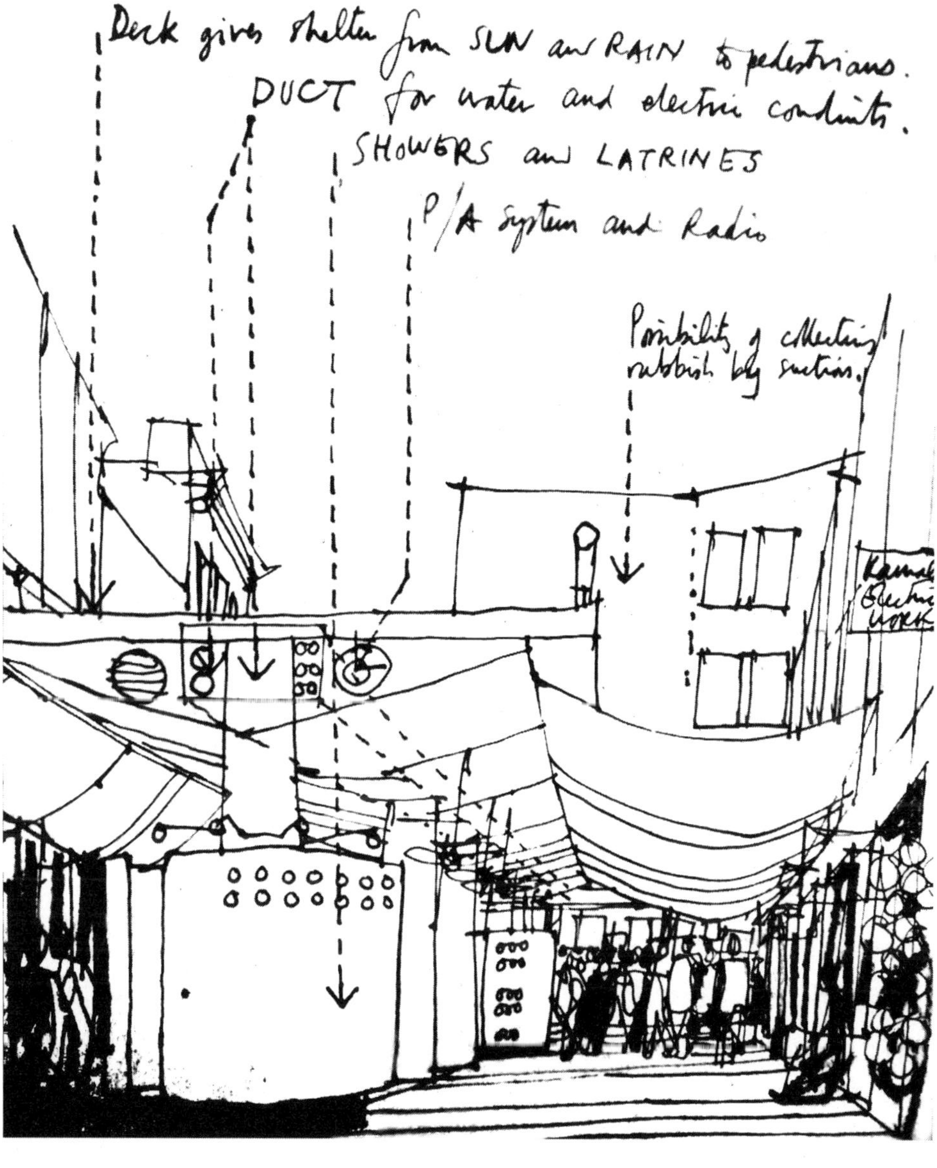

Figure 9.8
Cullen's idea for a typical pedestrian concourse in Kolkata with amenities for the informal economy and street people.
Source: Cullen (1966), B7. Courtesy of Santosh Ghosh.

the city. Today the Chowringhee "colonnade" continues with its chaotic urbanism, but the Grand Hotel has found a way to isolate itself by creating a new entry off a driveway from Chowringhee. The colonial river frontage of the city now has a major park as the warehouses and stevedores left with relocation of the port to Haldia some 20 miles down the Hooghly River. Today the BDP effort of the Ford team is faulted for being remiss of the vitality of the informal economy of Kolkata, and especially of the nexus between the formal and informal economies. Gordon Cullen's vision of Kolkata's civic design was similarly somewhat out of touch with social and economic reality, although he captured the potentials of informal economy in his visions.

10 The Spectacle of Poverty and Inequality

"Well now, my friend," volunteered the stranger. "You don't look too well!"

This friendly remark comforted Hasari. There were not many people who treated you like a "friend" in this inhuman city. He wiped his bloodied mouth with a corner of his vest.

"It must really be a tough job to have to pull one of those carriages when you're coughing your head off!" continued the stranger.

Hasari nodded. "You bet your ass!"

"What would you say if I were to offer you as much money as you earn in two months sweating between your shafts, without your having to do anything," the stranger then inquired.

"As much money as ..." stammered Hasari at a loss for words. "Oh, I would say that you were the god Hanuman in person." Then suddenly he remembered the middleman who had accosted him one day in the Bara Bazar. "If it's my blood you're after, you're on the wrong track," he announced sadly. "Even the vultures wouldn't want anything to do with my blood. It's rotten."

"It's not your blood I'm after. It's your bones."

"My bones?"

The puller's expression of horror brought a smile to the procurer's face.

"That's it," he explained calmly. "You come with me to my boss. He'll buy your bones for five hundred rupees. When you kick off he'll collect your body and take your skeleton."

—Dominique Lapierre, *The City of Joy*[1]

Dominique Lapierre's *The City of Joy* is a story of a Kolkata *bustee* (or slum). The dust jacket of the volume claims that it is about "the most fascinating experience a man can have at the end of the twentieth century," except perhaps that of "walking on the moon."[2] Marketing rhetoric aside, the existential distance between the everyday world of an average Western reader—for whom this message was intended—and the everyday experience of slum dwellers of Kolkata may be interplanetary indeed in a metaphorical sense. The spectacle of poverty may be as fascinating to some voyeurs as watching men walk on the moon.

In the new global economy poverty has become a tourist attraction these days. This is quite a change, considering that about a half a century ago when anthropologist Oscar Lewis published *The Children of Sanchez*, a story of life in poverty in a Mexico City colonia, the Mexican government took offense and treated him as *persona non grata*.[3] As the high-rent districts of prospering cities of the Global South increasingly look like the cities of the West—gated communities, shopping malls, skyscrapers—they seem to lose the novelty of their earlier urbanism of underdevelopment. Only the urban spaces of enduring poverty remain exotic. Organized tours of favelas and colonias are now available in Rio de Janeiro, Mexico City, and Mumbai, where a voyeur can enjoy the tableaux of poverty from a safe distance in the comfort of an air-conditioned limo or tour bus.[4]

The Spectacle of Poverty

The story of *The City of Joy* begins with the declining economic circumstances of a poor peasant family from rural Bengal and their migration to Kolkata. Soon after his arrival with his family of six, Hasari Pal, the central figure in the story, finds himself walking the streets of Kolkata looking for work and fighting for a little corner of a sidewalk where his hungry and tired family can sleep. The city seems unfriendly, conniving, and mean. Hopes of making a decent living fade quickly; survival becomes a major challenge. Finally, Hasari Pal gets a break and joins the ranks of the rickshaw pullers, and his miseries seem to be over.

But the pathos in Lapierre's story has only begun. We soon learn that the occupation of a rickshaw puller—a degrading, inhumane, and highly exploited form of labor—is often terminal. Few can survive the ordeal of pulling a rickshaw through the scorching sun and the hot, humid, and congested asphalt-melting or monsoon-flooded streets of Kolkata year after year (see figure 10.1). Hasari Pal falls victim to this cruel occupation and loses his health, and eventually his job. He cannot even sell his blood as he becomes too anemic. Economic redemption comes at the end as Pal consigns his body for a few hundred rupees[5] to the firm that supplies cadavers and skeletons to the medical schools of the West.

The setting is a fictional slum Anand Nagar (meaning "The City of Joy" in Bengali), based on a sprawling and crowded urban district in the industrial town of Howrah across the Hooghly River from Kolkata proper.[6] Here the poor are heroes, and their very survival is an act of heroism. The villains are anonymous agents of the state and capital. Inspirational, and only vaguely political, Lapierre's book is an important documentation of life in poverty—its images vivid and haunting.

Figure 10.1
Rickshaws are still plying in the streets of Kolkata, although they are limited to the older districts in the northern part of the city.
Source: Author, 2018.

The book became a Hollywood movie in 1992, produced and directed by Roland Joffé. Patrick Swayze played the lead role of an American doctor (replacing the Polish priest in the original story), and the well-known Indian actor Om Puri played the role of Hasari Pal.[7]

The filmic version of *The City of Joy* shifts the spotlight from the heroism, struggles, and sacrifices of the poor, to the altruism, commitments, compassion, and sacrifices of the Western world to help the poor. An American doctor and a British nun become the saviors and advocates of the slum dwellers, against the exploits of the rentier class in a Third World economy. This bit of cinematic adaptation seems inevitable, from the box office perspective—Hollywood needs its own hero, and its own brand of compassion.

The novel and the movie are an excellent pedagogic tool for illustrating some of the key concepts of urbanism and urbanization of underdevelopment—the classic rural-urban migration;[8] slum housing; widespread poverty; lack of infrastructure; informal economy; dualism; marginality; culture of poverty and the like.[9] The movie dramatizes the spectacle of poverty of the most debilitating kind, while sympathizing with the struggle of the poor, their handicaps, and their spirit of survival and their sense of community. The deformed human bodies—the lepers, the midgets, the lame and disfigured—symbolize poverty as a disability and deprivation.

This theme becomes further evident as the movie also places the character of Hasari Pal in a subaltern relationship with the American doctor and the British nurse, the saviors of the slum dwellers. Asserting the moral and spiritual superiority of the West, and the altruism of Christianity, the movie poignantly underscores the enduring dependency of the developing world and why its development remains an ongoing project of the West.

The tableaux of poverty have drawn artists, photographers, writers, filmmakers, and journalists to cities like Kolkata with a perverse urge of voyeurism. Poverty makes good human-interest stories, its images portraying the ultimate alterity from the Western perspective in the same way philosopher Julia Kristeva discusses abjection.[10] The horror, grotesqueness, and repugnance of poverty never run out of their novelty for the developed West. "Voyeurism," as Kristeva points out, is a "structural necessity" that "accompanies the writing of abjection." And further, "When that writing stops, voyeurism becomes a perversion."[11]

Examples like *The City of Joy* abound. The 2002 Brazilian film *Cidade de Deus*,[12] the ironic namesake of Saint Augustine's early-fifth-century treatise on Christian philosophy, is a story of real-life favela youths and gang violence played by a cast largely drawn from its residents. The movie would later inspire a Brazilian television series titled *Cidade de Homens*,[13] mirroring Saint Augustine's portrayal of the human history as an ongoing conflict between the City of God and City of Man, the tension between the spirituality and the secularity of human existence. Mira Nair's *Salaam Bombay* is a Bollywood epic about children in poverty in a big city. *Born into Brothels* is an award-winning documentary by Ross Kauffman and Zana Briski that documents the experience of growing up in a brothel, unsurprisingly, located in Kolkata. British filmmaker Danny Boyle's Oscar-winning movie *Slumdog Millionaire* offers glimpses of life in the Dharavi slum in Mumbai. Another Hollywood production, *Lion*, continues the refrain.

Perhaps one of the most fascinating examples of the voyeurism of abjection is the author Günter Grass's illustrated travelogue of India, and Kolkata more specifically. In the mid-eighties, Grass published *Show Your Tongue*, a collection of powerful narratives, sketches, and poems based on his travels in India, and his experience of Kolkata in particular. He visited every possible space of abjection—cremating *ghats*, pavement encampments, squatter settlements along railway tracks, slums and *bustees*, garbage dumps, and so forth. Grass displayed an indefatigable curiosity mixed with a sense of outrage and sympathy rooted in his leftist leanings,[14] but not necessarily one of guilt or shame for his voyeurism of abjection. Instead he sought an aesthetic redemption in the authenticity of poverty and abjection, where the poor are denied any claim or right to their dignity and privacy in such unabashed voyeurism.[15]

This argument about the aesthetics of abjection, however, is not very compelling, and gratuitous at best. In the face of his obsession with filth, excrement, stench, and waste, Grass fails to connect the sensorium of poverty to the history of the collapse of a rural economy, postcolonial refugee movements and the overcrowding and infrastructure deficit that resulted from decade of underinvestment. In a review for a Kolkata newspaper, a critic characterized the book as a "Drain Inspector's Report."[16] In another literary review, Ilija Trojanow,[17] a German writer, denounced the work of Grass along with that of the Italian filmmaker Pier Paolo Pasolini[18] as an "imperialist gaze" and inherently racist and supremacist under a veneer of empathic left-leaning progressive intellectualism.[19]

Images of Inverted Development

The spectacle of poverty is a reality, and it continues largely unabated today as a stubborn contradiction to growing global prosperity and wealth. Poverty keeps reminding us of the image of inverted development. This was not a part of the original script of development—the civilizing imperative—inspired by the images dear to the Western liberal democracies. Enduring poverty, in its extreme and abject form, continues to frustrate the project of development. Inability of the developing world to follow the script leads to a "blaming the victim" response—the culprits typically being corruption, cultural backwardness, absence of modern values, and so on—and the derision and sanctimony that go with it as in the case of Grass.

Perhaps the script of development was a bit utopian to begin with. Poverty, after all, has had a long history. There were mendicants and vagrants in the time of antiquity, and certainly in premodern times. There are at least four different Chinese words for mendicancy—*qiga, taofan, jiao huazi* or *huazi*, and *biesan*—that go back many centuries.[20] Historically just about every religion has glorified, if not celebrated, poverty that symbolized sacrifice, simplicity, rejection of material goods, and a higher moral status. The poor were considered closer to God; helping the poor served a spiritual and moral purpose. Vow of poverty is a ritual of the clergy in the Catholic church. In India, the traditional thread ceremony—the act of becoming a Brahmin, or *dwija*, meaning "twice born" in Sanskrit—requires the adolescent Brahmin child to emulate the life of poverty[21] and role-play mendicancy by asking for alms: "*Bhaban/Bhabati Bhikshan Dehi*" (in Sanskrit "Sir/Madam please give me alms"). Historically then, poverty was more than an epiphenomenon, it was an institution, and it was assumed to be one of choice or fate. Even today Buddhist monks sitting with their rice bowls by the main approach to temples waiting for their daily alms are a familiar sight in Laos, Cambodia, and Thailand.

In the liberal West, poverty is not an acceptable state or premise and certainly not to be celebrated as an institution or condoned even though it may remain embedded in the rites and decorum of religious practice. Indeed, Marx's famous observation that "religion is the opium of the people" captures modernity's rejection of any spiritual pandering to poverty. The communist ideology translated scientific modernism to egalitarianism as the means for eliminating poverty. Even in the modern capitalist economies eradication of poverty—for example, Lyndon Jonson's "war on poverty" or Indira Gandhi's "*garibi hatao*" (get rid of poverty, in Hindi)—have been the political catchwords in the oldest and largest democracies of the world in the second half of the last century.

Poverty, nevertheless, continues in the developing world in its most abject, wrenching, and undignified form. In 2005 development economist Jeffrey Sachs argued, optimistically, that among the 6.3 billion people of the world, at least 5 billion have reached what he calls "the first rung of economic development" and "at least one step above extreme poverty."[22] However, this means that more than a fifth of the world population was still living in extreme poverty, or below $1 a day (adjusted for purchasing power parity, or PPP) per capita, a measure commonly used by the World Bank. In addition to this 1.3 billion living in extreme poverty, another 1.6 billion lived in moderate poverty, between PPP-adjusted $1 to $2 a day per person. These numbers have improved significantly today, more than a decade later, thanks to trickle-down effects of the prospering global economy, and national policy initiatives. According to a UN report, today 783 million people live below $1.90 per day, the international poverty marker. In other words, 11 percent of world population are living in extreme poverty, concentrated mainly in southern Asia and sub-Saharan Africa, the latter group accounting for 45 percent of the extreme poor worldwide. While this is good news, we should reckon the fact that it has taken almost four decades for the number of those in extreme poverty to shrink from 1.5 billion in 1981, or a little over a third of the world population at that time, to the current level of 10 percent, or almost 800 million.[23] At the same time, it appears from the same study that the proportion of the population living in extreme poverty has increased in sub-Saharan Africa and Eastern Europe (and Central Asia) while barely changing in Latin America. The proportion of population living in moderate poverty has actually increased significantly in East Asia, Eastern Europe (and Central Asia), and South Asia.[24] Economists see this trend as a harbinger of good news and expect the share of people living in moderate of extreme poverty to decline to about 15 percent by 2025, as global economic growth continues apace. Still, the progress seems rather modest given the enormous growth in the total world production, which we have discussed previously.

The consequences of poverty—hunger, malnutrition, morbidity, stunted development, deprivation, illiteracy, and all the "unfreedoms" discussed by Amartya Sen—are well known and well documented, and the causes of poverty are also no mystery.[25] Simply put, poverty is associated with absence of development. Countries that fail to grow bear a greater burden of lingering poverty than countries that grow. This is the standard economic explanation for persistence of poverty. Recently Sachs has summarized in a rather lucid manner the circumstantial variables that explain historic underdevelopment and the failure to develop in recent times. These include, for example, what he calls "the poverty trap" which is characterized by low human capital, lack of infrastructure, very little savings, depletion of natural resources, and the fiscal inability of the national government to break out of the vicious circle. Second, as we have reviewed previously,[26] physical geography—the absence of natural resources, inhospitable climate or terrain, landlocked existence without access to a coastline—plays a role in retarding economic development. Here Sachs invokes geographer Jared Diamond's famous book *Guns, Germs, and Steel* in support of his argument.[27] There is also the "fiscal trap" which is somewhat related to the "poverty trap" and the failure of the national state to govern properly, failing to nurture the private and business sectors. Cultural barriers—that may include systematic denial of rights to women or minority groups—also play a role, as we see in many parts of the world today, along with geopolitics and systematic lack of innovation. But more critically, there is also a "demographic trap" or the failure to achieve a demographic transition that leads to declining fertility and birth rates that would ultimately help to push per capita gains of development on an upward trend, and thus triggering a virtuous circle.

The numbers in the aggregate, however, do not capture the existential reality of poverty. They do not tell us much about the experience of living in poverty, and the spaces and landscapes of abject poverty.[28]

Urban Poverty: Size and Regional Variations

A 2003 study by the United Nations Human Settlements Programme (UN-Habitat) estimated that one billion people worldwide live in slums—roughly a third of the total urban population. The study further suggests that in the absence of significant and aggressive policy interventions, the slum population in the developing world will double by around 2030 (from its 2001 base). The census undertaken by the study shows that during the 1990s the slum population in the developing regions increased by 30 percent, while the urban population increased by 40.5 percent. These figures vary by regions, but generally it appears that the growth of slum population has generally kept up with the urban population, albeit not quite on a one-to-one basis. But this is no solace, because in absolute numbers the increase in slum population is still quite phenomenal. In the 1990s the ranks of slum dwellers increased by over 200 million in the developing regions. Absolute variations in the slum percentage (of total urban population) show a slight decline across all the regions, the actual percentages remain remarkably high. In 2001 slum dwellers made up almost 72 percent of the total urban population in sub-Saharan Africa, followed by South Asia, where the number was 58 percent. Even in Eastern Asia, a region that includes many successful economies, the slum population was still 35 percent of the total urban population.

A report by UN-Habitat presents somewhat different but still dire numbers about population living in urban slums (see figure 10.2). The 1990 figure for the slum population in the developing regions of the world was 689,044, but by 2014 it had increased to 881,080, although as a percentage of total urban population it declined (from 46.2 percent in 1990 to 29.7 percent in 2014). In sub-Saharan Africa the share of slum dwellers as a percentage of total urban population in 2014 was 56 percent, followed by over 31 percent in Southern Asia and 28.4 percent in Southeast Asia.[29]

The distribution of the slum population by regions and countries is quite remarkable, and in many instances appalling. About 20 percent of all slum dwellers live in Africa, and another 14 percent live in Latin America. In 2001 slum dwellers composed a very large percentage of the urban population in several sub-Saharan African countries (although in many the percentage had declined significantly by 2015): 99.4 percent in Ethiopia; 99.1 percent in Chad; 97 percent in Somalia; 96.2 (70.0 in 2015) percent in Niger; 95.8 percent in Sierra Leone; 94.3 in Mauritania; 94.1 (80.3 in 2015) percent in Mozambique;

Figure 10.2
A squatter settlement in the urban commons—the bank of the Sabarmati River in Ahmedabad. It was razed in 2010 to be replaced by a riverside promenade.
Source: Author, 2009.

93.4 percent in Guinea-Bissau; 93.0 percent in Uganda; 92.9 (77.2 in 2015) percent in Madagascar; 92.4 percent in Central African Republic; 91.1 (66.7 in 2015) percent in Malawi; and 90.1 (74.8 in 2015) percent in Congo.[30]

Between 1990 and 2015, while the urban population has increased significantly, the percentage of slum population declined, albeit variably in different regions of the Global South. In northern African countries, the slum population as a percentage of total urban population declined from 34 percent in 1990 to 12 percent in 2015; in Latin American countries it dropped from 34 to 21 percent; in East Asia, from 44 to 26 percent; in Southern Asia, from 57 to 31 percent; and in Southeast Asia, from 50 to 28 percent. While it is encouraging to see such declines, it remains more than a quarter of the urban population in most instances.[31]

Percentages could be misleading, however. While it would seem that China and India should be commended for lowering their share of slum population by 5.8 percent and 5.3 percent respectively during the 1990s, suggesting some trickle-down effect of economic growth, in reality China has added 40 million and India 27.2 million more slum dwellers during this period because of their enormous population base and growth in urban population. Even in Sri Lanka, where the percentage has been halved, in absolute numbers the population of slum dwellers has increased by over 9 million.

While this report does not present data on the growth of slum populations by cities, a recent study by geographer Dhanaraj Gownamani and her colleagues documenting the growth of slum population in Chennai, India, from colonial days to the beginning of this century is quite telling.[32] According to the study, the slum population has grown from about 80,000 in 1933 to about one and a half million in 2001. While in 1961 the slum population used to be less than a fourth of the city's population, it grew to more than a third of the city population during subsequent four decades. During the economic liberalization of the nineties the city added a quarter million new slum dwellers. Similar trends are seen in larger metropolises in other parts of the developing world. According to the Brazilian Institute of Geography and Statistics, the proportion of Rio de Janeiro's population living in favelas has steadily increased from 7.24 percent in 1950 to 18.7 percent in 2000. The growth rate of the favela population had consistently exceeded that of the city's population through these decades. According to a 2005 study by the city's planning department, some 1.65 million people were living in Rio's 752 favelas.[33] This is particularly remarkable since rural-urban migration, which led to peripheral squatter settlements typical of earlier decades, had been in decline in Brazil for some time.

Tertiarization, Dualism, and Informality

As noted previously, much of the growth of the slum and squatter population is a result of rural-urban migration, both domestic and transnational. The urban poverty represented by these settlements is rural poverty transferred to urban areas. In the history of Western industrialization, the growth in the industrial economy absorbed surplus labor from rural areas with the growing productivity of the agricultural sector. But it is important to remember that in the West urbanization driven by industrialization also created massive slums, as captured in the well-known narratives of Dickensian London, or in the following description by Engels:

> Every great town has one or more slum areas into which the working classes are packed. Sometimes, of course, poverty is to be found hidden away in alleys close to the stately homes of wealthy. Generally, however, the workers are segregated in separate districts where they struggle through life as best they can out of sight of the more fortunate classes of society....

> The streets themselves are usually unpaved and full of holes. They are filthy and strewn with animal and vegetable refuse. Since they have neither gutters nor drains the refuse accumulates in stagnant, stinking puddles. Ventilation in the slums is inadequate owing to the hopelessly unplanned nature of these areas.[34]

The narrative of inverted development, however, is one of urbanization without industrialization. Because of the collapse of the rural economy with the rise of multinational agribusinesses and the growth of *latifundas* in Latin America, the rural poor came to the city only to be added to the ranks of the service sector. Urbanization of the developing world thus is associated with what is called *tertiarization*, or the growth of the service sector.[35] While the development of the West involved a growth in the formal-sector economy, Third World urbanization resulted mainly from a growth in the informal sector and the rise of what geographer Terence McGee referred to as *proto-proletariats*.[36] The emergence of an informal economy parallel to the formal economy has been characterized as a condition of dualism (see figure 10.3).

Figure 10.3
Spaces of informal economy in the peri-urban Delhi, India.
Source: Author, 2004.

The formal economy is guided by modern institutions of trade and commerce—taxes, land-use regulations, business licenses, insurance, labor laws, property rights, financial instruments, and the like—involving modern and technological means of production. Public-sector jobs and activities also are embedded in the formal economy. The informal economy, in contrast, exists outside these formal institutions of a market economy. Also referred to as the traditional (as opposed to modern) or bazaar and peasant (as opposed to firm) sector economy,[37] much of this informal economy is based on traditional modes of production, highly labor-intensive, often small and family-based, and usually operating outside the formal rules and regulations that define the formal economy. Until the later part of the last century the informal economy had not been part of any development economic policies. In the early seventies an International Labor Organization report pointed out that while largely neglected in mainstream development thinking, the informal sector played an important part in a nation's economy. Economist Hernando de Soto would argue later that for a country like Peru a large segment of the economy belonged to the informal sector, "in which 48 percent of the economically active population and 61.2 percent of work hours are devoted to informal activities which contribute 38.9 percent of the gross domestic product (GDP) recorded in the national accounts."[38]

This statement probably would be valid for other Latin American countries and certainly elsewhere in the developing world even today. While this may not be an across-the-board ratio for all developing economies, the numbers in all instances are nontrivial. The informal economy is an integral part of the development discourse today, and de Soto, a market libertarian, has argued that promoting informal economy by dismantling regulatory barriers—codes, ordinances, license fees—and promoting property rights, would unbridle the economy and help the poor.

Interestingly, however, the concept of economic dualism grew out of an earlier work by anthropologist Clifford Geertz.[39] Based on his work in Indonesia, Geertz proposed that there is a technological dualism in the production and consumption processes of the developing world. This involved a parallel use of traditional technologies along with modern technologies of large-scale manufacturing and other industrial developments. Others extended this metaphor to include cultural and social dualisms. Dependency theorists have argued further that this dualism is a direct outcome of hegemonic relationship between the West and the developing countries.

The link between a dualistic economy, dependent urbanization, and a dualistic urban form remains tenuous. First, it is not obvious that economic dependency necessarily produces economic dualism or dualistic urban form. As economist Deepak Lal has pointed out in his critique of the dependency theory, a country like Canada is profoundly dependent on the US economy but this fact has not produced underdevelopment, nor a dualistic urban form.[40] Second, it is not clear whether economic dualism leads to a dualistic urban form and why or how. Empirical evidence suggests that the formal and informal economies might be more closely entangled, and indeed may exist in an intractable continuum of economic, social, and spatial relationships.[41] In some parts of the developing world it might be difficult to tell where the formal sector ends and the informal sector begins.[42]

In this complicated social ecology of urban space one can imagine a peon or a janitor working for an upper circuit business or government establishment, but not earning enough income to afford formal-sector housing, and thus forced to live in informal-sector housing, such as the illegal structures inside the *hutongs* of Beijing or one of the *bustees* of Kolkata, or in the *kampungs* of Jakarta. For a family dependent on multiple incomes, the wife might have a formal-sector employment, while the husband might be working in the informal sector. Or, one could imagine a middle-class family living in an ancestral house in old Kolkata, having lost a formal-sector job, forced to look for a living in the informal sector, as often portrayed in the Satyajit Ray films on Kolkata.[43] Indeed, a geographical mapping of the informal-sector and formal-sector territories in urban space might be impossible in a city like Kolkata.[44] Even if possible, it is most likely to appear as blotches of informal sector spreading throughout the city. It may even be imagined as a Swiss cheese overlaid on the entire city grid and the public realm—which incidentally is an exhaustive matrix of formal sector where property rights and public infrastructure are formally delineated in cadastral maps, and where every square inch of land is spoken for in terms of ownership, if not purpose[45]—with "holes" or enclosures defined by gated and protected domains and enclaves of the formal sector, whether corporate or government. Even in contemporary Rio de Janeiro, after a decade of the Favela-Bairro Upgrading Program, when "all the traditional distinctions between *favelas* and the rest of the city have become useless as denoters of how and where to draw the boundaries," there remains a "distinction between *favelas* (often called *morros*, or hills) and the rest of the city (commonly referred to as the *asfalto*, or pavement)."[46]

While it might be an empirically daunting task to sort out and map the influences and the overall territorial coverages of the informal economy in urban space, there is no question that the quotidian of urban informality plays an important part in the transitional urbanism of developing cities.[47] It is certainly reflected in the spatial organization and urban form, where the supply of urban infrastructure did not keep pace with the informal-sector growth, thus creating a serious infrastructure deficit. This phenomenon of explosive growth of cities has led some observers to call these agglomerations "premature" or "incomplete" metropolis, or "cities of peasants."[48]

Spaces of Poverty

Although not all poor live in slums or squatter settlements these two categories account for a very large proportion of the spaces of poverty. Slums and squatter settlements are not exactly the same, although they are frequently conflated, as in the following definition: "Slums range from high density, squalid central city tenements to spontaneous squatter settlements without legal recognition or rights, sprawling at the edge of cities."[49] The UN-Habitat survey reported earlier is likely based on a similar definition; what is not clear is whether it also includes the sizeable urban population in abject poverty who may not be necessarily residents of slums or squatter settlements.

Seemingly there is a lack of consensus about what constitutes a slum, and there are interregional and interagency differences. Generally they are seen as informal or "spontaneous" settlements and lacking basic services, especially water, drainage, waste collection and toilet facilities, making the residents vulnerable to disease, disasters, and crime. Typically they also lack social infrastructure as schools, clinics, and community facilities.[50] Slums could vary in density, location, types of construction, age, legal status, and size. They might comprise tightly packed informal huts and shacks, as in the hills of Caracas or Tijuana, or old and squalid inner-city tenements like the *chawls* in Mumbai. Although squatter settlements are often conflated with slums, the former lack legal status because the settlements involve squatting on public or private land. Typically squatters occupy land that is considered either public easements, or simply unbuildable, undesirable, and unhealthy, with very little value in the real estate market. A 1981 World Bank documentary on "sites and services" projects[51] captures such features of a squatter settlement in Recife, Brazil. With the growing demand for new urban space in a global economy, even these settlements are becoming targets for eviction and redevelopment. Recent proposals aim to resettle the residents in high-density apartment towers concentrated within a small area, while releasing the bulk of the land for formal-sector development.[52]

Some of these slums could be quite large. With its three-quarters of a million residents, the Kibera district of Nairobi is considered the largest slum in the world. The Dharavi district in Mumbai and Orangi in Karachi are also notable for their size. Proving the impossibility that a part can be greater than the whole, the Ashaiman slum of the Ghanaian city of Tema apparently has exceeded the size of the original city.[53] While smaller slums might be vulnerable because of their size, some larger slums have managed to command political patronage if not political power.

The ubiquity of slums and squatter settlements throughout the developing world has been acknowledged in different countries by naming them in local languages with culturally distinct lineages. Thus, they are called *ranchos* in Venezuela, *callampas* or *campamentos* in Chile, *favelas* in Brazil, *barriadas* in Peru, *villas miserias* in Argentina, *colonias* in Mexico (and the local term *paracaidistas,* meaning parachutists, in Tijuana), *barong-barong* in the Philippines, *kevettits* in Myanmar, *gecekondu* in Turkey, *bustee* (Kolkata) and *jhuggi-jhopri* (Delhi) in India, *bidonvilles* in Morocco, *alagados* in Bahia, *kampungs* in Jakarta, and so on. The preponderance of these terms from Latin America suggests that the squatter problems have been around in the continent for a much longer period, as the urbanization process there had begun much earlier than the rest of the developing world.[54] In his important book on global poverty Mike Davis offers a more generic typology of slums defined by their location within the city—center versus periphery—and formal versus informal status.[55]

The place of slums and squatter settlements in the social ecology of cities can be quite different and paradigmatic for different regional contexts with different culture and history. The initial wave of squatter settlements in Latin American cities typically occupied spaces in the margin of the Laws of the Indies cities and their formal urban form. It is this marginal location, among a number of other social and economic characteristics, that earned the slum dwellers the term *marginalidad* (or marginality), a well-known Latin American concept to describe the poor.[56] Most favelas in Brazil are examples of this marginality (see figure 10.4).

In the latter part of the last century the suburbanization of the middle class occurred beyond the earlier squatter colonies that comprised the periphery. Thus the latter became more solidly embedded in the sprawling metropolis of today. What began as a collection of temporary jerry-built structures of plywood, tarp, and tin roof became a more permanent occupation where the owners slowly converted such structures to brick and mortar structures and concrete roof, as seen in some of the *villas miserias* in the Buenos Aires urbanized areas (see figure 10.5). Architect John Turner had famously described this process as "progressive development."[57]

In Asian cities the spatial distribution of slums and squatter settlements can be quite different. Historically they were dispersed in the metropolitan landscape, for example, as seen in the case of Kolkata. It is apparent that the slums are integrated at a much finer grain with the formal-sector urban form. The origin of this mix goes back to the colonial era, when the native "Black Town" that provided service and domestic labor for the Europeans consisted of a small cluster of huts grouped around a tank excavated for the purpose of raising the grade for construction purposes.[58] Later, with the opening of jute mills and other industrial activities, large slums or *bustees* were created to house industrial workers in the vicinity of the factories. Thus informal slums were inextricably linked with the formal manufacturing sector. The narrative of dualism does not quite capture such economic relationships. Under different circumstances many of the so-called slums are really rural settlements or villages that existed in the peri-urban areas of Delhi or Ahmedabad. With the expansion of the urban sprawl through these peri-urban areas these villages became

Figure 10.4
Cantagalo, a hillside favela in Rio de Janeiro.
Source: Courtesy of Frank Zerunyan, 2013.

engulfed by the formal sector urban land development. They became slums of informal economy but with a cheek by jowl relationship with formal economy providing domestic help and other services.

By 2001 about 1.5 million persons, or roughly a third of the Kolkata Municipal Corporation population, were living in 2,011 registered and 3,500 unregistered slums, much of this growth being located in greenfield land, or easements of roads, canals, and railroads, and other miscellaneous marginal land.[59]

The ecology of slums and squatters throughout the developing world has many different spatial patterns, and according to one report they can be classified into two broad types: (a) declining areas (such as older city center slums and newer "slum estates"); and (b) progressive settlements like squatter settlements and semilegal subdivisions.[60] Bogotá's inner-city slums, Durban's hostel areas, and Mumbai's *chawls* are some notable examples of the former type. This former type also includes the historic cores of the traditional walled cities, as in Lahore or old Delhi, or the casbah of Algiers or the medina of

Figure 10.5
Villas miserias on the outskirts of Buenos Aires, showing progressive development.
Source: Author, 2011.

Marrakech, which are increasingly deteriorating from disinvestment and illegal conversions, and the resulting overcrowding.[61] Many *hutongs* within the historic walled city of Beijing have also seen unauthorized conversions of the historic courtyard houses. It seems that over the years, the Beijing municipality government has allowed the informal mutations of courtyard houses through a policy of benign neglect intended to accelerate their deterioration so that these areas will be ripe for clearance and renewal. Informal settlements on the periphery of Durban, illegal subdivision of agricultural land outside Cairo, and peripheral settlements of Quito are also examples of the latter type.

The UN-Habitat study further categorizes the slums and squatter settlements in three groups based on their location characteristics: central; scattered slum islands; and peripheral,[62] thus confirming the variable ecologies of poverty in the developing world. For example, in the Indian urban context, Gownamani and colleagues' study of Chennai catalogs the distribution of slum locations by site characteristics, especially those that are considered "objectionable."[63] The percentage distribution of slum families in the marginal spaces of the urban commons is as follows: river margins (24%), road margins (20%), railway easements and rights of way (3%), accounting for about half of all—about 175 thousand-slum families in the city.[64]

Returning to Chandigarh, the modernist utopia we have considered previously,[65] we note from the study of urban scholars V. P. Dubey and colleagues that some 45 slums or "colonies"—19 of them "authorized" and another 26 "unauthorized"—house 227,372 persons, or roughly a fourth of the city's total population.[66] In this instance the ecology of slums resembles a "scattered slum island" (or archipelago more appropriately) typology as suggested in the United Nations Centre for Human Settlements (UNCHS) report. But this pattern was not entirely accidental. The authorized colonies were initially contained within certain sectors, usually in the periphery of the original layout proposed by Le Corbusier. Even today some of these colonies are carefully hidden, concealed by high walls, as in Sector 25 of the contemporary city. Over the years, however, most of the unauthorized colonies have sprung up outside the planned city.

Poverty and Slums in the Policy Landscape

How the poor are located in the policy landscape is a reflection of how poverty figures in our collective ethical and moral landscape. The latter in turn is shaped not only by dominant religious edicts about the poor and poverty, but also by cultural, historical, and political-economic traditions and realities of contemporary urban societies. Academic research and analysis also play an important role in shaping this moral landscape. Thus, for example, urban planner Janice Perlman's debunking of the concept of "marginality," which was a popular refrain for nonaction among the policy makers in the seventies, led to uses of an alternative language to discuss the poor and the slum dwellers.[67] In her well-known study of the favelas of Rio, Perlman had originally argued that the concept of marginality was socially constructed with specific social, cultural, economic, and political components of the slum life. Socially, marginality meant internal disorganization and external isolation; culturally it signified traditional ways of life and the "culture of poverty";[68] in economic terms, it suggested parochialism and parasitism; and politically marginality was tantamount to apathy and/or radicalism. As her study showed, these constructs were "empirically false, analytically misleading, and insidious in their policy implications."[69] Yet concepts like marginality or "culture of poverty" offered excuses for widespread clearance and removal of slums in Brazil and elsewhere, and "benign neglect" as the principal policy response toward the underclass.

In her study, Perlman has shown that in reality the favela residents are cohesive, well organized, and well connected to the larger urban context; culturally they subscribed to mainstream values and aspirations; economically they composed the low-wage labor pool that contributed to, if not subsidized, mainstream economic activities, by dint of their dismal wages and by consuming overpriced products; and politically, they were quite capable of working the system in order to improve their situation.[70] Similarly, others have contended that notions linked to the culture of poverty—such as dysfunctional family, alienation from the larger society, lack of self-esteem—are also not necessarily evident in slum communities.[71] Anthropologist Larissa Lomnitz's study of a Mexican shantytown and urban planner Ananya Roy's more contemporary inquiry into the peri-urban settlement colonies of Kolkata also attest to this fact.[72] Urban planner Matthew Westfall's award-winning documentary *On Borrowed Land* (about the squatter community of Manila's Tondo) and the World Bank's 1981 sites and services program documentary also document the community spirit, work ethic, and mainstream aspirations of people living in slums (see figure 10.6).[73] At a theoretical level, urban planners like William Goldsmith and Lisa Peattie have argued about the positive community and organizational resources of ghettos and slums.[74]

In a follow-up study of Rio's favelas some thirty years after the initial study, Perlman found significant economic mobility and material improvements in the lives of her original subjects and their children and grandchildren. The physical condition of many of the favelas has improved, with paved streets, running water, electricity, waste disposal, schools, health clinics, and public spaces like any other neighborhoods. Indeed, there are significant differences in the income and consumption levels within the favelas. Yet she found that, in contrast to the sixties, when their existence was denied and shown as empty areas, the favelas are no longer considered illegal and are included in the official city maps. However, they still carry the stigma of marginality and are seen as a social problem.[75]

The image of inverted development has been associated with two very different types of response: a voyeurism from the outside, especially from the Western developed world, as epitomized in the works of Günter Grass, and a sense of denial from the inside, especially among those of power and affluence. In both instances there is an underlying sense of alterity—the otherness—of the slums and the poor. This "otherness" is embedded in the Orientalist instinct in the case of voyeurism, or in a form of cognitive distancing through such culturally rooted belief systems as caste or such modern conceptual artifacts as marginality or culture of poverty in the case of the latter. Slums and poverty are always seen as a problem of the poor and not the system of which structurally they are a part.

It will be an unfair and incomplete portrayal of the moral and policy landscape of inverted development without discussing some of the ongoing efforts to improve the lives of the urban poor, and slums and squatter settlements in particular, at both the civil society and the state levels. These efforts can be best described as an ongoing "conversation," as planning theorist Donald Schön once observed,[76] between the squatters and slum dwellers and the city authority, a variant of the "spatial dialectic"—to invoke geographer Milton Santos—between the formal and informal city.[77] This dialectic is one of invasion, squatting, and illegal occupation on the one hand, and the conversion and transformation of urban land (including public spaces, infrastructure rights of way,

Figure 10.6
Satellite dish in the slum—a sign of income improvement? A slum adjacent to Sabarmati Ashram, Ahmedabad.
Source: Author, 2011.

abandoned or underutilized land, and depositories of waste) on the other. The dialectic evokes corresponding countermeasures that may begin with evictions, clearances, and closures, but that ultimately change to a phase of denial and neglect, and perhaps ultimately acceptance and integration. Many of these sites are patently dangerous and unsanitary, subjecting the squatters to biological and toxic hazards, underscoring blatant incidences of environmental injustice and social inequality. These settlements are also subject to occasional disasters and chronic unhygienic conditions. For example, in the Kiberia slum of Nairobi heavy rainfall routinely washes the area's accumulated garbage into its water sources, thus contaminating them with pollutants. Several years ago a fire in Tondo, a Manila slum, destroyed some 2,500 dwellings, rendering over 25,000 residents homeless.[78] Settlements like these are also vulnerable to natural disasters like earthquakes and tsunamis, as was the case in the 1972 Managua earthquake, the 2005 Indonesian tsunami, and the 2010 earthquake affecting Port-au-Prince in Haiti. The 1984 Union Carbide accident in Bhopal, India, also underscored the vulnerabilities of slums and squatter settlements to man-made disasters because of their locations near industrial and toxic sites.[79]

Nevertheless the conversation that continues today in the form of a spatial dialectic had begun around the middle of the past century. Housing expert Charles Abrams had described the early acts of squatting as a "conquest" of targeted areas by the poor.[80] But these conquests or "invasions" by squatters were often only provisional, as government bulldozers would frequently remove squatter huts. But where the squatters occupied residual, unclaimed, or unusable urban space, the response would be generally one of benign neglect and denial, as we have discussed previously. Meanwhile there was considerable advocacy for squatter settlements, as represented by the works of architects John Turner and Geoffrey Payne, who argued that autonomous and progressive improvements of squatter settlements should be looked at as an answer to the shelter crisis that the resource-poor cities of the developing world constantly face.[81] Urban experts further argued that the best type of intervention might involve infrastructure improvement—including water, electricity, drainage, sanitation, schools, clinics, and community public spaces—and "regularization" of the settlements by offering titles to the property occupied by the settlers.[82] In the 1970s and 1980s the World Bank began its sites and services program, which provided loans to municipalities to finance a variety of settlement improvement programs, such as the *bustee* upgrading in Kolkata, improvements for the squatter settlements in Recife, and low-income subdivisions with individual lots fitted with plumbing and utility cores in Dandora, Kenya. The World Bank's enthusiasm waned as local governments began to realize that sites and services projects were in fact locking in valuable real estate in good locations. In countries

Figure 10.7
The Ambani tower, a residence in Mumbai not too far from the vast expanse of the Dharavi slum.
Source: Dinodia Photo. By permission of Getty Images.

like Brazil, local initiatives were directed at the established favelas, most of which had already gone through progressive development and consolidation. The Favela-Bairro Project of Rio de Janeiro, which began in 1993 with funding from the Inter-American Development Bank, is a major ongoing project that is in the process of integrating some 620,000 favela residents into the fabric of the city in 143 established favelas and 25 irregular settlements. Still another phase is planned, with a target of reaching some two million residents. The program includes shelter and infrastructure improvements, the latter involving both the physical and the social kind.[83] A significant infrastructure improvement serving the poor in squatter settlements is the recently constructed escalator in Medellín, Colombia. (See Epilogue: Best Practices.)

Clearly the Brazilian initiative has moved the dialectic in a positive direction, from a state of denial and social exclusion to acceptance and inclusion. Such findings are coming from other countries also. In a study of informal settlements in five Iranian cities, urban designer Mahyar Arefi concludes that these Iranian initiatives with World Bank financing have produced significant positive welfare in the form of engagement, self-help, and capabilities among the dwellers in such environments.[84] At the same time in many other countries, the growing competition for urban land in a global economy is making informal settlements untenable. Squatters are being evicted, slums are uprooted as the juggernaut of real estate development—shopping malls, condominiums, office complexes, hotels and restaurants, entertainment centers—continues to transform the landscape of emerging markets like Brazil, China, India, Mexico and the like. Furthermore, these informal settlements are proving to be highly vulnerable and impermanent, as the claims of the informal sector are constantly contested and resisted, and occasionally denied by force, as evident in the history of squatters in Lima, Peru, where it involved government military response.[85] The removal of Tondo residents in Manila[86] or the recent incident of removal of informal settlements in Zimbabwe are cases in point.

There is also the larger question of whether the mix of the formal and informal sectors is changing as some developing cities are making rapid economic progress, and as the voracious appetite for land in real estate development and urban infrastructure are squeezing out the informal economy. Recent studies in contested urban spaces have captured some of the inherent tensions and conflicts arising from this dynamic.[87] The dialectic that began with colonial subalternity, continued as postcolonial benign neglect and denial has now turned contentious and hostile, as the gap between the formal and informal sectors, between the leading and the trailing edges of development continues to widen. This new spectacle of inequality is now apparent in the emerging cityscape of the Global South (see figure 10.7). The enduring spectacle of poverty and inequality in the landscapes of inverted development continue to deprave and frustrate the ideal image of development.

11 The Faustian Imperative

> The only way for modern man to transform himself, Faust and we will find out, is by radically transforming the whole physical and social and moral order he lives in. Goethe's hero is heroic by virtue of liberating tremendous repressed human energies, not only in himself but in all those he touches, and eventually in the whole society around him. But the great development he initiates—intellectual, moral, economic, social—turn out to exact great human costs.… Goethe's *Faust* is the first, and still the best, *tragedy of development.* (emphasis added)
>
> —Marshall Berman, *All That Is Solid Melts into Air: The Experience of Modernity*[1]

In the seventies and the eighties shimmering new cities marked the spectacular transformation of the traditional desert landscapes of Saudi Arabia and Gulf Emirates. These were icons of passage into modernity, fueled by massive wealth from oil revenue. Meanwhile, other countries have undergone similar changes, if not as spectacular.[2] Beginning in the eighties we saw the rise of China, perhaps the most breathtaking of these transformations. The unprecedented scale and pace of this transition can best be described as one driven by a Faustian obsession with development. In this chapter I will argue that this obsession is manifested in two parallel agencies of change—the authoritarian developmental state on the one hand, and the hegemonic order of the new global economy on the other. I will pursue this metaphor here to describe the contemporary transformation of cities in many parts of the developing world, focusing on Beijing and Shanghai in China, and Dubai in the United Arab Emirates.

The Growth Unbound

In the recent past the media reported stories about China's stunning economic growth—peaking to more than 10 percent growth in GDP per capita during the nineties and the two following decades. While China's growth rate has slowed somewhat—it has been between

6 and 7 percent since 2016[3]—it remains one of the leading engines of the global economic growth. Media reports of China's rise as a "global factory" abound. Detractors point to its voracious appetite for energy, its contribution to global warming, the economic impacts of its export on domestic markets and jobs in other countries, its economic colonization of primary-resource-producing countries in Asia and Africa, its domestic income inequality and rural poverty, its steadily growing consumer economy, the growth of its cities and the extensive investment in their infrastructure and architecture, and so on.

These occasional critical themes notwithstanding, typically the media coverage is adulatory, or at best one of deference and awe. In publications on finance, technology, engineering, architecture, and real estate such obsequious stories abound. In architecture trade magazines and glossy coffee-table publications homage is paid regularly to China's modern structures and infrastructure, the emerging skylines of its cities, and its growing collection of "signature architecture" produced by world-renowned architects and architectural firms. Today not just China, but also other "emerging markets" have offered a new sandbox for Western architects to play out their aspirations, fantasies, and imaginations under the indulgent auspices of authoritarian states and global capital. It will be recalled that in the immediate postcolonial years the craze for new capital and new town development provided opportunities for frustrated visionaries whose ideas were previously ridiculed in the West. The new global economy and its willing state partners are now creating new opportunities for such architectural fantasies to be built in the deserts of Saudi Arabia and the Emirates, and in the coastal plains of China. These projects have become the driving images of global development today.

Too bad Le Corbusier did not live long enough to benefit from this architectural bonanza. But his legacy of city design—the tenets of the *Ville radieuse* and the Voisin Plan—continue to play a major role in massive developments in China and elsewhere, if not in the modernist design of Le Corbusier, certainly in appearance. In a recent article critiquing the contemporary urban development of China, urban planner Daniel Abramson aptly invokes the legacies of Haussmann and Le Corbusier as the defining characteristics of the transformation of the Chinese cities.[4] But if Haussmann and Le Corbusier symbolize the planning and design, who or what is driving this change whether it is the Chinese, the Emirati, or the earlier Saudi urban development? The answer of course lies in the growing role of the state, especially the authoritarian state, in concert with global capital. To explain the role of an authoritarian state in urban transformation and development in the contemporary project of modernization, political theorist Marshall Berman's discourse on modernity is particularly relevant here.[5]

Although Berman's work predated this transformative change in the developing world and was mainly retrospective of nineteenth- and twentieth-century urbanism and urban development of the Western world, his treatise on "the experience of modernity" remains relevant today. His interpretation of the experience of modernity combines a Marxian vision of modernity with a more humanistic reflection drawn from Baudelaire and contemporary literary writings. Berman's interpretation of Goethe's Faust as a "Developer" is an important trope in his treatise on the transformation of cities and more broadly, the human consequences of the passage from tradition to modernity.

Of the many versions of the story of Faust told over some 400 years, Berman found Goethe's rendition most appealing because of the imperative of development intrinsic to Faust's desire for change. What appeals to Berman about Goethe's interpretation of Faust is that the transition to modernity can be achieved only through the parallel development of the individual and the larger society, a very republican idea that is embedded in many of the contemporary development theories we have reviewed previously. But the implications for such development are enormous, and tragic.[6]

If Goethe's Faust is a developer, and development is an intrinsic experience of modernity, who then is Faust and who is Mephistopheles in the contemporary development experience? The answer may not be immediately obvious. Berman places the "desire for *development*"[7] squarely on the imperatives of capitalism that requires growth, innovation, and change. Here he sees in the cultural transformation of modernity the rise of a consumer society and development pursued by "Faust-as-the-consumer" aided and abetted by "Mephistopheles-as-the-developer."[8] Although a scholar of Marxian following, he shuns a structural analysis, which may seem more compelling in its use here.[9] Berman reveals his own affinity with the experience of modernity—spectacles and beauty on the one hand, and the narratives of loss on the other. He refers to St. Petersburg as a symbol of modernity, as "the paradox of public space without public life."[10] The notion of agency that drives the development process—modernization from above—becomes apparent further when Berman expresses his own despair and disbelief at the way large-scale public works projects built under the leadership of Robert Moses—the Cross Bronx Expressway in New York to be specific—had demolished the core of the Bronx, the borough where he had grown up. The mid-twentieth-century cityscape of New York, according to Berman, had been "an image of modern ruin and devastation."[11] Berman does not invoke Faust here, nor does he suggest Robert Moses as the twentieth-century proxy for Faust, just as it would have been inappropriate to think of Haussmann as the Faust of late-nineteenth-century Paris. Yet the imperative of change and growth manifested in the routine clearance and renewal of urban spaces remains the essential experience of modernity in urban space. The principal agencies of change lie in the authority of the state and the capitalist economy itself. Contemporary theories of the political economy of urban growth have variously characterized the nexus between the state and capital as the "growth machine,"[12] as a "state apparatus,"[13] "primitive globalization,"[14] and in the "urbanization of capital."[15]

This intellectual position embedded in the literature of the seventies and the eighties allows us to imagine the state as the Faust figure and global capital as Mephistopheles prodding Faust toward his "desire to develop." However, this metaphor becomes untenable for two reasons. First, the experience of modernity was not limited to capitalist economies, it was aggressively pursued also in the socialist modes of production as we have discussed in an earlier chapter. Even in China, where contemporary development is seen largely as an outgrowth of its market economy, a form of Faustian development was underway after the liberation, long before its embrace of market economy and state capitalism. Second, this concept of modernity preceded the growth of global capital and the powerful and hegemonic role that it now plays in transforming cities of the Global South. Contemporary writings on the urban outcomes of globalization are beginning to capture the dynamics of development.[16] Particularly noteworthy is sociologist William Sites's account of the contemporary changes in New York, a sequel to Berman's account some fifty years later.[17]

Sites uses the term "primitive globalization" to describe the dynamics of redevelopment in Midtown and Lower Manhattan during the last two decades. He defines this process as one where "certain states, neither circumvented by globalization nor resistant to it, instead, actively facilitate globalization through the use of state power in highly destructive or 'disintegrative' ways."[18] The concept of "primitive globalization" captures the essence of what I have called the Faustian imperative, and also helps to locate Faust as the symbol of state power, and Mephistopheles—if we were to pursue the metaphor further—as the agent of global capital.[19]

We should note that this metaphor may not fully express contemporary drive for development captured by the notion of "primitive globalization." Goethe imagined Faust as a developer in the Western context and did not anticipate the larger world that is fragmented, differentiated, and specialized in numerous nation-states, many of which were controlled by megalomaniac state authorities. The Faustian world was a uniform and homogenous plane where the identities of city, country, nation, and beyond were obviated by a seamless space of continuity and tradition yet to be re-formed by imperatives of modernity and its inherent "desires of development." In this undifferentiated landscape there was no competition between nations or any ranking of nation-states by power and wealth. But in today's world, nations and cities are in competition with each other in the international marketplace,[20] all vying for global capital and "foreign direct investment," or FDI. Today there may be many Fausts competing for the attention and favor of one Mephistopheles: global capital. A country like China, it seems, is in a race with time and itself, to reach the number one ranking in economic power as quickly as possible. Indeed, not that long ago a forecast by Goldman Sachs, as reported in *The Economist*, showed China surpassing the United States in GDP by 2025, and just about doubling the US GDP by 2050.[21]

The recent devolution of the development authority in China shows that the provincial and local governments of very large cities also have aggressively pursued global capital, in competition with each other, and at times in defiance of the nation-state. The Chinese State has now bred many subnational state authorities that are all being driven by the same impetus, abetted by the central state. It is this frame of reference that could help us understand the unprecedented transformation of several cities in the Global South.

Shanghai: The Making of a World City

In an article published in the July 1988 issue of the *Atlantic Monthly*, writer James Fallows described his visit to Shanghai as follows:

> One big Asian city, though, does seem to have frozen in time. This is Shanghai, self-proclaimed "Paris of the East" in the 1920s and now more romantic, sort of, than Paris itself.... Along the sluggish Huangpu River, on the famous Bund (or "river embankment"), the foreigners built hulking colonnaded trading houses, graceful Art Deco hotels, consulates and apartments that could have been plucked from pre-war Paris or Berlin....
>
> ... From that point on it was as if the physical aspects of the city—buildings, streets, homes—had gone into suspended animation: nothing added and nothing taken away....
>
> ... Shanghai's appeal has little to do with Chinese history indeed anything Chinese. But the effect is entrancing, even magical. To visit Shanghai is like being able to walk into Manhattan or Berlin fifty years ago.[22]

Reminiscent of Naipaul's reactions to Kolkata of the early sixties,[23] Fallow's account did not include the historic old city, or the vast stretches of postcolonial socialist housing that surrounded the earlier colonial city.[24] Nor did he acknowledge that many of the Western-style buildings were designed by the Chinese architects and construction professionals, albeit in the Western colonial style.[25] (See figure 11.1.)

To a large extent, this reference to a "frozen" urban form, and to an absence of a vibrant urbanism[26] commonplace in capitalist economies, is a reflection of the earlier Maoist policy of achieving balanced development, where much more attention was given to rural industrialization and modernization, and relatively little investment was directed to cities.[27] Cities in general suffered from the postliberation Marxian belief system that considered cities as the center of capital accumulation and as exploitative of labor and the countryside. Shanghai in particular was an "unloved city"[28] from

Figure 11.1
The Bund in Shanghai. The colonial legacy continues.
Source: Author, 1987.

the time of liberation until the end of the Cultural Revolution, mainly because of its colonial heritage and its urbanism; it was sullied by the influences of foreign cultures. According to political historian Richard Gaulton, Shanghai's "neon lights, European architecture, modern utilities, and vice and corruption contributed to its reputation for evil; it seemed part of a cultural world thoroughly alien to a Chinese peasant."[29]

Immediately before liberation there were some 200,000 privately owned industrial and some 120,000 commercial establishments in Shanghai.[30] Although the private enterprises disappeared with the formation of collectives and state-owned enterprises, this allegedly decadent city continued to produce more than a third of the gross industrial output of the country years after the liberation. In the fifties there was an attempt to decentralize industries from Shanghai and its cohorts, before recognizing that slowing down the main economic engines of cities would not help grow the national economy.

The development trajectory of Shanghai began full steam in the early nineties, soon after Deng Xiaoping's visit to the city in 1992, when he ordained Shanghai to lead the regional and national speed up its reform and take the lead in regional and national development.[31] The most significant component of Shanghai's transformation has been the area called Pudong (east of the river), previously an estuarine land between the Yangtze and Huangpu rivers comprising small towns, villages, and farmlands (see figure 11.2).

Figure 11.2
A traditional Chinese junk on the Huangpu. The tree-lined Pudong shore of an earlier era can be seen in the background in stark contrast to the current Pudong (see figure 11.3).
Source: Author, 1980.

Although a plan for Pudong development had existed for some time, the official go-ahead came from the central government in April 1990. An area covering some 533 square kilometers, Pudong has emerged as the most significant icon of modern China and its growing economic prowess. By 2000, in a matter of a decade, the Pudong New Area had become the "showcase of Shanghai's all-round competitiveness" with a population of 1.63 million (it would reach 5 million just ten years later, according to the 2010 census), and more impressively boasting a GDP of 92 billion RMB yuan (roughly US $11.5 billion). Since then, almost two decades later, Pudong's GDP has grown almost eight times, to about 690 billion RMB (about US $100 billion). This amount is larger than the total GNP of many small and poor countries in the Global South.[32] Pudong's 2000 GDP amounted to one-fifth of the total GDP of the Shanghai area, and also a third of its export, and a third of its foreign investments. Meanwhile, infrastructure investment in the area—highways, bridges, a new airport, a maglev rail (the first and fastest commercial line in the world) connecting to the airport—amounted to 300 billion RMB (roughly US $40 billion).[33] By 2006 more than thirteen hundred foreign enterprises from more than one hundred countries had invested in the Pudong district.

Planned as the setting for an economic growth machine, the Pudong New Area plan organizes its proposed functions in discrete districts: Lujiazui Finance and Trade Zone; the Jinqiao Modern Industrial Park; Zhangjiang Hi-Tech Park; Waigaoqiao Free Trade Zone; and Sunqiao Modern Agricultural Park. The Lujiazui district is the largest planned area, comprising 28 square kilometers. Its dramatic skyline features many high-rise buildings, accentuated by a communications tower of futuristic design facing the colonial waterfront on the opposite side. By 2001 some 180 office buildings of various architectural designs were already completed or under construction, many of them occupied by financial institutions like major domestic and multinational banks, stock exchanges, and insurance companies, and including regional headquarters of some 28 multinational corporations (see figure 11.3).

Similar success stories were to be told for the other Pudong districts. About the same time 20-square-kilometer Jinqiao Modern Industrial Park district had already attracted more than 370 foreign companies, with some 150 manufacturing plants specializing in automotive, information and communication technology, and microelectronics. In 2000 the district's industrial output reached 45.667 billion RMB, or US $5.7 billion, and has grown to almost US $1 trillion today. Another 25-square-kilometer area, known as the Zhangjiang Hi-Tech Park, was trying to draw pharmaceutical and microelectronics companies.

In many ways the Pudong New Area epitomizes the notion of "space of flow," as suggested by Castells.[34] There are variations in the way spaces of flow are manifested, but

Figure 11.3
The skyline of contemporary Pudong as seen from the Bund, across the Huangpu.
Source: Author, 2017.

one dominant paradigm is the spaces created for a new industrial and information economy, to nurture a "milieux of innovation"[35] The previous incarnations of these planned "technopoles" have come in a "variety of urban formats"[36]—Silicon Valley near San Francisco, the 128 Corridor outside Boston, and the Research Triangle in North Carolina are obvious examples. A technopole is designed for facilitating the flow of people, goods, money, and information, serving as a node in the new global economy where buildings house corporate headquarters, financial institutions, research and development firms, and high-tech production centers.

As a technopole, the Pudong New Area, however, is certainly not a "space of places"—the obverse, as suggested by Castells.[37] Its Lujiazui district—the finance and trade zone—is an ensemble of discrete, isolated, and non-sequitur architecture, many of which bear the "signature" of internationally renowned architects and architectural firms who are commissioned worldwide by Western and multinational corporations. As the "downtown" Pudong, and also a second central business district (CBD) of Shanghai, it was seen as a "strategic site for China's entry into the global market."[38] According to its promotional literature, Lujiazui is "intended to be developed as the Manhattan of Shanghai."[39] In its rush to capture global capital investments, and in a classic Faustian gesture of modernity, the built form of Lujiazui district has shunned all linkage to the traditional Chinese city, where the streets, temples, and gardens had always served as the most significant public realm and social space. The format of the planned city is one borrowed from the American "edge city": reminiscent of Irvine in Orange County, California; Tysons Corner in the Washington, DC, Metropolitan Area; and Mountainview or Sunnyvale in the San Francisco Bay Area.[40] Detractors compared the experience of Lujiazui similar to that of "the decaying downtowns in American cities in the sixties ... as a boring place where diverse human activity was not encouraged, largely because of the single and monotonous architectural functions and aesthetics."[41] In other words, this well-planned new urban district that features signature architecture from around the world lacks the kind or urbanism that thrives in Nanjing Road across the river, in the contemporary Puxi.

The central urban design feature of the Lujiazui district is Century Avenue, a major east-west axis some 100 meters wide, connecting the Oriental Pearl TV Tower—the distinguishing icon of Pudong skyline on the east bank of the Huangpu—with Century Park, five kilometers to the east. This monumental axis is wider than the Champs Élysées but roughly about the same distance between the Louvre and Place de la Porte Maillot in Paris. This parallel is not entirely accidental, and the future design scenarios for the design of this axis are developed with the help of urban design and landscape consultants[42] from the West to emulate if not exceed the grandeur and elegance of the famous Haussmannian axis of Paris. The high-rise office and residential towers are to be concentrated along this axis in overlapping diamond-shaped districts, as the axis diagonally cuts through the larger grid of Lujiazui.

The second most significant feature of the urban design of the Lujiazui district is Century Park, which occupies a land area of 140.3 hectares. Designed by the LUC Company of Britain with an investment of some US $125 million, this huge open space is a major entertainment and recreation complex. It is not quite a Hyde Park of London, or a Central Park of New York. It is more of a green theme park that includes everything from a golf course to an outdoor music square to fishing spots. It has seven theme scenic spots: beach areas, pastoral areas, scenic areas, a bird sanctuary, a sparsely planted lawn area, an international garden area, and a mini-golf course. The attempt to bring nature is commendable, but it lacks the sense of place and repose typically found in traditional Chinese gardens, such as the Summer Palace in Beijing or the East Lake in Hangzhou. What is ironic about this grand and monumental gesture of bringing nature to the Lujiazui district is that it fails to connect to the endogenous tradition of Chinese garden and landscape design, the deep sense of landscape aesthetics that is captured in centuries of traditional Chinese paintings. This deep tradition was dismissed, emulating instead the Western landscape designed by a British consultant.

The Pudong New Area development, while drawing immediate attention because of the architectural icons that dominate the skyline across the Huangpu River, is but a part of the larger narrative of hyperdevelopment that Shanghai has come to represent. While in 1980 there were only 121 buildings over eight stories—mainly vestiges of the treaty era—by 1989 that number had increased sixfold to 748. During the next ten years, that number increased some thirtyfold, and by 2006 Shanghai boasted almost 12,000 high-rise buildings. It was reported in the late nineties that one-sixth of world's construction cranes were being deployed in Shanghai. Between 2000 and 2005, total investment in fixed assets in Shanghai was 169.7 billion yuan (roughly US $21.3 billion). Of this amount, 67.8 billion yuan (US $8.6 billion) was invested in real estate.[43] By 2018 the total fixed-asset investment was estimated to have reached 200 billion yuan.[44] Obviously, this level of development has required considerable investment in urban infrastructure and public utilities. Between 2000 and 2005 this amount totaled some 30 billion yuan (US $3.75 billion).[45]

This massive capital investment in the transformation and "remaking" of Shanghai is part of a larger effort by the Chinese state to make Shanghai one of the top four or five world cities.[46] As Sun Sheng Han has pointed out, this effort began in the mid-nineties with a vision of spatial restructuring of the entire Shanghai urban region that featured "one core, three circular belts, and eight medium-sized cities."[47] This plan integrated satellite towns of the socialist era—Jiading, Minhang, Jinshan, and the like—and six development corridors devoted to various industrial sectors. The implementation of the plan required major infrastructure investments that included a subway system, two bridges across the Huangpu, an inner ring road, and the expansion of the existing airport. Soon, additional projects were identified including a deep-water port, a new international airport, a communication network, an outer ring road, a fly-over, and sewage and power plants. These investments and undertakings are examples of how "the state plays a key role in determining the timing, the pace, and the economic and spatial configuration of Shanghai's development, while the market is an indispensable part in central and local state decision-making."[48]

According to scholars who have studied this phenomenon of hyperdevelopment, the relationship between state, market, and global capital has been a dynamic and nuanced one. In agreeing to develop Pudong during the Eighth Five-Year Plan (1991–1995), the Chinese state pledged 4.5 billion yuan (over US $500 million) in five years, expecting that $100 million of foreign direct investment for those five years would be forthcoming. Although anticipated as an equal partnership, by the end of the Plan period, foreign investment had already exceeded US $4 billion, with promises of much more in signed contracts.[49] By 2000 total overseas investment had reached US $34.3 billion. More recently, in 2016 Shanghai attracted over US $16 billion, an increase of 2.5 percent over the previous year.[50]

In the center of old Shanghai, not far from the Bund on the Huangpu is People's Square, formerly the site of the Shanghai racecourse, now a monumental square surrounded by a busy jumble of public edifices, museums, symphony halls, and city administration buildings. On the east side of People's Square stands a proud civic building called the Shanghai Urban Planning Exhibition Center, devoted not just to plans and projects but also to the urban history of Shanghai. The uppermost floor of this museum is occupied by a sprawling scale model of the future Shanghai—a breathtaking sight—the emergent "five-star" world city (see figure 11.4).

Figure 11.4
A model of a world city, Shanghai City Planning Museum.
Source: Photo by author, 2017. By permission of Shanghai Urban Planning Exhibition Center.

But this new urban form reveals little about the urbanism of the place, the quality of public realm and space, or any sense of the future habitus. Standing in the People's Square, I remembered my first visit to Shanghai, in 1980, when this space—the former colonial race course—was a public open space where people came to take strolls, families and friends met, children played, and people gathered around storytellers. Today one could still find small clusters of older people dancing to music, a tradition difficult to pursue in the crowded big cities today.[51] Obviously, this pace of growth and hyper-development has not reckoned with issues of livability and quality of life. It has not produced significant new space for street life and social activities. I should note, however, that Shanghai's statistics on green areas show impressive improvement. Coverage of green area increased from 8.2 percent in 1978 to 37.3 percent in 2006. The number of parks has increased more than threefold, with large gardens built at the edge of the district. Yet, a relatively meager number of these green spaces are set aside for parks and public spaces, and the growth has also been rather modest compared to other types of ceremonial green spaces, as in the easements of road infrastructure or large green areas devoted to "Special-Purpose Green Areas" or "gardens and nurseries." Even the green spaces have been squeezed by the imperatives of developing this Faustian metropolis.

Beijing: Denouement of the Canonical City

On a sultry July evening in 2001, a crowd started to gather in front of a large television screen in Shanghai's Nanjing Road, in anticipation of the Olympic Committee's announcement to anoint Beijing as the host of the 2008 summer games. As the announcement was made, the crowd—mainly young Shanghainese—exploded in spontaneous cheers and joy, and soon a public celebration began, waving Olympic and Chinese flags. The celebration did not last long and turned out to be unexpectedly ephemeral. As the crowd of young men and women swarmed toward the Bund, the police moved in and quickly dissipated the promise of a long party on the Bund and the normal quiet of the night returned.

This event signaled a shift in the exigencies of priorities of the Chinese state, as Beijing became the second city from the developing world to host the Olympic Games. Although the coming of the Olympics put the development of Beijing into high gear, the deconstruction of this city—the canonical Chinese city that many experts believe took the Chinese over a millennium to perfect has been underway for quite some time, going back to the Japanese occupation of the forties [52] The new imperative of the Olympics marked beginning of the final denouement of this historic imperial city, captured in the brass relief of the Qing-Ming dynasty Beijing (see figure 11.5).

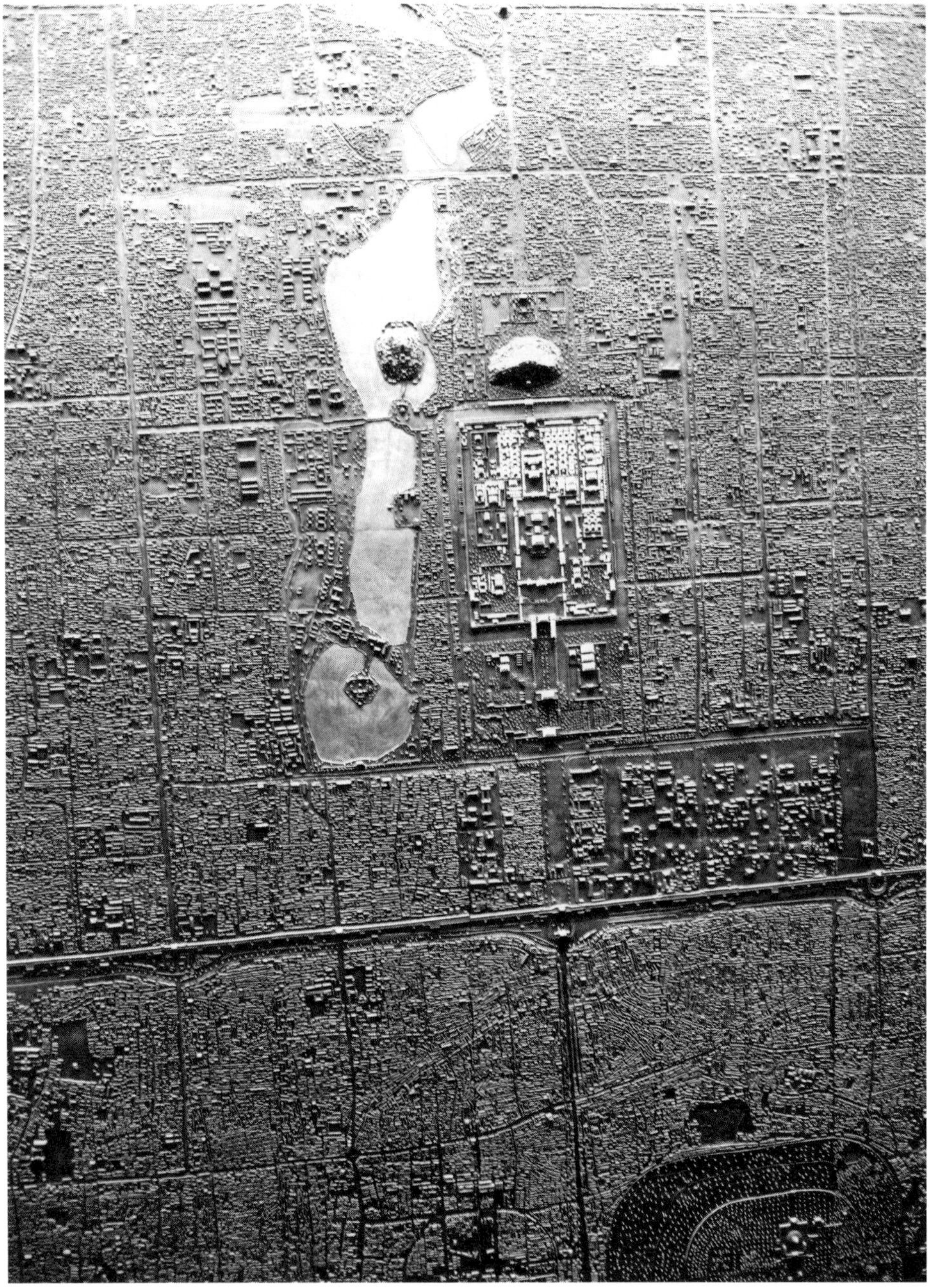

Figure 11.5
A brass relief of historic Beijing on display at the Beijing Planning Museum.
Source: Author. Photo taken at the Beijing Planning Exhibition Hall, 2009, with permission.

Selective removal of the historic walls in the vicinity of various gates began as early as the Japanese occupation. By 1961 the historic wall had been completely taken down by Chairman Mao's order and replaced by a ring road, a subway loop, and segments of high-rise buildings tracing the old wall. The opening up of Tiananmen Square was another act of socialist modernization of Beijing, along with the widening of Chang'an Avenue and the construction of the imposing People's Hall and the Cultural Museum flanking the new square, which was truly monumental in scale. The original north-south canonical axis—"the most magnificent urban axis of the premodern world"[53]—was reinforced by locating the Monument to the People's Heroes, and some years later Mao's mausoleum, on various points along that axis.

There were misgivings about making the historic canonical city the seat of the new People's Republic of China. Where to locate the new capital was discussed in two competing proposals: (a) redevelopment of the old city proposed by Zhu Zhaoxue and Zhao Dongri; and (b) a new site in the west suburb outside the walled city proposed by Liang Sicheng and Chen Zhanxiang.[54] The former idea ultimately gained strength on symbolic grounds—in fact, Tiananmen Square in the heart of old Beijing was chosen for the founding ceremony of the People's Republic—even though the west suburb proposal was based on sound planning strategies.[55] Architect Liangyong Wu underscores the Faustian rationality of this decision:

> There was little mention of the significance of the Old City or the historic architecture it contained. *The idea underpinning this proposal was that making way for a new world required destroying the old.*[56]

Furthermore, as he added:

> The Gate of Tiananmen had by then been confirmed as the symbol of the Neodemocratic Revolution, and its image was placed at the centre of the national emblem. The political significance could not have been more clear.[57]

Once the development imperative of the modern socialist state was established in the choice of the location of the capital, there was no turning back. The historic "T"-shaped space in front of the Tiananmen Gate that had served in many symbolic and official rituals during the Qing dynasty was demolished, along with flanking official buildings, to make room for the contemporary Tiananmen Square. The walls too came down despite controversy among preservationists and modernists. Presumably it was Mao who made many of these decisions.[58]

As Wu points out, the script for rebuilding the old city was already embedded in the 1951 Master Plan, heavily influenced by the Soviet approach to planning. The dominant rationale for rebuilding the old city was that since 80 percent of the building stock was single-storied and many very old, it would be easier to rebuild the entire old city than to build a new city. The Western rational mind failed to appreciate the magnificent heritage of *hutongs* and courtyard houses—the essential syntax and meaning of the text of the old city.[59] Notwithstanding its peasant-based revolutionary origin, seemingly the Chinese socialist state remained beholden to this Western image of modernity and change defined by style of architecture iconic of the Soviet Union. The imperative of change by rejecting the old and welcoming the new is well captutred in a contemporary poster (see figure 11.6). A parallel image is captured in the more recent

Figure 11.6
"Smash the old world & build a new one." A poster of the early communist era (dated April 1967).
Source: By permission of the University of Westminster Archive.

demolition of the existing building stock to make room for new office and residential towers and shopping malls (see figure 11.7).

In his critical commentary about the loss of the historic city, Wu continues,

> A grand renewal plan was set up to redevelop the entire old city within ten years, at a rate of 1 million square metres of demolition and 20 million square meters of construction each year.... redevelopment was emphasized and conservation ultimately neglected, although initially the two were to proceed hand in hand. Ironically the decision made in the early 1950s to redevelop the Old City destroyed much of the best of the city, including many grand mansions, and yet left much of the worst unchanged for forty years.[60]

The only problems with the rapid implementation of the Plan were that (a) the Chinese state was quite poor, its GNP per capita lower than that of India at that time of its liberation; and (b) in its egalitarian ideology it was committed to providing shelter for its citizens, including poor denizens of the old city. The rent was reduced several times in the 1960s and 1970s. According to Wu the minimum rent at "0.12 *yuan* per square metre per month, was equal to the price of a pack of cheap cigarettes."[61] So, while housing was almost free, there was also very little money available to repair the old housing stock or construct new housing to keep up with the demand as the population of the old city grew. Consequently, the original housing stock deteriorated further, and courtyards were gradually filled in with illegal additions and subdivisions. In the sixties and seventies, a limited amount of new housing was built in the form of three-to-six-story apartment blocks, many by collectives. Since much of this construction was for replacement housing, net addition to housing stock was fairly limited. Meanwhile demolition of historic hutongs and courtyard houses continued with the usual narrative of loss (see figure 11.8).

The script of redevelopment that stalled for almost forty years finally picked up steam with China's phenomenal economic growth in the nineties. Throughout the nineties and subsequent decades demolition of old courtyard housing and hutongs has been a common sight in Beijing in recent years, as streets are widened and new housing or office towers and large shopping complexes are being built. With the exception of public works projects involving infrastructure improvements and civic or government buildings, all other redevelopment projects are done by private investors and developers.[62] The entitlement scenario worked in the following manner: Municipality planners would show interested developers a blighted area of housing and hutongs, and stipulate certain conditions for new development. First and foremost would be a requirement for replacement housing for the residents in the area to be redeveloped, which was met either by building replacement housing on site, or by constructing new housing in designated areas in the peripheral suburbs, or simply advancing the

Figure 11.7
A parallel image of a person with a sledgehammer demolishing the historic building stock, Beijing, 2006.
Source: Courtesy of Fang Wang.

Figure 11.8
Demolition of hutongs and courtyard housing underway, Beijing, 2007.
Source: Courtesy of Fang Wang.

equivalent money in lien fee to the municipality who would then take care of replacement housing. Although land lease was priced fairly low to make the return appealing, developers ended up paying a variety of additional fees and were often required to take care of their power needs, waste disposal, and the like.[63]

As the denouement of the canonical city continued according to the Soviet script of the 1951 Master Plan, its historic hutongs (derived from the Mongolian word for "well") became a major casualty. Previously they had defined the internal structure, organization, and social life of historic Beijing. Hutongs were the east-west lanes of the city, main access routes to courtyard houses. They typically intersected major thoroughfares, which ran in the north-south direction. While the width of an arterial street or avenue was expected to be 24 paces or 37 meters, the width of a hutong was supposed to be 6 paces, or about 9 meters. Over the years the width of many hutongs became much narrower as residents expanded their compound walls into the public right of way. It was an organic way to accommodate growth, not unlike the autopoietic Muslim cities discussed previously.[64]

The hutongs of Beijing used to beget the urban sensorium, urban form, the essence of its urbanism, and the very habitus of the city. They were the settings of everyday social life, the public realm of the quotidian, and the historical and cultural vicissitudes of Beijing society. Hutongs were the essential text of the city that was written over many years in a language that urban planner Eric Heikkila metaphorically refers to as *hutonghua*.[65] Much of that text was inscribed in the naming of hutongs, which were named after people; or elements of nature and landscape; or to reflect the shape, size, or functions of the hutong. As one Beijing publication narrates:

> Names of Hutongs in Beijing seem to be all-embracing—They involve river, lake and sea ... ; mountain, the sun and the moon ... ; personage and family name ... ; market and merchandise ... ; factory and workshop ... ; flower, grass, fish, and insect ... ; cloud, rain, star, and sky ... ; chicken, duck, fish, and meat ... and so forth.[66]

Most of the hutongs are now gone; memories remain in books of photographs designed for the tourist market. In the 2002 foreword to one such book, Shu Yi, director of the Chinese Contemporary Museum, talked about how the hutongs provided a counterpoint to the hustle and bustle of a growing metropolis, and how these districts, with 800 years of history, are "brilliant showcases of China's glorious culture and traditions," concluding, "We must therefore preserve these architectural treasures instead of modern skyscrapers to replace them."[67] By 2002 this exhortation was already too late (see figure 11.9).

A few of the hutongs still remain as tokens of history catering to the tourist economy; they include Liulichang Culture Street and Dazhalan Shopping Street in the Qing addition; Nanluoguxiang, dating to the Yuan dynasty (see figure 11.10); Shishahai historic and cultural spot in the original Ming city; and reconstituted Ju'er Hutong.[68] The memory of this historic city is now reconstructed in computer simulations for future generations.[69]

The Faustian imperative of erasing eight hundred years of history of not just Beijing but the Chinese civilization more broadly is not over; it remains a challenge to some of the canons of historical city design. One aspect of the original imperial city that has always troubled Beijing planners and boosters is the absence of a "downtown," especially that of a skyline dominated by a cluster of high-rise buildings like in typical American cities. Even Shanghai today boasts an impressive vertical skyline befitting a world city. But modern Beijing remains a veritable urban sprawl—perhaps competing with Atlanta or Phoenix by any measure of urban sprawl—as a polycentric spread city without a dominant center.

When the plan proposed by Liang Sichen to locate the new capital in the city's western suburbs failed (including Liangyong Wu's modified west suburb plan), his last attempt to save the old city was to suggest a height limit to new buildings located within the walled

Figure 11.9
Large billboards announcing the changes to come.
Source: Author, 1996.

city so that they would not compete with the profile of the historic buildings. This was respected during the socialist years, partly because there was not a big impetus for redevelopment, and in the socialist economy the centrality driven by access considerations of a typical land market was largely absent, as the state owned all urban land.

The center, it will be recalled, was the canonical center where the Imperial Palace was located with a profile dominated only by royal palace structures.[70] In respect for this profile there was codification of height zoning that prevented any high-rise buildings to be constructed near the Forbidden City—the rule being that no man-made structures may be visible from inside the courtyards of the Imperial Palace complex. A few chimneys and unseemly buildings managed to intrude upon the pristine visual field. Consequently the tall buildings were consigned to the zones outside the original wall, now called the Second Ring Road, thereby maintaining the supremacy of the canonical center.

Figure 11.10
Restored Nanluoguxiang, one of the original hutongs preserved as a tourist attraction.
Source: Author, 2009.

There are competing and parallel plans for a new downtown. The Chaoyang district to the east of the Forbidden City from Wangfujing—a historical shopping street—to the Third Ring Road in the east has over the years accumulated major office, shopping, and high-end residential complexes, largely serving embassies and expatriate communities. In the late nineties the Chaoyang district was anointed as the site of the new downtown, and a competition was held for a plan for this area. The competition was won by the Los Angeles firm Johnson Fain and included a significant cluster of tall buildings, as expected in a downtown skyline. The whimsical CCTV tower, designed by the Dutch architect Rem Koolhaas, has become an iconic landmark (figure 11.11). Meanwhile, a second downtown flanking the Forbidden City in the Xicheng district to the west was also rising along another historical shopping street—Xidan Dajie—with a synergy drawn from the nearby linear financial district along the western alignment of the Second Ring Road.

Figure 11.11
The CCTV tower designed by Rem Koolhaas.
Source: Author, 2009.

These competing imperatives of modernity and change are now played out by the lower-order agencies of the Chinese state—in this instance, two district governments of the Beijing municipality, not the municipality as a whole. In her discussion of the development of the central business districts of Beijing, Shanghai, and Guangzhou, geographer Piper Gaubatz has argued that the opportunistic private development initiatives have often trumped the overall master plan and policy intents of local municipalities. In the case of Beijing, the district governments have come to play a major role in subverting the overall plan.[71] Thus, the canonical center is challenged by not one but two downtowns rising from the clearance of the historic city.

The story of the remaking—the "malling"—of Wangfujing, a historic shopping street immediately east of the Forbidden City, has been discussed in depth by architect Anne-Marie Broudehoux as part of her general arguments about the "making and selling" of post-Mao Beijing.[72] This popular pedestrian-only shopping street features familiar contemporary destinations like McDonald's and Starbucks (and why not, if the Galleria Vittorio Emmanuele Due in Milan can host them). Wangfujing, however, features full-size brass sculptures reminiscent of the street life that defined the essential concept of public space in China. Here I would focus on the "remaking," and "selling" of Xidan Beidajie (or north Xidan Street), which, as of the summer of 2005 was still flanked by many hutongs.

According to the current master plan of Beijing, Wangfujing, Xidan Beidajie, and the Qianmen shopping district to the south of the Qianmen Gate of the Ming city wall are the three primary commercial and retail districts in Beijing. The old shopping district south of the Qianmen Gate has been reconstructed—reinvented in fact—in the images of its preliberation urbanism, complete with a short streetcar line running through the middle of street (see figure 11.12). Meant for tourists, it is reminiscent of Main Street, Disneyland, in California.

Figure 11.12
Reinvented Qianmen district, Disneyland redux in historic Beijing.
Source: Author, 2009.

Development of the historic Xidan Street began in the early 1990s, ten years after the economic reform, although several department stores had located there even earlier. The intersection of Chang'an with Xidan Beidajie has defined the thrust of the subsequent development, with the headquarters of Bank of China located at the northwest quadrant. The north side of Chang'an is to be developed mainly as shopping, entertainment, and hotels for attracting "higher-level" customers. The southern side will be developed mainly as banking, financial services, and communications centers, as well as for hotel and entertainment uses. The planning, development, and management of this burgeoning district is overseen by a Functional Development Area Construction and Administration Committee that works with the local Chamber of Commerce, a Business Improvement District, and a Construction and Administration Committee for the Multi-Functional District. By 2005 the Xidan district had added some 1.44 million square meters of office and retail space with a target of 2.7 million by 2008.

Development has proceeded by widening the historic street, from 33 meters wide for a typical *dajie* to 70 meters, from Chang'an Avenue to Ling Jing hutong.[73] Many of the traditional businesses and stores serving the hutong residents are gone. The vision of the future Xidan is one of a "high-end" shopping district, where not all businesses or polluting industries will be welcome, according to the Xicheng district officials. Officials expect higher-quality international brand establishments and hope to develop a special zone for American products. The Xicheng district officials were very clear in their vision of drawing higher-income Beijing residents, as opposed to Wangfujing, which draws mainly Chinese and foreign tourists, or Qianmen district to the south, which caters to more moderate-income Beijing residents. Even though a new subway line is about to operate below Xidan Beidajie, off-street parking facilities are integral to these large mixed-use developments. Regarding the question of the future of the hutongs, the official view was that the "historical relics" are only worth saving if they have tourist appeal.[74]

Beyond the historic Ming-Qing city, the Faustian development imperative has led to large-scale Haussmannian urban surgery of street widening, and the building of successive ring roads. Most of the socialist-era walk-up apartments are now gone, replaced by tall residential towers in large superblocks reminiscent of Le Corbusier's Voisin Plan. The public realm has atrophied; the scale of development and growing auto ownership have made walking or biking difficult, if not impossible, near the major arterials in a city that used to be known for its millions of bicycle users. Large shopping malls—including the largest in Asia—are cropping up in the peripheral district along and beyond the Fourth Ring Road. Seemingly the new downtown of the Chaoyang district needs space for expansion. An international design competition in 2009 sponsored by

Beijing's CBD Forum invited ideas for the expansion of the existing downtown in the Chaoyang district. Most of the submissions suggested high-rise tower development, continuing the legacy of Le Corbusier (see figure 11.13).

Many major projects of civic, cultural, government, or private development, currently underway, or at planning stage, continue to advance the Faustian script of modernity and change carried out on a large scale and at a rapid pace. Almost all of these projects are planned and designed by internationally renowned Western architects, and many of them were chosen through international competitions.[75] The list of fourteen major master-planning projects (five in Beijing) conducted through international design competitions since 1993, as compiled by Gaubatz, is quite telling.[76] Western firms from Australia, France, Germany, Great Britain, Japan, Spain, and the United States won all these competitions, except one. The plan for the Beijing 2008 Olympic

Figure 11.13
Recent high-rise office and residential towers in the Chaoyang district, Beijing.
Source: Author, 2009.

Green involved the partnership of a foreign firm—Sasaki Associates (US)—and a domestic firm, Tianjin Huahui. In describing the proposed National Museum in Tiananmen Square designed by Gerkan, Marg und Partner of Germany,[77] architectural critic Layla Dawson comments that while a project of such cultural significance being designed by a Western architect may seem odd, "this decision is in line with China's policy of collecting international stars to add luster to their new found economic power."[78]

With a touch of irony the Olympic Green, planned by Sasaki Associates, immediately north of the Fifth Ring Road, is located at the top of the canonical north-south axis with a new railway station to the south. The master plan for this Central Axis was prepared by Albert Speer and Partner, which bears the legacy of his father, the older Albert Speer who helped Hitler conceptualize the north-south axial plan (called Germania) for redeveloping Berlin—a city that also has been described by urban historian Alexandra Richie as "Faust's Metropolis."[79] The saga of Beijing's transformation that began at a feverish pace in anticipation of the 2008 Olympics still continues unabated. A scale model occupying an entire floor in the Beijing Exhibition Hall attempts to capture this sprawling expansion of the historic city (see figure 11.14).

Dubai: Designer Islands, Global Malls, and the Tallest Building

In the 2007 Venice Biennale devoted to architecture and urbanism of the developing world, there was a wall plastered with blown-up satellite images of the Arab coast of the Persian Gulf. This impressive sweep of the coastal desert landscape of the United Arab Emirates displayed detailed renderings of several man-made islands attached to the straight coastline like peas in a pod. The islands are not all fully completed—some are in the planning stage—and are of different shapes and sizes. The most notable islands look like palm trees from above, the fronds being long peninsulas subdivided in linear strip of lots with water frontage served by an access road through the spine of each frond (see figure 11.15). Another island, more of an archipelago, is shaped in the form of the various continents—a veritable world map as seen from above, never mind that none of these land forms will be visible unless you are flying overhead or looking at a satellite photograph. Most of these islands are located off the coast of Dubai. Other variations on the palm theme can be seen further along the coast. This theme has been adopted elsewhere beyond the Emirates and proposed off the coast of the Qatar Peninsula and even the island of Bahrain. These new residential developments have attracted the wealthy, the retired, and the leisure class to rest, relax, and enjoy "the good life" on designer islands surrounded by pristine turquoise-blue waters.

Figure 11.14
A visitor trying to comprehend the transformation of the historic city.
Source: Photo by author, taken at the Beijing Planning Exhibition Hall, 2009, with permission.

Developed by Nakheel Properties, a Dubai land developer, the two Palm Islands—Palm Jumeirah and Palm Jebel Ali, the World Island and Deira Islands—are all located in the Jumeirah coastal area of the Emirate of Dubai. Deira development is the largest, and closest to downtown Dubai.[80] The Palm Island to the west is Palm Jumeirah (see figure 11.15), smaller of the two. Designed as a retreat and leisure-oriented residential area, Palm Jumeirah contains mainly large villas, but also apartments, cafes, and marinas. The westernmost of the three Palm Islands is Palm Jebel Ali, which is designed as an entertainment island that will feature six marinas, theme parks, and housing built on stilts—a "Waterworld" of sorts. The archipelago called "The World Islands" is located between Deira Islands and Palm Jumeirah. It will consist of 300 small private artificial islands, ranging from 23,000 to 94,000 square meters, divided in four different categories—"private homes, estate homes, dream resorts, and community islands"[81]—to be developed by independent private developers.

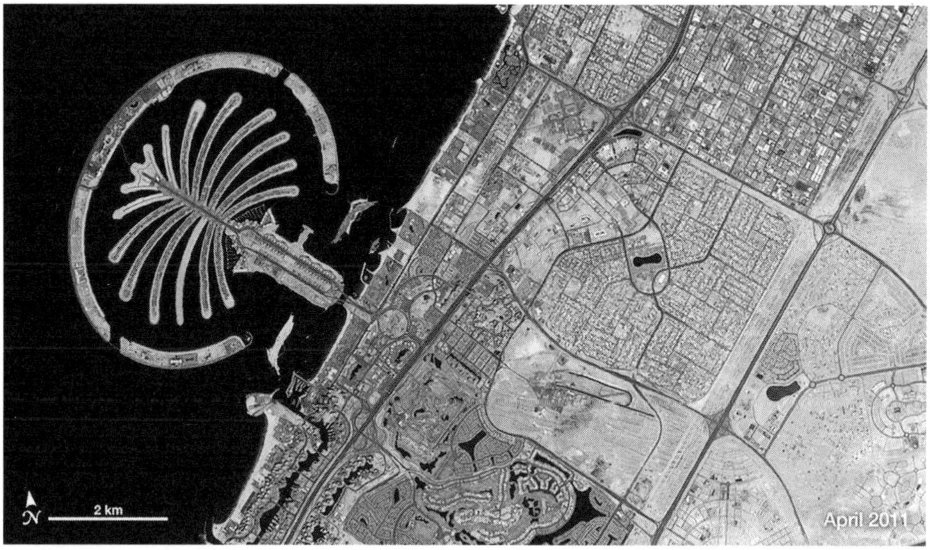

Figure 11.15
Palm Jumeirah, a new island development off the coast of Dubai.
Source: Courtesy NASA/JPL—Caltech.

These man-made islands under construction, some nearly completed, are only the opening narrative of a much larger and grander development script that Nakheel Properties has unveiled for the Emirate of Dubai. Dubai Waterfront is the vision for a huge development that will extend the current coastline of Dubai by 820 kilometers (or 492 miles), twelve times the current length of the natural coastline. This development will cover an area of 81 million square meters (266 million square feet) that will include more man-made islands in the shape of a partial crescent, and an artificial canal 70 kilometers (42 miles) long that will wend its course through the desert, creating new waterfront properties and inland developments. This grand vision will be carried out ten different areas involving 100 different waterfront communities and over 150 planned communities. Developers of this project see it as being the world's largest beachfront development.[82] The core of this new development is the Madinat Al Arab area, anchored by a 750-meter (2,460-foot) skyscraper, Burj Khalifa, the tallest building in the world.

It is not too difficult to interpret the symbolism of palm trees, a map of the world, and a giant crescent with a star used by Nakheel Properties to shape these megaprojects. They expect these forms to be visible from outer space, and to be the only man-made forms to reach that distinction other than the Great Wall of China. These icons of

Figure 11.16
The access to Palm Jumeira, lined with apartment complexes and featuring a light rail connection.
Source: Author, 2012.

Islam—now the faith of one-fifth of the world population—will be visible from outer space along with the Great Wall of China, perhaps the largest public works project undertaken during the Ming dynasty. Might the world map be also seen as an icon for the global city that Dubai is aspiring to be?

The development imperative in this instance comes from the former Emir of Dubai. While the United Arab Emirates—a consortium of seven emirates on the Gulf—is one of the wealthiest nations of the world, with a GNP per capita of $39,130[83] and the fourth-largest oil reserve after Venezuela, Saudi Arabia, and Iraq, albeit most of it concentrated in the Emirate of Abu Dhabi. The Emirate of Dubai had few oil reserves within its territory and could not count on the oil-based wealth that has driven the growth of other emirates. It could, however, count on the investments from its enormous wealth that was being accumulated in the region, and also on the emerging markets of the new global economy. Accordingly, the Emir of Dubai, in a strategic move and with a good deal of foresight, chose to make his emirate a global destination for material consumption and entertainment. Although the people of the Emirates are traditionally conservative orthodox Muslims, the Emir of Dubai decided to create a highly secular and permissive environment to make it a global city. The current Emir of Dubai has proposed to make Dubai the smartest city in the world through technological investments by the end of this decade. Earlier, Dubai had entered the competition for the tallest building in the world, and it now claims the winner, Burj Khalifa, a residential hotel tower of over 160 stories, with a height of 828 meters, located in downtown Dubai (see figure 11.17). Designed by Adrian Smith of Skidmore, Owings & Merrill, this building is now the principal landmark in the transforming desert landscape.

Figure 11.17
Burj Khalifa (under construction) in downtown Dubai.
Source: Author, 2007.

Today the Emirate is a shopping mecca for upper-middle- and upper-income families from the Arab world and the Southeast Asian countries, which also provided the cheap labor needed for the Emirate's blue-collar service jobs and construction projects. It has built on its historic role as a trading post on the Gulf. In the old Dubai harbor one sees many cargo *dhows*—traditional boats made of lumber—that may come from as far away as Sri Lanka, across the Arabian Sea, but more commonly from Karachi and other coastal cities of Pakistan and India. The *dhows* bring spices, tea, cotton, and other primary products, take back cheap electronic goods, and deliver goods to places south on the African coast in Yemen and Somalia.[84]

In the late nineties and in the first decade of this century the pace has quickened, as Dubai has become a successful destination, not just for shopping and entertainment but also for wholesale trade, finance, and professional services. An area called "Silicon Oasis" has been set aside for information technology development in the hopes of making Dubai a hub for software development.

With the overall boom in real estate and foreign investment, the "malling" of Dubai has continued apace. The Mall of the Emirates, measuring 6.5 million square feet (with 2.4 million gross leasing area), opened in 2005, is now one of the largest malls of the world.[85] Its large, cavernous halls are fully air-conditioned and complete with an all-season indoor ski slope, while the outside desert temperature exceeds 40 degrees Celsius (104 degrees Fahrenheit). There are many other malls, each with a different theme. The Il Mercato mall is designed with an Italian flair. The Ibn Battuta Mall, opened in 2005, is based on the theme of six countries—China, Egypt, India, Indonesia, Morocco, and Persia—that the famous Arab traveler Ibn Battuta visited several centuries ago.

One could argue further that the Ibn Battuta Mall, seemingly a creative and original expression of the Third World modernity by Nakheel Properties, in a way represents the worst form of Orientalism, by reproducing all of the romantic and imagined extensions of reality represented in the Orientalist paintings of the West. Other malls suffer from an ersatz hyperreality,[86] a Disney-like chimera, which includes malls designed like traditional souks. But the consumers in these spaces represent both a domestic and a global audience. The global audience is increasingly from the prosperous oil-rich Gulf countries, but also includes expatriates and visitors from the lately prospering countries such as China, India, Malaysia, and the Philippines. This repackaging of traditional cultures in the images of the Western mind could very well be what these consumers want.

Finally, efficiency and sustainability are certainly not a consideration in this Faustian script. Sustainability remains a major issue. The shiny glass towers in downtown Dubai are a case in point (see figure 11.18). The environmental costs of the man-made islands on the nearshore marine ecology are now being questioned in the blogosphere.[87]

Figure 11.18
Glass towers shining in a hot desert landscape.
Source: Author, 2019.

Groundwater depletion in nearby Bahrain has already caused salt-water invasion and loss of native groves of palm. Similarly, the impact of rising impact of desalination plants and their waste on marine and terrestrial ecologies are also beginning to be examined. Nevertheless, the largest desalination plant to date is now functioning off the coast of Fujairah, drawing water from the vast supply of the Indian Ocean. It is also interesting to see the way the urban landscape is being "greened"—with lawns and foliage-laden trees—mainly with recycled water that comes from desalination plants.

Concluding Thoughts

The examples of Shanghai, Beijing, and Dubai are but three epitome examples of Faustian development that have denied endogenous roots, culture, and presumptive moral order, but also their environments, their nature services, and their large carbon footprints. Along with its tallest structure, Dubai is considered the least sustainable place in the world. The dark side of this transformative development also hides the fact that the construction of the buildings and infrastructure are done by expatriate workers from South Asia, most of them living what amounts to labor camps carefully hidden from plain view.

The examples reviewed here thus are examples of what Berman saw as "tragedy of development," as captured in the epigraph for this chapter.

12 The Place of Medina

> Our country's beauty lies in its historic monuments, but its modern constructions detract from this great beauty. I am not referring to the bidonvilles but to our streets—to what is seen by foreigners and to what we ourselves see when we pass through an alley or a street. For example, if we lowered a blindfolded person from a helicopter into one of our cities, he would not recognize the city and would probably not realize that he is in Morocco.
>
> —His Majesty King Hassan II[1]

The archetype of medina—the old city of medieval vintage—was intrinsic to our discussion of the autopoietic city. The question that it begs, however, is where might we place the medina in our images of development. Can we imagine the medina to be an antithesis to modernity in an ongoing dialectic about development that began with the colonial era? In the precolonial, premodern time the medina was the endogenous and reigning thesis of community, place, and sustainability. The Western project of modernity introduced by colonial powers presented an antithesis to that inertia. Today, two centuries later, the urbanism of modernity has become the reigning thesis. The relevant discourse on the future of city design is now framed in a dialectic that includes a competing antithesis of authenticity, cultural continuity, identity, and sustainability. Accordingly, instead of considering the surviving historic cores of the developing world—Fès el Bali, Khan Khalili of Cairo, the Bazaar of Espahan, Chandni Chowk in old Delhi, and the like—as anachronism, we may think of them as antithesis to modernity. Perhaps an answer to sustainability may emerge from this dialectic between the medina and the modern metropolis.

The setting for this exploration is Morocco, with a focus mainly on the historic medina of Fès.[2] The planning agency of the Fès municipality (Agence Urbaine de la Wilaya de Fès et de Sauvegarde de Fès) and the agency created in 1992 to oversee the conservation and restoration of the architectural masterpieces of the Fès medina

(Agence pour la Dédensification et la Réhabilitation de la Médina de Fès, or ADER-FÈS) are facing the very questions posed above. The following narrative focuses mainly on the experience of Fès. Where appropriate, relevant examples and images are drawn from other medinas of Morocco—Rabat, Salé, and Marrakech—as well as more generally, from the experience of other historic cities of the precolonial genre.

The Medina as a Symbol

The medina today symbolizes many different values: continuity and community on the one hand, and counterpoint and contrast on the other. The medina in Moroccan cities is fundamentally a walled medieval city that has endured through centuries, and in the case of Fès, over a millennium. Oldest of the imperial cities of Morocco, Fès was founded toward the end of the eighth century and settled by families who came from such places as Baghdad and Arab Andalusian Spain to escape persecution or threats of expulsion. The history of medieval Marrakech and Rabat also goes back to the twelfth century.[3] The continuity of these medinas is not just a matter of the physical form, but also one of a mode of urbanism and habitus, which is integrally linked to the structure of their economy, institutions, activity settings, and uses of space. Much of the medina economy is still organized around artisan guilds similar to those of the medieval times, where traditional skills have been passed on from generation to generation.

To some observers the medina—its physical form, economy, institutions, and urbanism—is associated with underdevelopment and backwardness of the traditional societies and suggests the inability of some traditional societies to become modern. Even within some of the prosperous and modernizing Arab countries traditional settlements similar to the medina have been abandoned as backward, functionally obsolete, or not reflective of the prosperity and standard of living these countries can afford for their citizens. Thus, residents of traditional settlements in the Unayzah area in the Al Qassim province of Saudi Arabia, for example, were relocated to more modern settlements, leaving the old settlements as ghost towns.[4] Decanted of their original residents, historic cores of such major cities as Dubai, Kuwait City, Manama, and Riyadh have been and are now occupied almost entirely by the expatriate workers from the Indian subcontinent and other parts of the world.

The spatial dialectic[5] between the medina culture and modernity had begun during the colonial times, with the new European settlements distancing themselves from the traditional city. As Abu-Lughod pointed out, the original medina economy, although physically distinctive and usually walled, was closely linked to the agricultural hinterland.[6] The circulation system inside the medina was limited to pedestrians and pack animals, not unlike medieval cities of Europe. Even today some thousands of donkeys are registered with the Fès municipality to carry heavy loads in and out of the medina, underscoring its enduring physical form. "A common legal system," notes Abu-Lughod, "quite different from Roman law, regulated the relationships of neighbors within the smaller cells of the city."[7] The colonial city, *la ville nouvelle*, was built according to Western tenets of modern city planning, albeit influenced by baroque tradition of axial layouts and geometric form, as epitomized by Baron Haussmann's redesign of late-nineteenth-century Paris.[8] Seemingly more orderly, these settlements were less dense, with larger street blocks, and a very different "grain"[9] of development.

But the contemporary medina is more than just a symbolic counterpoint. It is also emblematic of income polarization, class differences, and marginality.[10] As Abu-Lughod argued, the medina in the precolonial times was not stratified by class; rather, it was organized along "clientage,"[11] kinship, and ethnicity, and in the case of Fès, along artisan and trade guilds, most of which still endure. She argued further that this traditional order and social organization of the medina started to break down with the colonial urban development outside the walls of the medina and the founding of the modern quarters. Seemingly, this was a case of both push and pull effects. The usual uneven spatial development and dependent urbanization[12] that ensued after the colonial arrival led to a massive influx of rural poor, who had been uprooted because of the collapsing rural economy.[13] While much of this explosive growth ended up in peripheral, uncontrolled settlements known as *bidonvilles*, many rural migrants found shelter in the medina. At the same time, original minority residents of medinas—the Jewish residents of Mellah in Fès or Salé—and some upper-class families, chose to leave because of the appeal of the new developments outside, and also to escape crowded quarters inside. Thus, the original order of the medina, which, according to Abu-Lughod, was "the antithesis of the cash nexus class segregation of the modern urban community,"[14] metamorphosed into class-based segregation of low-income population. The medina became the antipode to the modern postcolonial city.

Functions of Medina: The Case of Fès[15]

The contemporary functions of the medina obviously may vary from city to city, depending on their location, size, and age. In its reference class Fès medina stands out an epitome urban form, with a quintessential urbanism of community, place, and sustainability.

The map of the urbanizing areas of the Fés municipality captures the sprawling nature of its current growth, discontinuous and piecemeal. Discontinuities reflect the typology of the phases of North African urbanization as discussed by Abu-Lughod: the historic core, the colonial city, the contemporary *ville nouvelle* (the colonial city is now a center for the new urban extensions since the independence),[16] the *bidonvilles*, the peripheral suburbs, and the rural fringe (inexorably being transformed into a new type of "edge city"). There are large gaps in this urban sprawl, some explained by topography and productive farmland, but others are not so easily understood. In any event the metaphor of leap-frog development seems appropriate to describe the pattern of this urban sprawl.

Today the medina is only a small part of the larger municipality, but easily distinguishable in the larger urban context because of its compact and organic form. While it houses a total population of 156,000,[17] occupying about one-third of the total area of the city, it is ten times denser than the rest of the city. It is considered one of the largest car-free urban areas in the world. Located in a valley (see figure 12.1)—a hollow, more appropriately—the medina has a linear form that stretches for three and a half miles along an east-west axis.

It comprises two distinct parts, Fès el Bali, the older and original medina, and Fès Jdid, a later addition in the western part of the complex. The older section of the medina includes the historic Quaraouiyine mosque and the souks. A river, Wad Fès, mainly underground today, runs through the older medina along a north-south axis.[18] The newer section, added in the fourteenth century,[19] contains the royal palace, and the Mellah, the Jewish quarter. A continuous wall defines the boundary of the entire medina—Fès el Bali and Fès Jdid—punctuated by eight different gates as the principal entry points.

Figure 12.1
Urban form of the Fès medina.
Source: Author, 1999.

At its widest part the medina is no wider than a kilometer, and it is less than 4 kilometers in length. Although most of the medina is contained within the wall, it spills over in the northern edge in the form of newer settlements built immediately outside a major opening in the wall. The land outside the medina wall is generally vacant, with the exception of some farming, educational institutions, a hospital, and a few cemeteries; the rest is mainly rugged natural terrain. A major highway encircles the walled medina, providing access to the various gates. The medina thus remains isolated from the rest of the city, seemingly maintaining its physical distance and symbolic insularity from the larger secular and globalizing urban context.

Despite this apparent spatial insularity in its larger urban context, the medina's social and economic integrity—indeed, its very soul or habitus—is seemingly far from being secure, as we will see in the ensuing text. But in order to appreciate the nature of such threat, it is necessary to review the traditional functions of the Fès medina.

Community and Piety

Whether there is such a thing as an Islamic city or what constitutes an Islamic city has been a topic of considerable scholarly debate.[20] Some have suggested that the archetype is mythical and a figment of Orientalist imaginations. Nevertheless, it is reasonable to argue that while the medina serves many secular functions, an "Islamic essence," to use Abu-Lughod's term,[21] certainly pervades the medina. She identifies three defining characteristics: a juridical distinction between population classes based on their relation to the community of believers, gender segregation in space, and system of property laws. These are basically characteristics that pertain to the social ecology, urban form, and urbanism of the medina, but not necessarily the ethos and the spirit of the medina. These are the "soft city" attributes, to draw from Jonathan Raban, which I would argue are embedded in the ethical and moral foundation of the medina residents—their sense of responsibility toward their neighbors and the needy, and their acceptance of a larger social contract.[22] (See figure 12.2.) There is no doubt that their quotidian rituals and social contacts are facilitated by the spatiality of the medina, one that clearly obligates and privileges propinquity. But the sense of community and piety is also derived from the tenets of Islam and reinforced by its institutions. Repeatedly the residents of the medina who participated in our focus-group discussions pointed out that it was important to care for one's neighbors, for example, in the same way one would treat one's heir.[23]

Sense of Place

With the notion of piety and community comes the sense of place, an elusive quality that seemingly is in short supply in the environments of modernity. Invoking

Figure 12.2
Sense of place: a pedestrian street in the Quaraouiyine district in the Fès medina.
Source: Author, 1999.

Lynch's work on imageability, Abu-Lughod has suggested that the medinas are settings of strong imageability.[24] For the residents of the Fès medina their environment will no doubt score high on at least two of three criteria of imageability discussed by Lynch—identity and meaning. The third criterion, structure, may not be immediately apparent to a casual observer, because it lacks legibility and remains a complex, daunting maze. But it may be perfectly legible for the longtime residents who possibly have developed a coherent cognitive structure derived from familiarity and learning, and an

Figure 12.3
Urbanism of Fés medina.
Source: Author, 1999.

understanding of the essential syntax necessary to read the built form and the social ecology of the medina. Nevertheless, even to the visitor the medina will always remain a memorable experience. The visual form of the Fès medina has all of the properties of a good image, except legibility of its street pattern—a strong edge defined by the walls, paths defined by the main routes of travel between the gates, important landmarks of mosques and madrasas, nodes defined by convergence of paths and intensity of activities that occur around some of the gates and elsewhere, and districts defined by the souks, the guilds, and the residential areas (see figure 12.3). But the sense of place that medina residents have about their locality is a function not only of imageability of the physical setting, but also of a confluence of existential values related to community, identity, and propinquity. Sociologist John Gulick, who replicated Lynch's methodology to study the public image of Arab cities, concluded that quotidian life and social meanings are more likely to determine important landmarks in the collective images, than the visual dominance of buildings.[25]

Culture of Guilds

The institution of guild, a vestige of medieval times, still continues in the Fés medina, almost as a counterpoint to the global economy of mass consumption and production. The guilds are closely associated with the various artisans' districts—brassware, furniture and woodwork, pottery, tanning and leather goods, and the like—which have existed for many centuries (see figure 12.4). Even today the crafts produced by the various artisan communities remain the principal source of income for the medina population. The structure of the guild helps to protect traditional skills which are transferred from generation to generation through apprenticeship and family networks. And indeed the collective identity of the medina residents is in large part derived from their association with the guilds and the active practice of these traditional arts and crafts. The culture and institution of guilds also impart on these medina residents a heightened sense of aesthetics and a pride of ownership of the place. This in turn contributes to the formation of social capital, voluntarism, and grassroots activism that, as we will see later, has become an incipient force in tackling the growing problems of the contemporary medina.

Figure 12.4
Workers in a tannery in a leather workers' guild in Fès.
Source: Author, 1999.

Public Realm

Much has been written about the gendering of space by Islamic edict, and how the women are consigned to the confines of the house for maximum privacy.[26] In reality the transition from the private to the public space is more gradual, through the hierarchy of alleys, neighborhood streets, and the like, which serve as intermediate semiprivate and semipublic domains. For traditional and cultural reasons, the public realm is still dominated by male presence, but certainly not exclusively in the medina space. Indeed, as the medina becomes more crowded, and original courtyard houses convert to multifamily dwelling units, the quotidian life and activities certainly spills over to the public space. In these crowded and shared quarters domestic privacy is severely compromised, and families had to make do by hanging sheets or constructing temporary walls to block off parts of the shared courtyard space. Alleys and neighborhood streets are used for child's play and adult socializing.

Since the form of the medina was obtained in a precapitalist, and pre-market-economy era, the public realm is not sharply differentiated by the lines of property ownership. Rather it has evolved very much as a shared commons, with the institutional overlays of the guild, the mosque, and historical trading customs. The public realm of the souk is differentiated according to the practice of spacing land use according to their negative externalities and bulk of goods traded—those with high negative externalities (industries, wholesale, produce markets, etc.) away from the core, and closer to the gates, while the land uses that are more convivial, and of high positive externality, like food, pottery, jewelry, books, prayer rugs, and incense (the latter related to the religious customs) closer to the center of the souk, near the main mosque. The system of mosques, including the famous Quaraouiyine mosque and the madrasas, *hammams*, open squares, spaces inside or outside the gates, the fountains, all contribute to the social construction of the public realm, comprising a community of places.[27] (See figure 12.5.) It is different also from modern cities in the sense that it functions as a common resource pool, rather than one that is defined and managed by the state as an external entity.

Social Capital, Voluntarism, and Civil Society

These days we hear a lot about civic engagement, decentralized decision making, capacity building, social capital, and civil society as antecedents of development, especially after sociologist Robert Putnam made his case based on empirical work.[28] These virtues are seen as essential foundations of the Western liberal democracy, of modernity; in the absence of such institutions, it is seen as difficult to create democracy and to garner the bottom-up momentum necessary for successful development. What is striking about

Figure 12.5
Restored historic building in the medina, enhancing the public realm.
Source: Author, 1999.

the medina culture, as I have argued previously, is the strong tradition of *virtu civil*, or what the French call *sense civique* that has existed for generations and survived through colonial times and postcolonial modernity.[29]

This stock of the medina's social capital certainly did not accumulate through any history of democratic governance of the country; it happened mainly because of the cultural and spiritual institutions of the medina and its legacy of autopoiesis. As the circumstances of the medina are changing, which I will discuss in detail in the following section, the tradition of a strong civil society and an abiding sense of community have helped to develop new responses to new challenges. What was particularly striking was how the long-term medina residents, traditionally artisans and craftsmen with a heightened sense of aesthetics and appreciation of the built form, organized to act against the recent decline in the quality of life of the medina because of crowding, densification, and the arrival of a poor, migrant population uninitiated with the ethos and decorum of the medina.

Many of the medina residents are active members of an association that was founded in 1996 by a group of residents around an alley called Sbaa Louyat in the Quaraouiyine district, literally in the shadow of the famous mosque. The group called itself Association Pour l'Education sur l'Environment, dedicated to educate the recent migrants about the values about cleanliness and conservation of this precious environment and to train them to appreciate the long-standing decorum of the medina life, and have them cooperate in keeping their alleys, and the medina environment more generally, clean (see figure 12.6).

They began by a door-to-door campaign to enlist both merchants and residents to cooperate in raising the overall awareness about the aesthetic values of the medina. They expanded the campaign to recruit medina women—willing and enthusiastic participants—and succeeded in reaching children by introducing environmental awareness learning program to the schools. Activities of this association have now branched out to include various charitable functions, such as providing food to the needy families during holiday celebrations; covering rent, hospitalization, or funeral expenses for poor families; mediating legal issues; and providing assistance to the newly arrived migrants in getting identification cards. Other such voluntary organizations are now cropping up, adding new increments to the medina's existing stock of social capital.[30] According to a recent World Bank report, there are some sixteen such ad hoc groups within the medina, nine of which have some type of official status.[31]

The Bazaar Economy

The economy of the medina, which has its roots in precapitalist era, is also an institution by itself, and represents the "bazaar" or the "informal" sector of a classic dualistic economy. The medina economy of Fès shares many of the characteristics of informal economy prescribed by the International Labor Organization (ILO): labor-intensive, low overhead, low and substandard wages, family operation, and so on.[32] In the case of Fès medina, and generally for other medinas with substantial tourist trade, the bazaar economy maintains significant interface with the formal economy. In the early nineties it was estimated that about three-fourths of the medina residents were working

Figure 12.6
"Together for the sake of environmental protection"—a sign from a local civil society, Fés medina. *Source*: Author, 1999.

in the informal sector economy, and the medina employment comprised about two-thirds of all jobs in the city of Fès.

Threats to Medina and Official Response

The Fès medina is one of some thirty-three historic medinas (thirty-three medinas and historic archaeological sites)[33] in Morocco that have been undergoing steady decline since the early twentieth century, as new investments and urban growth have taken place largely outside their walls, following Lyautey's directives for new colonial development at the turn of the century.[34] This gradual decline has led to severe deterioration of historic and architectural heritage, urban services and infrastructure, and the overall quality of life. The cycle of disinvestment and neglect began as many original owners moved out and sold their houses to speculative buyers or just became absentee landlords. Meanwhile, as the rural poor continued their exodus to the city throughout the century, the medina became the host for many of these migrants, who managed to escape the *bidonvilles* and other peripheral settlements. By the late eighties some 20,000 migrants were arriving annually, leading to an annual growth rate of 2.5 percent. The medina population apparently had swelled to 250,000, forcing the government to relocate about 100,000 from the crumbling old structures.[35] By the late nineties the population figure was reported to be around 181,000 for the medina, including Fès Jdid. A survey conducted in 1995 reported that some 36 percent of the medina population was below the poverty threshold, much higher than the national average of 28.7 percent for rural and 10.4 percent for urban population.[36]

The supply of the low-income housing stock was created through a mutation of original courtyard houses, designed for habitation of a single family. Now three to four families share many of these houses in the medina by partitioning of the courtyard and corridors for privacy and other domestic functions. The dynamic of this transformation has at least three facets.[37] The first phase of this transformation began in the earlier part of the twentieth century with the development of the new colonial and modern city, as Abu-Lughod has pointed out.[38] Many of the families who were not Muslim, or who had money and secular orientation, were the ones to move out first. The new owners—and the children and heirs of original owners—of these houses as absentee landlords chose to convert some of these large courtyard houses for multifamily occupancy.

There were two other explanations for this transformation—the one sociological, and the other institutional—that may not have been fully documented in the previous literature, or in the more recent studies conducted for the World Bank. The former has to do with the nature of inheritance and transition from extended to nuclear family mores. When the patriarchs of some of these older medina houses died, the property was transferred to the children. When some of them chose to move out of the medina, property subdivision became inevitable. Today many of the residents of the medina housing are original residents now sharing the family house with renters. These are also the reasons for the continuing disinvestment and lack of maintenance contributing to the steady decline of the physical stock of the medina. Finally, the third factor that has further exacerbated this decline is the rent control policy of the postcolonial years. As common all over the world, property owners have very little incentive to maintain their properties under rent control.

The decline and neglect of the external public and semipublic spaces was also a function of this transformation, abetted by municipality taxation.[39] As some of the original residents moved out, the ethos and decorum of medina living also declined. Original residents knew about the collective responsibility of keeping the *derbs* (alleys) clean, painting and repairing them as needed, not littering the street, and the like. New residents were unaware of such ethos, or did not care. Furthermore, now that the residents are required to pay taxes, there is an expectation that the municipality will take care of such maintenance.

What is particularly noteworthy is that the transformation of the medina not only led to overcrowding, densification, and a decline in the physical structures and the quality of life, but also resulted in declining social capital. And it is this decline of social capital that led to the deterioration of important architectural heritage involving religious and institutional buildings, which otherwise would have been kept in shape through collective contributions and wealthy benefactors.

Today there is a major program for the conservation and rehabilitation of the Fès medina initially financed by the World Bank,[40] and based on a master plan (*Schema Directeur*) prepared in the early eighties by the Moroccan Ministry of Housing and Territorial Management.[41] It had taken over a decade to get the plan (*d'Aménagement*) implemented, but it is finally and currently underway. The mission of the Fès-Medina Rehabilitation Project (these are the only World Bank loan–financed components) is to conserve and rehabilitate the historic housing stock and the larger urban environment (see figure 12.7).

Possibilities for the Medina

What is the future of historic quarters like the Fès medina in the context of a globalizing and technological world order that is defining contemporary notions of development? What is the place of the medina in the images of development? Can the medina be seen as an antithesis to modernity, a sustaining argument in a spatial dialectic with the contemporary modern city? Authors commenting on the downside of globalization have pointed out that the global economic order has not mitigated poverty, in fact has exacerbated the income inequality throughout the world. Hence the dualism is likely to continue, in various subtexts of the old and the new, the modern and the traditional, and the like. We have a choice of either engaging in this dialectic, or just

Figure 12.7
Restoration of a historic structure underway in Fès medina.
Source: Author, 1999.

simply ignoring the medina as an anachronism. Depending on how we approach it we can come up with several scenarios.

Slums of Despair or Hope?

As the Fès example has shown, historic urban districts like the medina can easily slip into the status of an overcrowded and unhealthy slum. As long as rural-urban migration continues, and most of urban housing remains out of reach for poor residents, older districts will continue to draw poor families. As we have seen the dynamic of transformation inevitably leads to decline, dilapidation, and ultimately blight. Consequently, and because of their central location, these historic districts become targets for demolition and removal. In fact, it is perfectly sensible, from the urban land market point of view, for the blighting tendencies to accelerate so that the land can be recycled for modern development and higher use. This happened in colonial Algiers when parts of the casbah were cleared to make room for a new waterfront development and for major arterials to facilitate through traffic. And during the Shah's regime, traffic exigencies led to cutting through historic bazaar of Espahan, and the historic cores of such cities as Kashan and Kerman. The recent deconstruction of historic Beijing has followed a similar script.

Planning scholars have argued for the positive aspects of slum. Anthropologist and social planner Lisa Peattie and urban planner William Goldsmith have argued that slums or ghettoes can be a positive resource in community building and in mobilizing political activism.[42] Similarly, urban planner Janice Perlman had argued that the favelas of Brazil served as important setting for the migrants, and despite their "*marginalidad*" status they did not necessarily display the characteristics of marginality, as suggested by anthropologist Oscar Lewis's famous work on the "culture of poverty."[43] This is essentially the social capital argument, and as we have seen in the case of Fès medina, community-based initiatives and activism are on the rise. Also, one could argue, citing examples from the Gulf states, that the older districts have provided useful, affordable housing stock and community context for the workers from other countries. In this sense the medinas can be seen as engaging in a form of dialectic with the forces of globalization.

Living Museum

Probably a sensible approach to historical districts is to preserve the architectural heritage and the built form, and make the environment habitable for residents, and visitors. This instinct is guided by a sense of enlightened taste for history, culture, and educational values. The idea is to create a living museum, where tourists, visitors, and students can come to appreciate and understand cultural history, architectural masterpieces, and the endogenous urbanism of efficient consumption. Historic districts can be important tourist attractions, with benefits for the local residents, and certainly for tourist businesses and conglomerates. With the conservation and rehabilitation efforts such movements are already underway in the Fès medina. Older houses are being converted by owners to serve as restaurants or bed-and-breakfast places that are now advertised regularly on the Fès websites or on the online vacation rental site Airbnb, with an average daily rate of US $63 as of this writing. Indeed, the concentration of such lodging rental places in Fès is in the medina. Elegant courtyard houses have been converted to banks or shops, and as the tourist business picks up, there will be more of that development. But at some point the indigenous community is displaced, as in Venice, Italy, where very few of the workers who serve the tourists and depend on the tourist economy actually live in Venice; they commute from neighboring Mestre. The living museum scenario, one of a tourist destination, where the medina becomes a spectacle and its quotidian rituals become novel tableaux, is indeed quite attractive and plausible in the wake of globalization. There is money to be made. Local planners funded by World Bank planners are precisely interested in such returns on their investment from expanded tourist trade. But is that inevitable? What happens to the dialectic, as the medina becomes co-opted by the global tourist economy?

Gentrification

A scenario associated with the living museum is one of gentrification, as it has commonly happened in European cities, and in the US. It is possible that younger generations of locals or expatriates—educated and professional—might, like their tourist counterparts, find medina living attractive and appealing. In the beginning the medina might draw artists, sculptors, writers, and other creative professionals, but also attorneys, doctors, bankers, businesspeople, and the like. This scenario would invariably lead to displacement and removal of the poor class, and even some long-term residents, and their trades. Here too, we may see an abandonment of the dialectic. By the beginning of the millennium satellite dishes were already commonplace and adorned the roofscape of the medina (see figure 12.8).

Sustainable Community

If sustainability is the balancing act between the three E's—Economy, Environment, and Equity—historically the medina has managed to balance them well. But today the decline of the medina of the past decades has also affected the equilibrium that existed for many years. Today economic and environmental conditions have certainly deteriorated, and equity is also a major concern. In this final scenario a restored medina can achieve the continuing dialectic we want to see. Here the medina continues not only as an alternative to the modern urban form, but also as an alternative model of place and community imbued with a strong sense of the public realm and social capital. Thus, the medina can serve as a model of a compact city, of a walkable community, as an

Figure 12.8
The roofscape of Fès medina.
Source: Author, 1999.

antithesis to sprawl and automobile-dominated urban life. The medina can also serve as a model for balancing work and living, sustainability, and thus become a demonstration community. This is where experiments could occur in alternative ways of life, in building democratic institutions, in educating recent migrants from rural areas, and in creating social capital. The medina could be the setting for civic engagement, empowerment of women, and participatory governance. It could be an incubator for creative ideas. The dialectic that began in the colonial times thus may continue.

13 Looking Ahead from Vila Dunia

> The ideal of contamination has few exponents more eloquent than Salman Rushdie, who has insisted that the novel that occasioned his fatwa "celebrates hybridity, impurity, intermingling, the transformation that comes of new and unexpected combinations of human beings, cultures, ideas, politics, movies, songs. It rejoices in mongrelisation and fears the absolutism of the Pure. Mélange, hotch-potch, a bit of this and a bit of that is how newness enters the world." No doubt there can be an easy and spurious utopianism of "mixture," as there is of "purity" or "authenticity." And yet the larger human truth is on the side of contamination—that endless process of imitation and revision.
>
> —Kwame Anthony Appiah, "The Case for Contamination"[1]

In today's world of "fake news" and the spreading conflation of truth and lies, one is compelled to revisit Orson Welles's 1973 documentary *F for Fake* (or *Vérités et mensonges* in French, which translates to "Truth and Lies") about Elmyr de Hory, the famous art forger. In his masterful documentary Welles challenges the audience to discern the distinction between copies and originals and question the imperatives of authenticity. In today's world we are constantly challenged by the fake versus real in our everyday experience of the built environment: Is that wood paneling real or Formica with wood texture? Is that potted plant real or plastic? It seems that in our everyday experience of the built environment, the copy often looks or feels better than the original, to recall Umberto Eco's discussion of his "Travels in Hyperreality." The real can be uncertain and provisional while the copy is predictable and reliable. Simulacra thus obviate simulation since originals are not necessary.[2] One often hears today: Wouldn't you rather have a good copy than a bad original? In his essay "What's Wrong with Plastic Trees?" urban theorist Martin Krieger challenges conventional wisdom with the argument that plastic trees may even prove to be more sustainable in the long run.[3]

This book has been a retrospective journey, through the history of ideas, ideals, ideologies, and idiosyncrasies of development, which have defined the images in which human settlements and urban spaces were planned, designed, and created. It will be recalled that the scope of this book is defined by certain persistent narratives of loss, bewilderment, and awe about the contemporary scene of urban development and renewal in the developing world. Vila Dunia, discussed in the opening chapter of this book, is just one case in point. The essential premise is that in order to understand the process that led to the contemporary urban outcome we must necessarily explore the history of city design in the developing world, and specifically the images that have guided such design and development. The case is presented in three distinct phases.

This intellectual journey began with a consideration of the ideas and implicit ideologies of development, and also of urban form. The subject of the form and design of cities has not received much attention in the contemporary literature on development, and correspondingly, the literature on urban form and design remains distant from the ongoing discourse on the social, cultural, and political economy of development. We have had only limited understanding today of the consequences of development and underdevelopment on urban form and space, which makes it difficult for development analysts and design professionals to conceive autonomous, culture-specific, and humane "images of development." In the absence of such images, macroeconomic models of economic growth and liberal reform on the one hand, and global expressions of Western architectural forms on the other, have essentially scripted the operative "images of development" today. The aim of this book is to begin a synoptic conversation that interrogates current trends in development, urban form, and city design in the Global South.

I choose the term "image" advisedly, because it encompasses both the positive and the normative constructs of an existential or anticipated reality. These are then the images of development that are driving the transformation of the developing world. Unlike premodern times, these images of development are catholic and thus exogenous to the history and culture of any one particular land. The earlier chapters in this book addressed these topics.

In the chapters of the second section, I argued that through human history, development—whether manifested in settlement forms or in some abstract shared value of emancipation and transcendence—has always been driven by normative ideals. In premodern times, for example, the design of traditional human settlements was often based on idealized forms of spatial organization. Primitive villages were often laid out in the shape of human anatomy, the most developed form of living organism. The design of ancient Chinese and Incan cities derived their organizing principles from the larger cosmic order, and the Hindu cities relied on an organizational hierarchy of castes representing different parts of divine anatomy of Brahmā, the Creator in Hindu mythology. What is significant is that these images of ideal city were endogenous to the culture where they were conceived.

Devoted to historical antecedents of city design in the developing world, this section is not entirely about endogenous images of development and city design. It also includes a chapter devoted to the early roots of exogenous models of development imposed during the colonial rule. The colonial era brokered the transition to modernity, or at least the images and values of modernity championed by the West and embedded in industrialization and the rise of capitalism in the European homeland of the colonial powers.

The chapters of the third section focus on the postcolonial record of city design in the developing world, focusing specifically on the ideals and ideology of modernity, and its corresponding urban outcomes.

In the penultimate section, the three chapters present both the extreme contradictions in the state of contemporary development with its urban imageries and also the choices that we might face. The Faustian imperatives stand in dramatic contrast to the tableaux of growing inequality and poverty worldwide. A counterpoint to this scenario is presented in the personae of the medinas of North Africa, as a model of conservation and sustainability.

In reviewing the prospectus of this book, one reviewer had suggested that perhaps not everything that has happened in the recent past should be dismissed as grotesque or undeserving. Surely there must be some good examples—"best practices"—that can be showcased as models or paradigms. In fact, Janice Perlman's Mega-Cities Project attempted to do precisely that—to transfer experiences of endogenous best practices of urban innovations from different corners of the world to other locations with similar problems that might benefit from transfer of such experiences.[4] This can be seen as a sort of planned globalization using successful bottom-up planning and design efforts.

While writing this manuscript I have informally solicited nominations for best practices from experts, academics, and graduate planning and design students in different countries. Unfortunately, and not entirely unexpectedly, there were no such nominations of conviction. Consequently I present in the epilogue my personal choices, fully aware of the risks and liabilities associated with such unilateral decisions. I will, however, discuss these cases and my rationale for these choices along the way.

The agenda of this concluding chapter then includes the following themes. First, I begin by summarizing the major trends in contemporary city design and development in emergent market economies. Second, I present, in a speculative vein, what might be the alternative scenarios of city development given these trends. Third, I address the matter of best practices and how one recognizes a best practice when one sees one. I will present my choice of a sample of such best practices, with a discussion of the global rationale I have used to choose them. Fourth, I take up the matter of urban form and the performance criteria for good city form, and suggest two very broad and synoptic criteria derived from some of theories of development that I presented in the second section. Finally, I conclude this chapter and the book by considering the prospect of a seventh bell curve suggested by several scholars in response to the principal arguments presented in this book.[5]

Urban Outcomes of Becoming Globalized

The broad tendencies that can be culled from some of the previous chapters are that of the experience of the "disequlibria"of becoming global. If the colonial powers brokered the process of becoming modern, its inertia continued through the postcolonial years, including a provisional socialist variant, now sustained by the process of becoming global. The antecedents of this process began during the colonial period and continued through the postcolonial years initially, through technical assistance programs from the West, and now through the global capital investments, locally desired as FDI (or foreign direct investment). Although development and modernization generally, and becoming global more specifically, has been and remains a project of the West, we should note that we have entered an era of "the colony strikes back." The tourist economy of the European countries is becoming dependent on the *nouveau riche* tourists from the newly developing economies. Chinese capital is now financing infrastructure development in Ethiopia, Pakistan, Myanmar, and many parts of sub-Saharan Africa in return for its voracious appetite for natural resources. These countries in Africa are becoming a new version of the "periphery of the periphery" (the earlier version was being the supplier of slave labor to the development of European colonies of the New World).[6] Today an Indian industrialist, Lakshmi Mittal, has taken over the failing steel factories in Germany. The name Tata is becoming increasingly familiar in the UK, where the Indian conglomerate runs many steel plants and has taken over the manufacturing of the erstwhile British automobiles Jaguar and Land Rover. Flashy advertisements for Tata Communications are now plastered all over the walls of "Tube" stations in London, beginning with the concourse to the Paddington express at the Heathrow Airport.

Becoming global, however, is not just a matter of identity established through the emergence of global cities, as sociologist Saskia Sassen has suggested. It is a profound transition involving institutional, economic, and political transformations.[7] Becoming global also means getting connected, getting plugged in to the global network, becoming a member of the club. To be sure, it involves certain rites of passage.

The first and perhaps most important rite of passage is the formation of a strong market orientation and a commitment of the state to develop institutions that support a market economy. Recent history has shown that this transformation, initiated during the Thatcho-Reaganite era, had taken considerable goading by Western political authorities and financial institutions—the IMF, the World Bank, USAID, and possibly the Asian Development Bank (ADB)—to initiate structural reform, deregulation, dismantling of trade barriers, removal of subsidies, and the like.

The second rite of passage involves a transformation in the role of the state and the functions of governance. The shift to a market orientation often involves a shrinking of the modern welfare state and development of a corporatist state, which functions in close collaboration with business and global capital. Indeed, it is the corporatist state that becomes directly involved in attracting global capital and promoting the individual nation-state, China being a case in point.[8]

The third element of becoming global is the role of the corporatist state to become actively engaged in promoting the appearance and design of its cities in the images of the West. Often this involves clearance of older and often historic neighborhoods and districts to make room for multinational corporate investments in hotels, office towers, shopping malls, luxury condominiums, and the like.[9] (See figure 13.1.) This phase also involves infrastructure improvements, such as street widening and straightening in a Haussmannian fashion, as well as massive investments in freeways, parking structures, and transit systems. The aim is to make cities competitive in the global economy by mimicking the design of Western buildings and the form of Western cities.

Western architects and planners play a major role in this process of becoming global. The chapter titled "The Faustian Imperative" documented the process and impulse of becoming global. But this transformation comes with a rather steep price tag in terms of environmental and human consequences. These too can be considered a part of the rites of passage.

A fourth aspect of becoming global is that it is only partial. This transformation is paralleled by a growing polarization and income inequality, especially between the rural and urban population. The bright and shining edifices that represent the global face of cities cast a long and deep shadow of massive poverty and human misery, within cities and in their rural hinterlands. Many years ago economist Michael Lipton wrote about the "urban bias" in contemporary world development.[10] The process of becoming global has exacerbated this bias in unprecedented way. China is a case in

Figure 13.1
Rajarhat New Town, Kolkata. Global capital and corporations are exporting models of property development in the emerging economies in Asia.
Source: Author, 2012.

point. The bright new face of prosperous China represented by its impressive urban panorama is a veneer that obscures persistent rural poverty and growing pollution. Foreign scholars[11] and journalists typically are required to have "official approval to travel outside *Western-influenced* (emphasis mine) cities such as Beijing or Shanghai."[12] The inequality and polarization fester within cities that have come to represent the global faces of the developing world.

The fifth phenomenon is the exclusion of the poor or people of the traditional society from the new "Western-influenced" landscapes of global economy with modern amenities and facilities. Often the poor are carefully edited out from the ersatz spaces of globalization. They remain invisible in spaces outside the globalized territories. This exclusion obtains from subtle design features, gating, surveillance, or spatial isolation.[13] One of the rituals of becoming global is the construction of "alterity." This otherness not only defines the poor or the "marginals,"[14] but also immigrants from other countries. For example, the workers from the Philippines and the Indian subcontinent in the UAE or other Gulf states remain invisible and neglected in their expatriate ghettoes or labor colonies, separated by contemporary version of *cordon sanitaire*.[15]

Sixth, as the duality and polarization intensify, and the competition for urban space increases, we begin to see the rise of gated communities in these cities. In some instances the wealthy are gentrifying poorer neighborhoods and even encroaching into squatter settlements, as in the favelas of Brazil. Some economists have referred to this phenomenon as the "enclosure of the commons" and even celebrate its advent as an efficient social outcome, as the "public goods" conventionally purveyed by the state are now privatized, thus presumably achieving some overall efficiency.[16] As these neoliberal models of privatization become a part of the process of becoming global, there is a corresponding shrinkage of the urban commons from enclosures and "encroachment." The notion of a "voluntary city"[17] works only for those who can afford, but it exacerbates polarization as those who cannot afford to be a part of it suffer from simultaneous withdrawal of the welfare state.

Seventh, the encroachment of the commons is paralleled by a gradual shrinkage of the public realm in the global city. As we saw in the case of Chinese cities, the Haussmannian transformation of built form and the construction of the major road infrastructure have atrophied the traditional street and the social life of public space. Meanwhile, newly created open spaces are neither open nor accessible.[18] The tragedy of development here is that while the many cities of the West maintain an ethos of public realm and the possibility of flânerie, it is increasingly obviated by the new spaces of globalizing cities.[19]

Eighth, the scale and the speed of these transformations do not bode well for the environment. Very little of the built form planned and designed after the Western images of development seem to be "green," environmentally friendly, or sustainable in the long run. Furthermore, the development imperatives have led to the abandonment of the existing systems of ecologically sensitive and sustainable processes. For example, after the liberation the municipalities of China devised elaborate systems of waste recycling, and plans were formulated to preserve the rich agricultural hinterland of these cities. Millions of trees were planted and nurtured at the street level, thus reducing the "heat island" effect. Much of those policies are now defunct. As the urban sprawl of the new global economy expands to coalesce with other adjacent metropolitan regions, prospects for megaregions loom large. In China today there is talk about planning for nine or ten megaregions of 50 million people each in order to contain its future urban growth. Environmental consequences of such emerging mega-sprawls have yet to be fully fathomed or anticipated; ignorance continues as bliss.

Finally, there are also the contamination effects of becoming global. In varying degrees, the agencies of globalization—capital and information technology in particular—begin to influence not just the form and sensorium, but also the urbanism and habitus of the city. It leads to hybridity and a loss of identity, and to a precipitous decline in the authority and authenticity of local culture.[20] Philosopher Kwame Anthony Appiah has argued recently that contamination and hybridity need not be seen as a loss.[21] He suggests that it is precisely through contamination and hybridity that new expressions may emerge and defy the universalizing effects of becoming global. Indeed, this argument may be seen as embedded in the seventh bell curve argument, which I will present in the concluding section.

As I have proposed earlier in chapter 4, contemporary urban outcomes of development and the experience of becoming global can be mapped in the conceptual framework of the seven levels of urban experience I introduced previously in table 4.2 in chapter 4. Here in table 13.1, I elaborate on that premise.

Beginning at the bottom of the table, examples of development effects on ***nature services*** are evident in almost every major urban agglomeration of contemporary times. Today the valuable farmlands of the rich fertile coastal plains of China are being constantly gobbled up by the unrelenting peri-urban growth. The imperatives of development continue to overrule arguments for preservation of nature and ecosystem. Some years ago landscape architect Ian McHarg attributed the incessant loss of nature in development to the Judeo-Christian value system, in which nature was seen as wild, hostile, and to be tamed.[22] No doubt the colonial industrial development, especially the jute mills necessary for the colonial economy, began the process, but it certainly was not constrained by Hindu mythology about the holiness of the river *Ganga* and its partner *Yamuna*. These two rivers, which flow through the metropolises of Delhi and Kolkata, are long-standing examples of how industrial and human waste from their

Table 13.1
Urban outcomes of development mapped

Levels of urban experience	Urban outcomes of development in a global economy
Identity	Ersatz ("wannabe"), hyperreality
Habitus	Confused and declining
Urbanism	Transitional, provisional, missing
Social ecology	Evolving, situational, lumpy
Urban form	Fragmented (splintered) and polarized
Urban sensorium	Atrophying and debilitating
Nature services	Neglected, abused, irreversibly depleted, endangered

urbanized banks continue to pollute the valuable sources of water that serve millions of people living in the Indo-Gangetic Plain of India.

Along with the neglect, abuses, irreversible depletion, and perils to the nature services came the deterioration of the quality of the ***urban sensorium***. The legendary air pollution in Beijing, resulting from both industrial and vehicle emissions, is a case in point. Most large cities of the Global South that are going through a mobility transition—from people and animal-powered transportation to motorized vehicles—are now experiencing chronic air pollution from vehicle emissions. In India such pollution is exacerbated seasonally by the burning of the biomass of farmland detritus—for example, leaves, scrap wood, and cow-dung patties—by the urban poor for cooking or keeping warm in winter months. The seasonal winter fog in northern India is denser and lasts longer today because of this pollution. The urban sensorium becomes a major health hazard, as evident in the high incidence of chronic respiratory disease in cities of the Global South. People wearing breathing masks are a fairly common sight in Beijing and other large Chinese cities.

Among other effects on the urban sensorium are the "heat island" effects, which are lately being recognized and studied in various parts of the world, but less commonly in the developing world. Development brings with it an artificial sensorium of round-the-clock air-conditioned spaces of residences, cars, offices, and shopping malls, minimizing the exposure to heat, dust, and humidity for those who can afford it, while possibly exacerbating the "heat island" effect, increasing heat exposure for less fortunate residents or the unconditioned spaces of informal-sector commerce.[23] The sensorium thus gets partitioned and polarized into conditioned—occasionally fragranced and "muzaked"—spaces of the well-to-do, versus the naturally hot and muggy sensory experience of the excluded.

Although the link between development and urbanization is generally presumed and accepted, much less is known or accepted about how development influences the ***form*** of developing cities. The model of dualistic urban form has been around since the colonial project began. With the postcolonial development and underdevelopment the city has become fragmented, polarized, and even "splintered," as urban geographers Stephen Graham and Simon Marvin have suggested.[24] Although these authors have used the qualifier "splintering" to define the emerging urbanism of a global economy, their discussion and analysis pertain primarily to the geography of what has been characterized by Castells as "network society."[25] In this emergent urban form, new infrastructure investments have created hegemony of new "spaces of flow" over traditional "spaces of places," in some cases obviating the latter.[26] Discrete and territorially well-defined and well-defended spaces of technology, commerce, and residence—in the form of industrial or "high-tech" complexes, shopping malls, gated communities, and entertainment districts and complexes—have begun to transform the granularity of the existing cities into lumpy and delimited spaces of global economy and the residual subaltern spaces of poverty, informality, and underdevelopment.

With development the ***social ecology*** of the city begins to mirror the fragmented and splintered urban form of the city. The imperatives of global economy easily translate into demand for accessible, desirable, and large chunks of urban land. The ecology of developing cities often inherits patterns intrinsic to the endogenous models of development. Poverty often sullies the purity of nature services. Thus, floodplains, mangrove forests, estuarine lands, riverbanks, and steep hills and valleys—generally considered inaccessible and therefore undesirable locations for development—are typically targets of insurgent and spontaneous settlements of the poor. Unserviced or underserviced, they constitute an urban commons of poverty. With the demand for new land, these areas of the urban commons made habitable by the poor subsequently become targets of redevelopment for condominiums, shopping malls, and industrial parks. Gentrification and displacement necessarily follow, replacing the organic and autopoietic components of social ecology of the earlier years. In the large-scale redevelopment of the Dharavi slum in Mumbai, negotiations are underway to accommodate slum residents in high-rise towers ("vertical slums," according to some detractors) to be built in one corner of the vast district, thus opening up the remaining area for upper-income residential towers.[27] As the urban areas sprawl, aided and abated by the new infrastructure of highways and occasional commuter rail, a new ecology emerges in the peri-urban fringes. Here we might see the beginning of an urban sprawl characterized not necessarily by single-family low-density homes but also by higher-density housing and planned and gated communities served by commuter rail and shopping malls at the same time.

Along with the fragmented and splintered urban form comes a type of ***urbanism*** that is transitional and at best provisional. This transitional urbanism can be seen as one of a transition from informal to formal economy,[28] and possibly as one from the extreme inequality of dualistic economies to the low-income consumerism benefiting from the trickle-down effects of the global economy. Shoes on every pair of feet, wristwatches and cell phones, proliferation of street food, and the like become the early indicators of a changing economy and lifestyle. The global economy is aware of this emerging market and responds effectively, making detergents and soaps in small packets for prices affordable to the poor. With development comes mobility transition—bicycles and rickshaws give way to *tuk-tuks* (auto rickshaws), motor scooters, and eventually compact city cars (such as the widely acclaimed but not so successful Tata Nano). Urban streets and roadways in India known for their "democratic" tradition[29]—load-bearing camels, bullock carts, pushcarts, bicycles, bicycle-rickshaws and other such nonmotorized vehicles coexisting with cars, buses, and trucks—are increasingly becoming "limited access," thereby segregating the formal from the informal mode of economy and urbanism. Thus, one way to look at this transitional and provisional nature of urbanism is as an ongoing narrative of social exclusion and economic inclusion, growing inequality, and mass consumption. It is possible also to think of the new ersatz cities in the developing world as cities without urbanism, as sociologist Harvey Molotch has argued in the case of Dubai,[30] or as "un-cities," as urban planner Surajit Chakravarty has called Abu Dhabi.[31]

It can be argued that the ***habitus*** of these emergent cities could hardly retain any of the endogenous exigencies of climate, culture, or faith. With the easy access to cell phones, communication is no longer dependent on propinquity. Interventions of globalization through the ethnoscapes and mediascapes, to invoke concepts of anthropologist Arjun Appadurai,[32] facilitated by the Internet and international labor migration, make the endogenous habitus increasingly strained and confused. True, the rhythm of pausing for prayer five times a day is built into the official schedule of activities in Saudi Arabia, and the country strictly maintains gender separation in educational institutions along with mandatory hijab requirements in public spaces. At the same time, shopping malls there are fully stocked with all types of Western consumer products, including provocative displays at lingerie stores. In the complicated maze of new architectural spaces of development it is difficult to keep track of the cardinal orientation in interior spaces, much less the direction of the qibla. It is quite common that hotel rooms in the Emirates and Saudi Arabia come with a sign painted on the ceiling or the night table indicating the qibla direction to facilitate daily prayers.

Finally, we consider the matter of ***identity***, increasingly much sought after in the competitive global economy. In a 2009 CBD Urban Forum conference in Beijing organized by the Chaoyang urban district officials and stakeholders, a good part of the discussion focused on the future of high-rise buildings in the new extension of the downtown Beijing. In a definitive voice the vice-mayor argued that it is impossible to think of a CBD (central business district) without high-rise towers. It is a matter of identity, she seemed to imply. The irony is inescapable. The identity of the historic Beijing was embedded in its canonical form, its walls and gates, its classic axis and the dominant Forbidden City. While the walls are long gone, the axis, some of the gates, and the Forbidden City still remain in their majestic appearance through the near total deconstruction of the historic city. Now the city needs a CBD similar to the typical American downtown, which is a result of the centrality of location in a land market. In this search for identity, individual buildings of "signature architecture," such as Rem Koolhaas's CCTV building or Paul Andreu's new National Centre for the Performing Arts building, increasingly play a critical role. The Kingdom Tower in Riyadh, designed by Norman Foster; the Petronas Towers in Kuala Lumpur, designed by Cesar Pelli; or Burj Khalifa in Dubai, designed by architect Adrian Smith of Skidmore, Owings & Merrill, or "the Frame" in Jabeel Park,[33] an iconic tourist attraction, also in Dubai, all represent such a search for identity or "brand" in promoting the city in the increasingly competitive international marketplace.

What then are the possible scenarios for the future urban outcomes if the contemporary trend is to continue? In the following section I present some of the possibilities.

Possible Scenarios for the Future

The possible scenarios presented below are derived from contemporary trends that I discussed previously. These categories are not to be considered as exclusive scenarios. They could overlap in space and in time, and they may manifest in different cities in different parts of the world.

The Ersatz City

In this scenario we might see a rise of a genre of ersatz cities that Dubai or Abu Dhabi have come to epitomize. Variations of this type, on a smaller scale, can be seen in many other cities in the form of planned communities such as Kota Wisata or Kota Legenda outside Jakarta, or large entertainment complexes like the planned $19 billion theme park in Dubai, or major new increments to an existing city like Pudong in Shanghai, or nine new towns in its metropolitan region.

In their purest form, ersatz cities will be designed for the consumption and entertainment demands of the new global bourgeois and leisure class. They will serve as important destinations in the burgeoning tourist economy. They will be the classic "entertainment cities."[34] In Dubai today, four out of five residents are businesspeople, tourists, or expatriate labor in the service economy.

Ersatz cities combine fetish, hedonism, and hyperreality. A *New York Times* Travel Section story described Dubai as an "over-the-top" city and as "the Oz of the Middle East."[35] Cities like this will cater to fetishes such as having the tallest hotel, or the tallest office tower, or the largest man-made islands, or the largest indoor ski slope, and a never-ending script of one megaproject after another (see figure 11.15). City planner

Daniel Burnham's famous saying, "Make no little plan," will continue to inspire the planners of the city of fetishes.[36] At the same time these cities will serve as classic examples of "hyperreality," a concept author Umberto Eco used so effectively to describe the America of the seventies.[37] The aesthetics of the fake, of imitation, would serve the average imagination and taste, which in this case is likely to be globally cultivated, indeed "Americanized," via information and communication technology and the culture media. What Eco wrote about the "secondary America" may apply to these ersatz cities and their global bourgeois clients:

> The industry of the Absolute Fake gives a semblance of truth to the myth of immortality through the play of imitations and copies, and it achieves the presence of the divine in the presence of the natural—but the natural is "cultivated" as in the Marinelands....
>
> The ideology of this America wants to establish reassurance through Imitation. But profit defeats ideology, because the consumers want to be thrilled not only by the guarantee of the Good but also by the shudder of the Bad. And so at Disneyland, along with Mickey Mouse and the kindly Bears, there must also be, in tactile evidence, Metaphysical Evil (the haunted Mansion) and the Historical Evil (the Pirates).[38]

One hopes that this ersatz city scenario will be limited to a few locations in the developing world and not become a widespread phenomenon. After all, even Disneyland can get boring. Aspects of it, however, will surely be embedded on a smaller scale within other cities. Already other Gulf countries, such as Bahrain and Qatar, are emulating Dubai-like development, complete with "palm islands." Thanks to Nakheel Properties, the developers of the Palm Islands, these models are now being exported to other destinations along the Arab coast of the Gulf.

Away from the coast, in the middle of a barren desert landscape, many new developments are underway. Along the highway to the inland city of Al Ain lies the Dubai Silicon Oasis development, adjacent to the Dubai International Academic City, where information technology and institutions of higher learning are being located. Between the Emirates Road and the Dubai Bypass Road, the outermost peripheral highway that takes one to Abu Dhabi, lies a large chunk of desert called Dubailand that is being subdivided into smaller residential projects with such names as "Global Village," "Falcon City of Wonders," and "The Villa." Along the highway one sees recently completed development of Mediterranean-style architecture, or advertisement of future development (see figure 13.2). Elsewhere, along the highway to Bab Al Shams, a desert resort, are phantasmagoric futuristic mock-ups announcing future developments of various sorts, reminiscent of the Hollywood back lot of a Disney or Star Wars production (see figures 13.3 and 13.4).

Figure 13.2
A roadside billboard announcing a new residential development with promises of a modern Western lifestyle.
Source: Author, 2007.

Hybrid City

The possibility of a hybrid city has several intellectual roots. According to his taxonomy of African cities, geographer Anthony O'Connor suggested the hybrid city as a distinct type emerging from the colonial era as the Western European influence interacted with the indigenous urban form and urbanism.[39] Although O'Connor remains somewhat ambiguous about the specific properties of such a city, Ali Mazrui's discussion of the urbanism of cities like Dakar and Senegal, and the cultural transformations that have ensued since colonial times, offers a likely exemplar.[40]

Discussions of hybridity typically focus on food, music, art, and certainly architecture, when the cultural influences of an alien or exogenous culture permanently modify or redefine traditional expressions in some permanent and profound way. (See figure 13.5, which suggests resistance to such adaptations.)

One may wonder how much of the cultural core has to change for the outcome to be truly hybrid.[41] And what might be an appropriate example of a hybrid city? Before we consider a concrete example, let me present another intellectual thread about

Figures 13.3 and 13.4

The Ersatz city, Dubai. Two roadside phantasmagoric displays announcing a future development in the middle of a desert landscape.

Source: Author, 2007.

Figure 13.5
Retrofitting Western-style suburbia to meet cultural norms of privacy, Riyadh, Saudi Arabia. *Source*: Courtesy of Mohamad Alnowaiser, 1983.

hybridity rooted in the postcolonial discourse, some of which we have previously considered.[42]

It has been proposed that the postcolonial discourse that grew out of critical academic writings about the colonial rule and the subaltern role of the indigenous population and culture itself represents a profound form of hybridity. The academics who have led this discourse were trained in colonial language and Western intellectual tradition, and thus themselves are representatives of that hybridity. For the "postmodernist alienation" with postcolonial discourse, "the concept of hybridity makes supreme ideological and political sense," argues journalist-scholar Adebayo Williams, because "hybridity represents the ultimate denial of origin, subject, race, class and indeed nation."[43] Philosopher Kwame Anthony Appiah directly addresses the argument that globalization is contributing to homogenization—if not "Americanization"—of the developing world and the loss of plurality in identities and cultures. He makes a "case for contamination" that celebrates hybridity and personal choices and preferences focusing on the individual rather than race, ethnicity, caste, creed, or class (see the epigraph to this chapter).

The concept of hybrid urbanity, however, can be confounding. Aside from the ideological differences in the concept of hybridity, there are differences in meaning as well—in biology (crossbreeding), in literature (mix of styles and components), and in electronics (as in integrated circuits with different components). The metaphors may be variably appropriate at different levels of urban experience, returning to our overall schema for organizing urban experience (table 13.1). Thus, there might be hybridity at the level of urban sensorium (a mixture of signs and sounds), at the level of urban form (mixture of styles and components, as in literature), and at the level of habitus (from crossbreeding, albeit inchoate).

In a globalizing world where contamination is inexorable and celebrated, hybrid cities might emerge as the most common form. But whether these multicultural, multiethnic, multilingual cities could assert a collective identity remains to be seen. Of course, Hollywood offers one scenario, as captured in Ridley Scott's 1982 movie *Blade Runner*,[44] which imagines a diasporic scenario for Los Angeles of the future with a hybrid urbanism—a population of mixed racial identity and origin, consuming fusion food and speaking a pidgin dialect that combines English, Spanish, Chinese, and Tagalog. It is likely that urban hybridity will be captured in the multiple, competing, and contingent ethnoscapes of diaspora, as suggested in recent literature on multicultural cities.[45]

The concept of hybrid urbanism remains a contested topic among urban theorists. AlSayyad begins a discourse within the framework of the postcolonial dialectic, and seeks the spatiality of this discourse in the concept of "third space," but without engaging the arguments of urban planner Edward Soja and his definition of the concept that he coined earlier in his discussion of critical regionalism.[46] Instead AlSayyad imagines the third space as an outcome of the colonial contact and influence, not unlike King's discourse on "third culture," which he used to explain the new spatial organization and urban form of colonial India.[47] In response to AlSayyad's arguments and the examples he assembled, urban planner Ananya Roy presents nuanced discourse about the spatiality or hybrid urbanism as a tension between identity and power from the perspective of feminist theories.[48]

While the discussion of hybrid urbanism has yet to arrive at closure, explorations into hybrid urban form have also been rather limited. Examples are not readily available. One may think of such a hybrid city in the design and layout of Pujiang new town, one of several built under Shanghai's "One City, Nine Towns" planning initiative in the nineties. It will be recalled that this planning initiative became famous because these towns were designed to reflect different European themes—English, Canadian, Dutch, French, German, Italian, and the like. Pujiang was meant to be the Italian town, in fact to incorporate a Venetian urbanism. This choice was not entirely arbitrary, because the site—its nature services—included an existing grid of irrigation canals harnessed from existing streams and rivers to support farming in the alluvial coastal plane on the east bank of the Huangpu. Thus, a canal city designed by Italian architects in the images of Venice seemed logical. Accordingly, the renowned Italian architectural firm Gregotti Associati received the commission to design the Pujiang new town, completed in 2009. As can be seen in the following images of the original traditional settlement along a nearby canal system (figure 13.6) and the completed high-income housing (figures 13.7 and 13.8)—mostly inside gated communities—there is very little resemblance of the designed city to the historic organic form of Venice. While historic Venice was strictly pedestrian or navigable by boat, Pujiang is mainly auto-oriented but with dedicated rights of way for bikers and pedestrians. In fact, if anything the layout of Pujiang, with its long blocks and axial organization of important buildings, is vaguely reminiscent of the layout of historic Beijing.

It would seem that among the many representations of Venice,[49] Pujiang by Gregotti Associati is certainly not the kind of simulacra one finds in some of the other nine new towns. Instead it is designed in the Western images of modernity and to meet the consumption demands of the new bourgeoisie class in China, while seemingly accommodating traditional preferences for residential space that provides for open terraces and roofs where one can sleep in extreme summer nights or even dry the laundry, as customary in local culture.[50] Ignoring the organic form of real Venice, the architects

Figure 13.6
Historical Xincheng in the same regional context.
Source: Author, 2017.

Figure 13.7
The new Venice? Pujiang new town.
Source: Author, 2017.

Figure 13.8
Contemporary luxury housing, Pujiang new town.
Source: Author, 2017.

here chose a layout that is vaguely reminiscent of traditional Chines cities. The hybridity of the design inheres in the integration of canals with modernist house types and a layout of seemingly endogenous origin. (See figures 13.7 and 13.8.)

Palimpsest City

The concept of the urban palimpsest has been around for some time in the literature on architecture, urban design, and urbanism. The dictionary meaning of "palimpsest" refers to a parchment, usually sheepskin, that has been written on or redrawn several times, erasing the earlier writings and drawings, yet with their traces still barely visible. This image offers an immensely romantic metaphor for describing cities of the past, present, and future. It resonates with the notion of the city as a text, and the act of flânerie as a way of reading the text. The urban palimpsest of Mexico City as captured in Salvador Novo's *Nueva grandeza mexicana* is a case in point.[51] Writer Roxanne Davila describes it as "quite literally a textual stroll through the streets of Mexico City."[52]

Furthermore, the palimpsest metaphor evokes not only reading but also writing the text of the city. And who are the writers? Often they are anonymous and only responsible for writing short sentences than a whole passage. This anthology of urban text includes the professional work of not only architects, developers, urban designers, and planners but also individuals and communities, notwithstanding the fact that the overall script may be written by the people with power and money. Many of author Italo Calvino's narratives of "invisible cities" could represent the urban palimpsest. Calvino's description of Zaira captures the metaphors of both reading and writing text:

> The city … does not tell its past, but contains it like the lines of a hand, written in the corners of the streets, the gratings of the windows, the banisters of the steps, the antennae of the lightning rods, the poles of the flags, every segment marked in turn with scratches, indentations, scrolls.[53]

Typically cities with a long historic legacy are the candidates for such metaphors. Thus, one always thinks of Rome, although much of its text from various periods is carefully preserved. In addition to Mexico City, the metaphor has been used to describe Delhi (the site of nine different capitals), the Cairo of multiple dynasties,[54] and recently Beijing, as it goes through its dramatic transformation (see figure 13.9).[55] Geographer David Harvey, however, used the term to describe the constantly transforming cities in the era of globalization.[56]

It is this globalization context in which we should be considering the palimpsest city as a possibility. It is interesting to note that Beijing, even after near denouement of the canonical city that evolved through many years of the Yuan, Ming, and Qing

Figure 13.9
A palimpsest city—Luxor, Egypt. A mosque constructed inside the complex of ancient Egyptian temples of Luxor can be seen beyond the columns with a modern hotel farther back.
Source: Author, 1993.

dynasties, considers itself an urban palimpsest, making it a major display in the newly opened Beijing Museum of Planning. The palimpsest city carries with it broader challenges for city design and conservation, since there is nothing in the notion of a palimpsest that guides us about which text to erase and what the script for rewrite should be. The process through which we come to such decisions remains a major challenge, as captured in the following passage from philosopher and sociologist Maurice Halbwachs:

> Thus we understand why spatial images play so important a role in the collective memory. The place a group occupies is not like a blackboard, where one may write and erase figures at will. No image of a blackboard can recall what was once written there. The board could not care less what has been written on it before, and new figures may be freely added. But place and group have each received the imprint of the other. Therefore every phase of the group can be translated into spatial terms, and its residence is but the juncture of all these terms. Each aspect, each detail, of this place has a meaning intelligent only to members of the group, for each portion of its space corresponds to various and different aspects of the structure and life of their society, at least of what is most stable in it.[57]

Palimpsest cities, it can be expected, will be the likely model of urban development for older cities with historic layers of urban form that may or may not be rewritten by imperatives of new development in prosperous economies. An example is the old

Figure 13.10
The old walled city of Ahmedabad, a palimpsest city.
Source: Author, 2010.

sixteenth-century historic walled city of Ahmedabad, a living city, whose gates and walls and residential quarters have been overlaid with modern infrastructure (see figure 13.10).

A good example of a palimpsest city is contemporary Delhi, the seat of multiple dynasties in the history of India, including the capital of the modern democratic republic, "the Ninth Delhi." The capital of British India prominently featured in the map shown in figure 7.17 (chapter 7) is the Eighth Delhi (also referred to as Lutyens' Delhi). The old city of Shajahanabad of the Mogul era to the east separated by a *cordon sanitaire* is the Seventh Delhi, currently referred to as the old Delhi. Many of the locations of the earlier eras still exist as archaeological ruins (Tughlakabad, the Third Delhi, and Purana Kila, the Sixth Delhi, are cases in point). Others exist in name only (Indrapat, Firozabad, and Jahanpanah are relevant examples). (See figure 7.17, showing the plan of Lutyens on the existing palimpsest of the seven previous dynasties of Delhi.)

For the first fifty years of independence Delhi's postcolonial urban sprawl involved infill between these historic sites, engulfing them in most cases, and new suburban and peripheral growth. This peri-urban growth has bypassed the original villages, ensconcing them as permanent urban slums. Since the liberalization of the economy in the early nineties, the economy has globalized, and we now see a second layer of postcolonial growth characterized by new opportunities for consumption—mega-malls, auto dealerships, high-rise housing estates, and gated communities—claiming new peripheral territories and redeveloping some of the earlier postcolonial settlements. In this expansion, enclosure of the urban commons for private purposes has become quite commonplace. Most other cities of historic origin—Cairo, Mexico City, Beijing, and Shanghai, to mention a few—are also likely to display the characteristics of a palimpsest city.

Dualistic City

Dualistic urban form, as we have seen in out discussions in chapter 10, is a legacy of the colonial period.[58] The concept of dualism and its validity in the contemporary globalizing world has been called to question in light of empirical evidence. Yet, as we have seen in many scholarly reports discussed in chapter 10, income inequality has increased not only between countries but also within countries, especially in the emerging economies. The income gap between the urban and rural population explains much of that polarization, and as the rural poor have moved to cities, the microcosm of that polarization has appeared in cities becoming global. Indeed, more than a dualism of the native city versus European city of the colonial era, dualism has morphed into many islands of contrasts—between gated communities and slums, between wealth and poverty, between mainstream and marginality, between the privileged and the subaltern—in a finer grain of urban form.

While the Brazilian case shown in figure 13.11 may be an extreme juxtaposition of the polarities of urban form, this dualism will be a dominant, and probably the most common, form of urban development, as long as massive poverty remains a reality and urbanization of poorer countries—many in Africa—continues at a brisk pace. While the dualism continues, it also presents an opportunity for dialectic between the visible contradictions and polarization in the urban outcomes of globalization. In some instances it may reflect the enduring tension between tradition and modernity. A recent article in *The Economist* describes the growing hillside neighborhoods of *yurts*—traditional structures used by nomadic herders—cropping up the hillsides of the Mongolian capital of Ulaanbaatar and housing some 60 percent of its population. These settlements stand in stark contrast to the city's prosperous district of Zaisan, which shows off luxury villas, Western-style shopping malls, and even gated communities.[59] This duality will continue to be a challenge for urban planners and the local state, unless otherwise co-opted by the global agenda. Geographer Simon Marvin and planner Stephen Graham have described the emerging spatial outcomes as "splintered urbanism."[60]

Figure 13.11
Juxtaposition of the Cantagelo favela and the affluent housing of Ipanema.
Source: Courtesy of Frank Zerunyan, 2013.

The Bricolage City

By "bricolage city," I refer to the ongoing process through which built environment outcomes are obtained through community participation, engagement, negotiation, and even insurgency. The specific components of the bricolage city might be provisional and informal, and therefore formally illegal. Yet it can be argued that the vast majority of contemporary global cities contain aspects of the bricolage process. The street scene of contemporary Cairo in figure 13.12 shows an apartment building seemingly constructed in defiance of any engineering standards or building codes.

The dictionary meaning of "bricolage" usually refers to something like "(in art or literature) construction or creation from a diverse range of available things" (Oxford Dictionaries). In his book *The Savage Mind* anthropologist Claude Lévi-Strauss introduced the idea of *bricoleur* to describe the creativity of such mind to put together available pre-existing things, making do with whatever is at hand, in new, "devious" ways to create useful

Figure 13.12
Informal construction—a bricolage—in a formal city.
Source: Author, 1991.

products.[61] Lévi-Strauss contrasts the work of *bricoleur* with that of the engineer, a synoptic scientific mind that solves the problem in a systematic and synoptic manner with necessary technology and materials. We can argue here that the Western images of city design that are driving the urban transformation in the developing world are imagined as such synoptic projects with an engineering mind—projects that are permanent, efficient, and essentially top-down. However, against such projects we find many examples of urban settings that are products of *bricoleurs*, not engineers. They exist in the informal spaces and nooks and crannies of the modern city, and they significantly contribute to its urbanism. Furthermore, it can be argued that the bricolage promises the emergence of indigenous creativity in the future city design. The rock garden of Chandigarh, for example, is one such example of bricolage space that has become a popular place in the urbanism of modern Chandigarh (see epilogue).

The urbanism of the bricolage city involves technological adaptation and making-do that used to be commonplace in the early years of the postcolonial national poverty.

In the early years after India's independence, one would have seen in Kolkata make-do heavy rollers to compact the aggregates used for construction of new streets. The bricolage technology involved powering the rollers by borrowing transmission from a tractor mounted on a platform connected to roller axles. Similar contraptions could be found in the seventies, when the transmission from a two-wheel motorcycle was used to create a three-wheeler pickup truck. The scooter-taxis that provide affordable transportation in the streets of Indian cities are all examples such technological adaptation of two-wheeled scooters. And even today one might find in the Chao Phraya River in Bangkok passenger ferryboats using pickup truck engines, connected to the rotors by a long axle, as their outboard motor (see figure 13.13). In another example from India, the old townscape of Kolkata has been rewired in ad hoc jumbles of wires to provide cable and Internet access (see figure 13.14).

Megaregions and Mega Urban Sprawls

Finally, the principal challenges of city design and sustainable development will be to contain and manage what might emerge as mega-sprawl covering large geographical regions. Middle- and upper-class prosperity will lead to increased car ownership. The Chinese state has already identified the automobile industry as a growth industry, and

Figure 13.13

Truck engines converted to outboard motors to ferry commuters and tourists on the Chao Phraya River in Bangkok.

Source: Author, 2005.

Figure 13.14

Getting networked. Kolkata: accommodating modern communication in the old townscape.
Source: Author, 2012.

the domestic market in China is a major incentive for many international automobile manufacturers to locate there. In India, Tata Automotive recently set up a new plant in Gujarat to produce inexpensive cars for the Indian market. In the absence of a sustainable growth strategy, urban sprawl remains an inexorable outcome of becoming global. Indeed, as existing metropolitan regions continue to grow and expand in their edges, eventually touching another such area to become a megaregion—a process already underway in China, which has some ten of them according to one account—mega-sprawls are a likely outcome and a lingering planning concern.[62]

It is reasonable to assume that the examples of this possible typology of cities will be hosted within emerging megaregions and their inchoate and patently unhealthy mega-sprawl. Design thinking that should be guiding the internal organization of megaregions is still largely absent. This is one scale where nature services should be the principal focus, and sustainable urbanism guided by regional landscape and ecology should define the principal development objectives.[63]

Good City Form and the Images of Development

As we explore the future possibilities of a good city form and the principles of city design that would achieve such outcome, we must necessarily ask: What are the relevant images or notions of development that may guide such performance dimensions of good city form? One thinks of Kevin Lynch's seminal effort to identify the essential performance characteristics of good city form, which were culled from commonly stated goals and objectives in the master-plan or project-plan documents for American cities.[64] But how universal are these criteria? Are they linked to some larger, universally shared image or images of development? After all, one of the premises of this book is that there has yet to be a conversation about (a) development and urban form, and how they may influence each other; and (b) whether the form of cities should be linked to some universally shared images of development.

A careful reading of Lynch's prescription of the performance characteristics of good city form would suggest that he believed that the criteria for good city form represent universal values, although the catholicity of his normative criteria could be an issue, given that they are embedded in the fundamental beliefs of Western liberal democracies. But more importantly, the performance characteristics he was advocating were not explicitly linked to any specific image of development. In the following text I focus on alternative images of development in which the criteria for good city form can be embedded.

It will be recalled that in chapter 3 we considered several critiques of contemporary development theories. Two of these critiques are worth revisiting in this context, which, I believe, offers additional foundations for developing the normative criteria for good city form and effective city design. These images are one of "development as sustainability" and one of "development as freedom."

As I have noted previously, the concept of development as sustainability should be taken as a positive concept and should be seen as a moral order of development and a counterpoint to the technical order that has dominated contemporary history of modernization and development in the images of the West.[65] The moral order of sustainability is derived not just from concerns for environmental protection, global warming, and efficiency in the uses of land, water, and nonrenewable resources, but also from the continuity of communities, cultures, and localities that exist in and beyond urbanized areas. The moral order of sustainability is derived from a sense of shared values and ethos and people's ability to participate in making decisions about the future of their environments and quality of life.

It is true that the concept of sustainability, even as an environmental issue, remains a somewhat elusive and ambiguous concept. It is difficult to operationalize. Some may find this ambiguity vexing from a policy-analytical perspective. Some would consider it compelling because of its flexibility and inclusive agenda. Thus, from the environmental economics perspective, efficiency might be the guiding principle for sustainable development. Others may see it as a compromise between environmental determinism and economic determinism. A currently popular view is one of balancing the imperatives of economy, environment, and equity.

In the world of policy and practice, sustainable development goals are now being practiced in local, regional, and sectoral variants of best practices. Some are quite specific, such as obtaining LEED certification for buildings, or switching to CNG from gasoline (as has been done in Delhi and Beijing to curb air pollution), or pursuing a "smart growth" approach to planning and design, and so on. There have yet to be specific performance characteristics for good city form derived from these best practices. Yet it seems possible to convert the sustainable development goals to concrete planning objectives, such as shrinking the "ecological footprint" or reducing the sprawl index in the future urbanization process.

It can be argued further that endogeneity lies in sustainability, and in the tradition of historic urban form that evolved in response to the prevalent nature services. The example of Shibam, a desert city in Yemen, is a glorious example of urban form that emerged from cultural response to climatic condition and the available technology of construction. The result is a spectacular cityscape of tall buildings built with mud bricks (see figure 13.15). Constructed with thick walls, limited openings, and narrow pedestrian passages at the ground level, the buildings offer shade for each other and minimize

Figure 13.15
The urban form of Shibam, Yemen, featuring the world's first mud skyscrapers—a case for sustainable urban design.
Source: www.MaciejStangreciak.co.uk; maciejstan@gmail.com. By permission of Getty Images.

solar exposure. In addition to providing insulation and minimum solar exposure, their collective urban form creates natural cooling through the narrow passages and occasional squares and courtyards, a much-needed relief from the humidity imparted upon the region by the Indian Ocean.

The pursuit of the other notion of development—development as freedom[66]—also presents some operational difficulties. In this instance the problem is not so much one of definition, which is theoretically precise, a few lacunae notwithstanding. The difficulty is one of application of this particular image of development in practice. Since the basic premise of this image of development is to achieve freedom at the individual level—"freedom" defined as the capability to achieve the functionings one may desire—the question of aggregation across many vectors of functionings and also the purveyance of such functioning needs remain unresolved. To settle this impasse, Nussbaum has suggested a set of universal capabilities in the context of gender and development.[67] These capabilities might be a good place to start for exploring relevant criteria for good city form.

Currently my doctoral students and I are exploring how we can derive performance characteristics of good city form based on the concept of development as freedom and the capabilities approach more broadly. We have taken the position that the performance characteristics that Lynch had proposed over twenty years ago may be seen as the bridge that connects development theory to urban form, just the way Nussbaum had translated Sen's ideas about functionings and freedoms to basic universal capabilities.[68] So, it is possible then to begin with the Lynch criteria and check them against the goals of sustainability and development as freedom.

The Possibility of a Seventh Bell Curve

In the course of working on this book I had several opportunities to present the ideas contained in this volume in various academic forums. The discussion of the five bell curves followed by the sixth one (the environmental Kuznets curve) has on at least three separate occasions elicited the observation from my audience that perhaps there is a possibility of a seventh bell curve that connects economic and cultural developments.[69] There is quite a bit of merit, and hope, in this argument. So, we imagine a bell curve of cultural development where the horizontal axis, as usual, represents economic development, but where the vertical axis represents the dimension of city design trending from endogeneity (autonomy/sustainability) to exogeneity (Western dependency). (See figure 13.16.) The trajectory of this bell curve will suggest that at the early stage and lower level of economic development, the cultural expressions will be rooted in the customs and traditions of a country. However, with economic development that must necessarily involve globalization and modernization in the images of the industrialized West, external influences will increase. In the arts, architecture, consumption of goods, and urbanism, Western norms will be mimicked. With growing prosperity and the increasing ranks of the working and middle classes, preferences for Western commodities and lifestyle—consumerism, shopping malls, house types, automobile ownership—will increase and trump all other choices of authentic expressions and values. This may occur due to increased exposure to the entertainment media[70] and information and communication technology.[71] According to this trajectory, at some point there will be a leveling off of Western or exogenous tastes and preferences, and then there should be a revival of interest in endogenous cultural expressions, creativity, and imagination, and ultimately authentic tastes and expressions in architecture, urban design, fashion, industrial design, and so on. What will trigger this inflection point is not clear. Perhaps there will be public investment in education, creativity, and innovation. Perhaps this will emerge spontaneously from the "blooming, buzzing confusion"

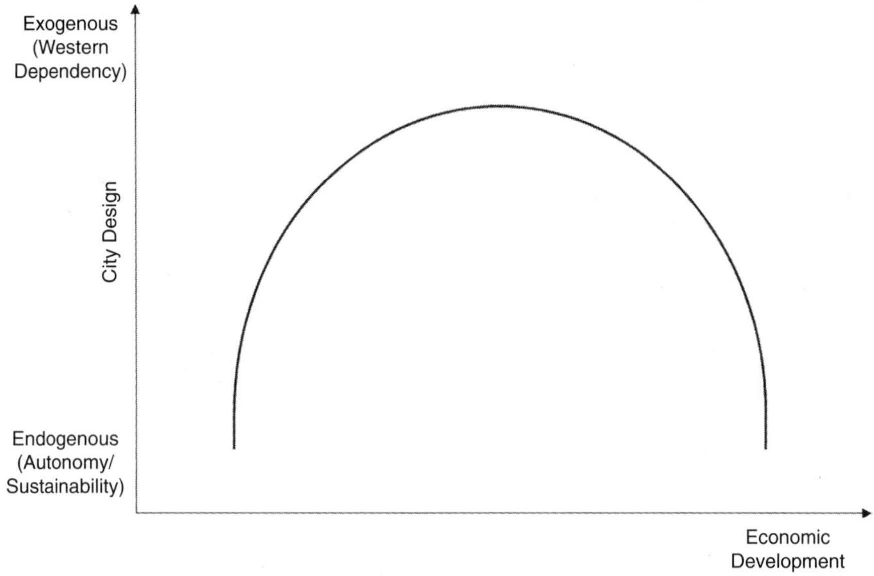

Figure 13.16
The seventh bell curve.
Source: Author.

(to invoke William James) of hybridity brought on by globalization. And this is perhaps what Appiah had in mind when he urged us not to worry about contamination, because historically cultural innovations and creativity have occurred precisely because of such culture contact.[72]

The preceding could very well be a plausible scenario. But I think that the real autonomy and authenticity in cultural values and expressions, especially in urban form and design, will evolve from the pursuit of freedom and sustainability as development goals. While some of the functionings and capabilities will no doubt be influenced—and perhaps irreversibly altered—by exogenous and globalizing forces in motion, one would expect many of such desired functionings to be rooted in local habitus and ethos. Emphasis on sustainability should bring the capacities and limitations of local environments to the fore, requiring innovations in the design of architectural and urban form. The autonomy and authenticity that this seventh bell curve promises must come from these alternative images of development.

Epilogue: Best Practices

> Another important goal of the Ju'er Hutong project is to create a new urban culture within the traditional urban context. Housing is not only for people's material needs, it also has an important role in people's social and cultural lives. Ju'er Hutong project tries to create a meaningful place which will enable the habitants to have their privacy as well as accesses to neighbourhood communication and contacts with nature within their neighbourhood. All these will (be) further considered in the extended 84 hectacre redevelopment Luoguxiang neighbourhood.
>
> —Liangyong Wu, "The Future Direction of the Experiments"[1]

What is a "best practice"? How it is defined remains theoretically unexplored, although it is used commonly in many different fields. In the area of urban planning and design, annual professional awards from various professional organizations or the internationally prestigious Pritzker Prize or Aga Khan Award for best design provide some benchmarks for excellence, although they may not necessarily mean best practices. The term "best practices" suggests that it may not be a unique and elite production like Frank Gehry's Guggenheim Museum in Bilbao, which would be typically honored in such professional awards programs. Rather, it can be seen as a way of achieving a good outcome, of serving the larger purpose of creating a good city. The idea of "best practices" thus must have a promise of transferability, applicability, or at least being an inspiration for other innovations and development, or even becoming "an accepted and established way" of doing things. Best practices may never be final, definitive, or deterministic, or entirely transformative. There may always remain a touch of provisional quality to the concept.[2]

The term "best practices" is well entrenched in the professional vocabulary of planning, public policy, and urban design, but a formal definition has yet to be proffered. One way of thinking of best practices is that they represent "accepted ways of doing things." Another view might see it as a project, an experiment, or a venture that has worked or been successful and thus is worthy of further application. One could also interpret this term as referring to culturally rooted, endogenously obtained skills and procedures that always seem to work in adaptive and innovative ways. In this sense it is probably close to what anthropologist James C. Scott would describe as *mētis*, a Greek word for a very similar concept.[3]

Winners of competition or recipients of prestigious awards may not necessarily claim the distinction of a best practice. Recipients of these projects may represent, for instance, excellence in design, exceptionalism in defying the norm, innovation in form, or application of technology. Frank Gehry's Guggenheim Museum at Bilbao, or Disney Hall in downtown Los Angeles, or a Taj Mahal or Hagia Sophia of earlier times may be a claimant of such distinction, but not of being best practice. In fact, there is very little in Gehry's exceptional design that can be replicable or taught as a general principle to students of architecture. How often does one get a chance to build a Hagia Sophia?

In other words, best practices need not be exceptional or unique but just a role model or even a paradigm for subsequent design. Best practices are exemplars that may inspire similar innovations in other geographical locations and cultural contexts. The examples presented in the following pages are nominations by this author. I don't expect all scholars and experts to agree with me in the choice of these examples. The list is not exhaustive; there must be many others that I have missed or not known about. I fully expect the list to expand, based on the current universe and the ones to come in the future.

Here I offer what I consider to be examples of best practices. Usually they are not a total concept of city design, but only vignettes of success that may serve as increments and building blocks that may lead toward achieving a good city. These examples are inspirational and certainly provisional. They are demonstration projects or models that show endogenous arguments of modernity and change as an antithesis to the Faustian imperatives of development and change aided and abetted by the globalization juggernaut. These are examples of local imaginations, initiatives, and innovations. They are not driven by desires of global identity or branding, or the compulsion for "selling" the city in the global marketplace. Rather, they represent thoughtful and sincere attempts to improve the livability of a city's inhabitants, and are based on local imaginations and innovations embedded in the endogenous culture, history, and tradition.

I admit further that many of these examples are ordinary, not designed by starchitects like Le Corbusier or Rem Koolhaas. Specific designers responsible for these projects may not be recognized or even identified; they are not products of architectural heroism indulged by wealthy clients and corporations and backed by global capital. I also recognize that scholars and experts will find many faults with some of these projects—that they caused displacement, or excluded the poor, that they are token achievements, or only serve the upper class, or are mere causes for soliciting a role in the global economy. I concede that all of these critiques may hold for many of these cases. But then, perfection is not what we are after, nor what we may achieve. It is appropriate to consider the Persian rug story here. Apparently the rugs woven by Persian crafts-persons were never perfect. There was always some fault, some error—but introduced deliberately, even in such architectural masterpieces as the Taj Mahal. Why? It is only Allah, the Almighty, who makes things perfect. After all, one does not or should not compete with Allah!

1. The Rehabilitated Bund of Shanghai

The Bund—a word of Indian origin, equivalent to the concept of a levee or embankment—is the waterfront promenade on the Puxi side of Shanghai. It is a major linear public space that was remade in the nineties to improve the stock of public amenities in the city. The Bund itself is a historical space that was used extensively during the colonial years for many functional, ceremonial, and recreational purposes. It is not unlike other such generic "bunds" common among the treaty ports of East Asia. As historian J. E. Taylor points out, "bunds" often "marked the site at which the segregation and violence that accompanied late nineteenth- and early twentieth-century imperialism made its presence felt in Asian ports."[4] Zhongshan Road was used for parades and later demonstrations. Seagoing ships and local ferryboats moored on the docks along the Bund. Indeed, the impressive buildings designed and constructed in classic European style presented the formal colonial face of the treaty port of Shanghai. Since China's liberation, the Bund has continued to be a place where locals gather and young couples huddle under umbrellas for romantic trysts on a rainy day, or perhaps practice their English with a few foreigners visiting the city. In the eighties the Bund was still bustling with fishing boats, junks with tattered sails, and larger ferryboats moored at the docks. The pedestrian promenade was narrow and congested. The new makeover of the Bund removed the old docks and created a wide, spacious pedestrian promenade at a higher level overhanging the old waterfront. It is a significant example of open space in a city that otherwise was falling behind in its supply of public space while becoming a global city. The space is used for early-morning exercise and late-evening strolls, especially on a hot and muggy summer day. There are kite fliers, jugglers, fortune-tellers, magicians, and musicians, very much in the manner of street scenes portrayed in the historical scrolls of Chinese cities. From the Bund one can take in a magnificent panorama of the city, with the colonial buildings on the Puxi side, reminiscent of the city's past, and the impressive futuristic skyline of Pudong across the Huangpu announcing the future yet to come. (See figures E.1 and E.2.) The rehabilitated Bund is truly a significant public realm, an example of a best practice.

Figure E.1
A model showing proposed reconstruction of the Bund in Shanghai.
Source: Photo by author, 2017. By permission of Shanghai Urban Planning Exhibition Center.

Figure E.2
The reconstructed Bund promenade.
Source: Author, 2001.

2. Ju'er Hutong, Beijing

In the previous chapter we considered what I referred to as the denouement of the historical and canonical city of Beijing, in particular the removal of the historical *hutongs*. If the Faustian clearance and redevelopment of the hutongs with high-rise buildings was the modernist antithesis of preservation and conservation values, the Ju'er Hutong redevelopment offered a synthesis that attempted to achieve a middle ground. The Ju'er Hutong project demonstrated how new courtyard housing at a much higher density can be achieved through innovative architectural and urban design. The project is the result of many years of patient work by Professor Liangyong Wu and his Tsinghua University colleagues, who began in 1978 to find an alternative idiom for the redevelopment of historic Beijing (see figures E.3 and E.4).

The project site is located outside the northeast corner of the Forbidden City, about 600 meters east of the Drum Tower. It is part of an 8.2-hectare superblock defined by the canonical principles that determined the spacing between east-west streets. The

Figure E.3
Ju'er Hutong, an exterior view of the complex.
Source: Courtesy of Daniel Abramson, 1995.

Figure E.4
Ju'er Hutong, view of an interior courtyard.
Source: Courtesy of Daniel Abramson, 1992.

southern boundary of the block is defined by Ju'er Hutong, but the northern and eastern boundaries are defined by two major arterials—Gulou Dong Dajie and Jiaodaokou Nan Dajie. Its eastern boundary is defined by an intermediate-size north-south road called Nanluoguxiang, after which the superblock is named. The antecedent policy that led to the Ju'er Hutong development is the 1982 Beijing Municipality Master Plan that designated the Nanluoguxiang superblock as a "Traditional Courtyard Housing Preservation District."[5] This overlay zone had rather sparing applications in the historic city, as evident from the extent of clearance that has taken place since that time. Nanluoguxiang, a historic street of old Beijing that serves as the spine from which hutongs branch out like fishbones, has become an attractive tourist destination that emulates the street life of old Beijing, albeit with contemporary consumer products and outlets. (See figure 11.10.)

The project involved clearance of existing courtyard houses, most of which were in dilapidated condition, with the courtyard spaces filled in by informal extensions of the units occupied by the residents. The project was planned in four phases and involved a new design of housing two- to three-story structures clustered around a new system of courtyards. The first phase included seven old courtyards on a site of 2,090 square meters, completed in 1990. The second phase involved a larger footprint of 1.14 acres, completed in 1994. The remaining two phases were on hold for political and bureaucratic reasons. The design of Ju'er Hutong, which is inspired by the traditional courtyard house architecture, has won international acclaim. "The use of traditional Chinese architectural elements," writes Liangyong Wu, "has helped to create a sense of belonging ... and support the continuation of traditions that are still common in the *hutong*."[6] In arguing for what he called the "organic order through organic renewal," and what we might consider the endogenous approach to city design, Wu further commented:

> The historic cities themselves can be thought of as works of art that are constantly in use. When parts are worn out patches have to made according to the intrinsic texture. Also they have to be washed and cleaned regularly. In time an artifact may be full of patches, but it remains a work of art all the same.[7] (p. 9, as counted)

This statement stands as an antithesis to all the Faustian imperatives in the denoument of the historic Beijing as discussed in chapter 11. The Ju'er Hutong project won many national and international awards incliding World Habitat Award in 1992.

3. The 798 Art District, Beijing

Also known as Dashanzi Art District, this 175-acre site, an abandoned industrial complex in Beijing, is a commendable reuse of a brownfield site. Originally built as a major electronic factory complex by Russian and East German engineers, the complex produced mainly military but also limited civilian electronics equipment for the earlier socialist incarnation of the Chinese state. With the embrace of the market economy in the eighties and corresponding retrenchment of the collectives and state-owned enterprises, the Dashanzi factory complex gradually lost state support and by the late eighties and early nineties was completely abandoned.

Members of the Beijing arts community, in search of a permanent home, moved into the complex, particularly the section known as the 798 zone. The arts pioneers began to use the cavernous factory spaces for studios, foundries, kilns, photo labs, and display spaces. The 798 space, a vaulted industrial structure, is now used as an art gallery, holding periodic shows and exhibitions. With available housing that was built as part of the original industrial complex, the district has become a live-work space for the artistic community. It is a creative urban space that is relatively rare in the developing world.

Within the short life span of the 798 Art District, it has become quite trendy and has begun to gentrify, with rent increasing dramatically in recent years. Furthermore, once considered to be on the outskirts of the city, this area is now within the Fifth Ring Road and adjacent to the expressway connecting to the airport. In 2004 the area was slated for demolition and new development—perhaps new industrial complexes—and despite appeals from the Beijing arts community and academics, its fate appeared to be sealed. It seemed that the success of the 798 Art District had proved to be only provisional, a characteristic I have noted previously in discussing the attributes of best practices.

But soon thereafter the 798 Art District escaped the wrecking ball because of considerable public outcry and intervention of important cultural institutions. Local planners were able to successfully make a case for an "adaptive reuse strategy" that could still achieve its real estate development potential for the landholder Seven Star Group.[8] By 2008 the US planning firm Sasaki had prepared a vision plan that emphasized four guiding principles: arts as the main theme; retaining industrial structures and their unique architectural features; increasing visibility and accessibility; and encouraging additional development. The Sasaki planning firm received the Pierre L'Enfant International Planning Excellence Award from the American Planning Association in 2018. The 798 Art District is now a very successful tourist attraction, ranking third after the Great Wall and the Forbidden City. (See figures E.5 and E.6.)

So what began as a space of insurgent activism of local artists and the creative class soon became globalized in its success story with the collaboration of the government, a Belgian philanthropist, and a local real estate developer, finally winning an award of excellence from an American planning organization. We don't know if the original artists are still there, or whether they have been displaced by the inexorable gentrification that comes with success. One may wonder why I have even chosen this as an example of "best practice." The case to be made here is the endogenous nature of the initiative and insurgent agency of a creative class exploring their identity within an authoritarian state at a time when the civil society in China was still very much in a prostrate state.[9]

Figure E.5
Entrance to the 798 Art District announcing an exhibition underway, Beijing.
Source: Courtesy of Fang Wang, 2007.

Figure E.6
An artists' workshop in the 798 Art District.
Source: Author, 2005.

4. Rock Garden of Chandigarh

The well-known, almost iconic, master plan of Chandigarh shows a large green area to the northeast of the capital complex (see figure 8.2 in chapter 8). A forested land along one of the several streams that flow through the urbanized area of the city today, it was meant to be a nature reserve—a commons under public ownership. In fact it still is, both in plan and reality, with one exception—the 175-acre Rock Garden, now a major attraction for residents and visitors alike. The Rock Garden is more intimate, intriguing, and engaging than the Capitol Complex designed by Le Corbusier, a rather sterile monotony of paved empty space separating the three architectural marvels of Le Corbusier (see figures 8.3 and 8.4 in chapter 8). What is particularly interesting about the Rock Garden is not only its spellbinding ensemble of sculpture, murals, landscaping, and sensorium, but also the process through which it came about. It is a story of agency, initiative, creativity, imagination, and ultimate ownership by the public and the institutions of the state.

The story is fascinating. When the site of Chandigarh, the new capital, was selected—in the foothills of the Shivalik mountains—it was dotted with some twenty villages and small settlements. In 1952, when the construction of a new city began according to Le Corbusier's master plan, most of these settlements had to be demolished, resulting in "piles of debris—pottery fragments; bottles; glass; tiles; rocks—littered the landscape."[10] These piles of waste and debris inspired Nek Chand Saini (1924–2015), a road inspector for the local government, to secretly imagine the possibility of a rock garden constructed from these detritus of demolition. The implementation of this rock garden began as a covert and even subversive act because no construction was permitted in this public land. Beginning in 1958 in his spare time and on weekends, Nek Chand collected the debris and rocks from these waste piles and transported them on his bike to a gorge in the forested commons, hidden from public view. In 1965 he began his sculpture garden—his own planned city with collection of abstract human and animal forms—still hidden form the public view or awareness. Eventually in 1972—fourteen years after he began his creative enterprise—the incipient garden was discovered by a government official and brought to the attention of higher-ups, including the chief architect of Chandigarh. The garden at that time had occupied some 12 acres of land.

Under normal circumstances illegal construction on public land planned as a nature reserve would have faced routine demolition and clearance under the state bureaucracy. But surprisingly that did not happen. With overwhelming public support and that of the chief architect, the rock garden received endorsement from the government and came under its supervision. Nek Chand became the supervisor, with some 50 employees working under him to continue implementation of his ideas. By 1976 it had sprawled over 30 acres, and officially became open to the public.

The rock garden is a visual feast of sculptures and forms that are all constructed from broken and discarded materials—colorful glass bangles, broken pottery, ceramic insulating pods used in transmission lines, bicycle frames, and so on. These sculptures are arranged as tableaux with cultural roots and mythology. Winding paths expose the observer to a varied sensory experience, leading one to a central town square with many behavior settings for children, families, and visitors. Although Nek Chand was not trained as an artist, his creative expressions are on par with such well-known architects as Antoni Gaudí or Paolo Soleri. (See figures E.7, E.8 and E.9.)

Figure E.7
Landscaped path in the Rock Garden with a waterfall along a natural gorge.
Source: Author, 2004.

5. The Public Realm, Buenos Aires

One of the casualties of development, one could argue, is the shrinkage and segmentation of the public realm. In precolonial and preindustrial times the urban commons was ubiquitous and accessible for common use. Property rights were loosely defined, unless established by walls forbidding the entry of the public, as in the case of Ming dynasty Beijing. But generally speaking, the boundaries between the private and public realms were less formally defined and allowed for overlaps, sharing, and altruism. One sees this even today in a city like Jaisalmer in Rajasthan, near the western boundary of India, where public easements interweave spaces of large *havelis* or mansions. Even for less sumptuous residences, the front porch traditionally had a semipublic status—accepted as a part of the commons, as it were—and could be seen used by kids, itinerant street vendors, or a cow or two belonging to the local milkman. Similar spaces and

Figure E.8
The ladies of the Rock Garden.
Source: Author, 2004.

uses of the urban commons still continue in the medinas of Morocco and other such surviving settings in the Middle East.

Elsewhere in the Global South, during the colonial era, as James C. Scott has noted, modernity brought modern institutions of governance, which included the cadastral regime and property rights.[11] The subsequent advent of neoliberal economic thinking emphasized the efficiency of market economy and strict allocation and enforcement of private property rights, supporting further enclosure of the commons.[12] Economic development thus inexorably leads to the partitioning of the commons and allocation of rights to individuals and organizations, leaving the residual land for public use. This space then becomes the public realm, nonexcludable and nonrival, to use the common definition of the public good. In Latin American cities the public realm has become a principal focus of city design, Buenos Aires being a case in point, and arguably a best practice to be emulated elsewhere in the Global South.

Figure E.9
Taking care of the Rock Garden's permanent residents.
Source: Author, 2004.

It seems that the principal city design strategy in many of Latin American cities—Buenos Aires in particular—is to enhance the overall experience of the public realm. In the words of architecture professor Silvio Macedo of University of São Paulo in Brazil, they consider public space as the principal "protagonist" in the larger city design,[13] and this view seems to capture the various public design initiatives in Buenos Aires undertaken by the local administration under the tutelage of the ruling political party. There are several components of these initiatives: preserving the public realm of the historic neighborhoods like San Telmo and La Boca (see figure E.10); closing off many central city streets to increase their stock of public space and pedestrian movement; a citywide public information system describing the immediate neighborhood or streets in graphically attractive maps, dial-in apps to listen to online commentary about the immediate urban space, and social media to connect many of the public spaces to their users and immediate neighbors and beyond. Thus, the Facebook signs (posted in these

Figure E.10
The historic and artistic neighborhood of La Boca, Buenos Aires.
Source: Author, 2011.

public spaces) connect a neighborhood park to a larger audience that includes not only immediate neighbors and users but also a larger "non-place" community (see figure E.11). Elsewhere, urban designer Ileana Apostol and her colleagues described this phenomenon as the "flânerie between the net and place" and discussed this initiative as a means for connecting the place and the non-place communities,[14] and thus hoping to achieve communities of propinquity.[15]

Thus, the awareness of an improved public realm—*espacio público*—pervades the entire city and is closely linked to the notion of sustainable development. It is expressed proudly in public works projects and even on city buses, reminding us that the medium of mass transit is also a public space (see figure E.12).[16]

6. The Pedestrian Escalator of Medellín

The city of Medellín, the second largest in Colombia, shares the characteristics of many Latin American cities: a historical colonial core surrounded by residences of the affluent and the space needed for business and commerce. Typically cities of such origin

Figure E.11
"Flânerie between net and place"—Plaza Diaz Vélez, Barracas district, Buenos Aires.
Source: Author, 2011.

Figure E.12
A reminder: transit is also public space. Buenos Aires.
Source: Author, 2011.

share very similar ecology. Perhaps the most distinctive part of this social ecology is the squatter settlements on the periphery of the city. In the case of Medellín, as in many other Latin American cities, they are all located on the steep terrains of the Andean foothill. The access to the settlements on the hillside was never easy and required climbing the stairs along the steep hillside.

For a long time Medellín was known for its drug trade and as the most violent city in the world with a murder rate of 380 per 100,000 people in 1991. Many of the hillside settlements were once the stronghold of guerrillas and drug traffickers. Comuna 13 is one such neighborhood of 12,000 residents. Settled on a steep hillside, residents had to climb a height equivalent to 28 stories after earning their livelihood in the city each day. Although Medellín had built a cable car system that provided access for different parts of the hillside settlements, areas like Comuna 13 lacked that privilege.[17]

This all changed in 2011 when the city authorities installed a 385-meter covered escalator system to connect Comuna 13 with the services and opportunities that the city offered below (see figures E.13 and E.14). Covered with a bright orange roof, and comprising multiple segments negotiating different rights of the way, this was a major innovation in transportation and met the criterion of access, one of the important performance characteristic of good city form.[18] In another sense, the initiative was, as Henri Lefebvre[19] would argue, a fundamental right to the city for the public that has been historically neglected, excluded, and marginalized. One could see this as an application of Amartya Sen's capability theory of development,[20] which argues that the capability to achieve one's functioning needs should be the aim of development. In this instance these escalators can be seen as contributing to access and mobility needs of the poor, thus serving to improve the functioning needs of the poor.

7. Transportation and Public Space, Bogotá

Another success story of improving the public realm also comes from Colombia—in its largest city, Bogotá. The success story of how Bogotá evolved was written over several decades under the leadership of three mayors, as insightfully discussed in a recent book by a planning academic, Rachel Berney.[21] The effort to transform Bogotá, a city notorious in the eighties for its crime, poverty, and violence, began in the early nineties when Jaime Castro, the third elected mayor of Bogotá, initiated major institutional reforms that included modernization of the tax code, collection of tax revenues from residents, and obtaining Bogotá's share of national tax revenues. These reforms led to a significant improvement in public finance available for physical changes in the city. The legacy of Castro's administrative reforms helped the two mayors who succeeded

Figure E.13
The Medellín escalator negotiating the existing settlement form.
Source: "New escalators, new life!" by Young Shanahan is licensed with CCBY2.0. To view a copy of this license, visit https://creativecommons.org/licenses/by/2.0/.

him, Antanas Mockus and Enrique Peñalosa. These two mayors focused on improving the public realm of Bogotá, which defined the everyday life experience of most Bogotáns, 80 percent of whom were low income or poor. Berney referred to Mockus and Peñalosa as the "public space" mayors.[22] Initially Mockus focused on "citizen culture" and became well known for his use of students of theatrical arts dressed as clowns to stand in busy street intersections and offer thumbs up or down to the drivers for their driving performance. And apparently this was highly successful and brought about more discipline in traffic performance. In the same spirit, he also tried to achieve the public culture that would make the existing public spaces—plazas and parks—more accessible and enjoyable. Public space was seen an integral part of improving the quality of life (see figure E.15). This ethos was developed even more vigorously by Peñalosa, seemingly combining a Lefebvrean right to the city with Sen's capability approach to make the city more accessible for all. This included providing mobility for the lower-income residents, while increasing the stock of public spaces by closing some major

Figure E.14

The escalator system negotiating the hillside settlement form.

Source: "Comuna 13" by Nigel Burgher is licensed with CCBY2.0. To view a copy of this license, visit https://creativecommons.org/licenses/by/2.0/.

streets for pedestrians and creating a network of designated rights of way for bicyclists called *ciclovías* and *ciclorutas*. In a documentary titled *Urbanized*,[23] a segment on Bogotá features a jubilant Peñalosa biking through these *ciclovías* and pointing out the miseries of car drivers. In this segment the mayor—he was reelected in 2015 for a third time—takes great pride in another of his major accomplishments—the TransMilenio bus rapid transit (BRT) system, a network of designated bus lanes through major arterials with stations designed after those in rail transit (see figure E.16). What is significant is that the BRT and its stations are well integrated with the system of public spaces. Thus access, mobility, and right to the city are all well integrated in a seamless system of BRT, *bike lanes*, pedestrian streets, and public spaces (see figure E.17). This is indeed a major achievement in city design serving people of lower-income strata, including the very poor, thus achieving the causes of equity and social justice.

Figure E.15
Existing public squares integrated with pedestrian streets in downtown Bogotá.
Source: Author, 2015.

Figure E.16
A TransMilenio station, Bogotá.
Source: Author, 2015.

8. Conservation of Fès Medina

Chapter 12 was devoted to Fès medina as an exemplar of traditional and historic settlements not only in northern Africa but also in the Middle East and Asia. The chapter was presented as a counterpoint to the imperatives of growth and change that have shaped the fate of many such magnificent examples of premodern, precolonial cities. The narrative of the demolition of the historic urban form in Beijing that we covered in some depth in chapter 11 seemingly is the script that confronts the broader public interest in heritage preservation. I have presented the case of Fès medina as a case of endogenous life experience and as a possible model of sustainable development. I have referred to its enduring sense of place and community, piety, social capital, and engaged civil

Figure E.17
Pedestrian street, public space, and TransMilenio right of way combined, Avenida Jiménez, Central Bogotá.
Source: Author, 2015.

society. I have only tangentially referred to the conservation and heritage-preservation efforts that have made Fès medina a candidate for a best practice example.

In a paper devoted to the project history of the conservation efforts in Fès medina, Radoine reviews the history of conservation efforts in Fès and argues that indeed a post-impact appraisal will support any claim for a best practice example.[24] In this article he reviews the history of Fès medina's preservation efforts, which began in the early seventies from a collective international effort. It received strong support from the national government, the local government, and international organizations like UNESCO, USAID, and the World Bank. To effectively undertake the conservation planning and management efforts, in 1982 the Interior Ministry of the Moroccan government established a Delegation for the Safeguard of the Medina of Fès to begin to identify the institutions for developing and implementing the conservation program. In 1989 a new institutional framework was created to shift the focus from research and analysis of the problems to implementation of the strategic projects. This organization, Agence pour la Dédensification et la Réhabilitation de la Médina de Fès (ADER-FÈS), is still functioning and takes credit for some major achievements in the thirty years since its inception. It has made 3,340 deteriorating buildings safe, restored 27 key monuments, restored the Quaraouiyine Library, and rehabilitated 4 *fondouks*, or inns.[25] (See figure E.18.)

The initiative had several components. First, it provided rehabilitation grant for the conservation of historic structures under private initiatives. Second, it provided access and critical links to emergency public services and medina entrances, improved mobility of people and goods, increased parking, and provided better traffic management. Third, it aimed to improve solid-waste collection and disposal of industrial waste and pollution through better management of traditional crafts workshops and the like. Fourth, it planned to rehabilitate the medina wall, provided emergency actions

Figure E.18
A restoration project underway in the Fès medina.
Source: Author, 1999.

for residents of dilapidated housing, and promoted labor-intensive job opportunities through local contractors. And finally, it aims at strengthening the capabilities of the local institution—ADER-FÈS is responsible for the conservation and rehabilitation of the medina and the Municipality of Fès-Medina.[26]

More significantly, what the conservation effort has succeeded in doing is to mobilize the local support, particularly the existing stock of social capital that goes back to the nexus of piety and community that I have referred to in chapters 6 and 11. In fact, it is this characteristic that ranks foremost among the six arguments that Radoine makes in support of his case for the Fès medina as "best practice" in heritage conservation:[27]

1. Participatory process and community development
2. Political structure and conflict resolution
3. Economic development
4. Environmental improvement
5. Restoration as urban rehabilitation
6. Infrastructure and facilities

9. Jan Marg, Ahmedabad

Arguably the city of Ahmedabad is one of the most progressive cities in India and has achieved major infrastructure improvements in recent years, thanks to urban redevelopment initiative funding available from the national government. Nevertheless, this is the city that hosted the works of some of the best-known modern architects: Le Corbusier and Louis Kahn. Noteworthy also are the works of Charles Correa and Balkrishna Doshi, two architects who worked in Le Corbusier's atelier when he was working on the Chandigarh project. So, the culture of modern architecture has been around for some time, albeit in the possession of wealthy patrons and institutions, with a clear view of nearby squatter settlements and extreme poverty. The spectacle of poverty was integral to the urban landscape, as customary in any city of the Global South. One of the infrastructure initiatives—the Sabarmati Riverfront development project—has been a major environmental improvement with a major addition to the public space, but the eviction and resettlement remains controversial.

The Janmarg ("people's way" in Hindi) BRT project is less controversial, although it has its share of detractors. This is an infrastructure improvement that addresses the issues of access and mobility in a growing city of some 6.3 million, particularly the vast majority of the lower-income population, whose travel options are limited for longer-distance travel. What is impressive about the system was that it was designed endogenously, by the faculty and professional staff of a local university. No foreign consultants were involved. Under the leadership of Professor H. M. Shivanand Swamy, the staff and students of CEPT University designed the alignment of the system quite skillfully to include exclusive rights of way of the buses along highways and arterials but also acquiring one-way easements through crowded inner-city commercial districts.

What is impressive is how quickly the system was operationalized, in a time span of three to four years. It was opened in the later part of 2009. The network had expanded to 89 kilometers by the end of 2015, with an ultimate coverage goal of 155 kilometers. The fleet consists of locally constructed buses, both air-conditioned and non-air-conditioned. The stations are well designed to serve passenger comfort and convenience. Recently the Janmarg added women-only buses.

Critics point to the high indolent ridership numbers, as is common in many transit systems throughout the world. This will perhaps change with planned and market-responsive development along the Janmarg corridors and stations. Nevertheless, it remains an early effort to serve access and mobility to a large segment of population who remain transit-dependent because of class or demographic reasons. (See figures E.19 and E.20.)

Figure E.19
Access to a Janmarg station, Ahmedabad.
Source: Author, 2011.

Figure E.20
A Janmarg station concourse and waiting area, Ahmedabad.
Source: Author, 2011.

10. The Legacy of Patrick Geddes

In responding to my discussion of what I call the "Geddes paradigm," one of the reviewers of the manuscript, while complimenting the idea of inserting Geddes into the contemporary discourse on city design in the Global South, suggested that this should have been done earlier in the book. Perhaps, but there were no obvious places in the flow of the text where that could have been achieved. In any event, a brief biographical sketch of Geddes is in order here before I discuss Geddes's contribution to town planning in India.

Geddes was a Scottish town planner at the turn of the twentieth century who earned renown in in the UK by introducing new ideas and arguments in the practice of town planning. Trained as a biologist but with interests branching out to include sociology and geography, he might have been one of the earliest practitioners of the social sciences who questioned the architectural and civil engineering orientation integral to planning. In his earlier work in Edinburgh he advocated the notion of "civic survey" as a fundamental step in undertaking a town-planning project. As Lewis Mumford, a renowned planning historian, noted, Geddes's background in biology and sociology made him interested in regional culture and regionalism, thus combining the parallel notions of ecology of places with the ecology of people. But it is his insistence on "diagnosis before treatment" in the Edinburgh plan-making that made him well known in the UK. Mumford calls Geddes a "global thinker" and argues that "one cannot appreciate Geddes's regionalism unless one also appreciates his internationalism, his universalism."[28] He thought that this was why Geddes's contribution to the Indian town planning became so poignant. Commenting on Geddes's work, Mumford notes further the two sides of Geddes:

> One aspect was systematic and rigorous to an extraordinary degree, it was based upon a cartography of life, mind, and society which he had created to facilitate his own thinking, so that his ideas would be related, in space, time, and function, to the concrete situation from which they were momentarily abstracted—unlike the thought of the specialist which treats the abstraction as it were self-sufficient.[29]

It is the former trait that would characterize much of Geddes's work in India.

Geddes arrived in India in 1915, during the final phase of the British colonial rule. After developing over several centuries, the colonial urban form had been finalized with such iconic landmarks as the Victoria Memorial in 1905 and Lutyens's plan for the British capital in Delhi in 1911. In the early twentieth century civil construction efforts were directed at the indigenous subaltern settlements, which had been previously ignored in the grand schema of colonial city building. The indigenous settlements were seen as messy and unclean, and as lacking sanitation and basic public health measures. Accordingly, the public works improvement projects were directed at drainage and sanitation, clearance of older buildings (particularly "*kutcha*"[30] structures), and straightening and widening of the crooked and organic urban form. Geddes's innate sensibilities—as captured in Mumford's comment noted previously—militated against such Haussmannian measures. He instead proposed schemes that would be done with sensitivity to local lifestyle, improving public health and sanitation measures, but also opening up the dense forms and creating more public spaces with trees planted in or around them.

During his several years' stay in India, Geddes was involved in many projects and proposed improvement schemes for many indigenous settlements, as well as for revitalization of compact and congested business districts, such as Burrabazar in Kolkata. Several of these former case studies are included in the book edited by architectural historian Jaqueline Tyrwhitt.[31]

So, what is the "Geddes paradigm," and why might it be considered a best practice? For one, in Geddes's own words: "Town-planning is not mere place-planning, nor even work-planning. If it is to be successful it must be folk-planning."[32]

The significance of the "Geddes paradigm" has to be understood in the context of the colonial project discussed previously in chapter 7. The narrative of the colonial project will remain incomplete and one-sided without acknowledging the contributions of Patrick Geddes to settlement planning and design in India. Unlike his other professional peers, who displayed little regard for or understanding of the local customs and practices—the *mētis* in Scott's term[33]—of settlement design and building, Geddes sought to bring endogenous rules and practices to the contemporary urban transformation. He understood and appreciated the urbanism in local settlements and offered many specific proposals that emphasized urban conservation rather than Haussmannian colonial projects of clearance and transformation commonplace then in many parts of the Global South. He emphasized "diagnostic surveys" that helped provide an understanding of the relationship between place, work, and folk (or, in the constructs presented earlier in this volume, between nature services, the sensorium, form, urbanism, the social ecology, and the habitus). In Geddes's schema the changes often lay in "conservative surgery" rather than wholesale redevelopment. His ideas for conservative surgery were often driven by considerations of public health—sanitation and waste disposal, locally grown healthy food, and landscapes of trees and foliage. In today's terms "sustainability" and "healthy cities" were the driving components of Geddes's notion of endogenous city design in the Indian context.

He saw the process as having several phases and normative components. Thus, it must begin with a "diagnostic survey," which "seeks to unravel the old city's labyrinth and discern how this has grown up."[34] In contemporary parlance, the aim is to understand the "urbanism" of the city. In developing this understanding, the planner or city designer must obtain "public co-operation" and draw from "local knowledge and understanding."[35] Geddes was opposed to the wholesale clearance of existing settlements. (Imagine how he would have reacted to the Faustian denouement of historic Beijing in recent years!) Instead he preferred what he referred to as "conservative surgery," which involved carefully selective demolition and rebuilding that would address issues of health and also public life by creating a system of small public spaces, all in consultation with the local community. Geddes was aware of the religious classes and caste differences, and thus of the need to create a multicultural urban life in India. Although Geddes did not explicitly address issues of sustainability that concern us today, it was implicit in his prescriptions for creating open space and tree planting and limiting the ecological footprints of developments. All of his ideas remain pertinent today, a hundred years later.

Notes

Preface

1. United Nations, Department of Economic and Social Affairs (2018).

2. See *The Economist* (2019b); Shephard (2015).

3. For an exchange over market versus planning, see Richardson and Gordon (1993) and T. Banerjee (1993).

4. Westfall (1990). Recipient of the 1991 Paul Davidoff Award from the American Planning Association.

Chapter 1

1. Eco (1986), p. 22.

2. When I had a chance to visit Indonesia—Jakarta and Bandung—in 2001 and 2003.

3. My travel companion was Wilan Oktavian, a transportation planner with the National Development Planning Agency (Bappenas). In Bandung we met Dr. Widiarto, a planning professor at ITB (Bandung Institute of Technology), who graciously offered to give me a tour of Vila Dunia.

4. All three were built by a real estate subsidiary of PT Duta Pertiwi Tbk, one of the most highly diversified public real estate corporations in Indonesia. Kota Wisata and Legenda Wisata are located in an area called Cibubur in the larger Jakarta metropolitan area, about an hour's drive from central Jakarta. Dr. Hadi Suprayoga, now Primary Planner for Regional Development at the Ministry of National Development Planning (Bappenas), graciously accompanied me during my first visit.

5. By this I mean a subtle change in the experience of one's relationship to her proximate environment.

6. Pizarro (2005).

7. A. King (2004), p. 28.

8. El-Shakhs (1997).

9. See *The Economist* (2019b).

10. Cowherd and Heikkila (2002).

11. Observers have referred to Dubai as "a city without urbanism" (lecture at USC by Harvey Molotch, March 2, 2017 https://calendar.usc.edu/event/cities_without_urbanism_lessons_of_money_and_power_in_the_gulf_region#.X1uTBWhKhyw) and to Abu Dhabi as an "un-city" (Surajit Chakravarty, 2019).

12. Piazzoni (2018).

13. See Piazzoni and Banerjee (2018).

14. See Pearlstine et al. (2019).

15. There is conjecture that Chongqing—an urban agglomeration with a population of some 34 million—may be the model for the future urbanization of China.

16. Many questions come to mind: Why are they here? Who is this for? Who would want to live here? Most of the housing units in Kota Wisata, I noticed, were still unoccupied or unsold. A representative of the developer confirmed that these places are mainly for the local market. Families currently living in Jakarta are buying them as second, weekend homes. Obviously well heeled, the residents are probably professionals and business executives, well educated and well traveled, who have bought into the culture of American-style low-density suburban living, which is not available within crowded Jakarta itself. It is reasonable to conclude that the same is true for Vila Dunia in Bandung.

17. Interview with Julius Keke, architect, previously director of the Real Estate Division of the Sinar Mas Group. I am grateful to him for arranging a second visit to these two developments and granting permission to take photos.

18. See Diamond (1997); Mellinger, Sachs, and Gallup (1999).

19. Frank (1966).

20. Said (1979, 1993).

21. Kuznets (1966).

22. Rostow (1975).

23. Inkeles and Smith (1974).

24. Several influential and widely read books have provoked broader public discussions of the appearance of our built environment. See, for example, Oldenburg (1989); Hiss (1990); Zukin (1991); Garreau (1992); Sorkin (1992); Kunstler (1993); Rybczynski (1995); Huxtable (1997); C. Boyer (1997).

25. See Mabin (2005); Pearce-Oroz (2005); Briggs (2005).

26. Piketty (2014).

27. Jain-Chandra (2018).

28. Kim (2016).

29. Do Lago (2001); Villaça (2001); O'Hare and Barke (2002).

30. O'Hare and Barke (2002); Perlman (2006).

31. United Nations, Department of Economic and Social Affairs, Population Division (2017).

32. WWF's *Living Planet Report 2006* offers the following definition: "The Ecological Footprint measures humanity's demand on the biosphere in terms of the area of biologically productive land and sea required to provide the resources we use and to absorb our waste" (WWF, 2006, p. 14).

33. See Ehrlich and Ehrlich (2009).

34. For some dystopic scenarios, see Lynch (1990b).

35. See Krieger (1987).

36. See Castells (1996).

37. Barber (2000); Stiglitz (2002).

38. See Peattie (1981) for a discussion of the moral order versus the technical order of development.

39. The Kyoto Protocol of 1997, 2001, and 2007 and the Intergovernmental Panel on Climate Change (https://unfccc.int/kyoto_protocol) report on climate change are cases in point. See Blanco et al. (2009).

40. See Lefebvre (1991); Gottdeiner (1985).

41. See Gunder (2011), for example.

42. In order to further such aims as citizenship and democracy, planners have increasingly conceded their normative authority to local political interests. The problem with this practice is that in the absence of any normative positions, planners and designers become mere functionaries of the inexorable juggernaut of profit motives, market liberalism, technological determinism, and narrow political interests. This is particularly true in the Western liberal democracies, especially the US. There is considerable literature on the contemporary role and responsibilities of planners, but none of it considers normative vision as one of these responsibilities. Kevin Lynch (1981) may have been the last planner to address the normative aspects of city design.

43. See Peattie (1987b); T. Banerjee (2014).

44. After the title of a seminal work by Lewis Mumford (1938).

45. See Alnowaiser (1983).

46. See Lynch (1981).

47. Fukuyama (1989).

48. C. Taylor (2001).

49. See Campanella (2008); Bosker (2013).

50. Sorkin (1992).

51. See Scott (1998).

52. See T. Banerjee (2009).

53. Embree (1971), p. 3.

54. See T. Banerjee and Verma (2003a, 2003b).

55. See Pizarro, Wei, and Banerjee (2003).

56. A. Thomas et al. (1994).

57. Said (1979).

58. Said (1993).

59. See Abu-Lughod (1987); AlSayyad (1991); Amirahmadi and El-Shakhs (1993).

60. Naipaul (1964).

Chapter 2

1. Bairoch (1981), p. 7.

2. See Lynch (1960).

3. The difference between a photograph and a sketch or between a cartographic map and a mental map are examples of such variable verisimilitude.

4. Hirschman (1988).

5. The Maslovian need hierarchy consists of five levels of human needs, where the higher levels become relevant only when the lower-level needs are fully satisfied. These needs, in ascending order, are basic needs such as food and shelter; safety and security needs; belonging and social needs; needs for self-esteem; and need for self-actualization. See Maslow (1954).

6. Rostow proposed that development takes place in stages, and he described five distinct stages through which a nation must advance in its quest for development: traditional society, pre-takeoff stage, takeoff stage, drive to maturity, and stage of mass consumerism. See Rostow (1960).

7. Croll (1994).

8. See Murphey (1980).

9. Since 1997/1998 the World Bank's annual development report has listed countries alphabetically, rather than by their GNP per capita rank, although the bank still classifies countries as upper, middle (with the subclassification upper-middle and lower-middle), and lower income based on GNP per capita cutoff levels, and it reports aggregate data for each of these groups. The

most recent reports group countries by six geographical regions and four income classes based on gross national income (GNI) per capita. See, for example, Table 1, World Bank 2012).

10. I thank Ferdinand Lewis for noting this point.

11. In the early 1990s the *New York Times* ran a series of editorials critiquing the state of affairs in New York City under the title "New Calcutta."

12. Reiff (1991).

13. Writes Sen (1999), "It is remarkable that the extent of deprivation for particular groups in very rich countries can be comparable to that in the so-called third world. For example, in the United States, African Americans as a group have no higher—indeed have a lower—chance of reaching advanced ages than do people born in the immensely poorer economies of China or the Indian state of Kerala (or in Sri Lanka, Jamaica or Costa Rica)" (p. 21).

14. De Soto (1990).

15. Arndt (1987).

16. See A. Smith (1999); Frank (1966).

17. Detractors of this view would argue that the colonial powers invested considerable resources in infrastructure and installing institutions of the modern state, education system, and health services, as the British seemingly accomplished in colonial India.

18. Colclough and Manor (1991).

19. Rostow (1975).

20. Said (1993).

21. Mokyr (1990).

22. Castells (1996).

23. Indeed, these ignored achievements may have been important antecedents of the Newtonian physical order, by most reckoning today. But the claim of the authority of the new scientific order is also an assertion of the inherent superiority of the Western worldview over the rest. It became a self-serving position that might have eventually influenced the political economy of contemporary development, as argued forcefully by Said (1993) in linking Orientalism with the colonial exploits of that world view.

24. Sachs (2001). Others have contested this view arguing that the "reversal of fortune" is more a case of introduction of institutions resulting from European colonialism and subsequent urbanization. See Acemoglu, Johnson, and Robinson (2002, 2005).

25. Of course, from the Marxian perspective, economic growth is inherent in the logic of capitalism, state or no state. The state in the Western liberal democracies is needed, according to this view, to maintain and sustain the capitalist system. The "state apparatus" is a necessary ingredient of the dynamic of capitalism (see Clarke and Dear, 1984).

26. Hirschman (1977).

27. See also Hirschman (1982); Heilbroner (1985).

28. Heilbroner (1985), p. 114.

29. Lowi (1969).

30. The "four laws of development"—Adam Smith's division of labor (1776), Thomas Malthus's principles of population growth (1798), David Ricardo's law of wages (1817), and Henry George's growth of real estate values (1879)—suggested specific misgivings about the notion of an automatic society assumed by the theory of capitalism. Indeed, the theories show the contrary and disruptive effects of laissez-faire capitalism and market competition on various aspects of society (see Lowi, 1969).

31. Lowi (1969), p. 19.

32. Lowi (1969), p. 27.

33. This twentieth-century variant replaced the vision of nineteenth-century market liberalism with "interest group liberalism" and "an amalgam of capitalism, statism and pluralism" (Lowi, 1969, p. 29), that believed in many sources of power and control other than the government itself (see also Lindblom, 1977). Today we are well aware of the concept of pluralism and the effect of statism in the contemporary politics of Western liberal democracies. The seeds for government intervention and guidance in shaping the economy were planted even before World War II, Arndt's earlier assertion notwithstanding. The New Deal programs ushered in by the Roosevelt administration following the Great Depression is the most eminent case in point.

34. Arndt (1987).

35. I am referring to the conflicts inherent in Islamic fundamentalism in the context of globalization. See Barber (1995); Naipaul (1981); Friedman (2000).

36. Arndt (1987).

37. Myint (1980).

38. World Bank (1978).

39. According to the World Bank's *World Development Report 2007*, the GNP per capita for fifty-four low-income countries was $580 in 2005, while for fifty-seven high-income countries (including twenty-four OECD countries) it was $35,151, or sixty times larger, and adjusted for purchasing power parity (PPP) it was thirteen times larger (World Bank, 2006, p. 289).

40. O'Brien (1982, 1990).

41. O'Brien (1990), p. 177, quoting Frank (1998), p. 42.

42. See Frank (1998).

43. Thomas et al. (1994).

44. The 1989 GDP of sub-Saharan Africa was $161,820 million. See World Bank (1991), Table 3.

45. Sen (2005), p. 335.

46. For associated charts and maps, see A. Thomas et al. (1994), pages 28–29 in particular.

47. A. Thomas et al. (1994), p. 28.

48. A. Thomas et al. (1994), p. 28.

49. Frank (1966).

50. Frank (1998). He writes:

> Indeed, the colonies did pay. They supplied not only almost free money, but also servile labor and the cheap sugar, tobacco, timber, cotton, and other goods produced in the Americas for European consumption.... Ernest Mandel (1968: 119–120) estimated the European colonial booty between 1500 and 1800 at 1,000 million gold pound sterling, of which 100 to 150 million reached Britain from India alone between 1750 and 1800. This inflow of capital facilitated if not financed Britain's investment in the new industrial revolution, especially in steam engines and textile technology. (pp. 195–196)

51. Mellinger, Sachs, and Gallup (1999). See note 26 for alternative positions.

52. World Bank (1984), figure 1.3.

53. World Bank (2002), Table 1.

54. A. Thomas et al. (1994).

55. Frank (1998), p. 168. The per capita difference, however, was more significant because the LDCs contained more than 70 percent of the world population

56. Note that the World Bank data used in table 2.2 did not reflect the purchasing power parity (PPP) that is commonly applied today in the analysis of comparative economic development.

57. Bairoch (1981). In fact, what Paul Bairoch had done a quarter-century ago is now a standard practice in international comparison of economic development: the PPP-based GDP.

58. Agreeing with the World Bank (1984) analysis.

59. Kuznets (1966). See also A. Thomas et. al. (1994); Darby and Fullard (1970).

60. See particularly Amin (1972); Frank (1967). For a strong and convincing argument in support of this premise, see Tharoor (2017).

61. See, for example, Bairoch (1993); O'Brien (1982); Landes (1969).

62. Castells (1996); Mokyr (1990), p. 7.

63. Issawi (1958), p. 93.

64. Sjoberg (1963).

65. Note that I have treated the Japanese and Turkish urban agglomerations as part of the more developed groups, because of developed status of the former and the European status of the latter, and also because both had imperialist pasts.

66. Gernet (1962). The following description by Gernet suggests the prosperity and influence of this city: "The space which nature had measured out to Hangchow in such niggardly fashion was occupied in the thirteenth century by the biggest urban concentration in the world at that time. The largest cities of Europe, with a population of several tens of thousands, were nothing but petty market towns in comparison with the 'provisional capital' of China" (p. 43).

67. Arndt (1983).

68. W. A. Lewis (1976), p. 76.

69. Kuznets (1966).

70. See Ahluwalia (1976).

71. Ahluwalia (1976), p. 335.

72. Piketty (2014), p. 14.

73. Arndt (1987) observes, "The touchstone, if not the essence, of economic development was taken to be growth in output and income per head in the less developed countries" (p. 53).

74. To the further chagrin of the Western liberalism, the Indian leadership assumed a strong "visible hand" approach to development, including a Soviet-style five-year planning process.

75. Frank (1966).

76. T. Banerjee and Schenk (1984).

77. Arndt (1983); ul Haq (1971).

78. Todaro (1989), p. 651.

79. Seers (1979), p. 9.

80. Seers (1979), p. 13.

81. It was a major breakthrough, considering that the World Bank is focused on economics, and economists tend to abhor the concept of "need" because it does not include the notion of "willingness to pay" and does not readily translate into a palpable market "demand."

82. See Sen (1999).

83. Chenery et al. (1974).

84. Not to be confused with the controversial work *The Bell Curve* by Richard Herrnstein and Charles Murray (1994), which makes claims about intelligence difference among ethnic groups.

85. Alonso (1980).

86. Kuznets (1955). Also see Annez and Buckley (2009), and Acemoglu, Johnson, and Robinson (2002).

87. See Annez and Buckley (2009).

88. I am paraphrasing Ed Soja of UCLA, in a seminar he gave at USC in 2007.

89. More generally, economic geographers, land and real estate economists, regional scientists, and urban and regional economists have constructed an impressive body of literature, albeit primarily on location of firms and economic activities, and mainly of the microeconomic ilk.

90. Lipton (1988).

91. See, for example, Friedmann (1969). I doubt, however, that Friedmann today would have agreed with his own position then.

92. Castells (1977) has defined the term as "a level of urbanization higher than that which can 'normally' be attained, given the level of industrialization" (p. 41). The idea of overurbanization, of course, was not fully accepted by all scholars. Sovani (1964), for one, questioned the relevance of the concept itself.

93. Annez and Buckley (2009). See also Quigley (2009).

94. Bairoch (1993).

95. Bairoch (1993).

96. Johann Heinrich von Thünen, an early-nineteenth-century (1783–1850) economist—considered amateur—advanced an economic model of agricultural land use that became the basis of bid-rent theory of land use.

97. French economist François Perroux (1903–1987) advanced the concept of "growth pole" in a sectoral context, but it was largely used in a spatial context as a basis for policies of decentralization.

98. Walter Christaller, a German geographer, proposed the central place theory of urban hierarchy based on the distribution of urban places in southern Germany in his 1933 dissertation *Die zentralen Orte in Süddeutschlnd* (*The Central Places in Southern Germany*).

99. Berry (1967).

100. Represented by a log-normal distribution of city populations. Log-normal distribution is typically used to plot the frequency distribution of cities by their size category. Since city sizes range from very large—over ten million—to very small—a few thousand—a logarithmic scale is used for showing this distribution. In a well-articulated system of cities, this distribution approaches a normal curve.

101. Urban primacy is a measure of urban concentration. The most common measure—called the four-city primacy index—is the ratio of the population of the largest city and the combined population of the second-, third-, and fourth-largest cities. A ratio significantly greater than unity implies a condition of primacy.

102. Apologists counter by saying that if India or China were seen as a collection of several smaller countries, one could find high primacy in those constituent regions. Similarly, if we consider Europe as one country, there would be very little urban primacy.

103. El-Shakhs (1972) had to drop the two major outliers—China and India—for this otherwise elegant relationship to hold.

104. Richardson (1977).

105. Williamson (1965).

106. World Bank (1992).

107. OECD (1991).

108. Shafik and Bandyopadhyay (1992).

109. D. Stern, Common, and Barbier (1996), p. 1151.

110. World Bank (1991).

111. Panayotou (2000).

112. Selden and Song (1994).

113. Grossman and Krueger (1991).

114. Bhattarai and Hamming (2001).

115. Antle and Heidebrink (1995).

116. Andreoni and Levinson (2001), p. 269.

117. Ezzati, Singer, and Kammen (2001).

118. Harbaugh, Levinson, and Wilson (2002); Millimet, List, and Stengos (2003); Arrow et al. (1995); Jha and Murthy (2003).

119. This measure remains more in the idea stage and has yet to be fully operational or widely used.

120. See Ahluwalia (1976).

121. Cf. Meadows, Randers, and Meadows (2004), where they revisit and update their original analysis of interaction between earth and human systems and the consequent limits to growth.

122. Panayotou (2000).

Chapter 3

1. Sen (1999), p. 15.

2. Banfield (1958), p. 8.

3. Portes (1976).

4. Portes saw this "as a direct continuation of the thesis Weber developed in *The Protestant Ethic and the Spirit of Capitalism* (1958)" (p. 68).

5. Durkheim (1933).

6. Tönnies (1974).

7. Redfield (1953).

8. Inkeles and Smith (1974).

9. Portes (1976).

10. Written and directed by Jamie Uys (1980).

11. Compared to less than 60 percent as customary in most presidential elections in the United States, the most recent 2020 election being an exception.

12. Barber (1995).

13. Horowitz (1982).

14. Scott (1998).

15. C. Taylor (2001), p. 173.

16. Castells (1996).

17. C. Taylor (2001), p. 186.

18. Indeed, this position can be seen as reconciliation between the advocates of modernity and its detractors, and it may help us accept the fact that there might be an "Indian modernity," a "Chinese modernity," and even an "Islamic modernity."

19. Hosagrahar (2005).

20. Escobar (1995), p. 221.

21. Said (1979).

22. Recall recent incidents at the Abu Ghraib prison in Iraq, where the prisoners were subjected to such shame so that they would mentally break down and cooperate with the military interrogators.

23. AlSayyad (1999).

24. Pizarro, Wei, and Banerjee (2003).

25. Castells (1996).

26. Fathy (1976).

27. See C. Taylor (2001).

28. See Steele (2002).

29. Writings on dependency and development represent dual perspectives of political economy (Amin, 1972; Arndt, 1987; Bagchi, 1982; Higgins and Nguyen, 1979) and sociology (Castells, 1977; Portes, 1976; Horowitz, 1982).

30. Frank (1966).

31. See also Amin (1972).

32. See Chilcote (1974).

33. Cardoso and Faletto (1979).

34. See Lal (2000).

35. Chilcote (1981).

36. Castells (1977).

37. See Peattie (1981).

38. Beier et al. (1975), p. 368.

39. Hardoy (1975).

40. "Hyper-urbanization" refers to a rate of urbanization exceeding twice the rate of industrialization (as historically the urbanization rate in Western developed countries has been roughly twice the industrialization rate).

41. Castells (1977).

42. As discussed by Beier et al. (1975).

43. A. Gilbert and Gugler (1982).

44. See Peattie (1987a).

45. Castells (1977), p. 54.

46. ILO (1972).

47. Castells (1977), p. 41.

48. Morse (1978).

49. See McGee (1977); Armstrong and McGee (1985).

50. Berry (1967).

51. Wallerstein (2011).

52. This argument considers Western industrialized developed countries as the core, and the developing countries as the primary-resource-producing periphery that services the manufacturing activities and serves as the markets for products of the West.

53. C. A. Smith (1985).

54. Castells (1977).

55. Singhal and Rogers (1999).

56. See Castells (1996).

57. Pizarro, Wei, and Banerjee (2003).

58. Jameson (1991).

59. See, for example, *American Beauty* (1999), written by Alan Ball and directed by Sam Mendes.

60. Pizarro (2005). While his study is limited to three Colombian cities—Cartagena, Medellín, and Bogotá—it is not unreasonable to assume that such tendencies are true elsewhere in Latin America.

61. C. Taylor (2001).

62. Said (1993).

63. See Campbell (1996).

64. Summers's memo was widely broadcast by *The Economist* in 1992 under the title "Let Them Eat Pollution." What follows are excerpts from the memo:

> "Dirty" Industries: Just between you and me, shouldn't the World Bank be encouraging MORE migration of the dirty industries to the LDCs [Least Developed Countries]? I can think of three reasons:
>
> 1) The measurements of the costs of health impairing pollution depends on the foregone earnings from increased morbidity and mortality. From this point of view a given amount of health impairing pollution should be done in the country with the lowest cost, which will be the country with the lowest wages. I think the economic logic behind dumping a load of toxic waste in the lowest wage country is impeccable and we should face up to that.
> 2) The costs of pollution are likely to be non-linear as the initial increments of pollution probably have very low cost. I've always thought that under-populated countries in Africa are vastly UNDER-polluted, their air quality is probably vastly inefficiently low compared to Los Angeles or Mexico City....
> 3) The demand for a clean environment for aesthetic and health reasons is likely to have very high income elasticity. The concern over an agent that causes a one in a million change in the odds of prostrate [*sic*] cancer is obviously going to be much higher in a country where people survive to get prostrate [*sic*] cancer than in a country where under 5 mortality is 200 per thousand. Also, much of the concern over industrial atmosphere discharge is about visibility impairing particulates. These discharges may have very little direct health impact....

The problem with the arguments against all of these proposals for more pollution in LDCs (intrinsic rights to certain goods, moral reasons, social concerns, lack of adequate markets, etc.) could be turned around and used more or less effectively against every Bank proposal for liberalization. (Summers, 1992, p. 66)

65. United Nations (1987).

66. Mazmanian and Kraft (2009).

67. Peattie (1981), p. 8.

68. Peattie (1981), p. 7.

69. Rodwin (1969); Peattie (1987b).

70. See Redfield (1953).

71. Banfield (1958).

72. Lansing (1991).

73. Scott (1998).

74. Sen (1999).

75. Sen (1999).

76. Berlin and Hardy (1991).

77. Sen (1999).

78. Nussbaum (2000).

79. Sen (1999).

80. Castells (1977).

Chapter 4

1. Mumford (1961), p. 544.

2. Nolli (1748). See also Verstegen and Ceen (2013).

3. Lynch (1974).

4. Calvino (1974); Raban (1974).

5. Milgram (1970).

6. Tönnies (1974); L. Wirth (1938).

7. Langer (1984).

8. Writings of Richard Sennett (1970, 1977, 1991) are cases in point.

9. A. Morris (1972); Mumford (1961); Eisner, Gallion, and Eisner (1993).

10. Abu-Lughod (1971, 1980).

11. Reps (1965); Gaube (1979); Kheirabadi (1991); Madanipour (1998); G. Wright (1991); AlSayyad (1994); Amirahmadi and El-Shakhs (1993); Rasmussen (1974); Abu-Lughod (1971, 1980).

12. Alexander (1977).

13. Krier (1979).

14. Cuthbert (1985).

15. It is also used in linguistics to refer to studies of the structure of language.

16. See Moudon (1995, 1997).

17. Bacon (1967); Blumenfeld (1953); Hegemann and Peets (1988); Sitte (1945); Spreiregen (1965). Critics reject this design nostalgia for older urban form as a type of urban romanticism (see Dyckman, 1962, for example).

18. See Handlin and Burchard (1967).

19. Summerson (1967), p. 166.

20. Garvan (1967), p. 178.

21. Lynch (1981).

22. Lynch (1981).

23. McHarg (1969), for example, argued that damage to nature resulting from past developments is basically a case of the Judeo-Christian value system, which essentially sees nature as subservient to man, unlike in some Eastern cultures where man is seen as subservient to nature.

24. Also see Peattie (1981).

25. Tzonis (1972).

26. In Hindu mythology the origins of castes were linked to different parts of Brahmā, the creator.

27. Lynch (1981).

28. Lynch (1981), p. 293.

29. About the time Lynch finished his work, his colleagues Donald Appleyard and Allan Jacobs (1987) also completed their well-known "manifesto" on urban design, which included and further embellished on some facets of Lynch's work.

30. Goodman and Goodman (1947).

31. Alexander (1977) had argued, however, that the composition of patterns will depend on the individual creativity of the designers.

32. T. Banerjee and Southworth (1990); Hall (1966).

33. See also Jones (1962).

34. Alonso (1964).

35. The concentric ring (by Burgess, Park, and McKenzie, 1925); the sector (by Hoyt, 1939); and multi-nucleated (by Harris and Ullman, 1945) are notable cases in point.

36. Lynch (1961).

37. Lynch and Rodwin (1958).

38. Webber (1963, 1964).

39. This was apparent in the development of urban design plans in many major cities. See Southworth (1989).

40. Lynch and Rodwin (1958).

41. Raban (1974); Webber (1963, 1964). Niraj Verma and I have made an argument for metaphors over models, inspired by Raban's work. See T. Banerjee and Verma (2003b).

It should be noted that the book *Notes on the Synthesis of Form*, by design theorist Christopher Alexander (1964), marked a major advance in design methods, nudging architects to think more systematically than intuitively and judgmentally about architectural design problems. In this "brave new world" of computers, systems, and mathematical algorithms, problems were seen as determinate and with a finite solution. The problem—like a village in India in Alexander's case study—can be decomposed into its component parts (which schematically looked like a tree) and restructured by a computer-based hierarchical decomposition and restructuring algorithm. Later he acknowledged that the city as a problem is more complex. The components of the city, if possible to decompose, would be interlinked like what he called a "semi-lattice," and would not be amenable to a hierarchical restructuring algorithm. Soon Rittel and Webber (1973) made their pithy but powerful argument that there are two types of social problems: benign and wicked. While benign problems might be complex, they are solvable. Planning problems—which happen to be the reference class for most social and urban problems—are inherently wicked and elude positivist methods, thus corroborating Alexander's concession, albeit from a different perspective.

42. Moudon (1995, 1997). Now there is a journal on urban morphology.

43. See Roe (2019); R. Jackson and Ferdman (2019); C. Chen (2018).

44. See Tyrwhitt (1947).

45. Lynch (1960).

46. Lynch (1960). Lynch (1985) himself was disappointed at the nonuse of his methods for the purposes he intended. See also T. Banerjee and Southworth (1990). Even today, after all this talk about communicative planning and "ballot box" planning, real conversation between the designers and the public remains elusive.

47. Tolman (1948).

48. For that matter, few of Lynch's followers seem to have been aware of Tolman's work; he is rarely cited in their academic publications.

49. Gulick (1963); Karan, Bladen, and Singh (1980); Appleyard (1976); Lynch (1977).

50. Gulick (1963).

51. Jameson (1991).

52. Tuan (1974); Relph (1976); Lynch (1974).

53. T. Banerjee and Baer (1984).

54. Armstrong and McGee (1985); Castells (1977); Abu-Lughod (1980); Sites (2003); Savitch and Kantor (2002); Stiglitz (2002).

55. See Lefebvre (1991).

56. Castells (1977).

57. O'Connor (1983); Roberts (1976); Mangin (1970).

58. Geertz (1963).

59. ILO (1972). For an earlier discussion of the formal/informal sector dichotomy, see McGee (1977).

60. De Soto (1990).

61. See T. Banerjee (1993).

62. I recall a conversation I had with Nirmala Banerjee of the Centre for Studies in Social Sciences, Calcutta, a well-known economist, who was at that time conducting an important study on women in the informal sector. When I asked her if anyone has mapped informal-sector activities in Calcutta, she pointed out what an impossible task that would be, given the intractable nature of the informal sector.

63. In chapters 8 and 13 we will address this issue in more depth in exploring how urban space is functionally transformed and differentiated with development and globalization.

64. As the proponents of dependency theory were called in those days.

65. McGee (1977); Armstrong and McGee (1985); Santos (1979).

66. Dumont (1970).

67. Rapoport (1969, 1988); Rykwert (1988).

68. Sennett (1970).

69. Meier (1962).

70. Castells (1996).

71. Mitchell (1995); C. Boyer (1997).

72. Abu-Lughod (1971, 1980, 1990).

73. A. King (1976).

74. G. Wright (1991).

75. Çelik (1997).

76. Holston (1989); Evenson (1966, 1969, 1973). Also, more recently we are seeing efforts to examine specific cultural icons and their significance in the palimpsest cityscape of many developing countries (see Nas, 1986; A. King, 2004).

77. See Polanyi (1958).
78. For additional discussions of this point, see T. Banerjee and Verma (2003a, 2003b).
79. See T. Banerjee (2001).
80. See Meinig (1979); J. Jackson (1984); K. Jackson (1984); Hiss (1990); Scott (1998).
81. See Bosker (2013); Campanella (2008); Friedmann (2005).
82. Roy and Ong (2011).
83. Benjamin (1999).
84. Buck-Morss (1989), Friedberg (1993), Jameson (1991).
85. Fraser (1990).
86. See Hayden (1984), for example.
87. See AlSayyad (1991, 1992, 2001); Caldeira (2013); Irazábal (2008); Roy (2001, 2003).
88. Said (1979).
89. See Cronon (1991) and Carl Smith (2013).
90. Cronon (1991).
91. Clemente (2015).
92. See Lynch (1976).
93. More on this in chapter 8.
94. Choudhury (2017), noted in the *New Yorker* (2018).
95. See Firey (1947).
96. See L. Wirth (1938).
97. See Barnett (2011).
98. T. Banerjee (1993).
99. Graham and Marvin (2001).
100. Ghertner (2019).
101. Longhofer and Winchester (2016).
102. See Cudny (2016).
103. Lynch (1972).
104. Lefebvre (1993).
105. Calvino (1974); Raban (1974); Mehta (2004).

106. Revol (2016).

107. Lynch (1960).

Chapter 5

1. A. Wright (1977); italics added.

2. A. Wright (1977).

3. Calvino (1974).

4. Calvino (1974), p. 164.

5. Sjoberg (1963).

6. Tzonis (1972).

7. Weber (1958).

8. Skinner (1977).

9. Skinner (1977). The author observes,

> Other analysts posit two, three, even four basic societal types where Sjoberg sees one, and at the very least his "preindustrial city" should be subdivided into the cities of agrarian civilizations (with literate elites) and those of primitive states (without them). Each of the three, or even four basic societal types might then be dichotomized into autonomous/ enclaved versus dependent/ integrated. These subtypes in turn could then be subdivided on a cultural/geographic basis, whereby the dependent/integrated category occurring in primitive states would be broken down into its New World examples (Inca, Aztec, etc.) and its African examples, and the dependent/integrated category in agrarian civilizations would be broken down (initially) into East European, Middle Eastern, Hindic, Sinic, etc. Finally, the Sinic grouping (to take the relevant case) would be at the next level down in the hierarchy subdivided into its Chinese, Vietnamese, Korean, Japanese, and other variants. (p. 4)

10. Redfield and Singer (1954).

11. Peattie (1981). See discussion in chapter 3.

12. Eck (1987), p. 2.

13. Eck (1987), p. 2.

14. Eck (1987), p. 2.

15. Eck (1987), p. 2.

16. Reynolds (1987).

17. Kostof (1991), plate 9.

18. Quoted in Kostof (1991), p. 38.

19. Correa (2012), p. 77.

20. B. Smith and Reynolds (1987).

21. See Wikipedia. Scott (1998) writes, "Broadly understood, mētis represents a wide array of practical skills and acquired intelligence in responding to a constantly changing natural and human environment" (p. 313). He observes further, "In a sense, mētis lies in that large space between the realm of genius, to which no formula can apply, and the realm of codified knowledge, which can be learned by rote" (p. 316).

22. Tzonis (1972).

23. Tzonis (1972), p. 20.

24. See Tuan (1974).

25. Alexander (1964).

26. Forde (1954).

27. Tzonis (1972) quotes Michelangelo:

> "Nè Dio, sua grazia, mi si mostra altrove Più che'n alcun leggiardo e mortal velo; E que sol amo, perchè in lui si specchia."
>
> (Nowhere does God, His grace, reveal Himself more clearly than in a lovely and mortal shape; which I love because it is mirrored on Him.) (p. 22)

28. Although Plato never explained the rationale for this number, Lynch (1981) thought it might have had something do with the fact that 5,040 is factorial 7. In a speculative vein Lynch observed, "we may guess that he thought a factorial number ideal because it could be divided so flexibly into various equal groups (and perhaps also for more mystical mathematical reasons) and that factorial 6 (or 720) was in his judgment too small, while factorial 8 (40, 320) was too large" (p. 239).

29. Lynch (1981).

30. Spreiregen (1965).

31. Spreiregen (1965).

32. Spreiregen (1965).

33. Spreiregen (1965); Kostof (1991).

34. Kostof (1991).

35. Kostof (1991).

36. Kostof (1991); Lynch (1981). In fact, Kostof (1991, p. 163) is dismissive of many utopian concepts, such as Thomas More's Amaurot and Tommaso Campanella's "Città del Sole" in the Western tradition, which he felt had very little connection with urban reality, as they were, in his opinion, often little more than exercises deriving pure geometric forms from Plato's *Republic* or Saint Augustine's *City of God*. I should note also that not all utopian ideas were canonical, nor did they represent any specific ideas of development, a view held by both Lynch and Kostof.

37. Lynch (1981).

38. Lynch (1981), p. 73.

39. There are debates as to whether the canons derived from the cosmic model were different or actually quite similar in these two ancient cultures, both in terms of their philosophical roots and their evolution.

40. Skinner (1977).

41. A. Wright (1977), p. 34.

42. L. Wu (1999).

43. N. Wu (1963); S. Chang (1970); Wheatley (1971); A. Wright (1977); Lynch (1981); Steinhardt (1990); Kostof (1991).

44. Steinhardt (1990).

45. Boyd (1962).

46. See Steinhardt (1990) for more details. Steinhardt also includes the "royal necropolis"—the imperial burial ground—as one of these paradigmatic components, albeit one located outside the city walls, but she does not mention anything about the burial spaces for the common people.

47. The four primary ones are Xi'an, Beijing, Luoyang, and Nanjing. The five occasional ones are Kaifeng, Hangzhou, Datong, Chengdu, and Ye (see Steinhardt, 1990).

48. S. Chang (1970).

49. See A. Wright (1977).

50. Gernet (1962).

51. A. Wright (1977).

52. A. Wright (1977).

53. A. Wright (1977), Lynch (1981), Steinhardt (1990).

54. Wheatley (1971), p. 416.

55. Frankfort (1948), p. 3 (cited by Wheatley, 1971).

56. Wheatley (1971), p. 418.

57. Eliade (1954).

58. Eliade (1954).

59. Wheatley (1971).

60. A. Wright (1977), pp. 39, 41.

61. A. Wright (1977), p. 42.

62. A. Wright (1977).

63. A. Wright (1977).

64. The images of the cosmic order, it will be recalled is one of Lynch's (1981) examples of the "cosmic model" version of normative planning theories.

65. Dumont (1970).

66. Long established and internationally renowned in the ancient world, Madurai is mentioned in Greco-Roman documents of the first and second centuries CE. Cited in Reynolds (1987), Majumdar (1960), and Maloney (1970).

67. Reynolds (1987), p. 15.

68. Reynolds (1987), p. 19.

69. Reynolds (1987), p. 19.

70. Eck (1987).

71. In discussing the representation of the cosmos in these *mandalas*, Reynolds (1987) notes further how the plots are allocated to different deities with Brahmā at the center, the Vedic gods representing three levels of the cosmos, the Naksatras (or constellations), and the guardians of cardinal and in-between directions. The cosmos represented by this grid of plots is overlayed on the body of purusa representing an anthropomorphic synthesis of these disparate elements and powers of the cosmos.

72. Meyer (1987) offers a typology of sacred cities: (a) "Cosmic City," Beijing, Chang'an, and Madurai being notable examples; (b) "City of Local Sacrality," such as Banaras, Jerusalem, and Mecca; and (c) "City of Saints," which may include "Mormon Salt Lake City or Calvin's Geneva" (p. 126).

73. Meyer (1987).

74. N. Wu (1963), p. 35.

75. N. Wu (1963), p. 35.

76. N. Wu (1963), p. 13.

77. N. Wu (1963), p. 30.

78. Eck (1987), p. 7.

79. Wheatley (1971), p. 450.

80. Wheatley (1971), p. 450.

81. See also Eck (1987) and N. Wu (1963).

82. But if taken seriously, and noting parenthetically, does this contrast offer another explanation for the 3 percent differential in the GDP per capita growth rate between these two countries, which otherwise was described as a democracy discount?

83. I prefer the term "settlement planning" to "town planning," a term commonly used (see Dutt, 1977) because many of the edicts involved site planning and village planning. Furthermore, the Sanskrit word *vastu*, which is in conjunction with such words as *vidya* (knowledge) or *silpa* (arts), is closer in meaning to "settlement" than "town."

84. Dutt (1977).

85. Quoted in Dutt (1977), p. 1.

86. Dutt (1977).

87. Dumont (1970), p. 67.

88. Dumont (1970). See Dutt (1977).

89. Some readers might find this term "planned social ecology" oxymoronic because the metaphor of ecology implies something organic and evolutionary. I would argue, however, that even in modern times the social ecology of our cities is more a product of public policy than pure market outcome.

90. According to Dutt (1977),

> In India considerations of efficiency in corporate life, and the principle of Varṇāśrama Dharma developing a social stratification of the people in general and of the functionaries of the state, led to a segregation of the classes following different pursuits; and the same caste or people of the same profession were congregated in the same ward so that a uniformity of life and consequent economic efficiency and progress were secured. Every ward was set apart for a caste or a trade guilt [*sic*] of note which enjoyed an autonomy of its own. Thus if the Sūdra class was numerically very large, a separate block or even a separate site was allotted to it. The goldsmiths, the artisans, the perfume-dealers, the Brāhmaṇs, or the soldiers would have distinct muhallas or a detached group of blocks of their own. (p. 147)

91. In India today a caste-based affirmative action program still remains in place, with considerable dissent over the opportunity outcomes.

92. Dumont (1970).

93. Bouglé (1958) quoted in Dumont (1970), p. 43.

94. See Eck (1982).

95. See Eliade (1987).

96. Kristeva (1982). For a similar argument related to the apartheid cities of South Africa, see Popke (2001).

97. Spivak (1999). See Dirks (2001), for example.

Chapter 6

1. Geertz (1989), p. 291. It can be argued that Geertz's description suggests an Orientalist view of a "classic" medina, from which of course Sefrou is an exception. Yet it is the very Orientalist stereotyping that is the focus of much of the ensuing discussion in this chapter. I am grateful to

Hussam Salama, a professor of architecture at German University in Cairo, for pointing out this distinction.

2. See Peattie (1998).

3. Goonewardena (2005).

4. Features that are also quite common in other medinas of Morocco.

5. See endnote 1 above.

6. The Fès medina is a major focus of contemporary domestic and international efforts for urban conservation. See Radoine (2011).

7. Alnowaiser (1983); Abu-Lughod (1987); Mernissi (1987).

8. See Hall (1966).

9. Burckhardt (1980).

10. Eliade (1987).

11. See, for example, O'Connor (1983); Drakakis-Smith (1987); Arnaud (1988).

12. In tracing the historiography of the concept of the "Islamic city," AlSayyad (1991) draws from Said's (1979) critique of the Orientalist scholarship and its subsequent critique by Abu-Lughod (1987). In a comprehensive review of this literature, AlSayyad points out that the earliest model of the Islamic city was actually constructed by Western scholars such as the Marçais brothers (W. Marçais, 1928; G. Marçais, 1957a, 1957b), Sauvaget (1934, 1941), LeTourneau (1961), and von Grunebaum (1955), with subsequent embellishments from authors such as Pauty (1951), De Planhol (1959), Roberts (1979), and Blake and Lawless (1980).

13. W. Marçais (1928).

14. G. Marçais (1957a, 1957b).

15. LeTourneau (1961); Berque (1958); AlSayyad (1991), p. 17.

16. Sauvaget (1934, 1941).

17. Von Grunebaum (1955).

18. AlSayyad (1991).

19. Gaube (1979); Noe (1981).

20. Eickelman (1974).

21. See AlSayyad (1991), for example, for a fairly comprehensive and critical review of this literature.

22. Built by Caliph Al-Mansour in 762 CE.

23. Hourani and Stern (1970).

24. Abu-Lughod (1987).

25. Abu-Lughod (1987), p. 155.

26. Abu-Lughod (1987), p. 156. The word *isnād* means "chain" in Arabic.

27. AlSayyad (1991). See also Said (1979) for the more general argument.

28. There is a common saying that the medieval cities were represented by three "M"s—monarchy, monasteries, and mercantilism. If we substitute mosques and madrasas for churches and monasteries, the spirit of the three "M"s seemed to remain the same.

29. Raymond (1994), p. 12.

30. E. Wirth (1982).

31. Quoted in Raymond (1994), p. 12 (emphasis added).

32. See also Jain and Jain (1994).

33. Hourani (1970).

34. AlSayyad (1991) and Kheirabadi (1991).

35. AlSayyad (1991).

36. AlSayyad (1991), p. 2

37. Brand and Lowry (1987).

38. Kathirithamby-Wells (1986).

39. Hourani (1970).

40. As discussed in the previous chapter.

41. Al-Hathloul (1996); Hakim (1986).

42. Abu-Lughod (1987).

43. Ardalan and Bakhtiar (1973); Bianca (1982).

44. AlSayyad (1991), p. 38

45. Al-Hathloul (1996) and Hakim (1986).

46. Chronologically, it should be noted, however, the work of Ardalan and Bakhtiar predates most of the anti-Orientalist scholarship. Also, they seemingly accepted, if unwittingly, the stereotype codified by the Orientalist scholarship.

47. In fact, in discussing the growth of cities, Ardalan and Bakhtiar (1973) use the analogy of the human body as an ideal form, like in primitive Dogon villages, and reminiscent of the organic analogy promoted by the International Congress of Modern Architecture (CIAM). Consider this description:

> Central to this system is the belief that man exists most wholesomely [*sic*] within a physical environment that is analogous to him. The city, in its disposition, is thus thought to emulate the human anatomy which, by inverse analogy, relates to the cosmos. As a governing concept, this is one that can grow indefinitely, with a multiplicity of geometric element developing from it, like cells in a body or leaves from the limbs of a tree. The bazaar traditionally begins at the palace precincts, which symbolize the spiritual head of the body, and grow cellularly [*sic*] in an apparent natural pattern in the direction of its symbolic heart—the Masjid-i-Jāmi—going on, then, to the opening of one of the city gates. As the city bazaar grows, the vital backbone of the city evolves, and the pedestrian streets leading into the city's body proper insert themselves as ribs. Within this structure and in proximity to the skeletal center, the vital organs of the city develop: bath houses, schools, carvanserais.... (p. 93)

Although there might be other more secular and technological explanations—such as walking range of pedestrians, for example—about the dynamics of this form, this description epitomizes a normative position on city development and design.

48. Ardalan and Bakhtiar (1973), pp. 87–88 (italics added). Referring to Herat, they wrote:

> The strong symbolism of this plan follows ancient cosmographic concepts embodied in the *mandala*, while the general identification of all these ancient plans with their numbers and geometry created their common linkage to the world of pure and constant form.

49. Ardalan and Bakhtiar (1973), p. 88. In interpreting the Baghdad plan, Ardalan and Bakhtiar wrote further:

> A positive centripetal motion toward the central medina provided the essential internal direction of the city. This movement may be viewed analogously as the motion of soul towards the Spirit—the hidden treasure within the body. Conversely, viewing the symbolic geometry incorporated in the square plans of the medina, representing man and the Earthly Paradise, there is a centrifugal movement outwards towards the all-encompassing circular walls, a movement corresponding to the spirit and the Heavenly Jerusalem. Further evidence of this inherent esoteric symbolism is to be found in the plan of the central palace, which is in the form of a *mandala* of nine squares. Thus within the rigid tranquility of axial composition the potential of endless cycles of motion was created.

50. AlSayyad (1991); Hakim (1986).

51. See Çelik (1996).

52. Rapoport (1988).

53. In a more recent article Hakim (1998) acknowledged the need to understand the role of institutions and laws concerning property rights, land tenure, land subdivision, and other such matters that dictate the overall urban form outcome.

54. AlSayyad (1991).

55. This ambivalence reflects an essential tension between the spiritual tenets of Islam that might command the possibility of a canonical archetype on the one hand, and the secular forces of culture, climate, geography, and the idiosyncrasies of history on the other that precisely militates against indoctrination of such an archetype.

56. To be fair, we should acknowledge that AlSayyad (1991) is aware of the lacunae involved in switching from Islamic to Muslim Cities as an operational concept, and more generally with the problem of ascribing a particular identity to cities that were built during the spread of Islam or

predominantly inhabited by Muslim population. It is likely that AlSayyad uses the term provisionally, rather than categorically.

57. In chapter 4 I have placed this particular work of Lynch and Rodwin (1958) as a classic example of what I referred to as the "positive analytic" approach to the study of urban form.

58. Typically of the medieval vintage.

59. Grabar (1983); Raymond (1994).

60. There are questions about whether Ibn Khaldun was a philosopher or more of an interpreter of history. Khaldun himself had some concerns about philosopers and found himself more comfortable as a social historian and commentator. The literature on Khaldun is also quite diverse—some saw his work as a major intellectual contribution, while others saw relatively little value-added in his work considering it too naive or lacking rigor (see Baali, 1988).

61. Baali (1988), p. 2.

62. Baali (1988), p. 6. A point originally made by Rosenthal (1940), whom Baali quotes in agreeing with him.

63. Khaldun (1958), vol. 2, p. 243.

64. Baali (1988); L. Wirth (1938); Durkheim (1933); Simmel (1950); Weber (1958).

65. Redfield (1953); Tönnies (1974).

66. See White and White (1962).

67. Khaldun (1958), vol. 2, pp. 243–244, 246–247.

68. See D. King (1985).

69. Referring to a Tunisian miniature that shows the four corners of the Ka'bah perfectly aligned to the cardinal directions, Bianca (2000) notes:

> Its simple geometric volume is a condensation, as it were, of the physical world, with its faces relating to the six primary directions of the earth—the zenith, the nadir and the four cardinal points. Symbolically, it represents the intersection of the human world with the celestial spheres, both being connected by the vertical "axis mundi" around which the rotation of the universe takes place. (pp. 32–33)

This interpretation is remarkably similar to the "cosmic model" that have guided city design in ancient Chinese and Indian cities, as we have seen in chapter 5.

70. "Turn your face toward the Sacred Mosque [the Great Mosque of Mecca]; wherever you may be, turn your faces toward it" *Qur'an 2:144.* (From Bonine, 1990, p. 50.)

71. D. King (1985); Bonine (1990).

72. Bonine (1990), p.70.

73. Or, alternatively the geodesic inaccuracies may suggest pragmatic approximation of the qibla direction to conform to the topography and slope.

74. Gaube (1979).

75. Galdieri (1979).

76. Bonine (1979).

77. See also Kostof (1991), p. 65.

78. Tavassoli and Bonyadi (1992). Also see figure 6.14 later in this chapter.

79. Bonine (1990).

80. Cf. Kathirithamby-Wells (1986).

81. Abu-Lughod (1987); Raymond (1994).

82. Abu-Lughod (1987), p. 162. She notes:

> Several cues seemed to trigger a subliminal response. First, the ratio of males to females on the street and public places were higher in Muslim than in Hindu areas. Second, butcher shops and trades related to hides and animal products were located almost exclusively in Muslim areas. Third, it seemed that the decibel level of sounds was higher and more animated in Muslim quarters, of which the call to prayer was only one of the added elements.

83. See E. Wirth (1982).

84. E. Wirth (1982).

85. Weber (1958).

86. Hourani (1970), p. 13.

87. Amirahmadi and El-Shakhs (1993).

88. See Brown (1973); Hourani (1970); Stern (1970).

89. Amirahmadi and El-Shakhs (1993); Bianca (2000).

90. Bianca (2000), p. 30.

91. Kuran (2001), p. 842.

92. Bianca (2000), p. 30.

93. Kuran (2001). Kuran offers a formal definition of *waqf*:

> A waqf is an unincorporated trust established under Islamic law by a living man or woman for the provision of a designated social service in perpetuity. Its activities are financed by revenue-bearing assets that have been rendered forever inalienable. Originally the assets had to be immovable, although in some places this requirement was eventually relaxed to legitimize what came to be known as a "cash waqf." The reason the waqf is considered an expression of piety is that it is governed by a law considered sacred, not that its activities are inherently religious or that its benefits must be confined to Muslims. (p. 842)

94. Kuran (2001), p. 863.

95. Kuran (2001), p. 843.

96. See Beito, Gordon, and Tabarrok (2002).

97. Bulliet (1975), p. 224.

98. Brown (1973). Never mind the fact that, as Bulliet (1975) argued, these street patterns are preindustrial in origin and the legacy of a "society without wheels" (p. 216).

99. *Ulama* refers to religious scholars.

100. Bianca (2000); Bulliet (1975).

101. Bianca (2000), p. 56.

102. *Palace Walk*, *Sugar Street*, and *Palace of Desire*.

103. Raymond (2000).

104. AlSayyad (1994), p. 74.

105. See Thiel (1970).

106. Lapidus (1996); Hodgson (1964).

107. Lapidus (1996), p. 9.

108. Lapidus (1996), p. 151. For a detailed account of this process, see also Hodgson (1964).

109. Hodgson (1964). In defining the nature of the populist characteristics of Islam, he writes:

> Early Muslim thinkers were unusually rigorous in eliminating any elitism from within the community; and this populist orientation was interpreted moralistically. In the Shari'ah, Muslims combined the hope for social justice with the stress on the ordinary man's moral status by vesting historical and social responsibility in each believer individually. In this spirit, social legitimacy of every kind was made to depend on the range of awareness, in principle, of the common believer; any insight not essentially accessible to the common man came readily to be suspect as antisocial.... Consistent with this moralistic populism, I think, was something that may be called factualism: a cultivation of common-sense and matter-of-fact reality, with low tolerance for abstractions or imaginative symbolism, subtle or profound. (p. 228)

110. Hodgson (1964).

111. Hodgson (1964), p. 223.

112. See Barrucand (1989).

113. Khaldun (1958), vol. 2, p. 268.

114. Taj Mahal being a notable example, where the adjoining mosque to one side of the main mausoleum mosque was completely subordinated to the main mausoleum in terms of placement and importance. The imperatives of aesthetics and symmetry of the site design required placing an identical mirror-image copy of the mosque to be placed on the eastern side of the complex.

115. Abu-Lughod (1987), p. 27.

116. Also see Akbar (1988).

117. Mernissi (1987), p. 138.

118. Mernissi (1987).

119. Mernissi (1987), p. 138.

120. See Fraser (1990).

Chapter 7

1. Fanon (1963), pp. 38–39.

2. Funk & Wagnalls (1963).

3. Urbinati (1998), pp. 370, 372. Many scholars have interpreted Gramsci's contributions to his own physical deformity and oppressed youth.

4. Germino (1986). Parenthetically, it should be noted that Gramsci himself saw a role for architecture in supporting and also overcoming the state apparatus of oppressive regimes.

5. In Sanskrit *varna* literally means "color" and also type, order, or class (see https://en.wikipedia.org/wiki/varna_(Hinduism).

6. Spivak (1999). See Dirks (2001), for example.

7. See Tzonis (1972), for example.

8. See AlSayyad (1992); G. Wright (1991); A. King (1976).

9. AlSayyad (1992).

10. Hosagrahar (1992).

11. Çelik (1997).

12. A. King (1976).

13. Prakash (1995), p. 199.

14. Prakash (1995), p. 199.

15. Blaut (1993), p. 11.

16. Blaut (1993).

17. Blaut (1993), p. 25.

18. See Foucault (1995).

19. Mazrui (1986).

20. At the time of India's independence, the life expectancy was around thirty-seven years, while in the metropole it was over sixty.

21. A case in point, for example, was Weber's dismissal of the traditional Muslim city as "non-city" because it lacked the administrative apparatus of a municipality in the West.

22. See Kinsbruner (2005).

23. Kinsbruner (2005), p. 24.

24. Hardoy (1975), p. 28.

25. Article 114 quoted in Kinsbruner (2005), p. 24.

26. Hardoy (1975).

27. Lynch (1981), p. 83.

28. Hardoy (1975).

29. Markman (1978).

30. Rykwert (1988).

31. Lynch (1981), p. 20.

32. Lynch (1981). He wrote:

> Not that the indigenes were wholly excluded from the new center. The Laws of the Indies propose that they be kept out during construction, and only admitted when it was splendid and complete. The strange new city is to awe them into submission, just as the first cities awed their peasants. (p. 20)

As we will see, Lynch's comments may also apply to the other colonial ventures and their city building and design.

33. Metcalf (1994).

34. Malinowski (1945).

35. A. King (1976). King thought Malinowski's obsession with the indigenous culture was not helpful to him, and also that he did not offer sufficient structural analysis of the exogenous culture. He framed his analysis instead from the perspective of "European colonial culture, which results from the transformation of metropolitan cultural institutions as they come into contact with the culture of the indigenous society" (p. 58).

36. A. King (1976), p. 25.

37. Metcalf (1994).

38. See Abu-Lughod (1980), G. Wright (1991).

39. Irving (1981). According to a recent story in *The Economist* titled "Where the Raj Lives On," the cantonment culture is alive and well in the Indian subcontinent, thanks to the defense establishment. India has 62 such areas occupying 200,000 acres of land. Pakistan has 43, and Bangladesh has 30. See *The Economist* (2019c).

40. Which King criticized; see endnote 35.

41. There are ample examples of such resistance involving rejection of the Western influence as part of political movements against the British—Gandhi's *Swadeshi Andolan* (independence movement) being a case in point.

42. See Dirks (2001).

43. Metcalf (1994).

44. Khilnani (1998).

45. The British rule, that is.

46. Metcalf (1994).

47. Suhash Chakravarty (2007).

48. Suhash Chakravarty (2007), p. 112. The quotation is from Leonard Woolf, "Pearls and Swine," in Saros Cowasjee's 1982 anthology *Stories from the Raj*.

49. Metcalf (1994). He wrote:

> To legitimate the conquest of India it was necessary, so Burke argued, not only to discipline Britain's agents in that country, but to reorder their activities. England, he insisted, could right the wrongs of the past, and so contain the guilt implicit in the colonial enterprise, by constructing a government that would rule India in the interests of the Indian people. (p. 19)

50. Metcalf (1994), p. 29.

51. Cf. Scott (1998).

52. Joyce (2003). He wrote, "India became an 'ethnographic state', anthropology supplanting history as the principal colonial modality of knowledge. It identified as a subject 'native' population that was to be ruled. Colonial history conceded to anthropology the study of an historical subject that had not yet become modern.... It was caste that articulated this legacy of tradition, standing in place of the historical mindedness that was seen to be absent from Indian sensibilities" (p. 246).

53. The Bengali term refers to the custom where a Hindu widow was expected to join the dead husband in the funeral pyre as self-sacrifice, but often not without coercion.

54. Child-marriage.

55. The intellectual and enlightened class of the Bengali society, under the leadership of Raja Rammohan Roy, founder of *Bramho Samaj* and a key protagonist of the Bengali renaissance of the early nineteenth century, had already begun to reform such ancient practices.

56. Metcalf (1994), pp. 199–200.

57. Levine (1994).

58. Metcalf (1994), p. 177. In reality, however, there was considerable contact with the native population who were service workers within these isolated enclaves.

59. Metcalf (1994); A. King (1976, 1984); Davies (1985).

60. Dutta (2003).

61. Indeed, after considerable deliberation the West Bengal state government has relocated the Calcutta port activities to a new site 78 miles south of the city, and notably, on the west side of the river. Actually, Charnock's decision may not have been all that wrongheaded considering this was preindustrial times, and most of the primary resource items for export—jute and lumber—were to be obtained from the hinterlands of Bangladesh and Myanmar.

62. Wilson (1906), plate VI, quoted in Sinha (1978), p. 5. Wrote Sinha, "The visual impression from the two maps underscores a sharp transformation in the physical mould of the city. The tiny squares, representing masonry construction in Upjohn's map, have been replaced by large dark blotches on Schalch's Plan of Calcutta. The more irregular gray markings on Schalch's Plan stand for innumerable pools mostly excavated to raise the level of land for masonry constructions" (p. 5).

63. Sinha (1978).

64. A. King (2004).

65. Named after Benoy, Badal, and Dinesh, three local heroes of the independence movement.

66. Dutta (2003), p. 60.

67. Dutta (2003), p. 60.

68. Dutta (2003), p. 132.

69. Naipaul (1964). He wrote:

> But nothing I had read or heard had prepared me for the red-brick city on the other side of Howrah Bridge which, if one could ignore the stalls and rickshaws and white-clad hurrying crowds, was at first like another Birmingham; and then in the centre, at dusk, was like London, with the misty tree-blobbed Maidan as Hyde Park, Chownringhee [*sic*] as a mixture of Oxford Street, Park Lane and Bayswater Road, with neon invitations, fuzzy in the mist, to bars, coffee houses and air travel, and Hooghly, a muddier, grander Thames, not far away. (p. 257)

70. "The word 'durbar' roughly means 'public audience'—the occasion on which a ruler presents himself as a visible (and, in theory at least, an accessible) figure before his vassals and subjects, who pay him homage and tribute. The British, in a characteristic and shrewd move, adapted this old custom of Indian kings to further their goals in India" (Nath, 2002, p. 18).

71. A. King (1976).

72. Irving (1981).

73. Irving (1981). He wrote:

> Unquestionably there are remarkable correspondences between the plans of Washington and New Delhi a system of grand diagonal avenues and rond-points delineating giant hexagons, interlocked with a grid pattern; a commanding capitoline acropolis from which radiates a patte-d'oie, including a broad two-mile parkway terminating at a monument at the river's edge; and a bold axis crossing the center of this leafy mall.... Evidently these similarities did not escape Herbert Baker: in 1930 he characterized New Delhi's "ingenious" layout as "a noble development of the germ of L'Enfant's plan of Washington and Wren's rejected design for the City of London." (pp. 83–84)

74. Khilnani (1998).

75. Irving (1981).

76. Overhangs and cupolas, respectively.

77. See Cullen (1960) and also Vale (2014).

78. Lutyens quoted in Irving (1981). See also note 73.

79. Irving (1981), p. 78.

80. Davies (1985). He noted:

> The socio-spatial layout of the city reflected the cultural values and relationships of a colonial society which had changed little for sixty or seventy years. The relative status and privilege attached to each rank were guarded jealously and set out in official publications.... Within the hexagonal grid pattern five areas were allocated according to race, occupational rank and social status—one for gazetted officers (fat whites), another for European clerks, a third for indigenous clerks and lower ranking officials, a fourth for Indian princes and nobility, and finally a discrete area for non-persons of the lowest rank. (pp. 224–225)

81. Abu-Lughod (1980).

82. Abu-Lughod (1980).

83. In a 1921 speech delivered at the Congress of Moroccan Higher Education, Lyautey proclaimed, "We wish to conserve in Morocco Beauty—and it is not a negligible thing. Beauty—as well as everything which is respectable and solid in the institutions and traditions of the country ... whether it be a question of antiquities, fine arts, folklore, history, or linguistics" (abridged quote from Abu-Lughod, 1980, p. 142).

84. Thus even today non-Muslims are not allowed inside a mosque according to the edicts of the French colonial rule, as the residents of Fès pointed out when asked about this restriction. In Egypt, Iran, and in the Indian subcontinent more generally such restrictions do not exist, and obviously it is not a religious requirement.

85. Çelik (1997), p. 37.

86. Quoted in Abu-Lughod (1980), p. 142.

87. Commenting on the urban outcome of this vision, Abu-Lughod (1980) wrote: "Yet out of the 'best intentions' in the world, Lyautey created a system of cultural and religious apartheid, segregating Europeans in new cities laid out on vast open spaces ... while confining Moroccans to the oldest cities, which, he decreed, should be touched as little as possible" (p. 142).

88. See note 18.

89. De la Casinière (1922), p. 88, quoted in Abu-Lughod (1980), p. 144.

90. Abu-Lughod (1980).

91. Abu-Lughod (1980). She summarized this paradigm as follows: "All have more or less the same stamp. If at all feasible, next to the convoluted medina was open land (the cordon sanitaire). Beyond was a widespread, regular, modified radial street system interlaced with perpendiculars of somewhat narrower widths arranged around central points of public and monumental focus, generally landscapes and attached to parks. Peripheral ring roads connected segregated industrial districts concentrated at ports, at railway exchanges, and on the outskirts. Articulation with the native city was kept to a minimum, using no more than the major streets on either side of the wall" (pp. 146–147).

92. Lynch (1960).

93. Gulick (1963).

94. Çelik (1996), p. 203.

95. Balbo and Moretti (1973).

96. Cited in Çelik (1997).

97. Çelik (1997), p. 38.

98. Çelik (1997), p. 38.

99. Fanon (1963).

100. Çelik (1997), p. 22.

101. Writes Çelik (1997): "Provoking associations between the curved lines of his projects and the "plasticity" of the bodies of Algerian women, Le Corbusier described at length his enchantment with these women and consistently represented the casbah as a veiled head in his reductive drawings ... The cover sketch of his *Poésie sur Alger* depicts a unicorn-headed, winged female body—supple-hipped and full-breasted—the city/poem caressed gently by a hand (the architect's) against the skyline of new Algiers, to be designed by Le Corbusier himself" (p. 22).

102. See A. Thomas et al. (1994). During the fascist dictatorship Albania, Dodecanese islands and Ethipoia were also added to the Italian colonial holdings (Ben-Ghiat and Fuller, 2005).

103. See Ben-Ghiat and Fuller (2005).

104. It will be recalled that the French used the same strategy in the case of Morocco.

105. Interview with Professor Ezio Godoli of the University of Florence School of Architecture. October 2005.

106. The introduction to a set of reports prepared by the faculty of Agricolo Coloniale of Florence, purportedly to document the role of the Italian technical expertise in the agricultural development in the colonies, made this point quite clearly:

> Among the various and complex aspects of the development of those territories, foremost has been the intensification and expansion of agriculture. Actually agriculture is of paramount importance to the economic life of all those territories, with the possible exception of Eritrea, where, notable though its agriculture is, industrial development and commerce undoubtedly offer greater opportunities.
>
> ...
>
> We scarcely need point out here to what extent the results of this work have been decisive also for the progress and welfare of the native populations, both in an indirect way by making higher and healthier their standard of life and, in a direct way, by founding farm-centers for natives, supplied with new technical equipment and directed by modern farming methods. Moreover, the planning and the completion of public works; the creation of new ways of communication; the introduction of modern means of transport, and, besides those economical improvements, the sanitary and educational services have caused a definite progress of the native African communities towards modern civilization. (from the Archives of Istituto Agronomico per l'Oltremare, Florence)

107. Ben-Ghiat and Fuller (2005), p. 3.

108. Fuller (2000).

109. Talamona (1993); also true for Mogadishu and Asmara (Gresleri, 1993).

110. Von Henneberg (2005), p. 156.

111. Morton (2000).

112. Morton (2000), p. 7.

113. Von Henneberg (2005), p. 158.

114. Morse (1978).

115. See Abu-Lughod (1980).

116. I borrow this expression from the title of an article by urban planner John W. Dyckman (1962).

Chapter 8

1. From an inaugural address given by Narayanan, then president of India, at the conference Celebrating Chandigarh, January 1999. See Narayanan (2002), pp. 20–21.

2. Holston (1989).

3. Vale (2014), p. 195.

4. Khilnani (1997), p. 28.

5. Quoted in Khilnani (1997), p. 30.

6. Khilnani (1997).

7. Khilnani (1997).

8. Punjab Government, undated, quoted in Kalia (1999), p. 12. A slightly different version is quoted in Nair (1950): "Let it be a new town, symbolic of the freedom of India, unfettered by the traditions of the past ... an expression of the nation's faith in the future" (p. 6).

9. Quoted in Kalia (1999), p. 47.

10. See Stein (1957); Parsons (1998); T. Banerjee and Baer (1984).

11. Quoted in Kalia (1999), p. 47.

12. Although originally promulgated by Ebenezer Howard as an antidote to the industrial city, the troika of the Garden City, the superblock, and the neighborhood unit concept became a formula for urban livability that was uniquely inspired by the antiurban writings of American intellectuals at the turn of the century (see White and White, 1962).

13. Evenson (1966).

14. Kalia (1999), p. 59 (emphasis added).

15. Previously discussed in chapter 5.

16. For details of their role in the selection of Le Corbusier and the Chandigarh planning process, see Kalia (1999).

17. Khilnani (1997), p. 32.

18. Jencks (1973), p. 12.

19. In presenting these ideas—typically modernist utopias of city design—he would often include the critical reviews like the following, in response to his 1937 Voisin Plan for Paris: "A megalomania worse than Ledoux's, a vandalism unique in history, the dreary uniformity, vanity and monotony of these skyscrapers ... have been proved spiritually and materially injurious, a contempt for historic and artistic tradition." Quoted in Jencks (1973), p. 179.

20. Some of which we have reviewed in chapter 7.

21. Kalia (1999) describes in depth the details of the financial arrangements.

22. Maurios (2002) points out that apparently the cardboard scale that Le Corbusier used to carry with him to make his argument for this proportion actually included wrong measurements due to an error made by his assistant.

23. Maurios (2002)

24. See Stein (1957).

25. See Birch (2011).

26. See White and White (1962).

27. See Takhar (2002).

28. Davey (2002), p. 203.

29. See Scott (1998).

30. Narayanan (2002), p. 20.

31. Quoted in Takhar (2002), p. 20.

32. This is the common impression, no doubt because the planning and architecture of Chandigarh are conflated into one paradigm. To keep the record straight, it was Mayer who had urged Thapar and Verma to look for architects from the West who could create the architecture of the new government complexes consistent with Nehru's desire for obtaining a new, modern, and progressive icon—a compelling image of development—in the new capital of Punjab (Kalia, 1999). While much credit is given to Le Corbusier to develop the basic concept plan for Chandigarh, in reality it adapted most of the original concepts of Mayer, the siting of the township, location of

the complex and the central business districts, a spatial organization by sectors, making sectors as the setting for the basic residential life, separation of fast-moving and slower traffic, and the like. (See T. Banerjee, 2009.)

33. When the new state of Haryana was created in 1966, Chandigarh became a shared capital of both Haryana and Punjab, and its administration and management was assigned to a Union Territory government—a special designation of territories under the control of the national government.

34. A lightweight portable cot strung with coir ropes is a common furniture in the villages and poorer neighborhoods of northern India, used both indoors and outdoors, especially in hot seasons.

35. Recall Dumont (1970), discussed in chapter 5.

36. For example, proximity of domestic and service staff is a necessity for the upper and middle classes even today.

37. As they are called in northern India.

38. Sarin (1982). *Dhabas* are roadside eating places of informal economy. Meanwhile, the official planning process continues to be remiss in anticipating the urbanism of informal economy, which remains intrinsic to the urban legacy of India.

39. See Eco (1986).

40. The Union Territory of Chandigarh reports the highest GDP per capita among all Indian cities.

41. See Barker (1968).

42. See Beinert (2002).

43. Beinert (2002). Under Beinert's guidance his students at MIT had explored interesting possibilities for "reurbanization" of the capitol complex by infilling new office buildings and the like.

44. Sorkin (2002).

45. As reported to me by Mr. Bahl, a retired economist and a longtime resident of Chandigarh.

46. See Frank (1966, 1967); Chilcote (1974); Epstein (1973).

47. Hirschman (1986).

48. Baran (1957); Frank (1967).

49. See Morse (1974, 1978), for example.

50. Holston (1989), p. 17.

51. Holston (1989).

52. Holston (1989), p. 20.

53. Evenson (1973), p. 145.

54. Evenson (1973).

55. Holston (1989).

56. In selecting the Costa scheme, the jury headed by Oscar Niemeyer stated that they were "seeking a well-knit project which would give the city grandeur through the clarity and proper ranking of its components; in the opinion of the members, the project which best integrates the monumental elements into the city's daily life as a federal capital, and which is presented as a rational, essentially urban composition—in fact a work of art— ... by Mr. Lúcio Costa." (Quoted in Evenson, 1973, p. 143.)

57. Vale (2014).

58. Quoted in Vale (2014), p. 134.

59. Espejo (1984).

60. Vale (2014).

61. Holston (1989).

62. Holston (1989), p. 85.

63. Both Costa and Niemeyer were associated with Le Corbusier in several projects; noted among them was the United Nations headquarters in New York. The Athens Chapter is a 1933 document published by Le Corbusier based on deliberations of the Congrès International d'Architecture Moderne (CIAM). The Charter was named after Athens, where the conference was held in 1933.

64. Le Corbusier (1957), quoted in Holston (1989), p. 31. See Boesiger, Willy, and Hans Gersberger (1960).

65. In the case of Brasília, however, Holston (1989) interprets its design as a reflection of the deeper ideologies of the CIAM tradition, which he lists as: "(1) anticapitalist and egalitarian basis, (2) machine metaphor and totalizing rationality, (3) redefinition of the social functions of urban organization, (4) development of building typologies and planning conventions as instruments of social change, (5) decontextualization and environmental determinism, (6) reliance on state authority to achieve total planning, (7) techniques of shock, and (8) conflation of art, politics, and daily life" (p. 43).

66. See Rawls (1974).

67. See Perlman (1976); Epstein (1973).

68. See "Inequality in South America" by Max Roser (2015). According to another report, by 2014 Brazil's Gini index had fallen to .49, still one of the highest in South America and the world (CIA World Factbook).

69. See Perlman (1976).

70. In 1980 the total urban population of the Federal District was 1,139,480, and in Plano Pilot it was only 246,360 (see Holston, 1989, table 5.8).

71. Holston (1989), p. 289.

72. Epstein (1973), p. 26.

73. Epstein (1973), p. 24.

74. Holston (1989).

75. Holston (1989), p. 101.

76. I have chosen the term "dialectic" over the word "discourse" used by Holston, because what is public and what is private is becoming increasingly contested in the social production of urban spaces. I draw from my previous work in making this substitution. See Loukaitou-Sideris and Banerjee (1998); T. Banerjee (2001).

77. As reported by Germano Johnson, a transportation planner who works and lives in Brasília.

78. J. J. School of Architecture, Mumbai, India.

79. The 1961 census of India reported a population of 361 million.

80. Scott (1998).

81. Recall Dumont (1970).

82. Predating Rawls (1974), however.

83. Francis Fukuyama (1989) is an articulate protagonist of this view. See for example the response to Fukuyama by James Atlas (1989).

84. Other members of the group wrote reports on Hangzhou, Nanjing, Zhengzhou, Luoyang, and Beijing.

85. *National Geographic*, May 2004, "On Assignment" (n.p.).

86. Almost every city had a horticulture department that were in charge of planting, maintaining, and pruning these street trees to allow the utility wires to pass through their lush foliage.

87. Szelenyi (1993).

88. "Urban primacy" refers to the concentration of urban population in one or two cities.

89. Defined as the rate of urban population growth surpassing the rate of urban job creation.

90. Szelenyi (1993), p. 47.

91. See Kunstler (1993), for example.

92. Szelenyi (1993), p. 53.

93. Szelenyi (1993), p. 54.

94. O. Lewis (1966a).

95. Heilbroner (1985).

96. Castells (1977).

97. A. King (1976).

98. See Geertz (1963).

99. See Santos (1979), for example.

100. Scott (1998).

101. C. Taylor (2001).

102. Berman (1982).

Chapter 9

1. Cullen (1960), p. 400.

2. See T. Banerjee and Chakravorty (1994).

3. See T. Banerjee (2005).

4. See Nilsson (1973).

5. Joseph Stein, a US architect practicing in India, is credited with initiating the first five-year professional degree program in architecture at Bengal Engineering College in Shibpur, with the degree granted by Calcutta University.

6. Largely because of the collapse of the rural economy.

7. CMDA (1986).

8. For example, the planned township of Kalyani, built near an abandoned World War II vintage airport, was meant to alleviate the settlement of the refugee problem and also the population pressure on Kolkata. Planned and designed by the civil engineers with public works expertise, the township did not serve its purpose because of its lack of industry and employment, and a fairly long commute to Kolkata proper. Most of the refugee population—several million—uprooted from the then Pakistani side of the state of Bengal eventually settled in the rural periphery of the existing city in what came to be known as the "refugee colonies."

9. Perroux (1955).

10. Readers will recall our discussion of the bell curves in chapter 2.

11. A measure of interregional economic disparity based on differences in the gross regional product as shares of national product (Williamson, 1965). Also see chapter 2.

12. Although in case of Paris these new towns were seen as a point to intercept new immigrants—especially from the developing world—and settle them there rather than creating immigrant ghettoes within Paris proper. As we have seen in recent street riots in France, both the satellite towns and the inner-city immigrant ghettoes have become theaters of dissent and insurgent citizenship.

13. See Osborne and Whittick (1969).

14. Willmott (1962).

15. See Alnowaiser (1983).

16. Today these new towns have come to function as successful affluent suburbs, as housing development catered to upper-income families, and the edge of expanding Cairo brought them closer to the city proper.

17. American Public Health Association (1948).

18. Vidyarthi (2015).

19. Holston (1989).

20. Castells (1996).

21. From *desa* (country) and *kota* (city) in Bahasa Indonesia. See McGee (1977).

22. On the role of architects, Doxiadis wrote: "He must become a scientist, carry out research, create a system of thought, devise a programme of action and carry out proper schemes of organization in government, in industry, in production, in design" (Doxiadis, 1963, p. 195; quoted in Nilsson, 1973, p. 150).

23. From conversations with Manuel Castells, fall 2004.

24. See Brenner (2014); also Ross (2009).

25. That included cruises in the Mediterranean off the coasts of Greek islands, reminiscent of earlier such events under the auspices of CIAM.

26. Karachi was the original capital at the time of Pakistan's independence.

27. Commenting on this feature of "dynapolis," architect Stan Nilsson wrote: "On the diagrams everything is very clear and simple; later the two cities are to serve each other, but Islamabad, of course, is to take the lead. In practice the capital has been protected against unwanted infiltration; on the road to Pindi there is a laconic sign: *Road closed for carts and tongas*." Nilsson (1973), p. 158.

28. Nilsson (1973).

29. Nilsson (1973), p. 156.

30. Nilsson (1973).

31. Nilsson (1973). Nilsson observed: "They fill out irregularities, strengthen unstable slopes with walls, and are sometimes faced by the impossible task of passing through a rock or of cutting right through a hill—which actually would have proved an asset in its context. They also clothe the fairly bare landscape in vegetation, a laborious undertaking under the difficult circumstances. The fertility of the soil is poor and the Pakistanis would rather see the slopes of Margala Hills covered in pink blossom than shaded by hardy trees that Derek Lovejoy Associates want to plant" (p. 156).

32. The two agencies were to serve under the administrative control of the chairman of Delhi Improvement Trust, previously involved with public works matters.

33. Reflecting Nehru's wishes according to a letter from Douglas Ensminger to Albert Mayer mentioned in Goodfriend (1978). We should note parenthetically that Mayer was also chosen initially to develop the Chandigarh master plan, but his plan was rejected (also by Nehru, as the rumors go), as discussed in the previous chapter.

34. Goodfriend (1978). Members included Gerald Breese, urbanization specialist; Edward Echeverria, physical planner; Archie Dotson, government and administration specialist; George Goetschius, urban sociologist (later replaced by Marshall Clinnard); Britton Harris, regional demarcator and industrial planner; Walter Hedden, traffic and transportation specialist; Bert Hoselitz, economist; and Gordon Cullen, civic designer.

35. See Ghosh (1968); Swamy (1971); Rai (1971).

36. Verma (1996).

37. C. Boyer (1983), from the title of her book.

38. This sentiment was no doubt influenced by the public health and hygiene concerns from an earlier era.

39. Jacobs (1961); Sennett (1970); Perin (1977).

40. We should note that the federal urban renewal program was still very much in its infancy in the United States, and the major community-based oppositions supported by academic writings were yet to happen.

41. Historically Delhi has been the capital of seven different dynasties. Shahajanabad or Old Delhi of the Mogul era was the seventh, followed by the British colonial capital (the eighth) and the current capital of the Republic of India (the ninth).

42. DDA (1961).

43. Arnstein (1969).

44. See Putnam (2000).

45. The idea of this urban community development program, which had an uncanny resemblance to the grassroots neighborhood council movement currently in vogue in many American cities (Los Angeles being the most eminent case in point), no doubt was pioneering, but the process was contrived at best. While India had a long tradition of self-governance in the rural communities (or *gemeinschaft*) in the form of *gram panchayats*, their impact in more socially heterogeneous and anomic urban areas (typical of *geselleschaft*) remained marginal and uncertain. Nevertheless, it reflected a belief that such top-down programs for social capital formation would make a significant dent in alleviating conditions of urban poverty and slums through self-help.

46. Ensminger (1972), p. 1.

47. See T. Banerjee and Schenk (1984).

48. In 1972 Nayan Saini, a town and country planner for the Ford Foundation, developed a methodology for integrated area development planning based on his earlier work. See Saini (1968).

49. For details see the Ministry of Housing and Urban Affairs website: http://mohua.gov.in /upload/uploadfiles/files/74th_CAA13.

50. See Cullen (1960)

51. See T. Banerjee and Southworth (1990).

52. Naipaul (1964).

53. See Loukaitou-Sideris and Banerjee (1998); Kayden (2000); Kohn (2004); Whyte (1988).

Chapter 10

1. Lapierre (1985), p. 391.

2. Lapierre (1985).

3. O. Lewis (1961). Based on this and other studies, including *La Vida* (1966b), Oscar Lewis wrote his famous but controversial article "The Culture of Poverty" (1966a).

4. Personal finding from a visit to Mexico City in the summer of 2006, and a similar account by Clara Irazábal about Rio de Janeiro. See also Dovey and King (2012).

5. About $20 in the sixties.

6. F. Thomas (1997).

7. See Joffé, Medoff, and Eberts (1992).

8. Without getting into the causes of such migration, although covered cogently in the original book.

9. Or more poignantly, the absence thereof for the Hindu poor, as suggested by Oscar Lewis (1966a).

10. Kristeva (1982).

11. Kristeva (1982), p. 46.

12. Meirelles (2002).

13. With a lighter touch intended for a domestic audience. Cidade de Deus (commonly known as CDD) is also the name of a West Zone neighborhood of Rio de Janeiro.

14. In a moment of outrage against capitalism (the target here being a capitalist institution of his own country), Grass (1989) writes:

> If you lent (for a fee) one of these slum hovels, created from bare necessity, to the city of Frankfurt am Main, and had it set down next to the Deutsche Bank highrise, where the hewn granite sculpture by the artist [Max] Bill ... is incontrovertibly beautiful and immaculately endorses the circulation of money stamped valid for eternity—if, I say, you replaced the granite celebrating its flawless self, and set down instead one single slum hovel, as authentic as want has made it, right next to the glassy arrogance of Deutsche Bank, beauty would at once be on the side of the hovel, and truth too, even the future. (p. 21)

15. Grass (1989) writes again:

> Once again the (unwritten) aesthetics of poverty shocks me: how every detail of the huts made of rags, sheets of plastic, cardboard and jute sacks, is so terribly palpable, cries out for a name. This ultimate beauty challenges every other canon of beauty. (p. 58)

16. Cited in Chopra (1998).

17. Trojanow (2001).

18. An outspoken Marxist critic, Pasolini published a book on India titled *L'Odore dell'India* (The Breath of India) in 1962.

19. Trojanow (2001) contrasts the works of Grass and Pasolini with that of V. S. Naipaul, who presents a more ground-level view of a slum derived from interviews with a slum dweller in his book *India: A Million Mutinies Now* (not unlike Oscar Lewis's seminal work, *The Children of Sanchez*).

20. Lu (1999).

21. The rituals also require the shaving of head, piercing of ears, wearing the sacred thread, covering oneself with a single piece of a toga-like cloth, and sleeping on the floor on a reed mat.

22. Sachs (2005), p. 51.

23. Shaohua Chen and Ravallion (2004).

24. Sachs (2005).

25. Sen (1992).

26. See chapter 3.

27. Diamond (1997).

28. Although much of urban poverty is rural poverty transferred to cities with the collapse of rural economy, as has been pointed out by many researchers previously (Mangin, 1970; Roberts, 1976; Carol Smith, 1985; Todaro, 1969).

29. UN-Habitat (2017). But there is also some good news: Sri Lanka almost halved the slum population percentage from 24.8 in 1990 to 13.6 in 2001. Thailand almost eliminated its slum population from 19.5 percent to 2 percent.

30. UNCHS (2003).

31. UN-Habitat (n.d.).

32. Gownamani et al. (2003).

33. Perlman (2005).

34. Engels (1958), p. 33.

35. See Peattie (1987a).

36. McGee (1977).

37. McGee (1977).

38. De Soto (1990), p. 12.

39. Geertz (1963).

40. Lal (2000). Indeed, one variant of dependency theory discusses the possibilities of dependency and development. See Chilcote (1974).

41. Abu-Lughod (1987) reports the difficulty of applying factorial ecology to indigenous cities of the Muslim world.

42. Perlman (2005).

43. See Roy and AlSayyad (2004).

44. As confirmed by Dr. Nirmala Banerjee of the Centre for Studies in Social Sciences, Calcutta, some years ago. See N. Banerjee (1981).

45. Land-use controls like zoning or subdivision regulation remain at a very inchoate state in many cities of the developing world.

46. Perlman (2005), pp. 1–2.

47. Berry and Rees (1969); T. Banerjee (1993).

48. Bose (1965); Frank (1966); Roberts (1976).

49. http://web.mit.edu/urbanupgrading/upgrading/whatis/what-is.html.

50. World Bank (2000/2001).

51. Financed by the World Bank, the "sites and services" projects focused on upgrading the infrastructure of slums—electricity, potable water, sanitation, paved walkways, and so on—rather than the structures themselves. In some cases, such as in Recife, Brazil, it involved "regularization" of illegal settlements by granting property ownership titles to slum dwellers in exchange for their assent to pay taxes for services, etc. World Bank (1981).

52. Dharavi in Mumbai is a case in point. See Mukhija (2003).

53. Whelan (2004).

54. A. Thomas et al. (1994).

55. See Davis (2006).

56. Perlman (1976).

57. Turner (1968).

58. F. Thomas (1997).

59. UN-Habitat (2003).

60. UN-Habitat (2003).

61. Craig S. Smith (2006).

62. UN-Habitat (2003).

63. Gownamani et al. (2003).

64. Gownamani et al. (2003).

65. See chapter 9.

66. Dubey et al. (2002).

67. Perlman (1976).

68. See O. Lewis (1966a).

69. Perlman (1976), p. 258.

70. Perlman (1976).

71. Urquidi (1963).

72. Lomnitz (1977); Roy (2003).

73. Westfall (1990). The documentary received the Paul Davidoff Award from the American Planning Association in 1991. World Bank (1981).

74. Goldsmith (1974); Peattie (1994).

75. Perlman (2005).

76. The late professor of urban planning at MIT—from a presentation he gave at a design symposium held at Pilchuk, Washington, by the Department of Urban and Regional Planning of the University of Washington.

77. Santos (1979).

78. Whelan (2004).

79. Lapierre and Moro (2002).

80. Abrams (1964).

81. Turner (1968); Payne (1977).

82. De Soto (1990).

83. H. Boyer (2005).

84. See Arefi (2018).

85. See Turner (1968).

86. See Westfall (1990).

87. See Cuthbert (1985).

Chapter 11

1. Berman (1982), p. 40.

2. Brazil, Indonesia, Malaysia, Singapore, and Thailand are cases in point.

3. See *The Economist* (2018), p. 84.

4. Abramson (2008). Also see Heikkila (2011); Friedmann (2005); F. Wu (2000).

5. See Berman (1982).

6. Berman (1982).

7. Berman (1982), p. 39.

8. See Piazzoni and Banerjee (2018), p. 6.

9. Piazzoni and Banerjee (2018).

10. Berman (1982), p. 189.

11. Berman (1982), p. 290.

12. Molotch (1976).

13. Clark and Dear (1984).

14. Sites (2003).

15. Harvey (1985).

16. See T. Banerjee (2007).

17. Sites (2003).

18. Sites (2003), p. 2.

19. See also Harvey (2006).

20. See Savitch and Kantor (2002).

21. According to a 2007 forecast of *The Economist,* by 2025 both China and the US will have about $20 trillion in GDP. In 2050 China will have a GDP over $70 trillion, compared to $40 trillion for the US. In that year India will also catch up with the US and will be poised to exceed the US GDP in the following decades. See *The Economist* (2007).

22. Fallows (1988), p. 77.

23. See Naipaul (1964).

24. I should note that when I included this Fallows quote in a paper (see T. Banerjee, 1993), I presented at the First International Urban Anthropology Conference in Beijing hosted by the Institute of Nationality Studies of the Chinese Academy of Social Sciences in 1989, I was challenged by a professor of geography from Shanghai, who pointed out that Shanghai was not "frozen," and that many construction projects were underway, including a subway system. Of course he was right, as we know today, that by the late eighties Shanghai's transformation was well on its way. Both Fallows and I were wrong.

25. Q. Chang (2005).

26. See Szelenyi (1993).

27. See T. Banerjee and Schenk (1984).

28. Bergère (2004).

29. Gaulton (1981), p. 40.

30. Rowe (2004).

31. Bergère (2004).

32. The numbers and the quote are taken from a report titled "Guide to Pudong" by the Press and Information Office of Pudong New Area (2002). Current numbers are from the official Pudong website (see Shanghai Pudong New Area Government, 2018).

33. Data from "Pudong, Shanghai (1990–2001)," published by the Press and Information Office of Pudong New Area, http://www.pudong.gov.cn.

34. Castells (1996).

35. Castells (1996), p. 419.

36. Castells (1996), p. 421.

37. Castells (1996), p. 409.

38. Huang (2004), p. 104.

39. Quoted in Huang (2004), p. 104; and Yeh (1996), p. 279.

40. See Garreau (1992).

41. Xue, Zhai, and Mitchenere (2011), p. 226.

42. Such as EDAW and RTKL, well-known US consulting firms.

43. Source: Table 25.4, Statistical Yearbook, Shanghai Statistical Bureau, http://www.pudong.gov.cn.

44. He (2019).

45. Source: Table 25.3, Statistical Yearbook, Shanghai Statistical Bureau, http://www.pudong.gov.cn.

46. Yeung and Sung (1996); Huang (2004); F. Wu (2000).

47. Han (2000), p. 2102.

48. Han (2000), p. 2091.

49. F. Wu (2000). Yet according to Yeung and Li (2000) these investments did not initially yield the kind of "local embeddedness" that is expected of local engagement of transnational corporations.

50. Yu (2017).

51. See C. Chen (2018).

52. See chapter 5.

53. L. Wu (1999), p. 12.

54. L. Wu (1999).

55. L. Wu (1999)

56. L. Wu (1999), p. 17; italics added.

57. L. Wu (1999), p. 18.

58. Meeting of the US planners with the Beijing Municipality Urban Construction Bureau, summer 1980. During this visit I asked Beijing planners why the walls had to go. We were told, after an awkward silence, that "the order came down from the very top."

59. Halbwachs (1980); Yucekus and Banerjee (1998); Heikkila (2011).

60. L. Wu (1999), p. 22.

61. L. Wu (1999), p. 50.

62. The land still belongs to the state and is made available to the private developers on a leasehold basis.

63. From interviews with representatives of developers of the Junefield Plaza, lower Xidan.

64. See chapter 6.

65. Heikkila (2011); also Yucekus and Banerjee (1998).

66. Beijing Photography and Publishing House (1993), p. 17.

67. Yi (2002), p. 3.

68. See Epilogue.

69. Wang (2011).

70. See chapter 6.

71. See Gaubatz (2005).

72. Broudehoux (2004).

73. The initial phase of the Xidan widening.

74. From a presentation by the Xicheng district officials in 2005.

75. Some noteworthy examples: Soho City Master Plan (Zaha Hadid with Patrik Schumacher, planned in 2003); Hua Mao Centre Masterplan (Kohn Pederson Fox Associates, completion 2005); Central Axis Masterplan (Albert Speer and Partner, study 2002–2003): China Natural Offshore Oil Corporation Headquarters (Kohn Pederson Fox Associates, in construction); Zhongguancun West, BSTP Lot 21 in Haidian District (Kohn Pederson Fox Associates, under construction); International Automotive Expo (Henn Architekten, completion 2007); German School and Partments (gmp von Gerkan, Marg und Partner, completed 2000); China Petro Headquarters (Henn Architekten, 2003 international competition winner); National Theatre, Chang'an Avenue (Paul Andreu, completion 2005); Chinese Museum of Film (RTKL Associates, opening 2005); Museum and Art Gallery, Tsinghua University (Mario Botta, in planning); 2008 Olympics Wukesong Cultural and Sports Center Burckhardt+Partner, completion 2007); Beijing Capital International Airport Termina 3 (Foster and Partners, completion 2008); Bank of China Head Office (Pei Partnership, completed 2001); CCTV Central Chinese Television Headquarters (OMA Office of Metropolitan Architects, completion 2008). All of these projects are described and illustrated in Dawson (2005).

76. Gaubatz (2005).

77. This firm has designed over one hundred projects in China (Dawson, 2005).

78. Dawson (2005), p. 146.

79. Richie (1998).

80. Initially planned as a palm-shaped development but later redesigned as a cluster of islands. https://en.wikipedia.org/wiki/Deira_Islands.

81. https://en.wikipedia.org/wiki/Nakheel_Properties.

82. https://www.skyscrapercity.com/threads/epic-architecture-and-development-projects-around-the-globe.392487/page-3; https://en.wikipedia.org/wiki/List_of_tallest_buildings.

83. World Bank (2017).

84. From personal conversations with the owner of a Pakistani *dhow* at Dubai harbor in 2004.

85. https://en.wikipedia.org/wiki/Mall_of_the_Emirates.

86. See Eco (1986).

87. See Butler (2005).

Chapter 12

1. In an address to the National Association of Architects, Morocco, 1986.

2. This chapter draws from the findings of a USC graduate planning laboratory/workshop conducted in Fès in the summer of 1999, in collaboration with the students and faculty of Al Akhawayn University in Ifrane, and under the sponsorship of L'Agence Urbaine of Fès. Professor Hassan Radoine, now the dean of architecture, University of Morocco, was the coinstructor and coordinator of this project.

3. Rabat's date back two millennia.

4. See Alnowaiser (1983), for example.

5. See Santos (1979).

6. Abu-Lughod (1980).

7. Abu-Lughod (1980), p. 203.

8. Çelik (1997).

9. See Lynch and Rodwin (1958).

10. Cf. Perlman (1976).

11. Abu-Lughod (1971) defines this relationship as follows: "Each important family was surrounded by its clients—retainers or families tied to it through service or through marriages and alliances which might have been forged in the countryside. These social units, by definition, encompassed persons at a variety of levels of status and wealth who were held together by a network of mutual interdependence" (p. 207).

12. See Castells (1976).

13. See Carol Smith (1985), for example.

14. Abu-Lughod (1971), p. 207.

15. The following observations are derived from field studies and from focus-group interviews with medina residents conducted with students from USC and Al Akhawayn University in Ifrane. They also reflect many conversations we had with professor and architect-planner Hassan Radoine, who was then working with ADER-FÈS, and the officials from L'Agence Urbaine.

16. As noted by Hassan Radoine (personal conversation), then working with ADAIR in the restoration of medina housing and important historic buildings. Also, see https://en.wikipedia.org/wiki/Fes_el_Bali.

17. This number today is significantly lower than the 181,000 registered at the turn of the century. Clearly the "dedensifcation" program initiated by ADER-FÈS with help from the World Bank seems to have had an effect in reducing the earlier overcrowding of the medina.

18. The main river is called Wad Fès, and its historic name was Wad el-jawahir. https://en.wikipedia.org/wiki/Fes_el_Bali.

19. https://en.wikipedia.org/wiki/Fes_el_Bali.

20. See for example, Abu-Lughod (1987); AlSayyad (1991); Amirahmadi and El-Shakhs (1993); Eickelman (1974). Some of these arguments have been included in chapter 6.

21. Abu-Lughod (1987).

22. Raban (1974).

23. From the notes of Alicia Kitsuse, which were based on English translations from Arabic by Hassan Radoine, who was serving as an interpreter in all our focus-group meetings. This saying is based on a hadith—tradition—of the Prophet.

24. Abu-Lughod (1987).

25. Gulick (1963).

26. Abu-Lughod (1987), for example.

27. See Suttles (1972).

28. Putnam (1993).

29. Koning (1995).

30. One of the participants in the medina residents' focus groups with whom we met was a physically disabled woman, who had just started an organization, the first of its kind in Morocco, dedicated to advocacy of the interests of people with disabilities.

31. World Bank (1998).

32. ILO (1972).

33. Source: Hassan Radoine.

34. See chapter 7.

35. According to Hassan Radoine, the government never succeeded through a formal program to relocate people, and the decrease of medina population was due to other social housing programs targeting residents of *bidonvilles*—or informal squatter settlements.

36. World Bank (1998).

37. As it became clear to us from our conversations with the medina residents.

38. Abu-Lughod (1980).

39. As also pointed out by the medina residents.

40. The World Bank did not provide any grant for the rehabilitation project of Fès. It gave a loan to the Moroccan government to cover some components of the whole project. (For more details about the components see the World Bank web page: https://projects.worldbank.org/en/projects-operations/project-detail/P005524.)

41. But this plan was not respected, and the project of the rehabilitation was mainly based on a Rehabilitation Plan, or Plan d'Aménagement de la Medina.

42. Peattie (1994); Goldsmith (1974).

43. Perlman (1976). Also O. Lewis (1966a).

Chapter 13

1. Appiah (2006).

2. Baudrillard (1994).

3. Krieger (1973).

4. See the organization's website at https://megacitiesproject.org.

5. This includes Jane Smith, a historian, and Shin Lee, a planning professor.

6. See chapter 2.

7. Sassen (2012).

8. Elsewhere I have referred to the Chinese state as "China, Inc." (T. Banerjee, 2006).

9. See Sites (2003).

10. Lipton (1988).

11. From personal conversations with Eugene Cooper, a USC professor of anthropology whose research involved rural China.

12. Landsberg (2007).

13. Cf. Huang (2004).

14. Cf. Perlman (1976).

15. J. Morris (1985).

16. See Webster (2007); F. Wu (2000).

17. Beito, Gordon, and Tabarrok (2002).

18. See Lynch (1990a).

19. Huang (2000).

20. AlSayyad (2001).

21. Appiah (2006).

22. McHarg (1969).

23. Salamanca et al. (2014).

24. Graham and Marvin (2001).

25. Castells (1996).

26. Castells (1996).

27. See Mukhija (2003).

28. T. Banerjee (1993).

29. See Sorkin (2002).

30. Lecture given by Harvey Molotch at the Department of Urban Planning and Spatial Analysis, USC Price School of Public Policy, March 20, 2017.

31. See Surajit Chakravarty (2019).

32. Appadurai (1991).

33. https://en.wikipedia.org/wiki/Dubai_Frame.

34. See Baudrillard (1994).

35. Sherwood (2005).

36. Moustafa (2005).

37. Eco (1986).

38. Eco (1986), pp. 57–58.

39. O'Connor (1983).

40. Mazrui (1986).

41. See Steward (1955).

42. See chapter 8.

43. Williams (1997), p. 827.

44. Based on the novel *Do Androids Dream of Electric Sheep?* by Philip K. Dick (1968).

45. See Appadurai (1991); Qadeer (2016); Sandercock (2003); T. Banerjee, Chakravarty, and Chan (2016).

46. See Soja (1996).

47. A. King (1976).

48. AlSayyad (2001), Roy (2001).

49. See, for example, Kunzmann (2004).

50. See Piazzoni and Banerjee (2018).

51. Novo (1967).

52. Davila (2000), p. 107.

53. Calvino (1972), p. 11.

54. See the famous Mahfouz (1956–1957) triology and also Abu-Lughod (1971).

55. Moller (2004).

56. Harvey (1988).

57. Halbwachs (1980), p. 130.

58. This is also one of the categories identified by O'Connor (1983) in his typology of African cities.

59. *The Economist* (2017).

60. Graham and Marvin (2001).

61. Lévi-Strauss (1962).

62. See Ross (2009).

63. Spirn (1984); Scheer (2011); Mostafavi (2010).

64. Lynch (1981).

65. Peattie (1981).

66. Sen (1999).

67. Nussbaum (2000).

68. Uhm, Lewis, and Banerjee (2006).

69. Historian Jane Smith, spouse of Carl Smith, a noted urban historian who was a fellow scholar-in-residence at the Rockefeller Center in Bellagio, had first suggested that one could imagine a seventh "derivative" bell curve that would capture the trajectory of cultural development and autonomy with economic development. At a talk I gave at Cardiff University Department of City Planning, Shin Lee, a member of the faculty there, raised an almost identical point. A few weeks later, as I presented a similar talk at the Faculty of Architecture at the University of Florence Giulio Giovannoni, a research associate there also made a nearly identical observation.

70. See Pizarro (2005).

71. Pizarro et al. (2003).

72. Appiah (2006).

Epilogue

1. L. Wu (1994b), p. 34 (as counted).

2. Verma, Banerjee, and Chaudhuri (2004).

3. See Scott (1998).

4. J. Taylor (2002), p. 125.

5. L. Wu (1999).

6. L. Wu (1999), p. 231.

7. L. Wu (1994a), p. 9 (as counted).

8. American Planning Association (2018). http://www.planning.org/awards/2018/798arts/.

9. See Scott (1998).

10. https://en.wikipedia.org/wiki/Rock_Garden_of_Chandigarh#:~:text=The%20Rock%20Garden%20of%20Chandigarh,40%20acres%20(16%20ha).

11. See Scott (1998).

12. See Webster (2007).

13. Personal conversation during his visit to Los Angeles in 2013.

14. See Apostol, Antoniades, and Banerjee (2013).

15. See Webber (1963).

16. Apostol, Antoniades, and Banerjee (2013).

17. This cable car transit has been replicated subsequently in cities like Rio de Janeiro (Brazil), Caracas (Venezuela), Ankara (Turkey), and La Paz (Bolivia).

18. See Lynch (1981).

19. See Lefebvre (1996).

20. See Sen (1999).

21. See Berney (2017).

22. Berney (2017), p. 172.

23. *Urbanized.* 2011. A documentary film by Gary Hustwith.

24. Radoine (2008).

25. S. Gilbert (2017).

26. World Bank (1998).

27. Radoine (2008), pp. 7–11.

28. Mumford (1947), p. 9.

29. Mumford (1947), p. 9.

30. Referring to structures made from nonpermanent building materials, lacking brick-and-mortar building technology.

31. Tyrwhitt (1947).

32. See Tyrwhitt (1947), p. 22.

33. Scott (1998).

34. Tyrwhitt (1947), p. 29.

35. Tyrwhitt (1947), p. 37.

References

Abrams, Charles. 1964. *Man's Struggle for Shelter in an Urbanizing World*. Cambridge, MA: MIT Press.

Abramson, Daniel B. 2008. Haussmann and Le Corbusier in China: Land control and design of streets in urban redevelopment. *Journal of Urban Design* 13 (2): 231–256.

Abu-Lughod, Janet. 1971. *Cairo: 1001 Years of the City Victorious*. Princeton, NJ: Princeton University Press.

Abu-Lughod, Janet. 1980. *Rabat: Urban Apartheid in Morocco*. Princeton, NJ: Princeton University Press.

Abu-Lughod, Janet. 1987. The Islamic City: Historic myth, Islamic essence, and contemporary relevance. *International Journal of Middle East Studies* 19 (2): 155–176.

Abu-Lughod, Janet. 1990. New York and Cairo: A view from street level. *International Social Science Journal* 42 (3): 307–318.

Acemoglu, Daron, Simon Johnson, and James A. Robinson. 2002. Reversal of fortune: Geography and institutions in the making of the modern world income distribution. *The Quarterly Journal of Economics* 117 (4): 1231–1294.

Acemoglu, Daron, Simon Johnson, and James A. Robinson. 2005. The rise of Europe: Atlantic trade, institutional change, and economic growth. *The American Economic Review* 95 (3): 546–579.

Ahluwalia, Montek S. 1976. Inequality, poverty, and development. *Journal of Development Economics* 3:307–342.

Akbar, J. 1988. *Crisis in the Built Environment: The Case of the Muslim City*. Singapore: Concept Media.

Alexander, Christopher. 1964. *Notes on the Synthesis of Form*. Cambridge, MA: Harvard University Press.

Alexander, Christopher. 1967. The city as a mechanism for sustaining human contact. In *Environment for Man: The Next Fifty Years*, ed. William R. Ewald, 60–102. Bloomington: Indiana University Press.

Alexander, Christopher. 1977. *A Pattern Language: Towns, Buildings, Construction.* New York: Oxford University Press.

Al-Hathloul, Saleh Ali. 1996. *The Arab-Muslim City: Tradition, Continuity and Change in the Physical Environment.* Dar Al Sahan.

Alnowaiser, Mohamad A. 1983. *The Role of Traditional and Modern Residential Rural Settlements on the Quality of Environmental Experience: A Case Study of Unyzah and New Alkabra in Saudi Arabia* [Doctoral dissertation, University of Southern California].

Alonso, William. 1964. *Location and Land Use.* Cambridge, MA: Harvard University Press.

Alonso, William. 1980. Five bell shapes in development. *Papers of the Regional Science Association* 45 (1): 5–16.

AlSayyad, Nezar. 1991. *Cities and Caliphs: On the Genesis of Arab Muslim Urbanism.* Westport, CT: Greenwood Press.

AlSayyad, Nezar, ed. 1992. *Forms of Dominance: On the Architecture and Urbanism of the Colonial Enterprise.* Aldershot, UK: Avebury.

AlSayyad, Nezar. 1994. Bayn al-Qasrayn: The street between the two palaces. In *Streets: Critical Perspectives on Public Space,* ed. Zeynep Çelik, Diane Favro, and Richard Ingersoll, 71–82. Berkeley: University of California Press.

AlSayyad, Nezar. 1999. Virtual Cairo: An urban historian's view of computer simulation. *Leonardo* 32 (2): 93–100.

AlSayyad, Nezar, ed. 2001. Hybrid culture/hybrid urbanism: Pandora's box of the "third place." In *Hybrid Urbanism: On the Identity Discourse and the Built Environment,* ed. Nezar AlSayyad, 1–18. Westport, CT: Praeger.

AlSayyad, Nezar, ed. 2004. *The End of Tradition.* London: Routledge.

American Planning Association. 2018. 798 Arts District Vision Plan. *Pierre L'Enfant International Planning Excellence Award.* Sasaki—Beijing, China. https://www.planning.org/awards/2018/798arts/

American Public Health Association, Committee on Hygiene of Housing. 1948. (1960 rev. ed.) *Planning the Neighborhood.* Chicago: Public Administration Service.

Amin, Samir. 1972. *Accumulation on a World Scale: A Critique of the Theory of Underdevelopment.* New York: Monthly Review Press.

Amirahmadi, Hooshang, and Salah El-Shakhs. 1993. Urban development in the Muslim world: Encounter with modernity and implication for planning. In *Urban Development in the Muslim World,* ed. Hooshang Amirahmadi and Salah El-Shakhs, 1–10. New Brunswick, NJ: Rutgers University Center for Urban Policy Research.

Anderson, Martin. 1964. *The Federal Bulldozer: A Critical Analysis of Urban Renewal, 1949–1962.* Cambridge, MA: MIT Press.

Andreoni, James, and Arik Levinson. 2001. The simple analytics of the environmental Kuznets curve. *Journal of Public Economics* 80 (2): 269–286.

Annez, Patricia Clarke, and Robert M. Buckley. 2009. Urbanization and growth: Setting the context. In *Urbanization and Growth*, ed. Michael Spence, Patricia Clarke Annez, and Robert M. Buckley, 1–46. Washington, DC: The World Bank.

Antle, John M., and Gregg Heidebrink. 1995. Environment and development: Theory and international evidence. *Economic Development and Cultural Change* 43 (3): 603–625.

Appadurai, Arjun. 1991. Global ethnoscapes: Notes and queries for a transnational anthropology. In *Recapturing Anthropology: Working in the Present*, ed. Richard Fox, 191–210. Santa Fe, NM: School of American Research.

Appiah, Kwame Anthony. 2006. The case for contamination. *New York Times Magazine*, January 1, 2006.

Appleyard, Donald. 1976. *Planning a Pluralist City*. Cambridge, MA: MIT Press.

Appleyard, Donald, and Allan Jacobs. 1987. Toward an urban design manifesto. *Journal of the American Planning Association* 53 (1): 112–120.

Apostol, Ileana, Panayotis Antoniades, and Tridib Banerjee. 2013. Flânerie between net and place: Promises and possibilities for participation in planning. *Journal of Planning Education and Research* 33 (1): 20–33.

Archer, John. 1997. Colonial suburbs in South Asia, 1700–1850, and the spaces of modernity. In *Visions of Suburbia*, ed. Roger Silverstone, 26–54. London: Routledge.

Archives of Istituto Agronomico per l'Oltremare, Florence, Italy. 2005.

Ardalan, Nader, and Laleh Bakhtiar. 1973. *The Sense of Unity: The Sufi Tradition in Persian Architecture*. Chicago: University of Chicago Press.

Arefi, Mahyar. 1999. Non-place and placelessness as narratives of loss: Rethinking the notion of place. *Journal of Urban Design* 4 (2): 179–194.

Arefi, Mahyar. 2018. *Learning from Informal Settlements in Iran*. London: Palgrave Macmillan.

Armstrong, Warwick, and T. G. McGee. 1985. *Theatres of Accumulation: Studies in Asian and Latin American Urbanization*. New York: Methuen.

Arnaud, M. 1988. *The Islamic City* [Videorecording]. Films for the Humanities. Princeton, NJ: RM Productions and TF1.

Arndt, H. W. 1983. The "trickle-down" myth. *Economic Development and Cultural Change* 32 (1): 1–10.

Arndt, H. W. 1987. *Economic Development: The History of an Idea*. Chicago: University of Chicago Press.

Arnstein, Sherry. 1969. A ladder of citizen participation. *Journal of the American Institute of Planners* 35 (4): 216–224.

Arrow, Kenneth, Bert Bolin, Robert Costanza, Partha Dasgupta, Carl Folke, C. S. Holling, Bengt-Owe Jansson, Simon Levin, Karl-Göran Mäler, Charles Perrings, and David Pimentel. 1995. Economic growth, carrying capacity, and the environment. *Ecological Economics* 15 (2): 91–95.

Atlas, James. 1989. What is Fukuyama saying? And to whom is he saying it? *New York Times Magazine*, October 22.

Baali, Fuad. 1988. *Society, State, and Urbanism: Ibn Khaldun's Sociological Thought.* Albany: State University of New York Press.

Bacon, Edmund. 1967. *Design of Cities.* UK: Thames & Hudson.

Bagchi, Amiya. 1982. *The Political Economy of Underdevelopment.* London: Cambridge University Press.

Bairoch, Paul. 1981. The main trends in national economic disparities since the industrial revolution. In *Disparities in Economic Development since the Industrial Revolution*, ed. Paul Bairoch and Maurice Lévy-Leboyer, 3–17. London: Macmillan.

Bairoch, Paul. 1993. *Economics and World History: Myths and Paradoxes.* Chicago: University of Chicago Press.

Balbo, Marcello, and Guido Moretti. 1973. La Casbah nello sviluppo di Algeri. *Parametro* 17:6–13.

Banerjee, Nirmala. 1981. The weakest link. *IDS Bulletin* 12 (3): 36–40.

Banerjee, Tridib. 1993. Transitional urbanism reconsidered: Post-colonial development of Calcutta and Shanghai. In *Urban Anthropology in China*, ed. Greg Guldin and Aidan Southall, 76–100. New York: E. J. Brill.

Banerjee, Tridib. 2001. The future of public space: Beyond invented streets and reinvented places. *Journal of the American Planning Association* 67 (1): 9–24.

Banerjee, Tridib. 2005. Understanding planning cultures: The Kolkata paradox. In *Comparative Planning Cultures*, ed. Bishwapriya Sanyal, 145–165. London: Routledge.

Banerjee, Tridib. 2006. China Inc. and the future of European cities. In *China and Europe: Implications of the Rise of China for European Space (Regions and Cities)*, ed. Klaus Kunzmann, W. A. Schmid, and M. Koll-Screzenmayr, 97–106. London: Routledge.

Banerjee, Tridib. 2007. Urban outcomes of globalization: Theory, research, practice. *Journal of Urban History* 34 (6): 1044–1054.

Banerjee, Tridib. 2009. US planning expedition to post-colonial India: From ideology to innovation in technical assistance. *Journal of the American Planning Association* 75 (2): 193–208.

Banerjee, Tridib. 2014. General Introduction. In *Urban Design: Critical Concepts in Urban Studies.* Vol. 1, *The Idea of Urban Design*, ed. Tridib Banerjee, 1–31. London: Routledge.

Banerjee, Tridib, and William C. Baer. 1984. *Beyond the Neighborhood Unit: Residential Environments and Public Policy.* New York: Plenum Press.

Banerjee, Tridib, Surajit Chakravarty, and Felicity Chan. 2016. Negotiating identity in the diaspora: Ethnoscapes of Southeast Asian communities in Los Angeles. In *Space and Pluralism*, ed. Stefano Moroni and David Weberman, 173–199. Prague: Central European University Press.

Banerjee, Tridib, and Sanjoy Chakravorty. 1994. Transfer of planning technology and local political economy: A retrospective analysis of Calcutta's planning. *Journal of the American Planning Association* 60 (1): 67–78.

Banerjee, Tridib, and Sigrid Schenk. 1984. Lower order cities and national urbanization strategies: China and India. *Environment and Planning* 16 (4): 486–513.

Banerjee, Tridib, and Michael Southworth, eds. 1990. *City Sense and City Design: Writings and Projects of Kevin Lynch*. Cambridge, MA: MIT Press.

Banerjee, Tridib, and Niraj Verma. 2003a. Probing the soft metropolis: From Chicago models to Los Angeles metaphors. *Planning Theory and Practice* 2 (2): 133–148.

Banerjee, Tridib, and Niraj Verma. 2003b. The Third World in Los Angeles: A metaphor within a metaphor. In *Southern California and the World*, ed. Eric Heikkila and Rafael Pizarro, 133–150. Westport, CT: Praeger.

Banfield, Edward C. 1958. *The Moral Basis of a Backward Society*. New York: Free Press.

Baran, Paul. A. 1957. *The Political Economy of Growth*. New York: Monthly Review Press.

Barber, Benjamin R. 1995. *Jihad vs. McWorld: How Globalism and Tribalism Is Reshaping the World*. New York: Times Book.

Barber, Benjamin R. 2000. Globalization and its discontents: Winners and losers in the new world order. *Los Angeles Times*, August 13, 2000.

Barker, Roger G. 1968. *Ecological Psychology: Concepts and Methods for Studying the Environment of Human Behavior*. Stanford, CA: Stanford University Press.

Barnett, Jonathan. 2011. A short guide to 60 of the newest urbanisms. *Planning* 77 (4): 19–21.

Barrucand, Marianne. 1989. The case of Sadi Qasaba of Marrakech. *Journal of the Islamic Environmental Design Research Center* 1–2:18–27.

Baudrillard, Jean. 1994. *Simulacra and Simulation*. Ann Arbor: University of Michigan Press.

Beauregard, Robert A. 2015. *Planning Matter: Acting with Things*. Chicago: University of Chicago Press.

Béguin, Gilles, and Dominique Morel. 1997. *The Forbidden City: Center of Imperial China*. Translated by Ruth Taylor. New York: Harry N. Abrams.

Beier, G., A. Churchill, M. Cohen, and B. Renaud. 1975. The task ahead for the cities of developing countries. World Bank Staff Working Paper No. 209. Washington, DC: The World Bank.

Beijing Arts and Photography Publishing House. 2003. *Hutongs of Beijing*. Beijing, China.

Beinert, Julian. 2002. Future options. In *Celebrating Chandigarh*, ed. Jaspreet Takhar, 143–163. Chandigarh, India: Chandigarh Perspectives.

Beito, David T., Peter Gordon, and Alexander Tabarrok, eds. 2002. *The Voluntary City: Choice, Community, and Civil Society*. Ann Arbor: University of Michigan Press [Oakland, CA: Independent Institute].

Ben-Ghiat, Ruth, and Mia Fuller. 2005. *Italian Colonialism*. New York: Palgrave Macmillan.

Benjamin, Walter. 1999. *The Arcades Project.* Translated by H. Eiland and K. McLaughlin. Cambridge, MA: Harvard University Press.

Bergère, Marie-Claire. 2004. Shanghai's urban development: A remake? In *Shanghai: Architecture & Urbanism for Modern China*, ed. Peter G. Rowe and Seng Kuan, 36–53. Munich: Prestel.

Berlin, Isaiah, and H. Hardy. 1991. *The Crooked Timber of Humanity: Chapters in the History of Ideas*. New York: Knopf.

Berman, Marshall. 1982. *All That Is Solid Melts into Air: The Experience of Modernity*. New York: Simon and Schuster.

Berney, Rachel. 2017. *Learning from Bogotá: Pedagogical Urbanism and the Reshaping of Public Space*. Austin: University of Texas Press.

Berque, J. 1958. Land ownership and social integration in North Africa. *Cahiers Internationaux de Sociologie* 25 (July): 38–74.

Berry, Brian J. L. 1967. *Geography of Market Centers and Detail Distribution*. Englewood Cliffs, NJ: Prentice-Hall.

Berry, Brian J. L., and Philip H. Rees. 1969. The factorial ecology of Calcutta. *American Journal of Sociology* 74 (5): 445–491.

Beverley, J. 1999. *Subalternity and Representation: Arguments in Cultural Theory*. Durham, NC: Duke University Press.

Bhattarai, Madhusudan, and Michael Hammig. 2001. Institutions and the environmental Kuznets curve for deforestation: A crosscountry analysis for Latin America, Africa and Asia. *World Development* 29 (6): 995–1010.

Bianca, Stefano. 2000. *Urban Form in the Arab World: Past and Present*. London: Thames and Hudson.

Bierman, I., Rifa'at Abou el-Haj, and Donald Presiozi, eds. 1991. *The Ottoman City and Its Parts: Urban Structure and Social Order*. New Rochelle, NY: Aristide D. Caratzas.

Birch, Eugénie L. 2011. From CIAM to CNU: The roots and thinkers of modern urban design. In *Companion to Urban Design*, ed. Tridib Banerjee and Anastasia Loukaitou-Sideris. 9–29. London and New York: Routledge.

Blakely, Edward, and Mary Gail Snyder. 1997. *Fortress America: Gated Communities*. Washington, DC: Brookings Institution Press.

Blanco, Hilda, Marina Alberti, Ann Forsyth, and Kevin J. Krizek. 2009. Hot, congested, crowded, and diverse: Emerging research agendas in planning. *Progress in Planning* 71 (4): 153–205.

Blaut, J. M. 1993. *The Colonizer's Model of the World: Geographical Diffusionism and Eurocentric History*. New York: The Guildford Press.

Blumenfeld, Hans. 1953. Scale in civic design. *Town Planning Review* 24 (1): 35–46.

Boesiger, Willy, and Hans Girsberger. 1960. *Le Corbusier 1910–60*. Zurich: Editions Girsberger.

Bogaers, E., and R. Peter. 1986. Ir. Thomas Karsten and Indonesian town planning, 1915–1940. In *The Indonesian City: Studies in Urban Development and Planning*, ed. Peter J. M. Nas, 71–88. Dordrecht, Netherlands: Foris Publications Holland.

Bonine, Michael E. 1979. The morphogenesis of Iranian cities. *Annals of the Association of American Geographers* 69:208–224.

Bonine, Michael E. 1990. The sacred direction and city structure: A preliminary analysis of the Islamic cities of Morocco. In *Muqarnas VII: An Annual on Islamic Art and Architecture*, ed. Oleg Grabar, 50–72. Leiden, Netherlands: E. J. Brill.

Bose, N. K. 1965. Calcutta: A premature metropolis. *Scientific American* 213 (3): 90–102.

Bosker, Bianca. 2013. *Original Copies: Architectural Mimicry in Contemporary China*. Honolulu: University of Hawaii Press.

Bouglé, C. 1958. The essence and reality of the caste system. *Contributions to Indian Sociology* 2 (1): 7–30.

Bourdieu, P. 1984. *Distinction: A Social Critique of the Judgment of Taste*. Cambridge, MA: Harvard Business Press.

Boyd, A. 1962. *Chinese Architecture and Town Planning: 1500 B.C.—1911 A. D.* Chicago: University of Chicago Press.

Boyer, Christine M. 1983. *Dreaming the Rational City: The Myth of American City Planning*. Cambridge, MA: MIT Press.

Boyer, Christine M. 1997. *Cybercities: Visual Perception in an Age of Electronic Communication*. New York: Princeton Architectural Press.

Boyer, H. 2005. Urban land and housing challenges in Brazil. *Land Lines* 17:8–11.

Brand, Michael, and Glenn D. Lowry, eds. 1987. *Fatehpur-Sikri*. Bombay: Marg Publications.

Brand, Michael, Glenn D. Lowry, Ziyaud-Din A. Desai, and Attilio Petruccioli. 1985. *Fatehpur-Sikri: A Sourcebook*. Cambridge, MA: The Aga Khan Program for Islamic Architecture at Harvard University and Massachusetts Institute of Technology.

Brenner, Neil J. 2014. *Implosions/Explosions: Towards a Study of Planetary Urbanization*. Berlin: Jovis.

Briggs De Souza, Xavier. 2005. Social capital and segregation in the United States. In *Desegregating the City: Ghettoes, Enclaves, and Inequality*, ed. David Varady, 79–197. Binghamton, NY: SUNY Press.

Broudehoux, Anne-Marie. 2004. *The Making and Selling of Post-Mao Beijing*. New York: Routledge.

Brown, Leon Carl, ed. 1973. *From Madina to Metropolis: Heritage and Change in the Near Eastern City*. Princeton, NJ: Darwin Press.

Buck-Morss, Susan. 1989. *The Dialectics of Seeing: Walter Benjamin and the Arcades Project*. Cambridge, MA: MIT Press.

Bulliet, Richard. W. 1975. *The Camel and the Wheel*. Cambridge, MA: Harvard University Press.

Burckhardt, Titus. 1980. Fez. In *The Islamic City: Selected Papers*, ed. R. B. Serjeant, 166–176. Paris: UNESCO.

Burgess, Ernest W., Robert E. Park, and Roderick D. McKenzie. 1925. *The City*. Chicago: University of Chicago Press.

Butler, Tina. 2005. Dubai's artificial islands have high environmental cost. *Mongabay*, August 23, 2005. https://news.mongabay.com/2005/08/dubais-artificial-islands-have-high-environmental-cost/

Caldeira, Teresa P. R. 2013. *City of Walls: Crime, Segregation, and Citizenship in São Paulo*. Berkeley: University of California Press.

Calvino, Italo. 1974. *Invisible Cities*. New York: Harcourt Brace Jovanovich.

Campanella, Thomas. 2008. *The Concrete Dragon: China's Urban Revolution*. New York: Princeton Architectural Press.

Campbell, Scott. 1996. Green cities, growing cities, just cities? Urban planning and the contradictions of sustainable development. *Journal of the American Planning Association* 62 (3): 296–312.

Cardoso, F. H., and E. Faletto. 1979. *Dependency and Development in Latin America*. Berkeley: University of California Press.

Castells, Manuel. 1977. *The Urban Question: A Marxist Approach*. Cambridge, MA: MIT Press.

Castells, Manuel. 1996. *The Rise of the Network Society*. Malden, MA: Blackwell.

Çelik, Zeynep. 1996. Colonialism, orientalism, and the canon. *Art Bulletin* 78 (2): 202–205.

Çelik, Zeynep. 1997. *Urban Forms and Colonial Confrontations: Algiers under French Rule*. Berkeley: University of California Press.

Central Intelligence Agency. 2014. Distribution of family income – Gini Index. *The World Factbook*. https://www.cia.gov/library/publications/the-world-factbook/fields/223rank.html

Chakravarty, Suhash. 2007. *The Raj Syndrome*. New Delhi: Rupa.

Chakravarty, Surajit. 2019. Un-cities: The urbanism of rapidly growing cities in the Gulf region. In *The New Companion to Urban Design*, ed. Tridib Banerjee and Anastasia Loukaitou-Sideris, 83–94. London: Routledge.

Chang, Qing, ed. 2005. *Origin of a Metropolis: A Study on the Bund Section of Nanjing Road in Shanghai.* Shanghai: Tongji University Press.

Chang, Sen-Dou. 1970. Some observations on the morphology of Chinese walled cities. *Annals of the Association of American Geographers* 60 (1): 63–91.

Chen, C. 2018. Designing the danceable city: How residents in Beijing cultivate health and community ties through urban dance. *Journal of the American Planning Association* 84 (3–4): 237–249.

Chen, Shaohua, and Martin Ravallion. 2004. How have the world's poorest fared since the early 1980s? *World Bank Research Observer* 19 (2): 141–169.

Chenery, Hollis, Montek S. Ahluwalia, C. L. G. Bell, John H. Duloy, and Richard Jolly. 1974. *Redistribution with Growth.* New York: Oxford University Press.

Chilcote, Ronald. 1974. Dependency: A critical synthesis of literature. *Latin American Perspectives* 1:4–29.

Chilcote, Ronald. 1981. Issues of theory in dependency and Marxism. *Latin American Perspectives* 9 (3–4): 3–16.

Chopra, Asok. 1998. The city of angst through Gunter's pen. *The Tribune,* September 13, 1998. https://www.tribuneindia.com/1998/98sep13/sunday/modern.htm

Choudhury, Kushanava. 2017. *The Epic City: The World on the Streets of Calcutta.* London: Bloomsbury.

Christalller, Walter. 1966. *Central Places in Southern Germany.* Translated by Carlisle W. Baskin. Englewood Cliffs, NJ: Prentice-Hall.

Clarke, Gordon L., and Michael Dear. 1984. *State Apparatus: Structures and Language of Legitimacy.* Boston: George Allen and Unwin.

Clemente Mendoza, Homero. 2015. *The Crisis of Potable Water in Mexico City: Institutional Factors and Water Property Rights as Conditions for Creating Adequate Metropolitan Water Governance* [Doctoral dissertation, University of Southern California].

CMDA (Calcutta Metropolitan Development Authority). 1986. *Development Need of the Calcutta Metropolitan Area: 1986–2011.* Calcutta: Calcutta Metropolitan Development Authority.

Cobban, J. L. 1992. Exporting planning: The work of Thomas Karsten in colonial Indonesia. *Planning Perspectives* 7:329–344.

Colclough, C., and J. Manor, eds. 1991. *States or Markets?: Neo-liberalism and the Development Policy Debate.* Oxford: Oxford University Press.

Correa, Charles. 2012. *A Place in the Shade: The New Landscape & Other Essays.* Bonn, Germany: Hatje Cantz.

Cosgrove, Dennis E. 1984. *Social Formation and Symbolic Landscape.* Madison: University of Wisconsin Press.

Costello, V. F. 1977. *Urbanization in the Middle East.* Cambridge: Cambridge University Press.

Cowherd, Robert, and Eric J. Heikkila. 2002. Orange County, Java. In *Southern California and the World,* ed. Eric Heikkila and Rafael Pizarro, 195–220. New York: Praeger.

Cox, Harvey. 1968. Restoration of a sense of place. *Ekistics* 25 (151): 422–424.

Croll, E. 1994. *From Heaven to Earth: Images and Experiences of Development in China.* London: Routledge.

Cronon, William. 1991. *Nature's Metropolis: Chicago and the Great West.* New York: W. W. Norton.

Cudny, Waldemar. 2016. *Festivalisation of Urban Spaces.* Switzerland: Springer.

Cullen, Gordon. 1960. IXth Delhi. *Ekistics* 9 (56): 399–408.

Cullen, Gordon. 1966. Calcutta: The linear city. *Annual of Architecture, Structure, and Town Planning,* ed. Santosh Ghosh. Volume 5, B1–B10.

Cuthbert, Alexander. 1985. *Architecture, Society, and Space: The High-Density Question Re-examined.* New York: Routledge.

Dandekar, Hemalata C., ed. 1998. *City Space and Globalization: An International Perspective.* Ann Arbor: College of Architecture and Urban Planning, University of Michigan.

Darby, H. C., and H. Fullard. 1970. *The New Cambridge Modern History Atlas.* New York: Cambridge University Press.

Davey, Peter. 2002. The critical view. In *Celebrating Chandigarh,* ed. Jaspreet Takhar, 203–212. Chandigarh, India: Chandigarh Perspectives.

Davies, Philip. 1985. *Splendours of the Raj: British Architecture in India, 1660 to 1947.* London: John Murray.

Davila, Roxanne. 2000. Mexico City as urban palimpsest in Salvador Novo's Nueva Grandeza Mexicana. *Studies in the Literary Imagination* 33 (1): 107–123.

Davis, Mike. 2006. *Planet of Slums.* New York: Verso.

Dawson, Layla. 2005. *China's New Dawn: An Architectural Transformation.* Munich: Prestel Vertag.

DDA (Delhi Development Authority). 1961. *Master Plan of Delhi (1962–81).* Delhi: DDA.

De la Casinière. 1922. Notes sur les plans d'extension des villes et l'urbanisme au Maroc. Document 754. Archives Outre-Mer, Aix-en-Provence.

De Soto, Hernando. 1990. *The Other Path: The Invisible Revolution in the Third World.* New York: Harper & Row/Perennial Library.

Diamond, Jared. 1997. *Guns, Germs, and Steel: The Fates of Human Societies.* New York: W. W. Norton.

Dick, Philip K. 1968. *Do Androids Dream of Electric Sheep?* Garden City, NY: Doubleday.

Dirks, Nicholas B. 2001. *Castes of Mind: Colonialism and the Making of Modern India*. Princeton, NJ: Princeton University Press.

Do Lago, Luciana Corrêa. 2001. Socio-spatial structuring in greater metropolitan Rio de Janeiro. Paper presented at the *International Seminar on Segregation in the City*. Cambridge, MA: Lincoln Institute of Land Policy. OCLC No. 49767706.

Dovey, Kim, and Ross King. 2012. Informal urbanism and the taste for slums. *Tourism Geographies* 14 (2): 275–293.

Downs, Roger M., and David Stea, eds. 1973. *Image & Environment: Cognitive Mapping and Spatial Behavior*. Chicago: Aldine Publishing.

Doxiadis, Constantin A. 1960. *Dynapolis: The City of the Future*. Athens: Doxiadis Associates.

Doxiadis, Constantin A. 1963. *Architecture in Transition*. New York: Oxford University Press.

Doxiadis, Constantin A. 1968. *Ekistics: An Introduction to the Science of Human Settlements*. New York: Oxford University Press.

Drakakis-Smith, David. 1987. *Third World Cities*. New York: Routledge.

Dubey, V. P., H. L. Kalia, Bindu Duggal, Ravinder Kaur, and Rarjay Vardhan. 2002. Socio-economic profile of slum dwellers in Chandigarh. In *Celebrating Chandigarh*, ed. Jaspreet Takhar, 436–452. Chandigarh, India: Chandigarh Perspectives.

Dumont, Louis. 1970. *Homo Hierarchicus: An Essay on the Caste System*. Chicago: University of Chicago Press.

Dumont, Louis, and David Pocock. 1958. Commented summary of the first part of Bouglé's *Essais*. *Contributions to Indian Sociology* 2:31–44.

Duncan, James S., and Nancy G. Duncan. 2004. Culture unbound. *Environment and Planning A: Economy and Space* 36 (3): 391–403.

Dunn, R. E. 1986. *The Adventures of Ibn Battuta: A Muslim Traveler of the 14th Century*. Berkeley: University of California Press.

Durkheim, Emile. 1933. *The Division of Labor in Society*. New York: The Free Press.

Dutt, Binode Behari. 1977. *Town Planning in Ancient India*. Delhi: New Asian Publishers.

Dutta, Krishna. 2003. *Calcutta: A Cultural and Literary History*. Oxford, UK: Signal Books.

Dyckman, John W. 1962. The European motherland of American urban romanticism. *Journal of the American Institute of Planners* 28 (4): 277–281.

Eck, Diana. L. 1982. *Banaras: City of Light*. New York: Alfred A. Knopf.

Eck, Diana L. 1987. The city as a sacred center. In *The City as a Sacred Center: Essays on Six Asian Contexts*, ed. Bardwell Smith and Holly Baker Reynolds, 1–11. Leiden, Netherlands: E. J. Brill.

Eco, Umberto. 1986. *Travels in Hyperreality: Essays*. San Diego, CA: Harcourt Brace Jovanovich.

Ehrlich, Paul R., and Anne H. Ehrlich. 2009. The population bomb revisited. *Electronic Journal of Sustainable Development* 1 (3): 63–71.

Eickelman, Dale F. 1974. Is there an Islamic city? The making of a quarter in a Moroccan town. *International Journal of Middle Eastern Studies* 5:274–294.

Eickelman, Dale F. 1989. *The Middle East: An Anthropological Approach.* Englewood Cliffs, NJ: Prentice-Hall.

Eisner, Simon, Arthur Gallion, and Stanley Eisner. 1993. *The Urban Pattern.* New York: John Wiley.

Eliade, Mircea. 1954. *The Myth of the Eternal Return.* New York: Pantheon Books.

Eliade, Mircea. 1987. *The Sacred and the Profane: The Nature of Religion.* San Diego, CA: Harcourt Brace Jovanovich.

El-Shakhs, Salah. 1972. Development, primacy, and systems of cities. *Journal of Developing Areas* 7 (1): 11–36.

El-Shakhs, Salah. 1997. Globalization and African cities. *Interplan (Publication of the APA International Division* 57 (September): 1, 6–7.

Embree, Ainslie T., ed. 1971. *Alberuni's India.* Translated by Edward C. Sachau. New York: W. W. Norton.

Engels, Friedrich. 1958. *The Condition of the Working Class in England.* Oxford: Blackwell.

Ensminger, Douglas. 1972. Why did the Foundation accept and respond to Dr. B.C.Roy's invitation to assist in the development of a Long Range Plan for the Greater Calcutta Area? [Ensminger oral history, B4] Unpublished holding of the Ford Foundation archives, New York.

Epstein, David G. 1973. *Brasília, Plan and Reality: A Study of Planned and Spontaneous Urban Development.* Berkeley: University of California Press.

Escobar, Arturo. 1995. *Encountering Development: The Making and Unmaking of the Third World.* Princeton, NJ: Princeton University Press.

Espejo, L. Arturo. 1984. *Rationalité et forms d'occupation de l'espace: Le projet de Brasilia.* Paris: Anthropos.

Evenson, Norma. 1966. *Chandigarh.* Berkeley: University of California Press.

Evenson, Norma. 1969. *Le Corbusier: The Machine and the Grand Design.* New York: George Braziller.

Evenson, Norma. 1973. *Two Brazilian Capitals: Architecture and Urbanism in Rio de Janeiro and Brasília.* New Haven, CT: Yale University Press.

Evenson, Norma. 1989. *The Indian Metropolis: A View toward the West.* New Haven, CT: Yale University Press.

Ezzati, Majid, Burton H. Singer, and Daniel M. Kammen. 2001. Toward an integrated framework for development and environmental policy: Environmental Kuznets curves. *World Development* 29 (8): 1421–1434.

Fainstein, Susan. 2010. *Just City*. Ithaca, NY: Cornell University Press.

Fallows, James. 1988. Shanghai surprise. *Atlantic Monthly*, July 1988, 76–78.

Fallows, James. 2007. Macau's big gamble. *Atlantic*, September 2007, 96–105.

Fanon, Frantz. 1963. *The Wretched of the Earth*. New York: The Grove Press.

Fathy, Hassan. 1976. *Architecture for the Poor: An Experiment in Rural Egypt*. Chicago: University of Chicago Press.

Fes-el-Bali. 2020. https://en.wikipedia.org/wiki/Fes_el_Bali

Firey, Walter I. 1947. *Land Use in Central Boston*. Cambridge, MA: Harvard University Press.

Fisher, Claude S. 1981. The public and private worlds of city life. *American Sociological Review* 46:306–316.

Fishman, Robert. 1977. *Urban Utopias in the Twentieth Century: Ebenezer Howard, Frank Lloyd Wright, and Le Corbusier*. New York: Basic Books.

Forde, Daryll. 1954. *African Worlds: Studies in the Cosmological Ideas and Social Values of African Peoples*. London: Oxford University Press

Foucault, Michel. 1995. *Discipline and Punish: The Birth of the Prison*. New York: Vintage Books.

Frank, Andre Gunder. 1966. The development of underdevelopment. *Monthly Review* 18 (4): 17–31.

Frank, Andre Gunder. 1967. *Capitalism and Underdevelopment in Latin America: Historical Studies in Chile and Brazil*. New York: Monthly Review Press.

Frank, Andre Gunder. 1998. *ReORIENT: Global Economy in the Asian Age*. Berkeley: University of California Press.

Frankfort, Henri. 1948. *Ancient Egyptian Religion: An Interpretation*. New York: Columbia University Press.

Fraser, Nancy. 1990. Rethinking the public sphere: A contribution to the critique of actually existing democracy. *Social Text* 25/26:56–80.

Friedberg, Anne. 1993. *Window Shopping: Cinema and the Postmodern*. Berkeley: University of California Press.

Friedman, Thomas L. 2000. *The Lexus and the Olive Tree*. New York: Anchor Books.

Friedman, Thomas L. 2006. *The World Is Flat: A Brief History of the Twenty-First Century*. New York: Farrar, Straus and Giroux.

Friedmann, John. 1969. The role of cities in national development. *American Behavioral Scientist* 12 (5): 13–21.

Friedmann, John. 2005. *China's Urban Transition*. Minneapolis: University of Minnesota Press.

Fukuyama, Francis. 1989. The End of History? *National Interest* 16 (Summer): 3–18.

Fuller, Mia. 2000. Preservation and self-absorption: Italian colonization and the walled city of Tripoli, Libya. *Journal of North African Studies* 5 (4): 121–154.

Funk & Wagnalls. 1963. Subaltern. In *Funk & Wagnalls New Practical Standard Dictionary of the English Language*. New York: Funk & Wagnalls.

Galdieri, Eugenio. 1979. *Espahan, Ali Qapu: An Architectural Survey*. Rome: Istituto Italiane Per II Medio Ed. Estreme Oriente.

Gallup, John L., and Jeffrey D. Sachs. 2000. The economic burden of malaria. CID Working Paper No. 52. Cambridge, MA: Harvard University.

Garreau, Joel. 1992. *Edge City: Life on the New Frontier*. New York: Anchor Books.

Garvan, Anthony. 1967. Proprietory Philadelphia as artifact. In *The Historian and the City*, ed. O. Handlin and J. Burchard, 177–201. Cambridge, MA: MIT Press.

Gaubatz, Piper. 2005. Globalization and the development of new central business districts in Beijing, Shanghai and Guangzhou. In *Restructuring the Chinese City: Changing Society, Economy and Space*, ed. Laurence J. C. Ma and Fulong Wu, 98–121. London: Routledge.

Gaube, Heinz. 1979. *Iranian Cities*. New York: New York University Press.

Gaulton, Richard. 1981. Political mobilization in Shanghai 1949–1951. In *Shanghai: Revolution and Development in an Asian Metropolis*, ed. Christopher Howe, 35–65. Cambridge: Cambridge University Press.

Geertz, Clifford. 1963. *Peddlers and Princes: Social Change and Economic Modernization in Two Indonesian Towns*. Chicago: University of Chicago Press.

Geertz, Clifford. 1989. *Toutes directions*: Reading the signs in an urban sprawl. *International Journal of Middle Eastern Studies* 21 (3): 291–306.

Geist, Johann F. *Arcades: The History of a Building Type*. Cambridge, MA: MIT Press.

Germino, Dante. 1986. Antonio Gramsci: From the margins to the center, the journey of a hunchback. *boundary 2* 14 (3): 19–30.

Gernet, Jacques. 1962. *Daily Life in China on the Eve of the Mongol Invasion*. Stanford, CA: Stanford University Press.

Ghertner, D. Asher. 2019. Improvised urbanism in the design of India's unauthorized colonies. In *The New Companion to Urban Design*, ed. Tridib Banerjee and Anastasia Loukaitou-Sideris, 355–367. New York: Routledge.

Ghosh, Bijit. 1968. Delhi 1981 AD—Promises for a better city. *Shakti* 5 (2): 19–26.

Gilbert, Alan, and Josef Gugler. 1982. *Cities, Poverty, and Development: Urbanization in the Third World*. London: Oxford University Press.

Gilbert, Sarah. 2017. Fez medina gets new riads, restaurants, and restored monuments. *Guardian*, July 25, 2017.

Goldsmith, William W. 1974. The ghetto as a resource for Black America. *Journal of the American Institute of Planners* 40:17–30.

Goodfriend, Douglas E. 1978. *The Delhi Master Plan of 1962: An Anthropological Analysis.* New York: The Ford Foundation Archive.

Goodman, Percival, and Paul Goodman. 1947. *Communitas: Means of Livelihood and Ways of Life.* Chicago: University of Chicago Press.

Goonewardena, Kanishka. 2005. The urban sensorium: Space, ideology and the anesthetization of politics. *Antipode* 37 (1): 46–71.

Gottdeiner, Mark. 1985. *The Social Production of Urban Space.* Austin: University of Texas Press.

Gouda, Frances. 1995. *Dutch Culture Overseas: Colonial Practice in the Netherlands Indies: 1900–1942.* Amsterdam: Amsterdam University Press.

Gownamani, D., U. Manimekaiai, V. K. Kumra, and N. Sivagnanan. 2003. Distributional patterns of slums and its environs: A case of Chennai metropolitan city. *National Geographical Journal of India* 49 (4): 59–72.

Grabar, Oleg. 1983. Reflections on the study of Islamic art. *Muqarnas* 1:1–14.

Graham, Stephen, and Simon Marvin. 2001. *Splintering Urbanism: Networked Infrastructures, Technological Mobilities, and the Urban Condition.* London: Routledge.

Grass, Günter. 1989. *Show Your Tongue.* San Diego, CA: Harcourt Brace Jovanovich.

Gresleri, Giuliano. 1993. Mogadiscio e "paese dei Somali": una identita negate. In *Architettura Italiana d'Oltremare 1870–1940*, ed. Giuliano Gresleri, Pier Giorgio Masaretti, and Stefano Zagnoni, 203–214. Venzia: Marsilio.

Grossman, Gene, and Alan B. Krueger. 1991. *Environmental Impacts of a North American Free Trade Agreement.* Princeton, NJ: Princeton University.

Guha, Ranajit. 1997. *A Subaltern Studies Reader 1986–1995.* Minneapolis: University of Minnesota Press.

Gulick, John. 1963. Images of the Arab city. *Journal of the American Institute of Planners* 29 (3): 179–198.

Gunder, Michael. 2011. Commentary: Is urban design still urban planning? An exploration and response. *Journal of Planning Education and Research* 31 (2): 184–195.

Gunnell, John G. 1983. Review of *All That Is Solid Melts into Air*, by Marshall Berman. *Political Theory* 11 (3): 455–459.

Gutkind, Erwin Anton. 1964. *International History of City Development,* Volume I: *Urban Development in Central Europe.* London: The Free Press of Glencoe, Collier-Macmillan Limited.

Hakim, Besim S. 1986. *Arabic-Islamic Cities: Building and Planning Principles.* London: Kegan Paul International.

Hakim, Besim S. 1998. Urban form in traditional Islamic cultures: Further studies needed for formulating theory. *Cities* 16 (1): 51–55.

Halbwachs, Maurice. 1980. *The Collective Memory*. New York: Harper and Row.

Hall, Edward T. 1966. *The Hidden Dimension*. Garden City, NY: Doubleday.

Han, Sun Sheng. 2000. Shanghai between state and market in urban transformation. *Urban Studies* 37 (11): 2091–2112.

Handlin, Oscar, and John E. Burchard, eds. 1967. *The Historian and the City*. Cambridge, MA: MIT Press.

Harbaugh, William, Arik Levinson, and David M. Wilson. 2002. Reexamining the empirical evidence for an environmental Kuznets curve. *Review of Economics and Statistics* 84 (3): 541–551.

Hardoy, Jorge E. 1975. *Urbanization in Latin America: Approaches and Issues*. Garden City, NY: Anchor Press/Doubleday.

Harris, Chauncy, and Edward Ullman. 1945. The nature of cities. *The Annals of the American Academy of Political and Social Science* 242:7–17.

Harvey, David. 1985. *The Urbanization of Capital: Studies in History and Theory of Capitalist Urbanization*. Baltimore: John Hopkins University Press.

Harvey, David. 1988. Urban places in the global village: Reflections on the urban condition in late twentieth century capitalism. In *World Cities and the Future of the Metropolis*, ed. Luigi Mazza and Georges Teyssot, 21–32. Milan: Electa.

Harvey, David. 2006. *Spaces of Global Capitalism: Toward a Theory of Uneven Geographical Development*. New York: Verso.

Hay, Richard J. 1977. Patterns of urbanization and socio-economic development in the third world: An overview. In *Third World Urbanization*, ed. Janet Abu-Lughod and Richard Hay Jr., 71–98. New York: Routledge.

Hayden, Dolores. 1984. *Redesigning the American Dream: The Future of Housing, Work, and Family Life*. New York: W. W. Norton.

He, Wei. 2019. GDP of Shangai's Pudong likely to have reached 1 trillion yuan. *China Daily*, updated January 2, 2019.

Hegemann, Werner, and Elbert Peets. 1988. *American Vitruvius: An Architects' Handbook of Civic Art*. Princeton, NJ: Princeton Architectural Press.

Heikkila, Eric. 2011. Beijing: Lost in translation? *Journal of Architecture and Planning Research* 28 (1): 76–90.

Heilbroner, Robert L. 1985. *The Nature and Logic of Capitalism*. New York: W. W. Norton.

Henderson, J. Vernon, Zmarak Shalizi, and Anthony J. Venables. 2001. Geography and development. *Journal of Economic Geography* 1 (1): 81–105.

Hernstein, Richard, and Charles Murray. 1994. *The Bell Curve: Intelligence and Class Structure in American Life*. New York: Free Press.

Higgins, Benjamin, and Nguyen Tri Dung. 1979. *Dualism, Dependency, and Continuing Underdevelopment: Experience in Indian Ocean Countries*. Nagoya, Japan: United Nations Centre for Regional Development.

Highmore, Ben. 2005. *Cityscapes: Cultural Readings in the Material and Symbolic City*. London: Palgrave.

Hillier, Bill, and Julienne Hanson. 1989. *The Social Logic of Space*. Cambridge: Cambridge University Press.

Hirschman, Albert O. 1977. *The Passions and the Interests: Political Arguments for Capitalism before Its Triumph*. Princeton, NJ: Princeton University Press.

Hirschman, Albert O. 1982. Rival interpretations of market society: Civilizing, destructive or feeble? *Journal of Economic Literature* 22:1463–1484.

Hirschman, Albert O. 1986. *Rival Views of Market Society and Other Recent Essays*. New York: Viking.

Hirschman, Albert O. 1988. *The Strategy of Economic Development*. Boulder, CO: Westview Press.

Hiss, Tony. 1990. *The Experience of Place*. New York: Knopf.

Hodgson, Marshall G. S. 1964. *Histoire de la philosophie islamique*. Paris: Gallimard.

Hodgson, Marshall G. S. 1970. The role of Islam in world history. *International Journal of Middle East Studies* 1 (2): 99–123.

Holston, James. 1989. *The Modernist City: An Anthropological Critique of Brasília*. Chicago: University of Chicago Press.

Horowitz, Irving L. 1982. The new fundamentalism. *Society* 20:40–47.

Hosagrahar, Jyoti. 1992. City as Durbar: Theater and power in imperial Delhi. In *Forms of Dominance: On the Architecture and Urbanism of the Colonial Enterprise*, ed. Nezar AlSayyad, 83–105. Aldershot, UK: Avebury.

Hosagrahar, Jyoti. 2005. *Indigenous Modernities: Negotiating Architecture and Urbanism*. London: Routledge.

Hourani, Albert H. 1970. Introduction: The Islamic city in the light of recent research. In *The Islamic City*, ed. A. H. Hourani and S. M. Stern, 9–24. Glasgow: Bruno Cassirer.

Hourani, Albert H., and S. M. Stern, eds. 1970. *The Islamic City*. Glasgow: Bruno Cassirer.

Howard, Ebenezer. 1946. *Garden Cities of Tomorrow*. London: Faber and Faber.

Hoyt, Homer. 1939. *The Structure and Growth of Residential Neighborhoods in American Cities*. Washington, DC: Federal Housing Administration.

Huang, Tsung-Yi. 2000. Hong Kong blue: *Flâneurie* with the camera's eye in a phantasmagoric global city. *Journal of Narrative Theory* 30 (3): 385–402.

Huang, Tsung-Yi. 2004. *Walking between Slums and Skyscrapers: Illusions of Open Space in Hong Kong, Tokyo, and Shanghai.* Hong Kong: Hong Kong University Press.

Huxtable, Ada L. 1997. *The Unreal America: Architecture and Illusion.* New York: New Press.

ILO (International Labor Organization). 1972. *Employment, Incomes, and Equality: A Strategy for Increasing Productive Employment in Kenya.* Geneva: International Labor Organization.

Inkeles, Alex, and David H. Smith. 1974. *On Becoming Modern: Individual Changes in Six Developing Countries.* Cambridge, MA: Harvard University Press.

Innes, Judith E., and David E. Booher. 1999. Consensus building as role playing and bricolage: Toward a theory of collaborative planning. *Journal of the American Planning Association* 65 (1): 9–26.

Irazábal, Clara. 2008. *Ordinary Places, Extraordinary Events: Citizenship, Democracy, and Public Space in Latin America.* New York: Routledge.

Irving, Robert G. 1981. *Indian Summer: Lutyens, Baker, and Imperial Delhi.* New Haven, CT: Yale University Press.

Issawi, Charles. 1958. *An Arab Philosophy of History: Selections from the Prolegomena of Ibn Khaldun of Tunis (1332–1406).* New York: Grove Press.

Jackson, John B. 1984. *Discovering the Vernacular Landscape.* New Haven, CT: Yale University Press.

Jackson, Kenneth T. 1984. *Crabgrass Frontiers: The Suburbanization of the United States.* New York: Oxford University Press.

Jackson, Richard J., and Rebecca Ferdman. 2019. Refocusing planning and design to maximize public health benefits. In *New Companion to Urban Design*, ed. Tridib Banerjee and Anastasia Loukaitou-Sideris, 425–435. London: Routledge.

Jacobs, Jane. 1961. *The Death and Life of Great American Cities.* New York: Vintage Publishers.

Jain, Kulbhushan, and Minakshi Jain. 1994. *Indian City in the Arid West.* Ahmedabad, India: AADI Center.

Jain-Chandra, Sonali. 2018. Chart of the week: Inequality in China. *IMF Blog*, September 2018. https://blogs.imf.org/2018/09/20/chart-of-the-week-inequality-in-china/

Jameson, Fredric. 1991. *Postmodernism; or, The Cultural Logic of Late Capitalism.* Durham, NC: Duke University Press.

Jencks, Charles. 1973. *Le Corbusier and the Tragic View of Architecture.* Cambridge, MA: Harvard University Press.

Jha, Raghbendra, and K. V. Bhanu Murthy. 2003. A critique of the Environmental Sustainability Index. Australian National University Division of Economics Working Paper. https://ssrn.com/abstract=380160

Joffé, Ronald, Mark Medoff, and Jake Eberts. 1992. *City of Joy: The Illustrated Story of the Film.* New York: Newmarket Press.

Jonas, Andrew E. G., and David Wilson. 1996. *The Urban Growth Machine: Critical Perspectives Two Decades Later*. New York: SUNY Press.

Jones, Barclay G. 1962. Design from knowledge not belief. *AIA Journal* 38 (6): 104–105.

Jones, Barclay G., Blane D. Lewis, and Jeffrey W. Cody. 1987. Chinese cities among the largest world agglomerations: An historical analysis. Paper presented at a conference on planning for human settlements: China and the United States. Tongji University, Shanghai.

Jones, Barclay G., with assistance from William A. Kandel. 1992. Population growth, urbanization and disaster risk and vulnerability in metropolitan areas: A conceptual framework. *Environmental Management and Urban Vulnerability*. World Bank Discussion Paper #168, pp. 51–76. Washington, DC: The World Bank.

Joyce, Patrick. 2003. *The Rule of Freedom: Liberalism and the Modern City*. New York: Verso.

Kalia, Ravi. 1999. *Chandigarh*. New Delhi: Oxford University Press.

Karan, P. P., W. A. Bladen, and G. Singh. 1980. Slum dwellers' and squatters' images of the city. *Environment and Behavior* 12 (1): 81–100.

Kathirithamby-Wells, Jeyamalar. 1986. The Islamic city: Melaka to Jogjakarta, c. 1500–1800. *Modern Asian Studies* 20 (2): 333–351.

Kayden, Jerold S. 2000. *Privately Owned Public Spaces: The New York City Experience*. New York: John Wiley.

Khaldun, Ibn. 1958. *The Muqaddimah: An Introduction to History*. 3 vols. Translated by Franz Rosenthal. New York: Pantheon Books.

Khanna, Madhu. 1979. *Yantra: The Tantric Symbol of Cosmic Unity*. London: Thames and Hudson.

Kheirabadi, Masoud. 1991. *Iranian Cities: Formation and Development*. Austin: University of Texas Press.

Khilnani, Sunil. 1997. India's theaters of independence. *Wilson Quarterly* 21 (4): 16–45.

Khilnani, Sunil. 1998. *The Idea of India*. New York: Farrar, Straus and Giroux.

Kim, Annette. 2016. The extreme primacy of location: Beijing's underground rental housing market. *Cities* 52 (March): 148–158.

King, Anthony D. 1976. *Colonial Urban Development: Culture, Social Power, and Environment*. London: Routledge and Kegan Paul.

King, Anthony D. 1984. *The Bungalow: The Production of a Global Culture*. New York: Oxford University Press.

King, Anthony D. 2004. *Spaces of Global Cultures: Architecture, Urbanism, Identity*. New York: Routledge.

King, David A. 1985. The sacred direction in Islam: A study of the interaction of religion and science in the Middle Ages. *Interdisciplinary Science Reviews* 10 (4): 315–326.

King, David A. 1997. Two Iranian world maps for finding the direction and distance to Mecca. *Image Mundi* 49:62–82.

Kinsbruner, Jay. 2005. *The Colonial Spanish-American City: Urban Life in the Age of Atlantic Capitalism*. Austin: University of Texas Press.

Kohn, Margaret. 2004. *Brave New Neighborhoods: The Privatization of Public Space*. New York: Routledge.

Koning, Hans. 1995. A French mirror. *Atlantic Monthly*, December 1995, 95–106.

Kostof, Spiro. 1991. *The City Shaped: Urban Patterns and Meanings through History*. Boston: Little, Brown.

Krieger, Martin H. 1973. What's wrong with plastic trees? *Science* 179 (4072): 446–455.

Krieger, Martin H. 1987. The possibility of doom. *Technology in Society* 9 (2): 181–190.

Krier, Rob. 1979. *Urban Space: Stadtraum*. New York: Rizzoli International Publications.

Kristeva, Julia. 1982. *Powers of Horror: An Essay of Abjection*. New York: Columbia University Press.

Kubler, George. 1978. Open-grid town plans in Europe and America. In *Urbanization in Americas from Its Beginnings to the Present*, ed. Richard P. Schaedel, Jorge E. Hardoy, and Nora Scott Kinzer, 327–342. Paris: Mouton Publishers.

Kunstler, James H. 1993. *The Geography of Nowhere: The Rise and Decline of America's Manmade Landscape*. New York: Simon and Schuster.

Kunzmann, Klaus R. 2004. Venice, Venice, and Venice: Three realities of the European cities. In *The Real and Virtual Worlds of Spatial Planning*, ed. Martina Koll-Schretzenmayr, Marco Keiner, and Gustav Nussbaumer, 31–41. Berlin: Springer.

Kuran, Timur. 2001. The provision of public goods under Islamic law: Origins, impact and limitations of the Waqf system. *Law & Society Review* 35 (4): 841–898.

Kusno, Abidin. 2000. *Behind the Postcolonial: Architecture, Urban Space, and Political Cultures in Indonesia*. London and New York: Routledge.

Kuznets, Simon. 1955. Economic growth and income inequality. *The American Economic Review* 45 (1): 1–28.

Kuznets, Simon. 1966. *Modern Economic Growth: Rate, Structure, and Spread*. New Haven, CT: Yale University Press.

La Casinière, H. de. 1924. *Les Municipalités Marocaines, leur Développement-leur Législation*. Morocco: Impr. De la Vigie marocaine.

Lal, Deepak. 2000. *The Poverty of "Development Economics."* Cambridge, MA: MIT Press.

Landes, David S. 1969. *The Unbound Prometheus: Technological Change and Industrial Development in Western Europe from 1750 to the Present*. London: Cambridge University Press.

Landsberg, Mitchell. 2007. Beijing accused of unfair play. *Los Angeles Times*, August 7. Los Angeles: A5.

Langer, Peter. 1984. Sociology–Four images of organized diversity. In *Cities of the Mind—Images and Themes of the City in the Social Sciences*, ed. Lloyd Rodwin and Robert M. Hollister, 97–117. New York: Springer.

Lansing, Stephen. 1991. *Priests and Programmers: Technologies of Power in the Engineered Landscape of Bali*. Princeton, NJ: Princeton University Press.

Lapidus, Ira M. 1967. *Muslim Cities in the Later Middle Ages*. Cambridge, MA: Harvard University Press.

Lapidus, Ira M. 1996. State and religion in Islamic societies. *Past and Present* 151:3–27.

Lapierre, Dominique. 1985. *The City of Joy*. New York: Doubleday.

Lapierre, Dominique, and Javier Moro. 2002. *Five Past Midnight in Bhopal*. New York: Warner Books.

Lefebvre, Henri. 1968. *Le droit à la ville,* 1996 (English translation as *The Right to the City*). Paris: Anthropos.

Lefebvre, Henri. 1991. *The Production of Space*. Malden, MA: Blackwell.

Lefebvre, Henri. 1993. *Elements Rhythm Analysis: Introduction to the Knowledge of Rhythm*. Paris: Syllepse.

Lefebvre, Henri. 2003. *The Urban Revolution*. Minneapolis: University of Minnesota Press.

Le Tourneau, Roger. 1961. *Fez in the Age of the Merinides*. Norman: University of Oklahoma Press.

Levine, Philippa. 1994. Venereal disease, prostitution and the politics of empire: The case of British India. *Journal of the History of Sexuality* 4:579–602.

Lévi-Strauss, Claude. 1962. *The Savage Mind*. Chicago: University of Chicago Press.

Lewis, F., and Tridib Banerjee. 2005. Development as freedom and good city form. 46th Annual Conference and the Association of Collegiate Schools of Planning (ACSP). Kansas City, Missouri.

Lewis, Oscar. 1961. *Children of Sanchez: Autobiography of a Mexican family*. New York: Random House.

Lewis, Oscar. 1966a. The culture of poverty. *Scientific American* 215 (4): 19–25.

Lewis, Oscar. 1966b. *La Vida: A Puerto Rican Family in the Culture of Poverty—San Juan and New York*. New York: Random House.

Lewis, W. Arthur. 1976. Development and distribution. In *Employment, Income, Distribution and Development Strategy: Problems of the Developing Countries; Essays in Honour of H. W. Singer*, ed. Anthony Bottomley, Alec Cairncross, and Mohinder Puri, 75–96. New York: Holmes and Maier Publishers.

Lindblom, Charles E. 1977. *Politics and Markets: The World's Political Economic Systems.* New York: Basic Books.

Lipton, Michael. 1988. *Why Poor People Stay Poor: Urban Bias in World Development.* London: Temple-Smith.

Lomnitz, Larissa A. 1977. *Networks and Marginality: Life in a Mexican Shantytown.* New York: Academic Press.

Longhofer, Wesley, and Daniel Winchester, eds. 2016. Pierre Bourdieu. In *Social Theory Re-wired.* 2nd ed. New York: Routledge. http://routledgesoc.com/profile/pierre-bourdieu

Lopez, Robert. 1963. The crossroads within the wall. In *The Historian and the City,* ed. Oscar Handin and John E. Burchard, 17–43. Cambridge, MA: MIT Press.

Loukaitou-Sideris, Anastasia, and Tridib Banerjee. 1998. *Urban Design Downtown: Poetics and Politics of Form.* Berkeley: University of California Press.

Low, Setha M. 2000. *On the Plaza: The Politics of Public Space and Culture.* Austin: University of Texas Press.

Lowi, Theodore J. 1969. *The End of Liberalism: Ideology, Policy, and the Crisis of Public Authority.* New York: W. W. Norton.

Lu, Hanchao. 1999. Becoming urban: Mendicancy and vagrants in modern Shanghai. *Journal of Social History* 33 (1): 7–36.

Lynch, Kevin. 1960. *The Image of the City.* Cambridge, MA: MIT Press.

Lynch, Kevin. 1961. The pattern of the metropolis. *Daedalus* 90 (1): 79–98.

Lynch, Kevin. 1974. *What Time Is This Place?* Cambridge, MA: MIT Press.

Lynch, Kevin. 1976. *Managing the Sense of the Region.* Cambridge, MA: MIT Press.

Lynch, Kevin. 1977. *Growing Up in Cities.* Cambridge, MA: MIT Press.

Lynch, Kevin. 1981. *A Theory of Good City Form.* Cambridge, MA: MIT Press.

Lynch, Kevin. 1984. Reconsidering *The Image of the City.* In *Cities of the Mind,* ed. Lloyd Rodwin and Robert Hollister, 151–161. New York: Plenum.

Lynch, Kevin. 1990a. Openness of the open space. In *City Sense and City Design: Writings and Projects of Kevin Lynch,* ed. Tridib Banerjee and Michael Southworth, 396–412. Cambridge, MA: MIT Press.

Lynch, Kevin. 1990b. *Wasting Away.* San Francisco: Sierra Club Books.

Lynch, Kevin, and Lloyd Rodwin. 1958. A theory of urban form. *Journal of the American Institute of Planners* 24 (4): 201–214.

Mabin, Alan. 2005. Suburbanisation, segregation, and government of territorial transformations. *Transformation: Critical Perspectives on Southern Africa* 57 (1): 41–63.

Madanipour, Ali. 1998. *Tehran: The Making of a Metropolis.* New York: John Wiley & Sons.

Mahfouz, Naguib. 1956–1957. *The Cairo Trilogy: Palace Work; Palace of Desire; and Sugar Street.* Cairo: American University of Cairo Press.

Majumdar, Ramesh C. 1960. *The Classical Accounts of India.* Calcutta: Firma K. L. Mukhopadhyay.

Malinowski, Bronislaw. 1945. *The Dynamics of Culture Change.* New Haven, CT: Yale University Press.

Mall of the Emirates, Dubai, UAE. https://en.wikipedia.org/wiki/Mall_of_the_Emirates

Maloney, Clarence. 1970. The beginnings of civilization in South India. *Journal of Asian Studies* 29 (3): 603–616.

Mangin, William. 1970. *Peasants in Cities: Readings in the Anthropology of Urbanization.* Boston: Houghton Mifflin.

Marçais, Georges A. 1957a. *Algérie médiévale, monuments et paysages historiques.* Paris: Arts et Métiers Graphiques.

Marçais, Georges A. 1957b. *Architecture Musulmane.* Rome: Istituto per l'oriente.

Marçais, William. 1928. L'islamisme et la vie urbaine. *Comptes-rendus des séances de l année—Académie des inscriptions et Belles-Lettres* 72 (1): 86–100.

Markman, Sidney D. 1978. The Gridiron Town Plan and the caste system in colonial Central America. In *Urbanization in the Americas from Its Beginnings to the Present*, ed. Richard P. Schaedel, Jorge E. Hardoy, and Nora S. Kinzer, 471–489. Paris: Mouton Publishers.

Marris, Peter. 1974. *Loss and Change.* New York: Pantheon Books.

Maslow, Abraham. 1954. *Motivation and Personality.* New York: Harper.

Maurios, Georges. 2002. Corbusier's architecture—Values and symbolism. In *Celebrating Chandigarh*, ed. Jaspreet Takhar, 121–126. Chandigarh, India: Chandigarh Perspectives.

Mazmanian, Daniel A., and Michael E. Kraft, eds. 2009. *Toward Sustainable Communities: Transition and Transformations in Environmental Policy.* 2nd ed. Cambridge, MA: MIT Press.

Mazrui, Ali. A. 1986. *The Africans: A Triple Heritage.* Boston: Little, Brown.

McGee, T. G. 1977. Rural-urban mobility in South and Southeast Asia: Different formulations ... different answers? In *Third World Urbanization*, ed. Janet Abu-Lughod and Richard Hay Jr., 196–212. New York: Methuen.

McHarg, Ian. 1969. *Design with Nature.* Garden City, NJ: Natural History Press.

McRobbie, Angela. 1984. Review of *All That Is Solid Melts into Air*, by Marshall Berman. *Feminist Review* 18:129–133.

Meadows, Donella H., Dennis L. Meadows, Jorgen Randers, and William W. Behrens. 1974. *The Limits to Growth: A Report for the Club of Rome's Project on the Predicament of Mankind.* New York: Universe Books.

Meadows, Donella H., Jorgen Randers, and Dennis L. Meadows. 2004. *Limits to Growth: The 30-Year Update.* London: Earthscan.

Mehta, Suketu. 2004. *Maximum City: Bombay Lost and Found.* New York: Vintage.

Meier, Richard. 1962. *A Communications Theory of Urban Growth.* Cambridge, MA: MIT Press.

Meinig, Donald. 1979. *The Interpretation of Ordinary Landscapes: Geographical Essays.* New York: Oxford University Press.

Meirelles, Fernando, director. 2002. *Cidade de Deus* [Film]. O2 Filmes; VideoFilmes.

Mellinger, Andrew D., Jeffrey D. Sachs, and John L. Gallup. 1999. Climate, water navigability, and economic development. CID Working Paper No. 24. Cambridge, MA: Harvard University.

Mernissi, Fatima. 1987. *Beyond the Veil: Male-Female Dynamics in Modern Muslim Society.* Bloomington: Indiana University Press.

Metcalf, Thomas R. 1994. *Ideologies of the Raj.* Cambridge: Cambridge University Press.

Meyer, Jeffrey F. 1987. Traditional Peking: The architecture of conditional power. In *The City as a Sacred Center,* ed. Bardwell Smith and Holly Baker Reynolds, 114–133. Leiden, Netherlands: E. J. Brill.

Michelson, William. 1970. *Man and His Urban Environment: A Sociological Approach.* Reading, MA: Addison-Wesley Publishing.

Milgram, Stanley. 1970. The experience of living in cities. *Science* 167 (3924): 1461–1468.

Millimet, Daniel L., John A. List, and Thanasis Stengos. 2003. The Environmental Kuznets curve: Real progress or misspecified models? *Review of Economics and Statistics* 85 (4): 1038–1047.

Mitchell, William J. 1995. *City of Bits.* Cambridge, MA: MIT Press.

Mokyr, Joel. 1990. *The Lever of Riches: Technological Creativity and Economic Progress.* New York: Oxford University Press.

Moller, Daragh. 2004. On the streets where you live. *Beijing This Month.*

Molotch, Harvey. 1976. The city as a growth machine. *American Journal of Sociology* 82:309–332.

Morris, A. E. J. 1972. *History of Urban Form: Prehistory to the Renaissance.* New York: John Wiley & Sons.

Morris, Jan. 1985. *Hong Kong.* New York: Vintage.

Morse, Richard M. 1974. Brazil's urban development: Colony and empire. *Journal of Urban History* 1 (1): 39–72.

Morse, Richard M. 1978. Cities and society in nineteenth-century Latin America: The illustrative case of Brazil. In *Urbanization in the Americas from Its Beginnings to the Present*, ed. R. P. Schaedel, Jorge E. Hardoy, and Nora Scott Kinzer, 283–302. Paris: Mouton Publishers.

Morton, Patricia A. 2000. *Hybrid Modernities: Architecture and Representation at the 1931 Colonial Exposition, Paris*. Cambridge, MA: MIT Press.

Mostafavi, Mohsen. 2010. Why ecological urbanism? Why now? *Harvard Design Magazine* 32 (Spring/Summer): 124–135.

Moudon, Anne Vernez. 1995. Teaching urban form. *Journal of Planning Education and Research* 14 (2): 123–133.

Moudon, Anne Vernez. 1997. Urban morphology as an emerging interdisciplinary field. *Urban Morphology* 1:3–10.

Moustafa, Amer A. 2005. Understanding Dubai: Creative dynamics of a city vying a global stature. American University of Sharjah, UAE.

Mukhija, Vinit. 2003. *Squatters as Developers? Slum Redevelopment in Mumbai*. Burlington, VT: Ashgate.

Mumford, Lewis. 1938. *The Culture of Cities*. New York: Harcourt Brace.

Mumford, Lewis. 1947. Introduction. In *Patrick Geddes in India*, ed. Jaqueline Tyrwhitt, 7–13. London: Lund Humphries.

Mumford, Lewis. 1961. *The City in History: Its Origins, Its Transformations, and Its Prospects*. New York: Harcourt, Brace & World.

Murphey, Rhodes. 1980. *The Fading of the Maoist Vision: City and Country in China's Development*. New York: Methuen.

Murray, Charles, and Richard J. Herrnstein. 1994. *The Bell Curve: Intelligence and Class Structure in American Life*. New York: Free Press.

Myint, H. 1980. *The Economics of Developing Countries*. London: Hutchinson.

Naipaul, V. S. 1964. *An Area of Darkness*. New York: Vintage Books.

Naipaul, V. S. 1981. *Among the Believers: An Islamic Journey*. New York: Knopf.

Naipaul, V. S. 1990. *India: A Million Mutinies Now*. New York: Viking.

Nair, L. R. 1950. *Why Chandigarh?* Simla, India: Publicity Department, Punjab Government.

Narayanan, K. R. 2002. Inaugural address. In *Celebrating Chandigarh*, ed. Jaspreet Takhar, 19–22. Chandigarh, India: Chandigarh Perspectives.

Nas, Peter J. M. 1986. The early Indonesian town: Rise and decline of the city-state and its capital. In *The Indonesian City: Studies in Urban Development and Planning*, ed. Peter J. M. Nas, 18–36. Dordrecht, Netherlands: Foris Publications Holland.

Nath, Aman. 2002. *Dome over India: Rashtrapati Bhavan.* Mumbai: India Book House.

New Yorker. 2018. Briefly noted. April 30, 2018, 73.

Nielsen, Marjatta, and Jakob Skovgaard-Petersen, eds. 2001. *Middle Eastern Cities 1900–1950.* Aarhus, Denmark: Aarhus University Press.

Nilsson, Stan. 1973. *The New Capitals of India, Pakistan and Bangladesh.* Copenhagen: Scandinavian Institute of Asian Studies.

Noe, Sam V. 1981. Old Lahore and old Delhi: Variation on a Mughal theme. *Urbanism Past & Present* 6 (2): 1–20.

Nolli, Giambattista. 1748. *Roma Al Tempo Di Benedetto XIV: La Planta di Roma.* Città del Vaticano: Biblioteca Apostolica Vaticana.

Novo, Salvador. 1967. *Nueva Grandeza Mexicana.* Mexico: Ediciones Era.

Nussbaum, Martha. 2000. *Women and Human Development: The Capabilities Approach.* Cambridge: Cambridge University Press.

Nyce, B. 1988. *Satyajit Ray: A Study of His Films.* New York: Praeger.

O'Brien, Patrick. 1982. European economic development: The contribution of the periphery. *Economic History Review,* 2nd ser., 35 (1): 1–18.

O'Brien, Patrick. 1990. European industrialisation from the Voyages of Discovery to the Industrial Revolution. In *The European Discovery of the World and Its Economic Effects on Pre-industrial Society, 1500–1800,* ed. Hans Pohl, 54–164. Stuttgart: Franz Steiner.

O'Connor, Anthony M. 1983. *The African City.* New York: Africana Publishing.

OECD (Organization for Economic Cooperation and Development). 1991. *The State of the Environment.* Annual Report. Paris.

O'Hare, G., and M. Barke. 2002. The favelas of Rio de Janeiro: A temporal and spatial analysis. *Geojournal* 56 (3): 225–240.

Oldenburg, Ray. 1989. *The Great Good Place.* New York: Paragon House.

"On Assignment," *National Geographic,* May 2004, n.p.

Osborne, Frederick J., and A. Whittick. 1969. *The New Towns: The Answer to Megalopolis?* London: Leonard Hill Books.

Panayotou, Theodore. 2000. Economic growth and the environment. CID Working Paper No. 56. Cambridge, MA: Harvard University.

Parsons, Kermit C., ed. 1998. *The Writings of Clarence S. Stein.* Baltimore: Johns Hopkins University Press.

Pasoloni, Pier Paolo. 1962. *L'Odore dell'India.* Milan, Italy: Guanda.

Payne, Geoffrey K. 1977. *Urban Housing in the Third World*. London: Leonard Hill.

Pearce-Oroz, Glenn. 2005. Causes and consequences of rapid urban spatial segregation: The new towns of Tegucigalpa. In *Desegregating the City: Ghettos, Enclaves, and Inequality*, ed. David Varady, 108–124. Albany, NY: SUNY Press.

Pearlstine, Norman, Robyn Dixon, David Pierson, David S. Cloud, Alice Su, and Max Hao Lu. 2019. Who's behind Huawei? *Los Angeles Times*, April 14, 2019, A1, A8–A11.

Peattie, Lisa. 1975. *Living Poor: A View from the Bottom*. Los Angeles: School of Architecture and Urban Planning, University of California.

Peattie, Lisa. 1981. *Thinking about Development*. New York: Plenum Press.

Peattie, Lisa. 1987a. The informal sector: An idea in good currency and how it grew. *World Development* 15 (7): 851–860.

Peattie, Lisa. 1987b. *Planning: Rethinking Ciudad Guyana*. Ann Arbor: University of Michigan Press.

Peattie, Lisa. 1994. An argument for slums. *Journal of Planning Education and Research* 13 (2): 136–143.

Peattie, Lisa. 1998. Convivial cities. In *Cities for Citizens: Planning and the Rise of Civil Society in a Global Age*, ed. John Friedmann and Michael Douglass, 247–254. Chichester, NY: John Wiley & Sons.

Perin, Constance. 1977. *Everything in Its Place: Land Use in America*. Princeton, NJ: Princeton University Press.

Perlman, Janice E. 1976. *The Myth of Marginality: Urban Poverty and Politics in Rio de Janeiro*. Berkeley: University of California Press.

Perlman, Janice E. 2005. The myth of marginality revisited: The case of favelas in Rio de Janeiro, 1969–2003. In *Becoming Global and the New Poverty of Cities*, ed. Lisa M. Hanley, Blair A. Ruble, and Joseph S. Tulchin, 9–54. Washington, DC: Woodrow Wilson International Center for Scholars.

Perlman, Janice E. 2006. The metamorphosis of marginality: Four generations in the favelas of Rio de Janeiro. *Annals of the American Academy of Political and Social Science* 606 (1): 154–177.

Perroux, François. 1955. Note sur la notion de pôle de croissance. *Économie appliquée* 1 & 2:307–320.

Piazzoni, Maria-Francesca. 2018. *Real Fake: Authenticity and Production of Space*. New York: Fordham University Press.

Piazzoni, Maria-Francesca, and Tridib Banerjee. 2018. Mimicry in urban design: The urban form of development. *Journal of Urban Design* 23 (4): 482–498.

Piketty, Thomas. 2014. *Capital in the Twenty-First Century*. Cambridge, MA: Harvard University Press.

Pine, Joseph B., and James H. Gilmore. 1999. *The Experience Economy: Work Is Theatre and Every Business a Stage*. Boston: Harvard Business School.

Pizarro, Rafael. 2005. *Suburbanization of the Mind: The Hollywood Urban Imaginarium and the Rise of American Suburbia in the Colombian Caribbean* [Doctoral dissertation, University of Southern California].

Pizarro, Rafael, Liang Wei, and Tridib Banerjee. 2003. Agencies of globalization and Third World urban form. *Journal of Planning Literature* 18 (2): 111–130.

Polanyi, Michael. 1958. *Personal Knowledge: Towards a Post-Critical Philosophy*. Chicago: University of Chicago Press.

Popke, E. Jeffrey. 2001. Modernity's abject space: The rise and fall of Durban's Cato Manor. *Environment and Planning A* 33:737–752.

Portes, Alejandro. 1976. On the sociology of national development: Theories and issues. *American Journal of Sociology* 82 (1): 55–85.

Prakash, Gyan. 1995. Orientalism now. *History and Theory* 34 (3): 199–212.

Press and Information Office of the Pudong New Area. 2002. *Guide to Pudong*. Beijing: China Intercontinental Press.

Putnam, Robert D. 1993. The prosperous community: Social capital and public life. *The American Prospect* (13): 35–42.

Putnam, Robert D. 2000. *Bowling Alone: The Collapse and Revival of American Community*. New York: Simon & Schuster.

Qadeer, Mohammad. 2016. *Multicultural Cities: Toronto, New York, and Los Angeles*. Toronto: University of Toronto Press.

Quigley, John M. 2009. Urbanization, agglomeration, and economic development. In *Urbanization and Growth*, ed. Michael Spence, Patricia Clarke Annez, and Robert M. Buckley, 115–132. Washington, DC: IBRD and World Bank.

Raban, Jonathan. 1974. *Soft City*. New York: E. P. Dutton.

Rabinow, Paul. 1989. Governing Morocco: Modernity and difference. *International Journal of Urban and Regional Research* 13 (1): 32–46.

Radoine, Hassan. 2008. Urban conservation of Fez-Medina: A post-impact appraisal. *Global Urban Development* 4 (1): 1–14.

Radoine, Hassan. 2011. Planning paradigm in the *madina*: Order in randomness. *Planning Perspectives* 26 (4): 527–549.

Rai, R. B. 1971. Functional integration of "old and new" in Delhi. *Journal of the Institute of Town Planners, India* 69:22–26.

Ramanujan, A. K. 1970. Toward an anthology of city images. In *Urban India: Society, Space, and Image*, ed. R. G. Fox, 224–242. Durham, NC: Duke University Press.

Rand, Christopher. 1955. City on a tilting plain. *New Yorker*, April 30, 1955.

Rapoport, Amos. 1969. *House Form and Culture*. Englewood Cliffs, NJ: Prentice-Hall.

Rapoport, Amos. 1988. Review of *Arabic-Islamic Cities: Building and Planning Principles*, by Besim Salim Hakim. *Journal of Architectural Education* 41 (2): 60–61.

Rasmussen, Steen Eiler. 1974. *London: The Unique City*. Cambridge, MA: MIT Press.

Rawls, John. 1974. *A Theory of Justice*. Cambridge, MA: Harvard University Press.

Raymond, André. 1994. Islamic city, Arab city: Orientalist myths and recent views. *British Journal of Middle Eastern Studies* 21 (1): 3–18.

Raymond, André. 2000. *Cairo*. Cambridge, MA: Harvard University Press.

Redfield, Robert. 1953. *The Primitive World and Its Transformations*. Ithaca, NY: Cornell University Press.

Redfield, Robert, and Milton B. Singer. 1954. The cultural role of cities. *Economic Development and Cultural Change* 3 (1): 53–73.

Reiff, David. 1991. *Los Angeles: Capital of the Third World*. New York: Simon & Schuster.

Relph, Edward C. 1976. *Place and Placelessness*. London: Pion.

Reps, John W. 1965. *The Making of Urban America: A History of City Planning in the United States*. Princeton, NJ: Princeton University Press.

Revol, Claire. 2016. Kevin Lynch and Henri Lefebvre, thinkers of the aesthetic experience of the rhythms of the urban environment. *Rhuthmos*, October 21, 2019. http://rhuthmos.eu/spip.php?article852.

Reynolds, Holly Baker. 1987. Madurai: Kōyil Nakar. In *The City as a Sacred Center: Essays on Six Asian Contexts*, ed. Bardwell Smith and Holly Baker Reynolds, 12–44. Leiden, Netherlands: E. J. Brill.

Richardson, H. 1977. *City Size and National Spatial Strategies in Developing Countries*. Washington, DC: World Bank.

Richie, Alexandra. 1998. *Faust's Metropolis: History of Berlin*. New York: Carroll and Graf.

Rittel, Horst W. J., and Melvin M. Webber. 1973. Dilemmas in a general theory of planning. *Policy Sciences* 4:155–169.

Roberts, Bryan R. 1976. *Cities of Peasants: The Political Economy of Urbanization in the Third World*. Beverley Hills, CA: Sage Publications.

Robinson, A. 1989. *Satyajit Ray: The Inner Eye*. Calcutta: Rupa.

Rodwin, Lloyd, and associates. 1969. *Planning Urban Growth and Regional Development: The Experience of Guyana Program of Venezuela*. Cambridge, MA: MIT Press.

Roe, Jenny. 2019. A new health urbanism. In *New Companion to Urban Design*, ed. Tridib Banerjee and Anastasia Loukaitou-Sideris. London: Routledge.

Rosenthal, E. I. J. 1940. Ibn Khaldun: A North African Muslim thinker of the fourteenth century. *Bulletin of the John Rylands Library* 24:307–308.

Roser, Max. 2015. Inequality in South America. https://www.maxroser.com

Ross, Catherine L., ed. 2009. *Megaregions: Planning for Global Competitiveness*. Washington, DC: Island Press.

Rostow, Walt Whitman. 1960. *The Stages of Economic Growth: A Non-Communist Manifesto*. Cambridge: Cambridge University Press.

Rostow, Walt Whitman. 1975. *How It All Began: Origins of Modern Economy*. London: Methuen.

Rowe, Peter G. 2004. Privation to prominence: Shanghai's recent rapid resurgence. In *Shanghai: Architecture & Urbanism for Modern China*, ed. Peter G. Rowe and Seng Kuan, 54–67. Munich: Prestel.

Roy, Ananya. 2001. The reverse side of the world: Identity, space, and power. In *Hybrid Urbanism: On the Identity Discourse and the Built Environment*, ed. Nezar AlSayyad, 229–248. Westport, CT: Praeger.

Roy, Ananya. 2003. *City Requiem, Calcutta: Gender and the Politics of Poverty*. Minneapolis: University of Minnesota Press.

Roy, Ananya, and Nezar AlSayyad. 2004. *Urban Informality: Transnational Perspectives from the Middle East, Latin America, and South Asia*. Lanham, MD: Lexington Books.

Roy, Ananya, and Aihwa Ong, eds. 2011. *Worlding Cities: Asian Experiments and the Art of Being Global*. New York: Wiley-Blackwell.

Rybczynski, Witold. 1995. *City Life: Urban Expectation in a New World*. New York: Scribner.

Rykwert, Joseph. 1988. *The Idea of a Town: The Anthropology of Urban Form in Rome, Italy, and the Ancient World*. Cambridge, MA: MIT Press.

Sachs, Jeffrey D. 2001. Tropical underdevelopment. NBER Working Paper No. 8119. Cambridge, MA: National Bureau of Economic Research.

Sachs, Jeffrey D. 2005. *The End of Poverty: Economic Possibilities for Our Time*. New York: Penguin Press.

Said, Edward W. 1979. *Orientalism*. New York: Vintage Books.

Said, Edward W. 1993. *Culture and Imperialism*. New York: Knopf.

Saini, Nayan S. 1968. Total systems approach to the metropolitan area planning in India. *Journal of the Institute of Town Planners, India* 55–56:66–73.

Salamanca, F., M. Georgescu, A. Mahalov, M. Moustaoui, and M. Wang. 2014. Anthropogenic heating of the urban environment due to air conditioning. *Journal of Geophysical Research* 119 (10): 5949–5965.

Sandercock, Leonie. 2003. *Cosmopolis II: Mongrel Cities of the 21st Century*. London: Bloomsbury.

Santos, Milton. 1979. *The Shared Space: The Two Circuits of Urban Economy in Underdeveloped Countries*. London: Methuen.

Sarin, Madhu. 1982. *Urban Planning in the Third World: The Chandigarh Experience*. London: Mansell Publishing.

Sassen, Saskia. 2012. *Cities in a World Economy*. Thousand Oaks, CA: Sage.

Satō, Tsugitaka. 1997. *Islamic Urbanism in Human History: Political Power and Social Networks*. London: Kegan Paul International.

Sauvaget, Jean. 1934. Esquisse d'une histoire de la ville de Damas. *Revue des études islamiques* 4:421–480.

Sauvaget, Jean. 1941. *Alep: Essai Sue le Développement d'une Grande Ville Syrienne des Origins Auxmiliey du XIXe Siècle*. Paris: Paul Guethner.

Savitch, Hank V., and Paul Kantor. 2002. *Cities in the International Marketplace: The Political Economy of Urban Development in North America and Western Europe*. Princeton, NJ: Princeton University Press.

Scheer, Brenda. 2011. Metropolitan form and landscape urbanism. In *Companion to Urban Design*, ed. Tridib Banerjee and Anastasia Loukaitou-Sideris, 611–618. London: Routledge.

Scott, James C. 1998. *Seeing Like a State: How Certain Schemes to Improve the Human Condition Have Failed*. New Haven, CT: Yale University Press.

Seers, Dudley. 1979. The meaning of development. In *Development Theory: Four Critical Studies*, ed. D. Lehmann, 9–30. Totowa, NJ: F. Cass.

Selden, Thomas M., and Daqing Song. 1994. Environmental quality and development: Is there a Kuznets curve for air pollution emissions? *Journal of Environmental Economics and Management* 27:147–162.

Sen, Amartya. 1992. *Inequality Reexamined*. Cambridge, MA: Harvard University Press.

Sen, Amartya. 1999. *Development as Freedom*. New York: Knopf.

Sen, Amartya. 2005. *The Argumentative Indian: Writings on Indian History, Culture, and Identity*. New York: Picador.

Sen, Siddhartha. 2017. *Colonizing, Decolonizing, and Globalizing Kolkata: From a Colonial to a Post-Marxist City*. Amsterdam: Amsterdam University Press.

Sennett, Richard. 1970. *The Uses of Disorder: Personal Identity & City Life*. New York: Vintage Books.

Sennett, Richard. 1977. *The Fall of Public Man*. New York: Alfred Knopf.

Sennett, Richard. 1991. *The Conscience of the Eye: The Design and Social Life of Cities*. New York: W. W. Norton.

Serjeant, R. B., ed. 1980. *The Islamic City*. Paris: UNESCO.

Shafik, Nemat, and Sushenjit Bandyopadhyay. 1992. Economic growth and environmental quality: Time series and cross-country evidence. World Bank Working Paper WPS 904. Washington, DC: World Bank Group.

Shanghai Pudong New Area Government. 2018. *Pudong's Economic Development Statistics (September)*. Updated March 13, 2018. http://english.pudong.gov.cn/2018-03/15/c_153333.htm

Shanghai Statistical Bureau. 2017. Shanghai Statistical Yearbook. https://www.chinayearbooks.com/wp-content/uploads/2018/01/shanghai-statistical-yearbook-2017.jpg

Shephard, Wade. 2015. *Ghost Cities of China: The Story of Cities without People in the World's Most Populated Country*. London: Zed Books.

Sherwood, Seth. 2005. The Oz of the Middle East. *New York Times*, May 8, 2005, 5–1, 8–9.

Simmel, Georg. 1950. *The Sociology of Georg Simmel*. New York: The Free Press.

Singhal, Arvind, and Everett M. Rogers. 1999. *Entertainment-Education: A Communication Strategy for Social Change*. Mahwah, NJ: Lawrence Erlbaum.

Sinha, Pradip. 1978. *Calcutta in Urban History*. Calcutta: Firma KLM.

Sites, William. 2003. *Remaking New York: Primitive Globalization and the Politics of Urban Community*. Minneapolis: University of Minnesota Press.

Sitte, Camillo. 1945. *The Art of Building Cities: City Building According to Its Artistic Fundamentals*. New York: Reinhold.

Sjoberg, Gideon. 1960. *The Preindustrial City: Past and Present*. New York: The Free Press.

Sjoberg, Gideon. 1963. The rise and fall of cities: A theoretical perspective. *International Journal of Comparative Sociology* 4 (2): 107–120.

Skinner, G. William. 1977. Introduction: Urban development in Imperial China. In *The City in the Late Imperial China*, ed. G. William Skinner, 3–31. Stanford, CA: Stanford University Press.

Smith, Adam. 1999. *The Wealth of Nations*. Edited by Andrew Skinner. New York: Penguin. First published 1776.

Smith, Bardwell, and Holly Baker Reynolds, eds. 1987. *The City as a Sacred Center: Essays on Six Asian Contexts*. Leiden, Netherlands: E. J. Brill.

Smith, Carl. 2013. *City Water, City Life*. Chicago: University of Chicago Press.

Smith, Carol A. 1985. Theories and measures of urban primacy: A critique. In *Urbanization in the World Economy*, ed. Michael Timberlake, 87–120. New York: Academic Press.

Smith, Craig S. 2006. The crumbling of the casbah. *New York Times*, July 23, 2006.

Soja, Edward W. 1996. *Thirdspace: Journeys to Los Angeles and Other Real-and-Imagined Places*. Malden, MA: Blackwell.

Sorkin, Michael, ed. 1992. *Variations on a Theme Park: Scenes from the New American City and the End of Public Space*. New York: Hill and Wang.

Sorkin, Michael. 2002. Infrastructure: The ecology of the new. In *Celebrating Chandigarh*, ed. Jaspreet Takhar, 273–275. Chandigarh, India: Chandigarh Perspectives.

Southworth, Michael. 1989. Theory and practice of contemporary urban design: A review of urban design plans in the United States. *Town Planning Review* 60 (4): 369–402.

Southworth, Michael, and Balaji Pathasarathi. 1996. The suburban public realm I: Its emergence, growth, and transformation in the American metropolis. *Journal of Urban Design* 1 (3): 245–263.

Sovani, Nilkanth Vithal. 1964. The analysis of "Over-Urbanization." *Economic Development and Cultural Change* 12 (2): 113–122.

Spirn, Anne Whiston. 1984. Designing the urban ecosystem. In *The Granite Garden: Urban Nature and Human Design*, 242–262. New York: Basic Books.

Spivak, Gayatri Chakravorty. 1988. Can the subaltern speak? In *Marxism and the Interpretation of Culture*, ed. Carey Nelson and Lawrence Grossberg, 271–313. Urbana: University of Illinois Press.

Spivak, Gayatri Chakravorty. 1999. *A Critique of Postcolonial Reason: Toward a History of Vanishing Present*. Cambridge, MA: Harvard University Press.

Spreiregen, Paul. 1965. *Urban Design: Architecture of Towns and Cities*. New York: McGraw-Hill.

Stanislawski, D. 1947. Early Spanish town planning in the new world. *Geographical Review* 37:94–105.

Steele, James S. 2002. *Orientalism and the Other* [Doctoral dissertation, University of Southern California].

Stein, Clarence. 1957. *Toward New Towns for America*. Cambridge, MA: MIT Press.

Steinhardt, Nancy S. 1990. *Chinese Imperial City Planning*. Honolulu: University of Hawaii Press.

Stern, David I., Michael S. Common, and Edward B. Barbier. 1996. Economic growth and environmental degradation: The environmental Kuznets curve and sustainable development. *World Development* 24 (7): 1151–1160.

Stern, S. M. 1970. The constitution of the Islamic city. In *The Islamic City: A Colloquium*, ed. A. H. Hourani and S. M. Stern, 25–50. Oxford: Bruno Cassirer.

Steward, J. H. 1955. *Theory of Culture Change: Methodology of Multilinear Evolution*. Urbana: University of Illinois Press.

Stiglitz, Joseph E. 2002. *Globalization and Its Discontents*. New York: W. W. Norton.

Stimmann, Hans. 2001. *City models—models for a city?* Berlin—Stadmodelle, City of Berlin.

Stimmann, Hans. 2002. *The City in Black: The Physiognomy of Central Berlin in Figure-Ground Plans and Parcel Plans*. Berlin: Nicolai.

Summers, Lawrence. 1992. Let them eat pollution. *The Economist,* February 8, 1992, 66.

Summerson, John. 1967. Urban forms. In *The Historian and the City,* ed. Oscar Handlin and John Ely Burchard, 165–176. Cambridge, MA: MIT Press.

Suttles, Gerald. 1972. *The Social Construction of Communities.* Chicago: University of Chicago Press.

Swamy, M. C. K. 1971. Blending old and new—a planning aspect. *Journal of the Institute of Town Planners, India* 69:28–32.

Szelenyi, Ivan. 1993. East European cities: How different are they? In *Urban Anthropology in China,* ed. Greg Guldin and Aidan Southall, 41–64. Leiden, Netherlands: E. J. Brill.

Tajbakhsh, Kian. 2001. *The Promise of the City.* Berkeley: University of California Press.

Takhar, Jaspreet, ed. 2002. *Celebrating Chandigarh.* Chandigarh, India: Chandigarh Perspectives.

Talamona, M. 1993. Citta europa e citta araba in Tripolitania. In *Architettura Italiana d'Oltremare 1870–1940,* ed. G. Gresleri, P. G. Massaretti, and S. Zagnoni, 257–279. Venzia: Marsilio.

Tavassoli, Mahmoud, and Naser Bonyadi. 1992. *Urban Space Design 1.* Tehran, Iran: Urban Planning and Architecture Research Center of Iran.

Tavassoli, Mahmoud, and Naser Bonyadi. 1993. *Urban Space Design 2.* Tehran, Iran: Urban Planning and Architecture Research Center of Iran.

Taylor, Charles. 2001. Two theories of modernity. In *Alternative Modernities,* ed. D. Gaonkar, 172–196. Durham, NC: Duke University Press.

Taylor, Jeremy E. 2002. The bund: Littoral space of empire in the treaty ports of East Asia. *Social History* 27 (2): 125–142.

Tharoor, Shashi. 2017. *Inglorious Empire: What the British Did to India.* London: Hurst & Co. Publishers.

The Economist. 2007. The hobbled hegemon. June 28, 2007, 29–32.

The Economist. 2017. City life in Mongolia: Villas v yurts. July 15–21, 2017, 35.

The Economist. 2018. Economic and financial indicators. May 5, 2018, 84.

The Economist. 2019a. Economic and financial indicators. March 16–22, 2019, 76.

The Economist. 2019b. Turkey's oddest ghost town. February 2–8, 2019, 45.

The Economist. 2019c. Where the Raj lives on. May 11–17, 2019, 33.

Thiel, Philip. 1970. Notes on the description, scaling, notation, and scoring of some perceptual and cognitive attributes of the physical environment. In *Environmental Psychology: Man and His Physical Setting,* ed. Harold M. Proshansky, William H. Ittleson, and Leanne G. Rivlin, 593–619. New York: Holt, Rinehart and Winston.

Thomas, Alan, Ben Crow, et al. 1994. *Third World Atlas.* 2nd ed. Washington, DC: Taylor & Francis.

Thomas, Frederic C. 1997. *Calcutta Poor: Elegies on a City above Pretense*. Armonk, NY: M. E. Sharpe.

Todaro, Michael P. 1969. A model of labor migration and urban development in less developed countries. *American Economic Review* 59 (1): 138–148.

Todaro, Michael P. 1989. *Economic Development in the Third World*. New York: Longman.

Tolman, Edward C. 1948. Cognitive maps in rats and men. *Psychological Review* 55 (4): 189–208.

Tönnies, Ferdinand. 1974. *Gemeinschaft and Gesellschaft*. East Lansing: Michigan State University Press.

Trojanow, Ilija. 2001. Imperial politics in the progressive gaze. *The Hindu*, December 2, 2001.

Tuan, Yi-Fu. 1974. *Topophilia: A Study of Environmental Perceptions, Attitudes, and Values*. Englewood Cliffs, NJ: Prentice Hall.

Turner, John C. 1968. Housing priorities, settlement patterns, and urban development in modernizing countries. *Journal of the American Institute of Planners* 34 (6): 354–363.

Tyrwhitt, Jaqueline, ed. 1947. *Patrick Geddes in India*. London: Lund Humphries.

Tzonis, Alexander. 1972. *Towards a Non-oppressive Environment: An Essay*. Boston: iPress.

Uhm, Jung A., Ferdinand Lewis, and Tridib Banerjee. 2006. Children's capabilities: Toward a framework for evaluating built environment. In *Children and the Capability Approach*, ed. M. Biggeri, J. Ballet, F. Comim, 304–328. London: Palgrave Macmillan.

ul Haq, Mahbub. 1971. Employment and income distribution in the 1970s: A new perspective. *Development Digest* 9 (4): 3–8.

UN-Habitat. n.d. *Slum Almanac 2015–2016: Tracking Improvements in the Lives of Slum Dwellers*. https://unhabitat.org/slum-almanac-2015-2016

UN-Habitat. 2003. *The Challenge of Slums: Global Report on Human Settlements*. London: Earthscan.

United Nations. 1987. *Our Common Future: Report of the World Commission on Environment and Development* (also known as the Brundtland Report). New York: Oxford University Press.

United Nations. 1989. *Prospects of World Urbanization*. New York.

United Nations, Department of Economic and Social Affairs, Population Division. 2017. *World Population Prospects 2017—Data Booklet (ST/ESA/SER.A/401)*.

Urbinati, Nadia. 1998. From the periphery of modernity: Antonio Gramsci's theory of subordination and hegemony. *Political Theory* 26 (3): 370–391.

Urquidi, Victor L. 1963. Los Hijos de Jones. Institute of Latin American Studies, University of Texas, Special publication.

Uys, J., director. 1980. *The Gods Must Be Crazy* [Film]. C.A.T. Films; Mimosa Films.

Vale, Lawrence J. 2014. *Architecture, Power, and National Identity*. 2nd ed. New Haven, CT: Yale University Press.

Verma, Niraj. 1996. Pragmatic rationality and planning theory. *Journal of the Planning Education and Research* 6 (1): 5–14.

Verma, Niraj, Tridib Banerjee, and Swati Chaudhuri. 2004. Towards a theory of best practices: Some cases of sustainable development. Grenoble, France: Association of European Schools of Planning.

Verstegen, Ian, and Allan Ceen. 2013. *Giambattista Nolli and Rome: Mapping the City before and after the Planta Grande*. Rome: Studium Urbis.

Vidyarthi, Sanjeev. 2015. *One Idea, Many Plans: An American City Design Concept in Independent India*. Abingdon, UK: Routledge.

Villaça, F. 2001. "Segregation in Brazilian Metropolis." International Seminar on Segregation in the City. Paper presented at the *International Seminar on Segregation in the City*. Cambridge, MA: Lincoln Institute of Land Policy. www.lincolninst.edu/pubs/dl/620_villaca.pdf

Von Grunebaum, Gustave E. 1955. *Unity and Variety in Muslim Civilization*. Chicago: University of Chicago Press.

Von Henneberg, Krystyna. 2005. Public space and public face: Italian fascist urban planning at Tripoli's colonial trade fair. In *Italian Colonialism*, ed. Ruth Ben-Ghiat and Mia Fuller, 155–165. New York: Palgrave Macmillan.

Wallerstein, I. 2011. *The Modern World System II: Mercantilism and the Consolidation of the European World Economy 1600–1750*. Berkeley: University of California Press.

Wang, Jun. 2011. *Beijing Record: A Physical and Political History of Planning Modern Beijing*. Singapore: World Scientific Publishing.

Webber, Melvin. 1963. Order in diversity: Community without propinquity. In *Cities and Space*, ed. Lowdon Wingo, 23–56. Baltimore: John Hopkins Press.

Webber, Melvin, ed. 1964. *Explorations into Urban Structure*. Philadelphia: University of Pennsylvania Press.

Weber, Max. 1958. *The City*. New York: The Free Press.

Webster, Chris. 2007. Property rights, public space and urban design. *Town Planning Review* 78 (1): 81–101.

Westfall, Matthew. 1990. *On Borrowed Land* [Film]. Amphion Productions.

Wheatley, Paul. 1969. *City as Symbol*. London: H. K. Lewis.

Wheatley, Paul. 1971. *The Pivot of the Four Quarters: A Preliminary Enquiry into the Origins and Character of the Ancient Chinese City*. Chicago: Aldine Publishing.

Whelan, Simon. 2004. One third of the world's urban population lives in a slum. World Socialist Web Site, February 17. https://www.wsws.org/en/articles/2004/02/slum-f17.html.

White, Morton G., and Lucia White. 1962. *The Intellectual versus the City: From Thomas Jefferson to Frank Lloyd Wright*. Cambridge, MA: Harvard University Press.

Whyte, William H. 1988. *City: Rediscovering the Center*. New York: Doubleday.

Williams, Adebayo. 1997. The postcolonial flaneur and other fellow-travellers: Conceits for a narrative of redemption. *Third World Quarterly* 18 (5): 821–841.

Williamson, Jeffrey G. 1965. Regional inequality and the process of national development: A description of the patterns. *Economic Development and Cultural Change* 13 (4): 1–84.

Willmott, Peter. 1962. Social research and new communities. *Journal of the American Institute of Planners* 32:387–398.

Wilson, C. R. 1906. *Old Fort William in Bengal*. Plate VI. London: John Murray, Albemarle Street.

Wingo, Lowdon. 1963. *Cities and Space: The Future Use of Urban Land*. Baltimore: Johns Hopkins University Press.

Wirth, Eugen. 1982. Villes Islamiques, villes arabes, villes orientales? Une problématique face au changemont. In *La ville arabe dans l'Islam*, ed. Abdelwahab Bouhdiba and Dominique Chevallier, 193–215. Tunis: Universite de Tunis.

Wirth, Louis. 1938. Urbanism as a way of life. *American Journal of Sociology* 44 (1): 1–24.

World Bank. 1978. *World Development Report 1978*. Washington, DC: World Bank Group.

World Bank. 1981. *The Neighborhood of Coelhos* [Video]. https://archivesholdings.worldbank.org/world-bank-films-neighborhood-of-coelhos-portugese-version-inter-negative-bono-reel

World Bank. 1984. *World Development Report 1984: Population Change and Economic Development*. New York: Oxford University Press.

World Bank. 1991. *World Development Report 1991: The Challenge of Development*. New York: Oxford University Press.

World Bank. 1992. *World Development Report 1992: Development and the Environment*. New York: Oxford University Press.

World Bank. 1998. *Morocco—Fes-Medina Rehabilitation Project*. Project Appraisal Document. Washington, DC: World Bank Group.

World Bank. 2000/2001. *World Development Report Attacking Poverty*. New York: Oxford University Press.

World Bank. 2002. *World Development Report 2002: Building Institution for Markets*. New York: Oxford University Press.

World Bank. 2003. *World Development Report 2003: Sustainable Development in a Dynamic World – Transforming Institutions, Growth, and Quality of Life*. New York: Oxford University Press.

World Bank. 2006. *World Development Report 2007: Development and the Next Generation.* New York: Oxford University Press.

World Bank. 2012. *World Development Report: Gender Equality and Development.* Washington, DC: IBRD/World Bank.

World Bank. 2017. *World Development Report: End Extreme Poverty – Boost Shared Prosperity.* Washington, DC: IBRD/World Bank.

World Bank. n.d. *Fes Medina Rehabilitation Project.* https://projects.worldbank.org/en/projects-operations/project-detail/P005524

Wright, Arthur F. 1977. The cosmology of the Chinese city. In *The City in Late Imperial China,* ed. G. William Skinner, 33–73. Stanford, CA: Stanford University Press.

Wright, Gwendolyn. 1991. *The Politics of Design in French Colonial Urbanism.* Chicago: University of Chicago Press.

Wu, Fulong. 2000. The global and local dimensions of place-making: Remaking Shanghai as a World City. *Urban Studies* 37 (8): 1359–1377.

Wu, Liangyong. 1994a. New model for integrated rehabilitation of courtyard houses in Beijing's Ju'er hutong. In *Beijing Ju'er Hutong New Courtyard Housing Experiment.* Institute of Architectural and Urban Studies, 4–9, Tsinghua University, Beijing, China.

Wu, Liangyong. 1994b. The future direction of the experiment. In *Beijing Ju'er Hutong New Courtyard Housing Experiment.* Institute of Architectural and Urban Studies, 34–40, Tsinghua University, Beijing, China.

Wu, Liangyong. 1999. *Rehabilitating the Old City of Beijing: A Project in the Ju'er Hutong Neighborhood.* Vancouver: University of British Columbia Press.

Wu, Nelson. 1963. *Chinese and Indian Architecture: The City of Man, the Mountain of God, and the Realm of the Immortals.* New York: George Braziller.

WWF (World Wide Fund for Nature). 2006. *Living Planet Report 2006.* https://wwf.panda.org/knowledge_hub/all_publications/living_planet_report_timeline/lpr_2006/

Xue, Charlie Q. L., Hailin Zhai, and Brian Mitchenere. 2011. Shaping Lujiazui: The formation and building of the CBD in Pudong, Shanghai. *Journal of Urban Design* 16 (2): 209–232.

Yeh, Anthony G. O. 1996. Pudong—The remaking of Shanghai as a world city. In *Shanghai: Transformation and Modernization under China's Open Policy,* ed. Yue-man Yeung and Yun-wing Sung, 273–298. Hong Kong: Chinese University of Hong Kong Press.

Yeung, Yue-man, and Xiojian Li. 2000. Transnational corporations and local embeddedness. *Professional Geographer* 52 (4): 624–635.

Yeung, Yue-man, and Yun-wing Sung. 1996. *Shanghai: Transformation and Modernization under China's Open Policy.* Hong Kong: Chinese University of Hong Kong Press.

Yi, Shu. 2002. Foreword. *Hutongs of Beijing Photography*. Beijing: China Travel and Tourism Press.

Yu, Ran. 2017. Shanghai attracts $18.5 billion in overseas investment in 2016. *China Daily USA*, January 3, 2017, 14.

Yucekus, Emel, and Tridib Banerjee. 1998. Xidan Street, Beijing: Reading and writing urban change. In *City Space and Globalization: An International Perspective*, ed. Hemalata C. Dandekar, 88–96. Ann Arbor: College of Architecture and Urban Planning, University of Michigan.

Zukin, Sharon. 1991. *Landscapes of Power. From Detroit to Disney World*. Berkeley: University of California Press.

Index

Urban and Industrial Environments

Series editor: Robert Gottlieb, Henry R. Luce Professor of Urban and Environmental Policy, Occidental College

Karen Chapple and Anastasia Loukaitou-Sideris, *Transit-Oriented Displacement or Community Dividends? Understanding the Effects of Smarter Growth on Communities*

Henrik Ernstson and Sverker Sorlin, eds., *Grounding Urban Natures: Histories and Futures of Urban Ecologies*

Katrina Smith Korfmacher, *Bridging the Silos: Collaborating for Environment, Health, and Justice in Urban Communities*

Jill Lindsey Harrison, *From the Inside Out: The Fight for Environmental Justice within Government Agencies*

Anastasia Loukaitou-Sideris, Dana Cuff, Todd Presner, Maite Zubiaurre, and Jonathan Jae-an Crisman, *Urban Humanities: New Practices for Reimagining the City*

Govind Gopakumar, *Installing Automobility: Emerging Politics of Mobility and Streets in Indian Cities*

Amelia Thorpe, *Everyday Ownership: PARK(ing) Day and the Practice of Property*

Tridib Banerjee, *In the Images of Development: City Design in the Global South*

Ralph Buehler and John Pucher, eds., *Cycling for Sustainable Cities*